4.88

DARROW

DARROW

A Biography

Kevin Tierney

THOMAS Y. CROWELL, PUBLISHERS

ESTABLISHED 1834

New York

PHOTO CREDITS

The Bettmann Archive: 10, 14, 17; Chicago Historical Society: 8, 11; Compix: 15, 19, 22; International Museum of Photography, Rochester, N.Y.: frontispiece; *The Story of My Life* by Clarence Darrow, courtesy of Charles Scribner's Sons, Mrs. Gordon Chase, Mrs. Burton Simonson: 1, 2, 3, 4, 5, 7, 20; Wide World Photos; 6, 9, 12, 13, 16, 18, 21, 23, 24, 25

FIRST EDITION

Designed by Stephanie Winkler

Library of Congress Cataloging in Publication Data

Tierney, Kevin.
  Darrow, a biography.
  Bibliography: p.
  Includes index.
  1. Darrow, Clarence Seward, 1857-1938. 2. Lawyers—
United States—Biography. I. Title.
KF373.D35T53   345'.73'00924 [B]   78-3319
ISBN 0–690–01408–2

79 80 81 82 83 10 9 8 7 6 5 4 3 2 1

Contents

PART THREE: FROM DISGRACE TO DISTINCTION

    Photographs follow pages 154 and 346.

PART ONE
From Village to City

1

Beginnings

"If I had chosen to be born I probably should not have selected Kinsman, Ohio, for that honor; instead, I would have started in a hard and noisy city where the crowds surged back and forth as if they knew where they were going and why." So Clarence Seward Darrow later commented on the circumstances of his birth—in Kinsman, Ohio, on April 18, 1857, the fifth child of Amirus and Emily Eddy Darrow. The prospects of a boy born to poor parents in a tiny village in Ohio just before the Civil War were, by any reasonable estimate, fairly limited. Kinsman, with only four hundred inhabitants, was so insignificant that its name did not appear on contemporary maps of the area.

The Darrow family left few traces of its doings prior to Clarence's appearance, and Clarence himself professed a studied indifference to ancestry, his own or anybody else's. "I have been told that I came of a very old family," he wrote. "A considerable number of people say that it runs back to Adam and Eve, although this, of course, is only hearsay, and I should not like to guarantee the title. . . . I am sure that my forbears run a long, long way back . . . but what of it, anyhow?" According to his own account, he could run his "pedigree . . . with reasonable certainty . . . back to a little town in England that has the same name as mine, though the spelling is slightly altered"; but his confidence in this may have been misplaced, since the standard authorities list the name Darrow as Gaelic rather than English, if they list it at all, and no little town of Darrow has as yet come to the notice of the English Place Name Society. However there seems no doubt that his maternal ancestry was English, and the Eddys were descended from William Eddye of Bristol. Both families had been in America since the seventeenth century: a Darrow had been holder of a royal grant of the town of New London, Connecticut, while two Darrows served in the Connecticut Navy during the Revolutionary War. John and Samuel Eddy landed at Plymouth, Massachusetts, on October 29, 1630. The families settled in Connecticut until, in the early nineteenth century —though they were not acquainted with each other—both of Clarence's grandfathers heeded the call of the frontier and headed west. First the Darrows and a few years later the Eddys traveled the arduous wagon route through upstate New York. The fact that they left Connecticut and then New York and

3

took the chance of continuing west is some evidence that, even if they were not actually failing in the East, they were not succeeding very well. This was a conclusion Clarence reached with respect to both his father's and his mother's forbears: "Both grandfathers were poor and obscure, else they would have stayed where they were." The Darrows stopped for a time in Henrietta, outside Rochester, and then pushed farther west to the extreme northeastern corner of Ohio, which at the time was unsettled territory.

Their grandson Clarence dwelt humorously upon the great risk that the Darrows and the Eddys might never have met: "When I visualize the paternal grandfather Darrow driving off on a thousand-mile trip to a near-wilderness I can hardly refrain from shouting to tell him that he has left Grandfather Eddy behind." Emily Eddy and Amirus Darrow attended the same school at Amboy, Ohio, which had a reputation for excellence sufficient for Henry Howe to have noted it as "a fine classical academy." There, according to the testimony of their son, they were drawn to each other by their shared love of books, respect for education, and independence of mind—and though this formidable high-mindedness sounds too good to be true, the pair's subsequent pattern of life lends it credibility. In particular Amirus, like many a child of the first great age of mass literacy, had swallowed hook, line, and sinker the terrible delusion that the truth on all subjects was to be found in books.

Neither of them had come from bookish families and it is something of a mystery where either acquired such tastes. Amirus's brothers and sisters showed no penchant for reading and Emily's family was "inclined to believe that a love of books was a distinct weakness, and likely to develop into a very bad habit." From a conventional standpoint, the Eddys' opinion was entirely vindicated by the way in which Amirus and Emily combined bibliophilia with a total lack of worldly success.

They married shortly after graduating from the Amboy school, in 1844. Emily's family was the richer of the two; the Darrows had no business of their own, but the Eddys were prosperous farmers. The family's husbandry was efficient and Emily's oldest brother, Lorenzo, who farmed 136 acres, came to be numbered "among the most substantial men of his community."[1] But there was not so much wealth that Emily could bring Amirus a dowry and from the start the couple had to fend for themselves. This was easier said than done, for Amirus was a singularly impractical man whose extraordinary devotion to learning left him little time for earning a living. "In all the country round, no man knew so much of books as he," observed his son, "and no man knew less of life. . . . One of my earliest recollections is the books in our home. They were in bookcases, on tables, in chairs, and even on the floor. The house was small, the family large, the furnishings meagre, but there were books whichever way one turned. . . . We children were brought up in an atmosphere of books, and were trained to love them." Amirus carried the apparent virtue of studiousness to such an extreme that it amounted to a vice. He was enslaved by his addiction to books, unable to resist them. From them he sought truth, but like a will-o'-the-wisp, it repeatedly eluded him just as he thought he had it in his grasp.

Yet still he searched, never becoming cynical or doubting that somewhere lay the key, if only he could find it. In an era before public libraries, faced with the choice of buying books or doing without them, Amirus bought them, then read them avidly over and over again. The result was that he knew more about the Roman Empire than Ohio and cared more for the classics than earning a living. Recalling that he had read Gibbon's *Decline and Fall* in the edition with Milman's notes, Clarence told a correspondent, "My father resented these notes being published with Gibbon. He did not like the idea of a preacher trying to correct and change the great author's work. . . ."[2]

Amirus was a religious young man who had been brought up as a Methodist. Because he was eager to learn and serve Christ, the newlyweds decided to move to Meadville, Pennsylvania, so that he could study at Allegheny College, a Methodist institution founded in 1815. He entered the college in 1845, poor but dedicated, on the threshold of adult life, giving even the doubting Eddys some hope that their impractical son-in-law might make his way in the world.

As a temporary expedient to support himself and Emily, he worked in a furniture shop while attending college, which was just as well, for within a year he had another mouth to feed; his first son was born on October 28, 1846. It is difficult to imagine a couple less ready for the economic difficulties of starting a family. They called their child Edward Everett, after the religious statesman of that name, whom Amirus greatly admired.

The Darrows' joy in their first-born was quickly overshadowed by another, very different event, which seemed to dash Amirus's hopes as a servant of the Lord and the Eddys' hope that he would do well by their daughter. On December 9, Amirus was expelled from Allegheny College, accused of having misused the key to the debating society hall. Amirus felt the disgrace keenly and appealed to the board of trustees, protesting himself to be wholly innocent of the charges against him. Though the trustees rescinded his expulsion on March 6, 1847, they did so not because they were satisfied of his innocence, but on the technical ground that his expulsion had not been in accordance with the college charter. They offered to reinstate Amirus as a student only if he acknowledged misconduct, promised future obedience to college rules, and received a reprimand from the college president. But by this time Amirus had suffered four months of uncertainty and indignity, and he apparently refused to accept the trustees' terms; he did not return to the college. Besides, at a recent General Conference of the Methodists the issue of slavery had caused a schism which led Amirus to doubt that he could any longer give the denomination his support. He enrolled instead in the new Unitarian seminary founded in 1844 which was Allegheny College's rival in Meadville, where he studied theology and became acquainted with the works of John Newman and William Channing. The latter was then enjoying great popularity, his *Works* already being in their eleventh edition, and he impressed Amirus so much that his second son, born in 1849, was named after him.

Amirus successfully completed his theological classes, and might in the ordinary course of events have made his living as a man of the cloth; probably that was his intention when he embarked upon his studies. He was already on the way to acquiring the wagonload of books and house full of children that are proverbially a minister's earthly reward. Unfortunately his graduation coincided with a loss of faith, which he never recovered, and ever afterwards he refused to preach. No record remains of the origin of Amirus's religious doubts; perhaps his wife, who was not a churchgoer and had not come from a devout family, encouraged them. His touching religious belief had always contained within it the seeds of disillusion, for there inevitably came a time when it appeared to his inquiring mind that what was taught was not always right; that even the best of scholars were incapable of explaining any but a small fraction of the universe; and that fallacy, superstition, and prejudice weighed with the common run of humanity at least as much as truth. His loss of faith had been accompanied by a reappraisal of conventional attitudes on almost every important subject. He was a Democrat amidst Republicans; a dreamer whose neighbors' efforts were devoted to the hard practicalities of making a living; an unbeliever surrounded by rural piety. In time, this loss of faith blossomed into a heterodoxy that was to be a profound influence on his fourth son, Clarence.

The gap between received opinion and Amirus's own widened until the Darrows (and a handful of other families outside the mainstream of belief on religious and social questions) stood apart from their neighbors, "strangers in a more or less hostile land." At first the result was that the family was ostracized to its discomfort, but Amirus made an appropriate psychological adjustment and turned adversity to strength. "My father was the village infidel, and gradually came to glory in his reputation," wrote Clarence. "I cannot remember that I ever had any doubt that he was right." He played this role with such adeptness that his son would seek to emulate it throughout his life, magnifying it to a national career. The effect on the boy was that he grew up with a deep moral commitment and the courage of his convictions. "I, like all the rest of the boys, inherited my politics and my religion," he confessed.[3] His suspicion of popular opinion, his attraction to heresy, and his dislike of established authority were all derived from his father. Clarence would show himself open and steadfast on all subjects, never concealing his point of view even when it was manifestly unpopular. He learned to stand firm, refusing to be intimidated or to compromise with error. His greatest inheritance would be the ability and resilience to stand up to the crowd.

Once Amirus's faith had deserted him, there seemed little reason to tarry longer in Meadville, and he and his family left for Kinsman, about 20 miles away, where Amirus had a sister. There Amirus, determined to make his way, set up as a carpenter and furniture maker. This choice of occupation seemed a sensible one since he had learned its skills while working his way through college and Kinsman had no local man already in the field. The neighbors and farmers round about were his customers and he made them sturdy beds, tables, and chairs.

By dint of Emily's careful housekeeping the family was just able to make ends meet, but it was a struggle. In 1852 the couple's first daughter, Mary Elizabeth, was born. Two years later another son, Herbert, arrived, but he died in infancy. No longer were the Darrow progeny given distinctively religious names, and when the fifth child arrived, he was named Clarence Seward:

> When it came my turn to be born and named, my parents had left the Unitarian faith behind and were sailing out on the open sea without rudder or compass, and with no port in sight, and so I could not be named after any prominent Unitarian. Where they found the name to which I have answered so many years I never knew. Perhaps my mother read a story where a minor character was called Clarence, but I fancy I have not turned out to be anything like him. The one satisfaction I have had in connection with this cross was that the boys never could think up any nickname half so inane as the real one my parents adorned me with.

But the older Darrows had followed their prior practice in name-giving in the case of Clarence's middle name: he was called Seward after William Henry Seward, the abolitionist, whom Amirus revered. Clarence Seward liked neither name, and in adult life he was known to his friends simply as "Darrow" and to his wife as "Dee." "I believe no one ever called him Clarence," reported Carl Sandburg.[4]

Clarence was followed by Hubert in 1860, Herman in 1863, and lastly Jennie in 1869, when Clarence was twelve. From the regularity with which new Darrows arrived, Clarence deduced that Amirus and Emily knew nothing of birth control, since his father could ill afford so large a family: that was an ignorance not curable by reading books, for contraception would remain a taboo subject for another half century. The adult Clarence had a characteristic observation to make of his parents' lack of information in this respect: "Perhaps my own existence, as fifth in a family, is one reason why I have never been especially enthusiastic about keeping others from being born; whenever I hear people discussing birth control I always remember that I was the fifth." Still he realized what a burden of support he and his brothers and sisters put upon Amirus. "He must have been puzzled and perplexed at the growing brood that looked so trustingly to the parents for food and clothes," recalled Clarence. "He must have wearily wondered which way to turn to meet the demand." Nevertheless meet it he did; the seven Darrow children who survived infancy grew up in a happy, bustling home.

The family lived first in a cottage in Farmdale, just outside Kinsman, and then in an octagonal house built in the 1850s to a design recommended by Orson Squire Fowler, located in Kinsman itself, which Amirus managed to buy in 1864. There Clarence spent his childhood. This choice of home was not, as has been suggested, a mark of eccentricity so much as a necessity of poverty. Fowler, who billed himself as a "Christian phrenologist," was a crackpot who in 1848 had published a book advocating octagonal homes as cheaper and more natural than those of the orthodox shape and whose stated aim was "especially to bring comfortable dwellings within reach of the poorer classes."

For the most part Clarence looked back on his childhood with fondness, remembering fishing in the little stream, baseball in the long summer evenings, and tobogganing down the snow-laden hills in winter. "My mind goes back to Kinsman because I lived there in childhood, and to me it was once the center of the world, and however far I have roamed since then it has never fully lost that place in the storehouse of miscellaneous memories gathered along the path of life." The family was large enough to provide him with playmates of a wide variety of ages. He grew up with the guidance and inspiration of three older children—two brothers and a sister—who played ball and joked with him, teased him, and did all the frivolous things brothers and sisters normally do together; but there was a serious side to their influence too. Even when he was a small boy, Edward and Mary took him to the Friday night meetings of the Literary Society, where he sat enthralled by its debates and lectures. Channing, the second brother, had no interest in intellectual pursuits and did not join in these visits; but the taste for speaking that Clarence acquired at the Literary Society never left him. He conceived a lifelong admiration for Edward and Mary and later followed in their footsteps, attending the same school as they had and then settling in Chicago. It was they who later encouraged him to pursue his legal studies at the University of Michigan, which both had attended briefly.[5] Edward was a rather grand big brother, ten years older than Clarence, and always the example to the younger children. When Clarence was seven, Edward left Kinsman for the University of Michigan and could thereafter only be admired from a distance except on his return home during vacations. Of Channing, almost nothing is known. Clarence saw more of Mary because she was younger, and because she relieved her mother of some of the duties of looking after the younger Darrows.

Happy though family life was, there were serious influences at work upon young Clarence, for the reverberations of the Civil War could be felt even in Kinsman. The boy grew up in a part of the country that knew at first hand of the terror and determination of many of the abolitionists. The underground railway took its course directly through the area in which the Darrows lived. To a man, the citizenry was abolitionist in sentiment. Ever afterward Clarence would be an outspoken champion of black Americans. His fame brought in its wake myths purporting to explain his tenderness toward Negroes, as when Clarence True Wilson reflected a common delusion by reporting that John Brown, the abolitionist, had laid his hand on five-year-old Clarence's head, saying to him: "The Negro has too few friends; you and I must never desert him." Brown had been hanged when Darrow was only two years old and the story is therefore quite impossible.[6] What is true is that John Brown had mustered his men in West Andover, only 15 miles from Kinsman, just prior to the attack on Harpers Ferry; Amirus, a known supporter, may have met Brown personally. Certainly Amirus shared in the abolitionist ferment:

> As a little child, I heard my father tell of Frederick Douglass, Parker Pillsbury, Sojourner Truth, Wendell Phillips, and the rest of that advance army of reform-

ers, black and white, who went up and down the land arousing the dulled conscience of the people to a sense of justice to the slave. They used to make my father's home their stopping place, and any sort of vacant room was the forum where they told of the black man's wrongs.[7]

Clarence was old enough to have a vivid memory of the company of Union soldiers, some no more than boys themselves, recruited to serve in the Civil War:

> I hear a drum and fife coming over the hill, and I run to the fence and look down the gravelly road. A two-horse wagon loaded with men and boys, whose names and perhaps faces I seem to know, drives past me as I peer through the palings of the fence. They are dressed in uniform, and are proud and gay. In the center of the wagon is one boy standing up; I see his face plainly, and catch its boyish smile. They drive past the house to the railroad station, on their way to the Southern battle-fields.

And to that picture was shortly added another one, sad and stark:

> I recall a great throng of people, and among them all the boys and girls from school, and we are gathered inside the burying-ground where they are carrying the young soldier who rode past our house a few months before. I cannot remember what was said at the funeral, but this is the first impression that I can recall of the grim spectre of Death. What it meant to my childish mind I cannot now conceive. I remember only the hushed awe and the deep dread that fell upon us all when we realized that they were putting this boy into the ground and that we should never see his face again.[8]

Many other glimpses of death would be added to that first experience the young Clarence remembered so vividly, the combined influence of which tinged his character with morbidity and fatalism. For his happy childhood was overshadowed by the fact that Amirus, finding carpentry to be an insufficient livelihood by itself, had followed the path of many country cabinetmakers of his age and become the village undertaker.

Amirus's undertaking work was done in a shed next to the house. Clarence knew by childish intuition that his father dealt with death, and the wooden caskets made by his father were silent reminders of the fact. Like Oliver Twist, who slept in Mr. Sowerberry's workroom, Clarence was greatly fearful:

> I know that the sale of a coffin meant much more to him and his family than any piece of furniture that he could make. My father was as kind and gentle as anyone could possibly be, but I always realized his financial needs and even when very young used to wonder in a cynical way whether he felt more pain or pleasure over the death of a neighbor or friend. Any pain he felt must have been for himself, and the pleasure that he could not crowd aside must have come for the large family that looked to him for bread. I remember the coffins piled in one corner of the shop, and I always stayed as far away from them as possible, which I have done ever since. Neither did I ever want to visit the little shop after dark.

As he lay in the dark after being sent to bed, the shadows seemed to the boy's childish imagination full of phantoms and bogeymen, menacing, sinister, and malignant, who had escaped from his father's workshop. "All of us boys had a weird idea about darkness, anyhow. The night was peopled with ghosts and the wandering spirits of those who were dead," he recorded. Familiarity with mortality did not diminish his horror of it; "time and years have not changed or modified it, or made it any easier to reconcile or understand." Indeed Clarence's adult utterances were to be redolent with images of death and decay. He had an acute consciousness of mankind's mortality, viewing life as but a slow and somewhat tedious progress toward what he referred to as "the waiting grave." Essentially it was the resigned attitude of a religious, but without the expectation of salvation.

At six Clarence was sent to the district school, embarking upon a formal education most notable for its lack of distinction. His record gave no hint of promise for the future. "Never was there a time when I did not like to go to school," he said. "I always welcomed the first day of the term and regretted the last. The school life brought together all the children of the town." He loved the new friendships and games that school provided, and there learned to play baseball, which he described as "the only perfect pleasure we ever knew." "I have snatched my share of joys from the grudging hand of Fate as I have jogged along," he recalled, "but never has life held for me anything quite so entrancing as baseball; and this, at least, I learned at district school." Even the battles at Wrigley Field could not rival the purity and intensity of the Saturday afternoon games that Kinsman played against teams from surrounding villages. "When we heard of the professional game in which men cared nothing whatever for patriotism but only for money—games in which rival towns would hire the best players from a natural enemy—we could scarcely believe the tale was true. No Kinsman boy would any more give aid and comfort to a rival town than would a loyal soldier open a gate in the wall to let an enemy march in."

Clarence had his first taste of the approbation of a crowd thanks to baseball. One long afternoon when the Kinsman team stood a point from winning the game, it was his turn to bat:

> After one or two feeble failures to hit the ball, I swung my club just at the right time and place and with tremendous force. The ball went flying over the roof of the store, and rolled down to the river-bank on the other side. I had gone quite around the ring before anyone would get near the ball. I can never forget the wild ovation in which I ran around the ring, and the mad enthusiasm when the home-plate was reached and the game was over.

He recorded that his greatest regret at growing old was the fact that he had to give up playing ball; but he would never stop trying to repeat that triumph when he "knocked the ball over the dry-goods store and won the game."[9]

The young Clarence did not show a similar devotion to the subjects on the district school curriculum. He learned to read and write, but found the finer points of grammar impossible to master, and was not a diligent student. The antiquated syllabus of school stifled the boy's naturally inquiring spirit and made learning appear to be one of those unwelcome afflictions of youth, like acne, from which only time would bring relief. Luckily, though stifled, it was not destroyed and would reappear with added force once formal education had finished; the very paucity of his schooling made him eager for the real thing when it came his way.

Clarence's experience in district school was to be repeated at every level of formal education through which he passed—high school, college preparatory school, and law school. He never achieved academic distinction; nor did he desire to. His mature conclusion was that his school days were "an appalling waste of time," and he often disparaged the value of schooling, even though his brother Edward and his sisters Mary and Jennie all made teaching their careers and he himself was a teacher for a short while before practicing law.* His disparagement sprang from more than natural laziness and dislike of discipline, though he had both characteristics. He believed that schools pandered to orthodoxy by destroying independence of mind and that education suppressed the natural inclinations and spontaneity of children for no good purpose. He also had some suspicion that schools were institutions of establishment propaganda. He recognized on whose side the schools were in the continuing warfare between parents and children. "In our pieces and in our lessons a great deal was said about the duties that children owe to their parents, a great deal about how much our parents had done for us, and how kind and obedient we should be to them," he observed. "But I cannot recall that there was a single line about the duties that parents owe to children, and how much they should do for the child who had nothing to say about his own entrance into the world."[10]

School was the first of many institutions Clarence was to encounter that seemed to him far from perfect. Above all his objection to educational institutions was that they narrowed the mind, not widened it. Instead of encouraging thought they encouraged parrot-fashion learning; instead of originality they spawned unwarranted respect for the errors of a previous generation. He saw that the main function of schools was to keep children out of their parents' way during the day, and accepted that reason for their existence; but he did not approve of the skills schools taught, or the morality they preached. In his view the aim of all learning should be to make life easier, which he found mathematics (beyond simple arithmetic), ancient history, Latin, and Greek ill-suited to achieve. Most of all, however, Clarence later castigated the McGuffey Readers, which were the mainstay of his district school classes and followed him to the local academy. He was bitterly contemptuous of the complacent morality they taught. Yet their morality was not McGuffey's invention; it was simply the morality of his age. Like many other mid-Victori-

*Mary became principal of the James McCosh School, Chicago.

ans, McGuffey believed that virtue paid, and in this his books differed little
from the Horatio Alger tales. "Not one story in the book," Clarence recalled,

> told how any good could ever come from wilfulness, or selfishness, or greed, or
> that any possible evil ever grew from thrift, or diligence, or generosity, or
> kindness. And yet, in spite of all these precepts, we were young savages, always
> grasping for the best, ever fighting and scheming to get the advantage of our
> playmates, our teachers, and our tasks. . . . We were such striking examples of
> what the books would not do that one would almost think the publishers would
> drop the lessons out.[11]

Clarence reacted with no more favor to two other banes of his young life.
Neither Amirus nor his wife was totally unorthodox; they were loving but not
permissive parents who, raising their children in reliance on feeling rather than
logic, unconsciously followed most of the conventions of child-rearing even
while believing themselves unconventional. So they took their children to
Thursday prohibition meetings and Sunday school, and expected them to
behave like other little children. This orthodox side of his parents' regimen did
not please Clarence. On Thursday there was a ritualistic denunciation of the
demon drink:

> . . . up to the time when I was ten years old, I used to be dragged to church on
> Thursday night to listen to a Prohibition Meeting, and I will bet I signed the
> pledge a thousand times. There wasn't anything to drink within fifty miles of me,
> but I signed the pledge and everybody else did. The meetings were always held
> in churches, Presbyterian, Baptist or Methodist, as a rule. I am not crazy about
> them—I might just as well admit it.[12]

Sunday was undoubtedly the worst day of the week. It started with the ignominy of a thorough scrubbing: "Every Sunday morning our mother washed
our necks and ears; and no boy could ever see the use of this. Nothing roused
our righteous indignation quite so much as the forced washing of our necks.
The occasion, too, was really less on Sunday than on any other day, because
then we always wore some sort of stiff collar around our necks."[13] Once he had
been reduced to an unnatural state of cleanliness, Clarence was subjected to
a succession of exercises in godliness. Dressed like Little Lord Fauntleroy, he
was forced to endure two horrors—Sunday school and church. Church particularly repelled him by bringing out his morbid fears. "The church and the
graveyard were closely associated in my mind," he admitted. "It seemed to me,
as a little child, that the church had full jurisdiction of the yard, and that the
care and protection of the graves and their mouldering tenants were the chief
reasons why the church was there." That aside, he was not keen on prayers
or sermons. He remembered the prayer that was trotted out by the minister
every week:

> I could not have sat through that prayer, but for the fact that I learned to find
> landmarks as he went along. At a certain point I knew it was well under way;
> at another point it was about half-done; and when he began asking for guidance

and protection for the President of the United States, it was three-quarters over, and I felt like a shipwrecked mariner sighting land.[14]

Sermons, if anything, were worse. "I can never forget the horror and tortures of listening to an endless sermon when I was a child. Of course, I never understood a word of it, any more than did the preacher who harangued to his afflicted audiences."[15] Even after the service had ended, he was not free from tribulation, for "often on Sunday evening my father gathered us about the family table in the dining room and read a sermon from Channing or Theodore Parker or James Martineau."[16] By bedtime the consolations of religion seemed to young Clarence small indeed.

In this respect, as in many others, the child was father of the man. The deep-seated resentment of religion that gripped him when he was young burgeoned into the militant agnosticism of Darrow's prime. His childhood resentment of the demands of institutionalized piety became the basis of a lifelong theological irreverence which, coupled with his lack of enthusiasm for school, gave his mind its distinctive cast. Indeed his repudiation of religion was linked to his detestation of formal education, for McGuffey's Readers were, after all, mostly Sunday school fare that happened to be dished up on weekdays. His young mind lumped together the precepts of school and church, and he pretty well concluded that institutions organized for the supposed good of young boys were really devices for curbing their freedom.

Clarence did not hesitate to inform his parents that he saw no reason why he should suffer the travails of devotion and learning, and in arguing against them exploited to the full the incompatibility of his parents' advanced views on some matters with their entirely conventional attitude to others. Amirus and Emily probably did not see any clash between their radical views and the orthodox upbringing they gave to their children, but a child's mind is fresh and sensitive to such contradiction. Clarence was bewildered by the pattern of parental authority and, spotting its inconsistencies, sharpened his mind for the profession he was later to join: he was able to analyze, compare, and dissect most courses of conduct in the light of stated principles with such incisiveness that after he had finished there was no rhyme or reason to the affairs of life at all. "I was very young when I first began to wonder why the world was so unreasonable," he confessed. "It seemed to me as if our elders were in a universal conspiracy against us children; and we in turn combined to defeat their plans."[17] As he improved his skill by practice, contrariness became a game to be played for its own sake and in due course would be his hallmark. Indeed his defect was that he enjoyed this exercise so much that he rarely felt the need to go beyond it, with the consequence that one who followed his logic was, as it were, left dangling on the horns of a dilemma. In his maturity, his best argument was *reductio ad absurdum,* which—though refined through fifty years of practice—had its origins in the cunning tactics of a child fighting a rearguard action to delay and avoid the implementation of parental edicts.

Like all parents, Clarence's were convinced that they knew best. It was inconceivable to them that their son should not profit from his schooling. The guiding force of Amirus's life was the desire to study—so much so that in 1864, the year following Clarence's introduction to the district school, his father made one more determined effort to conquer the world of learning. He made the journey west to enroll in the law department of the University of Michigan, which had been established just five years before, and stayed there one academic year, 1864–1865. He was already forty-six years old, the father of six living children, and it seems extraordinary that he could afford the enterprise.

Amirus did not graduate, but he returned from Michigan with a fortified faith in education and a determination that Clarence should imbibe the wisdom of the ages. Why his ambition focused upon Clarence is not clear. Possibly his older sons had all, one way or another, proved unsuitable for what he had in mind. Perhaps Clarence already manifested signs of the marked talent he was to show as an adult for gaining attention, upstaging all his brothers and sisters. Clarence made his own view of the matter clear when he wrote, only half in jest: "I was only one of a large family, mostly older than myself; but while I was only one, I was the chief one, and the rest were important only as they affected me."[18] In any event it was Clarence for whom Amirus wished those successes that he himself had been unable to attain, and the more he saw with dismay that his favorite son was a long way from the top of his class at school, the more he resorted to home remedies, insisting that Clarence study away from school even if he did not study in it. He eagerly transferred to Clarence his thwarted ambition, hoping that fate would be on his son's side as it had not been on his.

Amirus set about supplementing his son's education at the village school by a prescribed course of home instruction. It was unfortunate for Clarence that one of the profoundest orthodoxies to which his father subscribed was that country children should strive to master the classics and ancient history, though they knew nothing of crop rotation, irrigation, the care of livestock, or any other practical skill. Amirus was not the last parent to hold up the prodigious example of John Stuart Mill, reputed to have had a knowledge of Greek by the age of three and Latin by the age of ten. "I shed many a tear and complained bitterly over the precocity of John Stuart Mill," Clarence recalled.[19] But misguided though he at first thought his father's efforts to be, Clarence later came to understand why he set so much store by them:

> I know that, all unconsciously, it was the blind persistent effort of the parent to resurrect his own buried hopes and dead ambitions in the greater opportunities and broader life that he would give his child. Poor man. I trust the lingering spark of hope for me never left his bosom while he lived, and that he died unconscious that the son on whom he lavished so much precious time and care never learned Latin after all, and never could.[20]

Fortunately his father encouraged other types of reading besides the classics, and so saved Clarence from remaining an ignoramus for life. His dislike of formal education was ultimately counterbalanced by his parents' inculcation of a love of books, and from them he made good many of the deficiencies of his formal education. Once he got over his initial reluctance to do his father's bidding, books became a major influence in his life, familiar companions of his leisure that fired his intellect more than anything except debate. Bookishness is often accompanied by a certain distance from reality, but Clarence came to combine it with a passionate interest in the world around him. He bridged the gap between study and action, thriving on controversy, no matter on what subject, so that the reflective calm of the library complemented the cut-and-thrust of argument. When he grew to maturity, his greatest addresses were derived in large part from book learning. Clarence's mind was not, as some admirers claimed, an original one—his ideas were clearly traceable to the authors most in circulation in his day—but he had the art of lifting ideas off the page and applying them directly to the real world. He was born too late to be called a child of the Enlightenment, but he was its grandchild; he had the energy, rebelliousness, and spirit of free inquiry of a Rousseau. Most of his convictions had clear antecedents in the rationalism of the eighteenth-century *philosophes,* with whom he shared a distrust of priests and kings as well as a yearning to overturn orthodoxy. In particular Voltaire exercised a strong influence on him, as interpreted by Robert Ingersoll, who established his fame during Clarence's formative years as "the American Voltaire." This rationalism remained his intellectual foundation, though in time it was supplemented by an overlay of Marxist economics and Darwinian determinism, also culled from books. What was unusual about Darrow was the synthesis he made of these various intellectual streams; he was a popularizer, whose intellectual disposition was immediately related to the world around him, and who became one of the best read men of his time, not only because of the quantity of books he had consumed but also because of his capacity to retain their ideas. In spite of his resentment of his father's prodding, the strength of his adult reading came to be that it was voluntary and enthusiastic, not compelled. "I do not recall ever having heard a book mentioned in his presence with which he was not thoroughly familiar," wrote George Leisure, who became an associate and friend in Darrow's later years.[21] This familiarity was to be a resource of extraordinary value in the construction of subtle arguments to which so much of Clarence's professional life was to be devoted.

The backdrop against which his schooldays were played out was therefore one of insistence on the value of education without any parental, but with much childish questioning of its utility—a skepticism that did not diminish with the passing years. At twelve Clarence left the district school and went to the local high school, known as "the academy on the hill." Enrolling at the academy brought him a new sense of importance, some new clothes, and greater opportunities for self-assertion. A sprawling, lanky youth, whose most striking features were his piercing blue eyes, Clarence felt for the first time the dawning of sexual interest in girls and became self-conscious in their presence, "but this was quite easily and rapidly overcome." Still the boys felt the difference from their relationship with the girls in the district school: "Now, we stood before them quite abashed and awed. They had put on long dresses, and had taken on a reserved and distant air; and much that we said and did in the Academy was with the conscious thought of how it would look to them."[22]

As in the district school, few of the pupils at the academy took their studies seriously. The system's precepts were almost totally irrelevant to the needs of the boys and girls of Kinsman, and they and their parents knew it. The terrors of Latin and algebra replaced English grammar and arithmetic on the syllabus, and Clarence responded negatively to both, though he did not communicate his lack of enthusiasm for the classics to his father, knowing that he set great stock by them. He did, however, once become the hero of his classmates by expressing his exasperation when faced with a technical problem of grammatical rectitude: he told his teacher that grammar did not matter much as, "When I have something to say, I can always say it." The statement proved prophetic, for though he never did learn grammar, Lincoln Steffens would admiringly agree sixty years later that Clarence's foremost characteristic was that "he can say anything he wants to say."[23] Experience did not temper the harsh judgment of Clarence's schooldays. "I have used language extensively all my life, and no doubt have misused it, too," he wrote. "In a way, I have made my living from its use, but I am convinced that I was rather hindered than helped in this direction by the public schools."

Clarence proceeded in regular but undistinguished course through the academy, but in his final year a pall hung over the normally happy Darrows, sapping the high spirits of all the children and conjuring up once more the boy's morbid nightmares. His mother, Emily, lay ill for months at home, courageously waiting for death. On June 14, 1872, a day when Clarence happened to be away, she died at the age of forty-eight, three years after bearing her last child, Jennie. "I never could tell whether I was sorry or relieved that I was not there," wrote Clarence at seventy-five, "but I still remember the blank despair that settled over the home when we realized that her tireless energy and devoted love were lost forever."

2

Becoming a Lawyer

Perhaps because his sister Mary had taken over the responsibility of supervising the younger children, Clarence's memory of his mother was scanty; "her figure has not that clearness and distinctiveness that I wish it had," he later wrote.[1] She had contended successfully with her husband's dreamy impracticality and inability to make money, not only attending to the household but helping out in the furniture business besides. Clarence admired the way in which, in spite of the press of practical necessity, she had always managed to share in her husband's interests and keep abreast of current politics: "I look back to my childhood and see the large family that she cared for, almost without help, I cannot understand how she did it all, especially as she managed to keep well-informed on the topics of the day, and found more time for reading and study than any of her neighbors did."[2] She was a supporter of female suffrage and Clarence remembered her as "an ardent woman's-rights advocate."

Although she was not religious, she was buried in the Kinsman churchyard. Clarence was deeply upset by her death and never afterwards liked to visit her grave, which he did only once. The references to his mother contained in his reminiscences smack somewhat of the conventionalized tributes that nineteenth-century sons paid to the ideal of motherhood. He portrayed her as a selfless, firm, but kindly parent. After her death, he felt guilty that he had taken her too much for granted and an "endless regret that I did not tell her that I loved her and did not do more to lighten the burdens of her life."[3] In an effort to make up for his dereliction, in his adult years he was inclined to pay tributes to her that went well beyond what custom required and perhaps ignored the resentments that lurked below. After all, it was she who had insisted that the children attend Sunday school and church; she who had made them sign the pledge, and even her parsimonious but efficient domestic economy—which Clarence identified as her major virtue—he scoffed at elsewhere as Ben Franklin's foolish precept of thrift.

As he grew to maturity, he came to feel that he had been insufficiently appreciative of both his parents:

> The world seems to take for granted that every parent is a hero to his children, and that they look to the father and mother as to almost superhuman beings whose power they cannot understand but can rely upon with implicit faith. ... But I cannot remember that in my youth either I, or any of my companions, had the feeling and regard for our parents that is commonly assumed. In fact, we believed that, as to wisdom and general ability to cope with the affairs of life, we were superior to them; and we early came to see their shortcomings rather than their strength.[4]

His mother's death strengthened this inclination and stifled any tendency to adolescent rebellion, for it was evident that without her his father was incapable of the simplest practicalities and needed the guidance of his elder children on the basic aspects of survival. In this condition, he was too gentle and unworldly to excite antagonism and too unsuccessful to excite envy. Instead, his vulnerability brought forth his son's love, and Clarence changed from boy to man in perfect harmony with his father. "More and more he made clear to us his intense desire that we should reach the things that had been beyond his grasp."[5]

This aspect of his maturing years had important consequences for Clarence's attitude as an adult, for it robbed him of a personalized form of rebellion such as most boys go through with their fathers. He avoided the frustrations of a father-son conflict, but suffered the equal frustration of having no one conveniently close at hand against whom to rebel. His spirited noncomformity in his mature years was in part the consequence of having to transfer this rebellion to a paternalistic society instead. The specter of his father's failure and inability to cope with the practicalities of living became a spur to his ambition. He did not reproach his father for lack of success, but rather blamed the society that kept a virtuous man poor and without influence. His father had failed because he was unworldly, but was that not a virtue in an imperfect world? Did the world's prizes in fact go to the good? Was integrity rewarded in this life? Clarence compared the qualities of the successful men of his age with those of his father and thought not: "sheer bunk," he called the theory.

As Clarence observed, his father had "neither by nature nor by training ... any business ability or any faculty for getting money." To his son, he came to be both an example and a warning. His father's unworldliness, naïveté, and faith appeared to be weaknesses, and the young Darrow was determined not to be like him. Consequently a dramatic reversal of the normal roles of father and son took place over the years. The father bowed to his son, and in his son's eyes became childlike: innocent, gentle, without guile. Taking pride in his son's success, and acknowledging his own knack of failing, Amirus later willingly became his son's pupil.

Emily's death did not lessen Amirus's efforts on behalf of his fourth son; on the contrary it seemed, if anything, to have intensified them. He continued his faith that "the magic wand that would free the Darrow brood of their parents' poverty was education."[6] At the end of the school year, in 1873, Clarence left the local academy and was sent away to the preparatory department of Allegheny College, his father's alma mater. Ambitious parents in the locality generally dispatched their children either to Oberlin or Allegheny, both of which advertised in the local newspapers, the latter declaring that there was "no better college in the country for poor boys and girls" than itself.[7]

It was a relief for Clarence to put the sorrow of death behind him and leave for the college at Meadville, even though its syllabus reflected a strongly classical preoccupation, not only continuing the hated Latin but adding Greek. He concluded, predictably, that "Greek was even more wasteful of time and effort than Latin." Other new subjects were geometry, botany, and zoology, the last two of which he enjoyed. But the emphasis in the curriculum was on the ancient world, mainly as revealed in the works of Virgil, Cicero, and Caesar, and he did badly. His appraisal of what he had learned at college coincided almost exactly with that of his professors: "I came back a better ball player for my higher education," he said. His lack of sympathy with the subject matter led him to neglect his studies, and he learned to despise the ancient languages even more. "Since I left Allegheny College I have never opened the lids of Virgil or any other Latin author, except in translation," he said. "I am inclined to believe that the age-long effort to keep the classics in schools and colleges has been an effort not to get knowledge but to preserve ignorance."

Possibly Clarence would have been forced to tell Amirus all this if his college education had been prolonged, but the depression of 1873 convinced him that it was unfair to allow his father to continue to meet his expenses, and he left Allegheny after a single year. Of the several Darrows who attended Allegheny College, only his sister Mary ever succeeded in graduating. According to Clarence:

> We left the school as ignorant of life as we commenced, nay, we might more easily have learned its lesson without the false, misleading theories we were taught were true. When the doors were opened and the wide world met us face to face, we tested what we learned and found it false, and then blundered on alone. We were taught by life that the fire and vigor of our younger years could not be governed by the platitudes of age.[8]

At the age of sixteen the formalities of his general education had ceased forever, and he was thrust onto the none-too-welcoming labor market of Kinsman with no practical skill in the midst of a depression. In the long run he would have no cause to regret leaving college; indeed in one way his lack of a college education would be a major intellectual asset. One of the reasons that Darrow's nimble mind came to be viewed as original, and seemed so unpredictable in debate, was that, not having been molded by the conventions of a college curriculum, it retained a fresh perspective. He often congratulated himself on having avoided a college education.

But in the short run he was caught without any notion of what he wanted to do. Like all boys, he had dreams: "How many dreams we dreamed, how many visions we saw,—visions of our manhood, our great strength, and the wonderful achievements that would some day resound throughout the world!"[9] Of great achievements he was sure, but their shape lacked definition, and until that was settled, he had to do something. So he was set to work in his father's furniture store, which at least was better than farm work. (He had worked one summer for a farmer for $15 a month and not liked it at all.) But carpentry was not to his taste either: "I was never fond of manual labor," he recalled. "I felt I was made for better things. I fancy all boys and girls harbor the same delusion." His stay in his father's business was short, though that did not stop local folk from claiming to have furniture made by Clarence Darrow once he was famous.

In fact he apparently spent most of his energies during his sojourn in his father's workshop trying to get out rather than producing tables and chairs. To escape it, though pedagogy was unappealing, he became a schoolteacher at Vernon, a village about 7 miles south of Kinsman. Darrow got the job because there were no other takers and he came cheap. It must have occurred to him that there was small hope of improvement in the school system if teachers were recruited in the way he was. From his own account of his schooldays, and from his mediocre record at the preparatory school of Allegheny College, it is hard to imagine that any of his own mentors could recommend him with enthusiasm. The pay was poor even by the prevailing standards of the teaching profession: $30 a month plus room and board. During the week he stayed at different houses of the local residents, returning to Kinsman only at the weekend. This suited him well: "Boarding around was not so bad. I was 'company' wherever I arrived, and only the best was set before me. I had pie and cake three times a day."

The arrangement was satisfactory enough to both sides to be continued for three successive winters, even though the new teacher—giving a glimpse of what his future might hold—defied convention by abolishing corporal punishment and lengthening the lunchbreak. He made no claim that he imparted much knowledge to his young charges, regarding it as a sufficient justification of his unorthodox methods that they enjoyed themselves. The most momentous aspect of Darrow's years as a teacher was that they provided him with time to embark upon the study of law: "Every Monday morning, as I started off to teach my school, I took a law book with me, and having a good deal of time improved it fairly well."

Clarence Darrow was never able to identify what impelled him to enter the legal profession, though he acknowledged that its showy aspects attracted him. The decision was one that he often doubted to be wise in the light of his subsequent experience, believing that law practice was sterile and confining and had prevented him from developing talents more admirable than those the law required. Periodically throughout his later life quite different ambitions would surface to distract him from the duties of his chosen profession, the most notable being his recurring desire for literary laurels. "I have always wanted to write a book," he confessed:

> I remember when I was very small, and used to climb on a chair and look at the rows of books on my father's shelves, I thought it must be a wonderful being who could write all the pages of a big book, and I would have given all the playthings that I ever hoped to have for the assurance that some day I might possibly write down so many words and have them printed and bound in a book.[10]

He would come in time to resent the law for making it impossible, as he believed, to take his rightful place as a man of letters. But as a boy on the threshold of a career, none of these conflicts were apparent to him and he did not recognize that by plumbing for one aspect of his diffuse ambitions, he was unconsciously suppressing others. Later he concocted a humorous answer to inquiries by journalists and earnest admirers about the secret of his success, based upon the memories of his $15-a-month summer. Most people attributed their success to hard work, he was told. "Put me down for that too," he responded. "I was brought up on a farm. When I was a young man, on a very hot day I was engaged in distributing and packing down the hay which a horse-propelled stacker was constantly dumping on top of me. By noon, I was completely exhausted. That afternoon, I left the farm, never to return, and I haven't done a day of hard work since."[11] Darrow appreciated the value of a good myth, such as the fictitious meeting with John Brown, or the pieces of furniture he had allegedly made; but his story was an amusing embroidery of his experience of harvesting. In fact the reason most strongly propelling him was the desire of his father and Edward and Mary to see him become a lawyer. Edward and Mary, who had both spent some time at the University of Michigan, were now teaching school and bringing in money regularly. They knew that their father's ambitions had set upon Clarence, who had become the apple of his father's eye, and that he was keen that Clarence should follow him to the law department at Ann Arbor. Besides, they liked Clarence and had faith that he could succeed if given the chance. So, after the third winter that he taught the Vernon school, they encouraged him to enroll at the University of Michigan at their expense, and he entered in 1877.

The days were still far off when bar associations laid down minimum requirements of college and law school credits; bar admission was given simply upon passing the bar examination. This meant that even boys of poor families could, by diligence and sacrifice, meet the standards. University study was neither required nor usual for prospective lawyers, and as the university's catalogue expressed the law department's standards of entry: "The sole requisites for admission are that the candidate should be eighteen years of age, and be furnished with certificates giving satisfactory evidence of good moral character. No previous course of reading is required. . . ."[12] That very year, however, the department felt it wise to add that it was "expected that all students will be well grounded in at least a good English education, and capable of making use of the English language with accuracy and propriety." Apparently Clarence was not the only one among the 384 students enrolled in the Michigan law department to whom the finer points of grammar caused difficulty; in 1889 the dean was to write, somewhat defensively: "if the reader

is here disposed to criticize, let him remember that the other law schools
throughout the country were then no more stringent in their requirements
governing the admission of students. . . ."[13]

Michigan boasted some distinguished professors while Clarence Darrow
attended it, including Cooley and Campbell, successively Chief Justices of
Michigan. Cooley was the American editor of a much-used version of Black-
stone's *Commentaries,* and his *Constitutional Limitations* was already in its
third edition by the time Darrow went to Ann Arbor. Yet Clarence followed
the precedent he had set at Allegheny College by matriculating but not graduating. After one year he decided to prepare for the bar examination by studying
in a lawyer's office. He was acutely conscious of the financial burden his
attendance at Michigan imposed upon Edward and Mary, and knew it would
be far cheaper to become an apprentice. In any case his generation still regarded clerking in a law office as the proper preparation for practice at the
bar.* The changeover to institutional education took place only after the
longhand copying work that an apprentice could do was eliminated by the
typewriter, and when part-time law schools could be run at night after the
invention of the electric light bulb.

Darrow's departure from the University of Michigan marked the end of his
formal education. Its most notable aspect was that, without exception, he had
done badly. In spite of his fierce desire for truth, his avid reading, and his
consistent pursuit of the pleasures of the mind, he was no scholar. This was
to have profound consequences for his future, for the fact that he had not been
through the educational mill explained both his strengths and weaknesses as
a controversialist. His brilliant mind was unconfined by convention, with the
result that he was capable of extraordinary flashes of insight while simultaneously revealing huge blind spots. His thirst for learning was never quenched
—but he was unmethodical and partisan in his lines of inquiry. To the end he
remained ill-disciplined and untrained; a teacher would have admonished him
for "lack of application." In this respect the pattern of his schooldays turned
out not to be greatly different from the pattern of his life. His failure to prepare,
to do the plodding, unexciting work that assured success, relying instead on
inspiration, luck, and his ability to "rise to an occasion," was notorious among
his colleagues. When he worked at all, it was in short bursts. His successes were
pulled off by improvisation, not solid groundwork. At school, where what was
tested was the accumulation of knowledge over a semester, Clarence did not
shine because he had not applied himself consistently. The verdict of his term
reports was therefore unfavorable, but that did not mean, as he himself was
wont to say, that it had been a total waste. If he had not learned much, he had
learned something; and if it had not been a welcome education, it had been

---

*In so doing, he acted contrary to the intention attributed by the school's dean to the taxpayers
of Michigan, who, by establishing the law school, "discarded the old notion that the place to learn
law is in the lawyer's office, rather than in a University. A law school was established because
it was thought that there the law could best be learned"—Henry Wade Rogers, "The Law School
of the University of Michigan," 1 Green Bag (1889), p. 190.

an influential one, which provided in embryo all the targets that he became a celebrity by attacking.

He determined to do his law office studying during 1878 in Youngstown, Ohio, the nearest community of any size in his part of the state, with a population of about 20,000. It is not known with whom he studied, but the likelihood is that arrangements were made for him by his cousin, Burdett O. Eddy, who was official stenographer in the Youngstown courts and who had attended the Michigan law department only three years before Clarence.

After some months of study Clarence felt that he could face the bar examiners, and together with a dozen others he presented himself to the committee of lawyers who were entrusted with the job of testing applicants. The proceedings were entirely oral, and the decision was reached on the spot, so that candidates were not held in suspense. There was a jocular and sympathetic spirit to these occasions. "The committee did not seem to take it as seriously as examiners do today," he reported. "I was not made to feel that the safety of the government or the destiny of the universe was hanging on their verdict." He remembered the bar examiners with some fondness—no doubt because they passed him. "They were all good fellows and wanted to help us through," he said. His recollection was that they passed everyone who presented himself on that occasion. If that is so, his experience was unrepresentative; on other dates the bar examiners of Ohio turned out not to be wholly good fellows and had the audacity to fail some applicants.[14] For him they came up trumps, and he was admitted to the bar at the age of twenty-one.

When Clarence emerged triumphant, a licensed lawyer, it must have been a poignant day for Amirus, prompting wistful thoughts of what might have been. But no hint of self-pity spoiled his son's glory: "He was delighted and possibly surprised, at my good luck. Poor man, he was probably thinking what he could have done had Fortune been so kind to him. But, like most parents, the success of his son was his success."

Now that Clarence had a profession, if not a practice, he felt himself on the verge of adulthood. He could have remained a bachelor, unencumbered by the problems of supporting anyone but himself. Instead, he got married less than two years after his admission to the bar. He had taken a fancy to Jessie Ohl, the daughter of a modestly prosperous local family, whom he had known through the years of adolescence and whose company he sought out at the Saturday night dances that were the highlight of Kinsman's social calendar. The Ohl family fortunes had been founded by Michael Ohl, who had built the local grist- and sawmill near Warren, a business that had grown enough for it to be the most noteworthy in the immediate area and to justify calling the settlement around it Ohltown. This enterprise had provided capital that was invested in farmland around Crookston, Minnesota, and managed with much aplomb by Jessie's parents, who spent more time there than in Ohio. Clarence was sufficiently interested in Jessie to make the journey of 800 miles to visit her in Crookston, where she spent her summers, soon after his admission to the bar. On April 15,

1880, Clarence and Jessie were married in the home of Jessie's brother in Sharon, Pennsylvania. In view of the circumstances and the times, his choice of Jessie as a wife was entirely appropriate. By northeastern Ohio's modest standards, it was a good match; and as his father had done before him, Clarence had married into a family more prosperous than his own.

Yet, the exhilaration of his newly acquired status as a lawyer was punctured very quickly by the attitude of friends and neighbors. They congratulated Clarence on his success, but they did not give him work. In their eyes, he was still a boy with no more wisdom than local boys normally had. "They could not conceive that a boy whom they knew, and who was brought up in their town, could possibly have the ability and learning that they thought was necessary to the practice of law." He saw that to gain the esteem of his locality, it was necessary to move away. At first he considered going far afield, moving westward. The pioneering era was still within living memory and young men of Darrow's generation felt the romance of pressing on toward yet newer settlements. Northern Ohioans of the period looked to Kansas as a land of promise, and Clarence scouted the possibility of settling in McPherson.[15] "I looked the town over, and thought it was all right; so I rented an office, but did not take possession," he wrote much later. ". . . I never did go back to take that office. I don't know whether they have held it for me all these years, but I have been a little afraid to go back for fear I would be sued for the back rent."[16] Instead of crossing the Great Plains to McPherson, he decided to stay much closer to home and set up in Andover. It was a distance of only 10 miles from Kinsman, but that was far enough to get away from immediate neighbors. Here, he hoped, he would be accepted as an attorney to whom professional business could safely be entrusted. He had considered setting up shop in Youngstown, where he had done his apprenticeship, but it intimidated him: "it was a city of twenty thousand people, and I felt awed by its size and importance."

As it turned out, Andover was not a good choice of location, for the opportunities it offered to a lawyer were extremely limited; it had never had any substantial economic basis and its chief claim to fame was that it had been an early center of abolitionist settlement. As Clarence observed, "it would not have been possible to build up what lawyers call 'a good practice' where my name was first posted on an office door." Although in 1883 the Ashtabula *Sentinel* devoted three columns of its first page to describing "the thriving town of Andover" in a manner that might persuade a reader unfamiliar with the area that a great city was arising, the truth was that Andover was too small to provide regular remunerative work. It did not even have a bank until 1884, four years after Clarence and Jessie moved there. The few businesses in Andover and the neighboring farmers provided only a modest and erratic living to a young lawyer and in consequence, as he admitted, "I did not succeed at first." When, as he put it, he flung his shingle to the breeze, he had had to borrow money from the Ohls to pay for the books he needed. Nevertheless he began to build a reputation. "My business, as it slowly opened up, grew out of the horse trades, boundary lines, fraudulent representations, private quarrels and grudges, with which the world everywhere is rife. There were actions of debt, actions of replevin, cases of tort, and now and then a criminal complaint." In other words, his practice had all the ingredients that combine to keep a country practitioner moderately busy without letting him become rich. For the first two years in Andover his home, a small apartment above a shoe store, doubled as his office. His earnings were less than he had made teaching school in Vernon and after a few months the Darrows took in a boarder, a young lawyer by the name of James Roberts, with whom Clarence planned to practice as well as live. Roberts, eighteen months younger than Darrow and only recently admitted to the bar, was the son of Kinsman's blacksmith. But the arrangement lasted only a short time, because Roberts stole Clarence's lawbooks and disappeared.

In spite of this setback to his ambitions, Clarence persevered and within two years he had a separate office, which he shared with another lawyer, J. S. Morley. The local newspaper was able to report that "Lawyer Darrow now has a pleasant and comfortable office in which to entertain callers. . . . Messrs. Morley and Darrow look cozy as you please in their new quarters."[17] Cozy they might be, but busy they were not, and Clarence was forced to advertise his availability, attempting to exemplify the rule laid down by a contemporary periodical by which "it is the sons of poor men who become eminent in the legal profession." In those days the art of oratory was considered an essential attribute of a lawyer, more important than a command of the dry technicalities of pleading. Times had not changed much since, thirty years before, Abraham Lincoln had advised law students to practice speaking: "It is the lawyer's avenue to the public," he said. "However able and faithful he may be in other respects, people are slow to bring him business if he cannot make a speech."[18] There was a chance to be flamboyant on the special occasions of the country calendar on which a speech was in order. "When I was still quite young," Darrow recalled, "the lawyers from the county seat always visited our town on all public occasions. On the Fourth of July and on Decoration Day, in all political campaigns and on all holidays, they made speeches and were altogether the most conspicuous of the locality." And he frankly admitted to finding that aspect of the bar appealing; "young men are ambitious to get into the law game largely because it is a showy profession, and is one that lets a man enjoy the limelight."[19] Something impelled him to addressing crowds rather than being part of them. In *Farmington,* a fictionalized account of his childhood, Darrow described the glamour he found in these opportunities and his desire to emulate the grandees who addressed the crowds on these days, especially the local squire, who read the Declaration of Independence:

> We thought it was something Squire Allen wrote, because he always read it, and we did not think anyone else could read the Declaration of Independence. . . . When Squire Allen finally got through the reading he introduced the speaker of the day. This was always some lawyer who came from Warren, the county

seat, twenty miles away. I had seen the lawyer's horse and buggy at the hotel in the morning, and I thought how nice they were and how much money a lawyer must make and what a great man he was and how I should like to be a lawyer and how long it took and how much brains. The lawyer never seemed to be a bit afraid to stand up on the platform before the audience, and I remember that he wore nice clothes, and his boots looked shiny, as though they had just been greased. He talked very loud and seemed to be mad about something, especially when he spoke of the war and the "Bridish," and he waved his hands and arms a great deal, and made quite a fuss about it all.[20]

Darrow determined that he should be the one who spoke rather than listened, and he deliberately imitated the rococo bombast then thought to be the highest state of the speaker's art. By 1881 he began to obtain engagements around the locality. He was scheduled to deliver the Fourth of July oration at Jamestown, Pennsylvania, which was just that year planning to celebrate the aniversary for the first time. But on July 2 Guiteau made his attempt on the life of President Garfield, so the program of the Fourth was overshadowed and Darrow missed his chance of being reported. Amends were made in August, however, when he received high praise for his performance at the Third Annual Wayne Harvest Home. The Ashtabula *Sentinel* commented that "his eulogy on the man who lives in the home of his fathers was beautiful and worthy of consideration and we think was appreciated. His speech was good throughout. Although a young man, he had evidently given his subject thought and presented it in such a manner as to create a very favorable impression."[21] Evidently he was still imbued with most of the values and assumptions of his rural upbringing. In the midst of a nation peopled by immigrants who had traveled from afar, whose history was a restless migration from East to West and from the country to the city, the young Darrow assured his audience that the highest virtue was to remain where their families had been before them. He was unabashedly feeding the small-town appetite for windy oratory to which Buncombe gave its name; but in this taste Buncombe County was not discernibly different from Jamestown or Andover or any other rural American community in the same era, and mere chance singled its name out for the dubious honor of passing into the language as a synonym for hot air. Still the pat on the back from the *Sentinel,* which was edited by Joseph A. Howells, brother of William Dean Howells who edited the *Atlantic Monthly,* must have pleased Darrow considerably. Chance served him well in presenting this connection with the distinguished Howells. Later the famous brother and he were both to plead for clemency for the Haymarket anarchists—sentenced to death in Chicago—and Darrow was to impress acquaintances by laying a somewhat dubious claim to having the editor's ear on literary matters.

The confidence gained from these early appearances fed upon itself, and from this time on, Darrow was established as a speaker of ability. In both 1883 and 1884 Andover itself honored him by choosing him to give the Memorial Day address. Granted that he was an embattled Democrat in a Republican stronghold, this was itself a considerable achievement, for such occasions as gave an opportunity for oratorical display tended to be regarded as Republican monopolies. "Lawyers, of course, were Republicans," attested a native of northern Ohio, "else how could they deliver patriotic addresses on Decoration Day and at the reunions of the 66th regiment?"[22] At first Darrow did not flaunt his political heresy, and steered clear of overtly partisan topics. He took all the opportunities he could to spread his fame, even addressing the Andover Temperance League on one occasion—though what he said has not been preserved. These early platform appearances were, of course, one of the few means of self-advertisement open to a young lawyer and were worth making for that reason alone; but aside from that, Darrow's yearning for public attention impelled him to seek speaking engagements for the sheer pleasure they gave him, regardless of the occasion or the subject to be discussed. In so doing he adopted the canting, platitudinous style of the times, dwelling upon the beauties of nature, the happiness of the farmer's lot, the perfection of the American Republic, and the excellence of northeastern Ohio just as his peers did. Few of those who sat on the grass eating their box lunches at a harvest picnic as they listened to Darrow declaim would have dreamed that he was destined to become the most outspoken radical of his generation, who would hold Chicago and the nation enthralled by his daring attacks on nearly all America's sacred cows. Later he acknowledged the shortcomings of his early efforts: "In those days I was rather oratorical. Like many other young men of that day, I did the best, or worst, I could to cover up such ideas as I had in a cloud of sounding metrical phrases." But people listened, even to commonplace themes, if expressed with enough orotundity.

There were not enough public holidays to assuage his appetite for speaking; so the main outlet of his histrionic abilities automatically became politics. And politics rapidly became an avocation, which Brand Whitlock characterized as "the fate of most Ohioans"—not to talk politics, he observed, "in Ohio dooms one to a silence almost perpetual."[23] Darrow, already loquacious, became active in the Democratic Party. It was unthinkable to him that he should work for the Republican interest, but he espoused the Democracy only as the lesser of two evils, believing that of the two major parties it stood for a fairer distribution of wealth. "Living in the North, and holding these views, I have always been driven to the support of the Democratic party, with few illusions as to what it meant." He was casting his lot with the minority of Ashtabula County, but there was no harm in that, since even though nearly all the locality's lawyers were Republicans, party differences did not prevent professional cooperation.

By 1884 Darrow had become secretary of the Ashtabula County Democratic Convention and was elected its delegate to the district convention in neighboring Warren after a "spicy and interesting discussion."[24] From that time forward, party-sponsored functions provided him with an outlet for his abundant energies, and Democratic meetings seem to have been among the liveliest of the countryside's diversions. On October 3 he addressed a meeting at Smith's Opera House in Ashtabula at which "the house was crowded to

excess and many were turned away unable to gain admittance." Free trade was
a major issue in Grover Cleveland's campaign for election and one of the main
bones of contention between the protectionist Republicans and the Democrats
in 1884. Darrow debated the subject with one of the locality's leading Republicans: "We hope everyone will attend as such a discussion cannot but do good
to the Republican cause," declared the Republican *Sentinel.*[25]

As it turned out, Grover Cleveland and free trade won the election. Darrow
was a lifelong admirer of Cleveland. He would later say:

> As political questions have come and gone I have clung in my political allegiance
> to the doctrines of states' rights and free trade. To me they are as true and almost
> as important as they were in the historical campaign of 1884, when Cleveland
> was elected President of the United States. . . . For a young man I took considera-
> ble part in each of the three campaigns for Grover Cleveland, and then, and ever
> since, this President has been one of my idols. His courage, independence and
> honesty have always seemed far above those of most of the political figures of
> his time, or since his day.

In view of the Democrats' failure to win a national election since the Civil War,
Cleveland's success was an occasion for a "grand jollification" in Ashtabula,
at which Darrow again spoke. "Democratic enthusiasm which had been put
up for 24 years' past, burst out and the town was painted a bright crimson."[26]

In the midst of all this political activity Clarence and Jessie became parents
of a son. Paul Edward Darrow was born on December 10, 1883, in Andover.
The event no doubt impressed Clarence with the need to consolidate his career
and indirectly led him to reevaluate his position. One of the consequences of
his political involvement had been to focus his activities more and more in
Ashtabula, though he was still living in Andover. Ashtabula, some 30 miles
northwest of Andover, was by far the more important community, with a
population of 5,000, and nearly all significant meetings were held there. The
contacts he made through the Democratic organization tended to be concentrated there and its opportunities of all sorts were larger than Andover's. But,
most important, Darrow had acquired confidence from his immersion in politics and by now felt that he "was too big" for Andover. So, immediately after
the elections, the Democratic *Standard* reported that "C. S. Darrow, Esq., of
Andover, is contemplating moving to Ashtabula to engage in the practice of
law there."[27] Within five months he had made the move pay.

His reappraisal of Andover as a forum for his talents had further significance. Ashtabula was the hub of northern Ohio's commerce, being a railroad
stop of some consequence and a Great Lakes port. Settled by Yankees, it had
been known for its enlightened and literate politics since before the Civil War;
when William Dean Howells's family moved there in 1852, he noted that
"everyone in town that summer seemed to be reading a new novel entitled
Uncle Tom's Cabin."[28] Within Darrow's terms, the move was an important
step toward the fulcrum of politics and commerce. His achievements there
were what emboldened him three years later to make another move without

which America would probably never have heard of him. He was still feeling his way, setting his sights on targets at close range. He was torn between two models of success: one, conservative and sensible, dictated steady, moderate progression by well-considered moves; the other, which easily took hold of a young man's imagination in his expansive moments, dictated one giant stride to the forefront of national life. As Darrow grew to maturity, the latter possibility seemed to be part of America's promise. The young were catapulted into the public eye as captains of industry, inventors, and political and religious authorities, so that it seemed that for some the gap between rags and riches could be swiftly closed. The time was not far off when William Jennings Bryan, three years younger than Darrow, would become known—in a popular phrase of the age—as a "boy wonder," having achieved the Democratic nomination for the presidency at the age of thirty-six. The move from Andover was a sign, not only of Darrow's inner will to succeed, but of the restless impatience for recognition with which his entire generation had been imbued.

His name and ability were already known in Ashtabula. He had often visited it for political meetings and had litigated in its Court of Common Pleas, whose Judge Laban S. Sherman had been a successful practitioner in the town for many years prior to his election to the bench. Sherman recognized both Darrow's nascent talent and his pressing need for income. Although a Republican, Sherman used his considerable influence on Darrow's behalf, introducing him to the leading Republicans of the Ashtabula bar and recommending him to run for the office of Ashtabula borough city solicitor, which paid $75 a month and left its incumbent with enough free time to take cases on the side. Modest though this office was, it was an auspicious first step for one so young. It could mean one of many victories at the polls to come as he trod an established path to distinction. With minor variations, the pattern was clear: "It was natural for a young man to be a lawyer, then to be elected prosecuting attorney, then to go to the legislature, then to congress, then—governor, senator, president."[29] Darrow was elected without contest on Monday, April 6, 1885, and from then on appeared regularly in the local courts.

The petty disputes of the courts of Ohio were fought with cunning and imagination by the local bar, and Darrow's experience in those backwoods forums would stand him in good stead in his subsequent career. Indeed he was to look back on those days as an invaluable training ground, proving the saying that Chicago lawyers were made in the country:

> Much of the business of the country lawyer in my day was the trial of cases before justices of the peace. These often seemed to be exciting events. And right now I am not sure but that the old-time country lawyers fighting over the title to a cow were as clever, and sometimes as learned, as lawyers now whose cases involve millions of dollars, or human lives. The trials then were not such a matter of rote. A lawsuit, then, before a justice of the peace, was filled with color and life and wits. Nor was the country lawsuit a dry and formal affair. Every one, for miles around, had heard of the case and taken sides between the contending parties or their lawyers. Neighborhoods, churches, lodges, and entire communi-

ties were divided as if in war. Often the cases were tried in the town halls, and
audiences assembled from far and near. An old-time lawsuit was like a great
tournament, as described by Walter Scott. The combatants on both sides were
always seeking the weakest spots in the enemy's armor, and doing their utmost
to unhorse him or draw blood.

The young Darrow learned his lessons well in those country courts. There he
gained the confidence to face the world, dealing with replications and replev-
ins, assumpsit and trespass, and the technicalities of pleading. But perhaps the
greatest lesson of all was the recognition that lawsuits, no matter how trivial,
engaged the emotions of the parties and their attorneys, sometimes leaving
wounds that never healed. He did not believe in dispassionate advocacy. He
knew that he must fight hard, meaning to win, and that he was most effective
when his heart was in his client's cause so that, as he put it, "it seemed as if
my life depended upon the result." Not only did he not believe in dispassionate
advocacy: he was incapable of it. Once possessed by an emotion, he could not
rid himself of it; there was an obsessive aspect to his make-up that would not
let him rest after his feelings were engaged. "His power and his weakness is
in the highly sensitive, emotional nature which sets his seeing mind in motion
in that loafing body," Lincoln Steffens remarked.[30]
Darrow was by nature a partisan, unable to detach himself from the plight
of his clients, and the motive power of his advocacy was always feeling more
than intellect. "I have unconsciously and perhaps even consciously tried to
make life worth while by seeking to work out my strongest emotions," he
confessed, knowing that there was no other way for him.[31] It was a realization
that was to have profound consequences for his career, for ever afterward he
tried to avoid arguing cases in which he did not believe. Conversely, he
deliberately argued cases in which he did believe even though the amount at
stake was trivial, and the earliest example dated from his days in Ohio. The
son of a prosperous family, a notorious drunk, had ordered a harness on credit
and omitted to pay for it, in consequence of which an attempt to repossess it
from an innocent third party was made. The value of the harness was only $25,
but Darrow was incensed at the principle that an innocent person should suffer
because of the default of a rich drunk. He fought the case through the courts
twice, and with E. B. Leonard, a leading local Republican as co-counsel, finally
prevailed in the Supreme Court of Ohio, paying the costs himself. (Perhaps
Judge Jacob F. Burket, who delivered the opinion of the Court, understood
the determination of the young attorney who finally won the case; he shared
much the same background as Darrow, and was in a position to know the
intensity of feeling engendered by a country feud.) The case—*Brockway* v.
Jewell—is still occasionally cited in Ohio as an authority on the rights of a
creditor to repossess and it stands as an early monument to Darrow's personal
commitment to a client's cause.[32]
The move to Ashtabula meant that for the first time Darrow was soundly
based financially; his part-time job paid from the public purse gave him security that made private practice viable. He was not specially interested in office

for its own sake but he wanted the income it provided, realizing that a pay-check was a cushion against lawyering's fluctuating and sometimes uncollect-ible fees. (He would contrive to be on a public payroll for a considerable portion of the next decade.)

Apart from attending to his official duties, Darrow was now able to take cases on his own account, and managed to do well at it, especially while acting in concert with another local attorney by the name of Charles Lawyer, Jr. Lawyer, the son of a doctor, was a Republican, but the different persuasions of the two men did not prevent their amiable professional cooperation; rather, rivalry between them in seeking party favor was conveniently avoided. When Darrow had visited his in-laws in Minnesota in 1883, Lawyer occupied his office while he was away, and the following year they engaged in some modest real estate speculation together. Both of them had started out in Andover, but when Darrow left for Ashtabula, Lawyer moved to Jefferson, the county seat. Nevertheless they continued to share cases, and appeared together on behalf of the wife in a divorce case that aroused some local interest. The ground of the wife's suit was gross neglect and extreme cruelty, and the witnesses in-volved numbered about a hundred. The wife was successful and obtained alimony of $1,200. In addition, both Darrow and Lawyer defended indigent prisoners, for which they were paid by the county.[33] Lawyer, like Darrow, made his way in the world and later became an Ohio state senator.

Darrow was able to take even more interest in Democratic politics than he had before. In August 1885 he represented the county at the party's state convention in Columbus. In October he ran for Senate seat in the General Assembly, but was soundly beaten by the Republicans. The following year he ran as Democratic candidate for the post of Prosecuting Attorney, but again the Republicans won with ease. By running he kept the party flag flying and his own name before the voters; he was a party stalwart doing his duty. In neither of these contests can he have had any faith that he had a chance of winning—the Republican vote in Ashtabula County had outweighed the Democrats by about three to one from time immemorial—but it showed willingness, he enjoyed it, and it provided him with further local fame. He had only managed to become city solicitor by running on a nonpartisan basis, and because no one else wanted the job; but these experiences built up his confi-dence, and gave him the sangfroid essential to a public figure.

At the same time his horizons were being further expanded through reading. He had persisted in the bad habits of a bookworm, and in this he was not alone. Backwater though northeastern Ohio might be, it nurtured men of intellect with the will to explore social issues. There were lively minds to be found in the small towns dotted among the farms. The very isolation of such communi-ties meant that the lessons taught by books were well learned; in fact the foundations of all Darrow's thinking on political economy and criminology were laid through books to which he was introduced at this time by Ashtabula companions. It was the cashier of the Farmer's National Bank, Amos Fisk Hubbard, who advised him to read Henry George's *Progress and Poverty,* first published in 1879. The book's influence on Darrow was to prove enormous. Not only did he build upon George's views ever after, but it encouraged him to seek wider audiences than Ashtabula could offer. To a young man born into a farming community of propertyless parents who, in spite of all endeavors, remained poor, it seemed self-evident that a tax on the increase in value of land would set many social evils to right. Besides, the main themes of George's work were ideally suited to platform presentation; their logical outlines were clear and the data upon which they relied were, as George himself proclaimed in his introduction, derived from "common experience and observation." Darrow soon incorporated them into his growing repertoire.

The writings of John Peter Altgeld also reached Darrow in Ashtabula through another friend, Judge Richards of the local police court. Altgeld, a German immigrant who had made a considerable amount of money in the New World, had brought with him some political assumptions traceable to his interest in the unification of his native land. He used the printing press and the mails to build up grass-roots support. Like most immigrants, Altgeld had found his success in the city, but he had not forgotten that the rural vote was decisive in obtaining statewide elective office. (His life in America had started in Mansfield, Ohio—some 100 miles west of Darrow's birthplace—to which his parents had brought him from Prussia.) He thus invested in a continuing program of pamphleteering to scattered communities throughout the Midwest, where he believed his ideas might find support.

The first of his works to come to Darrow's attention was *Our Penal Machinery and Its Victims.* At the beginning of 1887 Altgeld, having been elected a judge of the superior court of Cook County the previous November, had sent 10,500 free copies out through the Middle West, including one to Judge Richards. "Of public officials, clergymen, writers and lecturers, group leaders of one kind or another of any prominence anywhere, there were few who did not receive a copy," wrote his biographer. "He handled most of this work himself, mulling over lists of names as industriously as a mail-order advertiser."[34] And, in a sense, Altgeld was a mail-order advertiser. By distributing his book, he was advertising himself in order to further his political ambitions by attracting into his fold just such bright young spirits as Darrow. Altgeld's instinct was sound, for in rural areas where books were scarce, people were liable to read anything that was sent to them free, regardless of its subject. The book was an attempt to change prevailing attitudes toward crime, modern in its concern with etiology and its rejection of explanations of crime predicated upon the innate sinfulness of criminals. Like his transatlantic contemporary Samuel Butler, looking over Erewhon, he saw the futility of punishing men for things over which they had no control. He impressed Darrow: ". . . up to that time I had the conventional view of crime and criminals. In a vague way I believed that a criminal was somewhat different from other men. He was evil and malignant, because he deliberately chose that way of life. I never had reflected that his composition and environment had any share in this conduct."

Altgeld's book changed Darrow's commonplace view to one more progressive, but its importance in Darrow's personal development was at once more subtle and profound, for it served to focus his attention, as nothing previously had done, upon metropolitan America. Altgeld's facts and figures were from Chicago, Milwaukee, and Boston, and were suggestive of the problems and challenges of America's future in a way that no crime statistics of Ashtabula could be. From this and other works came the dawning realization that the age-old assumptions of continuity might not be applicable to his generation of Americans; perhaps, in spite of his own Harvest Home oration, the virtue of dwelling in the home of one's father depended on where his home was.

Toward the close of his life, looking back over the span of half a century, Darrow conceded that Altgeld's work was "rather crude," but maintained, "in that little book written more out of the heart than the head, you will find the beginnings of what later our heads have worked out."[35] At the time it first came into his hands, it had a pleasing and stimulating freshness. The germs of all Darrow's later thinking were planted in Ashtabula, not Chicago, and the move there was the effect of, not the cause of, Darrow's radicalism. Through the medium of books Darrow had been spiritually transported to America's great urban center long before he arrived there physically: he had "read himself out" of the countryside.

As he read more, and gained more experience in his profession and in politics, he became attuned to the notion that he must move on from Ashtabula, just as he had moved on from Andover. The placid life of an up-and-coming Ashtabula lawyer did not satisfy him. The very tranquility of existence there became hard for him to bear and its distractions seemed petty and inconsequential. As he observed,

> . . . almost anything attracts attention in a little village. If a horse fell down on the street it drew a great audience. If a safe was lowered from the second story, the entire Main Street came to a standstill to watch it swung by ropes and pulleys to the sidewalk below. After that, we eagerly looked for something else to satisfy our curiosity and interest.

As often as not, the "something else" in Darrow's case was a game of poker, which by now had replaced baseball as his major sporting activity. "With congenial companions, a deck of cards and a box of chips, and a little something to drink, I could forget the rest of the world until the last white bone had been tossed into the yawning jack pot."

Yet poker could only assuage his smoldering discontent in brief fits and starts. Unconsciously he was preparing himself for bigger things than northern Ohio could offer. He knew what lay in store for him if he lived out his days in that small town. He knew that farmers rarely prized intellect or its fruits. As he later said, "The part of Ohio where I lived and dreamed was of course a farming section with farmers' ideas, if farmers can be said to have ideas." Unless he moved, the world would never hear of him. There could only be one solution—he must escape.

3

Moving to the Boss City

Darrow's escape from Ashtabula was a narrow one—made just as he was about to weave himself further into the fabric of the town's society by buying a house. As the breadwinner of a family, who by now had $500 in the bank, he decided the time had come to own a residence. He had found a suitable house on sale by the local dentist at $3,500 and had arranged to give his savings as a down payment, the balance to be paid over a period of years. But when the day for closing came, the embarrassed dentist appeared at Darrow's office to explain that he could not consummate the deal because his wife, a co-owner, refused to sign the deed of assignment. Darrow set forth with the dentist to see whether she could be persuaded to change her mind.

"Why will you not sign?" he asked when they reached the house.

"Because, young man, I don't think you'll ever earn thirty-five hundred dollars," she snapped.[1]

Darrow fought to control the flash of annoyance he felt at this slight, concealing his disappointment by refuge in a white lie: "All right. I don't believe I want your house anyway, because"—the words rushed from him before he could stop them—"I'm going to move away from here."

Until that moment his dissatisfaction with Ashtabula had remained below the surface; now it welled up in the irritation of being balked at the final fence. Investment in a house of his own would have marked his reconciliation to the fact that Ashtabula was where his life was to be led. Only in the nick of time did destiny rescue him.

Having blurted out his secret desire in the form of a polite lie, Darrow compounded it, for within the day he had given out that he was going to Chicago and transformed his wish into action. The sudden turnabout must have come as a considerable surprise to Jessie, but she dutifully acquiesced in it. Perhaps she had an inkling of what was in store from her husband's envy of his brother Edward, who was now teaching in Chicago and whose letters describing the wonders of that city were read and reread avidly. It was agreed

34

that he would go on ahead, with Jessie and Paul to follow once necessary arrangements for winding up their modest affairs in Ohio were made. The $500 were destined to support a far greater speculation than buying a house.

The sudden announcement of Darrow's departure coincided with a depression that had put the rural economy into an unhappy state. Although his livelihood in Ashtabula was not directly dependent on agriculture, farming determined the level of the community's prosperity. Throughout the 1880s farm products had commanded poor prices on the market, causing farming to become only marginally profitable, and plunging thousands of farmers even further into debt. It seemed as if America's staple industry was no longer one in which a man could make an honest living, and a generation brought up on the land was leaving for the cities as agricultural prices plummeted and the level of debt mounted. In this, the great age of migration to the cities, many a country-dweller looked across the plains to see a new city on the skyline where none had been before. Its new shape on the horizon lured many a son of the soil away from his birthplace. A lawyer did not need to ask about economic conditions; the default notices, assignments in favor of creditors, and foreclosures told their own story. Darrow was not alone in believing that the future belonged to the cities.

By moving to Chicago in 1887, then the most bustling, exciting city in the United States with already close to a million inhabitants, Darrow was realizing an ambition that he had harbored, dormant, for several years.[2] He forsook rural life with only momentary hesitation and never showed any desire to return except for brief visits to bask in the glory of a hometown boy made good, which he kindled periodically by sending back accounts of his triumphs in the city. From the vantage point of a small town in Ohio in 1887, Chicago, ever the Mecca of Midwestern ambition, seemed to be *the* big city of America, and Darrow was eager to take it on. No other place challenged its pre-eminence in actuality or prospects. America's young hopefuls assessed Chicago as the city of the future; its growth was the marvel of the industrial age. William Stead, referring to Chicago as "the future capital of the United States," a "great city which has already secured an all but unquestioned primacy among the capitals of the New World," and "the capital of the Western World," envisioned its position at the dawning of the twentieth century:

> Even New York no longer dreamed of contesting the supremacy of the younger city. The workmen were putting the finishing touches to the magnificent series of state buildings which were reproducing in marble the architectural glories of the World's Fair, in order to provide accommodation for the Federal Government which was shortly to be transferred from Washington to the continental center.[3]

This did not seem fanciful in the last quarter of the nineteenth century. The balance of advantage had not yet been located on the East Coast, and for many of the newly formed national organizations of the period it was a close question whether they should set up their headquarters in Chicago rather than New

York or Washington, D.C. Chicago was a city for audacious aspirants to all
types of success, the visible sign of burgeoning industry for miles around, and
a traveler could measure his pilgrimage from afar:

> From whichever direction he comes, he crossed level country which, though
> dotted with towns, still has the horizon, the tints, and something of the grand
> freedom, of the Mid-western steppes. Soon the windy open spaces fall behind.
> Into the picture move the shapes of industrial plants, a legion of monsters that
> smoke and hiss on the city's border.[4]

Clarence Darrow arrived in Chicago just as the Haymarket "martyrdom"
had given unprecedented impetus to the liberal and reforming element of its
citizenry, and from then until 1896, successive events that stirred the liberal
conscience would provide a focus for the exercise of a young man's idealism.
Relays of radical causes ran in the wake of the Haymarket martyrdom: the
American Railway Union strike against Pullman; the trial and conviction of
Prendergast, Carter Harrison's assassin; and finally the Democratic National
Convention in 1896, providing practical object lessons to the reformers upon
which political and theoretical suppositions could be tested.

The memory of the Haymarket bombing of May 4, 1886, was still vivid—
the rights and wrongs of everything had to be discussed by reference to it and
the subsequent trial of the alleged offenders. On that evening a public meeting
had been held by a group of anarchists in the Haymarket Square. Though there
had been some inflammatory speeches, it had been peaceable. The mayor,
Carter Harrison, had attended it as an onlooker, and seeing that it was not
unruly, went home before the meeting came to an end. The police were under
orders to let the meeting proceed, but after the mayor left some disagreement
arose between a speaker and the police officer in charge. It would have been
unworthy of historical notice as one of the minor conflicts with authority to
which such occasions have always been susceptible, but for a sudden, huge
explosion. Somebody had tossed a bomb. The carnage was dreadful, killing or
injuring policemen and bystanders alike. In the chaos that followed, those
police who were unscathed arrested a large number of the anarchist leaders,
whom they suspected, without direct evidence, of complicity in the bombing.
Soon, on May 27, thirty-one of them were charged with the incendiarist
murders, and were shortly after tried in a highly charged atmosphere of public
prejudice. On August 20 a verdict of guilty was brought in against eight men,
seven of whom were sentenced to death.

In the year between the verdict and the hearing of their appeals, the public
outcry against them subsided and many thinking citizens began to doubt the
justness of their convictions. No conversation could long stay off the subject:
in truth, there never had been a case that so connected law and politics as this
one did. Discussion had an edge to it as the date for execution of those
sentenced to death drew nearer. Their appeal was rejected by the state Supreme
Court, which held, in a lengthy opinion, that the defendants' trial had been
fair and that there was no ground for reversal. This determination was widely

praised. A leading periodical of the day grudgingly conceded that "even they" were entitled to a fair trial, "although since the days of the primeval murderer Cain, there have been few homicides less worthy of sympathy than the Chicago anarchists." Commenting upon their doctrines as tantamount to incitement to crime, it continued on a later occasion: "It is noteworthy that with very few exceptions the men who figure in this style of agitation, on the rostrum and elsewhere, are of foreign birth and recent importation, who have been attracted to these shores by the laxity of the laws, and who hope to find here a suitable field for the promulgation of their peculiar doctrines."[5] The decision of the state Supreme Court was felt to be an appropriate warning that America was not, after all, a suitable field, and it was with general satisfaction that the news was heard that, on November 2, the Supreme Court of the United States refused to interfere for want of a federal question.

There was, however, a thoughtful and influential minority who were perturbed at the anarchists' treatment. Their doubts were cogent enough that, on the very eve of the execution, Governor Oglesby commuted the hanging sentences on three of the men—Fielden, Neebe, and Schwab—to life imprisonment. There was a great surge of public sentiment in favor of saving the remaining men; but it was too late, and they were hanged the next morning. Among the various opinions two main schools of thought could be discerned: those who sympathized more with the policemen killed by the bomb, and those who sympathized more with the men executed for complicity in throwing it. With splendid impartiality, Chicago erected monuments to both sets of martyrs—one to the police in Union Park, and one to the convicts in Waldheim Cemetery. From the start, Darrow knew where he stood: against capital punishment; against the police; and against the conspiracy law. Ever afterward his sympathies would lie in Waldheim Cemetery rather than Union Park, and he was an active member of the Amnesty Association formed to seek pardons for those convicted who had not already been executed.

At once Darrow plunged deep into the controversy, steeping himself in its every aspect. He derived his first knowledge of the law of conspiracy from the case and later this expertise would prove his trump card in the defense of many important labor cases. He read the court's decision avidly for, as the staid *Harvard Law Review* commented, the case was destined to become "a source of permanent interest to lovers of the sensational, while the points of law involved will render it worthy of the attention of the legal student."[6] Chicago radicals deduced from the anarchists' conviction that radicals and police were natural enemies. In turn the police, believing that radical talk led to radical crime, began compiling lists of subversives and developed a system of spying and informing. This aspect of the Haymarket affair, as much as the allegations of impropriety in the trial itself, mobilized advanced opinion against the authorities. The police attitude was clearly demonstrated by a book published in 1889 by Captain Michael J. Schaack of the Chicago police department, entitled *Anarchy and Anarchists.*[7] Captain Schaack, a police captain who had been personally active in the investigations leading up to the trial of the conspirators, saw radicalism as an international conspiracy and was too zealous in his investigations for the comfort and taste of many Chicagoans. Some of them —Darrow included—believed that the growth of police forces was not an unmitigated blessing, for it put more power in the hands of the government, tipping the balance of advantage yet further against the accused.

Despite his pent-up eagerness to embark upon an urban odyssey, Darrow did not escape either trepidation or sheer funk. The city's dynamism affected all those who visited it, and he exhibited every small-town boy's susceptibility to big city wonders. Sherwood Anderson recalled how as "a raw boy just out of my Ohio town . . . I first came to Chicago. What city man, come out of a small town, can forget his first hours in the city, the strangeness and terror of the tall buildings, the human jam?"[8] And Darrow never forgot:

> From the very first a cloud of homesickness always hung over me. There is no place so lonely to a young man as a great city where he has no intimates and companions. When I walked along the street I scanned every face I met to see if I could not perchance discover some one from Ohio. Sometimes I would stand on the corner of Madison and State Streets—"Chicago's busiest corner"—watching the passers-by for some familiar face; as well might I have hunted in the depths of the Brazilian forest.

But thousands of young men, like Darrow, have stood on some such corner in the midst of a bustling city and experienced the monumental indifference of the populace; most search for fame yet find only obscurity. One of the astonishing aspects of Darrow's life was that he achieved his ambition and conquered the great city. Having arrived without money or friends, he became within ten years one of the best-known lawyers in the city, to whom journalists turned for opinions and politicians for advice. Soon those very crowds would turn their heads and take notice.

In the meantime the realities of existence were harsh. He applied to the first division of the appellate court on the Friday of the first week of its new term for admission to the Illinois bar and was granted a license with a minimum of trouble.[9] This was no great achievement for, as in Ohio, Darrow had arrived in Illinois before there was a general tightening of standards. A Western legal periodical regretfully described conditions at the bar: "Every thin-brained student is, with the utmost candor, advised to 'turn his face toward the setting sun' as the West is the only field where a lack of intellect is profitable."[10] No one could justly accuse Darrow of a lack of intellect in its literal meaning; but in the sense of knowledge of the law and in particular, Illinois law, there was then and subsequently some reason to doubt his ability. However, the hurdle of getting licensed having presented no great problem, he at once rented "a very modest apartment" and took desk room in an office on the third floor of 94 La Salle Street. "I had no money to waste and never liked to borrow or be in debt, so I tried to live within my means, but in this I did not fully succeed. . . . In that first year, all told, I did not receive in fees, or any other way, more than about three hundred dollars."

In the beginning Darrow was overawed, but soon he recognized that many city slickers were but sophisticated hayseeds with even less to offer than he. In a few short months the Windy City had blown the straw out of his hair. He realized that it was necessary to "make a name," that fame started with getting to know people, so that they in turn knew you. So he embarked upon an intensive program of self-advertisement, appearing at numerous meetings and public occasions in the hope of being "noticed." He saw at once that Chicago had considerably more lawyers than it needed or was willing to support. In Ashtabula there had been competition, but it had been restrained and good-natured. Here it was ferocious. As Darrow put it later to a friend, "We have seven thousand lawyers in Chicago. One thousand could do all the work, and probably the world would be better off without them."[11] In these circumstances it did not seem likely that his newly acquired license to practice law in Illinois would be a passport to success. Something else was needed. Darrow decided that this might well be a political connection. Becoming active in the Cook County Democratic Party, as he had been in Ashtabula County, might be a means to obtaining some badly needed legal business. With that insight he was already on the way to success.

Nowhere else was competition among young hopefuls so intense as in Chicago; they flocked from every part of the nation to capture the city's prizes. It was no place for the reticent. Looking about him, Darrow felt an overwhelming need to make up for lost time, as though his years in Ohio had been a write-off, and he became the typical young man in a hurry, impatient to embrace the golden future that was rightfully his. In his efforts to gain recognition he became pushy, struggling to the front of the crowd to shake the hand of some notable, or writing out of the blue to the famous. He set about finding the men whose words in print had thrilled him. In part, his move to Chicago was a homage to intellect—the city was, so to speak, a library of authors and not merely their books, in which he could browse at will without fear of exhausting its bountiful collection. Some opportunities came without effort. For instance, he met Lyman Trumbull, whom Usher Linder described in 1879 as "a man whose name is familiar to every school-boy in this nation," through the mundane chance of renting an office in the same building from which Trumbull practiced law.[12] Darrow did not undervalue this acquaintanceship, which was to make a decided difference to his career. Other revered names, known only from books and newspapers, were to be heard in Chicago every day; the only problem was to find time to listen. Nearly all of them were radicals, whether in or out of politics. Among others he sought out Henry Demarest Lloyd, Henry George, Robert Ingersoll, and John Peter Altgeld— a veritable Pantheon of progressives and freethinkers. He lost no time. He had only been there a few months when he read a letter of Henry Demarest Lloyd's in the Chicago *Record-Herald* for January 3, 1888, on the subject of "Labor and Monopoly." Darrow immediately wrote direct to Lloyd congratulating him on the letter: "It will do much good. Organized labor is fortunate in having such a champion."[13] His sights were set upon industrial concerns and progressive causes from the moment he arrived in Chicago; long ago he had familiarized himself with its great issues and aligned himself with its most advanced opinions. His espousal of urban preoccupations was, of course, part of the adjustment Darrow made to his new city. Not wishing to appear a country bumpkin, he tried especially hard to show familiarity with its concerns, becoming in his eagerness *plus royalist que le roi.*

He attended meetings at which the famous spoke, doing his best when the occasion allowed to introduce himself afterwards and congratulate the speaker in person. These expressions of admiration, though sincere, were part of Darrow's plan to further his own career; he saw no harm in a little sycophancy. At first his efforts were unsuccessful. Although he spoke at all sorts of occasions, the newspapers never printed a word he said. The difficulty was that the audience for most such addresses was made up of young men just like himself, eager to get ahead and impatient for him to finish so that they in turn could have the chance to speak. One of the consequences of this strategy for "getting on" was that Darrow cultivated more friends of the older generation than among his contemporaries, for their fame was more likely to have penetrated to the small settlements of Ohio. Knowing the power of flattery, he deferred to his elders, who responded by helping him in all sorts of ways, whereas he could not help but be in competition with men of his own age. Darrow was not so artless as to believe that ability alone allowed a man to get ahead. On the contrary, he recognized that Chicago was in many respects much like the communities of northern Ohio, in that advancement came from political preferment. He told the *Record-Herald* that success came from "money, pull and luck."[14] Without money, and unsure of luck, he was doing what he could to give himself a little "pull." But self-interested though his cultivation of the famous was, it was not hypocritical: he was a genuine disciple of those whom he got to know and remained in all fundamental respects faithful to their convictions.

When, after the first few anxious months, he began to make a little headway in his ambition to be recognized, some of his regrets about the time spent back in Ohio dissolved. He realized that it had been of some advantage to him to have taken his initial steps outside the city and to have made his elementary mistakes in the decent obscurity of Andover. He had learned much that could be put to advantage from his small-town experience; even the politics of the big city were not a mystery after his apprenticeship in Ohio. Although the scale of Chicago was vastly greater than anything he had encountered before, its machinery of government was in all essential respects like that of Ashtabula. "To a very large extent Chicago is an overgrown village," wrote the Constitutional commentator Andrew Bruce. "With the machinery of a village and a combination of ward, township, and county government, it is attempting to govern a city of over three million inhabitants, a suburban area of a million more, and a daily list of visitors numbering into the hundreds of thousands."[15] Darrow's understanding of village politics allowed him to cut through the thicket of political intrigue in a way that impressed seasoned politicians in Cook County, and won him their patronage. Country wisdom and no-nonsense insight into the affairs of mankind combined with the vitality of a burgeoning city to create in him a kind of spontaneous combustion. When the city was still young, its sole source of inherited political experience was rural Jeffersonian democracy. Only native ingenuity could overcome the problems of the new urban colossi; though the European immigrants who flocked to Chicago had known big cities in the Old World, they were not descended from the burgermeisters of Europe and were without political proficiency. Besides, Chicago was not an old, wise, staid city like those of Europe. Darrow's capacity for political insight was therefore much more in demand than his legal talents, and it was his political acumen rather than legal ability that initially won him a living in the city.

True, the scale on which politics were conducted in Chicago was a factor. The stakes were higher, the spoils greater, and the competition fiercer than they had been in Ashtabula, breeding in the Windy City a corruption that was unknown in northern Ohio. He was not blind to these problems, accepting them as a feature of city politics not within his power to stop, and in time he developed a marked tolerance to graft. He came to see that—whether what they did was legally theft or not—there was larceny in the hearts of many of those in public life, which was morally indistinguishable from the crimes for which poor men were sent to jail every day. The conduct of politics in Cook County was to be a profound influence upon Darrow's mature attitude toward crime in general, for he came to regard the mainspring of political chiseling as exactly the same as any other form of crime. Not being able to see any distinction between dishonesty in public life and ordinary criminality, and not wishing to punish the politicians, whom he liked and with whom he had daily contact, he ended up desiring to see no one punished. He was therefore warmly sympathetic to the views of John Peter Altgeld.

Altgeld had moved from Ohio to Missouri as a boy, and then to Chicago, where he had rapidly advanced as a shrewd businessman and a lawyer of talent. By 1884 he was already influential enough to obtain the Democratic nomination for Congress for the fourth district of Illinois, a Republican district which he lost, but lost honorably. Along the way he picked some admirers who, like Darrow, would prove themselves loyal helpmates in furthering his political ambitions. One was John W. Lanehart, his first cousin, who was also an attorney. Another was George Schilling, a socialist who was organizer of the Eight Hour Day Association. Yet another was Joe Martin, a professional gambler who met Altgeld originally in the course of the latter's practice of law. These, along with Darrow, would form the nucleus of what the Chicago *Tribune* somewhat unfairly called the "whole motley crew of malcontents serving under Captain Altgeld" who were to witness one of the most remarkable sagas of American politics of any generation.[16] Each among this "motley crew" had claims at different times to be dominant influences upon Altgeld: Lanehart was a relative; George Schilling was the earliest to enlist; Joe Martin was considered by Carter Harrison to be Altgeld's "closest friend and adviser." But there can be no doubt that Darrow's influence as Altgeld's Chicago connection would often be most decisive in the years to come.

Having failed to win the congressional seat, Altgeld looked around for another elective office in which he could bide his time until the chance of entering national politics arose again. He found it in a superior court judgeship in Cook County, for which he became a candidate in August 1886, won in November, and assumed in December. He had no particular enthusiasm for the office, and considered the law—though it provided his livelihood—boring. It was a trivial job in his eyes, far too local in its importance to be a stepping stone to what he had in mind. He therefore determined to spread his fame as best he could through the medium of the mails, which was how Judge Richards of Ashtabula had received *Our Penal Machinery and Its Victims* "with the compliments of John P. Altgeld."

The book had so impressed Darrow that the first person that he sought out after his arrival in Chicago in 1887 was Altgeld, whom he went to see in his chambers. There a friendship was struck up that would only be broken by Altgeld's death. It was to have important consequences for both men. Altgeld obtained a shrewd adviser, who was to accomplish many missions on his behalf. Darrow had the direction of his career in Chicago shifted in a way that otherwise he might not have considered. For Altgeld pointed to a future in politics, not law. The acknowledged influence of Altgeld's advice at several crucial stages of Darrow's establishment in the city leaves no doubt that Altgeld's blueprint for Darrow's success was but a carbon copy of his own. He discouraged Darrow from footling his time away with the mundane practice of law. He used his influence first to get him an appointive position at City Hall; then to place him with a great corporation, so that he could accumulate capital that would later pay for his political campaigns; and then to try the route that he had tried in vain, and run for Congress.

As a first step to their intimate association Darrow moved into offices at 115 Monroe, just down the corridor from John Lanehart, the cousin to whom Altgeld had entrusted his practice when he went on the bench. Darrow knew perfectly well what the move entailed. As he later admitted, Altgeld "in his appointees had an essentially political point of view. If you want to do something, put your friends on the job."[17] Darrow, as a friend, was frequently called upon—and received reward in the customary manner. At once, therefore, his practice experienced a turn for the better.

In throwing in his lot with Altgeld, Darrow plunged into the mire of Chicago and Illinois politics at the deep end. Altgeld belonged to the most radical wing of the Democratic Party, aligned with the most extreme elements in the city. He was the most feared, hated, and maligned radical of his age— "the reigning hobgoblin of the United States," as H. L. Mencken described him:

We have had, in these later years, no such communal devil. The La Follette of 1917 was a popular favorite compared to him; the Debs of the same time was a spoiled darling. What I gathered from my elders, in the awful years of adolescence, when my voice began to break and vibrissae sprouted on my lip, was that Altgeld was a shameless advocate of rapine and assassination, an enemy alike to the Constitution and the Ten Commandments—in short, a bloody and insatiable anarchist. . . . When I dreamed, it was of catching him in some public place and cutting off his head, to the applause of the multitude.[18]

But this reputation developed only after Altgeld, by a peculiar mixture of idealism and ruthlessness, had fought his way up to become the most important man in the Illinois Democratic machine. There was in him all the compulsiveness, madness even, of political ambition—"other men get recreation from playing cards. Or they bet on horse races. Or they have their children," he told a friend. "Politics is my recreation."[19] Altgeld played politics as a game, but he played it without humor and with a frightening intensity. He risked his self-made fortune upon his political career and ultimately lost it. But at the peak of his power as governor of Illinois, he was one of the influential Democrats in the nation who almost controlled the Democratic National Convention of 1896. Beatrice Webb, the English socialist, thought him "a man who is clearly not to be intimidated or put into the background by anyone. . . . He was not the skilled brainworker: he was the skilled maker of things, brooding magnificently in his leisure about ultimate principles, speaking weighty words to his fellow workmen, exciting them to discontent."[20]

Darrow, surveying the political scene in Chicago, saw none of Altgeld's characteristics as a disqualification. On the contrary, he regarded them as especially desirable in the circumstances. If improvement were to come, it must be through a candidate for political office with a strong, even rigid, sense of public duty who was nevertheless familiar enough with the ways of politics not to be outsmarted. He must be both incorruptible and intensely ambitious. Darrow thought he had found such a man. He told the socialist George Schilling about it: "What ought to be done now is to take a man like Judge Altgeld, first elect him mayor of Chicago, then governor of Illinois."[21]

Soon Darrow was in frequent contact with Altgeld, familiar through Lanehart with both his public and private affairs, and knowing that Altgeld sought high office. It did not take long for realization of that ambition to become their mutual aim. From then on, as much as Darrow's time was spent as Altgeld's agent as it was on anything; other projects were made to bow to Altgeld's plans. His years in Chicago, until Altgeld's death in 1902, would be lived in Altgeld's world of idealism coupled with political intrigue, as his confidant, adviser, backstairs negotiator, and the manager of his political machine.

There was such respect and loyalty between the two that Darrow became almost the older man's alter ego. Nothing of moment was done by Altgeld without Darrow's being privy to it, and his turbulent political activities were, at times, almost joint enterprises. Though they were very different, they understood each other spiritually and intellectually to such an extent that each could

take solace from the mere presence of the other; sometimes there was commun-
ion though no words were spoken between them. Altgeld took the young
Darrow, fresh from Ohio, and drew him to the center of radical Democratic
politics in Chicago, the state of Illinois, and the nation. He gave Darrow an
unforgettable insider's view of power, its brokers and wielders, how it might
be used and abused. This was an education that Darrow never forgot, any more
than he forgot the man who gave it him. As he acknowledged: "Altgeld made
my life what it is."[22] Even more significantly, Altgeld made Darrow in his own
image. William H. Holly, who later became a federal judge, commented that
Darrow "was feared and hated almost as much as Altgeld was."[23]

   "Altgeld was like Danton," recalled Darrow. "He would gladly take money
from aristocrats and give it to poor people to buy guns to shoot the aristocrats.
He was absolutely honest in his ends and equally as unscrupulous in the means
he used to attain them."[24] Not the least significant aspect of Altgeld's influence
over his young protégé was that he induced him to accept and even admire
this strain of character. From Altgeld, too, Darrow would absorb a very
ambivalent attitude toward democracy: it was good to be on the side of "the
people," but they were not to be left to their own devices, because they were
not capable of judging their own best interests. Altgeld was as manipulative,
even conspiratorial, once in power as he was in seeking it, leaving as little as
possible to the free rein of elections. He not only accepted the political "fix"
but thought it necessary and himself attempted it several times. In this respect
his idealism had much in common with the whiskey-sodden ward-heeling of
less self-righteous Cook County Democrats. All this Darrow came to understand and approve. Although he protested that "the scheming and dickering
and trading for political place never appealed to me," in reality he loved the
backstairs, behind-the-scenes maneuvering that accompanied politics, and
himself engineered many of the most unholy alliances between reformers and
the Democratic Party machine that Chicago had ever seen.

   There is little doubt that Darrow, when faced with a predicament in later
life, often asked himself, "What would Altgeld have done?" He answered with
as little scruple about means as he would if he had asked, "What would Danton
have done?" And he found out the hard way, as Altgeld did, that acting upon
the principle that the ends justify the means brought trouble in its wake. But
Altgeld's strength lay in his steadfastness of purpose and the refusal to be
diverted from his goals, even when these entailed private agony, near bankruptcy, and the hatred of the multitude. Indeed he took a certain perverse
pleasure in standing alone that made him invite unpopularity; he had a streak
of arrogance that would not allow him to be conciliatory though he could have
been without loss of face. There was a style to Altgeld's public career that
Darrow translated into his own: he gave no quarter and received none. Darrow
learned from Altgeld that democracy did not connote mature deliberation. The
crowd was fickle and the mob cruel, and one whom the public had raised could
just as easily be smitten down. "I know the crowd," said Darrow toward the
end of his life. ". . . In a way, I despise them."[25]

Darrow's initial plan—to make Altgeld mayor—was never implemented because the ultimate intent to make him governor of Illinois was realized directly without the necessity of a detour through Chicago's City Hall. A false start was made in 1891, when Altgeld tried unsuccessfully to wrest John H. Palmer's Senate seat away from him. At that time, when senators were nominated through state legislatures, Darrow personally went to Springfield on Altgeld's behalf to see whether the vote could be swung in Altgeld's favor by the Independents. This plan aborted, but it was only a minor setback in the bid for power, and Altgeld was elected state governor in 1892. It was a startling achievement in so short a time; he had entered politics only four years before, with his election to the superior court bench. But he had one advantage that speeded his rise—he could pay his own way at the hustings. His real estate ventures had made him rich. As his biographer observed: "Altgeld, a 'man with a barrel,' could pay for his own campaign! That seemed an irresistible qualification to the politicos."[26] Actually the "barrel" was not as large or as full as the politicos thought, but they were not to find that out for some years. As long as they believed it substantial, Altgeld, with Darrow's advice, parlayed it into a remarkable political success by obtaining his election to the state's highest office. For this Darrow deserved much of the credit; it was his acumen that had originally identified Altgeld as a viable candidate for great office, and it was his advice and strategy that gave Altgeld his prize.

This, however, did not come until 1892. In the meantime Darrow had to make a living, and it was Altgeld who ensured that he did. Once under Altgeld's wing, Darrow was no longer simply one of the hundreds of aspiring young attorneys in Chicago waiting for clients; instead he was the recipient of, first, a patronage job with the city, and then, an even more lucrative position with one of the best-connected and profitable railroads in the nation. In these positions it was well understood that he should be free to devote time to political affairs that were not directly part of his responsibility as an employee. Altgeld had ensured that his lieutenant should not be in need, and so Darrow prospered in those early years.

4

"Getting On"

When Darrow first plucked up courage to visit Altgeld, he could not, of course, foresee the benefits his acquaintance would bring in its wake. He regarded the event as only one of many steps he was taking at the time to become known around the city. He was doing all he could to meet prospective clients and friends and became an inveterate joiner of clubs and attender of meetings.

There was no shortage of opportunities, for every evening some group met; in a burgeoning city, ideas burgeoned too. Over fifty years before, de Tocqueville had remarked:

> In no country in the world has the principle of association been more successfully used, or applied to a greater multitude of objects, than in America. . . . In the United States, associations are established to promote the public safety, commerce, industry, morality, and religion. There is no end which the human will despairs of attaining through the combined power of individuals united into a society. . . .[1]

In the Chicago of 1887 the number of different debating associations, lecture and discussion groups, and the diversity of their views entranced Darrow. On any given night it was possible to congregate in support of free trade or against capital punishment; in praise of Walt Whitman or Leo Tolstoy; in protest against labor injustice or poverty and for dispute over any matter under the sun. The difficulty was to choose among them, for all were in some way desirable. On the other hand, he found it difficult to give his complete support to any one organization, being inclined to see weak planks in every platform. Nevertheless the associations represented an *embarras de richesse* by comparison with Ohio, providing a diversion for almost every moment. Naturally Darrow gravitated to those meetings held in furtherance of causes with which he was already somewhat familiar, such as the ones held in the Democratic wardrooms, the reform clubs, and the free trade leagues. There were, however, two organizations that he came to attend with special fidelity: the newly established Sunset Club; and, because he had read Henry George while still back in Ashtabula, the then-flourishing Single Tax Club. The membership of these two organizations, like many in Chicago in this era, overlapped to some extent, but from Darrow's point of view their important characteristic was that they gave young hopefuls such as himself the chance to meet the rich, the powerful, the famous, and the infamous on informal terms.

Darrow, like almost every liberal of his generation on either side of the Atlantic, was strongly influenced by Henry George's blend of economic radicalism and Jeffersonian democracy. George's "single tax" program, with its emphasis on the "unearned increment" of landlords as a social evil, provided the impetus to many a young radical in the 1880s not merely because of its criticism of the landowning classes but because, as H. G. Wells said, it was "an easy argument to understand."[2] Darrow had first read *Progress and Poverty* in Ashtabula and his reaction was wholly favorable: "I had found a new political gospel that bade fair to bring about the social equality and opportunity that has always been the dream of the idealist." Later he would drift away from George's teaching, saying:

> The error I found in the philosophy of Henry George was its cocksureness, its simplicity, and the small value that it placed upon the selfish motives of men. I grew weary of its everlasting talk of "natural rights." The doctrine was a hang-over from the seventeenth century in France when the philosophers had given up the idea of God, but still thought that there must be some immovable basis for man's conduct and ideas. In this dilemma they evolved the theory of natural rights. If "natural rights" means anything, it means that the individual rights are to be determined by the conduct of Nature. But Nature knows nothing about rights in the sense of human conceptions. Nothing is so cruel, so wanton, so unfeeling as Nature; she moves with the weight of a glacier carrying everything before her.

The Single Tax Club worried Darrow by the very enthusiasm and faith of its members; in time it came to be a hallmark of his thinking that the more adherents a belief had, the more he doubted it. The undertones of fanaticism in such groups put him off, for speakers at their meetings were preaching to the converted: "In due time I realized that at every meeting the same faces appeared and reappeared, week after week, and that none of them cared to hear anything but a gospel in which they all believed. It did not take long for Single Tax to become a religious doctrine necessary to salvation." These circumstances were unpropitious for the conduct of anything but rather circular and repetitive debate—and it was this, among other considerations, that led to the formation of the Sunset Club. Organized in March 1889, just as Darrow was beginning to catch the eye of prominent men, it catered exactly to his tastes; of all early influences, this was to be the most profound. Its object was stated to be "to foster rational good fellowship and tolerant discussion among business and professional men of all classes," and its requirement for membership was simple: "any genial and tolerant fellow may become a member on approval of the executive committee."[3] The club held a dinner every other Thursday at 6:00 P.M., nearly always drawing more than a hundred people to the Sherman House, the Grand Pacific, the Palmer House, or Kinsley's restaurant. This last, conveniently located downtown on Adams Street, was a favorite rendezvous, "especially for us younger lawyers in meeting the older ones. . . . In season, he served a whole teal duck with dressing, mashed potatoes, bread and butter and coffee for thirty cents, and half a mallard for fifty cents with the like trimmings."[4] At these gatherings every current controversy was aired by paper speakers on both sides, followed by speeches from the floor, and it was rare that Darrow was not in attendance. Among the figures who addressed the club from time to time were Altgeld, Charles T. Yerkes, and Jane Addams.[5] From the start Darrow was a ready contributor to the discussions, either from the floor or as a paper speaker. His earliest contribution was at the fourth meeting, held at the Sherman House on Thursday, May 2, 1889, when, bridging the gap between the Single Tax Club and the Sunset, he spoke from the floor on "Land Taxation as Proposed by Henry George." At the sixth meeting, four weeks later, he was a paper speaker on "The State—Its Functions and Duties" before an assembly of 126 people, and took the opportunity to speak out strongly against the recent execution of a young Negro as an example of the misuse of governmental power. At the ninth meeting he was a floor speaker once again on "Nationalism as Proposed by Edward Bellamy," and at the twelfth he answered "Yes" to the question: "Should the Municipality Furnish Heat, Light and Intramural Transportation as well as Water?" Soon he became one of the club's most familiar figures, always ready to address any issue, deft in argument. When he acted as chairman of a meeting, he jokingly referred to his persistence in seeking to be heard: "I will say in advance . . . that speeches will be limited to eight minutes, and I shall enforce that rule. I have had it enforced on me a good many times. But you can console yourselves as I have often consoled myself, that while the time may seem very short to the speaker it seems long enough to the audience."[6]

The Sunset Club was a microcosm of the city that he found irresistible. No organization could have been devised that was better suited to his taste for combining instruction and entertainment. At those Thursday meetings Darrow sharpened his oratorical skills, exchanged political banter, and forwarded his career—all at the same time. The Sunset Club constituted the greatest education of his life, far surpassing the academy on the hill and the preparatory school of Allegheny College. In many respects the club turned out to be Darrow's university.

Nearly all the issues that were to preoccupy Darrow throughout his life were given an airing at the Sunset Club, and its debates made a lasting impression upon him. Long after the minutes of the meetings had yellowed with age, the issues remained as fresh and clear in Darrow's mind as if they had been discussed yesterday. He became an example of his own adage: that it is difficult to get an idea into anyone's mind, and impossible to get it out once it is in. Until the end of his life he would debate the same themes that were before the Sunset Club in almost identical terms. The comments at the meetings of October 22, 1891, and December 29, 1892, in answer to the question: "Should the World's Fair Be Open on Sunday?" could be reproduced with only minor modification in a speech upon the propriety of prohibition laws in 1909, or an attack on the Lord's Day Alliance in 1928.[7] His discussion of "Realism versus Idealism in Literature and Art" under the club's auspices provided material for a pamphlet on the same subject in 1899, and stated the critical standpoint from which he was to greet the novels of his friends Sinclair Lewis, Theodore Dreiser, and Upton Sinclair a quarter century later.[8] Nearly all of the topics with which Darrow's name would become associated in the public mind were on the agenda of the club. He had not stolen his material from others, but the stock-in-trade of his lifetime of public speaking was developed there and from 1900 on would simply be polished rather than expanded.

The Sunset Club normally provided audiences of between one and two hundred—a respectable size, but not big enough to satisfy Darrow's ambition. For already he wanted to speak to the masses, to face one of Chicago's great halls packed to capacity. That opportunity came to him through Henry George.

In 1888 Darrow was still a "pronounced disciple" of George's. The Single Tax Club was a focal point for radicals of many differing shades of opinion, attended by luminaries of the Democratic and Progressive parties alike. At these congregations of the great and would-be great, young men like Darrow attended in the hope of catching the eye of a man of influence. Chicago had grown too fast yet to have achieved the snobberies of the East, and access to the rich, powerful, and intellectually brilliant was available to those who sought them out. Thus by dint of faithful attendance, it was possible for Darrow to speak on the same program as Henry George himself on the topic of Free Trade, and he seized the chance. He had prepared for this moment. "As a matter of fact, I had taken great pains to prepare my speech. The subject was one that had deeply interested me for many years, one that I really understood," he recalled. Furthermore it was a subject upon which he had given addresses several times before: it had been rehearsed at least twice in Andover three years before, when he first became acquainted with George's writings.

When Darrow stood up at Central Music Hall, he was inspired with evangelical zeal. It was then, conclusively, that he knew he could cast a spell. No matter that he had other skills; his ability to hold an audience was paramount. He could entrance, move, and convince its members at least for the moment, and he liked doing so. It was not merely that he enjoyed having an audience —though undeniably he did—but that he functioned best before one; it was as if he was wholly alive only when facing a crowd. At that point a psychological switch was pulled that allowed the thoughts to come, the words to flow, and a harmony of sound and gesture to be achieved. In that auditorium Darrow learned for sure that he could take on the big city. And there, for the first time since his arrival in Chicago, he saw that he had achieved what he most yearned for—the attention of the press. "I had long wanted the newspapers to notice my existence," he confessed, "but the reporters refused to even look at me." Now it was different. As reporters scribbled down his words, and the audience hushed to the ebb and flow of his oratory, he saw that the magic that had worked on a few in Ashtabula worked also on Chicago's many. The momentum of his speech would carry all who could be gathered in one place to listen. His uprooting from the country, the months of hardship, loneliness, and disappointment, were washed away. The decision to move was vindicated. Now he knew for sure that his talents were as big as Chicago—that even the boss city of the universe would pay him attention. At the end of his speech, as he sat down to tumultuous applause, Henry George himself came across to shake him by the hand. The taste of success was as sweet that night as it had been when, back in Kinsman, he had hit the ball over the dry-goods store and won the game. Darrow felt as if he could conquer the world.

Rising early next morning, he went out and bought all the morning newspapers. To his immense gratification he was front-page news, quoted at length. He read the reports over and over again: "It was exceedingly pleasant to my senses," he admitted. But he realized that oratory itself was ephemeral. Unless a speech was reported, there was nothing to show for it after the applause had died away. In future he would make it a condition of his more important speaking engagements and cases that his words should be transcribed and published as a pamphlet, so that they were preserved for a wider audience.

Still savoring his new-found celebrity, Darrow happily carried the collection of newspapers to his office, assuming that with his speaking ability now proven, the world's litigants would beat a path to his door imploring him to take their cases. He discovered the reality was otherwise: "Some of my Single Tax friends and Socialist companions began coming in to congratulate me on my speech. This was pleasing but not profitable. Single Taxers and Socialists never come for business; they come to use your telephone and tell you how the world should be organized so that every one could have his own telephone." As the day wore on, it became apparent that, while it was an advantage for a lawyer to have the gift of the gab, it did not guarantee that he would attract paying clients. Yet, though his need for paid employment was considerable, he was for the moment as delighted to have admirers as clients; at the outset, he had been drawn to the legal profession because it was "showy" more than out of love of the law. He had become a lawyer as a means of making his mark in the world, and as a stepping stone to other things rather than an end in itself. And the result of his triumph on the platform at the Free Trade convention was to attract the interest, not of professional clients but of professional politicians.

Not long after the meeting at Central Music Hall, DeWitt Cregier was elected mayor of Chicago. At the behest of Altgeld, Darrow had spoken on his behalf in the campaign though he had never met the candidate. His campaigning confirmed his usefulness in Altgeld's eyes and won him the approval of other powerful men within the Democratic machine, including Cregier himself. By the morality of Cook County politics (and there was such a thing, though it differed from the everyday precepts of good conduct) he was entitled to a leg up. A change of mayor in Chicago meant a changing of the guard at City Hall: a new administration fired most of the people already on the city payroll and replaced them with political supporters as a reward for their loyalty. Then as always, political survival demanded a lively recognition of favors anticipated and received.

When Altgeld suggested to Cregier that Darrow might deserve city employ- ment, it was hardly likely that Cregier would refuse. The circumstances of Cregier's election throw light on how Darrow "got on" and how, from the first, he was beholden to Altgeld. Cregier had come to office entirely as a result of Altgeld's remarkable manipulation of the city election of 1889. Cregier had great merits: he was an honest servant of the public interest, who as Commissioner of Public Works was described by the *Tribune* as "the hardest-working man at the City Hall; in fact, . . . the only head of a department who does more than sign his name. . . . He has great executive ability and keeps track of everything done, being so systematic that nothing escapes him."[9] But these sterling qualities were only incidental to the singular reason Altgeld had for promoting him to mayor. The fact was that Altgeld had schemed for his election to spite the incumbent, Mayor John A. Roche, against whom he had conceived a passionate grudge. His hatred revealed a darker side of his character and methods, which were to be so influential upon his young protégé Darrow.

Shortly after the election, therefore, Darrow received a hand-delivered message from the mayor-elect, asking him to go and see the mayor when he had time. Darrow's practice not having bloomed, "the latter part of the sentence sounded like a joke. I had time right then. So I put the letter into my pocket and went to see the mayor. The hall and offices were crowded with politicians looking for jobs. I sent in my name and was not kept waiting. After a little preliminary conversation Mr. Cregier asked me if I would take the position of special assessment attorney." Darrow asked him how it was he was being offered the job, in view of the fact that they had never met before.

"Don't you know?" replied Cregier. "Why, I heard you make that speech that night with Henry George."

It was enough for Darrow to learn that the job paid "the fabulous sum" of $3,000 per year. He accepted on the spot. Although he had very little idea of his duties, that was $3,000 a year more than he seemed likely to make if he stayed in his law office waiting for the phone to ring. It is inconceivable that Cregier's opaque reply to his inquiry fooled Darrow into thinking that it was his oratorical talent alone that had brought forth a disinterested offer of a job. He realized that he was being rewarded in the orthodox manner of Chicago politics. But he accepted the system's offer of help at a time when he needed it. As for his ability to handle the job, he considered what he knew about the workings of City Hall and came to the conclusion that no one got a job with the city simply because he was able. Now he was truly in the thick of things in Cook County, as much a politician as a lawyer. He was, in his own words, "getting on."

Darrow might reasonably be excused for being somewhat vague about the duties of a special assessment attorney to the city of Chicago. The organization of its law department was so haphazard that in a celebrated litigation only then

making its way through the appellate courts, a major point at issue was
whether the city attorney or the city corporation counsel controlled the city's
labyrinthine legal staff. In fact the special assessment attorney was an important figure, who superintended the legal work arising out of the city's efforts
to improve its roads and build new ones. In 1889 almost none of its thorough-
fares were paved; the heavy downtown traffic trundled over rutted, muddy
streets that became quite impassable when it rained, and its sheer volume was
such that the existing roads were quite insufficient. Darrow's job was to condemn the land necessary for street building and to deal with the disputes that
arose when property owners along the way were surcharged for the cost of
paving roads. In this exercise of governmental power he showed his mettle:

> Of course many questions came up for immediate answers which I did not fully
> understand, but I used the best judgment I had and always answered promptly.
> Seldom did I find that I had guessed wrong. I thought, then, that it was my
> natural judgment and wisdom that led me to always answer right. Since that time
> I have modified my opinion. I was working for the city of Chicago. I had all the
> strength of a large city behind my decision; few were able to contest my opinion,
> and even if they did, the tendency of the courts was always to decide for the city.
> All my experience in life has strengthened this conclusion. Every advantage in
> the world goes with power. The city, the State, the county, the nation can
> scarcely be wrong. Behind them is organized society, and the individual who is
> obliged to contest for his rights against these forces in either civil or criminal
> courts is fighting against dreadful odds.

Thus he came empirically to the truth that "You can't beat City Hall,"
recognizing early the self-validating tendency of officialdom.

Nevertheless there were bold spirits who battled the city until they had
exhausted all avenues of appeal, as the case of *Springer* v. *City of Chicago*
demonstrated. Shortly after Darrow's arrival in Chicago the city constructed
a bridge on Jackson Street. Warren Springer owned property on Canal Street,
past which the bridge approach lay. He claimed that the value of his property
had been diminished by the work, but the city refused to pay him compensation, because it knew that Springer had been able to sell the property at a
higher value only a few months later to a nominee of the street railway tycoon
Charles Tyson Yerkes, whose business adventures were to inspire Theodore
Dreiser's novel *The Titan*. Darrow became part of the city's law department
just in time to resist Springer's claim, which he did successfully in both the
intermediate appellate court and the Supreme Court of Illinois, giving Springer
an energetic legal trouncing. The trial judge had allowed the jury to go and
look at the property in question to see how far, if at all, the city's improvements
had harmed it. Springer claimed this was improper. In the Supreme Court the
city prevailed on both counts, the Court holding that the prices at which
Springer was prepared to sell before and after the city's works provided competent evidence of value, and that it was proper and sensible to allow the jury
to view the property, thereby obtaining "a much better understanding of the
issue presented by the pleadings."[10]

These and other achievements won Darrow approval at City Hall. The position offered considerable scope for graft, but he avoided all appearances of impropriety even though, during his tenure in office, the amount of street annexation by the city increased substantially; in 1889, 254 miles were annexed, in 1890 there was a drop to 99 miles, but then 117 miles were annexed in 1891 and another 107 in 1892. As special assessment attorney, Darrow legally and metaphorically helped pave the way to the Columbian Exposition of 1893.

Three months after Darrow's appointment Altgeld recommended him as assistant corporation counsel. This recommendation was not based upon Darrow's legal skills any more than the initial appointment had been—Altgeld, though a lawyer himself, was contemptuous of the qualities that made a "good" lawyer—but upon his extraordinarily useful political aid. For while managing the city's legal problems, Darrow had become increasingly active in fashioning the strategy by which Altgeld's political ambitions might be advanced. He was rapidly entering that inner circle of advisers around Altgeld for whom influence was generously exercised; soon he would be the single most important adviser of them all, playing Cromwell to Altgeld's Henry VIII. The salary of assistant corporation counsel was $5,000 a year, but when, only ten months later, the chief corporation counsel resigned for reasons of ill-health, Darrow was appointed acting corporation counsel in his place. "When luck began to change everything seemed rapidly to come my way," he recorded, although of the trilogy of factors by which Darrow explained success—money, pull, and luck—he might more candidly have credited "pull." Whatever the term that best described why he achieved his swift promotions, there was no doubt that he was rapidly becoming an important figure. As he reported laconically: "Nothing could be done without the advice of the Corporation Counsel's office." In this position he learned much about law and politics: "As acting corporation counsel I was in daily conference with the Mayor, and we came to be good friends."

His advice to the city while he was corporation counsel reflected the many political concerns of the day. By reason of its extraordinarily rapid growth, the corporation counsel's office was constantly faced with intriguing legal questions as to whether the march of progress was entitled to trample vested rights, even if they were inconvenient and anachronistic. As city attorney he became a familiar figure in the Cook County Circuit Court, protecting the interests of his employer in its multifarious suits—"this position kept me in court a great deal in contested cases," he recalled. Having frequently to appear at short notice with scant preparation, he became quick and adept at putting the city's position. Some litigations under his care did of course need and receive careful preparation. During his association with the office, for example, a major litigation tested the right of the city to insist upon the removal of a private tollgate, lawfully authorized by the Illinois legislature, from the corner of Milwaukee and Fullerton avenues. The state Supreme Court, and finally the United States Supreme Court, decided yes. There were other concerns. In particular, the streetcar franchises had become the butt of nearly all criticisms of municipal administration. "The sordid, tragic tale of their domination of municipal politics is now universally known," wrote Brand Whitlock in 1914, "and in the tale may be read the causes of most of our municipal misrule."[11] It was not the pioneers of streetcar lines against whom reformers' wrath was directed, but those who came after them, who by mergers and the natural expansion of the municipal lines' profitability came to have enough incentive and money to bribe state legislatures into extending the franchises and granting perpetual rights of way. Each time an existing franchise came near to expiration, there was in every municipality an orgy of political bribery as the companies attempted to gain renewals. The daily imposition of fares upon the working population was regarded as a form of tax upon the working class—and to the extent that it included bloated profits, it was regarded as an unjust one. The sentiment of urban areas moved toward public ownership of the street railways as the century drew to a close. In the meantime questions constantly arose as to the legal constraints there might be upon rate increases, expansion of lines, and control of services, the suspicion being that the city's franchises, whether public utilities, streetcars, or suppliers of goods under municipal contracts, were bilking the public.

Darrow demonstrated great legal acumen in juggling the complex of constitutional mandate, legislative sanction, and municipal regulation. He needed to, for the interests ranged against him could well afford excellent legal advice and would take advantage of his slightest slip. It was this experience working for the city which, more than anything else, persuaded him that his profession was almost inevitably the servant of wealth, not justice—one of a series of conclusions that was to lead him to disenchantment with his profession in later years. His legal opinions were exceedingly clear, identifying roadblocks to city action, suggesting appropriate means toward desired ends, and generally advising the city well. The erstwhile city solicitor of Ashtabula showed no sign of being daunted by Chicago's problems; on the contrary, he thrived on them and his office in Room 41 of City Hall became one of the most flourishing political centers Chicago had ever seen.

The city's business had to pass through that office. In addition, Darrow was managing Altgeld's campaign to become state governor. The tentacles of his influence were probing in all directions, so that even seasoned Cook County political managers were impressed by his rapid rise to prominence. He always admitted that he had supported the Democratic Party somewhat reluctantly, "with few illusions as to what it meant." Now any remaining illusions dissolved, for in the thick of things he saw daily "what it meant" to support the Democracy. Its members made a motley parade through the corridors of power, ranging from high-minded, top-hatted patricians to rather lower-minded, cigar-chomping Irish-American fixers like "Bathhouse" John Coughlin. Even the Chicago *Herald,* the leading Democratic paper, wrote despairingly:

> The average Democratic representative in the City Council is a tramp, if not
> worse. . . . [W]hether from the west, the south or the north division, he is in nine
> cases out of ten a bummer and a disreputable who can be bought and sold as hogs
> are bought and sold at the stockyards. Do these vicious vagabonds stand for the
> decency and intelligence of the Democratic party in Chicago?[12]

But Darrow was not squeamish about the seamier side of politics and struck
up amiable working relationships with most of its more picturesque representatives, whom he found congenial if not virtuous. The pursuit of politics
became a way of life, to be lived in the customary haunts of officeholders and
office-seekers, exchanging gossip and speculation between occasional frantic
attempts to catch up with the backlog of work. It seemed that he had found
his niche in life, round and about City Hall. He certainly enjoyed the corporation counsel's office. He shared it with several fellow members of the Sunset
Club, notably Morris St. P. Thomas (with whom he would later set up private
practice), and there were many occasions on which discussions started at the
club on Thursday evening were continued the next morning in Room 41.

City Hall provided a remarkable acquaintance with the denizens of democracy with a small *d* as well as a large one: indeed it would have been hard to
find a more extraordinary bevy of people in those days. The place was a
constant hive of activity. A vivid contemporary account was given by William
Stead: "I have never seen a city hall so thronged by loafers during the day
time," he wrote:

> The politician out of a job, the office-seeker waiting impatiently for his turn, the
> alderman and his string of hangers-on, the ex-official, the heeler, the jobber, swell
> the throng of those who do business until the air in the corridors is heavy with
> smoke, and the pavement is filthy with the mire of innumerable boots and stained
> with the juice of the tobacco plant—for not even the American allowance of
> spittoons can suffice for the need of the citizens in their Civic Hall.

Nor did the evening bring any cessation of activity, for during the winter:

> In this building, crammed with invaluable documents, the seat and center of the
> whole civic machinery, for want of any better accommodation, there were housed
> night after night . . . from one to two thousand of the most miserable men in
> Chicago. . . . They were allowed to occupy the spacious well-warmed corridors,
> and make such shift as they could upon the flags. . . . It seems strange, but it
> appears to be undisputed that the habit of allowing the homeless to shelter in the
> corridors of the City Hall is no new thing in Chicago.[13]

Thus Darrow was gaining a dual education there—in the problems of the
masses who congregated within its walls and the workings of the political
machinery that might solve them. But as he watched, he doubted gravely
whether such problems could be speedily solved.

From his vantage point as corporation counsel, he observed at first hand the
political legerdemain that both shocked and fascinated outsiders. Chicago's
politics was the archetype of all that idealists sought to avoid—muckrakers
made lifetime careers out of "exposing" it. Chicago had grown too fast to build

effective safeguards against corruption. Turning out fabulous amounts of wealth, it became a fabled city, attracting those whose enterprise was larger than their morality and who were indulgent of their fellow citizens' peccadilloes for fear that their own would be discovered. Its sudden accumulation of population and industry contributed to the magnificence of its municipal improbity, generating a private wealth that could buy favors from government never intended by the electorate to be for sale.

Eugene Debs, who was to give Darrow his first opportunity in a big case, described the city as uninhabitable because of the danger of typhoid and the rapaciousness of its politics, and strongly implied that one might as well have a mosquito suck one's blood as a Chicago politician:

> . . . Chicago is the product of modern capitalism, and, like all other great commercial centers, is unfit for human habitation. The Illinois Central Railroad Company selected the site upon which the city is built and this consisted of a vast miasmatic swamp far better suited to mosquito culture than for human beings.[14]

Debs's extreme statement was typical both of him and of the spirit of the times, for the muckraking school of journalism and the municipal reform movement alike were products of the rural conscience at work in the city. Debs spoke for a wider constituency than the readership of the socialist periodical *Appeal to Reason* when he denounced Chicago; he spoke to all those who knew that such goings-on would not be tolerated in Terre Haute or Kinsman. A generation later, muckraking was to degenerate into platitudinous and reactionary piety; but when Debs condemned Chicago, his words struck a chord of sincere and righteous indignation in America's heartland. The venality of politics in Chicago was symbolized by the City-County Building, which Darrow's office overlooked, and which, although only twenty years old, was gradually sinking into the earth because of the inadequacy of its foundations.[15] Whether this structural failure resulted from poor engineering or corrupt contracting was never established beyond doubt, but many saw in the sinking edifice a warning that if Chicago did not reform, it would be swallowed up by the earth as a piece of divine justice.

Yet, in spite of the howls of the reformers about the dire state of city politics, divine disapproval did not bring the politics of Cook County to a standstill. It seemed, on the contrary, that its political life had never been busier or more intriguing. Darrow was rapidly proving to be one of those people who thrive on perpetual distractions, loving to have a hundred different things going on around him and to be at the center of activity. At City Hall the decisions to be made, the plots to be hatched, the gossip to be circulated and received, and the innumerable petty crises of government made up an entrancing milieu, in which he developed an appetite for action and involvement that many onlookers predicted would sustain a lifetime in politics. He showed every sign of being delighted with his position, and it looked as though he was set up for life. And so he might have been if he had taken care to cultivate Mayor Cregier's successor. The regular wing of the Democratic Party had planned carefully for the next mayoralty campaign to ensure that Altgeld would not trip it up again, as he had by getting Cregier elected. At the election, Cregier was replaced by another Democrat unfavorable to Altgeld and his favorites. Darrow knew that he would shortly be out of a job. Hence the position gained by "pull" was lost for the lack of it. But Altgeld had other spheres of influence. In mid-1891 he suggested another lucrative job that Darrow could take while helping prepare for the gubernatorial campaign coming up in the following year. Darrow was not sure that it was to his taste, but he did Altgeld's bidding. The ambitious radical found himself installed in the unlikely setting of the Chicago & Northwestern Railway's substantial law department.

5

The Chicago &
Northwestern Railway

The Chicago & Northwestern appointment marked the beginning of the most frenetic period of Darrow's life. He was involved in much besides the business of the railroad. While there, he was the strategist and manager of Altgeld's successful campaign to become governor of Illinois. Afterwards he was to become Altgeld's intimate adviser on many aspects of the governorship and worked with him to realize their mutual ambition to put a Democrat in the White House in 1896 who was populist enough to secure the rural vote without being anti-urban. Darrow was also continually engaged in the political life of Cook County, and apart from his political concerns, struck up a deal with the Chicago & Northwestern by which he was entitled to engage in private practice simultaneously with his employment by the road, as long as no conflict of interest developed, and this practice flourished. Finally he continued to indulge his speaking and literary ambitions during these years. All in all he was drastically over-committed, so that no minute of his day was unfilled. He left himself no time for contemplation or repose; he did his thinking "on the run" and his work in a desperate hurry. It was a pace that would have broken most men, physically and mentally. But it was in these years that it became apparent that he enjoyed living with distraction on every side, with a hundred calls upon his time, and in a perpetual rush. His appetite for action and involvement anticipated the existentialism of a later generation, for it was not merely for love of work that he endured his punishing schedule; he also hated and feared inertia. He threw himself into work to ward off introspection and what he called "self-consciousness." He dared not allow himself the leisure to get depressed.

The many pursuits brought havoc to his domestic life, but Jessie bore it with good grace at first. She did not like seeing her husband so little; nor did she like his irregular hours; nor, on the few occasions when she met them, was she altogether taken with his colleagues and companions. Still there were consolations, including the undeniable fact that he was a success. He had prospered well enough to build a family home at 4219 Vincennes Avenue. Jessie appreciated this outward sign of success. Yet ultimately it was to be the cause of the breakdown of their marriage. Jessie wanted a normal bourgeois domestic life, entertaining visitors to tea and giving polite dinner parties as her neighbors did; but her husband gave her precious little chance of it. He spent so much time downtown that his visits to Vincennes Avenue were mainly for the purpose of sleep. In 1892 the conflict between his values and hers was not yet starkly apparent, but the next five years of frantic involvement were to make it unmistakable.

From Jessie's simple perspective, the move from City Hall to the railroad was for the better. It seemed to mean that her husband had at last turned his back upon the seedy politicians with whom he had associated in preference for a stable, respectable appointment with a solid business; this was the kind of progress she understood and wanted for Clarence. There was much justification for her view: Darrow was a rising star in the nation's most expansive industry, and his appointment was a golden career opportunity. At the head of the business was Marvin Hughitt, one of Chicago's most prominent men, whose elegant house at 2828 Prairie Avenue symbolized to the residents of Vincennes Avenue what Chicago might ultimately offer. The company Darrow had joined had a large and well-financed law department with an annual budget of nearly $125,000 a year,[1] and his position in it was one of the utmost respectability. "The principal officers of the Chicago and North Western remain as they have been for many years, which is the best evidence as to their trustworthiness and good management," wrote the authors compiling the *History of Chicago* in 1892, and there followed a list of the officers that included "C.S. Darrow, atty." Could there be any doubt that he had arrived? When he joined the railway, it already controlled 4,273 miles of track, of which 1,211 miles were proprietary lines, and still it continued to grow. He was in the midst of a hugely successful business, managed with all the brutal efficiency that unbridled competition demanded. And in those days there was competition: in 1893 a passenger could choose to travel any one of six routes owned by six different railroads from Chicago to St. Paul and Minneapolis, and even so, the competition was intensifying; by 1909 yet another had been opened. There was every prospect that Darrow could remain with the company for life, prosperous and esteemed, a pillar of the community.

But Jessie misconstrued the implications of the new job. For the move, far from being an abandonment of politics, immersed her husband still further in them. The Chicago & Northwestern had important assets at stake that gave it a lively interest in the political affairs of the city. Its legal department was a hotbed of political influence and intrigue, and Darrow's appointment there was as much political as his appointment to the city attorney's office. Railroading was a business in which the big operators found it desirable, if not palatable, to tolerate politically active employees on their payroll. Darrow's new job made him a colleague of William C. Goudy, one of the leading Democrats in the state, who, after being a state senator, became general solicitor of the

C. & N.W. He had been chief representative of the Vanderbilt interests at the time when Vanderbilt, charged with the illegalities daily committed by his railroad, had protested: "You don't suppose you can run a railroad in accordance with the statutes, do you?"[2] Altgeld owed a great deal of his success in the realty business to Goudy, who in the eighties had passed Altgeld inside tips on good investments and generally fostered his career. "Though not ostensibly an active politician," reported the *Chicago Law Times,* "his influence is widely felt in the politics of the democratic party of the City and State, and even of the nation."[3] Another contemporary recalled that Goudy and Frederick H. Winston "were the two men who largely controlled for years the principles and policies of the local Democratic Party."[4] In short, Darrow's employment by the railroad represented as much a continuation of his political avocation as it did his employment as a lawyer.

Goudy's position of behind-the-scenes influence in the Democratic Party was immensely attractive to Darrow; yet from the first, he was uncomfortable in his new employment. It seemed to compromise his integrity. In his coterie, working for a railroad was equated with working for the Devil. To be beholden to the industry even in a trivial way was a millstone around the neck of anyone with radical pretensions. Railroads were such anathema in populist circles that William Jennings Bryan refused on principle to accept fees or cases from railroading interests and had even briefly advocated their nationalization. Nowhere was the sentiment against the railroad interests stronger than in Illinois. A review of a book entitled *Railroads and the Courts* in a leading legal periodical reflected the contemporary opposition:

> We take it for granted that no lawyer will have the hardihood to cite it to the Supreme Court of Illinois in any pending cause; because, from beginning to end, it is little else than a bold arraignment of the course of decision in that court in favor of the railroad company against people who sue the railroad company for damages. . . . We think it will be found that the decisions of one or two other states present a similar concurrence of results in favor of railroad companies, and the people may well begin to reflect seriously whether their courts of last resort, whose judges are put there by the elective system, are not mere putty in the hands of these corporations.[5]

Hatred of the railroads was so widespread that Goudy lost his chance of achieving a lifelong ambition because of his association with them. He had managed Cleveland's campaign in Illinois and adjacent states, and had a substantial claim upon the President's favors. But according to one reliable source, Cleveland passed him over for appointment to the position of Chief Justice of the United States after he was told that Goudy "was probably the ablest Democratic lawyer in Illinois, but that he was a railroad attorney, and it would probably not be a good thing to appoint him."[6] It is therefore not surprising that Darrow was reluctant to join the railroad, for whatever might be gained materially, it meant a blot on his radical credentials that would take much to erase. Many lawyers would have been proud to serve the Chicago &

Northwestern, but to Darrow, his employment was a badge of shame, which declared that he had sold himself to the highest bidder. To him there was a stark contradiction in being a railroad lawyer by day and a radical by night; the more radical causes he adopted, the more intolerable his position seemed.

From the start there were aspects of the business that its new recruit did not like, including the necessity to turn down personal injury claims against the railway by employees and members of the public. The days of workmen's compensation and the railroad workers' equivalent of social security were still far off, and an injured employee might be left with nothing. As a legal periodical described the position in a corporation comparable to the Chicago & Northwestern:

> To a very great extent, the duties of a railway lawyer would seem to partake more of the character of those of a judge than those of an advocate . . . a great portion of the time of the members of the law department of this railway must have been consumed in investigating claims, with the purpose of avoiding litigation by paying those that were just. . . . We half suspect, however . . . that the efforts of the attorneys are largely directed to the compromising of claims upon the lowest basis attainable for the railway.[7]

Darrow's sympathies were with the claimants and their families, and he tried to pay them something if he could. He knew where the moral responsibility lay when members of the public suffered dreadful injuries from railroads crisscrossing the streets of Chicago at street level because the railroad companies were too mean to build bridges. The carnage attributable to this parsimony was horrifying, as an exact contemporary observed:

> If a stranger's first impression of Chicago is that of the barbarous gridironed streets, his second is that of the multitude of mutilated people whom he meets on crutches. Excepting immediately after a great war, I have never seen so many mutilated fragments of humanity as one finds in Chicago. Dealers in artificial limbs and crutches ought to be able to do a better business in Chicago than in any other city I have ever visited. On inquiry I found that the second salient feature of Chicago was the direct result of the first. The railroads which cross the city at the level in every direction, although limited by statute and ordinance as to speed, constantly mow down unoffending citizens at the crossings, and those legless, armless men and women whom you meet on the streets are merely the mangled remnant of the massacre that is constantly going on year in and year out.[8]

Darrow hated to have to contest the claims of these people. He knew that to allow the railroads to avoid the cost of building bridges and to avoid paying compensation to those injured as well was in the highest degree unconscionable. There were 257 people killed at level crossings within the city limits in 1889; 294 in 1890; 323 in 1891; 394 in 1892; and in 1893, 431—and these figures did not include those who, though seriously injured, escaped with their lives. Stead concluded that "No other great city in the world has allowed its streets to be taken possession of to a similar extent, and the massacre resulting therefrom is greater than that of many battles."[9]

Yet although his sympathies were with the poor, Darrow was not so one-sided as to believe that all those of the railroad fraternity were evil men. On the contrary, he frequently referred to the kindness and understanding shown him by his railroad colleagues and praised their abilities; even for those with whom he disagreed there was often friendship, always respect. He was able to follow his conscience to some extent by the grace of the general claim agent of the railroad, Ralph C. Richards, and its president, Marvin Hughitt, both of whom were enlightened and humane men. In spite of differences of politics and social status, Hughitt and Darrow worked well together: "we remained the best of friends to the end of his life," recalled Darrow.[10] In consequence, under Darrow's guidance many claims were compromised that otherwise would have been rejected entirely. On the other hand, while Darrow tried to settle claims so far as possible, the Chicago & Northwestern did not give up disputing claims for personal injuries during his tenure of office. Reported cases indicate that the railway was as frequently in court during Darrow's employment as it was before and after. It is seemingly true that Darrow tried to avoid being attorney of record in the cases in which a claim was disputed. Instead, at least on appeal, he lent his name to disputes about injuries to cattle and horses, boundary disputes, and eminent domain proceedings, in which his conscience was less troubled, appearing with Goudy and his assistant A. W. Pulver, both of whom were old hands at the game.

Quite aside from his distaste for some of the litigation arising from the Chicago & Northwestern's business, Darrow early on needed all the help he could get so as to have enough free time to advise Altgeld on his campaign for election as governor in 1892. He was, in effect, a campaign manager working with one or two other of Altgeld's acolytes on a most difficult task. Altgeld's victory would be a triumph of strategy, not a foregone conclusion, and it would be won only at the price of some considerable compromise among various groups of supporters whose interests diverged in certain crucial respects. The final achievement, in no small measure due to Darrow, can only be assessed with reference to Altgeld's major disabilities. First, Altgeld had found such favor as he had with the Democratic machine because he was wealthy. But the political managers greatly overestimated—perhaps because they had been misled—the size of his fortune. Altgeld had indeed done well. The Unity Building, his most visible asset, was a magnificent early skyscraper lauded as a Chicago landmark. Standing eighteen storeys high on Dearborn Street, it was one of the earliest developments in the Loop, costing over $2 million to build; he had put his entire savings of $600,000 into it. And there was the rub—for Altgeld was mortgaged up to the hilt. His wealth was so over-committed in realty ventures that there was little or nothing to spare for political purposes. This was not apparent in 1892, but by the middle of 1894 Altgeld's finances were in a critical condition from which they were never to recover. One of his primary appeals to the politicos, therefore, was based on an illusion. Second, even with the reputation of being rich, Altgeld never commanded the entire loyalty of the Democrats. The frank truth was that he was not naturally gifted with the attributes of a popular figure. Many people disliked him. He had neither an easy manner nor a lovable inarticulateness; in consequence there was opposition to his advancement from within his own party at every stage in his political career. Only the most careful plotting allowed him to come to prominence. It was here that Darrow's counsel was most useful, for he devised the means that piloted Altgeld to victory even without control of the entire Democratic machine.

Surveying the political scene statewide, Darrow concluded that his patron could only achieve the governorship by a coalition of disparate interests. Since he could not depend upon solid Democratic support, he must count only upon the sure votes of a Democratic faction, and supplement them elsewhere. It was decided that there were three sources of potential votes for Altgeld besides the Democratic machine: third parties, reform leagues, and the German-American community, regardless of its previous party affiliation. It was this daring combination, itself extremely precarious, that would bring off the prize for Altgeld.

As a beginning, Altgeld had some solid Democratic votes; indeed he became a dominant force in the party by combining the support of a large faction of the Democrats with third-party and independent support. Darrow himself described the strategy: "Altgeld always stayed in the democratic party and worked there; he thought that the best way to get his ends. But he was extremely sympathetic with third party movements. And the third parties always voted for him. There never was a third party when Altgeld was running anything."[11] The third-party vote, comprising most notably the populists, the single taxers, and the socialists, was a great untapped resource in the electoral system which Darrow harnessed to Altgeld's campaign. Darrow's rueful support of the Democrats stemmed from his recognition of the importance of the "machine." The divisiveness of radicals was too apparent to him to pretend that anything could be achieved without organization; they lacked the binding force of economic interest—and he knew that ideas could not hold men together unless in blind fanaticism. He did not believe that the natural tendency of humanity was cooperation or compromise. He saw the bitter feuds within and between liberal organizations and realized how, not being bound together by interest, they were divided by ideas. A party had finally to guide the way if there was to be any hope at all so that the ill-disciplined left might be coordinated at the only time it really counted—Election Day. When the moment of decision came in the election booth, many a populist and single taxer marked his ballot for Altgeld.

Other votes were culled for Altgeld by the so-called voters' leagues, whose members put aside party affiliation and voted for any candidate thought to be honest. Nearly all of them were dedicated to removing "rogue" politicians from office. The corruption of city government was such a well-recognized fact that a whole new vocabulary had been developed for it: bossism, graft, pork barrel, and boodle. Many of the members of voters' leagues believed that honest government could be achieved. This naïve belief was rejected by Darrow, though he constantly rubbed shoulders with those who shared it, for he knew that high-mindedness and good intentions were not enough. Compromise and even guile were necessary in order to achieve desirable objectives. And therein lay an inherent contradiction: once a reform candidate adjusted to the system by making compromises and using cunning, the line between good and bad men became severely blurred. Indeed the difficulty of making the distinction was later demonstrated by Altgeld's administration; for though his personal honesty was unquestioned, the same was not true of those under him. Shelby M. Cullom, senior senator from Illinois during Altgeld's governorship, whose political persuasion was very different from his, remarked on the contrast between the man and his subordinates:

> Of his honesty, his integrity, his seriousness of purpose, his determination to give the State a good administration, I never had the slightest doubt. The mainspring of the trouble, I believe, was an inability to select good men for public office. He was not a good judge of men; he surrounded himself with a coterie that betrayed his trust and used the State offices for personal gain.[12]

The weakness that Senator Cullom identified was not merely to be explained on the ground that Altgeld was a poor judge of character. More fundamentally, it was explicable only by the coalition of disparate interests that put him in the governor's mansion to begin with, and to which he perforce owed favors. By combining reform league votes with those of the regular Democrats, his young lieutenant had persuaded the reformers to join hands with the very interests they most abhorred; he must have seen its grim humor as he arranged it.

The third source of additional votes which Altgeld's campaign tapped was that of the substantial German-American population of Illinois. Here Altgeld dealt a master stroke of Machiavellian proportions in focusing on the issue of the Edwards Act and "the little red schoolhouse." In 1889 the General Assembly had passed a school bill on a nonpartisan vote that had been sponsored originally by the Chicago Women's Club. The bill, which Governor Joseph W. Fifer, Altgeld's opponent in the election, had signed into law, provided that all basic instruction must be given in English and that state truant officers should inspect both public and private schools. These provisions had annoyed two different religious groups: the Lutherans, staunchly in favor of instruction in the German language, disliked the provision for teaching in English; and the Roman Catholics (whether German or not) disliked the idea of state inspection of private schools, nearly all of which were Catholic and parochial. When this bill was proposed, Altgeld, as unpaid counsel to the Chicago Women's Club, had expressed his own personal support for the bill's provision and "probably helped draft it."[13] It therefore came ill from him to criticize the bill once it had become law, still less to blame Fifer for signing it. That, however, did not stop him from doing so. This rank hypocrisy was known to George Schilling, Mike McDonald, and John Lanehart, as well as Darrow, but they did not blanch. Altgeld made his whole attack upon Fifer rest upon the horrors of the Edwards Act, and though the *Tribune* discovered before polling day that the act was "the child of Altgeld's brain," it was by that time too late to reverse the swell of public sentiment that had arisen against Fifer. If this were not enough, Darrow compounded his complicity in this fraud on the electorate by providing yet another duplicitous reason for the adoption of this platform: "Making the campaign in that way it was unnecessary for him to reveal his standpoint on labor," he explained with satisfaction. "He would never have got in on his labor point of view."[14]

To give Altgeld success, it was necessary to persuade Roman Catholics to vote side by side with German Lutherans; for reformers who wished to purge politics of corruption to join hands with Bathhouse John; for anarchists and socialists both to see their best hope in the same man. But Altgeld pulled it off, and unseated the unfortunate Fifer, polling 425,558 votes to his 402,672. Perhaps Altgeld was indeed the better man, but his victory was hardly fairly won.

Yet that victory was still sweet. Illinois had its first Democratic governor since the Civil War and Darrow was to savor plaudits not only from Altgeld, but also from his superior at the Chicago & Northwestern, by whose indulgence he had been allowed to skimp on his attention to company affairs while engineering Altgeld's success. Goudy, though usually a stalwart of the Democratic Party line, was for Altgeld in 1892 and had actively used his influence to help him. His relations with Altgeld had been increasingly cordial since he had appeared in a will litigation against Altgeld in which Altgeld's handling of the case had pleased him—the newspapers had hinted at a corrupt deal between the two ostensible opponents. Though nothing was ever proved against Altgeld in this respect, it is certain that Goudy himself was not above suspicion of using influence, or more, in furtherance of his clients' interests. Starting on the path to success as a Vanderbilt lawyer, he knew that respectability was only skin-deep and that railway interests were among the strongest forces of corruption in political life. His counterpart, a lawyer for another railroad, told William Stead: "There are sixty-eight aldermen in the City Council, and sixty-six of them can be bought. This I know because I have bought them myself."[15] Darrow had not impaired his chances with the railroad in any way by bringing off his plan to the satisfaction of Goudy.

On the other hand it was surely true that Altgeld, with the patronage of the entire state of Illinois at his fingertips, was in a position to offer something in government if Darrow wished. But Darrow declined the opportunity. He remained on in Chicago, content to act as Altgeld's city agent, while Altgeld left for Springfield and the governor's mansion. Notwithstanding his reservations about employment with the Chicago & Northwestern, this was surely a wise decision. Over-dependence on Altgeld might have left him without any distinct persona of his own, so fatally easy is it to be swallowed up by somebody else's fame. Besides, a move to Springfield, even if only for the duration of Altgeld's governorship, would have been a regressive step—in Darrow's eyes

it was almost like backtracking to northern Ohio. By now he had acquired a
taste for the city's bustle, and was on his way to becoming a man of property.
His interests, professionally, intellectually, and personally, were centered in
Chicago and nowhere else. With the sole exception of John Lanehart, he was
Altgeld's major contact in Chicago, in itself a guarantee of continued political
importance. As the excitement of the gubernatorial victory subsided, a new
goal loomed on the horizon: control of the Democratic National Convention
in 1896, already scheduled to be held in the Windy City. Darrow had scarcely
finished being an unofficial campaign manager before he had started upon the
new task of being Altgeld's advance man for the convention of 1896.

6

Governor John P. Altgeld— "A Communal Devil"

The camaraderie of battle dissolved upon victory. With Altgeld's removal to Springfield, Darrow was no longer privy to the older man's musings or used as a sounding board upon whom new policies were tested. As Altgeld became embroiled in the obligations and privileges of the governorship, Darrow's relationship with him changed from one of intimacy to something approaching remoteness. It seemed as if he had been supplanted as Altgeld's confidant by those of his circle who had followed him to Springfield; almost, indeed, as if he had been "dropped." Quite unthinkingly, Altgeld was neglecting Darrow and other trusty lieutenants in favor of reveling in the reflected glory of his office, as he appeared exuberant and self-important at the numerous social occasions accompanying his inauguration:

> Nor were they working class affairs; far from it. They called for the starched shirt and swallowtails. Night after night immediately after the election, he decked himself out in such plutocratic garb to spend the evening shaking hands, consuming banquet food, making and listening to fatuous speeches, and in dancing. And he did those things because he enjoyed them, not from a sense of duty.[1]

Now that he had won the election, Society was wooing him. In spite of his radicalism he was a willing suitor; there was enough of the parvenu in him to be flattered greatly by its attentions.

Those who had supported him looked indulgently upon Altgeld's weakness for high society at first, but as weeks and then months passed without any progress being made in the direction of reform, many of them became impatient and disillusioned with their erstwhile hero. Darrow, as Altgeld's unofficial agent in Chicago, had to make excuses so often for his friend's remarkable political inactivity that it became quite embarrassing. As the architect of the coalition of interests that had put Altgeld into office, Darrow appreciated full well the need to appease each of them with some political benefaction or another at an early date—and such did not seem to be forthcoming. In particular, as the winter turned to spring, there was a group of supporters, among whom Darrow himself was prominent, who became dismayed at Altgeld's failure to pardon the Haymarket anarchists who were still in jail.

Altgeld's campaign had been conducted with something less than candor; his true position on the Edwards Act had been concealed, as had his advanced opinions on labor. But there was yet another matter upon which the vast majority of the electorate had been kept in the dark: many of Altgeld's inner circle of helpers during the election campaign were ardently in favor of pardoning the surviving Haymarket anarchists, and aided him largely because he was expected to grant such a pardon. Some, including Darrow, were members of the Amnesty Association formed specifically for the purpose of obtaining one. There was a certain irony about high-minded campaign workers working on an assumption that involved calculated deception of the electorate; in recognition that the vast mass of voters who might vote for Altgeld were clearly not in favor of such a move, the Amnesty Association had decided not to raise the pardon issue in the election, and "this policy was adhered to strictly."[2] Nevertheless, in Darrow's own words, "it got to be quietly understood that he would free the anarchists. This information was passed on from mouth to mouth where it could be trusted, but it was not publicly understood that way."[3] So a group that included some of the chief proponents of honesty in government practiced dishonesty in electioneering, and supported a candidate who they hoped would, on this question at least, fly in the face of public sentiment. Such was politics. It was true that there had been some softening of the public attitude, but it was by no means universal. Five years after the events in the Haymarket the Illinois Supreme Court held that to call a man an anarchist was libel, and to suggest that he was in any way associated with those who perpetrated the bombing was to bring him into "hatred, ridicule and contempt."[4]

Now the Amnesty Association wanted Altgeld to rectify some of the injustice done by pardoning those men who had not already been hanged. He had the power to do it, he knew the facts; there seemed nothing to hold him back. "Most of those who had been working for their release thought that the pardon would be his first official act," Darrow recalled. But it was not. The mood of expectation turned to puzzlement, then impatience; Altgeld's supporters felt betrayed by his inaction.

In fact supporters of the Amnesty Association who placed their faith in Altgeld made the same mistake as the politicos who had done so because he was "a man with a barrel"—they overestimated the extent to which Altgeld could be relied upon. Neither publicly nor privately had Altgeld committed himself to pardoning the anarchists, nor had he given any public sign of sympathy with the men at the time of their conviction. Subsequently he had refused to sign the petition that circulated asking for their pardon, though he gave money to their families; but this was done privately and could be interpreted as an act of compassion, not indicating any belief that the anarchists had been wrongly convicted. Altogether the assumption that Altgeld would use his official prerogative to free the men who had not already been hanged was based upon very slim grounds. As events proved, the question was not one Altgeld regarded as having high priority or upon which he had made up his mind when he came to power.

The compelling force that finally caused him to act was not idealism but a personal grudge against the trial judge, Joseph E. Gary, which had arisen in 1888. Just as a vendetta against Mayor Roche had been the mainspring of his successful campaign on Cregier's behalf, so his pardoning of the remaining anarchists was his way of settling an old score; once aroused, he was incapable of keeping his private feelings from influencing his public acts.

While Altgeld was still a judge, he had himself litigated in the courts of Cook County over a piece of land he owned in downtown Chicago, and in the course of the case had conducted himself so badly that the trial judge, Judge Waterman, found him guilty of contempt and fined him $100 notwithstanding that he found in Altgeld's favor in point of law. It was an unsavory scandal that a judge should be found guilty of contempt of court and afterward Altgeld appeared duly contrite. "It was exactly right," he said, referring to his punishment; "I was angry, acted foolishly and was treated according to the [trial] judge's duty and my own deserts."[5] But the statement belied his true feelings. He was still seething with emotion over the lawsuit, and when it went on appeal he was once more guilty of a most unjudicial outburst. The three-judge appellate court of the first division reversed the trial decision and remarked in conclusion, not in relation to the contempt, but as to the propriety of Altgeld's claim: "it appears that the course pursued by the appellee [Altgeld] was fair, open and free from any just grounds of censure."[6] When he read these words, Altgeld exploded in a totally intemperate fashion and at once wrote to the judges who had heard the appeal telling them: ". . . when you render a decision which some people would regard as a moral outrage, and you in the same opinion undertake to patronize me, then I protest. . . . I do not want your praise and ask you to strike it out."[7] The judges, not unnaturally, refused to strike the words from their opinion, and the passage appeared in the official reports.

Altgeld never forgave the first appellate division for what he regarded as a personal slight. In particular he seemed to hold one of its number, Judge Gary, who had three years previously presided over the trial of the anarchists, primarily responsible for the opinion, though it appeared under the name of the presiding judge and was subscribed to by all three judges. It is entirely possible, in view of the fact that he was a member of the judiciary himself, that Altgeld had inside information that Judge Gary was the true author of the opinion; in any event he treated him as such. Upon its publication, Altgeld saw that for the moment he was bested. But it was his characteristic never to forget a grudge: as Darrow admitted, he was "a hater and this was really his great weakness. . . . The truth was he hated Gary. . . . His feeling on this whole matter of his reversed judgment was very intense." So he bided his time, waiting for the chance to retaliate against Gary and anyone else who could be regarded as responsible for the decision against him. The lengths Altgeld went to were extraordinary: "For example, he used his political influence to remove the head clerk in the office where the opinion had been prepared—a man of fifteen tried and true years of experience," recalled Darrow. "He even tried to remove the next man, but that had to be done through me, and I wouldn't connive at it."[8] Little wonder that Altgeld was feared and hated. But it was not until five years later that he managed to strike a blow at the man whom he regarded as the real villain of the piece. And it was part of his peculiar, sinister genius to use the occasion for publicly flaying Judge Gary in circumstances that gave the judge no chance of redress.

By March of 1893, members of the Amnesty Association were reaching a fever pitch of indignation at Altgeld's inactivity and Darrow was profoundly worried. It was difficult for him to explain the delay to the influential Chicagoans who daily asked about it, and he himself had got to the stage of wondering "if we could have been deceived in Altgeld." With heavy heart he traveled down to Springfield and confronted the governor with the dissatisfaction of his supporters. Altgeld listened silently to Darrow's complaints, then tried to pacify him by offering him a piece of state patronage. But Darrow was insulted; he was not a dog to be distracted by the offer of a bone. "If that's your attitude, I'm through with you," he shouted. "I want nothing more of you until you do something about those anarchists. It is plainly the proper and popular thing to do."

Altgeld, retaining his composure, turned to face Darrow calmly and revealed for the first time how unpersuaded he was on the issue: "Go tell your friends that when I am ready I will act. I don't know how I will act, but I will do what I think is right. . . . I have not yet examined the record. I have no opinion about it." Thus, at a stroke, he had corrected the misconception that he was committed to pardoning the anarchists. He held out only the prospect that he would consider the case, and even as he did so, he warned Darrow of the political unpopularity that would come in the wake of a pardon if he chose to grant one. "When I do examine it I will do what I believe to be right, no matter what that is; if I conclude these anarchists ought to be freed I will free them. But make no mistake—if I do it I will be a dead man politically."[9] Darrow returned to Chicago disappointed and chagrined, wondering how he could keep the Amnesty Association at bay a while longer.

At the beginning of April Altgeld was staggered to find that the current issue of *The Century Magazine* contained an article by Judge Gary on the Haymarket trial, concluding that the trial had been entirely just and that the complaints made about it were without merit. No explanation ever appeared of why Judge Gary had chosen to break his proper judicial silence upon the case in the pages of *The Century,* but the timing of his article galvanized Altgeld. He saw immediately that, with renewed public attention focused upon the case, he could discredit Gary by the exercise of the prerogative of mercy for the remaining prisoners. At once the matter he had put off for months in the face of Darrow's protests became his first order of business. His eagle eye scanned the transcript of the trial proceedings and Gary's article, and mused over their implications. Then he decided upon his strategy: under the guise of correcting an injustice to the hapless survivors of 1886, he would arraign Gary in his pardon message. At last he would have his revenge.

In this matter he acted alone, consulting nobody, least of all Darrow. "If he had done it differently he might have gotten away with it better," Darrow later lamented, "but that bitter hatred of his got mixed up in it." Slowly and painstakingly, Altgeld went through the documents relating to the trial, reading every line carefully. He took his time, never heeding the complaints of his supporters, drafting a lengthy pardon message, measuring every word. Finally he was satisfied. On June 26, he called Brand Whitlock and told him to make out pardons for Fielden, Neebe, and Schwab. As Altgeld signed them, a supporter who had campaigned for exoneration of the men looked on and wept, but Altgeld brushed aside his halting gratitude with an impatient gesture. He was too proud to accept praise, just as he was too vain to take criticism. After the pardons were dispatched to the warden of the jail, Whitlock remarked to him: "Well, the storm will break now."

"Oh yes," he replied, with what Whitlock saw was a not wholly convincing air of throwing off care. "I was prepared for that. It was merely doing right."

The storm was indeed about to break, but the cause was not the act of pardon itself so much as the sixty-page statement of reasons Altgeld appended, which consisted of a detailed attack on Judge Gary's competence, fairness, and integrity. Its argument was divided into five parts:

> First—That the jury which tried the case was a packed jury selected to convict.
>
> Second—That according to the law as laid down by the Supreme Court, both prior to and again since the trial of this case, the jurors, according to their own answers, were not competent jurors, and the trial was, therefore, not a legal trial.
>
> Third—That the defendants were not proven to be guilty of the crime charged in the indictment.
>
> Fourth—That as to the defendant Neebe, the State's Attorney had declared at the close of the evidence that there was no case against him, and yet he has been kept in prison all these years.

These were serious enough allegations themselves, for all of them reflected upon Judge Gary. But that was not enough. Last of all Altgeld turned his knife in the wound:

> Fifth—That the trial judge was either so prejudiced against the defendants, or else so determined to win the applause of a certain class in the community, that he could not and did not grant a fair trial.[10]

He then proceeded to a detailed discussion of the evidence and principles of law involved in the Haymarket trial, on every point concluding that Gary had been wrong.

That pardon message was the measure of its author, reflecting at once his best and worst talents. It was analytical and well constructed; but it was also petty, malicious, and vain, and its attacks on Judge Gary were a scandal. Altgeld was lambasting Judge Gary for his conduct of a trial the result of which had been affirmed by the Supreme Court of Illinois, and which the Supreme Court of the United States had refused to reverse. To use the occasion

of pardon in this manner was an unprecedented outrage, shocking even to
those who were not opposed to the pardon as such. "There is no great cause
for complaint that three misguided men who now doubtless see the error of
their way are pardoned," wrote one commentator.

> Certainly the Governor is clothed with absolute power to pardon; but when he
> in exercising the pardoning power—the remission of a penalty inflicted by a court
> of justice—usurps judicial powers, and in his official capacity declares that the
> Supreme Court of the State and of the United States have affirmed the sentence
> of men who have not committed a crime, then it is that society must, by its duly
> constituted machinery, brand as untrustworthy such utterance. . . .

The article went on to suggest Altgeld's impeachment, on the ground that
"The Anarchists' case had become *res judicata,* and therefore, could not
properly be questioned by the Executive Department."[11]

Darrow was absolutely horrified at the pardon message, both for its content
and its political effects. He disagreed entirely with Altgeld's vindictive procla-
mation. "Gary was not so much to blame," he recorded;

> in fact, he was better than the majority of Chicago judges. He did only what any
> other judge in Chicago would have done and generally he was a great deal more
> unprejudiced than the majority. In this case he wasn't a big enough man for his
> job, but he did the best he could. The supreme court was much more to blame;
> although Altgeld condemned them, he did not mention them by name, pick them
> out and go after them as he did Gary."[12]

But quite apart from the unfairness of it all, Darrow saw what a catastrophe
the pardon was for Altgeld's future prospects. Now he finally understood what
Altgeld had meant by saying that if he pardoned the anarchists he would be
a dead man politically. It had never dawned upon Darrow that the pardon
would have taken this form, which inevitably meant that the wrath of press
and public descended upon Altgeld as much for the reasons he gave for the
pardon as for the pardon itself. If the pardon had been announced in the
normal way, it would not have created a furore. "Had Governor Altgeld
accompanied the pardon with a perfunctory official message, stating in the
general way that the pardon should be issued, comparatively little would have
been said about it."[13] Altgeld had, in an effort to stir up sentiment against Judge
Gary, actually stirred up sentiment against himself. Judge Gary was a well-
known and respected figure in Chicago, whose record was no worse than many
and considerably better than some. It was quite impossible for Darrow to
prevent a strong shift of city feeling against Altgeld as a result of the way the
pardon had been explained.

In point of law, Altgeld was not all wrong; there were legal grounds for
doubting the propriety of Judge Gary's conduct of the trial, especially his
rulings on jury selection. In an effort to show Gary wrong, Altgeld cited the
Cronin murder case, in which the defendant's conviction for murder had been
reversed by the Supreme Court of Illinois because the jury that tried him,
selected along the same principles as used by Gary in the anarchists' case, was

regarded as inherently biased.[14] Altgeld sought to show, by reference to the Cronin case, that the anarchists had not had a fair trial. But in this endeavor he was wading into deep water legally, and his reliance on the case was ultimately unconvincing. First, the state and federal supreme courts had approved Judge Gary's management of jury selection, and therefore he was practically vindicated. Second, the Cronin decision had not been rendered until three years after the Haymarket trial and was not retroactive. And third, the Cronin case had itself been the subject of much criticism. It was therefore far from obvious that the strictures of the pardon message were justified. Altogether Altgeld had behaved rashly in allowing his personal animosity to show through his official action so clearly. Darrow's verdict upon this action of his political master has stood the test of time: "It was the way he wrote that anarchist pardon which got him as much as anything; he was simply uncompromising. . . . He did it too flatfootedly and he played right into [his enemies'] hands."[15]

The reaction of the public to the announcement of the pardon was swift and unforgiving. At last, it was felt, the wicked governor of Illinois had shown his true colors. It was this event in 1893 that persuaded Henry Mencken's parents —and many others of their generation—that Altgeld was "an enemy alike to the Constitution and the Ten Commandments" and constituted "a communal devil." His reputation would never recover in his lifetime. Subsequent apologists have maintained that Altgeld was cruelly misjudged; that the public fell upon him unfairly, and that his nemesis was the tragic fate of an idealist in politics. But this is whitewashing the man. True, he had some excellent qualities; true, also, that the storm of protest following the pardon was an overreaction. Nevertheless the pardon message *did* show him as he really was. Carter Harrison was guilty of understatement when he observed: "it was not in his nature to forgive or forget."[16] No one who knew him, least of all Darrow, denied his malicious, even unscrupulous tendencies, or could be blind to his uncontrollable temper, his pettiness, and his abuse of the public trust. He showed more of these traits after 1893 when he became unashamed, imperious, and proud. Once he had managed to be elected he did what he, not the public, wanted. The consequence of the pardon was that the possibility of reassembling that strange coalition of interests which had brought him to power had been destroyed. From June 1893 he was effectively a lame-duck governor. He did not perceive this at first, believing that the storm would pass, and when he experienced defeat at the next election he was bitter.

Darrow for his part understood all too well that Altgeld had become the victim of his own vices and committed political suicide, but he did not desert his friend. On the contrary, he admired Altgeld's contempt of popular opinion, his willingness to baulk the madding crowd, his ability to face the music. Darrow loved Altgeld because of his faults, not in spite of them. When Darrow acknowledged that "Altgeld made my life what it is," he was referring to his sheer staying power more than any other characteristic. Darrow was to resist the mob with the same dogged courage, often for better reasons than Altgeld,

but never without the inspiration of Altgeld's example to strengthen his re-
solve. Darrow forgave Altgeld's many defects for the one virtue he respected
above all others: the psychological strength to stand alone in the face of the
contempt and loathing of the majority. In the first blush of urban democracy
in America, it was Darrow who resisted its excesses, striking a romantic figure
as he toiled against the vagaries of public prejudice. Darrow had found in
Altgeld a man who combined the moral honesty of his father with a much
more dramatic ability to influence affairs. Poor Amirus had had the right
instincts, but remained insignificant—a man too gentle to be a leader. Darrow
described his father as "the village infidel," who "gradually came to glory in
his reputation." Darrow, like his father, earned and valued such a reputation,
the difference being the size of their chosen villages. Amirus had moved to
Kinsman, but his son went to Chicago, perceiving, with Andrew Bruce, that
"to a very large extent Chicago is an overgrown village." His approach to all
matters reflected this understanding. People were everywhere the same, concluded Darrow; only the scale of operations in Chicago was greater. As to
dealing with politics on a grand scale, it was Altgeld who showed him how.
"John P. Altgeld was the biggest man Illinois ever produced," Darrow asserted. "Absolutely fearless—absolutely honest."[17] This was not mere hero
worship; beneath it lay a Nietzschean philosophy. Darrow was a follower of
Nietzsche, whose views were wholly compatible with Altgeld's course. "There
was almost no accepted truth that he [Nietzsche] did not challenge," wrote
Darrow:

> His idea was that whatever a majority believed must necessarily be untrue.
> . . . He defined good as power. The things that made strength were good; the
> things that were great were good. . . . Nietzsche has helped men to be strong—
> to look the world in the face. He was the manly philosopher who swept away
> the cob-webs of superstition, which ignorance and fear have ever been weaving
> around the minds of men![18]

When Darrow praised Altgeld's strength and immovability, he did so because
he was the embodiment of Nietzschean principle. Nietzsche struck a chord of
theoretical sympathy in Darrow just as Altgeld did in practice. Indeed Altgeld,
magnificent in adversity, was in Darrow's eyes a man made to Nietzsche's
blueprint. He was a superman, spurred by a psychological compulsion shared
by Darrow to place himself in situations that provided a chance to stand firm
against opposition, to test himself. In the face of this example Darrow was
developing a dangerous taste for tumultuous confrontation. It was to give him
fame and unique professional success but it was almost to destroy him, as it
actually destroyed Altgeld's prospect of political advancement and had left
Nietzsche a pitiful lunatic. In the next twenty years Darrow was to grow bolder
and bolder in defying public opinion: worrying, taunting, needling as he became the very incarnation of iconoclasm. Much later again, in the twilight
years of retrospect and dying passion, he was to have second thoughts about
Nietzsche and his influence, when he saw that his philosophy was a dangerous

intoxicant to the young and impetuous, as it had been to him. Meanwhile in 1893 he was to learn at first hand the meaning of Altgeld's suffering.

Startling though the public opposition to the pardon was, Altgeld did not neglect his gubernatorial duties. With Darrow acting as his Chicago agent, watching the maneuvers of various vested interests in getting favorable legislation through the Illinois legislature, Altgeld stood ready to exercise his power of veto to prevent the grosser frauds upon the public from becoming law. There were attempts to corrupt him, which he always fiercely resisted; this, too, meant that he would encounter more opposition when he sought a second term. If he had been a complaisant governor, who accepted the rewards that politics could bring, he might have continued in office, remained rich, and finally had more influence on the Democratic Party. But that was not his way. Instead of courting the forces of corruption, he exposed them. The pardon of the anarchists distracted him not one bit from continuing steadfastly, even recklessly, along a course of political self-destruction.

Now that his political base was smashed, his enemies set about eroding Altgeld's financial viability. His money was tied up in real estate, notably the Unity Building. "I am childless, and I look upon my buildings as children which will survive me and benefit the generation to come," he told a friend.[19] Now the Unity Building, the biggest and best of them, was taken away from him. His entire savings had gone into the project. It had started with high-quality tenants, but they left after he pardoned the Haymarket anarchists, to be replaced by well-meaning but less prosperous tenants who could not be relied on to pay the rent. Of course Altgeld's building fell victim to Gresham's law of tenancy—the bad tenants drove out the few remaining good ones. The result was that the income from the building dropped drastically and it became a haven of defaulters. "Any one not able to pay office rent moved to the Unity Building," Darrow recalled. His building came to be the address of young lawyers, radicals, and idealists who knew that Altgeld disliked exercising his right as a landlord to evict them. Every shade of liberal opinion was represented somewhere under its roof so that it became a veritable radical Tower of Babel, in which the only unity displayed among its tenants was the inability to pay rent. Altgeld, preoccupied by affairs of state in Springfield, let matters go from bad to worse, and the mortgage on the building was foreclosed for nonpayment of interest. Thus an age in which politics made pliable men rich made Altgeld poor.

It was a further blow to his battered psyche. But Altgeld did not falter. As Darrow observed, there was something magnificent about his resilience. In spite of the loss of his fortune, he resisted temptation; he was not corrupt. If he had wished, he could have saved the Unity Building. He could have sold his gubernatorial prerogative for profit. The street railway and other public utilities would have paid more for his signature to the famous "eternal monopoly" bills than his total indebtedness. He told Edward F. Dunne that he was offered half a million dollars to sign; but he refused and vetoed them.[20] He would not be bought. The days had gone forever when he would be wined and dined by polite society, or be a welcome guest in the mansions of Prairie Avenue. He gritted his teeth and did his duty as he saw it. The occasion of the temporary breach between him and Darrow passed and their reconciliation was complete. Altgeld turned his attention back to affairs of state, with three and a half years of his term still to run. And as the storm subsided, Darrow continued as his Chicago agent, determined to be more faithful than ever.

7

Exploring Downtown

With the pardon of the Haymarket anarchists Darrow was at last relieved of pressure from the Amnesty Association, but that did not bring him peace. The slackening of pace as the pardon furore ran its course brought back to him the awareness, more acute than ever, that he was temperamentally and intellectually unsuited to being a railroad attorney. It had been easy to forget his unhappiness at the Chicago & Northwestern while gripped by the cathexis of the amnesty; it was not so easy now.

Soon after his appointment he had attended a meeting at the Cavalry Armory protesting police brutality to some unionists. There Henry Demarest Lloyd spoke in a vein that reached to the depths of his sensibilities. He wrote to Lloyd the next day on the letterhead of the Chicago & Northwestern about the speech: "It was great. In logic and law it cannot be disputed. It made me feel that I am a hypocrite and a slave and added to my resolution to make my term of servitude short. I am glad you dare say what is true and know so well how to say it."[1] Unable to ignore his discomfort as an employee, Darrow asked himself whether a man with a paymaster whose business and attitudes he disapproved could ever truly be free—and knew, in his heart, that he could not. "It is hard enough to maintain an independent stand and freely express one's self without being handicapped by the desire for office or money," he concluded. Besides, the fruits of his skill necessarily went to his employers, whose interests led them to take positions unacceptable to Darrow. Yet he was well enough paid to make it difficult to give his job up. So Darrow stayed on, but sought distraction by throwing himself with great zeal into all sorts of extracurricular activities, as if to prove his independence.

The most obvious avenue of distraction was to exercise the option granted under his contract with the Chicago & Northwestern to undertake private practice of his own. This he did, beginning intermittently and alone in early 1893, by dealing with entirely conventional cases. He took pains to ensure that accounts of his successes reached Ashtabula: thus, that same year it was reported in northeastern Ohio that "Clarence Darrow is now a leading lawyer of Chicago, who recently came to notice by his winning a long contested land case involving $455,000."[2] But it was only a matter of months before he decided to form a partnership with some other attorneys.

He did not need to seek far for partners. His political contacts allowed him to join with three other well-respected lawyers, all considerably older and more experienced than he. Indeed he was the only one who had not held judicial office. One, Lorin C. Collins, was a former circuit court judge and speaker of the Illinois House of Representatives; another, Adams A. Goodrich, was a former state judge; and the third, William A. Vincent, was a former Chief Justice of the territory of New Mexico. Goodrich and Vincent were already practicing law together, so Darrow and Collins joined a going concern. The political magic carpet had carried Darrow much further than a man of his experience could otherwise have expected, and his familiarity with the workings of power meant that he was well on the way to a prosperous career at the Chicago bar. Henceforth this was to be the unbroken pattern of his career. His partners were to be party stalwarts and much of the lucrative business of his various law firms was to come because of political connections. Offices were taken in the Rookery Building—then the most lavish accommodation available in Chicago, though a little further from City Hall than Darrow liked—with the intention to practice business and corporation law, and with no expectation that the firm would engage in any but high-class bread-and-butter work. It was a prestigious address for lawyers. After the Great Fire of 1871, the original Rookery had served as a temporary courthouse, with the consequence that many of the older established law firms had offices there. Collins, Goodrich, Darrow & Vincent seemed to offer stability and respectability. Truly, the most revealing part of Darrow's plunge into private practice was its orthodoxy: his first Chicago partnership was constituted from the most respectable and sober elements of the commercial bar. Although history has dwelt upon Darrow's trials of special public interest, colorful and exciting litigations were always the exception rather than the rule. It was impossible to stray too far from the beaten path and make a good living as well. And Darrow, though veering politically toward the left, being at this time a populist in sympathy, had no inhibitions about setting up an ordinary law firm taking ordinary cases. He did not reason that because he was uncomfortable as house counsel to the Chicago & Northwestern he would be uncomfortable as a private practitioner serving clients whose interests were similar. His conception of "getting on" had many Victorian attributes, reflected in his vigilance in advancing his professional interest.

He found that there was an advantage to having learned the complications of pleading well as a prelude to practice in the big city. "In Chicago," wrote the Englishman James Bryce at the very time Darrow arrived there, "a place which living men remember as a lonely swamp, special demurrers, replications *de injuria,* and various elaborate formalities of pleading which were swept away by the English Common Law Procedure Acts of 1850 and 1852 flourish and abound to this day."[3] By the Illinois state constitution of 1870 nearly all the creaking machinery of the common law was maintained, including forms of action "usually stated in a rigid combination of Latin, Norman French, and archaic English."⁴ Altgeld had recognized the absurdity of the prevailing situation, observing in 1889: "in the mercantile world, in the manufacturing world, in agriculture, in medicine, in fact, in nearly every field of knowledge or human activity, there has been an advance . . . an honest effort to keep abreast of the spirit of the nineteenth century; while in our methods of administering justice we seem rather to have retrograded. What changes we have made in this State have tended to complicate rather than simplify."⁵

Darrow, like Altgeld, was impatient with all this, but nevertheless moderately skilled in its manipulation. He found the outmoded principles of pleading and practice a mere obfuscation of the real issues of a lawsuit—and in his strenuous efforts to get to these "real issues," he came to despise technicalities of all kinds. It irritated him to know that, as Maitland put it, "the forms of action are dead and buried, but they rule us from their graves," and he did his utmost to avoid their tyranny. He consoled himself with the view that trapped in every piece of legal rigmarole was a worthwhile issue trying to get out. His conviction that formalism in the law was a charade, disguising what courts and lawyers do and what litigation was really about, anticipated to some extent the school of "legal realists" that was to emerge in the generation succeeding his; and had he been interested in jurisprudence, he might have endorsed it. The fact was, however, that he had no abstract intellectual commitment whatever to law as such, and except as an incident to politics and government, he never turned his attention to legal philosophy. Rather, he shared an assumption with the worldly-wise luminaries of the Chicago & Northwestern's law department that law was to be used in furtherance of political aims and that lawsuits were extensions of political battles. If an enemy could not be outwitted through political intrigue, or defeated at the polls, then he might be restrained by the courts. If a policy could not be defeated because it was unwise, perhaps a court could be persuaded that its implementation was illegal; no political question was ultimately settled until it was litigated. "Nothing in the varied history of municipal government is more absurd and preposterous than the record of political quarrels carried into, and through, the courts from this city during the past two years," a leading journal had remarked in 1876.⁶ Regardless of whether a political motive was discernible from the record, or on the face of the pleadings, there was a good chance that a suit brought in Cook County had a political implication. Often the name of W. C. Goudy, or some other lawyer associated with him, could be found among the attorneys involved. Service with Goudy had reinforced Darrow's inclination to look behind the ostensible issues of a case to the real interests that underlay it, until in time he came to ignore almost entirely the way in which a case was framed in legal terms, and to concentrate solely on its social and political implications. Observation of Goudy's tactics and of the shrewd mixture of litigation and political intrigue with which business was conducted at the C. & N.W. did much to set him on this path.

Yet the glimmers of realism in Darrow's approach to the law did not make him a modernist in either his skills or attitude. If Illinois practice was old-

fashioned, Darrow was comfortable with it and never learned anything different. It so happened that throughout the entire span of his practice in Cook
County, the ancient system was preserved. From the state constitution of 1870
until the passing of the Civil Practice Act in 1933, by which time Darrow was
retired from the law for good, the forms of action at law and suits in equity
survived almost unmodified. In its tenacious conservatism Illinois was going
against the tide: "Led by New York, one state after another adopted a civil
practice act, until Illinois was one of only two states which clung to the
centuries old formalities at law and in equity. . . ."[7] By the time Illinois
capitulated, Darrow was an old dog not inclined to learn new tricks. In his
attitude toward practice, too, he reflected the older rather than younger generation. Even though he was principal in a succession of law firms, he acted
throughout as if he were an old-fashioned sole practitioner. It was Darrow's
misfortune to belong to an age in which office practice would eclipse litigation
in its economic importance.

Robert Ingersoll, one of Darrow's spiritual mentors and reputedly the most
successful lone practitioner in the nation, did not come close in financial terms
to lawyers like Joseph Choate, who were in substantial firms. Already the
professional ideal of standing alone economically was falling behind the times,
and it was becoming unusual for the leaders of the bar in any but small places
to be practicing on their own account. Darrow would live to see and lament
the domination of bar associations by lawyers who were members of firms that
were, like their major clients, corporate juggernauts. But even that was better
than being a mere employee of a business enterprise, serving for a salary, as
Darrow was. He believed that a lawyer should be true to the causes he supported, not hire himself out to inimical interests, and later had the temerity
to criticize Ingersoll for using his oratorical gifts in the service of bad causes.
Much of the disillusionment Darrow ultimately felt with his profession
stemmed from his frustration as one who, wishing to be independent, found
himself embroiled in the complicated mutual dependencies of partnerships.
Yet, if he was to have the economic success that he desired, he needed partners
and associates to carry him along.

Nevertheless he persisted in running his practice as if he were a country
lawyer. His filing system was nonexistent, his methods unbusinesslike, and
there was, in his dependence on the details of the local scene, much of the
village in him still. Though he appeared in cases all over the country, his
greatest strength in his home territory was "knowing his juries." Attorney Ben
Short reported that "he knew Chicago so well he could divine how the juror
would react to his theories by the part of the city he came from."[8] Such a skill
depended entirely upon knowing Chicago like Ashtabula or Kinsman. This
human, gossipy side of the law interested him; the other side did not.

Darrow's unduly casual attitude toward time-keeping, filing, and book-
keeping was to lead partners and clients alike to believe that, whatever his
politics, he subscribed in business to the purest form of anarchism. His first
attempt at big-time private practice found him totally inexperienced in the

running of a substantial law firm with a regular flow of business. The problems
of such a practice were unfamiliar to him and he adjusted poorly. To begin
with, most days found Darrow doing what his partners did: dictating letters,
interviewing clients, drafting pleadings, making court appearances, and drum-
ming up business, though he was inevitably hamstrung by his obligations to
the railroad. But soon his efforts in all these respects slackened off; psychologically, he regarded his office as a prison, keeping him from the important part
of life that took place outside its four walls. As in Ashtabula, his mind wan-
dered wistfully to the doings of the world while he sat with a client's file open
before him. The chores of law practice never held allure for him and he passed
many a professional hour waiting and hoping for a distraction. He was not
often disappointed, but when he was he all too often went out in search of one,
leaving his partners in the lurch.

Darrow's highly individualistic temperament rendered him incapable of
making the compromises and accommodations necessary to a satisfactory
partnership. He suffered from the not uncommon flaw of acting as if he were
boss, causing his partners consternation when they heard of his various unilat-
eral decisions. He had acquired the habit of command in City Hall, where, as
he said, he "had all the strength of a large city" behind his decisions—and
though that cause for respecting his wishes had gone, the imperial manner
remained. Success had taught him to expect implicit obedience to his will; any
intellectual question was open to free discussion, but on practical matters his
decision was not.

Darrow never made a satisfactory and lasting arrangement of his professional affairs. He did not manage to found a firm that would last throughout
his life and perpetuate his name thereafter and, ominously, this first partnership did not last long. It was to be the pattern of his professional life that he
never settled into one firm and stayed with it. The firms with which he was
involved showed a marked tendency to disintegration, and their shifting composition diminished his financial security, ultimately leaving him much poorer
than he might have been.

Soon he was seeking distraction from the railroad's business and the run-of-
the-mill clients of his new firm by sorties into more colorful areas of the law.
He raised some eyebrows by exercising his talents in a number of attention-
getting but entirely unpolitical cases during this period. He was retained to
defend three massage parlor proprietors, who had been charged under an
ordinance passed by the City Council on May 9, 1893, by which it was
unlawful for any female employee "to bathe, treat, manipulate, operate upon
or attend any male patrons." This ordinance, it was hoped, would diminish
the great number of massage parlors being used for immoral purposes. "The
only licensed houses of ill-fame in Chicago are the massage parlours," reported
William Stead, "fully 90 percent of which places are nothing more nor less
than houses of prostitution."[9] Darrow scored a considerable victory for his
clients by citing in their defense the provision of the Illinois penal code by
which no person could be convicted of a crime on the testimony of one who

participated in the offense, bringing out the fact that the complaining police officers had all submitted to massage in order to procure evidence against his clients. Upon hearing this, the jury returned verdicts of not guilty. The state's attorney, seeing that the ordinance had been rendered a dead letter by this tactic, complained: "Clarence, you have a way of massaging all of us."[10]

The prosecutor spoke the truth, for an element of Darrow's character that was coming increasingly to the fore was his love of confounding authority. There was nothing he liked better than setting the cat among the pigeons by dreaming up inconvenient arguments or causing well-laid schemes to fail. He was never so happy as when he tripped up the powers-that-be. Hamlin Garland put his finger on this when he said of Darrow: "He is on the 'off' side of everything."[11]

His iconoclasm was not merely intellectual; it reflected his emotional make-up as much as his convictions and was psychologically derived from a streak of awkwardness. He would adopt almost any opinion if it was likely to irritate enough people, being, as Garland surmised, "on the rampage." There was scarcely a group with which he did not disagree on something and his contentiousness was fabled. He liked to needle people. He was always putting his feet on the furniture, or stubbing out his cigarette on his dinner-plate. As he admitted, "I can be against anything." This natural tendency was aggravated by his dual dislike of his railroad job and his part-time practice; his financial prosperity seemed to him purchased at the expense of the spirit. And a rift was beginning to appear between himself and Jessie. The new house on Vincennes Avenue was the scene of the first overt signs of marital discord between them. Jessie complained, with reason, how seldom he was at home. In order to evade her complaints he stayed away still more, seeking distraction downtown even after putting in a long day of lawyering.

Distraction was not hard to find in the Chicago of 1893. The World's Fair had attracted every kind of huckster to the city and disguised the economic recession from which the rest of the Midwest was suffering. Chicago, a boom town since the Great Fire of 1871, reached greater heights still as the Fair displayed the fruits of American know-how. Business competed for the dollar by catering to every taste while assembly halls were let to every sort of organization. Visitors from all over the world converged on the city, which had become the marvel of the New World. Darrow did some speaking on the Exposition's official program, together with a mixed bag of progressives and eccentrics including Albion Winegar Tourgee of the National Citizens' Rights Association, John R. Commons, Frederick Douglass, and Susan B. Anthony. His most notable appearance was at the Labor Congress held to coincide with the Exposition; on August 30 he spoke with Henry George, Samuel Gompers, Thomas Morgan, Bishop Samuel Fellows, and Kate Field to an audience of 25,000. He found smaller but more permanent audiences in the new "settlement houses," most notably at Hull House, located in the steaming slum of Halsted Street, and also at Graham Taylor's similar—and, it must be said, rival —establishment called Chicago Commons, at which Darrow spoke occasionally. In addition, he also presided over the "Sunday Forum" held at the Institutional Church Settlement by the Reverend Reverdy Ransom. But it was Hull House, located less than five minutes' walk from either his office in the Chicago & Northwestern headquarters or the law practice in the Rookery Building, which most fascinated him. To its gates came every sort of visitor. When the English socialists Beatrice and Sidney Webb visited, Darrow gave a luncheon in their honor. But Darrow did not go there merely to cultivate the famous; soon he became an habitué of the settlement, participating in its discussion groups and lecturing to its assembled audience of self-improvers, enthralled by the variety of humanity to be found there. Like O. Henry in his "Bagdad on the Subway," Darrow was fascinated by the minutiae of city life, its characters and its secret sins, even to the degree that his enthusiasm was provincial. He became fond of lecturing to the multitude of tramps to whom Hull House ministered under the matriarchal management of Jane Addams, and his efforts were ultimately to bear fruit in the formation of the "Hobo College." With the Reverend Preston Bradley of the People's Church, he recognized that "many of the hoboes . . . were men with fine minds. They just did not believe in working regularly."[12] He ignored complaints that

> the tramp nuisance is becoming one of the most formidable of the lesser evils which afflict the Republic. The papers all this winter have been full of reports all pointing to the gradual evolution of the labourer in search of work into the mendicant tramp, and the still further evolution of the mendicant tramp into a species of banditti.[13]

His main advice to his audience when he lectured at the Hobo College was that they should never give in to any temptation they might feel to take a job. He believed, like the courageous Governor Lewelling of Kansas, who had admitted to having been a tramp in Chicago himself at the end of the Civil War, that "Even voluntary idleness was not a luxury forbidden to American citizens. The habit of fining tramps for being vagrants, and compelling them to work out those fines as municipal slaves on rock piles, was a flagrant violation of the Constitution."[14] Darrow therefore encouraged their calling, warning that whatever the travails of their chosen profession, the alternative of work was worse. In one of his most popular lectures he held up Walt Whitman as an example to be emulated: "As a man, he was classed by many people as a loafer—and largely he was. He knew better than to work when it wasn't necessary."[15] It did him no harm before the populist and proletarian audiences that he addressed to use the word "work" as if its only legitimate application was to manual labor. Yet this was not merely a pose; cerebration required much less effort from him than a day at harvest or in his father's carpentry shop. His own dissatisfactions with work in mind, he waxed eloquent on the desirability of avoiding it; from his more extreme pronouncements it would be easy to deduce that he thought the work ethic a mental illness. "Working people have a lot of bad habits," he was to say, "but the worst of them is work."[16]

This sentiment was, of course, entirely incompatible with the ideals of the settlement house, which was designed for the lofty but somewhat condescending purpose of uplifting the masses by teaching them skills with which to better themselves. Thorstein Veblen was soon to publish *The Theory of the Leisure Class,* condemning settlement houses as instruments of propaganda for the rich. Darrow was far from believing in their aims. As Gertrude Barnum, a young Hull House worker, recalled: "for years it was nip and tuck between Jane Addams and Clarence Darrow in a tug of war for young souls like mine." To her eternal credit Jane Addams tolerated and even encouraged Darrow's presence at the settlement, recognizing his talent even in his prevailing mood of discontent. The subversive nature of his contribution to Hull House at this period was reported by Miss Barnum. Darrow asked what she did there.

"I am helping to furnish legitimate amusement for the people," she replied seriously.

Darrow affected surprise: "Do they like that kind?" he asked.[17]

It was a fair question in the year of the World's Fair, during which Chicago catered liberally to all sorts of exotic tastes without regard to the law, and the most successful performances in town were those of the Park Theatre, described as "the antechamber of a lupanar." "Chicago May," a veteran of the booming days of the World's Fair, recalled "what dreadful things were done by some of the girls! It always made me sick even to think of them. The mere mention of the details of some of the 'circuses' is unprintable. I think Rome at its worst had nothing on Chicago during those lurid days."[18]

Behind the amusing interchange between Miss Barnum and Darrow lay real differences of opinion about the good that the settlement houses might do. For the impetus of the settlements was a desire to recreate the conditions of village life in the neighborhoods of the city, an effort to reimpose the restraints against which Darrow had rebelled in Ashtabula. He could not endorse their stated aim, though he found them amusing places of consort for bohemian company. The premise upon which they were run was anti-urban and their philosophy was doomed to eclipse. The cities would not disappear. In concentrating upon the slums, Jane Addams and Graham Taylor overlooked the signal reason for the expansion of Chicago: "despite its failures, the American city still held out the promise not only of life, but of the good life; it was the place a man went to in order to become the person he wanted to be."[19] Darrow was just such a man, beholden for his success to the city, and already it had his loyalty more than the "healthy natural community" from which he had come. Within a decade Theodore Roosevelt's Country Life Commission was to challenge the belief in such "healthy natural communities" by concluding that "drudgery, barrenness and heavy drinking characterized rural regions."[20]

It was not simply the social assumptions of settlements that Darrow could not accept. Beneath the settlement movement lay the theology of the American rural church. The morality preached by the settlement houses was an outgrowth of pastoral Christianity; settlements were set up by domestic missionaries, who plied their faith upon those whom they conceived to be domestic savages. They were, as Veblen perceived, evangelicals on behalf of a class ideal supported by theological justifications. Religious sentiment was inextricably tied to the village ideal of the unchanging, harmonious pursuit of a settled way of life by a small and homogeneous group of people sharing common values. Darrow did not share this vision of pastoral bliss. Indeed he saw the relationship between village and church as perpetuating nearly all that he challenged by a mutual endorsement of complacency. He sought stimulation, not the security of unquestioned tradition. He rebelled, just as his father had rebelled, against the narrow preachments of "do-gooders." He came to suspect, like Marx and Veblen, that religion in its emphasis upon social harmony was the opium of the people, deliberately administered to keep them quiet. He regarded Christianity as a "slave religion," encouraging acquiescence in injustice, a willingness to make do with the mediocre, and complacency in the face of the intolerable. Neither theologically nor politically did Darrow believe in turning the other cheek.

Nevertheless, for all his objections to settlement houses, Darrow could not ignore them; they were an integral part of the Chicago that he knew and proliferated to such an extent that by 1911 the annual Lakeside Directory listed over twenty-five of them in inner Chicago under a separate classification of "Social Settlements." Although Darrow did not believe in them they, more than any other single factor, shaped his world view—not by conforming it with theirs, but by acting as a sounding board for many of the ideas that were to make him notorious. And, although he never recognized it, he was at ease at their functions and among their supporters precisely because he was a product of the same tradition. He was rapidly coming to prefer the parlor of Hull House to his own home as a place of resort and solace.

There was much of the village in Darrow's fascination with the slums. His interest, like Hull House's, in the immediate locality of Halsted Street was a throwback to the village where neighbors knew each other's business and exerted moral pressure upon one another. The approach to the city's ills adopted by the sponsors of settlement houses and urban reformers generally was derived from the rural religious inheritance; their pronouncements on social conditions, industrial warfare, international relations, and racial justice were replete with biblical references. Many radicals of the 1890s saw themselves, not as leaving the church, but as returning to "true" Christianity, and this aura permeated the settlement house discussions. The perspective from which urbanism was judged was in many instances Christian, or professed to be; critics as various as Charles E. Russell, Lincoln Steffens, and William Stead all laid claim to being Christian radicals. When reproached for having a "Jesus complex," Upton Sinclair asserted that "the world needs a Jesus more than it needs anything else."[21] Almost no political tract of the times was complete without an admonition to follow the Golden Rule, an axiom favored by intellectuals such as Brand Whitlock and practicing politicians such as Toledo's "Golden Rule" Jones alike. A whole generation was unable to extricate itself from the influence of the Sunday school maxim, "Do as you would be done by."

Darrow, remembering the tedium of Sunday school and its humiliating neck-washing prelude, was less willing than Russell and Steffens to concede the similarity of Christianity and socialism: "I never saw any Socialist who could be a Christian, or any Christian who could be a Socialist, because either dope is enough to fill anybody. If a man is drunk on whisky he does not need morphine; if he has morphine he does not need whisky."[22] Notwithstanding these clear disavowals, he was plagued by allegations that he was "really" a Christian, and to the end spurious reports were circulated by religious zealots that he had finally "seen the light." The truth was that he remained as consistently an unbeliever as the evangelicals were devout.

In his many discussions in the parlor of Hull House Darrow was searching for a secular alternative to Golden Rule platitudes. He had moved to the city to escape from their stifling influence. He could not accept that the Golden Rule was either an appropriate or a realistic axiom for human conduct; certainly it did not accord with the prevailing mores of Chicago, where William Stead reported that the current version was: "Do your neighbor as he would do you—if he gets the chance."[23] Stead thought Chicago could be cured by spiritual regeneration, while Darrow on the contrary thought practice of the Golden Rule incompatible not only with commercial practice but with human nature. He believed in it in the same sense as a witty reverend gentleman opposing "Golden Rule" Jones, who said: "I am for the Golden Rule myself, up to a certain point, and then I want to take the shotgun and the club."[24]

But many of the radicals in Darrow's circle who clustered round the settlements were believers in a Christian socialism not greatly different from Charles Kingsley's. Some of them, indeed, treated them as identical. Charles Edward Russell, Darrow's lifelong friend, explained of socialism that "the essence of its doctrine is merely the practical application of the doctrine of Jesus Christ."[25] So objectionable was this view to Darrow that he felt himself unable to support any group of progressives wholeheartedly, even in the city, for fear of being contaminated by the conventions of piety. He was caught up in a fallacy: because many socialists claimed to be exponents of Christianity, socialism must be wrong; because the church laid claim to a monopoly of virtue, and the church was the enemy, it was wrong to be virtuous. And so it was with the other faiths that were debated at Hull House in those years. All of them had some fatal defects, none of them was completely acceptable. Religion was bunk, but so, in large measure, was socialism, or communism, or syndicalism, or anarchism—for that matter any other "ism." The difficulties were in human nature, not the system under which human beings lived. Having come from a background steeped in religion, it did not seem to Darrow as important to espouse an alternative dogma as to loosen the stranglehold that Christianity had upon the masses. The first task was to demolish before rebuilding. Like Robert Ingersoll, he felt such a necessity to undermine the grip of religion that the task of pointing out error and stimulating doubt was his highest priority. He became, in these years, a wrecker, who relished destruction of old values without having any clear idea what would replace them. He displayed on an intellectual level what the artist-builder of Cleveland, Kermode Gill, had observed in the exercise of brute strength:

> While it is difficult to get men to carry on any large construction, and carry it on well, and necessary to set task masters over them to have the work done at all, there is a wholly different spirit in evidence when the work is one of demolition. If a great building is to be torn down, the men need no task masters, no speeding up, they fly at it in a perfect frenzy, with a veritable passion, and tear it down so swiftly that the one difficulty is to get the salvage.[26]

This nihilism did nothing to bring Darrow spiritual peace. As he gradually worked through his negative attitude of mind, he became overwhelmed by a sense of purposelessness, brooding about the way in which he was caught up in railroad affairs for which he had no enthusiasm, and coming close to despair. Well-meaning friends asked him what the matter was, as often as not posing their question in the very religious terms against which he was in revolt. No, he did not regard the gift of life as a blessing from above, he would patiently explain. "Had I known what life would be like when I was born, I'd have asked God to let me off," he told them.[27] Downcast, he felt the mundane burdens of the day weigh heavily upon him, as he fought off self-pity and gloom. What he needed, though he only half-realized it, was a cause to take the place of the anarchists' pardon, another event like Altgeld's gubernatorial campaign that would keep him preoccupied and provide some excitement to lift him out of his depression. It could only be a matter of months before he found one. In fact, he found two.

8

Prendergast and Pullman

Darrow was first jolted into activity by a bizarre event that rocked Chicago politics. On October 28, 1893, a demented young man by the name of Eugene Prendergast assassinated Chicago's current mayor, Carter Harrison, his grievance being that he was entitled to have been appointed corporation counsel in the administration and that Harrison had deliberately cheated him out of the position. Darrow felt a personal interest in the case. Having occupied the position under Mayor Cregier, he might in a lighter moment have observed that it was a symptom of madness to want it, let alone to kill the mayor out of recrimination for not being appointed. On a more serious level, he must have reflected that if his plan for Altgeld's career had been followed, it might have been Altgeld, not Harrison, who was assassinated.

The public greeted Prendergast's act with horror: Harrison had been a popular figure and the very senselessness of Prendergast's garbled explanation added to its outrage. Almost inevitably the mob would be against him when he came to trial. Darrow's mind went back unhappily to the prejudice that had surrounded the trial of Guiteau, the mad killer of President Garfield, and to the fate of the Haymarket anarchists in the face of the crowd. "In all these cases the people of course wanted the killer put to death," he remarked sorrowfully, "and the voice of the people is the voice of their God." Still, although Darrow saw that the odds were against Prendergast, he consoled himself with the fact that a high-minded if not totally skilled lawyer, Captain Black, had offered to defend Prendergast in the criminal proceedings. So Darrow watched from the sidelines, in between his work at the Chicago & Northwestern, at Collins, Goodrich, Darrow & Vincent, and his trips to Halsted Street. The machinery of the criminal law ground slowly. It was not until well into the New Year that Prendergast came to trial. Then the prosecutor represented public sentiment every bit as accurately as Darrow feared he would, trying hard for a conviction and the death sentence, pouring scorn on the somewhat lame efforts of the valiant Captain Black to prove the insanity defense. There was no doubt that Prendergast was deranged, but the prosecution did not want him to avoid conviction by using the plea. Darrow followed the case closely, buying the latest editions of the newspapers, discussing the

case at Hull House, even occasionally dropping into court. Sometimes, perhaps, he wished that he was in Captain Black's shoes; but there was nothing
he could do, and no one doubted Black's energy and earnestness in representing his client. Besides, 1894 brought other concerns to Chicago.

The World's Fair of 1893 had brought Chicago unparalleled prosperity—
indeed it had staved off the effects of a national depression. The city had lived
in an economic fools' paradise during the year, oblivious to what was happening elsewhere; "the depression of 1893, the worst in the country's history,
demoralized business everywhere," recalled the younger Carter Harrison, "but
due to the 1893 World's Fair it by-passed Chicago until 1894."[1] While the rest
of the country was experiencing serious economic problems, the influx of
visitors to the Fair had kept every business in Chicago temporarily prosperous.
This was true even for professional criminals: "The World's Fair was a gold-
mine for me and my friends during the years 1892 and 1893," recalled Chicago
May. "The first of these years we nicked the builders, the second the visitors."[2]
And so it was also for legitimate business. But who was left to be nicked in
1894? The answer, as Chicago May and many other entrepreneurs found out,
was nobody—the boom had boomed. The consequences then were extremely
serious. Chicago suffered high unemployment, which rose during the severe
winter until a massive social problem had brewed. Manifestly, something had
to be done; some observers feared rioting. However hard the settlement houses
tried, they could not cope with want on this new scale. Fear was not confined
to radicals; Darrow's moderate partners saw the danger. In February 1894 the
Civic Federation was incorporated, which was designed to take care of some
of the most acute needs of the poor. Lorin C. Collins of Darrow's law firm was
one of its incorporators and trustees, along with many other entirely respectable and unextreme citizens who realized that something must be done. The
Federation set to work with a will, but it could only take care of a small
proportion of the acuter needs of the unemployed. Comprised of many of those
selfless volunteers in the settlement houses, including Miss Addams, it was in
essence merely a super-settlement, trying to fight the inexorable laws of economics. The unhappy realization of how little could be done came late to that
generation, but it came finally even to the indomitable Jane Addams. "In the
social and academic honors lavishly showered upon Miss Addams," wrote
Miss Barnum, "she found scant consolation for her utter failure to lessen
poverty even in her own settlement neighborhood."[3] If Hull House could not
cure the poverty of Halsted Street in forty years, the Civic Federation could
not cure Chicago's poverty in a few months. So in spite of the best efforts of
the many charities in the area, things got worse as 1894 unfolded. More and
more Chicago businesses laid off workers, leaving men and whole families
suddenly destitute, and scattered labor violence became common as wages
declined.

Darrow personally was not adversely affected by the depression. He was in
the pink of prosperity, with income from the railroad and his practice. Still,
the ugly mood of the workers did not pass unnoticed in the boardroom of the

Chicago & Northwestern; with good reason its principals apprehended the possibility of riot. In the early months of the year William Stead sensed imminent conflagration. "I have had some little experience of agitation in the Old World," he wrote,

> and I must say that I have never seen a condition of things in an English-speaking land where the signs point so unmistakably to change, and it may be to violent change. Evils often exist which are keenly felt but whose origin and source is so obscure that it is almost impossible for the sufferers to place their finger on the cause of their trouble, nor do they know how to redress it.[4]

In June 1893 a union of railroad men had been formed by a populist from Indiana named Eugene Debs. Marvin Hughitt and the other moguls of the industry knew that labor unrest in railroading would hit Chicago hardest of all since the entire system was centered upon the city. It became their constant concern that, in the current economic gloom, the railways should not develop into a focus of labor discontent. In fact the railroads had been successful thus far in avoiding major trouble and might have avoided it altogether but for the actions of the Pullman Palace Car Company and the pigheadedness of its proprietor, George M. Pullman.

George Pullman was a man of unquestionable business genius. He controlled a massive plant on the outskirts of Chicago and had built a "model village" next to his factory to accommodate his workers. He had prospered by supplying luxury sleeping and dining cars to be tacked onto the major railroads' trains. No one doubted that the Pullman Company had set a new standard of railroad travel which did it great credit; it had transformed long journeys from an ordeal into a pleasure. But in 1894 the Pullman Company's revenues declined, as fewer people could afford to travel by Pullman and demand slackened. George Pullman reacted by successively reducing the wages of his employees. This was standard practice of the time: painful, but not so out of the ordinary as to occasion much comment. In the six months preceding May 1894, wages had been reduced by approximately 25 percent. But there was the additional aggravating factor in the case of the Pullman employees that their employer was also their landlord, and while their wages went down, their rents stayed the same. Finally a delegation of workers requested that Mr. Pullman reduce rents in the village of Pullman or restore wages to their June 1893 level. Mr. Pullman did not even deign to meet with them.

There was considerable irony in the discontent of the Pullman workers, for they were supposedly living in a perfect environment. The trouble was that it was Mr. Pullman's concept of perfection, not theirs:

> Mr. Pullman's ambition was to make the city which he had built an ideal community. In order to do so he proceeded in entire accordance with the dominant feeling of most wealthy Americans by ignoring absolutely the fundamental principle of American institutions. The autocrat of all the Russias could not more absolutely disbelieve in government by the people, for the people, through the

people, than George Pullman. The whole city belonged to him in fee simple; its very streets were the property of the Pullman Company.

There had been a sign of the residents' unhappiness before, when they had by vote annexed Pullman to the city of Chicago. This had loosened the grip that the Pullman Company had over its employees, but George Pullman still held the whiphand. As a contemporary observed, "no annexation can destroy his control over the town."[5]

Pullman was held up to the outside world as a model facility. When the American Bar Association attended its annual meeting in Chicago in 1889, an excursion there by the delegates had been one of the high points of the program. But Pullman employees who actually lived there found conditions less ideal than visitors were led to believe, and considerable ill-feeling existed about the situation by mid-1894. When some of the men who had presented the workers' petition were dismissed, morale reached rock bottom. At that, the union local at Pullman declared a strike, and the Pullman Company in turn laid off all its remaining workers and closed its shops. Inflammatory as this sequence of events was, it would probably still not have touched off a major crisis had not the American Railway Union (ARU) before these happenings coincidentally scheduled its first annual convention in Chicago in the week beginning June 9. By the time it opened, the local railroad workers were already in sympathy with the Pullman employees, whether they were strikers or simply laid off. Naturally, being on the spot, they were profoundly influential with the delegates who assembled in Chicago, and when a motion was presented that all ARU members should refuse to handle trains to which Pullman cars were attached, it passed unanimously, to be effective June 26.

This turn of events transformed a local dispute with one company—not even a railroad company in the strict sense—into a national dispute between the major railroads and the emerging railway union. The directors of the railroads had no intention of uncoupling Pullman cars from their trains at the behest of the ARU even though many of them privately considered George Pullman to have behaved absurdly. Of course legal advice was taken by the Chicago & Northwestern no less than any other—but the legal position was a foregone conclusion. The boycott was illegal. And it was doubly illegal, not only as a conspiracy against the railroads, but also against the federal government—for the union had expressly declared that its boycott would extend even to those trains that carried U.S. mail, if they also included Pullman cars.

All this was not lost on Darrow, who could see that an historic confrontation between capital and labor was looming. Normally it would have riveted his attention night and day, and given spice to his work at the railroad. But by now he was already up to his neck in an extracurricular activity of consuming interest: a frantic, last-ditch attempt to save Prendergast from the gallows. For in the very week that the Pullman workers' demands had been rejected, Prendergast had been convicted of the murder of Carter Harrison. In spite of Captain Black's efforts, it appeared that the mob would have its way.

Darrow had been expecting just such a result, but still he was shaken when it was announced. His mind went back to that Independence Day fourteen years earlier, when the speech he had prepared for delivery at Jamestown had never been reported because of the news of the palpably insane Guiteau's assassination attempt on President Garfield. He felt sick as he recalled that Guiteau was convicted amid great applause in court after the jury had deliberated for less than an hour. Even then, his childhood horror of death had flooded back at the thought of the execution of Guiteau. Now, more than a decade later, the hanging of the mad Prendergast was a waking, vivid nightmare to him. In the years that separated the death of Garfield from that of Harrison, Darrow had read Altgeld's book on the treatment of crime, had become a firm opponent of capital punishment, and was already moving toward a view that accountability before the law was predicated upon a fallacious assumption of moral blameworthiness. That view was most clearly applicable to the mad—though he was later to extend it to the sane as well—and he now took the opportunity, in the midst of what he considered the slavery of his railroading employment, to pay his liberal dues by trying to save the poor, muddled wretch that was Prendergast. Dropping all his other commitments, he consulted two of Chicago's best-known lawyers, Stephen Strong Gregory and James S. Harlan, son of the Supreme Court Justice, about what could be done. Gregory, later to become a president of the American Bar Association, knew Darrow from the Sunset Club. He was a studious and careful lawyer whose work always bore the signs of good judgment and painstaking research; a man of pronounced liberal tendencies, yet "in spite of all this," recalled Darrow with grim humor, "he had a fine practice."

All three agreed that the only hope for Prendergast was to open civil proceedings to challenge his sanity. Under Illinois law, no one who was insane could be executed. On May 22, Darrow and Harlan became front-page news across the country by announcing that they would challenge Prendergast's sanity at a special inquest.[6] Between that date and June 21, the day set for opening the inquest, crucial developments took place in the Pullman dispute, but Darrow scarcely noticed them as he concentrated his efforts on the fate of one man. It needed no dissimulation on his part to take time to help Prendergast since his employers accepted his independent views without cavil. Tolerance of liberal opinion amongst its younger attorneys ensured the railroad friends in high places if some of them later chose political careers, as Darrow well knew; but his conscience was not troubled by this compared with the enormity of the injustice he feared Prendergast would suffer.

The legal situation was odd. Captain Black was at the point of nervous breakdown when his efforts to get Prendergast acquitted failed, but it was not clear that he had withdrawn from the case, or that Darrow and Harlan acted with Prendergast's authority. Even with the prospect of execution daily growing near, Prendergast was insane enough not to want to be found insane. He had not, of course, paid any fee or retainer to them. The two new counsel had to press on without Prendergast's cooperation acting, practically speaking, in the capacity of intervenors. When the inquest opened, Prendergast was the beneficiary of a galaxy of legal talent, for besides Darrow and Harlan, Gregory also appeared. They used their best efforts to prove to Judge Payne that Prendergast was too mad to hang. But things went badly. Prendergast became so unruly that at one point he was removed from the courthouse by Judge Payne, apparently protesting his sanity and repudiating the words of those who were trying to help him. As the hearing continued over several days, Darrow became almost totally immersed in its problems and would not have been conscious of any other events except the most momentous. But as luck would have it, simultaneously with Prendergast's hour of need Darrow's duties at the Chicago & Northwestern became more engrossing, if not congenial, than they had ever been before, as the railroads implemented their counter strategy against the American Railway Union.

The first major legal development was an application to the federal court, granted on June 29, for an injunction against the officers of the ARU, including Eugene Debs, by the receivers of the Atchison, Topeka & Santa Fe. This railroad had been run by receivers appointed under court order since the previous December, and it was well settled by court decision going back to 1877 that actions interfering or anticipated to interfere with the discharge of court-appointed receivers' duties were enjoinable. There was no question that this injunction was valid so far as it restrained interference with the A.T. & S.F.'s trains, but it did not cover the majority of the railroads affected which, of course, were not in receivership. An application for an injunction by those railroads not in receivership would need some different justification, and the legal advisers to the railroads had wracked their brains to develop a theory by which interference with the operations of all major railroads could be enjoined. In the face of the ARU boycott, the General Managers' Association, representing the major American railroads, decided on an overall plan by which they hoped to defeat it.

They did not merely litigate in the courts like any normal complainant. Through the use of their massive influence in Washington, they managed to get Edwin Walker, general counsel for the Chicago, Milwaukee & St. Paul Railway, appointed special government attorney, and on July 2 he obtained from the federal circuit court of the Northern District of Illinois an injunction against the ARU and its officers from interfering in the railroads' interstate operations or obstructing the carriage of the U.S. mails by railroad.

Of course no such thing could have been done had not railroading interests been stronger than any other lobbyists in the nation, and had not Pullman himself had some substantial claims to attention. Three months before the Pullman strike (when the observation could not have been colored by knowledge of it) it was recorded that he was "well known in Washington, and much esteemed by party treasurers, to whose campaign funds he has been a liberal contributor."[7] Darrow personally had no part in the formulation of this strategy: he had been nominated to the managers' committee, but when he told Marvin Hughitt that he could not serve on it in good conscience, he had been permitted to withdraw and do less soul-searing legal work. But Walker's appointment as a special attorney did not merely shock Darrow, it incensed him. "The government might with as good grace have appointed the attorney for the American Railway Union to represent the United States," he observed. The logic of his position appeared to be that an attorney who had recently been in the employ of the railroad interests ought to be disqualified from becoming a government attorney, at least one dealing with the government's interests during a railroad dispute, on the apparent premise that he would not put aside his allegiance to railroading interests in the discharge of his government duties. Darrow was possibly right in thinking that the government's credibility as an impartial agency between capital and labor was seriously impaired by making the appointment, though there was no law against it. But in his outrage with the appointment he slipped into error in suggesting that the government was not entitled to get an injunction, and that but for the appointment of a railroad lawyer as special U.S. attorney, no injunction would have been issued. Whether he personally ever believed that as a proposition of law may be disputed, but indisputably many unionists to whom he talked understood him to mean that there was no legal justification for issuing the injunction at the government's behest. In fact the U.S. government had the right to apply for and get an injunction on its own behalf to protect public order, during a labor dispute, or in any other circumstances. It had been done in New Orleans the previous year, and was done pursuant to the ARU boycott in St. Louis. Any notion that the federal government was barred from applying for an injunction in its own courts was legally quite absurd, though Darrow undoubtedly gave it currency among workingmen.

The three weeks following the issuance of the injunction were the most hectic in his life. The very next day, Prendergast was found sane and his hanging set for July 13. As the finding was announced, the poor lunatic agreed with it loudly. Darrow's efforts with Gregory and Harlan had been in vain. And on that day, too, the decision was made by President Cleveland, at the request of Edwin Walker, to send federal troops into Chicago ostensibly for the purpose of keeping order and preserving government and railroad property from the strikers but, as Darrow thought, really for the purpose of strikebreaking. The day after that was the Independence Day holiday, but Darrow was destined not to take a holiday for many days more.

On July 4, he rose early. Any hope on Jessie's part that Paul and she would have an uninterrupted day with him was doomed to disappointment. As usual he went downtown. The shops and offices were closed and the Loop's normal denizens were not there, but it was not deserted. Amazingly, federal troops were marching through its main streets. Along the shores of Lake Michigan hundreds of men were bivouacked, their tents making a strange contrast with the grandeur of Chicago's skyline. The General Managers' Association was determined not to stand by fiddling while Chicago was, as its members thought, in danger of burning.

Darrow knew that he must see Altgeld at once. He had anyway intended to travel to Springfield to beg for mercy on Prendergast's behalf, but the presence of United States troops in Chicago raised the most extraordinary political issues. On what possible legal ground were they there? Surely the managers had gone too far in requesting military protection for their property. There was no evidence that the local authorities were unable to maintain public order; Chicago was peaceful, having suffered almost no strike-related violence. Not for the first time, it became a matter of controversy whether the arrival of troops helped or hindered public order. William Holly, afterwards a law partner of Darrow's and a federal judge, thought it was a serious mistake to send troops in: "An examination of the files of the Chicago *Record*, a conservative and reliable newspaper . . . proves this. There is not a headline indicating organized violence or mob disturbances or serious injury to person or property until July 6, three days after the Federal Troops had been ordered to Chicago."[8]

Darrow's loyalties were oddly distributed. He was an adviser to Altgeld, who was sympathetic to the unionists, and at the same time he was an admirer of Grover Cleveland, who authorized use of federal troops. Still, he knew perfectly well that this was an occasion to support Altgeld and the unionists. As Altgeld's unofficial agent in Chicago, he had a special responsibility to stand by him. He took a train to Springfield at once, encountering no difficulty in doing so, and on the journey scanned the newspapers' accounts of what had happened. He flinched as he read on their front pages that Prendergast had been found sane and would hang within two weeks. But for the moment the strike news was more important. He saw with dismay that the newspapers were supporting the federal action, and portraying Altgeld as an upholder of anarchism in all its forms: "remember," they exhorted their readers, "his pardoning of Spies and all the rest."

On arrival at the state capital, he went straight to the governor's mansion. There he found Altgeld already preparing a protest to President Cleveland at what had been done. In fact the newspapers' allegation that Altgeld could not be trusted to keep order was entirely misplaced; Altgeld was by disposition autocratic and would readily have called out the state militia had it been necessary. His pardon message, far from giving any ground for suspecting his reliability in upholding the law, was on the contrary extremely severe. "Government must defend itself," he had written, "life and property must be protected, and law and order must be maintained. . . ." And he had since practiced what he preached in dealing with labor unrest. While governor he had called out the state militia to quell the disturbances during the quarrymen's strike in Lemont in June 1893, and only six weeks before the Pullman strike he had dispatched troops to all regions affected by the violence arising out of the strike of the soft-coal miners. As Waldo Browne justly observed: "No previous Governor of Illinois ever made such general and liberal use of the militia as did Altgeld at this time. . . . [T]he biennial report of the adjutant-general of Illinois for 1893–94 . . . reads almost like a record of war operations, so constantly and extensively was the State militia employed during those troubled days."[9] If any suspicion of nonfeasance were justified (and there was no evidence for it), it would have been better directed against the incumbent mayor of Chicago, John Patrick Hopkins. Hopkins was a critical ex-employee of Pullman who belonged to a wing of the Democratic Party unfriendly to Altgeld and who had the reputation of being "a trifle vindictive."[10] Browne dismissed as "a fantastic theory" the idea that Hopkins, "to satisfy an ancient grudge against the Pullman company, was working toward the latter's discomfiture in the strike"; but it did not appear fantastic at the time. Actually Hopkins was not being vindictive so much as engaging in buck-passing. He was waiting until the sheriff of Cook County, who was a Republican, acted—"each wished to throw upon the other the onus of an act that was bound to be unpopular with working-class voters."[11]

As Altgeld and Darrow discussed the matter at length, they pieced together the text of Altgeld's telegram of protest, which was sent to the White House on July 5:

> We have stationed in Chicago alone three regiments of infantry, one battery and one troop of cavalry, and no better soldiers can be found. They have been ready every moment to go on duty, and have been and are now eager to go into service, but they have not been ordered out because nobody in Cook County, whether official or private citizen, asked to have their assistance, or even intimated in any way that their assistance was desired or necessary.[12]

Caught up in the moment, Darrow felt the same exhilaration as when the two of them had planned the gubernatorial campaign together; the occasion brought recognition that his taste for the intricacies of politics should not be starved any longer. Feeling the old sense of camaraderie between the governor and himself once more, he took the chance to sound Altgeld out on the prospect of a pardon for Prendergast even as they worked at the draft of the telegram. Altgeld's reply was heart-rending. He would not exercise his prerogative of mercy in Prendergast's favor; he had learned his lesson about pardons from the anarchists' case. Darrow did not argue. The time was not propitious and he could see that Altgeld's mind was set. He turned back to the telegram and tried to concentrate on immediate problems. He worked until late that evening, when he took his leave of Altgeld and caught the Chicago & Alton's midnight train back to Chicago, promising to report developments in the city to Altgeld as they occurred. He slept fitfully in his seat until the train reached Chicago at 4:00 A.M. Realizing that there was no point in going home if he intended to do any work at all on the fifth, he stumbled out into the dawn streets, took breakfast, and then proceeded to investigate on Altgeld's behalf as the sun was rising. First he visited the stockyards, where he sounded out popular sentiment among the workers. Then he paid a visit to the cause of the present woes: the village of Pullman.

As he looked at the neat, standardized exteriors of the row houses at Pullman, Darrow must have doubted that they incarnated the highest vision of human happiness. They were attractive in their way, he could see. But inside those bijou residences what was there for the average family? He was repulsed by the antiseptic, orderly, and essentially dull routine that Pullman must impose on its inhabitants. As one who now spent more and more of his waking hours away from home, he was anyway not in the mood for the ideals of Pullman.

He left to return to Chicago and look over the huge marshaling yards of the railroads. And there he found what had scarcely existed before federal troops had arrived: arson, pillaging, and assault. Now the railroads' property was truly in danger. "As I stood on the prairie watching the burning cars, I had no feeling of enmity toward either side," he recalled. "I was only sad to realize how little pressure man could stand before he reverted to the primitive." Fatigued from his efforts in the last twenty-four hours, depressed by the outcome of Prendergast's sanity inquest, and torn between his affiliation with the Chicago & Northwestern and his sympathy with the strikers, it was a sight he never forgot.

That night he slept off the strain of the previous days and the next morning returned to the Chicago & Northwestern. Refreshed, he was open in his sympathy with the workers. When he saw in the newspapers Cleveland's reply to Altgeld, refusing to withdraw federal troops, his mind was completely made up about the affair. Florence Kelley was trying to arrange a protest meeting on behalf of the strikers at Central Music Hall and approached Darrow, who agreed to speak and contribute $25 toward the cost.[13] Still the C. & N.W. remained remarkably tolerant of his dissent and although tension in the strike was mounting, Darrow felt perfectly able to remain in its employment. Besides, he was not directly concerned with the legal response to the strike by the railroads, and was thinking more about Prendergast than any of the Northwestern's business.

Darrow knew that Altgeld would not pardon Prendergast, but he was not quite without hope yet. Prendergast's execution had been set for July 13. Darrow knew that Altgeld must go out of state on business in the next week, and it was then that he hoped to try once more to save Prendergast. According to the Illinois constitution, whenever the governor left the state, the lieutenant governor was entitled to exercise all the governor's powers in his absence. Relying on this provision, Darrow determined to ask the lieutenant governor, Joseph Gill, to pardon Prendergast as soon as Altgeld left. So the next week he made yet another visit to Springfield. While he was waiting for an audience with the lieutenant governor, another visitor was ushered in. It was Brand Whitlock, then a Chicago journalist and unknown to Darrow, who had come down to Springfield for the selfsame purpose. The lieutenant governor's secretary asked Whitlock what his business was, and he replied, "the Prendergast case." Whitlock described what followed.

"What interest do you have in the Prendergast case?" asked Darrow.

Whitlock replied, "None, except that I don't want to have him, nor anybody, hanged."

Whitlock was impressed by Darrow's reaction, though as yet he had no knowledge of who he was:

> On the man's face, tired, with the expression of world-weariness life gives to the countenance behind which there has been too much serious contemplation of life, a face that seemed prematurely wrinkled, there suddenly appeared a smile as winning as a woman's, and he said in a voice that had the timbre of human sympathy and the humor of a peculiar drawl: "Well, you're all right, then."

They introduced each other and got talking. Whitlock admired the fact that "He had taken it upon himself to neglect his duties as attorney of some of the railroads and other large corporations in Chicago long enough to come down to Springfield on his own initiative and responsibility to plead for the lad's life. ...." In the afternoon a hearing on the pardon was held, of which Whitlock recorded that Darrow "made one of those eloquent appeals for mercy of which he is the complete master."[14] Everyone present was moved, but the lieutenant governor refused to succumb.

A sad pair of men traveled back to Chicago that night. The very last hope had gone. On July 12—by which time Altgeld had returned to the state—there was an "eleventh hour" plea made for Prendergast's life, but it was *pro forma* and Altgeld refused reprieve peremptorily, saying that every opportunity had been given to prove Prendergast's insanity, without success, and now justice must take its course. On the thirteenth the trapdoor opened beneath Prendergast and he hanged until he was dead.

Meanwhile the conflict between the railroads and the ARU had reached critical proportions. The injunctions obtained by Edwin Walker, directed against the union's officials and expressed in the widest terms, were obviously not preventing trouble. There was some question whether it was within the officials' power to stop what was now a national confrontation; feeling ran so high among the rank-and-file that they could do little to restrain the skirmishes which were taking place as troops moved the mail trains. But the General Managers' Association nursed the not wholly unfounded suspicion that the leaders of the union movement were not even trying to stop the violence. Eugene Debs, in particular, seemed to wish to enter a trial of strength between labor and capital and settle labor grievances in one fell swoop, and even favored a general strike in sympathy with the striking railroaders. This was resisted by Samuel Gompers of the American Federation of Labor, but the ARU was not a member of the A.F. of L. and its claim upon the machinery of the latter was small. Already the newspapers were referring to the strike as Debs' Rebellion. So, using its strength with the federal government, whose legal machinery the Association by now effectively controlled in Chicago, the General Managers' Association went one step further in escalating the battle. On July 16 it had Debs and three other union officials arrested not only for breach of the terms of the injunction, but also in pursuance of a federal indictment charging them with criminal conspiracy. It appeared to the unionists that Judge Peter S. Grosscup, who was closely connected with the General

Managers' Association, believed unionists to be criminal conspirators almost by definition. But there was no doubt that many supported Judge Grosscup. His charge to the grand jury was hailed in the legal press as "undoubtedly correct" and "a clear and forcible declaration of principles which, though not new, have modern application."[15]

Up to this stage the ARU had been relying upon the advice of its regular counsel, William W. Erwin of Minneapolis, but the arrests of July 16 made it dramatically clear that more legal talent was needed. The decision was made to approach James S. Harlan. After thinking the matter over overnight, he refused to accept the job, telling his would-be clients that he could not afford to be identified with the case, "for you will be tried upon the same theory as were the anarchists, with probably the same result."[16] Only after this refusal was Lyman Trumbull, author of the thirteenth amendment to the Constitution abolishing slavery, consulted. Trumbull, one of the organizers of the American Bar Association in 1878 and already past eighty years old, was asked whether he knew of any lawyers who might be idealistic enough to represent the union. He thought of the valiant efforts of Stephen Gregory and Clarence Darrow in trying to save Prendergast. There was idealism. He knew Darrow because for a brief period Darrow had taken professional offices in the same building—115 Monroe Street—from which he practiced. Why not try those two men?

Trumbull's suggestion was taken up at once, and both Gregory and Darrow were contacted the same day. The union could not afford to pay them fees, and the battle would be long. Darrow did not want to commit himself to this thankless task, but he knew that he would regret it for the rest of his life if he did not take up the challenge. It was an ideal opportunity, as he saw it, to do penance for the work put in on behalf of the railroad; having worked for capitalism, he could now redress the balance by undoing some of the benefits his railroad work had conferred on the employer class. He believed in the cause. When he heard that Gregory was willing, he gave in: "I did not want to take it up knowing about what would be involved. I knew that it would take all my time for a long period, with no compensation; but I was on their side, and when I saw poor men giving up their jobs for a cause, I could find no sufficient excuse, except my selfish interest, for refusing."

It remained for him to give the Chicago & Northwestern notice. He went to see Marvin Hughitt to tell him of his decision. Hughitt listened attentively to the reasons Darrow gave for going to the aid of the strikers. He did not share Darrow's political sympathies, but he understood his sincerity and agreed with him that he should do what he believed to be right. Whatever bitterness the litigation caused in the outside world, it did not sour the relationship between these two men. Hughitt liked and respected Darrow, and to ease his path as a private practitioner offered to send him railroad work and continue his salary at half rate, which he did for a number of years. Thus, by a generous gesture, Hughitt subsidized Darrow's opposition to his railroad interests.

Estranged though he was from the corporate philosophy of the Chicago & Northwestern, Darrow had gained by his experience there. Having worked for a railroad, he ever afterward appreciated the arts of running one. And through-out his life men of practicality, who could get things done, commanded his allegiance far more than "dreamers." There was no great distance between Hughitt and Altgeld in their qualities of management, for though Altgeld might dream, he had also been a successful businessman. Darrow admired the spirit that could translate an idea into practice, whether in politics or in business. He was in many ways a good railroader, in the golden age of railroads when the ability to run a railroad was accounted an infallible benchmark of social utility. As he left Hughitt's office, he stammered out his thanks for the kindness and indulgence that his superior had always displayed. Hughitt and he both understood that he was at a crossroads and that his career could never be the same after that July day. He stepped out of the railway offices having found his true destiny at the age of thirty-seven.

PART TWO

From Success
to Disaster

9

In Re Debs

Having decided to aid the striking railroaders, Darrow threw himself into the preparation of their case with all the fervor that he had displayed back in Ohio when pursuing Brockway's claim against Jewell, the guardian of the drunkard Clark. As he said then, "it was as if my life depended upon the result." He worked with almost demonic enthusiasm, seeking to make up for the time he regarded as squandered in the service of the Chicago & Northwestern. The case served as a penance for his past, now that his strong emotions and abundant energy were at last harnessed with his ideological sympathies. His years with the city and the railroad had reinforced an opinion nascent within him that law and politics were inseparable; that, indeed, the one was the product of the other. He carried that conviction back with him into private practice, displaying it conspicuously in his approach to the problems of his new-found clients. It seemed natural to him that the political aspects of their situation should be the central point of discussion, and if the law deemed them irrelevant, so much the worse for the law. Brushing aside mere technicalities and looking to the substance as no lawyer representing labor had ever done before, he was determined to get to the real matters at issue between capital and labor. The effect was startling to the employers and invigorating for the workingman: it was as if a great fog had been lifted so that things were seen for what they really were.

Up to this time attorneys had stood apart from the labor clients they represented, translating their cause into the terminology of the courts so that it was impossible for unionists to sustain the impetus generated by the original dispute. But from the beginning Darrow showed himself an advocate not merely of the legal arguments in favor of the workmen, but of the political and economic ones as well. In fact he was more vitriolic than even the most militant of the ARU leadership. He regarded the litigation as a continuation of the dispute, not its ending. Writing with the Pullman strike in mind, he said: "Industrial contests take on all the attitudes and psychology of war, and both parties do many things they should never dream of doing in times of peace. Whatever may be said, the fact is that all strikes and all resistance to strikes take on the psychology of warfare and all parties in interest must be judged from that standpoint." This viewpoint did not originate with Darrow—it was a commonplace of radical labor organizers, often articulated by Debs, his own client—but what was distinctive was Darrow's serious attempt to carry it into court.[1] Once he had entered the Pullman case, he conducted himself as a belligerent, giving no quarter and expecting none.

He began by concentrating on the criminal charges that had given Eugene Debs a memorable taste of the Cook County jail. Debs recalled:

> I was given a cell occupied by five other men. It was infested with vermin, and sewer rats scurried back and forth over the floors of that human cesspool in such numbers that it was almost impossible for me to place my feet on the stone floor. These rats were nearly as big as cats, and vicious. I recall a deputy jailer passing one day with a fox-terrier. I asked him to please leave his dog in my cell for a little while so that the rat population might thereby be reduced. He agreed, and the dog was locked up with us, but not for long, for when two or three sewer rats appeared, the terrier let out such an appealing howl that the jailer came and saved him from being devoured.[2]

Debs for his part was glad to have found Darrow to defend the union. Both men were populists by sympathy, but there was more than merely political agreement between them. Debs approved of Darrow's uncompromising style. Much later there would be a parting of the ways, but for the moment they were a perfect match as attorney and client. Darrow's perception of the prosecution as a virtual deliverance of the powers of government into private hands had a lasting effect upon his attitude toward power, kindling the notion in him that lawful authority deserved no special respect, for it had no spiritual or secular justification except the habit of obedience imbued into the populace and the ultimate threat of force. *Authoritas* was only "what you can put over," its effective component being audacity rather than legitimacy. In time Darrow would come to regard almost any exercise of authority as pretentious, and to take a particular delight in challenging its tribunes and pricking its balloons. Tensions between men and groups were, he thought, solely trials of strength and bluff to see who could get away with what. This theory of politics had an essential unity with Darwin's theory of natural selection in nature, from which in the course of time it became almost indistinguishable in Darrow's mind. Those who sought and gained control over the organs of government were hardy predators, seeking to be kings of the jungle, who survived in a cruel state of nature because they were stronger, more cunning, and ruthless than the rest. Only by challenge from some equally ruthless group could they be unseated.

From July 1894 until the opening of the criminal proceedings the case maintained absolute first claim on Darrow's time. His partnership with Goodrich, Adams, and Vincent became a dead letter as he concentrated upon the union work. Without resigning from the partnership, he had entered the case on his own behalf, an action his partners treated as one more sign of Darrow's unmanageability.

But Darrow was not contrite. On the contrary, he even felt that, having found his true vocation, he should gather his relations around him to share his experience. This was the role for which his father had spawned him; now at last he had found something of which he could be proud, and he wanted Amirus to share in it. There was nothing to keep Amirus in Kinsman any longer—Emily was long since dead and all their children had grown up and gone away, several of them, like Clarence, to Chicago. Just as in his earliest years in the city Clarence had taken pains to send back news of his triumphs to Kinsman, so now he was anxious that his father should see at first hand what promised to be his greatest success so far. Edward Everett and Mary were both schoolteachers in the city, and Herman, the youngest son, had arrived the previous year. Once the battle with Pullman had begun and Amirus was brought to Chicago to see the fireworks, it was as if a family reunion had been convened to mark Clarence's emergence as labor's champion. Amirus, already seventy-six years old but still sprightly and remarkably unbent by age, followed every step in the proceedings with keen interest. He watched in amazement the assurance with which Clarence faced the big city, seeing that his fifth child displayed a power, an aggression, a determination, that had certainly not been learned from him.

The criminal case against Debs called before Judge Grosscup on January 26, 1895, was met with a fighting defense by Darrow. Indeed it was remarked that as between Debs and his counsel, "it was the young lawyer in his first big case whom one could pick as the fiery 'rabble-rouser' rather than his dignified client." It was a penetrating observation, which went far to explaining the reasons both for Darrow's success and for his ultimate downfall as a repre-sentative of labor: passionately involved in the proceedings, he would neither give quarter nor bow to the majesty of the law. It was not merely that he adopted the political aims of his clients; he became more radical than the radicals, taunting, infuriating, and goading authority to paroxysms of annoy-ance. He showed his scorn for the proceedings in every possible way, slouching in his chair with a disdainful expression and a characteristic posture described as "sitting on the back of his neck."[3] His very demeanor as the prosecution presented its case was factually, if not legally, contemptuous, a silent reproach to authority. His emotions as well as his intellect were engaged, and his sharp, bitter words conveyed all the pent-up resentment of clients who felt sorely misused. He was a good hater, with a capacity for courtroom hostility that few advocates have rivaled.

From the start of the case Darrow was ready to spew out all his venom on the prosecution, which he perceived as such a misuse of government power as to amount to a conspiracy against the public interest. He railed against the crime of conspiracy, which had been the darling of the prosecutors in the Haymarket anarchists' case, telling the jury:

> This is an historic case which will count much for liberty or against liberty.
> . . . Conspiracy, from the day of tyranny in England down to the day the General
> Managers Association used it as a club, has been the favorite weapon of every

tyrant. It is an effort to punish the crime of thought. If the government does not, we shall try to get the general managers here to tell what they know about conspiracy.... These defendants published to all the world what they were doing and in the midst of a wide-spread strike they were never so busy but that they found time to counsel against violence. For this they are brought into court by an organization which uses the government as a cloak to conceal its infamous purposes.

Then he went on to say some hard words about the fact that, although the prosecution was brought in the name of the United States, it had been instigated by the General Managers' Association entirely for the benefit of its members. He made much of the special position of Edwin Walker and Attorney General Richard Olney, both of whom were ex-railroad attorneys.

After this powerful beginning Darrow came to the particular accusations against his clients. "Where," he asked, "does wrongdoing really lie?" At this juncture he summarized the grievances of the Pullman Company workers. How his clients rejoiced as their cause reverberated round the courtroom in Darrow's vigorous language. This was the fighting talk they wanted to hear; at last they had found a lawyer who was not mealymouthed, and had the courage to speak plainly on their behalf. The new unconciliatory note that Darrow had sounded did not escape the notice of either the judge or the prosecutor. They recognized that Darrow was a man to be reckoned with, more than a match for some of the pompous witnesses for the prosecution whom he might be expected to cross-examine. Altogether the members of the prosecution became rather less enthusiastic about the criminal proceedings than they had been earlier. As it was, he mauled several of their witnesses; he had the capacity, indispensable in a good cross-examiner, to be really nasty.

Darrow later protested that his quarrels were with ideas, not with men; but that was not the whole truth. Many of those whom he attacked for their ideas were people he did not like: to believe that his trial performances were mere playacting was to misunderstand the man. He used argument and invective not merely to prove a point but to flay and diminish his enemies. Arguments were weapons of psychological warfare and cross-examination became an instrument of personal cruelty in his hands. Many of those with whom he disagreed took personal offense at the vitriolic way he attacked. His cross-examinations frequently left scars upon the pride of the recipients that never healed. Darrow was not so incapable of divorcing political disagreement from personal animosity as Altgeld, but he was far from being unaffected by his likes and dislikes among men. Antipathy gave an edge to his speeches and an added subtlety to his tactics. Even if he had no instinctive dislike for his legal opponents, he would deliberately pick a "goat" to be the brunt of his attacks.

It did not need much imagination for the powers behind the prosecution to guess who the "goat" in this particular case would be. Darrow had already told the jury that if the government did not call members of the General Managers' Association, the defense would. There was one goat above all that Darrow was going to torment: George M. Pullman. The government knew perfectly well that Pullman would not come out of the ordeal well. Already a subpoena had been issued for his appearance, and Darrow was flaying himself into ever greater feats of indignant cross-examination with each passing day. Unless something was done quickly, certain disaster for the railroad interests lay ahead. Either Pullman himself, or his advisers, decided that discretion was the better part of valor and that the unpleasantness of facing Darrow's tongue-lashing counterbalanced any possible benefit that the prosecution could confer. Behind the scenes, the right people (including Judge Grosscup) were spoken to about avoiding Pullman's imminent humiliation. It was decided that, rather than risking not only Pullman's personal discredit but also the possibility of an acquittal of Debs and the other ARU officials, it would be better to abandon the prosecution altogether.

The opportunity came when a juror fell ill. No alternate had been selected to carry on in such an event, and Judge Grosscup adjourned the case without making provision for resuming it. In theory, the suspension of the prosecution was only temporary until the juror recovered his health, but Darrow suspected with good reason that this was a covert way of abandoning the prosecution. He moved unsuccessfully to empanel another juror and get the record thus far read to him, and he made repeated inquiries about the resumption of proceedings, either when the juror recovered or with a new jury—but of course nothing happened and the charges were quietly "buried." Thus a prosecution instigated by private interests in the name of the United States was likewise terminated by those same private interests.

Naturally Judge Grosscup's adjournment of the criminal case was very frustrating for Darrow; apart from any other factor it deprived him of the jury, before whom he was at his best. By comparison, the later civil proceedings were calm and unemotional. But Darrow knew that his approach had discomforted the opponents of labor very greatly and that his chance would come again. The venomous frontal attack was to become his classic strategy in defending labor and he bided his time until other cases came his way in which the technique could be used again. In other words *United States* v. *Debs* gave Darrow the chance to develop, but not perfect, the style for which he was to become noteworthy in the defense of labor. The criminal case marked an important turning point in the legal relations between management and labor, which was largely engineered by Darrow; his defense had introduced an entirely new tone into court, carrying the resentments of acute industrial warfare to law as had never been done before. In pointing an accusing finger at the employers, he had opened a new era in labor litigation that was to make lawsuits overtly acrimonious. He refused to put aside hostility in court, thus making any "peacemaking" function of the legal process yet more difficult to achieve. In this respect Darrow's stance in the Debs case drew up the battle lines of labor litigation that were to prevail for the next twenty years, on which neither side gave quarter, and over which a delirious intensity was reached in successive cases until World War I. His determination not to compromise, his "duel to the death" mentality, verged upon fanaticism of the kind that, in other areas, Darrow himself was to disparage. If every strike was a conspiracy, then every prosecution of a laboring man was a persecution. Neither side gave the other credit for good faith—and, of course, bad faith turned out to be the result.

As Darrow regretfully turned his attention away from the criminal charges, he determined to sustain, so far as possible, the same vigor in defense of the civil proceedings as there had been in the prosecution. Inevitably some impetus was lost. The contempt proceedings were necessarily less dramatic, but Darrow knew that he had the General Managers' Association running scared by his belligerence, while simultaneously he had done wonders for the morale of the union's rank-and-file. Always previously when a labor dispute had got to court, the workingmen lost. Now, even though they had not technically won, the most unsympathetic newspaper accounts admitted that Darrow gave as good as he got and even better. So, with slight modifications, Darrow tried to translate his criminal defense strategy into the injunction case. There, however, he ran into difficulties. Whereas in the criminal trial he had undoubtedly dominated the defense, in the civil case he did not have the same primacy; indeed he was theoretically subordinate to both the other attorneys. William Erwin, who remained the ARU's "official" attorney, had the advantage of being much better known to the unionists outside Chicago than Darrow and having their implicit trust. Stephen S. Gregory had a different edge over Darrow by being senior to him in years and experience, and already highly regarded in his profession (he was later to be a president of the American Bar Association). Furthermore Gregory was already engaged with Erwin in the injunction case against the ARU that had been started in St. Louis, Missouri. Professionally, therefore, Darrow was in some ways the junior counsel in the team.

This triumvirate of lawyers fighting for the ARU was, like many a litigation team, an ad hoc coalition of different temperaments and persuasions. One of its difficulties was that its members never completely agreed on the theory and strategy by which they would defend the case. This was not wholly their fault, for they had to challenge an injunction issued hurriedly and with only cursory explanation in the first place. When Edwin Walker had applied for it on July 2, it had been granted with a minimum of argumentation so that the legal rights and wrongs never got a full airing. Because of this, the litigation that followed was in large measure a process of *ex post facto* rationalization for both sides; Walker had deliberately acted first, leaving argument until later. By the time of the contempt proceedings the issue before the court was not merely whether the injunctions were properly granted but whether, since they had been granted, they had been disobeyed. Much of the difficulty for the defense was that it consisted largely of a direct challenge to the injunctions themselves rather than a showing that their clients were not contemptuous. Had the case to be decided by a jury, with which logic might not have been decisive, this approach could have been effective; but the civil proceedings required reasoning on paper, not oratory, and the persuasion of judges, not a jury.

Notwithstanding the great legal difference between the criminal and civil proceedings Darrow persisted in regarding them as all of a piece, and his attack on both was very much the same. He criticized the U.S. government for bringing the prosecution, and when the prosecution was buried, he criticized the government for seeking and obtaining an injunction. In consequence, a large part of the legal wrangling during the next year related to the question of whether the government had a right to obtain an injunction, upon which the response of the courts was a foregone conclusion. Darrow would not adjust to the dropping of the criminal case and continued to use the same argument in the civil case that he had prepared for the criminal one. No matter that the course of litigation did not appropriately raise the issue he wanted to talk about, he talked about it anyway, with the result that false hopes were raised in his clients.

The defense put forward was finally a mishmash of none-too-consistent propositions. Darrow persisted in the suggestion that the government was in some way prohibited from obtaining an injunction, but he also objected that the injunction was too broad in its terms and that anyway neither Debs nor the other officials of ARU had violated it. His position here was most strange. "Mr. Debs and all the members of his board were enjoined—enjoined from what?" he demanded. "Of course no one could tell. It depended upon how many inferences could be drawn from other inferences, and to what degree." He seemed to assume that since it was (according to his view) impossible to tell what the injunction meant, it meant nothing; but he never explained how, if that were true, his clients could deny that they had violated it. Actually the injunctions were clear statements that they should stop interfering with the business of the railroads as common carriers in interstate commerce. But the real weakness of the defendants' case was that the facts did not fit their counsels' arguments, and here it is necessary to set forth a record that has often been misinterpreted and misrepresented by highly partisan accounts.

The injunctions against Debs and the other officers of the ARU had been issued without the defendants having an opportunity to argue against their issuance, on the assertion by the government that imminent harm was expected to arise from the strike, which had by then turned into a collateral industry-wide boycott. Thus it was perfectly true that the merits of the unionists' side of the case had not been considered when the injunctions were first issued; the procedure was essentially one for an emergency. But the correct legal course of action for the officers of the ARU would have been to apply to the court at once to set aside the injunction on the ground that it was improperly or improvidently issued. Had they done so, their application would have had an almost absolute priority in the court docket, since they had admittedly been enjoined without a hearing. By this means it would have been possible for them to avoid all subsequent litigation. But they did not do that. Instead, they ignored the injunction without taking any steps to have it set aside. On July 4, Debs said: "I have done nothing unlawful . . . and I shan't change my course of conduct in any way by reason of the service of this injunction."⁴ Subsequently he said many similar things; but at no stage did he move to get the injunction dismissed until he was arrested for contempt of it. In other words the ARU leadership deliberately refrained from using the avenue available to them to obtain a court adjudication of their rights, preferring instead to decide what their legal rights were for themselves. Clearly they did this at their peril. And there was necessarily in these circumstances a suspicion that they did not want to apply to court for an adjudication because they knew the law was against them.

Debs, in fact, did not want to lose the momentum of the strike by applying to the courts, for he knew that the young ARU was fighting for its life in the dispute. He was also disposed to refuse to recognize the authority of the courts at all—twenty years later he openly exposed the position that courts had no legitimacy and would not even hire attorneys or present legal defenses, because to do so was to recognize their authority. He preferred the law to be in his favor, but if it was not, he carried on regardless. A client like Debs would of course tend to link arms with a like-minded attorney if he could find one, and Darrow, more than Erwin or Gregory, was such a man. Darrow gave Debs the advice in the face of the injunction that he wanted to hear. According to the answer to the contempt proceedings filed in court, as soon as the injunctions were served upon them, "they forthwith consulted competent counsel . . . and were advised by him as to what they might rightfully and lawfully do . . . without violation of the order of the court or contempt of its authority. . . ."⁵ It is understandable that, as the subsequent proceedings ground through the federal courts up to the Supreme Court, the judges were somewhat impatient with litigants who preferred the advice of a sympathetic attorney to an authoritative decision from the court. In fact through three levels of federal court, with the attention of thirteen judges addressed to the case, not one would find in the union's favor.

In the circuit court the case was fought largely on the question of whether the injunction had been properly issued under the Sherman Anti-Trust Act of 1890, which declared illegal "every contract, combination in the form of trust, or otherwise, or conspiracy" in restraint of trade or commerce among the several states. The famous antitrust law did not explicitly include labor unions in its ambit, but it did not exclude them either. The record of so-called legislative intent was muddy; during its passage through Congress, a representation had been made by one of the bill's sponsors that it did not apply to unions; but on the other hand an amendment offered expressly to exclude them had been defeated. As a dispassionate scholar wrote, "the burden of amplification [of the Sherman Act] laid upon the courts is enormous. . . . In the main, the determination of what is and what is not condemned by the statute has been made, *ex post facto,* by the Supreme Court."⁶ Knowing the latitude for interpretation the act gave to the courts, Attorney General Olney had suggested in an annual report of his office published six months before the Pullman dispute that the scope of the antitrust law should be tested by litigation, and had pledged himself to seek definitive opinions on the exact ambit of the statute from the Supreme Court. It was scarcely surprising, therefore, that the United States entered a vigorous appearance in the Debs case, which seemed a golden opportunity to fight the question up to the Supreme Court. The fact that the Attorney General had announced his interest in such litigation many months before the Pullman strike was yet another reason why Darrow's objection to the appointment of Walker was somewhat misplaced. The actual position of the United States remained entirely consistent throughout, and there was no evidence that Walker had any success in changing it.

It was far from clear that labor should have been so keen to join battle on the correct interpretation of the statute. The whole litigation had a great potential for embarrassing the union movement if the result was against the ARU. The Sherman Act had been hailed as a great victory for the opponents of monopolistic capitalism. Nearly every lawyer sympathetic to labor had been in favor of it; crusaders against the "trusts" and in favor of unions were very much the same group. They had supported its passage thinking its main use would be against the robber barons, but the Pullman litigation raised the distinct possibility that the act would also be found applicable to unions. Much had been heard from radicals of "holding the public to ransom" and the evils of predatory capitalism; it was dogma of the pro-Sherman Act lobby that the price of maintaining business monopoly and oligopoly was ultimately paid by the public. But did not this logic apply equally to predatory unionism tit for tat? And if it succeeded in forcing up the price of labor in the marketplace, was not that extra cost likewise paid by the public? Already labor leaders like Debs had become just as ruthless in the pursuit of their objectives as the boldest captains of industry. The evils inherent in market domination were manifest for all commodities, including labor. The case was therefore one in which the radical populists were dangerously close to being hoist on their own petards.

And in the circuit court that was what happened. Circuit Judge William A. Woods held that the Sherman Act applied to all combinations of capital or labor alike; that the injunction had been validly issued under it and the officials of the ARU had violated it; and that Debs's claim that he had neither countenanced nor encouraged violence was untrue. Debs had relied heavily upon the fact that he had periodically sent out orders against violence. But the court regarded these self-serving declarations as inconclusive and hypocritical:

> Such admonitions against violence were sent out occasionally by the defendants, but it does not appear that they were ever heeded; and I am not able to believe on the evidence that, in the fullest sense, it was expected or intended that they should be. I am able and quite ready to believe that the defendants not only did not favor, but deprecated extreme violence, which might lead to the destruction of property or of human life. But they were not unwilling that coupling pins should be drawn; that Pullman cars should be "cut out" and side tracked; that switches should be turned and trains derailed; that cars should be overturned and tracks obstructed. . . .[7]

This was the second time within six months that a federal circuit court had expressed publicly its doubts about Eugene Debs's honesty; William Howard Taft, sitting in Ohio, had been caustic about him in July. Judge Woods did not stop there, however. He saw that from the time of his undertaking to advise the ARU, Darrow had been every bit as much responsible for what had happened as the union's leaders. Under the guise of legal advice Darrow had encouraged them along their course, and Judge Woods publicly doubted that good faith existed in either Debs or his attorney:

> By just what theories of law and duty they were governed might be better understood, perhaps, if in that part of the answer which alleges "that upon the service of the injunction of defendants consulted competent counsel, learned in the law, and upon a full and fair statement of facts in the premises, they were advised what they might rightfully and lawfully do without violating the order of the court, and that since that time they have in all things proceeded in accordance with that advice," they had disclosed, as they ought to have done, just what statement of the facts they made to counsel, and what advice they received. Without such disclosure, either in the answer or the proof, the alleged advice neither justifies nor mitigates a wrong or error committed in pursuance of the advice, but raises, rather, a presumption that a full statement would not be advantageous.[8]

It would have been no defense to the contempt even if the ARU had satisfied the court that it had acted in accord with legal advice given and received, and Judge Woods was giving a scarcely veiled warning to Darrow of where his course might lead. This was the first of several warnings from the bench that his view of the lawfulness of resort to violence in labor disputes was not an excuse for his clients. Like all of them, it went unheeded. The Debs case was notable in articulating Darrow's premise—to be developed much further later on—that no blame or legal liability attached to those who resorted to violence for political ends. Nevertheless the seeds of a philosophy that countenanced and even praised industrial violence are to be found in the Pullman litigation.

The union's defeat in the circuit court was so resounding that it was decided the defense team should be augmented on petition of the Supreme Court for habeas corpus by Lyman Trumbull. Trumbull, who had not felt able to undertake the strenuous effort of defense in the lower courts, was prevailed upon to argue Debs's case in the Supreme Court in the hope that he would commend himself to the justices more than the younger attorneys already engaged. In the three months between the decision of the circuit court and appearance before the Supreme Court on March 25 and 26, the argument of the union was refined down to the proposition that the government derived no power from any source to enjoin the acts of the defendants—an argument that depended on several different sub-arguments. First, the defendants continued to urge that the Sherman Act did not apply to unions. Second, it was argued that the defendants had done nothing unlawful by urging the membership of the ARU to quit their employment: "Refusing to work for a railroad company is no crime," Trumbull asserted, deducing that encouraging such refusal was therefore likewise no crime. Third, the government had no right to apply for an injunction to restrain interferences with the private property of the railroads rather than public property. And fourth, if what the defendants had done was criminal (which was not conceded), the only remedy available to the government was to prosecute; there was, Trumbull claimed, no right to enjoin a crime.

It was two months before the Supreme Court announced its opinion in the case, which went unanimously against Debs and the union. It can be inferred that such delay was occasioned not by the Court's difficulty in resolving the issues presented, but by its doubt about how best to announce its decision so as to give due notice to the militant unionists of their true legal position. They ought never again to think they had the excuse of relying on the advice of counsel who told them only what they wanted to hear. The opinion, announced by Justice Brewer for the entire Court, was carefully constructed to show the fallacies in the ARU's argument while at the same time explaining what unions were entitled to do and emphasizing that the decision did not treat unions as unlawful organizations or prohibit their activities. With this in mind, the Court's prime concern was to disabuse the unionists of any notion that the right to issue an injunction turned on the proper construction of the Sherman Act; on the contrary, the right of the government to obtain an injunction was inherent and not dependent on mere statute. The circuit court's opinion had dwelt so heavily on the Sherman Act that, if not qualified, it might be read as conceding the statute to be the only basis for issuing an injunction. The Supreme Court therefore chose its words carefully. "We enter into no examination of the act of July 2, 1890 . . . upon which the Circuit Court relied mainly to sustain its jurisdiction," wrote Justice Brewer. "It must not be understood from this that we dissent from the conclusions of that court in reference to the scope of the act, but simply that we prefer to rest our judgment on the broader ground. . . ."[9] This was the single most important announcement of the opinion, because it meant that the union's strategy had doubly backfired. The Supreme Court had by implication sanctioned the application of the Sherman Act to unions, but gone further by approving other bases for issuance of the injunction in the Pullman dispute.* Quite apart from any statutory right to an injunction, the Court ruled that the government had the inherent right under the Constitution to prevent interference with the federal mails or interstate commerce by injunction or otherwise—it could have taken direct action to protect its interests in these matters. "Indeed," said Justice Brewer, "it is more to the praise than to the blame of the government, that, instead of determining for itself questions of right and wrong on the part of these petitioners and their associates and enforcing that determination by the club of the policeman and the bayonet of the soldier, it submitted all those questions

*Later decisions of the Supreme Court, such as *Lowe* v. *Lawlor* (the Danbury Letter's case), 208 U.S. 274 (1908), would be explicit in holding unions to be within the statutory prohibition of combinations in restraint of trade.

to the peaceful determination of judicial tribunals. . . ."[10]

In passing to the second contention, Justice Brewer pointed out that obstruction of the U.S. mails and interstate commerce had in fact taken place. The injunction had not prohibited men from quitting their work, but only from obstructing the movement of trains carrying mail in interstate commerce. Undoubtedly there had been attempts, partly successful, to do this. Justice Brewer dealt especially with the admiration that Darrow had argued was due to the self-sacrifice of the striking workers:

> A most earnest and eloquent appeal was made to us in eulogy of the heroic spirit of those who threw up their employment, and gave up their means of earning a livelihood, not in defense of their own rights, but in sympathy for and to assist others whom they believed to be wronged. We yield to none in our admiration of any act of heroism or self sacrifice, but we may be permitted to add that it is a lesson which cannot be learned too soon or too thoroughly that under this government of and by the people the means of redress of all wrongs are through the courts and at the ballot box, and that no wrong, real or fancied, carries with it legal warrant to invite as a means of redress the cooperation of a mob, with its accompanying acts of violence.[11]

Once more Darrow's attitude had been marked out for condemnation by an appellate judge; rarely in the annals of the law has an advocate twice been reproved for his arguments on appeal in the same case without actually being held in contempt. But though most of the judges disagreed with Darrow's arguments and loathed his politics, they liked him as a character; even at his most cantankerous, he disarmed friends and enemies alike with that smile Brand Whitlock described as "winning as a woman's." For Darrow's strength as a litigator was not merely intellectual; he had a charm that usually ensured that the reprimands he often deserved were mild.

The third and fourth contentions of the petitioners were the ones most strongly refuted by the Court. It was untrue, declared Justice Brewer, that the government had no power to protect private property by way of injunction; when interstate commerce was being obstructed, the government had a right and a duty to protect it. Besides, the government had a property in the mails that would justify its intervention. In case the point should be missed, he went on:

> We do not care to place our decision upon this ground alone. Every government, entrusted, by the very terms of its being, with powers and duties to be exercised and discharged for the general welfare, has a right to apply to its own courts for any proper assistance in the exercise of the one and the discharge of the other, and it is no sufficient answer to its appeal to one of those courts that it has no pecuniary interest in the matter.[12]

Having made the point—somewhat obvious to everyone except the unionists —that the government had a general power to keep order, not confined to protecting its own property, the Court went on to deal rather lightly with the petitioner's final argument, that there was no right to enjoin a crime. The power existed and had often been used, the Court declared, citing the classic instance of an injunction to restrain the keeping of a house of ill-fame. It cannot have failed to influence the Court, however, that the injunctions had been effective in stopping the strike and its concomitant violence. Eugene Debs himself had testified before the President's Commission:

> It was simply the United States courts that ended the strike. Our men were in a position that never would have been shaken, under any circumstances, if we were permitted to remain upon the field, among them. . . . The men went back to work, and the ranks were broken, and the strike was broken up . . . not by the army, and not by any other power, but simply and solely by the action of the United States court in restraining us from discharging our duties as officers and representatives of our employees.[13]

In other words, the union was complaining of the very success of the injunctions in stopping the interference with interstate commerce. It was unlikely that the Court would take away from the government what was, on the union leader's own testimony, the only technique of ending what would otherwise have been an unshakable position.

Concluding, the Court announced that "We have given to this case the most careful and anxious attention, for we realize that it touches closely questions of supreme importance to the people of this country." But on not one point had the contentions of the ARU been upheld. *Debs* was, and remained, the fundamental Court ruling on the subject of enjoining a strike until it was partially superseded by statute half a century later. For all the union's claim of "consultation of competent counsel," the fact was that the Debs case represented a major defeat for extreme unionists—and one that had been precipitated by its own litigation strategy. The propositions advanced had been far too extreme for it to be conceivable that a court would adopt them; and several of them were completely at loggerheads with existing authority. Trumbull was too out of touch with the times to be held responsible for formulating the arguments he presented in the Supreme Court; the major responsibility clearly lay with Darrow. The union's posture had essentially been determined by him. He had put up a magnificent fight, but it had been on unwinnable terrain, for he had sought to use the passionate tactics suitable for use at trial in the appellate courts. In his first appearance in the Supreme Court, he had undoubtedly made an impression—but not of a kind that aided his clients. Politely, obliquely, he had been reprimanded. In fact the subsequent history of Darrow's appearances in the Supreme Court would be an unhappy one; he never attuned himself to addressing a deliberative body of judges rather than an impetuous body of jurors, and a number of his appearances in labor causes were disastrous. It took him and the labor movement a long time to recognize that he was at his best at trial level.

Long after the Supreme Court had spoken in the Debs case, union sympathizers continued to object that it was wrongly decided, often reiterating the arguments put forward by Trumbull and Darrow without also giving the

Court's rebuttal of them. Edgar Lee Masters—poet, radical, and later unhappy partner of Darrow in the practice of law—in one of his earliest published essays, "The New Star Chamber," trotted out the argument that a crime could not be enjoined. It was said that labor actions in the Pullman strike harmed interstate commerce:

> But does the fact that a crime injures business furnish legal warrant for enjoining its commission? Burglary, larceny, arson, forgery, cheating, counterfeiting and many other crimes injure business just as much as a strike does; and yet no one pretends that these crimes can be enjoined by a court of chancery. . . . No one carries the argument that far. For if it should be carried that far then the criminal courts would yield that no one could be fooled on the subject.[14]

This argument had been put forward and rejected in the Supreme Court, but that did not stop the question being brought up time and again in unionist circles as if it were still undecided legally. Probably, the Debs decision was legally correct at the time it was rendered. It was never subsequently overruled.

The union had lost the legal point at stake in the Debs case, but personally and professionally Darrow had gained much. He had set a new, more strident tone in labor litigation than had ever previously been seen, one that had attracted widespread attention and was to influence the course of future skirmishes profoundly. More important from his own point of view, his representation had a distinctness of approach that few other lawyers could match even if they had cared to. His strategy on Debs's behalf had set the pattern by which all his subsequent labor cases were governed. He had found his métier in the use of attack as defense, in his forceful, provocative method of speaking, his hostile, even menacing demeanor, and the constant imputations of bad faith against his opponents. Only the scale and intensity of his effort and the refinement of his technique were to change.

From the unionists' perspective, the fact that the litigation has been unsuccessful did not diminish their counsel at all. It was merely another proof that the Supreme Court was the tool of capitalism. By defeat, Darrow had become something of a romantic hero of the labor movement, thrust to the forefront for his conspicuous service in the case. It did not displease Darrow that he was in consequence emerging as a political figure in his own right.

10

The Congressman
That Might Have Been

By the end of March 1895 Darrow's unpaid work on behalf of the ARU was substantially complete. The case had been argued in the Supreme Court and all that was left was to wait for a decision. Between argument and judgment Darrow's stock with radicals all over the country and particularly with those in Chicago was very high indeed; he had become something of a hero of the unionists, from whom he was to receive many return favors for his altruism in the years to come. Now he had forged a political base in his own right, apart from Altgeld's patronage, and the temptation was very strong to abandon the practice of law for politics. During 1895 and 1896 a major part of his efforts were devoted to trying to convert the national publicity and union goodwill generated by his handling of the Debs case into a congressional seat. He had never allowed the political contacts accumulated through service in City Hall to evaporate; so, for example, when his younger brother Herman came to Chicago in 1893, he had been able to get him a job in the sewer department through political "pull." Apart from this, he retained massive influence at state level by reason of his relationship with Altgeld, and had also cultivated the support of "clean government" reform leagues in Chicago. In unconsciously ironic contrast he had taken pains to court the substantial Irish population, whose agitation for a free Ireland gave him scope for picking up votes and simultaneously exercising his taste for fiery dispute.

Darrow's first pamphlet, *The Rights and Wrongs of Ireland,* was published in 1895. It displayed a lasting characteristic of his—an empathy for extreme conflict. He performed best in a thoroughgoing confrontation, when reconciliation was neither desired nor practicable. The troubled Irish situation provided the kind of battleground Darrow liked—one where two sides were at opposite poles, compromise was impossible, and wholehearted commitment to one side or the other was a political necessity. That was Darrow's chosen way. He did not obfuscate differences, he pinpointed them. Of course it did him no harm politically to identify somewhat with the Irish cause; most of the

Democratic machine was controlled by Irish-Americans, as were many of the unions like the Teamsters. "I am aware that in America the Irish cause is a popular theme; all our political conventions for years have passed resolutions favoring Irish independence," he confessed. "I know that with this audience, and perhaps in this country, Irish independence, either with or without force, is a favorite theme."[1]

Yet while retaining the support and even affection of a good number of the Chicago Irish, he avoided being identified too closely with them by opposing "Bathhouse" John Coughlin's machine in the aldermanic elections in the first ward. Bathhouse John's record of corruption was distinguished even by Chicago's standards. The major part of an alderman's job in the first ward was to decide who should be allowed to run the saloons, brothels, and gambling houses of the area without interference. Since Billy Skakel, an underling of Coughlin's, was not satisfied with the cut Coughlin allowed him he determined to challenge him in the election, and for this purpose he formed the Independent Democratic Party, under whose banner his name was entered on the ballot. The Independents were independent of the official Democratic Party, but entirely dependent on Skakel and his supporters. When it looked as though Coughlin might be defeated by Skakel, the Democrats resorted to a legal ruse: the law said that no one convicted of an offense could run for office, and Skakel had been convicted of a gambling offense. The Coughlin forces applied to the court to get Skakel's name struck off the list of candidates, and succeeded. The Skakel forces, led by Darrow, were much incensed at this and launched their own legal proceedings, successfully arguing before County Judge Frank Scales that the striking of Skakel's name from the ballot was illegal. Judge Scales held that a man should not be barred from seeking office by a conviction for a minor violation some years before the election, and reinstated Skakel as a candidate. Notwithstanding this, Coughlin managed to get reelected through intimidation and bribery; like many another attempt to challenge the boss, Skakel's had failed. It was the power of the boss that most reform Democrats wanted to overcome, but it seemed insurmountable. On the evening of March 16, 1896, Darrow, speaking to fifteen hundred people interested in the Municipal Voters' League at the Central Music Hall, addressed them acidly.

"By this time I suppose it is fair to assume that this audience is not in favor of electing aldermen who sell their votes," he said. "The next thing, I suppose, will be to call a meeting to discuss the multiplication table. It is a reflection on civilization that we have to call a meeting to stir up sentiment for honesty."[2]

The League stood for clean government and was committed to support honest candidates regardless of their party affiliation or their lack of one, in order to diminish the influence of political machines. Throughout the country organizations were set up to fight Tammany or its equivalent. Darrow's friend Charles Edward Russell was a supporter of the Non-Partisan League, another similar endeavor. The corrupt state of politics was blamed by Brand Whitlock upon "that elementary germ or microbe, the partizan, the man who always voted the straight ticket in municipal elections, the most virulent organism that ever infested the body politic and as unconscious of its toxic power as the bacillus of yellow fever," and he lamented "the foul culture this organism blindly breeds—the political machine, with its boss."³ Indeed the nonpartisan leagues were a response to political thievery. The theory was that the leagues, by starting their own uncorrupt and incorruptible machine, could clean up politics. They had some success. In the twenty-eighth ward, the Municipal Voters' League managed to have Charles H. Rector elected for several terms on the council, and Darrow campaigned vigorously for him. The difficulty was an age-old one. The boodlers had large funds available to corrupt the electoral process. By contrast the leagues were poor. Rector's total campaign fund was only $400.

For all the good intentions of the reform clubs and in spite of his support of them, it cannot be said that Darrow was a true believer. The voters' leagues were but another side of the coin of journalistic muckraking; both proclaimed the outrage of "the people" being bilked by their elected representatives. But Darrow saw through this: he realized that "the people" got the government they voted for and deserved. Yes, he was on the side of "the people" as against the trusts, or (in some instances) Tammany, but he understood too well that democracy was a form of tyranny—the tyranny of the majority—which could be every bit as oppressive as any other form of government. So he built up an armamentarium of antidotes to the excesses of democracy. To him, crowds were the ultimate enemy of justice. Each member of a crowd reinforced the bad side of the others' characters—and human nature was bad to begin with. He regarded crowds not as sheep, stupid and easily led, but as wolves, predatory and savage in a pack but cowardly alone. One of the few things he shared with Bernard Baruch was a rueful awareness of "how easily the masses have been led astray."⁴ In fact Darrow exploited the voters' leagues with some cynicism; for example, it would not have been any great victory for good government to put Billy Skakel in Bathhouse John's position. How, if at all, Darrow quite managed to reconcile his political actions with his political beliefs is difficult to imagine. His views on the alternatives available in Cook County approximated those of Henry Mencken: "If experience teaches us anything at all it teaches us this: that a good politician, under democracy, is quite as unthinkable as an honest burglar."⁵ This was the political blind spot of a whole generation. It was why the critics were such failures as improvers and why the practical tendency of most of their political endeavors was toward a despotism disguised behind a facade of popular representation: "the muckrakers could be complicitly lawless; they recognized that democracy was slow to purge or reverse itself, and consequently they often looked with favor on strong men who set themselves above the law."⁶

What counted in politics was not honesty, or integrity, or popularity, but control of the machine. And one of Darrow's strengths as an emergent politician in 1895 was that through his friendship with Altgeld, he had a large measure of influence upon the state and even national machinery of the Democratic Party. True, Altgeld had suffered some very hard knocks over his pardoning of the anarchists and the Pullman strike—but he was still governor, with the patronage of the state behind him. The state party machinery was at Darrow's disposal, and his grip on it became stronger with the announcement that the Democratic national convention would be held in Chicago in 1896. Both Altgeld and Darrow determined that their weight would be felt there.

As governor of Illinois, Altgeld might easily have been a serious candidate for presidential nomination were it not for the fact that he had been born of foreign parents in Germany. After interviewing him in July 1894, Nellie Bly said: "I shouldn't be surprised if he were nominated for President of the United States some day." (Since Altgeld was notorious for his "foreignness," it can only be assumed that Miss Bly was ignorant of the constitutional prohibition.) She was not alone in seeing the potential in Altgeld; the Republican Senator Cullom believed that Altgeld would have been the Democrats' 1896 candidate but for his ineligibility. As it was, Altgeld had to confine himself to running for reelection as governor of Illinois. But so much did he wish to influence the nomination that he devoted too much time to preparing for the convention and too little to his own campaign.

Illinois was destined to play a pivotal role in determining the direction that the Democrats would take. After much sectional bickering the national party was divided between those who advocated the gold standard and those in favor of silver. This split was regarded as one between the rich and the poor, and Darrow and Altgeld sided with the poor. Darrow put the matter quite simply: "I was for the debtor rather than the creditor." He and Altgeld were keenly interested in seeing the Democrats put on a sound footing nationally by the same strategy of conciliation and fusion of third-party movements that had brought Altgeld the governorship of Illinois. As a microcosm of the nation in its mixture of urban and rural interests, the prairie state was thought to be a testing ground of the voting alliances likely to bring national strength. Populism had grown as a political force without fixed affiliations with either traditional party in the early nineties, and it was indispensable to success that its votes should be harvested for the Democratic cause. Indeed it was becoming of unparalleled importance nationally as the "free silver" movement swept the West's debt-ridden farmers, who blamed Eastern gold interests for their plight. The big question was whether the juggling act Darrow and Altgeld had performed in Illinois in '92 could be repeated nationally in '96. In the campaign to get Altgeld elected governor, a temporary alliance of rural voters and the growing bands of industrial labor had been brought about through labor's continuing support of populism. It was by no means clear that this could be relied upon in 1896—and oddly enough the Pullman strike with which Darrow had been so closely identified had put it in doubt. The most momentous effect of the adverse decision in the Debs case was not legal but political, in that it propelled the labor movement, hitherto somewhat unideological, away from populism toward socialism. It made union leaders more insistent upon the overall unity of working-class interests, as they urged solidarity not merely in concerted action against their own employers but against employers in related industries. Eugene Debs himself was converted by the experience from populism to socialism, and long afterward the alliance was to cause trouble on the left, so that the Democrats were nearly always in danger of losing the labor vote where a socialist candidate ran. The possibility that the union movement would become entirely Marxist was among the fears that added fuel to the opposition to the growth of unions. Unionism itself excited less dread in the public than unionism dominated by socialism. The Debs trial had been one of those events that had jolted the left into new directions; even Trumbull, a magnificent relic of the Civil War, sensed that times were changing. When Trumbull died in 1896, Darrow correctly identified the shift of his thinking when he told the Chicago *Times* that: "the socialistic trend of the venerable statesman's opinions in his later years sprung from his deep sympathies with all unfortunates; that sympathy that made him an anti-slavery Democrat in his early years, and afterwards a Republican. He became convinced that the poor who toil for a living in this world were not getting a fair chance. His heart was with them."[7] Trumbull was not alone. The division between the old and new radicals was the emphasis they placed upon the Debs case. But the exact dividing line did not appear as clearly to most people as it did to Darrow, and 1895–96 was a period of flux as realignments took place.

Shrewdly, Darrow did not commit himself on the doctrinaire splits in the Democratic Party, working instead within the party as a populist. He often indicated in those years that of all political persuasions, socialism was the one for which he had most sympathy, but never did he positively endorse it or take his anti-capitalism to extremes. Eugene Debs refused to use a bank account, believing it to be immoral; Darrow not only used banks but at one stage became a heavy investor in bank stock. As the election approached, he was careful to remain on friendly terms with all potential Democratic voters, exploiting his extraordinarily wide membership in political groups. He did belong to many organizations, but the impression that gave was misleading. Many of them were mere fronts for some Democratic or populist splinter group. The Eight Hour Day Association was not much different from the Amnesty Association, or the Single Tax Club, or the Municipal Voters' League, or the Secular Union, or the Personal Rights League; all these, and many more, had the same sorts of people as members and overlapped each other in interests and composition. Darrow's extraordinary range of memberships in all sorts of organizations, especially around Chicago, gave him great aid in flushing out votes for the Democrats at election time, by allowing him to build bridges of understanding among many groups. In the shifting sands of third-party radicalism, Darrow found a precarious foothold for the Democrats. Though it was never precisely calculable how many votes that would mean, he was good at dealing with a wide spectrum of the left in working for the Democratic cause. His skill at remaining on good terms with people of many different persuasions was unmatched during the crucial months before the state and national conventions. In fact his ability not to lose his balance in the shifting sands of politics sometimes meant that his shrewdness blended into guile. He managed to rally around him a great many dogmatists, true believers, and Utopians who were fully aware that he was not wholeheartedly with them but did not seem to mind. He successfully trod the path of skepticism while commanding the respect and support of many who were not skeptics, providing a healthy corrective to the credulity of the "committed" by denying the efficacy of political panaceas while building a political base.

There were two obstacles in the way of Darrow and Altgeld as 1896 approached. The first was that the majority of Illinois Democrats were not in favor of free silver; insofar as the state might be regarded as representative of national sentiment, it suggested that the gold standard would prevail. Altgeld knew that if Illinois rejected free silver, it would have no chance of adoption as a national platform, so he determined to force the policy through the Illinois state convention. It says much for Altgeld's influence within the state that he could swing so many votes to the "silver" candidate, although without his intervention, as Darrow put it, it was "very doubtful whether Illinois would have endorsed free silver." Altgeld engineered the timing of the Democratic state convention so that he could steam-roller a "silver" platform. Although Darrow protested that this did not give the people a chance to express themselves, Altgeld replied that that was exactly why he had timed things as he had.

"Would the people give *me* a chance?" he asked Darrow.

"No, sure they wouldn't," replied Darrow.

"Well," concluded Altgeld, "we will treat them the same way."[8]

The other problem was to find an appropriate national candidate. The party was in disarray, having no decisive frontrunner. Furthermore there was the necessity if the Democrats were to win of picking a ticket which the populists would support. Darrow and Altgeld went to the national convention knowing which policies they supported; yet the electorate at large needed not policies but a candidate, and strong candidates were few indeed. The preferred free silver candidate as the convention loomed was the little-known Richard P. Bland of Missouri, who had few supporters outside his home state; he was the preference of Darrow and Altgeld only as the lesser of two evils, as he was challenged by a more flamboyant Westerner, William Jennings Bryan.

Bryan, a Nebraskan, had developed a remarkable following in the West running on the leftward edge of Democratic principles so as to incorporate the rising populist movement. He had plowed the same furrow as Altgeld would have done if he had been an eligible candidate. Bryan had made a name for himself as a radical attorney, fighting the hated railroads; in the early 1890s he had been plaintiffs' counsel in several personal injury claims against the Chicago, Burlington & Quincy and the Rock Island & Pacific railroads, and had litigated in the Supreme Court two years before Darrow got there with the Debs case. Since Darrow and Altgeld could sway a substantial number of convention votes toward their preferred candidate, Bryan wooed them as best he could. In early 1896 Darrow was one of those trusted Democrats to whom Bryan wrote asking for advice on the political climate and whether he should throw his hat into the ring. Darrow prevaricated; neither he nor Altgeld was impressed with Bryan. They thought him too young at thirty-six, and far too attached to the rural origins of populism to be an effective leader of the new class of urban workers who were so visibly militant in Chicago and other great cities of the North. In Altgeld's terms, the rural element of the proposed coalition was properly to be subordinated to the interests of industrial workers, and one of Bryan's drawbacks was that he was wedded to the countryside and the past. For this reason neither Darrow nor Altgeld looked on Bryan with any kind of enthusiasm. They suspected him of being ill-informed and narrow-minded on many important contemporary issues, and out of touch with the modern, urban wing of the Democrats. Subsequent history was to show the suspicion to be well founded, but for the moment he was the only candidate who seemed capable of uniting the diverse factions of the national party.

If Altgeld and Darrow had reservations about Bryan, Bryan was likewise cautious about seeking their endorsement. To get the nomination it was necessary to have Altgeld's support, for he effectively controlled the entire Illinois delegation, whose votes held the balance in the convention. Yet Altgeld's support, with his reputation for radicalism, was nationally a liability amounting almost to the kiss of death. "Altgeld was a kind of political albatross that the young candidate could not cast off," observed one historian.[9] Without Altgeld's machine no aspirant could get the nomination; but with Altgeld's machine there was the real danger that at election time, voters would baulk at supporting Altgeld's man. So when the convention opened at the Coliseum on July 7, no firm commitment had been made by Altgeld in favor of any potential nominee.

Of one thing Bryan could be certain: he would not win the nomination because he was rich. He had almost no campaign funds. Although the convention was held in a city famous for its elegant hotels, he stayed at the rundown Windsor-Clifton on the corner of Monroe Street and Wabash Avenue, where the price of rooms ranged from 75 cents to $2. This did not necessarily harm him in view of the sympathies of the delegates—Senator David B. Hill lamented the predominance of populists "who never voted the Democratic ticket in their lives."[10] Of course that was the price that the Democrats had to pay for the populist vote. If Senator Hill was not prepared to pay it, Bryan was. He had seen the potential importance of populist support years before and when he announced his candidacy for the Senate in 1894, the platform he chose to run on was, in the words of his biographer, "an outright pilferage of all the major planks of Populism."[11]

Bryan's theft of the populist platform enabled him to muster enough support at the convention to force Altgeld finally to commit the Illinois delegation's votes to him. Altgeld did not wish to do so, but he had no alternative if he wanted to back a winner. There were several roll calls at which Bland received the Illinois votes, but as time wore on it became increasingly apparent that Bryan was the man of the hour. In spite of his unpopular acts as governor, Altgeld was still a powerful figure behind the scenes, able to influence the convention: "he was the brain and will of the Convention, as Bryan was—very literally—its voice."[12] But he was not strong enough to turn back the tide once Bryan had delivered his famous "Cross of Gold" speech on July 9, which had a stupendous effect on the convention and was widely credited with winning him the nomination. Darrow was sitting with Altgeld in the midst of the Illinois delegation and recorded his reactions:

> I have enjoyed a great many addresses, some of which I have delivered myself, but I never listened to one that affected and moved an audience as did that. Men and women laughed and cheered and cried. They listened with desires and hopes, and finally with absolute confidence and trust. Here was a political Messiah who was to lift the burden that the oppressed had borne so long. When he had finished his speech, amidst the greatest ovation that I had ever witnessed, there was no longer any doubt as to the name of the nominee.

Bryan's climax drew upon Christian imagery: "Having behind us the producing masses of this nation . . . we will answer their demands for a gold standard by saying to them: You shall not press down upon the brow of labor this crown of thorns, you shall not crucify mankind on a cross of gold." This theme struck a chord with farmers, who had suffered from a severe agricultural depression in the two preceding years, as well as with local Chicago residents, for Chicago had suffered a recession as the Columbian Exposition was dismantled and the tourist crowds along its great Midway dwindled.

The speech united the diverse elements supporting free silver at the convention, but as Louis W. Koenig remarked, Bryan "was ingeniously unspecific." Altgeld watched glumly—he had less faith in words than deeds, and believed that Bryan was the wrong man for the campaign. "It takes more than speeches to win real victories," he told Darrow the next day. "Applause lasts but a little while. The road to justice is not a path of glory; it is stony and long and lonely, filled with pain and martyrdom. I have been thinking over Bryan's speech. What did he say anyhow?" It was part of Bryan's skill to have avoided saying much; he had thought out carefully what he could not afford to say, as well as what he could. Actually the speech, even down to its striking references to the cross of gold and the crown of thorns, had been tried and tested by Bryan on several previous occasions, including in the House of Representatives in 1894. Darrow was right to deduce that "Doubtless he had gone over it many times in his home on the prairies of Nebraska"—it was one of Bryan's standard addresses, originally committed to memory for use at rural county fairs back in his home state. But its origins did not prevent its tremendous success at the convention. The speech had its desired effect, and Altgeld was finally forced to cast the forty-eight votes of the Illinois delegation for Bryan on the fifth ballot, which turned out ultimately to be unanimous.* The nomination of Bryan was a backfiring of the Democratic machine: "his nomination was received first as a joke and then as an outrage."[13]

---

*Darrow said in *The Story of My Life* that Bryan "did not get the vote of the truest and the bravest of them all, John P. Altgeld," but this can only be true of his personal vote in the election, for the delegation of which Altgeld was leader undoubtedly ended up supporting him.

Outrage it possibly was, but it was not a joke. For better or worse, the Democrats had to run with him. Altgeld and Darrow knew that unless they supported Bryan actively, McKinley would win the election and their party would remain out of office. Bryan himself was able to gain the nomination from the many smaller parties whose support was necessary for any Democratic victory—the National Silver Party, the Single Taxers, some of the Prohibitionists, and even the populists. But these were, predictably, uneasy alliances; in particular, the populists split the ticket by nominating their own vice-presidential candidate. In the convention's horse trading, the Democrats had nominated Arthur Sewell, a wealthy Eastern railroad director who was quite unacceptable to populists. The populists preferred Thomas Watson, a Georgia radical who was a reluctant candidate, but one who stood for what populists believed in.

Bryan's nomination was momentous for Darrow personally, for he was closer than ever to a career in politics in 1896, and had it not been for Bryan's defeat by McKinley in the November election he would have become a member of the House of Representatives, as a congressional candidate in the third district of Illinois. He expected to win: "The district was overwhelmingly Democratic, and I felt sure that with Bryan for President and Altgeld for governor there would be no doubt of my election." If elected, he stood a good chance of becoming a national figure politically, as Robert La Follette and William E. Borah did. Nine years after his arrival in Chicago he was by no means stuck there; he could picture a future in Washington, D.C., as long, effective, and interesting. True, it was difficult to make a lifetime political career in the House, because of the frequently recurring need for reelection. But there were many who had used election to that body as a stepping stone to other things, and Darrow was surely likely to have the chance as they did. He had all sorts of credentials that qualified him for politics—and as the fall of 1896 approached, he was so confident the new year would find him in the District of Columbia that he did not even trouble to enter into regular legal practice again in Chicago, preferring to spend the few months between the convention and the elections in November as a virtually full-time party worker. He had been favored with the Democratic endorsement in a seemingly safe district; to enhance his chances further, he ran not only as a Democratic candidate, but with the full endorsement of the People's Party.

Darrow's mistake was overconfidence. So sure was he of election that he devoted his time to aiding the campaigns of Bryan and Altgeld, and other Democrats, while neglecting his own constituency. As one of the party's best platform speakers, he was here, there, and everywhere but the third district, performing excellently at the hustings and proving himself effective in every way except his own interest. It was a massive miscalculation for a man otherwise so shrewd, explicable less by altruism than by Darrow's considerable underestimation of his opponent, Hugh Reid Belknap, an ex-superintendent of Chicago's South Side Rapid Transit Railroad to whom he disparagingly referred as "a clerk in a railroad office who had never taken any interest in

politics and was not known outside his small circle of friends." Small though
his circle of friends might have been, Belknap managed to poll 22,075 votes
against Darrow's 21,485. It was a remarkably close race, especially in view of
the fact that the district's population was over 300,000, and therefore a substantial proportion of the electorate must have stayed at home on Election
Day.[14] Only the latter part of Darrow's statement was honest when he said:
"I cared too little for the position and felt too sure." The result of the election
was a grave blow to him personally. He had looked forward to the excitement
of the change being sent to the House would have brought. He did care about
not being elected and all the evidence points to the fact that he was totally
unprepared for defeat. He had allowed his practice to dwindle to almost
nothing since the end of the Debs case, and had dissipated such savings as he
had manged to accrue while with the city and the Chicago & Northwestern.

All told the elections of 1896 were a disaster for Darrow and his friends.
No shrewd observer had any doubt that the election result was important for
the nation—not merely because of the immediate differences between Bryan
and McKinley, but because Bryan would have been young enough to have had
a profound influence upon Washington for years to come. Indeed Senator
Shelby M. Cullom of Illinois, remarking upon the fact that Bryan was defeated
only because some influential Democrats found Bryan's free silver platform
totally unacceptable, thought that otherwise he "would probably have been
elected and the history of this country would have been written differently."[15]
For Darrow it meant a change in the direction of his career. He often protested
that he did not want a career in politics; but he stood for election several times,
and in 1896 might easily have been shaken loose from Chicago. Until 1912 he
remained a man to whom political opportunities came constantly. He was a
political "natural" from many points of view. Had the Democrats swept the
ticket, his course, like the nation's, might have been very different.

Darrow had run for the House partly because Altgeld, though he had not
disclosed the fact, continued to nurture a desire to become a senator. This
desire had lain dormant since his abortive attempt in 1892 to snatch John
Palmer's seat from him, when he had used Darrow as his emissary to the
Illinois legislature. Had Altgeld been reelected to the governorship, he would
have used his patronage to persuade the legislators to vote him a senator, thus
joining forces with Darrow in Washington. If all had gone well, therefore, he
would only have served a further three months as governor even if reelected.
Now that he had been defeated in the gubernatorial election, his hold upon
the legislature was fatally diminished, but the fires of his ambition still burned
brightly and he insisted that his name go forward. Defeat followed swiftly: on
January 20, 1897, the Illinois legislature voted upon whether he should be sent
to Washington as senator, and he was defeated by 125 votes to 78. Having been
twice rejected within three months, all hope of his immediate return to office
was dashed. Darrow and Altgeld had gambled with big stakes in 1896 and both
had lost.

It did not take long for a postmortem on the election to be held, and like most inquiries into the causes of defeat, it became an occasion for the placing of blame. To Darrow and Altgeld, the author of their misfortune was clearly Bryan, who was the wrong man in the wrong place at the wrong time. They had supported him only reluctantly, believing that his leadership would probably deviate from their own conception of what the Democrats should stand for. Now, both having been beaten in the campaign, they had even less cause to want him as the head of their party. Darrow had blamed the corrupting influence of Republican gold for his own unhorsing in the campaign, but he knew that that alone was not the explanation. Increasingly he came to see Bryan as a weak, shallow candidate, who, instead of elevating the people, spoke at a level of unconscious mediocrity, without a vision of the future to inform his policies. He expressed his exasperation a few months later in a revealing encounter with Bryan at a banquet at the Tremont Hotel commemorating Jackson's birthday. "You'd better go back to Lincoln and study science, history, philosophy, and read Flaubert's Madam something-or-other, and quit this village religious stuff," he exploded. "You're head of the party before you are ready and a leader should lead with thought." It was the first skirmish of a lifelong feud.

Bryan, who was surrounded by a group of party faithfuls including Edgar Lee Masters, turned to them and said, ignoring the thrust of Darrow's outburst:

"Darrow's the only man in the world who looks down on me for believing in God."

"Your kind of a God," snapped Darrow, who turned tails and left in a huff.[16]

Darrow's smoldering dislike of Bryan and what he stood for would become a lifelong passion. His pique with Bryan was unfair; the reason for the defeat of 1896 lay not so much in Bryan's personal failings as in the inherent difficulty of melding rural and urban interests in one national program. Only by trial and error was it discovered that the rural vote was not easily persuaded in favor of a platform that industrial workers would support. Bryan was not personally responsible for being the candidate through whom that process of trial and error was implemented. Darrow, as the country boy made good in the city, might have seen this, but he was unwilling to acknowledge it, his political and social interests being by now totally urban. For the moment, anyway, the game of politics was played out for him. And by March 1897 Darrow was to be distracted from politics into an unpleasant personal and financial crisis.

11

"The Awful Compulsion of the Age"

After their successive defeats of 1896 and 1897, the primary concern of both Darrow and Altgeld was financial. Darrow had earned very little in the period from July 1894 to March 1897 and had allowed his connection with Collins, Goodrich, and Vincent to wither away. In defeat, he found out just what it meant to be an "out" instead of an "in" in politics; the flow of business that came directly or indirectly from political control of government had dried up.

Having impetuously thrown himself into protracted litigation on Debs's behalf for expenses only and then spent a further five months on campaigning, he was beginning to feel the pinch so badly that after the elections it was urgently necessary to regularize his finances. For six years he had been accustomed to the security of a paycheck—and at that, a substantial one—and now he was thrown back upon a fluctuating, unpredictable, sometimes uncollectible income from fees. His altruism had been costly, and he learned once more how tough a city Chicago was in which to earn a living through the practice of law. For all his contacts, private practice was to be much more arduous than employment at the Chicago & Northwestern. Marvin Hughitt's kind offer to continue to send Darrow railroad work after he had quit was not a promise to pay him for doing nothing. Darrow realized that he must start up a new firm. He set up practice anew with Morris St. P. Thomas, the colleague from his days in the city corporation counsel's office, and William O. Thompson, who had been an associate with Collins, Goodrich, Darrow & Vincent. First they took offices in the Chicago Title & Trust Building at 100 Washington Street; then shortly afterward they moved to the Ashland Block on the corner of Clark and Randolph. In setting up his headquarters in downtown Chicago, soon to become "the Loop," Darrow was within walking distance of friends and enemies alike. He could take heart from the tenants of the Unity Building, many of whom were sympathetic to labor, and enjoy proximity to the city's newspaper industry. On the other hand, he no doubt grimaced when he passed the national offices of the Women's Christian Temperance Union in the Temple on the corner of La Salle and Monroe, only three blocks away.

Having been at the center of a momentous litigation and a momentous election, Darrow could by no stretch of the imagination be regarded as novice in the ways of Chicago. He knew its raw, ugly aspect as well as its glories, but there was no hint of self-doubt in his decision to set up practice once more in the great city; he was where he wanted to be. Yet it might have been otherwise. His good friend and fellow Ohioan Brand Whitlock had been sufficiently repelled by the events of 1896 to wish to escape back to Ohio. "I am resolved to quit politics and a public life," he wrote to a fellow lawyer, confessing his dislike of Chicago, "but prefer some smaller city where life is less intense. . . ."[1] Not so Darrow; it was precisely the "intensity" of Chicago that he enjoyed. Whitlock explained the peculiar feeling that overcame him there when he confided to another correspondent: "That city has come to exercise a strange fascination for me, and yet it possesses for me, too, a certain vague inexplicable horror. The hardest work—until it came to waiting for a law practice—that I ever did in my life I did there, the hardest blows I ever received I got there, the heaviest things I ever had to bear, I bore there."[2] This was its heady effect on a man of relative stability and calm; its hold on Darrow's erratic, emotional nature was much greater.

The most important aspect of the new firm of Darrow, Thomas & Thompson was that Darrow was its senior partner. The frictions that had developed from his relationship with Goodrich and Vincent and to a lesser extent with Collins had taught him that he could not be anything but boss. By 1897 his senior position could be justified by his business-getting potential if not by age. His fame brought offers of legal work from all quarters. Of course his most valuable asset was the guarantee of business from the Chicago & Northwestern, which provided a cushion for the new practice that many a lawyer would envy. Most of the cases sent by the railroad involved personal injury claims by ex-employees, passengers, and passers-by, all of which provided conspicuous opportunities for Darrow to exercise his skill as a trial lawyer. As a result he soon attracted work of the same kind on behalf of both plaintiffs and defendants from other industries besides the railroads. He was in demand in civil suits, and won many a verdict for $10,000 in the circuit court of Cook County. He took cases that were the forerunner of workmen's compensation cases, acting as administrator to the estates of deceased workmen; typical was one (which he lost) involving a man who, working late in a laundry one night, fell down an elevator shaft. Such cases made him as familiar in the local courts as he had been in his heyday as corporation counsel.

But the most conspicuous and interesting development of his practice arose out of the great goodwill that he had built up with the labor movement. Had he wished, Darrow could have become salaried house counsel to any number of unions. But by the time he had cut loose from the Chicago & Northwestern he had developed a deep antipathy to being an employee, which he regarded as only slightly preferable to being a slave. Indeed he equated the two conditions, believing that the work of the thirteenth amendment had only been partially accomplished as long as wage labor was still permitted. "Clarence Darrow is one of the few men prominently before the public who have consciously and completely accepted the idea that slavery exists," wrote Hutchins Hapgood. "To him this fact is of supreme importance. Everything else he thinks negligible, of secondary moment."[3] In consequence of this attitude Darrow had a positive phobia against bosses and henceforward would maintain his own formal independence, often at great cost. But he learned the hard way that there was no such thing as complete independence for a man who had to earn his living, whether as a hired hand or by self-employment; for the demands of clients could be as strident as any foreman's and as difficult to resist.

It did not take long for the new legal office to attract a lot of union business. Unionists had not forgotten Darrow's impassioned defense in the Debs case. They had admired his technique of counterattack, which had focused attention upon the strikers' grievances, his refusal to bow in the face of vested interests, his unapologetic justifications of what his labor clients had done, and his excellent understanding of labor questions. Above all, his sincere sympathy with workingmen made him an attractive lawyer for unions in trouble. He spoke the unionists' language, he thought their thoughts, he shared their emotions. He was neither censorious nor distant in his attitude toward the great struggles from which labor litigation grew, accepting without condemnation even the ugly, inconvenient facts of his labor clients' cases. Most lawyers advised unionists against violence, but there was nearly always violence of some kind. Darrow was different; he accepted it. When it had to be admitted, he did not prevaricate or indulge in pretenses of regret. Yes, he acknowledged, violence happened—the wonder was that it did not happen more often. He regarded violence as the inevitable outcome of provocation, a reflexive action for which only the provoker, not the provoked, bore the blame. Violence was not the responsibility of labor, but of management, which had by its actions provoked workers into such acute frustration. Darrow's legal advice was sought out by unionists because it was what they wanted to hear, and in this there was a grave danger for lawyer and client alike. Darrow was incautious, even reckless, in forgiving the sins of his clients, and too often his natural sympathy encouraged them along dangerous paths. In his support of their aims, he sometimes failed to distinguish between what the law said and what he thought it ought to say, with the result that counsel and client seemed to combine in the fray, and the former's professional objectivity (if he had any) was lost. He almost seemed to say, "Go ahead. In your position, you are entitled to fight."

Darrow, unlike most lawyers, gave expression to union officials' own pent-up resentments against the status quo. If he did not win his case, at least he did not stand submissive and apologetic before the law. Even where the fight did not take on the dramatic qualities of the Pullman strike, Darrow's bellicosity translated itself into stonewalling noncooperation. When Darrow's firm was engaged on behalf of the Teamsters in 1897 during their strike against the Chicago street railways, Mayor Carter Harrison claimed: "I had more trouble calming his truculent obstinacy than with Mahon, Quinlan, Tabor and the whole strike committee," and when finally he got the opposing sides together, it was Darrow alone who held aloof.[4] His success in capturing labor business had the ironic result that his firm prospered by tapping an entirely new source of lucrative work. Trade unions had always been in need of legal advice, but usually it had been given almost as a charity by those few members of the legal profession who sympathized with union aims. In the 1890s any lawyer who announced an intention to specialize in labor cases was regarded with incredulity. Darrow certainly did not chart his course as a labor lawyer; he achieved a labor practice not through any conscious plan, but by chance. Probably no one was as surprised as he when well-paying cases started to come his way through union referral. Darrow, Thomas & Thompson and its successor firms had a claim to be the first modern specialists in labor law to practice profitably, and between 1897 and 1911, the practice was very profitable indeed.

As a result of his association with the labor movement and his political stance, an ever-increasing flow of entreaties to provide defenses for the poor and the oppressed came Darrow's way. He constantly received referrals from other lawyers, and pleas for help from penniless supplicants. Often these cases were accompanied by some such admission as "frankly, I do not see what you could do. . . ."[5] But even sifting through such cases cost Darrow money by distracting him from paying business. As with all lawyers, the only commodity Darrow could sell was his time. Yet he never rationed his charity according to the amount that the hours involved would cost. Throughout his life he spent much time in company with and doing things for people who by no stretch of the imagination could pay him for his work.

For the most part those who sought his charity were in genuine need, and there were far too many of them for him to help them all. He tried to sort them out on a fair and intelligent principle: he would only help the poor with cases in which he thought there was a reasonable chance he could achieve a satisfactory result. This eliminated 90 percent of the requests he received, for they involved truly hopeless cases—literally lost causes, in which a conviction had already been entered and there was no basis for appeal. Even this principle caused Darrow great effort; for learning enough about the cases to reject them took huge amounts of time. But he remained personally accessible to almost anyone who asked to see him throughout his practicing life, and although he took the precaution of having his home telephone unlisted, and when on his travels appreciated being shielded from casual inquiries, he rarely took evasive action or turned anyone away when he was in his Chicago office.[6] The most singular testimony to his altruistic side was that through fifty years of law practice, he always found time to listen.

Temperamentally Darrow found it difficult to refuse any request for aid, but he knew he must, realizing that an independent must still pay his bills and support his practice; even radicalism must have its paymaster. No one knew better than he that starving clients meant starving lawyers. So from the beginning he had to find some further means of cutting down the number of cases he took *pro bono publico.* His task was not made any easier by the fact that, if he accepted one, the news spread like wildfire so that twenty others would soon be at his door. He learned the hard way that a professional man who got the reputation of doing work free was liable to be taken for a sucker. He laced his genuine charity with a practical streak by guarding against being a dreamer like his father, who "never had the art of making or keeping money." There were too many people emerging from Chicago's teeming streets into Darrow's office who started out as paying clients and then tried to convert to charity status. With these, he stood no truck; he sued for his fees. He made a clear distinction between those cases he chose to do free and those in which an ostensibly fee-paying client tried to take advantage of him. Often he took a promissory note from a prospective client at the outset, as some assurance of payment, but even so he frequently received less than he bargained for. The records of Cook County's court clerk show that Darrow had to sue many defaulting clients before he got paid. His ruthlessness in pursuing these default-ers was thought by some to be inconsistent with his professed charity, but on that score, at least, he was maligned. Since the good causes he took up were usually incapable of paying anything, every time he espoused one it reduced the potential gross income of his firm. So his habit of taking deserving cases for nothing made the routine work even more indispensable; in order to take cases *pro bono publico,* paying clients had to subsidize the nonpaying ones.

His dilemma was that of all professionals who do good works: sooner or later he ended up robbing Peter to pay for work done for Paul. As a result the vast majority of his practice consisted of matters no more or less interesting than the average—mundane, except to the immediately affected parties, and accom-panied by public indifference. Dealing with clients of means, he adopted the policy of the railroads and charged what the traffic would bear. Had there been a government agency for the investigation of lawyers' fees as there was an Interstate Commerce Commission to regulate the railroads, it would probably have ruled Darrow's modus operandi unlawful. What especially outraged some critics was that he did not exempt labor organizations from paying what they could afford. He explained his theory very bluntly to Wendell Willkie when Willkie's father, a labor union agent, sought Darrow's help. Darrow named such a high fee for his intervention in the case that the young Willkie was visibly shocked. Darrow turned to him: "It's a good thing for you to learn, son, that there is nothing unethical in being adequately compensated for advocating a cause in which you deeply believe."[7] In the abstract, he might at times give qualified approval to socialism. But practically, he was neither economically nor temperamentally a leveler; he expected to prosper just as he expected to be boss. And on that premise he was not wrong to charge the labor unions high fees when they had the money to pay them. By paying heavily they became patrons, admittedly involuntarily, of good works.

Aside from the undoubtedly large number of cases that Darrow handled free, there was no reason to suppose that he was inclined to work cheaply.

Those who accepted his public pronouncements in favor of socialism as a statement of intent to conduct his law practice upon altruistic principles severely misunderstood the man and his generation. He was like his contemporary Louis D. Brandeis of Boston, of whom it was said that he was "determined to become 'the people's lawyer,' and to fight case after case without reward. This did not prevent him, however, from carrying on a large and lucrative private practice"—and as one commentator somewhat slyly pointed out, when Brandeis died, he left over $3 million.[8] Darrow's estate fell far short of that, but only because of mischance rather than any dislike of wealth. Although he advocated cooperation and collectivism as political ideals, he had an individualist's sense of self-interest. He did not believe that he could bring about heaven on earth through the practice of law, nor did he intend to try. He was proud of his ability to attract paying clients and boasted of his entry into law practice in Chicago after the Debs case that "neither then nor for any considerable time thereafter did I need to worry over business prospects." Darrow was deeply imbued with the Victorian assumption that the accumulation of wealth was strong if not conclusive evidence of success. Always he had his eye on the main chance. He explained the gap between precept and practice to a young associate who asked him what should be charged to a client for whom a debt had been collected by attachment.

"How much time did you spend on it?" asked Darrow.

"Two and a half days," was the reply. "But the main thing was that I beat the other creditors to the assets."

"Make a charge of five hundred dollars," Darrow ordered without hesitation.

This fee seemed rather large to the associate. "But Mr. Darrow, that's inconsistent with your idea about correcting the existing evils of compensating people for their labor," he objected. "The other day you told me that every individual should receive for his work a certificate for each hour of labor, and no matter what kind of work men did, their labor-hour certificates should be of equal value. You illustrated your point by saying that you should receive a certificate for an hour's law work, and the Rookery elevator men should receive an equally valuable certificate for an hour's work. The elevator man gets fifty-five dollars a month, and here you are charging five hundred dollars for two and a half days' work!"

"To hell with the elevator men," grunted Darrow; "we're practicing law."[9]

It is a revealing story. The truth was that there was even a certain coarseness in his attitude to fees. His unpaid labors on behalf of the ARU had left him "hungry," so that for the most part the altruistic side of him was subordinated to his financial ambitions. Visiting him in January 1898, Brand Whitlock found avarice rather than altruism the dominant mood. "He is deeply interested in letters, and should have devoted himself to literature, but he has been under the awful compulsion of the age, to make money," he wrote privately to a lady friend. "Have you ever reflected that we of this time are kept so busy making a living that we never find time to live?"[10]

Darrow had seen Altgeld reduced from riches to virtual pauperism within five years and knew all too well that what Chicago gave, it could take away. He knew also that the legal profession was a hard taskmaster and that many less fortunate lawyers would gladly take over the business of Darrow, Thomas & Thompson. He did not want to spend his time in practice, but he wanted even less to starve. So he spent much more time "minding the store" than his own accounts revealed. Yet he persevered with law practice reluctantly, feeling himself trapped and unfairly diverted from the literary and other interests that Whitlock correctly discerned within him. The ordinary run of legal business did not interest him. He preferred giving a speech or reading a book to preparing a memorandum or writing a brief. Much of the burden of doing the dross work fell upon his hapless partners and associates. He wanted the regular income of a practice while only working for it intermittently—a recipe for low morale and bad relations with those who had to do the work. And on the occasions when he did devote himself to clients' business, he was easily distracted by a visitor, a telephone call, or an invitation to lunch with a friend.

The creeping effect of Darrow's resentment of the need to practice—which was really simply the necessity to earn a living—was to set him against the legal profession and to some extent the law itself. He felt himself enslaved and to an increasing extent took to criticizing the bar. This criticism took many forms. Although he acknowledged that the profession was overcrowded, he nevertheless chastised it for being monopolistic. He followed Altgeld in believing bar associations to be largely devoted to keeping out competition: ". . . [T]he lawyers who already are admitted to the bar go to all kinds of trouble to keep others out, making preliminaries difficult, and examinations harder than ever," he complained.[11] He had tried desperately to prevent application of the recently enacted antitrust laws to trade unions, yet he applied the Sherman Act's theory of conspiracy to his own profession, in the process conceding the kindred desire of both unions and great corporations to create monopolies. "The Lawyers' Union is about as anxious to encourage competition as the Plumbers' Union is, or the United States Steel Co., or the American Medical Association," he grumbled, without pausing to explain why the anticompetitive tendencies of U.S. Steel deserved control although those of the Plumbers' Union did not. It was but a short step from his dissatisfaction with the profession to a dissatisfaction with the law which it professed. Increasingly, familiarity bred contempt as he became convinced that the legal system promoted injustice. In consequence he began to fight the system through his clients' causes, becoming unwilling to invoke the law against anyone. In particular, he positively refused to lend his skills to the prosecution. Alice Hamilton (a doctor whose interest in the control of typhoid led her to spend much time in the slums of Chicago) told a story of the outrage of the residents of Hull House when a Polish policeman shot two Italians, one of whom died from his wounds, because they failed to move on at the policeman's order:

When a delegation of Italians came to us to appeal for some sort of action we asked Clarence Darrow, then living not far from Hull House, to bring charges against the Polish policeman, and we collected, in nickels and dimes, some four hundred dollars for a retaining fee. But nothing came of it. Darrow never pushed it: he explained that his role was that of defender, not prosecutor, and the policeman was not even suspended.[12]

It did not need a particularly radical mentality to be against prosecution in Chicago, where the criminal courts were notoriously discriminatory instruments of oppression of the poor. There were many independent testimonies to this fact. In 1876 a Cook County lawyer had suggested that "no man of even moderate wealth or influence can be convicted in this country." Eighteen years later things had not changed much—"Criminals 'who have a pull' can usually escape in Chicago," reported William Stead.

Over and over again I have had to ask myself whether I was really in an American city or whether I had been spirited away and dropped down in some Turkish pashalik, so entirely has the very conception of impartial justice died out in the police courts of Chicago. That is a strong statement to those who do not know Chicago, but those who know the city will only wonder and be surprised that I should regard it as a subject interesting enough to talk about.[13]

Darrow embroidered upon this theme during a lecture in 1902:

If the courts were organized to promote justice the people would elect somebody to defend . . . criminals, somebody as smart as the prosecutor—and give him as many detectives and as many assistants to help, and pay as much money to defend you as to prosecute you.[14]

And in fact his attitude toward prosecution, which was one shared by many in his circle, was tied to his denigration of his own profession. There was the feeling that lawyering was essentially a sordid business, which enabled the rich to prey upon the poor. Lawyers as hangmen, as the voices of vindictiveness, as doers of dirty work, were by this view as criminal as those whom some of them prosecuted. The profession seemed incompatible with idealism and human sympathy, and it is a fact that many of the men who practiced law in Chicago in the 1890s felt that they were cut out for better things. Darrow, in 1897, was chief among them.

Yet there was in this attitude an enormous self-delusion. It was not really the legal profession that enslaved him, but his own ambition. He might encourage bums to be bums and admire Walt Whitman, but he had no intention of taking to the open road himself; he could not have tolerated the obscurity of a tramp's calling. His picture of the hobos as independent free spirits was crassly romanticized, and ignored the horrendous conditions in which such men slept and ate. Darrow's idea that he was trapped by legal practice laid blame entirely at the wrong door. He was, whether he admitted it or not, a bourgeois, who would have strained to support his by now excellent standard of living in some other way if law practice had not been the most convenient.

But Darrow's ruminations did not take account of this reality; instead, he refused to acknowledge that he was a family man with a house and a mortgage, whose economic path was indistinguishable from that of many thousand other Chicagoans of his age.

The years from 1894 had been lived at a hectic pace. He appeared at Vincennes Avenue rarely and usually only when he was too exhausted to do anything but go to bed. Jessie had quite understandable reason to complain. She neither knew much about nor cared deeply for the matters which had taken such a viselike grip of her husband's imagination, so that the wear and tear upon their marriage was severe. The single-mindedness with which Darrow pursued his interests downtown was both an evasion of her and an escape from a marriage that he found constraining. When he wanted to appear sophisticated and emancipated, he felt he was undercut by his simple, conventional domestic circumstances. In short, he found it difficult to be a fearless radical by day and a meek bourgeois by night.

Faced with the realities of Chicago, Darrow drifted from his wife, who had been chosen for a different world and a different style of living. The women of Chicago had no counterpart in Ashtabula; they were gay, they were intellectual, they were free. Not even his mother, whose memory he much revered, could touch these young things sparking with emancipated ideas. It was true, as Lincoln Steffens's second wife, Ella Winter, put it, that Darrow "had a great interest in women," being both flirtatious and adulterous from time to time— though in the latter pursuit he exercised considerable discretion.[15] The occasion of his open breach with his wife was a passing affair with another woman, but its cause was more fundamental: Jessie had lost her husband not to another woman but to a city. If there was a seducer in the case, it was Chicago, whose vitality and brazenness stole away Clarence's evenings and his weekends, leaving no time for the domestic attention Jessie desired. Ashtabula had at least left Sunday as a day of tranquil family relaxation. There it had been a day for piety in which all distractions except religion were suppressed, so that even wayward husbands were encouraged to stay home. But in Chicago, a man who would not suffer a sermon might go and hear an atheist instead, and all manner of other entertainments clamored for attention as on every other day of the week. Faced with so many allurements, Darrow succumbed to the temptation of them all, relishing the chance to congregate with like-minded spirits. The good companionship of the city was seemingly inexhaustible; almost every evening brought a new lecture, debate, dinner party, or similar diversion. It did not take great insight for Jessie to realize that even when her husband forced himself to stay at Vincennes Avenue for the whole evening, he was fretting to be elsewhere. He had new friends with whom to share his life, new people to impress, and he had the talent, charm, and will to do it. He was already a figure in Chicago who knew and was known to its leading citizens. They were his kind of people—but not his wife's. She entertained them because they were her husband's friends, not because she liked them.

Clarence for his part was uncomfortable with Jessie's lack of sophistication and distinction. It hurt his pride to be married to a woman who was a living reminder of his past. Like many country-born men making their way in the city, he felt self-consciously afraid that city-slickers would see through to the hayseed lurking beneath his confident exterior. In truth, his departure from Ohio and his parting from Jessie were spiritually closely related, for Jessie had become in his eyes a mere remnant of that rural past he was repudiating. It was not that Jessie begrudged him success; on the contrary, she was as loyal a wife as any man could hope for. The trouble was not that he had succeeded, but that he had succeeded upon such a grand scale. When they had married, Clarence was already a young man with prospects; he had the talent and the will to get ahead. But Jessie had measured those prospects by the standards of hamlets like Kinsman, where national eminence was undreamed of by most young men. When the setting of their marriage changed as a result of the move to Chicago, the impact of urban life, socially disruptive in so many ways, prized Clarence and Jessie apart. While he changed, she remained the same.

If any one factor may be singled out as decisive in casting Jessie and Clarence asunder, it must surely have been the publicity he received from the Debs case. Inevitably this widened the gulf between them. The irregular hours and the notoriety that it generated further dispelled any remaining hope she might have of a settled, quiet married life. Jessie was a private woman who, disliking the harsh, searching light of public attention, recoiled from her husband's open repudiation of "respectability" at the very time when he felt himself emancipated from it. July 1894 must finally have shattered her expectation of an unruffled, bourgeois family life in Chicago that approximated to what was considered proper in Ashtabula. Where Clarence felt pride in his fame, Jessie mingled with it shame; neither knowing of nor caring much for the social issues raised by the Pullman strike, she would have preferred to remain on the sidelines, occupying herself with less explosive matters. Clarence deprived her of that option, thrusting the family name beyond the pale of her conception and ideal of refined gentility. Some women might have basked happily in the reflected glory of their husband's fame, however achieved. Jessie was not one of them. Even the presence of Clarence's gentle father in Chicago became a divisive rather than unifying influence, for Amirus naturally identified with his son. Latterly, his father's apartment became a refuge from Vincennes Avenue for Clarence.

The long and irregular hours away from home were part cause and part effect of the deterioration in Clarence's relationship with Jessie. Paul, his only child, was just entering his teens, with all the problems of a boy brought up as the son of a celebrity—especially one who had taken positions in politics that were anathema to most of his schoolmates. Home life seemed less and less enticing to Clarence, until it came to be something he avoided rather than cherished. At last the strain of building up a practice and the fact that he had fallen out of love with Jessie led him to the painful decision—arrived at only after much procrastination and with considerable guilt—that he must seek a divorce. It took him a long time to find the courage to broach the subject to her; communication had been strained between them for years, confined to conventional platitudes and with no enthusiasm on Clarence's side. Finally he told her that he felt he could face the future better without her than with her, and that he wished her to start proceedings against him for desertion.

Knowing that divorce was still regarded as a disgrace to the guilty party, Jessie generously suggested that it would harm Clarence less professionally and politically if he started proceedings against her, which—subject to a satisfactory property settlement—she would not contest. Although Jessie did not want the divorce, she recognized that their marriage now existed only in form. Darrow's ex-partner Collins filed suit on March 12, 1897, alleging that Jessie had "wilfully deserted and absented herself without any reasonable cause" from the matrimonial home for the last two years, though of course in truth it was Clarence who had not been there. Jessie was represented by Samuel McConnell, a judge who had supported Darrow in his efforts with the Amnesty Association, and who was now back in private practice. The case, tried in the chancery division of the Cook County courts in April, was left uncontested by Jessie and a decree of divorce issued accordingly. Darrow agreed to pay her $150 per month for the rest of her life, to make over the fee simple of 4219 Vincennes Avenue to her, and to pay taxes on it for as long as she kept it.[16] So it came about that he celebrated his fortieth birthday, almost to the day, by getting a divorce. Although Darrow lost most of the material trappings of his success in the city, he made them over gladly, relieved that the tensions of his unloving marriage had been dissolved. Had not that house, built from the fruits of his early success in Chicago, rankled a little in showing him to be conventional? It was the visible sign of his *embourgeoisement,* giving the lie to his liberated self-image. He divested himself of it willingly.

But, free of the restraints of marriage, he found himself no happier, learning the hard way that he was no more content outside marriage than in it. Divorce had solved no fundamental problem: he was still under the necessity of earning his living and there were still no perfect answers. His divorce became a subject of remorse and there were even occasions on which he sought reconciliation. His general feeling of dissatisfaction had been only partly attributable to his domestic affairs; nevertheless the divorce was a landmark in Darrow's spiritual development. Having broken loose, he was determined to try bohemianism as he understood it—to prove, as it were, that his spiritual address was not on Vincennes Avenue. But it was not the new lifestyle he adopted that was really significant. What really counted was the fact that the period following the divorce would allow him to develop the extreme views that were finally to get him into a great deal of trouble.

12

"Free Lovers
as Well as Socialists"

As soon as the divorce was agreed upon, Darrow moved out of the Vincennes Avenue house to stay temporarily at the home of his mother's sister's family, the Fishers, who lived at 1321 Michigan Avenue. After that, he moved into the Chicago Athletic Club for a short time; but these were only makeshift arrangements and within a few months he had found himself less orthodox quarters. The Langdon Co-operative Living Club was putting up an apartment building on the corner of Desplaines and Bunker streets just when he was getting divorced. Darrow moved in shortly after it was completed, sharing a large apartment with Francis S. Wilson, a young cousin of Jessie's who was also a lawyer.

The period following upon his divorce marked an experiment with bohemianism for which Darrow had never previously had the opportunity. He sought and found distraction in the many "proper" organizations to which he already belonged, hurling himself even further into the city's abundant cultural life. Almost as soon as his divorce was granted, he was elected to the steering committee of the Sunset Club. But he had an appetite too for less staid entertainment. The alacrity of his plunge into the *demimonde* of Chicago showed that he had nursed a desire to enter it for some time, and that it might have contributed to his dissatisfaction with Jessie. It was as if the opportunities of youth came to him rather late and he was determined to take advantage of them. In the advanced circles in which he moved, free love was regarded as a desirable social concomitant of anarchism. At 2238 Calumet, Parker H. Sercombe headed a free love colony while he edited the magazine *Tomorrow,* with which Darrow was associated and which for a time he co-edited. Unattached, Darrow preached free love to associates like Gertrude Barnum rather more than he found opportunity to practice it, but still found more chance to philander than he had as a youth. The Langdon apartments were only a few hundred yards from Hull House, where advanced young ladies were easy to meet. Darrow and Wilson were both frequent guests there, and selected residents of Hull House were often their guests at the Langdon. The building was designed as a model tenement, but Darrow and Wilson managed to live better than typical tenement dwellers; for one thing, they had combined two apartments into one so that their floor area was considerable, and for another, both of them made considerably more money than any of their neighbors. The result was that their quarters became a focal point of the local community of settlement house workers and intellectuals. Many of the Hull House girls, like Gertrude Barnum, found Darrow "the center of attraction in our leisure hours."[1]

Darrow's relationships with women have left little evidence from which to draw conclusions. His dalliances have not been chronicled for posterity, but the permissive spirit of the circle in which he moved attained a notoriety that gave some credibility to allegations later made as part of smear campaigns against him that he and his friends were "free lovers as well as Socialists."[2] The truth was that Darrow was about as much a free lover as a socialist—which is to say not much at all. He was attracted by all sorts of nonconformity, but not committed to any in a steadfast intellectual sense. Indeed one of his great qualities was his ability to savor the diverse convictions of Chicago's *avant garde*. Chicago's bohemian smart set combined the low life and the law in a heady concoction. The offspring of good families like Gertrude Barnum's and Helen Todd's mingled with all classes of folk without stuffiness or inhibition at the settlement houses. He was maturing into an age remarkably tolerant of mavericks, who defied the conventional restraints of Victorian society intellectually and socially. There was something attractive about the lack of inhibition with which Darrow belabored the mighty. His primitive energy in attacking the established order had meaning even for those who did not share his views, but who nevertheless secretly rebelled against the straitjacket of convention. His anarchic views harmonized well with this emancipated interlude in his personal life, providing an added dimension to his desirability as a dinner guest.

The fascination of Darrow's intellectual interests for the young women of the settlements was somewhat counterbalanced by the way in which he became exceedingly careless of his appearance once he was divorced. Possibly this was a deliberate advertisement of his nonconformity, but it is equally likely that he simply did not know how to groom himself without Jessie's guidance. In any event, the chorus of female voices lamenting his appearance in these bachelor days is too large to be ignored. Fanny Butcher remarked that "his clothes fitted like a popular model from the U.S. Tent & Awning Company," and Gertrude Barnum herself was quite explicit that, in spite of her admiration for Darrow's mind, she found him physically repulsive "because of his dirty fingernails and rather greasy hair."[3] These and other women accused Darrow of being untidy, dirty, and smelly; but in spite of that—or perhaps because of it, in an age that associated sex and dirt more strongly than later generations —he never lacked female companionship. Certainly he made a strong impression on women, who became either loyalists or enemies, rarely remaining indifferent.

These six years as a single man had much more significance than merely providing Darrow with the sexual opportunities he had never known as a youth. They supplied an ambience of tolerance that allowed many interests which had been suppressed to come to the surface. One of the most significant of these was his espousal of the cause of the Negroes. On this question he was quite extraordinarily outspoken by the standards of his time. W. E. B. DuBois recollected that "he was one of the few white folk with whom I felt quite free to discuss matters of race and class which usually I would not bring up."[4] Darrow's role was not confined to mere speaking; he was, in the 1890s, one of the supporters of the foundation of Chicago's Provident Hospital, billed as "the world's first interracial hospital," whose board he later joined, and his personal physician was a so-called voluntary Negro, Dr. Daniel Williams. Unlike many of his generation, Darrow did not believe that emancipation had ended the difficulties of black Americans; on the contrary, he saw that it had had deleterious as well as beneficial effects. Of all the causes with which he was associated in his lifetime, the most constant was that of Negro Americans. He gave more of his time and money to their organizations than any other white man of the period. He understood that slavery was not merely a legal status, but an economic condition, and that though the Negroes no longer suffered its legal status, they were not free of the less discernible but equally desperate sort of economic slavery. He even, in occasional moods of despondency, pictured himself as a slave side by side with the blacks of Chicago, downtrodden by the need to make a living. Darrow's rebellion against law practice, his repudiation of his marriage, and his sympathies with the oppressed were all emotionally, if not logically, related.

It was true that while in the Langdon apartments he continued to attend his law office every day, walking the 2 miles with Francis Wilson, and stopping for breakfast on the way at Race's Fish Restaurant. But the frantic pace of his social life made it difficult for him to focus on the chores of law practice when he got there. Besides, he was also combining business with pleasure as a polemicist and was able to make some progress toward the emancipation he desired on other fronts, in particular in cultivating his artistic side. By now Darrow was in the forefront of platform speakers, developing the essentially colloquial style that was to mark him as a modernist. A natural speaker, who could capture and hold an audience seemingly without effort, politics had already given him much practice both in speaking and in listening to speeches. He had rejected histrionic affectation, acquiring by experience the platform poise of one used to being in a minority. He was not a clever orator in the sense of producing elegant turns of phrase. He spoke plainly in an age still given to purple prose. It was the total effect of his speeches that was telling rather than any carefully planted quotable quotes. Darrow was among the first great public speakers to abandon the stilted mannerisms of public speaking and turn to a more natural style. He came to recognize that the nineteenth century's attention to style was often at the expense of substance and that, as he wrote to a correspondent: "Oratory is played out with sensible people. It has no place with brains or thought. . . . The first thing for a young man to do if he proposes to be a public speaker is to have something to say. That is the last thing that the orator thinks is necessary."[5]

As a young man himself Darrow had imitated the current models of oratorical complexity including, among others, Robert Ingersoll. His original stylistic standards were those of the country fair whereas his final conclusions about oratory were the result of tried experience. His impatience with William Jennings Bryan was in part engendered by their different styles: the "Cross of Gold" speech did not communicate anything intellectually, however effective it was emotionally. Darrow's mature conclusions about speaking were a wholesale repudiation of what had been current when he was growing up:

> For years, before juries, on the platform, in conversation, I have first of all tried to know what I was talking about, and then to make my statements clear and simple, and the sentences short. I am not at all sure that this is the best method for writing and speaking. The reader has time to consider, and go over the pages if he will; if he misses a word or does not understand one, or even an idea, he can look things up in the dictionary or encyclopaedia. But the listener has but one chance, and that is as the information or opinion hastens along; so the words must not be too long, or too unfamiliar, nor spoken too rapidly for assimilation. Some grasp spoken matter quickly, and some need time to catch what they are not accustomed to hear. The speaker must aim to reach practically every person in his audience; therefore he must not speak too fast or use too many uncommon words.

Here spoke the authentic voice of one who had engaged in electioneering among the poor immigrants of the first ward, where command of English was almost nonexistent; for them, simplicity and directness were his greatest virtues. But his adoption of a less bombastic form of address was not purely pragmatic; he had read extensively on the art of oratory and was able to supply a bibliography on the subject to young hopefuls. Neither was the style which he adopted and of which he became the chief exponent truly "natural" in the sense that it was unrehearsed. On the contrary, his effects were carefully contrived and in his years living round the corner from Halsted Street he took special pains to cultivate a platform image as a tortured intellectual in an imperfect world. How pleased he must have been to be billed as "the intellectual and fearless" Clarence Darrow when he appeared in Wendel's Hall at 1504 Milwaukee Avenue in 1899. That was how he wanted the public to think of him, and he went to great pains to ensure that they did.

With this in mind, he confined himself to relatively few platform themes, which he repeated again and again, each time polishing them so that far from being "natural" they were in their way just as theatrical as the themes of exponents of the older school. It was all very well for Darrow to jeer that Bryan's presentation to the Democratic National Convention of 1896 had been gone over many times on the prairies of Nebraska, but it was equally true that most of Darrow's speeches had been gone over many times in Chicago meeting halls. Both Darrow and Bryan were members of the last generation in which it was possible for a public figure to use the same material repeatedly without being detected by most of his audience, and both of them did. They did not have to cope with the insatiable appetite of electronic media until they were old men, by which time they were not affected by it. Darrow admitted that his effectiveness was in part the result of the predictability of public debate in his time, both as to subject and approach:

> My public talks have been mainly about politics, economics, labor, religion, prohibition, crime, and now and then on literary celebrities and what they have said and done. My debates have been on prohibition, religion, politics, and science. . . . In these debates, most of the speakers, whoever they were, have very nearly echoed each other's sentiments. This of course saved me from varying my arguments to any great extent.

The cadences of his great speeches were beautiful and compelling, with a touch of evangelical ebb and flow about them. There was so much rhythm to them that he was able to quote poetry as he talked without losing the audience; his words and the poets' seemed to merge naturally. Indeed the only thing on the surface of his addresses that dates them is his quotation of verse. This foible was not only the mark of a more poetic age than later ones, but had special significance to Darrow personally; it was an attempt to use his debating and speechifying as a bridge to literary fame. His quotation of poetry on all occasions was partly designed to give him the literary credentials he otherwise found hard to garner.

In spite of the obvious affinity between the skills of speaking and writing, Darrow was never able to reach the distinction in print that he regularly achieved as an advocate. Apparently he only half understood why he could not convert his magnificent command of the spoken word into literature. The fact was that he needed the immediate stimulus of a live audience, which only speaking could give; without it, his words were undistinguished and uninspired. His muse was not suited to the solitary work of writing, and though he tried his hand at it many times the result was nearly always disappointing. Whether he turned to autobiographical fiction, to belles lettres, or to political satire, his work bore the marks of imitation of current fashionable models and a consequent flatness. He was not without talent—he was able to reproduce several different modes of writing with recognizable accuracy—but it was of a minor and somewhat unoriginal kind.

Still, he persevered at establishing for himself some literary standing, and during his years at the Langdon produced two major attempts at literature. The booming Chicago in which Darrow had settled was ideally suited to this interest, since it cast off opportunities galore for young, talented men like himself who had literary ambitions. The first and most contrived piece Darrow completed was *The Skeleton in the Closet,* an essay in the style of Victorian occasional prose that even then was a little *passé.* It was apparently prompted by his recent divorce, the theme being that it was better to acknowledge what had happened frankly than try (inevitably unsuccessfully) to hide it, thereby encouraging gossip and scandal that would probably be much more salacious than the facts. The essay was competent, and bore traces of Darrow's antipathy to formal education; but it was not specially distinguished and might comfortably have been included in an anthology of short pieces such as the *Home Books,* which had been popular twenty years before. Essentially it was a moral homily, exhorting readers to face life fearlessly, of the sort that might almost have been written by an advanced cleric.

His other major effort at this period was more substantial. Entitled *Realism in Art and Literature,* it put forward the critical thesis that realism was the proper aim of literature. "Most of the art and literature the world has known has been untrue," Darrow proclaimed. It portrayed beauty and light, though "not all the world is beautiful, and not all of life is good." He deplored the way in which art suppressed and distorted the sordid reality, drawing an analogy between the position of an artist and a lawyer in capitalist society, a subject which had been much on his mind since he took up residence at the Langdon: "Of course an artist would not paint the poor; they had no clothes that would adorn a work of art, and no money nor favors that could remunerate the toil. An ancient artist could no more afford to serve the poor than a modern lawyer could defend the weak." Behind this statement were many hours of anguished pondering by Darrow on whether he should abandon law practice altogether in favor of the literary life. He would have loved to do so. His boyhood experience made him give authorship immensely more prestige than lawyering, and now that Amirus was in the city, the image of his father's passionate reading was constantly refreshed. More and more he became convinced that the triumphs of platform speaking and advocacy were ephemeral by comparison to literary success. Darrow was an inveterate reader, not only for the purpose of understanding what writers had to say, but also to teach himself how to write. In the years between his divorce and the turn of the century, he was constantly on the brink of giving up his law practice in favor of letters, and had he achieved even one substantial literary success would undoubtedly have done so. But in spite of all his efforts and a cultivation of the literati of Chicago so assiduous that he gave the impression to younger men that he was their doyen, he was in fact accumulating a large collection of rejection slips. Certainly he took in Brand Whitlock, who as a journalist should have known better. "Mr. Darrow is an intimate friend of Mr. William Dean Howells," confided Whitlock eagerly to a correspondent, "and he asked me to send him several of my MSS that he might send them to Mr. Howells, with a view to interesting him in them, and enlisting his powerful influence in their acceptance and production."[6] There was a certain irony in Darrow's acting as unofficial broker of Whitlock's writing while himself having difficulty in placing his own.[7]

Whitlock thought highly of his literary criticism, even though Darrow had to resort to a kind of expensive vanity publishing to get his essays on the market. Whitlock was one of those favored with a copy of a lavishly produced collection of his works. He wrote off to a friend:

> I recently received from my good friend Mr. Clarence Darrow of Chicago a volume of essays written by him, beautifully bound and printed, with attractive rubrics good enough to eat, on hand-made paper with deckle edges and wide margins—one of which was on "Realism in Literature and Art." His thesis is that realism has been ancillary in its growth to liberty, and it is one of the most remarkably convincing and scholarly philosophical discussions of the subjects I have ever found. I wish you could read it. If the opportunity presents itself do not fail to do so."[8]

If any experience brought home to Darrow that his literary avocation would not support him, the necessity of subsidizing the publication of his serious critical work from the profits of his law practice ought to have done so. It revealed to him an unwelcome truth: evidently society valued his legal opinion more than his opinion on literary matters. It was an immensely frustrating lesson to him, but he was not such a fool as to ignore it and give up law practice. However much he wanted to be a literary man and enjoyed posing as a tortured intellectual, he did not want to starve in a garret. As a result his literary ambitions had to exist side by side with his profession as a means of earning a living.

Judged by his actual literary products, this must be regarded as a merciful deliverance. Notwithstanding Whitlock's lavish praise of *Realism in Art and Literature,* the essay revealed Darrow's severe limitations as a critic. His often expressed view that the highest art was "realism," not "idealism," was another way of saying that art should imitate life rather than vice versa. He wanted experience to be reflected in literature as a narrative that evoked the feelings of real life. "Realism" denied the status of literature to works of pure imagination. Consequently his preferred literature was historical, and usually a reflection of the recent past. All the novels he most admired were pieces of near-contemporary reportage: Sinclair Lewis's *Arrowsmith* and *Main Street,* Theodore Dreiser's *American Tragedy* and *The Titan.* Just as socialism was a response to the rise of industrialism, so the literature of the industrial age reflected an iconoclastic debunking of the businessman as hero. And this was a fallacy of which Darrow was egregiously guilty. His essay proclaimed that "The greatest artists of the world today are telling facts and painting scenes that cause humanity to stop, and think, and ask why one should be a master and another a serf; why a portion of the world should toil and spin, should wear away its strength and life, that the rest should live in idleness and ease."[9] It was a classic statement of art as propaganda: that the proper purpose of literature is a political awakening of the reader, and that the writer's mission is to stir dissatisfaction with the social order. And indeed, Darrow's tastes in literature were almost exclusively polemical, as Hutchins Hapgood perceived:

> . . . to my surprise I found him incapable apparently of appreciating literature and poetry except that of revolt. He seemed to feel like so many men who want

to change the world, that everything that has happened in relationship with the development of unjust institutions is evil; in that literature, poetry, morality, which has developed side by side with an unjust political and economic order, is there only to give support to this injustice, and therefore merely aids and comforts the devil. I have had many opportunities to observe this tendency.[10]

The prospect was that even if he had worked full time at being an author, Darrow's literary output would have been didactic and tractarian. Nevertheless he remained remarkably faithful to the desire for literary recognition. Even after he had retired and was past the age of seventy, he constantly sought to promote his earlier writings and to sell new ones. He had little more success in old age than he had in his years at the Langdon, though by then his fame helped to interest editors in his by-line.

He did manage one compromise that gave him solace. If he could not achieve large sales by setting pen to paper, it was possible that transcripts of his speeches would sell. Of their quality, there was no doubt; and after the death of Robert Ingersoll in 1899 there was no public figure to rival him except William Jennings Bryan. If his speeches and jury addresses were published in permanent form, he could achieve the satisfaction of authorship by seeing his name and words in widely circulated print. And from that possibility Darrow developed a special appetite for legal cases that for one reason or another would attract publicity. These he would handle free, or almost free, if they would generate a pamphlet or book based upon his advocacy. No matter that his tendency to take poorly paying cases was a constant source of friction with his partners, he would bend the practice of law to his purpose to achieve literary distinction.

As an *auteur manqué* who happened to practice law, he did not need to wait long for the chance to put this inspired plan into action. In mid-1898 Darrow was approached with a request to defend Thomas I. Kidd, general secretary of the Amalgamated Woodworkers' International Union, against a criminal conspiracy charge brought against him in Oshkosh, Wisconsin, as a result of his strike-organizing efforts at the Paine Lumber Company. The Woodworkers' Union had almost no money to pay Darrow. But the legal issue was one on which Darrow was exceptionally well informed as a result of his experience in the Debs case, and the events in Wisconsin promised him a chance to follow to its conclusion a prosecution of unionists for conspiracy of the kind that the United States attorney had dropped against Debs. The press was bound to pay it much attention. Darrow asked how much the union was in a position to pay. The answer was only $1,000, although the defense would require weeks of his time away from Chicago to the consequent detriment of his practice. The fee was much less than he could make on other business, but Darrow saw a way to feed his literary and legal ambition at the same time. He would defend Kidd and the woodworkers for only $250, he said, on one condition: that the union would promise to underwrite the expense of issuing his final address to the jury as a booklet after the trial, whatever the verdict. The union officials willingly agreed. It seemed and was a very generous offer. With that the deal was clinched. Darrow had successfully built a bridge between his two divergent ambitions, and the pattern of his future trial work was fixed.

In spite of Brand Whitlock's impression at the beginning of 1898, Darrow was not completely under "the awful compulsion of the age"; the fact that he took the Kidd case in the fall of that year proved that his conception of success was not wholly mercenary. Had he been a hardnosed lawyer on the make financially, he would never have bothered with Kidd, whose pitiful defense fund did not equal the profit from even a week of office practice with Darrow, Thomas & Thompson. On the other hand, neither could it be claimed that his entry into the case was born of pure altruism. If he had merely wanted to practice philanthropy, literally dozens of chances to aid the faceless poor emerged in Chicago every week, most of which he ignored. The truth was that his pay in the Kidd case was the assurance of public attention: he liked money, but he preferred fame. By 1898 Darrow did not need to worry about earning a living. As head of a burgeoning law firm in an era before income tax, he was in an enviable financial state. He was well on the way to becoming a rich man by channeling to his law firm the abundant legal business provided through his political contacts. Having lost his chance to go to Congress in 1897, Darrow knew that a lawyer's road to high public office frequently started with being conspicuous in the litigation of some public question. While he had mixed feelings about his narrow defeat in the congressional race and sometimes thought of it as a blessing in disguise, he did not wish to foreclose the possibility of entering the hustings once more. He could be a sure winner—he would not repeat the error of failing to campaign in his own district again. The Kidd case would revive the public memory (by now in danger of growing dim) that he had been labor's spokesman in 1894. If ever he decided to make a fight for the Senate, he knew this would stand him in good stead. Whether employers or employees won in court, the latter held the whiphand at the polls. Politically he was on the right side. He was tormented by conflicting urges regarding a political career, having neither decided in favor of it nor rejected it entirely. In many ways it was a more attractive prospect to him than a lifetime in the law. So, not knowing his own mind, he steered an indeterminate course. He undertook the Kidd case, which was the kind of practice he enjoyed most and which would also keep his political irons in the fire.

13

The Kidd Case

By the time of the Kidd case the initial trauma of Darrow's divorce had passed, but the lingering social discomforts of his reversion to a single status may have contributed to the attraction of the chance to get away from Chicago. The trip to Oshkosh had the dual benefit of laying to rest any remaining question that he controlled his own destiny, besides putting enough distance between him and Jessie to enforce his breach with her, which Darrow needed to do. For apparently the decision to go to Wisconsin was made only shortly after he had, in a moment of pathetic weakness, sought reconciliation with her. Following the awkwardness and hurt on both sides, he thought it good to get away so that he would not be tempted to repeat that performance.

The Kidd case was the first of many odysseys beyond Chicago that were to build Darrow's reputation as a lawyer of national stature. He enjoyed the implied compliment—that he was the only lawyer available who could do an adequate job—of being sent many miles from Chicago to defend clients. And as he became used to the role of peripatetic attorney to the labor movement, he often capitalized upon the drama of being a dragonslayer brought in from afar. The aura he sought to create around himself stood his clients in good stead; for in the outreaches of the continent, the mere fact of his visit imparted a certain importance to his clients' case which no local attorney could have given it. In Oshkosh, Wisconsin, a visit by Darrow was an Event.

Although there was an element of lawyerly calculation in creating this effect, Darrow's passionate commitment was beyond doubt: he believed in unionism as strongly as Debs or Gompers. And although his spellbinding abilities in court brought him many labor cases, union officials were just as much influenced by the sincerity he showed in his private talks with them. So it was with Thomas I. Kidd. Kidd first became familiar with Darrow when in 1894, during the Pullman strike, he had signed a message to President Grover Cleveland in his capacity as a member of the executive council of the A.F. of L., which had been meeting in Chicago. From then on, Kidd had frequently come to Darrow with the legal difficulties of the Woodworkers' Union, each time becoming surer that he was a true friend of labor. Here was no cynical paid mouthpiece, but an uncompromising believer. Hence, when the dragonslayer from Chicago arrived, he was breathing real fire.

Undoubtedly some of the bitterness accompanying the current strike arose from the fact that it had been inspired and organized by an "outsider" come to stir up trouble. The employees of the Paine Lumber Company had not spontaneously struck; they had been organized by Kidd, whose full-time job was, in effect, labor agitation. Informally, a decision had been made back in Chicago to fight the Wisconsin prosecution as a frontal attack on the unions. Kidd, with George Zentner and Michael Troiber, two local men who had acted as picket captains, had been indicted for criminal conspiracy to injure the Paine Lumber Company's business. The Woodworkers' Union saw this change as potentially more dangerous to the labor movement than even the prosecution of the ARU had been. Although both prosecutions had involved a challenge of conspiracy, the unlawful act charged against the railroaders was interference with interstate commerce, an accusation largely chosen to provide a jurisdictional basis upon which the federal government could proceed. But the Wisconsin prosecution was a much more direct attack on the right to strike, since the unlawful act charged was conspiracy to injure the business of the union's target company. If this was held to be a crime, it would amount to holding that a strike per se was criminal in Wisconsin, with the prospect that the decision would be copied in other states as the occasion arose. Furthermore this prosecution had only been brought after an unsuccessful application for an injunction had been made to the Wisconsin courts; in other words, the employers had resorted to the criminal law to get what the civil law had denied them. Small wonder, in these circumstances, that the Woodworkers' Union was anxious to repel the criminal charges.

The Paine Lumber Company made sashes, doors, and blinds, and was a substantial employer in the small town of Oshkosh. Darrow reported that, "As in all places outside of big cities and industrial centres, the feeling was very bitter on both sides." He would do nothing to diminish that bitterness: he believed that a fight was a fight. Any union that employed him as its lawyer had a guarantee that its position would be asserted with strength and fervor, if not always with tact and compassion. In the intensity of advocacy, he discarded these latter qualities as irrelevant, to the delight of his clients and often the chagrin of his opponents. The Kidd case was to be no exception.

The Paine Lumber Company was in the hands of the family that gave it its name, and George M. Paine and his son Nathan had done everything they could to prevent unionization of their plant and to discourage the strike. The senior Paine refused to negotiate, but it would have been unlikely that any compromise would have been reached if he had, for the workers had grievances against too many aspects of Mr. Paine's management of his business. Paine was like Pullman in being guided by a business philosophy that regarded unions as an unmitigated evil and refused to recognize them or accede to their demands, but he showed somewhat less wisdom than Pullman in submitting himself to cross-examination by Darrow, with disastrous results for his reputation.

Thus, in spite of its differences from the situation in Chicago in 1894, the Kidd case gave Darrow an opportunity to use many of the tactics he had prepared in vain for the criminal prosecution of the American Railway Union four years before. Darrow valued this chance particularly since any hope he had continued to harbor of confronting Pullman himself had been dashed by Pullman's death in 1897. Once again he made the dramatic accusation that the prosecution was a misuse of government power, and just as he had argued in 1894 that the federal prosecution of Debs was engineered by the General Managers' Association, so he argued in 1898 that the prosecution of Kidd was inspired by George Paine. Never one to look a gift horse in the mouth, Darrow built up the argument even further in Oshkosh. "Let us understand exactly who are the parties to this case," he entreated the jury.

> Counsel for the prosecution will stand before this jury with hypocritical voice and false words, and say it is the great state of Wisconsin on the one hand and these three defendants upon the other. I say that this is not true, and every person in the hearing of my voice knows that it is not true.
>
> Who is the state of Wisconsin, and how does the state of Wisconsin act? It moves only through its officers, ordinary men, strong in some ways, weak in others, subject to all those influences that move you and me and every other man that lives. Mr. Quartermass, the District Attorney, represents the state of Wisconsin. . . . I know that Quartermass filed this information because George Paine told him to do so. . . . He has made an assignment of the state of Wisconsin—not for the benefit of creditors, but for the benefit of Paine's lumber company.[1]

The four years intervening between the two cases added edge to Darrow's effectiveness in putting this point, which had the virtue, like all of Darrow's mainstays, of being usable in almost all labor cases interchangeably without regard to their particular facts. The Kidd case demonstrated that Darrow was building up an inventory of original ploys, usable and reusable throughout his long career with only a minimum of modification. Once he had developed an appealing argument, it was called into aid in all sorts of contexts subsequently. However much he used it, it would be new to the majority of his audience. And even when he repeated himself almost word for word in court during his long career, he had a way of making his points appear so apt to the occasion that it did not seem to matter that to a few of his listeners they had a vague ring of familiarity.

Even Darrow's central legal argument was derived from his ARU experience. There were minor variations in the law of conspiracy among the several states and between federal and state laws, but in outline the situation was the same. Darrow came to have a thorough understanding of this crime, and the law of conspiracy became one of his few strong suits as a lawyer. In most matters of technical law he was disinclined to do the necessary research to acquire any thorough understanding of the subject, leaving such work to associates. But having initially tackled the subject of conspiracy in a flush of enthusiasm to help the ARU, he afterward kept up with it.

Now, in addressing the issue in the Kidd case, he poured scorn on the principle of "guilt by association":

> Now, there is one beauty about a conspiracy case; there is one thing that made it valuable to ancient tyrants, and that makes it equally valuable to modern tyrants, and that is that you do not need much of any theory to carry it on, and this makes it possible for [the prosecutor] to try the case. If there is somebody you want to get, as there always is, because most of us have enemies, excepting Paine—but if there happens to be someone you are after, then you make a charge of conspiracy, and you are allowed to prove what the defendant said and did over any length of time that you see fit to carry it, and there you get your conspiracy. Conspiracy is the child of the Star Chamber Court of England, and it has come down to us, like most bad things and many good ones, from the remote past without much modification. . . . But today I take it that every intelligent person who has investigated this question, outside of the counsel for the State, understand [sic] that workingmen have the right to organize; understand that if laborers are not satisfied with their conditions, they may stop work; they may stop work singly or collectively, exactly as they please, and no court will say them nay. That is the law today, and if it is not the law, it ought to be. This hideous conspiracy in Oshkosh, where sixteen hundred of your fellow-citizens were plotting in the dark, was a labor union; that is all.[2]

The real conspiracy in the case, he maintained, was the prosecutor's conspiracy "to take away the liberty of his fellow-men under the sanction of law; and if there is any darker and deeper one, it is hard for me to imagine it."[3] Darrow made much of the fact that before prosecuting him, Paine had tried to bribe Kidd:

> Ordinarily men are brought into a criminal court for the reason that they are bad. Thomas I. Kidd is brought into a criminal court because he is good, and they understand it well. If Thomas I. Kidd had been mean and selfish and designing, if he had held out his hand to take the paltry bribes that these men pass out wherever they find one so poor and weak as to take their dirty gold, this case would not be here today.[4]

As before, his method of defense was to attack by turning the tables on the prosecution; his great success with his labor clients came in part because he magnified their bellicose spirit. The argument of the "real" conspiracy went down especially well in defense of Kidd, Troiber, and Zentner because the charges were not inherently serious. Although there had been some violence in the fourteen-week strike, it had been more accidental than intentional and Kidd had not been directly involved in it. Darrow was to encounter rather more difficulty in utilizing this technique in later cases where the charges were of murder or arson, but here the argument was both appropriate and appealing. In a real sense Paine, like Pullman earlier, had brought the strike upon himself, for the major grievance against him was his determination to lower his workers' living standard. Pullman had sought to do this by reducing wages directly, while charging the same rents at his model village. Paine had done so by even more insidious means: he had, from 1897 onward, started replacing the men in his factories by cheaper female and child labor so that by the time of the strike they constituted one-quarter of the work force. Of course, as those women and children were employed, men were thrown out of work; and since Oshkosh was a small town, the women and children were the families of the very men rendered unemployed. Thus did the Paine Lumber Company reduce its payroll costs. Although Oshkosh's economy was too diversified for it to be properly described as a company town, the Paine Lumber Company had a profound influence on its economy.*

In the Debs case Pullman had wisely avoided submitting himself to Darrow's questions. George M. Paine was not so wise and as a result suffered greatly. Darrow asked him if he employed girls in his factory and Paine answered reluctantly that he did. Even among the most unrepentant of capitalists, the employment of women and children at hard physical labor was recognized as undesirable. Pullman had boasted that of his 5,250 operatives, "only a few are children (perhaps 200 in all), and still fewer women, of whom only 150 are employed."[5] Pullman had in some ways been a more enlightened capitalist than Paine, who seemed to bear out Karl Marx's assertion a quarter century before that child labor was unavoidable in a capitalist society. Still, in consequence of the prevailing attitude of general disapproval, Paine understated the duties of his young employees. "They take little bits of sticks and saw them up on little saws," replied Paine. Darrow then called evidence to show that they in fact sawed heavy hardwood doors.

The workers had written to Paine to request a meeting to discuss their grievances, and had asked politely for four things: (1) a wage increase; (2) a weekly payday; (3) that he should cease to employ women; and (4) that the union should be recognized. Paine had not answered them at all. "Why not?" asked Darrow.

"It was an unbusinesslike letter," explained Paine, meaning that he regarded unions as unbusinesslike entities and their supporters as unworthy of attention. Darrow made much of this reply in his summation. "He is a nice man, is he not? . . . Here is this man, the monarch of fourteen states in the sash and door business, and he is paying his men the paltry pittance of a dollar a day, and he refuses to reply to their communication because it is unbusinesslike."[6]

Darrow was clearly a master of invective and insult, at his most eloquent and fascinating in moods of denunciation and scorn. His métier was character assassination—prolonged, cruel, and deadly. Under the protection of courtroom privilege, he was able to say things about opposing counsel or witnesses all the more shocking because they could be said nowhere else with impunity;

*Ironically, Oshkosh might have been much larger if, in the 1870s, there had been better rail communications, but "although manufactured products were turned out in such volume that there was a shortage of railroad cars to export them, the Chicago & North Western Railway [Darrow's ex-employer] resisted all attempts to bring a competing line into the city. Though in 1871 the lumbermen themselves financed a short railroad . . . Oshkosh had already lost the opportunity to become an important terminus."—Writers' Program, Works Progress Administration, Wisconsin. New York: Duell, Sloan and Pearce, 1941, p. 217.

only the immunity from suit for slander of words spoken during legal proceedings saved him from effective challenge. His unmerciful venom poured out, contemptuous yet magnificent. He reviled his adversaries as if inspired by hatred. It was in this mood, above all others, that he was memorable, as several of his clients recorded. When the mask of civilization had been put aside, and savagery possessed him, the innermost Darrow appeared. Then, the casual friendliness and the philosophical acceptance of human frailty discarded, he struck out against the enemy in every way he knew.

In the Kidd case he hammered away at the infamy of Paine's business methods—the inhumanity and contempt he displayed toward the men who worked in his factory, his hypocrisy and rapaciousness in dealing with his workers. As one of his discerning clients was later to say of Darrow: "When he was calm, which he nearly always was, he reminded me of a lion. That majestic bearing, that leonine mane of hair. Truly the king of beasts. But when he was excited he turned instantly into a tiger—a fierce, raging tiger. I'll wager that witnesses who have been raked by his fierce irony would not dispute my metaphor."[7] (Paine did not record his sentiments after Darrow had dealt with him.)

Darrow's choice of a butt for his venom among the personnel of the prosecution was another recurrent trial technique of his that was first exercised in the Kidd case. But perhaps the most important addition to his repertoire was his blunt admission that he intended to range well beyond the facts of the particular case in his jury address. He had done this to some extent in the Debs injunction case, but that was a civil proceeding, in which counsel was traditionally allowed leeway, it was not heard before a jury, and in any event his political and philosophical views were heavily interlarded with the minutiae of the evidence. Since then Darrow had made a considerable advance in technique. He had realized that the facts were often a hindrance to putting the union point of view clearly and that effective argument depended on avoiding getting bogged down in the evidence. *Kidd* was a major rhetorical experiment in that Darrow argued from theory and principle, dealing with the evidence almost incidentally. That this was a conscious choice was indicated by his introductory words to the jury, which explained his determination, never afterward abandoned, of discussing not only the evidence but the social context in which the case arose:

> While you have been occupied for the last two weeks in listening to the evidence in this case, and while the Court will instruct you as to the technical rules of law under which this evidence is to be applied, still it is impossible to present the case to you without a broad survey of the great questions that are agitating the world today. For whatever its form, this is not really a criminal case. It is but an episode in the great battle for human liberty, a battle which was commenced when the tyranny and oppression of man first caused him to impose upon his fellows and which will not end so long as the children of one father shall be compelled to toil to support the children of another in luxury and ease.[8]

A firm judge, on hearing Darrow's announcement that he intended to address the jury on "the great questions that are agitating the world today," might have stepped in smartly and reproved him for irrelevance. But the judge in the Kidd case was the first in a long line before whom Darrow appeared who let him continue in this vein. Darrow almost never encountered obstruction from a judge, although he adopted such arguments to juries time and again. Many of his justifications of famous clients were of no relevance to the law, indeed they amounted to virtual admissions of his clients' guilt. It was this, more than anything else, that made him so effective with juries; once he was allowed to discuss general questions, he was off and running.

It is difficult to know how far Darrow's disdain for legal relevance was the result of a practical recognition that there was little to say on behalf of many of his clients. It is a commonplace of advocacy that one of the best tactics of counsel in cases where the client is guilty is to distract attention from him and talk about something else. In many instances Darrow was in that position. But there was more to it than that, for he actually preferred to talk about the wider issues. He was masterful at rationalizing his broad view to the jury and genuinely chose the general considerations as his ground of combat. In defense of many clients, Kidd included, he told the jury that his client was not his main concern, asking for an acquittal as a vindication of general principle rather than justice in the individual case. Many a rogue sought protection under this umbrella, some with success.

The technique was a useful one in some cases, but Darrow would become too fond of it and use it too often. Its pitfall was that it degenerated too easily into an excuse for not preparing, which Darrow was always rather prone to. The risk of having him as a lawyer was that he would use one of his seemingly impromptu defenses, which was in fact an adaptation of what he had said hundreds of times before, so that one case merged into another and the same thing was said without reference to the particulars. Not that he ever got confused on his facts; his factual grasp was his greatest strength, and only rarely was he caught out in misstatements. But the all-purpose defense came to be divorced from the client's actual position, and thus somewhat threadbare. It diminished in force with the passing of each law term, as judges, journalists, and even juries came to see it for what it was—a device for excusing anything and everything.

As he gained experience, Darrow realized that the similarities among his defenses were greater than their differences and that, *a fortiori,* some arguments applied equally to all defendants. Having had many cases that genuinely shared many characteristics in common, he moved to the assumption that all cases were alike in many essentials, and argued accordingly. The same figures of speech, oratorical tricks, and illustrative anecdotes came up time and again and were called in aid of all sorts of criminal. Their sure-fire effect added credibility to those who complained that he had constructed the universal defense.

In making his wide-ranging addresses during cases, Darrow relied upon the

1. *Clarence Darrow's mother, Emily Eddy Darrow.*

2. *The earliest known picture of Clarence Darrow, age 4, 1861.*

3. *Clarence Darrow's picture when he entered the law department of the University of Michigan in 1877, age 19.*

4. *Clarence Darrow, with his father, Amirus, and only son, Paul, c. 1890.*

5. *Darrow and his son, Paul, c. 1896.*

6. *Darrow's patron and mentor, Gov. John Peter Altgeld of Illinois, c. 1890. "He made my life what it is," said Darrow.*

7. *Darrow as he appeared in 1903, shortly before his second marriage.*

8. *Henry Demarest Lloyd, John Mitchell of the United Mine Workers union, and Darrow at the time of the anthracite arbitration, 1903. There was much disagreement behind the scenes about hiring Darrow, but he was finally chosen because, as Lloyd said, "Mr. Mitchell is very anxious to have him."*

9. *Darrow, c. 1903, when George Bernard Shaw wrote of him: "With that cheekbone he wants only a few feathers and a streak of ochre to be a perfect Mohican...."*

10. *Clarence Darrow, c. 1920, age 63.*

11. *Darrow (right) with his client, Fred Lundin, during his trial for conspiracy to defraud the Chicago school board of more than a million dollars, 1923. "He was a man to whom politics was a game, like bridge or golf to others," said Darrow. After Lundin's acquittal, a journalist remarked that "only with the help of God and Clarence Darrow did he escape the penitentiary."*

12. *With his co-counsel, Walter (left) and Benjamin Bachrach, in the Leopold and Loeb case, 1924. His young clients can be seen in the background. He wrote afterward: "From that day I have never gone through so protracted a strain, and could never do it again, even if I should try."*

13. Darrow addresses his plea for Leopold and Loeb to Judge John Caverly, August, 1924.

fact that court discipline was lax and, later in life, on the indulgence shown to him by judges out of deference to his enormous reputation. But even as he developed his technique in the Kidd case, his audacity was startling, for not only did he insist on reviewing the world's "great questions" but he persistently refused to review the actual evidence. The "great questions" were used to distract the jury from the very matters upon which they were supposed to ponder. Kidd's defense was a remarkable first example of this. According to Darrow, the issue before the jury was not whether Kidd and his co-defendants were guilty of conspiracy, but whether labor unions were good things. On this premise, he ignored or belittled the significance of nearly all the prosecutor's case. One of the allegations against Kidd was that he had engineered the strike. Darrow dealt with this in summation by saying:

> You have heard a great deal of evidence as to whether Thomas I. Kidd provoked this strike. I do not care whether he did or not. . . . We have spent considerable time on this evidence, discussing the question as to whether Mr. Kidd or someone else brought on this strike, and Brother Houghton [a prosecutor] will split hairs upon the question whether Mr. Kidd spoke before the resolution to strike was passed by the Local Assembly or after the resolution was passed. A fig for all that. I do not care.

He took up the question of local assembly meetings again: "Mr. Kidd came from Chicago, and after they took the vote, as nine tenths of these witnesses say, although a few say it was before. But I do not care whether it was before or after." Another matter in dispute was the part played by Troiber and Zentner in picketing and in particular promoting violence. The evidence on this received a similar treatment:

> What were the pickets to do? Their duties were plain. They were well-understood. They were to keep track of their members to know who was working. They were also to go to the mills and implore others not to work when their brethren were on a strike. This they had the right to do. It may be, gentlemen, that here and there someone did more. I do not know, and I do not care.

With the same abandon Darrow passed over more specific allegations of violence against Michael Troiber. "Now, gentlemen, I do not care whether Michael Troiber struck the blow or not. It does not make the slightest difference on this case either to Kidd or Troiber. . . . So I am not going to waste my time or yours arguing as to whether he did this or not. I do not care who did it."[9] All in all, Darrow so often told the jurymen that pieces of evidence against his clients were immaterial, they might have wondered why the defendants had bothered to enter a defense at all. Their attorney spoke as if there was no case for them to answer.

The *pièce de résistance* of this defense was one that required some hardihood from Kidd, which Darrow required of all his clients. It was Darrow's announcement that he was unconcerned about his client's fate as he started upon his peroration:

Gentlemen, I leave this case with you. Here is Thomas I. Kidd. It is a matter
of the smallest consequence to him or to me what you do; and I say it as sincerely
as I ever spoke a word. . . . I do not appeal for him. That cause is too narrow
for me, much as I love him and long as I have worked by his side. I appeal to
you, gentlemen, not for Thomas I. Kidd, but I appeal to you for the long line
—the long, long line reaching back through the ages, and forward to the years
to come—the long line of despoiled and down-trodden people of the earth.

It might be thought that, having thus revealed to the jury the true nature of
the case, Darrow would rest content. Yet for good measure he also added an
appeal for "those women who are offering up their lives, their strength and
their womanhood on the altar of this modern god of gold"; for the "little
children, the living and the unborn, who will look at your names and bless
them for the verdict you will render in their aid"; and finally for "the dumb,
despairing millions whose fate is in your hands."[10]

An advocate of a later generation might have been squeamish about making
such an appeal. But Darrow had correctly gauged an Oshkosh jury of men
whose tastes were simple and whose senses had not been bombarded by commercial entertainment. To them, his appeal did not seem tawdry or commonplace but fresh and new. Himself the product of a small town, Darrow understood well the necessity as a spellbinder come from afar to tug a jury's
heartstrings.

This speech invited the jury to ignore two weeks of evidence in favor of the
higher good of vindicating the right to strike. The expectation of later publication made his summations more than just occasional pieces, designed to persuade the jury in the interests of his client; he spoke to a wider constituency
on a generalized plane considerably removed from the facts in litigation. What
he said was propagandist in intent and content, often at the expense of his
immediate client's interest. One cannot help but suspect that Darrow was
prompted to treat his major clients' interests as too narrow for his attention
partly because of his knowledge that his words were to appear in a pamphlet
that would give no hint of the immediate setting. If he had paid heed only to
the reactions of the men in the jurybox, he would have spoken more cautiously
and more briefly than he did in his major trials. Contemporary newspaper
reports indicate that he often failed to hold the attention of the juries before
which he pleaded and that their members showed boredom, irritation, and
indifference in about equal quantities.

Undoubtedly Darrow sometimes rose to extraordinary flights of oratory,
during which everyone was spellbound, but these were intermittent; for the
most part he was an average-to-good jury counsel with a marked tendency to
long-windedness. His reputation was based less on the impressions of those
who actually saw him in action than on the fact that he made good "copy."
Tributes to his extraordinary ability before the courts have come mainly from
partisan sympathizers with his point of view and from anthologists who have
depended on the final printed versions of his perorations.

In some ways the circumstances of Darrow's approach were propitious, for

the Kidd case involved the least serious charges of those in which Darrow was
to be involved over the years. Still, the proofs were not inconsequential. The
strike had been accompanied by a riot which it had been necessary to quell
by use of the militia and a young striker had been killed. While the jury might
legitimately find that Kidd, Troiber, and Zentner were not personally responsible for these, it could scarcely be complacent in the face of this social disrup-
tion. Thinking jurors might also have been both concerned and puzzled by
Darrow's assurances that the pattern of the future was preordained. The motif
of destiny that appeared in his summation would recur subsequently in nearly
all his major criminal trials. In discussing the position of Kidd, he made clear
that he believed that if Kidd had not acted as he had, someone else would have,
telling the jury: "George M. Paine is not wise enough to know that if he should
send Kidd to jail another man will take his place. He does not know that he
is sowing the wind." And he subscribed to the same theory again on a grander
scale:

> You may send these men to jail tomorrow if you will, and you may destroy
> George M. Paine and Nathan Paine, whose malice have [sic] made them pursue
> these defendants into the very temple of injustice. Aye, if all the chief actors
> should be numbered with the dead and the conditions still remained, the same
> babbling overflowing threatening sea of men and women would gather once
> again.[11]

The inference the jury was invited to draw was that it was pointless to convict
and punish the defendants, who were mere agents of fate. Darrow would
return to this theme time and again from 1898 onward, adapting it with minor
variations to all cases, but why the jury was not similarly inexorably bound
to reach its verdict, he never explained. If the course of history was already
decided, it was rather pointless for Darrow to be making such an obvious effort
of advocacy on behalf of his clients. The trouble with his fatalism was that only
his clients got its benefit—they were in the grip of fate. Employers, detectives,
and prosecutors were to be reviled for their reprehensible actions, a point on
which Darrow became positively sanctimonious. But if the defendants could
not have stopped themselves, how could their accusers? Such speculations did
not apparently trouble the jury in the Kidd case, for within fifty minutes of
retiring, it returned with a verdict of not guilty.

Nothing succeeds like success. Darrow's popularity in the labor movement
rose greatly on the verdict, though no one could ever be sure that it was his
efforts that made it favorable. What was certain was that he had brought the
case a great deal of attention it would not otherwise have obtained. His liking
for big issues and marked skill in arguing points of principle had given general
interest to an otherwise local trial. Like most lawyers, he exaggerated the
importance of his case. Unionism would not have died even if Kidd, Troiber,
and Zentner had been convicted. But Darrow left Oshkosh knowing that, as
a result of his performance there, his name would automatically come to mind
whenever the labor movement needed a lawyer in the future.

By bargaining in advance for the publication of his address to the jury, Darrow set a pattern in the Kidd trial he was to follow throughout his subsequent career. The Kidd pamphlet was distributed to members of the Woodworkers' Union itself and sold by Charles H. Kerr of Chicago to the general public.[12] It achieved a wide general circulation, and its pamphlet form meant that readers tended to treat it as a self-contained work, to be read and evaluated without regard to particulars of the trial itself. Thus William Dean Howells, editor of the *Atlantic Monthly,* said it was "as interesting as a novel" —and no doubt read it as such.[13] The foundation of Darrow's renown was laid by such an approach, so that his words were read and quoted for their own sake.

Yet the reputation obtained from the circulation of his pamphlets was not altogether fairly won precisely because the speeches appeared out of context. Posterity was unaware or forgot that many of his jury addresses were inappropriate to their occasion and ill-received at the time they were delivered. The gap between the high-minded idealism of Darrow's jury addresses and the accusations against his clients was sometimes so extreme that they must have suffered by the contrast. By pitching his arguments on an idealistic level, he must sometimes have prompted the jury to think how low the defendants had sunk; the heavy emphasis on his clients' virtuous purposes was prone to underline the viciousness of what many of them had done. The separate publication of Darrow's noble words ensured that they would be quoted long after the occasion of their initial delivery had been forgotten and was a potent force in spreading his fame. In some of his most famous cases he was speaking to the press, not the jury, and making a plea to posterity, not for the present. Certain it is that some of his clients were glad to have a case presented to posterity; but nearly all of them would have liked to win their cases too, and Darrow's arguments were not always well chosen to do that. When he disclaimed that his immediate client was his major concern, there was the danger that the jury would take him at his word.

The fact that Darrow's speeches were printed alone, without opposing counsel's speeches or the evidence, made them look altogether more convincing than they actually were. Moreover, while Darrow rarely appeared in a case by himself and journalists not infrequently thought his co-counsel did a better job than he, it was his speeches alone that were printed in the booklets after the trial. Unflattering comparisons were therefore not conveniently available, and Darrow appeared to stand alone in defending the right of workingmen to band together.

There was another, even less creditable, explanation for the fine impression made by the pamphlets: the speeches had received substantial aid between the time of trial and publication in permanent form. Several of those for which he became famous were edited and "tidied up" by Darrow before they were issued for mass circulation. Sometimes the published version of what was said differed in substance from what was said in court, and in one instance Darrow was publicly shown, over his own denial, to have made very material alterations of his own speech before it was released for publication by the socialist periodical *Appeal to Reason*.[14] Darrow, like a number of his contemporaries, falsified the record in order to enhance his chances with posterity and was much given to *ex post facto* improvements without troubling to bring his polishing to the reader's attention, thereby doing wonders for the flow of the original. The labor movement would become a rich source of business for his law practice for the next thirteen years.

14

Altgeld Joins the Practice

It was nearly Christmas by the time of Darrow's triumphant return from Oshkosh, and Darrow, Thomas & Thompson thrived as more and more union business came in on the waves of his well-publicized success. The Kidd case was the last labor case in which Darrow appeared for only a nominal fee; once he saw that the unions could raise legal defense funds, he insisted that they do so. He was not in the slightest abashed to ask for large fees and even larger expense accounts. Although he undertook many charity cases for individuals, he did not feel that union-backed defenses were the proper subject of charity. In latter battles, he more than once put the finances of a union in jeopardy to further its legal interests. Although he told the Industrial Commission that there was "no money in litigating on labor's behalf," his practice belied that. In several union cases the "war-chest" provided to him exceeded by far the annual budget of the entire legal department of the Chicago & Northwestern, itself a very active litigator with a huge amount of legal business. What Darrow meant was that there was other legal work which, after deductions for overhead, was arguably more profitable than the labor kind, and no doubt in that sense his statement was true. But even this was a somewhat skewed opinion; in the first decade of the twentieth century, little litigation on behalf of any interests whatever was better bankrolled than the big labor cases. Only a few of the major American businesses approached the legal expenditures of some of the large unions. Darrow was in fact doing very well in this new and expanding legal field.

Yet any remaining hope of his partners that Darrow would henceforward devote himself to the practice of law was soon dashed. He had no intention of working to dispatch the new business he had himself engendered. Rather, the Kidd case had fueled his appetite for Chicago's political and social life anew as he capitalized upon his celebrity. He wanted to be seen around town as much as he could before the public memory of the headlines faded. Almost at once he embarked on a round of speaking engagements that left none too much time for practice. Some of these were casual appearances, but others were devoted to a last effort to salvage Altgeld's political career.

Since the Illinois legislature's refusal to nominate him to the Senate, all had not been well with Altgeld. Lassitude had overcome him. Depressed and disillusioned by his defeat in the gubernatorial race of 1896, he had adopted the mentality of defeat, no longer confident of his ability to change the course of events. His views had not changed but his spirit had gone. Darrow saw the malaise that had come over his friend and sorrowed not only for him, but for the state of politics. The combination of Altgeld's insolvency and political vanquishment had humiliated him. An honest man doing his best, he had not been tough enough to take the body blows that politics had dealt him. Altgeld mused upon his fate: if survival in politics required men to be so tough, was it not inevitable that the only survivors would also be ruthless? He looked around at what he saw and found no rebuttal. He told Darrow that he wanted to crawl under a sidewalk and die like a stricken animal, such was his state of shocked inaction. His malaise was compounded by the lack of anything to turn his dwindling energies to once he ceased to be governor. He had not even his law practice to return to. When he had ascended to the bench in 1886, he had turned over his practice to his cousin, John Lanehart, who had preserved and even enhanced its business. But Lanehart had died of appendicitis unexpectedly in July 1896, leaving the practice high and dry.

Darrow used various strategems to rouse Altgeld from his inertia and redeem his political career. In an effort to produce a groundswell in favor of Altgeld's reentry into active politics, he organized a "Bryan and Altgeld club," supported by Jane Addams and other prominent Chicagoans, which would only endorse candidates for public office if they would "swear to work for the perpetuation and promulgation of the principles advocated by William J. Bryan and John P. Altgeld as enunciated in the platform adopted by the Democratic Convention in July, 1896."[1] Darrow waxed eloquent on the theme that in politics persistence paid and that just as public opinion had swung against Altgeld, it might swing back to him in the course of time. With the encouragement of his friend, Altgeld started to mend his political fences. In September 1898 he attended the Democratic state committee meeting and, for the first time since his defeat in 1896, persuaded the press that he was still politically alive. "The most significant feature of that gathering was the remarkable activity displayed by ex-Governor Altgeld in renewing friendships with party managers," reported the Chicago *Evening Post.* "His unusual amiability would have thawed even his opponents, and the word was passed round 'that the old man is getting ready to run the party machine again.' "[2] He could not hope for the Democratic nomination, but there seemed some chance that if he ran as an Independent, he would command a good number of third-party and dissident Democratic votes, and on this surmise he was persuaded to run for mayor of Chicago. Darrow had much enthusiasm for the move—it had been part of his original scheme for Altgeld's advancement ten years before. Darrow could now help Altgeld by his considerable influence in the ranks of the Municipal Voters' League. There seemed no reason to think that Altgeld's political career was at an end. After all, he was not—in spite of his appearance of being weighed down

by the world's woes and the sobriquet attached to him by the *Evening Post*
—an old man; in 1899, he was only fifty-two.

Altgeld cooperated with these plans, speaking all over the city and displaying some of his old vigor. He campaigned every night for several weeks, but
the brunt of the campaign was taken by his supporters. Broadsheets advertised
mass meetings at which "the intellectual and fearless" Clarence S. Darrow
would speak. But all these efforts turned out to be in vain; Altgeld ran a poor
third in the election. Thus, although Altgeld had enjoyed some success in
politics, Darrow's original plan to "make him mayor of Chicago" was never
implemented and Altgeld felt once more the fickle ingratitude of the public.

After that he reverted to his melancholic state, seemingly unable to pick
up the pieces and get on with life. He had lost none of his ideals, but
seemed convinced he was finished; politics had discarded him and he had
no strength or fight left. He seemed happiest in commiserating with those
who had been victims of political corruption, chatting about the monumental forces of evil that were pitted against the honest citizen. There
were always plenty of people willing to pass the time of day this way, including many who worked in the Unity Building, like Miss Margaret
Haley, business agent of the Chicago Federation of Teachers, who went to
Altgeld to ask his advice on how to persuade the state board of equaliza-
tion to levy taxes upon corporations honestly. Altgeld nodded knowingly
and recounted how he had tried in vain to have the board calculate and
assess the proper taxes on many of Chicago's large businesses without success. He knew the problem—it was the solution of which he was no longer
confident. Bilking the people was so easy.

Altgeld had seemingly played himself out, reaching a stage of almost total
inactivity—the ultimate sign of despair. The only work for which he showed
any enthusiasm was upon the manuscript of a proposed book on oratory, a
subject he had of necessity studied deeply at the beginning of his political
career when trying to overcome the disadvantages at the hustings of a certain
inarticulateness. The book was an academic exercise, for he was never again
to practice the art of oratory himself: the mayoralty campaign of 1899 was his
last attempt to gain office. Yet the stark fact was that Altgeld could not afford
to luxuriate in nonproductive pursuits. In May, a foreclosure on the Unity
Building stripped him of the last vestiges of his capital and manifested to the
whole world that he was in debt. Altgeld, having nowhere else to go, moved
to the Ashland Building, though not immediately to Darrow's offices. He could
scarcely pay the rent and needed to earn much more money than even the best
book on oratory was likely to bring in. Knowing this very well, Darrow in an
effort to help his friend proposed that Altgeld should join his law firm. This
was a kind but risky invitation, which could not have been altogether welcome
to Darrow's partners and associates, however well they regarded Altgeld.
There was no doubt of his legal competence; both as a practitioner and later
as a Cook County judge, he had shown a superior ability as a lawyer. Nor was
there any doubt that the firm was shorthanded; Darrow had tried unsuccess-

fully to recruit another lawyer* to help with the load in 1898. But whoever was hired needed to be a workhorse, and the difficulty with Altgeld was to know whether he would pull his weight for, as Darrow himself put it with utter simplicity, "he didn't like the law."[3] He regarded legal work as a chore, and there was no assurance that he would turn out to be an asset rather than a liability. Certainly his co-option into the partnership was a gamble, but Darrow wanted to have Altgeld and the firm was really his. Besides, it seemed a possible way to move along the backlog of work Darrow brought into the partnership but did not take care of himself. Altgeld, who was definitely not a business-getter, might get down to the paperwork. This was becoming an ever more urgent need as another factor was added to Darrow's already crowded life: now that he was divorced, Darrow was spending a much larger amount of time with his son Paul than he had devoted before to Paul and Jessie combined. So, with an optimism born of desperate overwork, Darrow's colleagues in the law firm acquiesced in Altgeld's rescue from the bands of the unemployed.

In the meantime Darrow was discovering the joys of fatherhood rather later than most fathers. Now that Paul was in his teens, he was coming to dote on the boy. Upon his return from Wisconsin, he took to introducing Paul to all his friends around Chicago, and brought him along on all sorts of occasions, giving him the chance to meet famous people on equal terms. But Paul, a somewhat awkward teenager, was not precocious enough to deal with the leading politicians, lawyers, and literary men of Chicago as equals, nor was he a chip off the old block. He reflected his mother's character much more than his father's—the subsequent course of his life would show that his disposition was far different from his father's. Besides, however hard Paul had tried, he could not help but be outshone by his father. By now, Darrow was a Personage who commanded attention by his mere presence; as Sherwood Anderson described his effect:

> "Who is that man?" they were asking. There are men like that. Clarence Darrow was one. When such a man comes into a room everything in the room changes. The very air of the place seems to change. People in the room begin to come alive in a new way.[4]

If Darrow's aim was to make Paul a worthy son and heir, he acted too late; by this time the contours of Paul's character had been molded on very different maternal lines. Lacking either an inclination or a moral basis for acting the stern disciplinarian toward his son, Darrow veered to the opposite extreme of exaggerated paternal pride and absurd indulgence. It was not for want of conflict between father and son that Darrow refused to assert himself. But this was a conflict deeper than the passing tensions of his growth to manhood, for Paul was destined to become the businessman son of a father who belittled business, the conservative offspring of an outspoken radical.

*It was Edgar Lee Masters.

As Paul was drawn into his father's circle, he achieved acquaintance with the leaders of Chicago politics and commerce effortlessly where once his father had had to strive mightily. The effect on Paul was not, apparently, to interest him in their pursuits; he did not absorb their enthusiasm for either law or politics. Although he was a proud and affectionate son, this early exposure to his father's professional affairs convinced him that he did not want to follow in his footsteps, or to inherit his father's mantle in any sense. Darrow nursed the hope that Paul would join him in his practice, serve the same ideals, and share the same burdens and triumphs. But his hope was in vain. Possibly it was this slight prospect that had made Darrow reluctant to recruit additional manpower for his practice, in case Paul showed any inclination to join in. But Paul's first job, between school and college, was with the McClurg Publishing Company.*

Neither father nor son ever fathomed the complexities of their loving but difficult relationship. On the father's side there was too much pride in his progeny for adult attention to be anything but an ordeal for Paul. And on the son's side was the embarrassment of having a father famous for standing for unpopular causes. Like his mother, Paul found Clarence's notoriety a burden rather than a blessing and became reticent in proportion to his father's assertiveness. Paul had no brothers and sisters with whom to share this burden and hence was under constant pressure from his peers to repudiate his father. His father's celebrity weighed heavily on him, but the taunt that he was a "class traitor" was worse. Paul had to disassociate himself from his father to be accepted by the rest of the world. From the start he was overshadowed, and it was a struggle to achieve and maintain a separate identity. In consequence, at the age when most youths turned radical as a rebellion against paternal conservatism, Paul had to move in the other direction—for not even the most vivid adolescent imagination could dream up subversions to compare with his father's. Darrow, himself an *enfant terrible,* could not inspire the fires of insurrection in his offspring.

As these peculiar inverted psychological battles were worked out, it became certain that Paul wanted neither to follow in his father's footsteps nor to live in his shadow. Darrow did not reproach his son for this, but it hurt and mystified him to the end. While his father courted publicity, Paul hid from it, valuing the ability to pass unnoticed through the crowd. Sufficiently far removed from the necessity of building a fortune to recoil from the brashness of his father's career, Paul chose to remain a very private citizen, outside the reach of his father's celebrity. Darrow retained the tenacity and courage of a self-made man, but Paul had all the reticence of one born to social position; the gulf between them was one of class as much as temperament. Amirus and Clarence had belonged to the same class—they had attended the same schools and they had remained the same because Amirus had not advanced himself. But Clarence had advanced so far that his son started out from a different level,

*The company published *Farmington* in its original 1904 edition.

already in the embrace of success. Many a young man unfamiliar with the difficulties of being Clarence Darrow's son might have looked enviously upon Paul as the heir apparent to a prosperous law practice; but such envy ignored Paul's emotional predicament.

In the face of Paul's determination not to be a lawyer, Darrow's enthusiasm for his practice was still further diminished. It would have sustained him spiritually through some of the dross work of his firm if he had known that Paul would ultimately be the beneficiary of his empire-building. His ambition to found a legal dynasty was considerable, but certain that his only child would not join him in the firm, he became more and more reckless in his professional conduct and relations, feeling that he need only look to his own interests without regard to longer-term results. And here, too, could be seen a side effect of his divorce; for by leaving Jessie, he had lost a touchstone of moderation, an adviser whose views were not less prudent because they were conventional. The absence of such a restraining influence was to have dire consequences on Darrow's future career. As it was, his renewed intimacy with Altgeld made him more and more contemptuous of his profession. As always Darrow, in general very independent in thought and conduct, was under Altgeld's spell, and by now Altgeld was soured on the law, as on most other things, to an irredeemable extent. Though practice was the only remaining way open to him to earn a living, Altgeld felt no gratitude to his profession for that. On the contrary, he inveighed against "the lawyers" (a category from which he excluded himself and a privileged few friends) as parasites, earning a living from others' misfortunes. He had never had the art of fraternizing easily with his professional colleagues even in the best of days. Now, smarting from his political defeats and the foreclosure of the Unity Building, he was totally alienated from the bar. His attention to legal business was desultory. Darrow described how "He sat in his office, day after day, receiving visits from the poor, the dreamers, the unadjusted and unadjustable, who were not only of Chicago but from all parts of the land. For several years the pathetic idealists, with their haunted and far-away gaze, came to his office, as the devout anchorite would visit a shrine." Instead of taking care of business, Altgeld devoted much of his time to the formation of and the affairs of the Cook County Bar Association. It was not that there was not already a bar association in Cook County—the Chicago Bar Association was already well established—but Altgeld regarded it as "one of the many aids to monopoly" which the profession sponsored and whose insidious power was growing.[5]

Altgeld was right to sense that a new restrictiveness was gripping the profession. He had entered it when it was influenced by a Jacksonian democratic impulse to allow an applicant to advance in the profession with as few obstacles as possible. But at the end of the nineteenth century the process reversed itself and more and more requirements had to be met before admission to the bar —many of which neither Altgeld, Darrow, nor many of their generation could themselves have satisfied. The attraction of the law in the formative years of the Republic had been that it counted as a learned profession while insisting on very little learning at entry, and indeed there had always been a certain spuriousness in lawyers' pretensions. But at the beginning of the twentieth century the law was ceasing to be a career open to talents and beginning to insist, if not on learning, then at least on credentials. Soon the days when young schoolmasters like Darrow with little formal education could become lawyers without a protracted institutional training would be gone. Many attorneys seized upon the imposition of educational requirements as a plausibly respectable way of cutting down competition; but Altgeld and Darrow refused to demonstrate in their own profession the very solidarity they admired so much among unionized workingmen. In their resistance to new restrictions, both remained true to their origins. They sensed that the established bar associations were by nature exclusionary, designed to aid the "ins" rather than the "outs," and that they would lobby for restrictions of a kind that would exclude from the profession just such young men as they had been.

Yet attacking the Chicago Bar Association and trying to start a rival one was no way to attract business or gain professional goodwill. Altgeld was simply isolating himself still further from his confreres. He did not care. It is probable that he already knew what others discovered only later, that he had not long for the world. But it was no favor to younger men, who had a life in the law before them, to put them out on a professional limb. In the practice of law in Chicago much depended upon mutual trust and respect among leading practitioners. Altgeld was forfeiting this. Indeed the establishment of Cook County Bar Association was virtually a declaration of war upon the local bar.

But the prospect of unpopularity no more stopped Altgeld in 1900 than it had in 1894, and he busied himself with legal details on behalf of the new association that he would have disdained if they had been done for ordinary, paying commercial clients. His main helpmate in this labor of love was Edgar Lee Masters, a young, struggling lawyer in the Ashland Block as yet unknown as a poet, who with Altgeld drew up the association's articles and by-laws. Masters was even more in agreement with Altgeld than Darrow, who had been a member of the Chicago Bar Association since 1892 and the State Bar Association since 1896, and remained enrolled continuously until his death. Still Darrow, attracted by Altgeld's iconoclastic notions, threw his weight behind the new organization as an alternative which, in his own words, was "meant to combat the capitalistic ideas of conventional Bar Associations."[6]

Probably Darrow would have come to be an antagonist of his own profession without Altgeld's encouragement, for he had no love of the law outside its dramatic and controversial aspects. But Altgeld acted as a catalyst to open opposition at a crucial time in Darrow's professional development. Up to 1900 it would still have been possible for Darrow to have retained the respect and cooperation of acknowledged leaders of the bar whose political persuasions were different from his; but the turn of the century marked the beginning of an undercurrent of rumor about him that impugned his integrity and created a gap between him and many powerful elements. "In his lifetime he was denigrated by leaders of the bar," wrote Morris L. Ernst. "Many called Darrow a turncoat."[7] Some called him worse—and they were not only the conservative or "capitalistic" lawyers: both Albert de Silver, the founder of the predecessor to the American Civil Liberties Union, and Moorfield Storey, the founder of the National Association for the Advancement of Colored People, would entertain dark suspicions of Darrow. De Silver saw in Darrow's challenges of prospective jurors on the ground of bias against labor unions "only cheap and futile charlatanism"; and Moorfield Storey declared that he had "no sort of respect" for criminal lawyers like Darrow. "I suppose he naturally sympathizes with the class to which his clients belong," he wrote disapprovingly.[8] Altgeld's legacy to Darrow in those final years of practice together was to draw to the law firm a group of malcontents and to ensure that Darrow's coming battles would increasingly cut himself off from professional support.

However much Altgeld influenced Darrow in this respect, the final responsibility for his continued disenchantment with the bar was Darrow's personally. In his hostility to the exclusionary practices of the legal profession, he undoubtedly followed his mentor; but there was, besides, an element of carping criticism injected by Darrow himself that was none too consistent. On the one hand, he disliked the tendency to monopoly which he saw growing in the restriction of entry to the bar; but on the other, he acknowledged that there was a surplus of lawyers, most of whom were economically marginal. Commenting in 1914 on the "seven thousand lawyers in Chicago," he wrote to William Kent,

> The great mass of these lawyers are making a very precarious living, and I have no doubt that under conditions of life where labor had anything like its fair tools, most of these lawyers would be at work. I hope I wouldn't have to, but I might.[9]

He even defended the lawyers who resorted to tricks to keep above water economically. When told by a journalist that he was doing an article on shyster lawyers, Darrow snapped back: "What do you mean by shyster lawyers? You mean poor devils who can't make a living? If we were in their condition we wouldn't be any better than they are."[10] Thus he acknowledged the profession's economic plight and bemoaned the evils of professional competition while complaining of attempts to restrict the supply of new lawyers and thereby reduce the surplus. It was not a recipe for professional popularity.

For the moment, though, it did not seem to matter that Darrow's firm was losing allies among the staider members of the bar. Apart from a growing amount of union work, it acquired important corporate clients, notably when William Randolph Hearst asked Darrow to incorporate the *Evening American,* the newspaper he hoped would give him a base of political power in Chicago. It was a measure of Darrow's priorities that he used this connection as a chance to get into print once again, by contributing a column entitled "Easy Lessons in Law." Actually these "easy lessons" were mere repetitions of the commonplaces of plaintiffs' attorneys, advocating widening the areas of liability an employer had to his employees. Two of them—dealing with the doc-

trines of fellow servants and of assumed risk—put the case for abolishing these
defenses, which would have been very advantageous to a law firm such as
Darrow's, though within a very few years workmen's compensation acts
removed such issues from the courts altogether.[11]

The only cases Darrow sought with a view to working upon them personally
were the attention-getting kind that held out the prospect of spanning the
borders of law and politics. And for these he came close to the unethical
practice of soliciting clients. He could claim with truth that "I have never had
to look for clients, they have come to me,"[12] but the clients that came were
not always the ones he wanted, and the ones he wanted did not always come.
When President McKinley was assassinated in Buffalo by the anarchist Leon
Czolgosz in September 1901, the head of state did not command unanimous
sympathy. Carry Nation, the somewhat eccentric ax-woman of the Women's
Christian Temperance Union, was ecstatic that McKinley had been killed and
described the late President as "a whey-faced tool of Republican thieves,
rummies and devils."[13] Another lady, speaking from a different political perspective, took sides with the criminal rather than his victim: Emma Goldman
expressed sympathy with Czolgosz, with the result that the district attorney
of Erie County tried to extradite her from Chicago for conspiracy to murder
the President. Darrow was not interested in defending Carry Nation, but he
was interested in defending Miss Goldman. He sent an associate to caution her
that she was in peril of being held as an accessory to the mad Czolgosz's act;
but this warning did not have the effect, which Darrow must have desired, of
obtaining Miss Goldman as a client. On the contrary, she took his overture
decidedly amiss, writing afterward that "it seemed strange that he should send
me such reprehensible advice, that he should expect me to join the mad chorus
of howling for the life of Czolgosz."[14] In fact Darrow had not asked her to
condemn Czolgosz, but merely to refrain from praising him. The distinction
seemed to escape Miss Goldman and, though she had frequent well-publicized
brushes with the law, Darrow was never invited to represent her.

The exact circumstances of Darrow's overture to Emma Goldman cast
light on the reasons for the ambivalence Paul felt toward his father. At the
very time of the McKinley assassination Darrow was with Paul in Hano-
ver, New Hampshire, where the boy was enrolling as a freshman at Dartmouth College. In spite of his oft-expressed doubts about the value of education, Darrow was giving Paul a far more expensive and exclusive
education than his own. He wanted to do well by the boy and to avoid
reproach for any neglect of parental duty following on his divorce. There
was some tendency for the grandees of Chicago to send their offspring east
for education, but that did not account for the choice of Dartmouth
which, of the many suitable institutions there, was rather less convenient
to reach from Chicago than most. Possibly Darrow was influenced by its
prominence in the law as a result of the leading constitutional case to
which the college gave its name. Another possibility is that Altgeld's
cousin, John Lanehart, a Dartmouth man, had recommended his alma

mater. Possibly also Paul wanted to go there because he had met many Dartmouth alumni at the McClurg Publishing Company. In any event, if there were such a thing as a college for the sons of radicals, Dartmouth was not it. And it must have been embarrassing for Paul that, while still green and unsure of himself in his first days there and on the eve of his first protracted absence from home, his father was doing all he could to defend a notorious female anarchist for defending an obscure male one who had killed a President.

Within the two years before Paul enrolled, his father had taken a leading part in several public memorials to Robert G. Ingersoll, to whose anti-Christian beliefs and platform technique Darrow owed much. Ingersoll had been a brilliant, fiery apostle of the unorthodox, whose persistent Christian-baiting was one of the early formative influences on Darrow: "I heard him twice, and with everyone in the audience I was entranced." His attitude toward religion was so bitter that it held him back from advancement that would otherwise assuredly have been his, and the same was coming to be true of Darrow. He could not escape from himself, and he had a self-defeating strain as potent as Ingersoll's. He was a man to whom responsibility, office, and public recognition would in the ordinary course of events naturally have come. But there was reluctance to give him a chance. His opposition to so many movements had gone too far in its destructiveness without offering any constructive suggestions. Darrow disappointed those who tried to treat him as an oracle; what went against him was not that he offered no solutions, but his scorn for those who did. He deeply offended people and groups that had believed him an ally. Sometimes this was the unhappy and inadvertent result of tactlessness. For example, at a conference on the status of the Negro, he asked rhetorically, referring to William Lloyd Garrison, a champion of civil rights, "Where are the Garrisons of the present generation?" This annoyed Garrison's nephew Oswald Villard, who was carrying on his uncle's work and sitting on the platform as Darrow spoke.[15] But often there was a deliberation in Darrow's disclaimers that went beyond mere tactlessness. Anarchists who had counted him as a supporter became irate when he described their belief as "a far-off dream having no relation to life." It did him no good with socialists when at a public meeting he was asked why he did not join the Socialist Party and replied that it was because there were so many unsocial people in it. He rather dampened the Jews' enthusiasm for him when he told a group of them that the characteristic Jewish crime was swindling because they were not brave enough to kill or burglarize. And not all Negroes—to whom he gave more support than any other group—were prepared to hear that "without slavery your race would never have had its chance for civilization. You might still be savages in Africa. . . ."[16] Every group dealing with Darrow finally had to learn that his support was tentative and conditional and never involved a total commitment; always he kept a corner to himself. He never pretended otherwise, but when the truth was revealed it frequently came as a shock and was interpreted as treachery, which hurt more than open total opposition would have. Darrow would not temper his opinions or lard them with tact. Once a lady remarked to him, "You must have suffered terribly from being misunderstood."

"Yes," he replied with a deep sigh, "but I should have suffered far more if I had been understood."[17]

The truth was that Darrow rather liked to shock people by gaining their confidence and then saying something he knew to be unpalatable. He even awaited the chance to do this with a certain glee. The tendency could be seen in his dealings with Ingersoll's admirers: when, on August 26, 1900, he addressed a meeting to mark the first anniversary of Ingersoll's death, he poured lavish praise on him, but managed to rouse the audience to booing and hissing by accusing Ingersoll of prostituting his talents on behalf of unworthy causes and being a reactionary on political questions. "The older and more venerable a political superstition, the more he would cling to it," he said. This so infuriated a bearded member of the audience that he rose crying "outrage."

Like Altgeld, Darrow was isolating himself by his boldness, so that if and when catastrophe struck, there would be many who would revel in his discomfort and few who would feel it their part to give him any help.

15

The Death of the Hobgoblin

As long as they were comrades in arms in the battle against injustice, the growing isolation of Altgeld and Darrow alike was scarcely noticed. But on March 12, 1902, Altgeld died shortly after giving a speech in Joliet in opposition to the Boer War. It was, as Darrow remarked, "a dramatic fitting death" for a determined political crusader. There were few mourners. Attempts were made to provide a conventional ceremony at Altgeld's grave. "Two invitations were sent to clergymen, supposed to be liberal-minded, asking them to conduct the farewell ceremony, but both found reasons for not being able to come," Darrow noted. The consequence was that Darrow himself made the funeral arrangements and gave the memorial address at Altgeld's grave:

> We who knew him, we who loved him, we who rallied to his many hopeless calls, we who dared to praise him while his heart still beat, cannot yet feel that we shall never hear his voice again. . . . The heartless call has come, and we must stagger on the best we can alone.

It was this address that Darrow chose, above all his speeches, to reproduce "whether it is good form or not" as an appendix to his autobiography. Perhaps he rather enjoyed taking the place that had been offered to two clerics. He was himself a preacher, though without faith or a church, and his panegyric to Altgeld would not have looked out of place in a book of sermons.

The period following Altgeld's death wrought a number of changes in Darrow's professional and private life. It was indeed difficult for him to contemplate Chicago without Altgeld; during his fifteen years there he had been in almost daily consultation with the man on politics and law. They had shared each other's triumphs and nursed each other's wounds: in 1896 Darrow had consoled Altgeld over his defeat in his bid to be reelected governor, and in 1897 Altgeld had seen Darrow through the trauma of his divorce. Right up to the end they had made a common cause of their opposition to the Boer War, practicing law together by day and campaigning together in the evening. Since his arrival in Chicago, Darrow had relied upon Altgeld as a sounding board for his opinions and a supporter for his ideals. Now he was gone.

The loss of Altgeld's counsel was the most profound intellectual and emotional deprivation that Darrow ever suffered. Darrow was not one to undertake any project unless he predominated. The only exception had been Altgeld, to whom he gave precedence, and no one would replace Altgeld in his life. He suffered other upheavals, but none matched this in its intensity or continuing significance. In choosing to reproduce his address at Altgeld's funeral as an appendix to his autobiography Darrow acknowledged this. From the time of Altgeld's death until World War I he lived his political life vicariously, through the memory of Altgeld and in furtherance of Altgeld's ideals. His own world view scarcely changed until the rude shocks of the European catastrophe. It was as if, by Altgeld's death, he had lost the capacity to advance intellectually, and to the end he remained in most respects wedded to the ideals of Altgeld's generation.

Altgeld's political mantle seemed likely to fall upon his shoulders if only he would let it. No one knew Altgeld's machine better than Darrow; he could have cranked it up for his own use if he had been so minded. Altgeld's contacts were his and he was as well known and better liked than his patron had ever been. Competent and respectable, though a radical, he could have had a career in politics that would have ensured prominence—even distinction—for the rest of his days. Darrow was well placed to achieve, as Altgeld had before him, a coalition of reform and third-party movements and the rank-and-file Democratic voters. It was extraordinary how many of them he belonged to. He was a natural as a political candidate, and within weeks of Altgeld's death he was besieged by offers to run for all sorts of offices, from senator to mayor of Chicago. He knew the temptations, but he also knew from the example of Altgeld that there was no gratitude in politics.

The political life would be in many ways congenial to him. Darrow was entirely happy among politicians in smoke-filled rooms. "As a rule," he observed, "the politician is a 'good fellow' who is generous, kind and liberal"— the fact that he might also be boorish and corrupt did not put him off. His love of playing politics continually brought him opportunities of elective office, yet he preferred appointive jobs. Always he resisted the offer of a political career; some inner voice told him that if he went further his independence and credibility would be lost. Always he fluttered close to the flame, like the proverbial moth, but never did he allow it to consume him. Instead he stood behind governors, mayors, legislators; he whispered in the ears of aldermen; he horse-traded at nearly every Democratic National Convention; he advised Presidents. So he became powerful by not running for office, frequently equating his independence with objectivity. "Who could understand this question better, a capitalist who was a part of it, or the working man who was a part of it, or I, who am looking on?" he asked a socialist meeting rhetorically, convinced that on political questions he, outside the system, had the best view.[1]

Nevertheless he finally succumbed, and in November 1902 was elected to the Illinois House of Representatives for the forty-third session of the general assembly as an Independent representing the 17th District, backed by the Legislative Voters' League. The League adopted the tactics of machine politics to get its candidates elected. Illinois allowed "cumulative voting," by which each voter had three votes, and there were three representatives to be elected. If a voter wished, he could cast all three of his votes for one candidate. The League encouraged its supporters to do this, and it was by such means that several "reform" candidates, including Darrow, were returned. The system was designed to give a determined minority the chance of having at least one representative in the legislature—and that purpose was achieved by Darrow's election.

Darrow had by this time reached a position of such importance on the left that he was invited automatically to become a founder of nearly every new reform organization. Thus, in 1899, he had joined with a number of prominent Chicagoans, including Frank O. Lowden, future governor of Illinois, to form the Illinois Industrial Arts League, the purpose of which was to provide artists and craftsmen with facilities to work in. It was successful, and by 1902 it ran a book bindery and two furniture shops. But even this organization had its political side, and it entertained Prince Peter Kropotkin, an anarchist, when he visited Chicago in 1901. Similarly in 1905 Darrow, with Jack London, Upton Sinclair and seven other sponsors, signed the call to found the Intercollegiate Socialist Society (later to become the League for Industrial Democracy), to promote "an intelligent interest in socialism among college men and women, graduate and undergraduate, through the formation of study clubs in the colleges and universities, and the encouraging of all legitimate endeavors to awaken an interest in socialism among the educated men and women of this country." Its organizational meeting was held on the top floor of Peck's Restaurant at 140 Fulton Street in New York, and included a number of present and future luminaries of the socialist movement, such as Morris Hillquit, later to be socialist candidate for mayor of New York. Jack London was its first president, with Upton Sinclair (then only twenty-six) as one of its vice-presidents.

By the time of his election, Darrow knew enough of politics to have tempered whatever idealism he had left with some practical realization of how politics worked. The Illinois legislature was not an edifying forum, even if it had its entertaining side. Brand Whitlock, who covered it as a journalist, recalled: "I shall never forget those scenes of riot, the howling and drunkenness and confusion and worse I have witnessed in the legislatures of Illinois and of Ohio the last night of the session."[2] And another contemporary observed: "To be an elected representative of the city of Chicago in the municipal council is counted a disgrace, and it is even worse to sit in the state legislature." This was confirmed by the testimony to William Stead of an ex-official of the city, who feared that if, by some miracle, Chicago was cleaned up, Springfield would get worse:

> Congressmen are not only a more disreputable lot than the aldermen, but their price is much lower. You can buy up the Legislature of Illinois at much less per head than you can the City Council of Chicago. It is ludicrous, if it were not a

matter for indignation, to see the kind of men who are considered fit and proper persons to represent this great city in the Legislature of the State.[3]

Because of the press of legal business, Darrow was not able to take his seat until three weeks after the legislative session opened on January 7, 1903. He served with a number of members who were to play an important role in the future politics of Chicago, among them Anton Cermak, Democratic representative of the 9th District. Darrow was tied to neither major party and listed himself as a "public ownership" member, along with the few others who did not choose to run on a major party label, such as the odd prohibitionist. In such circumstances, free of a party whip, he was able to devote his efforts to a number of favorite themes.

Among the bills that Darrow supported was one designed to restrict the courts' power to issue injunctions in labor disputes and punish disobedience as contempt. Its major provisions were to make contempt triable only by jury, not a judge sitting alone; to distinguish "direct" and "indirect" contempt; and to limit the power to issue an injunction to a temporary one valid for forty-eight hours, for good cause shown. It was, of course, defeated.

He had not expected to be elected and the event was not completely welcome, for having rashly agreed to submit himself to the electorate for a seat in the Illinois legislature, he found his position greatly weakened in refusing to allow his name to go forward for other elective offices. Now that he had entered politics directly, he had great difficulty in discouraging those who supported him. When he was asked to run as a late-entry candidate for mayor of Chicago in the election to be held on April 7, Darrow, more level-headed than his third-party supporters, declined. He saw that he had no chance of winning against the Democratic machine, which was backing Carter H. Harrison for a fourth term and that he might split the progressive vote by running so that the Republican got in. Events proved that this fear was not unreasonable, for in a hard fight, Harrison won by only 6,948 votes over his Republican challenger.

This was yet another illustration of how close Darrow was to becoming a politician. He refused the entreaties of his admirers, for he knew he could never ignore the pathetic requests for help that a mayor must ignore if he was to get on with the business of running the city:

> I had been in the City Hall connected with Mayor Cregier long enough to know and pity the hordes of hungry office-seekers clamoring for jobs. Some would go to the mayor's home in the morning before he could get away, and they were still arriving after he left the office in the evening; and all day the rooms and halls outside the main office were crowded, all on the same errand, most of them with families at home, many of them in actual want.

This was not Darrow's imagination; it had ever been the way in Chicago. As a well-known Chicago journalist commented of Mayor Thompson: "Job-seekers gathered around him like hungry little sucklings about a sow."[4]

The fact that Darrow was so much in demand as a political candidate was not wholly a compliment. He was wanted not because he was a good man, but because he was a sure-fire hit with the electorate. In Chicago, as elsewhere, the greatest political virtue was having the ability to win, which party managers translated as putting someone over on the public; if the man they chose to run for political office was honorable, it was purely coincidental. And he had a further advantage as a political candidate: in spite of his reputation as a fire-eating radical, he was surprisingly uncommitted. It was easy to know what he was against but more difficult to know what he was for. Most of his public pronouncements had been made to oppose policies, not to propound alternatives, and such ambiguity was an immense political asset. Together with his gift of gab, it made him almost irresistible. As a result, overtures were made to him time and again to accept nomination as political candidate for a variety of situations—alderman, governor, mayor, and senator. Unhampered by a program, his election would amount to *carte blanche* to do just what he wanted; and during his short period in the Illinois legislature, that is what he did.

Darrow took the opportunity his election provided to further his practical political education. He delighted in learning the strategems of political compromise and pursuing some of his own pet themes—notably preventing bills for increasing criminal penalties from being passed. This essentially negative use of his power was forced upon him by the circumstances of his election on a nonpartisan ticket. "I soon discovered that no independent man who fights for what he thinks is right can succeed in legislation. He can kill bad bills by a vigorous fight and publicity, but he can get nothing passed," he remarked. Springfield reinforced his disbelief in the ability of reformers to withstand the challenges to integrity that politics daily provided. He knew that all too often politics debased ideals. He knew the inherent dangers of democracy—that the majority might abuse its power and subjugate minorities, and that a politician with nothing good to report had a great incentive to tell his electorate a lie it wanted to hear.

There is no doubt that he could have gone on, possibly to national success, but in the final analysis he did not want to. He was neither willing to toe the party line, nor respectful enough of "the people" to devote his life to democracy. Faced with the opportunity to take over Altgeld's place in public life, Darrow came face to face with himself. He was a backstairs politician by temperament, not a front man. He and Altgeld had worked together so well for so many years because Darrow had been happy to act behind the scenes, exercising power without the public accountability that elective office entailed. He liked to be in the know and to be known by influential people, whom in turn he tried to influence. But he did not want to lose his independence in the scramble for power. So he chose to reject the inheritance he could have had from Altgeld, leaving others to pursue Cook County's titles of honor while he remained free to criticize and advise as part of the inner circle that gathered round every elected administration. The result was that others, who put a different emphasis upon Altgeld's significance, claimed to be his heir and his name became a rallying cry for Democrats with whom Darrow himself did not see eye to eye. The John P. Altgeld Memorial Association, founded "to keep alive the inspiring memory of John P. Altgeld, volunteer soldier, jurist, states- man, publicist and humanitarian, and to inculcate the principles of Free Gov- ernment to which he heroically dedicated his life," did not count Darrow among its officers or members, for by 1907 it had become a preserve of the Bryan wing of the party.

Instead of running for office again after his term in the legislature, Darrow made a determined effort to build a law firm with a "good" practice, not hesitating to use his political contacts as a means of expanding the firm's business. Now that he was not an office-seeker, the spoils of politics reached him indirectly. In the fat years of the first decade of the new century much of the commercial business of his firm came because of political contacts; and Darrow and his partners were not the first lawyers to use their practice as a dropbox for political favors. Within five days of Altgeld's death, he had written to Brand Whitlock in Toledo about the possibility that they would become law partners. "I would like you with me if it could be properly arranged. We need a good man who can do all kinds of work. I do not know whether you can or not. Literary men and dreamers are not generally the ones who can. Still, I think so much of you that I wish you could."[5] Whitlock, embroiled in Toledo's municipal politics, replied that the proposition was quite unrealistic as he was unable to leave Ohio for the time being. Still Darrow persisted in his attempt to put together a firm of lawyers who had not only legal skill but also literary distinction. With this in mind, he formed a new partnership with Edgar Lee Masters and Francis Wilson, a partnership that would for a time be one of the most successful in Chicago.

Darrow and Masters had a great deal in common—too much, so that their relations later became soured by an undercurrent of jealousy and competitive- ness. They had found common cause in opposition to labor injunctions in 1894. On a wider spectrum of issues both held radical views: both approved Altgeld's pardoning of the Haymarket anarchists; both were friendly with Altgeld per- sonally; both were sympathetic to the labor cause. They shared a common interest in literature, both being admirers of Walt Whitman. Even before they became partners, their legal practices had much in common—Masters had handled several cases involving factory, railroad, and industrial accidents, and had taken a noteworthy criminal case to the Illinois Supreme Court. He had even been involved in an important union arbitration involving the Chicago streetcar companies.

In 1898 Masters had arranged for Darrow to be appointed receiver of a bankrupt loan association, and at that time, Darrow had first suggested that Masters join his firm, an invitation that was refused. But in the spring of 1903 it was renewed, and Masters accepted. Then followed an exceedingly unhappy partnership that lasted eight years, until 1911. If proof were ever needed that Darrow, contrary to the statements of his well-wishers, was not universally loved, Masters's account of his relationship with Darrow is refutation enough.

It is a savage diatribe, which impugns Darrow's sincerity, honesty, and competence, and its reliability cannot be fairly judged without consideration of Masters's own faults. His autobiography maligns nearly every lawyer with whom he ever had an association in Chicago, and it is clear that he was something of a legal prima donna. His relationships with other lawyers and his clients were often poor because of his unwillingness to bend. He obviously resented the restraints and duties of a legal practice and believed that he did not get enough credit for his legal work; one of his major criticisms of Darrow was that he spent the money that Masters earned. But what is most surprising of all is that he joined Darrow's firm apparently already convinced that Darrow was disreputable. "He posed as an altruist and as a friend of the oppressed, but I doubted him. He was not in good odor in Chicago, and that made me fearful about listening to his proposal to join his firm," Masters wrote later. His father-in-law disapproved strongly of Darrow and his wife disliked and feared him. Yet Masters chose to join the firm. It was not for respect of Francis Wilson, either, of whom Masters said: "He seemed an old-fashioned soul, easy and lounging and full of generosities. As a matter of fact, he was penurious, grasping and shrewd."[6] These views did not bode well for the firm of Darrow, Masters & Wilson, and in the circumstances it is a wonder that the partnership lasted eight years. Altogether, the uneasy alliance of strong personalities within the new-formed partnership did not bode well. The combination of Darrow and Masters was described by a contemporary journalist as "an alliance calculated to greatly instruct a man or to land him in nervous prostration."[7]

The explosive alchemy of these strong personalities was not immediately put to the test, however, because of an event announced only two months after the new partnership was agreed. In the summer of 1903 Darrow remarried and embarked for a lengthy honeymoon in Europe, so that the battles royal in which the principals of Darrow, Masters & Wilson were destined to engage were deferred for a few extra months.

16

"We Both Love Darrow"

Darrow met Ruby Hamerstrom at a meeting of the White City Club in the spring of 1899, to which he had gone to deliver one of his stock lectures on Omar Khayyám. After his talk he was introduced to her by his friend John H. Gregg, whose shorthand system was rapidly gaining favor. Ruby, an itinerant journalist sixteen years younger than Darrow, was then engaged to be married to a New York stockbroker. Darrow was greatly attracted to her from the first and he at once asked her to join him for dinner. Since he exhibited a lifelong indifference to food, being an intermittent and unenthusiastic eater, it can safely be assumed that he had some more substantial purpose in view in making the invitation. After much entreaty she agreed, and from then on they were regular companions.

Sometime between 1899 and 1903 their affair turned into a courtship. Darrow had often proclaimed to his boon companions, including Ruby, that he would not marry again. He knew that there was as much to be said against marriage as for it; that it was likely that for each occasion when he would congratulate himself on his choice there would be a time when he would regret it. He had been dissatisfied with his first marriage, but not altogether happy alone, and concluded that matrimony was one of the many reluctant compromises a man had to make in a manifestly imperfect world. Neither of Darrow's marriages would prove the realization of the Aristotelian ideal of pairing with his "other half." Things were not so simple for him—fate had not provided a female counterpart and he never was to achieve a total harmony with any woman. He was once asked at a public meeting, "Is marriage to be considered a lottery?" and he replied, "Yes, if only there were prizes." On her side, Ruby doubted that she wished to marry him, finding his attention flattering but a little overwhelming.

Ruby's true attitude toward her new admirer can only be the subject of surmise, but it is possible to make certain assumptions. Her initial reluctance to take up with Darrow was not hard to understand. Her suitor had already been a party to one marriage that had foundered. It did not need much knowledge of his nature to deduce that the domestic life he offered would be demanding and that he could be tetchy, selfish, and unreliable, as well as brilliant, witty, and kind. Then, too, there were disadvantages as well as advantages to living in the reflected glory of a celebrity: the lack of privacy, the rushed schedule, the constant flow of guests, wanted and otherwise. A woman who had been heading for life as wife of a New York stockbroker needed to make some considerable adjustments before she could consider marrying Clarence Darrow, whose name was usually linked with some bitter epithet when it was mentioned on Wall Street. Subsequent events were to show that she was by disposition unable to bear the burden of her husband's anguish at the moments of extreme pressure in his turbulent career. The delay between their meeting and marriage is in part explicable by the necessity for her to extricate herself from the engagement made with her previous fiancé, but also gives some credibility to the assertion that she was a reluctant bride.

As for Darrow, perhaps the marriage to Ruby was evidence that the pace of bohemian life was getting too much for him; he was, after all, forty-seven. He begged off obligations because of fatigue more often now and was beginning to feel the clinkers of middle age. Ruby, with her domestic bent, offered a refuge from the day's battles. When both finally overcame their reservations and plunged into matrimony, they did so without fanfare and the event was anticipated only by a few. The Chicago *Evening Post,* for which Ruby had worked, recorded: "News of Mr. Darrow's marriage was a complete surprise to most of his friends and to nearly all of his relatives."[1] On Thursday, July 16, 1903, Clarence and Ruby repaired to the house of Mr. and Mrs. John Gregg, at 5401 Indiana Avenue, and were married in a private ceremony conducted by Judge Edward Finley Dunne, one of the coterie of Democratic insiders to which Darrow belonged.

The following Saturday they sailed from Montreal for an extended honeymoon in Europe. The choice showed how much prosperity and sophistication Darrow had culled from his years in Chicago. Ruby was marrying a man already well established, whose work on the anthracite arbitration* had recently brought him national attention; he was a member of the Illinois legislature, and his writings and speeches were much quoted. With these distinctions came connections with the rich, the famous, and the powerful. As they passed through France, Germany, and Switzerland the couple were able to turn the contacts Darrow had made through the network of international socialism to convivial use, taking a meal here and staying a weekend there in distinguished company. Besides making an impression on Ruby, Darrow's international contacts emphasized the gulf between the intellectuals and ideologues of the labor movement and the rank-and-file. Nearly all American unions paid lip service to internationalism in their titles—as often as not in recognition of the Canadian interests they hoped to represent—but their membership was generally interested in strictly immediate issues. The real focus of attention was on the "local," the very name of which suggested the gap between international-

*Described in the next chapter.

ism of the type Darrow espoused and the practical meaning of union membership in most workers' lives.

But this was an age when socialists felt themselves to be truly international.
National differences were ignored or brushed aside in pursuit of the common
goal. A visit to European socialists was as natural to American radicals as a
grand tour had been to an eighteenth-century aristocrat. Darrow visited literary and intellectual figures, not lawyers, while he was away; unlike Rufus
Choate, the American ambassador at the Court of St. James, he did not find
his greatest social pleasure in fraternizing with the English bar, but looked
instead for the unconventional doyens of the *avant garde.* In London, while
staying at the Langham Hotel, they met George Bernard Shaw and Henry Salt.
Shaw was exactly the kind of radical intellectual Darrow admired—a man who
gave literary form to contemporary political, social, and economic controver-
sies and was a commercial success. The two men hit it off together. "For some
instinctive reason I like him," wrote Shaw, "perhaps because he is a genuine
noble savage—with that cheekbone he wants only a few feathers and a streak
of ochre to be a perfect Mohican. . . ."[2] To speed him on his honeymoon, Shaw
gave Clarence a copy of his latest play, *Man and Superman,* the main theme
of which is that women are man-hunting predators to whom men inevitably
succumb. He must have felt much in common with Tanner, the determined
bachelor of the play who, on the eve of his nuptials, explodes: "But why me?
me of all men! Marriage is to me apostasy, profanation of the sanctuary of my
soul, violation of my manhood, sale of my birthright, shameful surrender,
ignominious capitulation, acceptance of defeat."[3] Had he not made much the
same sort of statement to his bohemian circle at the Langdon apartments? Yet
he had been snared just the same.

After London the couple went on to stay for a weekend at the Marxist Henry
Mayers Hyndman's country estate in Brasted, Kent. Darrow owed his introduction to Hyndman to the Single Tax Club. Though Hyndman had no direct
affiliation with Henry George, his writings on the Indian famines of the 1870s
had impressed George very much and been quoted in *Progress and Poverty.*
In consequence a cordial transatlantic connection had been established for the
increasing number of Anglo-American radicals who crossed the waters, and
Hyndman frequently offered weekend hospitality to Americans in England.

The honeymoon was a kaleidoscope mixture of pleasures, providing as it did
a change of scene and company, and an interval away from the pressures of
law practice and political intrigue back in Chicago. But even his honeymoon
did not provide Darrow with much respite from the driving fire of his ambition, and it says much about his abundant energy and restlessness that he did
not idle the time away. Instead, he snatched nearly every free moment to write
Farmington, his fictionalized account of his youth which he rated higher than
did the public. Darrow was prouder of this than any of his other works, and
was convinced to the end that it had literary merits not recognized by the
established critics. It was originally published by the McClurg Company of
Chicago, where his son Paul worked, but though it went through seven edi-

tions under the imprints of five different publishers during Darrow's lifetime, he was never satisfied with its sales. He took a wearisome interest in the details of marketing, complaining of one publisher: "They did not advertise *Farmington* according to the agreement. They searched their files . . . and to their seeming surprise found nothing except one ad. in the *Chicago News.*"[4] He was afraid that people were not reading it because they did not know of its existence, but that was not the real reason for its limited success. Granted that *Farmington* was written in idle moments snatched during a two-month honeymoon, it was a creditable accomplishment. Yet critics and public judged it without regard to how quickly it had been produced, and as such it was wanting. He did too much at breakneck speed, unable or unwilling to give painstaking attention to his work. He enjoyed living at fever pitch, but the result was detrimental to all his endeavors.

Ruby had married a man who had already made his mark on the world, and who was assured and self-reliant. He discouraged her from interesting herself in his business affairs, neither believing that she understood them nor wanting her to do so. Darrow was willing to make concessions to her tastes in domestic matters, but in his practice he would not be crossed. He was used to standing alone and never consulted her on decisions affecting his public life. Rather, he simply announced what he intended to do, expecting—and for the most part receiving—her loyal acquiescence.

When they returned to America in September, Darrow was also master in his own home, expecting and getting his own way. Although he periodically complained of Ruby's desire that he should be neater, cleaner, better organized, and tidier than he was, the pattern of his life after 1903 suited him well enough that he made little effort to alter it. Their relationship was a close one. There were no children to distract them—Paul was already a college senior by the time they married—and their social position in Chicago was already assured. The marriage was destined to be one of remarkable stability and cohesion. Its thirty-five years were spent under the same roof, except for some absences when Clarence was debating or litigating and the couple's world travels all over Europe and the Middle East during the palmy twenties. Home life remained an island of calm and reassurance in the midst of Clarence's battles in court, lecture halls, and with the press. The six years of single life between his divorce and remarriage had persuaded him of the benefits of a stable domestic background to his affairs.

If indeed Ruby had been a reluctant recipient of her husband's courtship, she became a possessive and jealous mate. Ruby may have been more fashionable in dress and manner than Jessie, but in other respects she shared many qualities in common with her predecessor. Ruby's devotion was no different from that which Jessie had faithfully provided—but it was given in a relationship that incorporated and accepted Darrow's perpetual involvement with affairs outside the home. Not having known the Darrow who had existed in a small Ohio town before his services were forever in demand, Ruby accepted both the trappings and the penalties of his success. She was no less domestic than Jessie, but she accepted that life with Darrow was inevitably peripatetic, and that the normal consolations of home and hearth were only rarely to be enjoyed.

Once, Lincoln Steffens asked, "How are you getting along with Ruby?" and Darrow summed up the situation, "Fine, because Ruby and me, we both love Darrow."[5] That appeared to be a fair description of the position to others who knew them both. Her devotion was so manifest that James Weldon Johnson, recalling occasions when Darrow had read from his own works to the assembled company at a private dinner party, imagined Ruby's attitude as "How lucky I am to be married to this wonderful man."[6] Granted Darrow's interest in the literary scene, Ruby may have seemed especially glamorous in his eyes because she was a journalist. But that was not sufficiently important to either of them to continue after marriage. Ruby had done well in her career, contributing to the column "Woman and Her Ways" in the Chicago *Evening Post* for several years. She had thrown off the restricted life ordained by the teachings of the Lutheran church in which she was brought up, and was by the standards of the time an emancipated and daring young woman. But in her relationship with Darrow after marriage, she contributed moral rather than intellectual support. She left journalism behind her when she married and there is no evidence that she had regrets about it. She made no effort to go back to writing on a reduced or free-lance basis and seems to have written nothing for publication after 1903, though she and Clarence knew literary people throughout their married life and Clarence was a frequent contributor to the public presses. The Darrows' acquaintanceship must have provided amusing anecdotal material (from the conversations of H. L. Mencken and Sinclair Lewis, for example), but she did not take up her pen to record it.* Even if Ruby had the capacity to be Clarence's intellectual sparring partner, she did not choose to be, and slipped quickly into a conventional place in his life. Probably it was just as well that she had no ambition to mold his mind, for he was notoriously unable to agree with anyone else for long and liked to get his own way. Ruby was glad that he should have it.

She was a loyal, protective, possessive woman, clever enough to marry a clever man, but not clever enough to keep up with him. Darrow remarked to Thomas Massie after a conference on trial strategy with him in her presence, "You know, she doesn't understand one thing we've said all evening."[7] Adela Rogers St. Johns remembers her as a twittering sparrow, whose identification with her man was almost total:

> This was a not very attractive woman who had by the turn of events become the heroine of a great love story. The wife of a famous man. His devoted and adoring wife, his very rib. A center of drama, tragedy, melodrama, violence. Like most women who had in themselves no possibility of such a full life, she was more Clarence Darrow than Clarence Darrow. Her god, religion, principles, activities

*The wives of several luminaries whom they knew published reminiscences—Marcet Haldeman-Julius and Ella Winter, Lincoln Steffens's widow, being examples.

all channeled through him, as him, he was the object of her affections, her *raison d'être.*[8]

In time Ruby lived and felt only vicariously, through her husband, savoring his successes and suffering his disappointments more keenly than he did himself. She knew no interest but his welfare. "She listens when he wants to talk, effaces herself when he prefers to think, suggests when he needs a sounding board," observed Marcet Haldeman-Julius; "even to those of us who admire him most he would seem finer were he to be a little more free with well-deserved acknowledgements to the gentle person who, herself, would be the last to ask for them."[9] But it was difficult for Darrow to be gallant in this way when her failure to keep pace with his intellect frequently reduced him to impatience. She had neither the intelligence nor the powers of expression to present a case convincingly; but her heart was in the right place.

If Marcet Haldeman-Julius's reproach of Darrow's treatment of his wife was justified, it reflected a general method of dealing with people—a method that was not confined to the home. Precisely the same attitude was the subject of much discord within the law practice to which he returned after the honeymoon. While Ruby set about looking for an apartment that would suit them both, Darrow was plunged once more into the practice he had so suddenly interrupted to go on honeymoon. The discord within the practice had not yet solidified, but the harmony of the office was not improved by the fact that Darrow had left unfinished several important pieces of business. One of them was tidying up the final settlement of the anthracite arbitration, which had drawn national attention upon him in the months immediately preceding his marriage.

17

The Anthracite Arbitration

By 1902 Darrow was nationally known as an advocate of the principle that the workers should have a larger share of the pie. His position in the Kidd case had impressed many unionists, including John Mitchell of the United Mine Workers' Union. Darrow had long been interested in the plight of miners, particularly anthracite miners, of whom he had said in the Kidd case:

> Down in the dark coal mines in the anthracite regions of Pennsylvania where those human moles burrow in the earth for the benefit of great, monstrous, greedy corporations that are corrupting the lifeblood of the nation, there they work men in chain-gangs, and put an Italian, an Austrian, a German, an American and Bohemian together so that they cannot understand each other when they speak, so that they may not combine and conspire because in combination, and in combination alone, is strength.[1]

In retrospect Darrow appears a natural choice as counsel to the United Mine Workers in the arbitration of the strike in the Pennsylvania coal fields which had begun in May 1902; but from contemporary perspectives, that was not so. Although John Mitchell warmly supported Darrow's appointment, it did not go uncontested. Walter E. Weyl, a statistician who was aiding preparation of the case before Darrow entered it, was not in favor of Darrow's appointment. And Henry Demarest Lloyd, who had suggested Darrow's name in the first place, had to acknowledge the soundness of Weyl's reservations. A month after Darrow had been appointed officially, Lloyd wrote to his wife: "Darrow seems to have made a favorable impression. Weyl frankly admits that he tried to have another lawyer, and says, as is true, that this is not a Darrow case."[2] Samuel Gompers believed that the miners should conduct their own case, without relying upon legal counsel. He advised John Mitchell that he "ought to insist that he and his colleagues conduct the miners' side before the commission because the introduction of lawyers into the hearing would becloud and befog the investigation and minimize its industrial effectiveness."[3] The dispute about whether to hire Darrow or not came to a head on October 29, when Weyl told Lloyd: "I left Washington last night with [John R.] Commons, and [Issac] Hourwich and Mitchell, and have spent the greater part of to-day on the problem of the lawyer. After considerable deliberation, we have practically decided to have Darrow, especially as Mr. Mitchell is very anxious to have him." Mitchell confirmed the selection by telegram on October 30.[4]

The strike was a protest against the general conditions prevailing in the mines, but differed from the Kidd case in that it was directed against all the mine operators in the area, not merely an isolated employer. As the area produced virtually all the hard coal consumed by the United States, the strike completely cut off new supplies, and neither the employers nor the union would compromise. Once the strike was under way, the usual legal responses were set in motion and there was an attempt to enjoin it. But the unions were in no mood to obey a court order; even Samuel Gompers advocated ignoring it. He wrote to Darrow on August 9:

> At my meetings I have said substantially that rather than surrender one jot of my constitutional and natural rights of free thought and free expression of my judgment, I would not only disregard the injunction of Judge Jackson, but I would violate it and trample it under foot and bear whatever consequences which such an act might entail; that after all the whole world is but a very narrow cell if a liberty loving man cannot explain his opinions—his honest convictions—and help his fellow man.[5]

Tensions were such that it was feared the very institution of private property was at stake. Even the conservatives were no longer sure that the courts could be relied upon to uphold its sanctity in the face of the mine owners' initial refusal to arbitrate. It was therefore with relief that the announcement of arbitration arrangements was heard. As one contemporary commentator put it:

> ... to many of us the situation had seemed most dangerous in the possibility that some attempt might be made by some violent process of law to wrest the mines from their owners; that in the then exasperation some court might be found to wrench the law out of its regular course and award some extraordinary remedy. Therefore those of us who maintained that there must be no overturn of private rights, even in so trying an exigency, feel a great sense of relief in this settlement without any resort to the courts by any of the three parties in interest: the miners, the operators, or the public. . . . To open the mines by any legal processes whatever, as that business now stands, would be to override private rights as they are established in our system. . . . The consequence of a decision that all business is subject to public operation in any way that temporary expediency might dictate would be socialism.[6]

Finally President Roosevelt intervened, suggesting an arbitration before a board of arbitrators appointed by the President. The union agreed to this proposal, but the operators did not, until J. P. Morgan urged them to do so after he met with Roosevelt as their representative. Roosevelt's suggestion was not met by unqualified approval in the labor camp; it was looked at suspiciously as a crafty political device to defuse labor unrest: "There is something fishy about this arbitration Commission," wrote Henry Demarest Lloyd privately.

Some things indicate that it is not to be an arbitration commission at all. It has
been scandalously packed against the miners—two of the members, [Thomas H.]
Watkins and [E.W.] Parker, are coal company partisans, and common decency
would demand that if partisans are to be on the board at all there should
be partisans of both sides. If Mitchell and the miners get the slightest idea that
they are being unfairly dealt with—tricked—they won't vote on Monday to go
back to work. It makes me boil with indignation to see how implicitly it has been
taken for granted that the workingmen are an inferior class, not entitled to the
treatment which business people, or any others, would demand as a matter of
course. . . .[7]

Darrow had never previously been connected with the United Mine Workers
when Mitchell asked him to represent them. It turned out to be a sound choice,
for Darrow's interest in social conditions made virtually certain that he would
present an effective case to the board of arbitrators. In arbitration he could give
full vent to his views, for he would not be bound by rules of evidence or the
other formal restraints of a court. Lloyd, though a lawyer himself, had never
practiced, and besides suffered from deafness. Indeed when Darrow asked him
to aid in its preparation and give the opening address on behalf of the miners,
Lloyd observed: "no more stirring case could ever come and this is my *first*
case."[8]

Darrow's appearance in the arbitration was historically important for several reasons. It showed him as a labor lawyer engaged in a cooperative forum,
the main purpose of which was to bind up differences between employers and
employees. He was not to appear in that stance in any subsequent case; the
remainder of his labor law career would be spent in the defense of labor heroes
accused of terrorist murder, in which the outcome would not be the peaceable
adjustment of labor relations. So, the anthracite arbitration was the last occasion upon which he stood up for labor with the direct purpose of obtaining a
reconciliation. The verdict of posterity has been that the anthracite arbitration
buttressed capitalism rather than destroying it, by taking the wind out of the
militants' sails. The arbitration has even been regarded as the model of all
subsequent collaborative developments in labor relations. Darrow's later statements and actions up to 1911 showed that he was not satisfied with the
compromise his efforts in the anthracite case achieved and that he abandoned
faith in compromise, desiring instead to heighten the conflict. This important
shift in his efforts was not perceived by the public with clarity, though some
of the press saw it and warned against it. Most men tend to become more
conservative as they reach their middle years. Not so Darrow; as he reached
middle age, he moved from working within the system to working for its
downfall. In effect he succeeded in bringing about the downfall, not of the
system but of himself.

From the start, the miners had a tactical advantage—they were united,
whereas the mine operators were not. Darrow led a relatively small team of
lawyers, all of whom except himself had once been miners themselves; but the

operators were represented by twenty-three different lawyers. Darrow recognized this: "The mine owners were handicapped by too many lawyers. A large number of corporations and individuals were involved, and most of them came into court. Of course many of the lawyers were of the first rank, but few of them had ever had any experience in labor arbitrations, or knew much about the common man and his needs and desires." It was not Darrow's opinion alone, either, that the mines' lawyers had not been as effective as the miners'; it was shared by the chairman of the arbitration commission, Judge George Gray of Delaware. At one stage Darrow remarked, "The operators are smarter men than we are. They say so, and we will admit it and save any proof on that question. . . . They can hire good lawyers and expert accountants, and they have got the advantage of us in almost every particular, and we will admit all that." Judge Gray interjected: "Except the lawyers"—he knew which side was better represented.[9] The miner-lawyers assisting Darrow, James Lanahan and the two O'Neil brothers, were familiar with the miners' work and conditions, and the technicalities of mining.

In addition Darrow successfully solicited the aid of Louis D. Brandeis, then a liberal young attorney. Brandeis offered his services free and they were gratefully accepted; he was able to provide important expertise on the legal status of the railroads, which he had studied carefully, and he wrote Darrow several letters on the subject.[10] The railroads were interested parties in the anthracite dispute for three reasons: some of them were owners or part-owners of mines; some of them derived a substantial portion of their revenues from the freighting of coal; and all were consumers of anthracite in the course of their railroading business. In consequence, railroads such as the New York, Ontario & Western were represented at the arbitration hearings. To balance this, President Roosevelt appointed as a member of the arbitration board E. E. Clark, Grand Chief of the Order of Railway Conductors. There was a natural affinity between the railroading and mining industries by virtue of the fact that they were among the first to be unionized. Brandeis was able to explain the ways in which railroads achieved and maintained their franchises and rights of way, and the legislation under which they operated, and like Darrow he was in favor of a greater measure of public control in railroading. Darrow had been involved in the same question on a smaller scale in his fight against the street railroad franchises in Chicago, which involved much the same issues of principle.* Brandeis never came into the arbitration as an official part of the miners' team because the commission found that the relationship between the mines and the railroads was not one that should be explored in the context of the miners' wage arbitration. But his help was valuable, and the acquaintanceship resulted in mutual respect; nine years later, Brandeis was one of very few who publicly sided with Darrow regarding the McNamara case.

The anthracite arbitration, held in Scranton's City Hall, showed how well

*Darrow's later finanicial and legal acumen in discussing the Chicago streetcar franchies clearly showed the influence of Brandeis's opinion on the railroad in 1902.

Darrow could dramatize the particular issues that were raised by the proceedings. In most of his criminal trials he avoided discussion of the simple facts of the case, preferring instead to discuss the larger context. But in the anthracite arbitration the tables were turned: it was the mine owners who wished to introduce evidence of the wider context—arson, threats, murder, which had accompanied the six months' strike—and it was Darrow who refused to do so. "A large part of the evidence in this case has no bearing upon the issues in the case," he told the board.

> So far as the demands of the Mine Workers are concerned, it makes no difference whether crimes have been committed or not. If John Smith earned $600 a year, it is no answer to say that Tom Jones murdered somebody in cold blood. That does not relieve you. It is no answer to say that someone's house was burned. It is not an answer to say that some person has been boycotted. The question is what has he earned? Are these men entitled to more money? Are they entitled to shorter hours?[11]

Darrow was using exactly the arguments that many prosecutors had made against him: Your client is accused of a crime. The issue is whether or not he committed it; it is irrelevant whether his social conditions were poor. Prosecutors were more justified in their position in court, where rules of evidence laid down standards of relevance, than Darrow was in his, during an arbitration in which rules of evidence did not prevail. But Darrow was a professional, well capable of seizing the advantage of the moment. His refusal to regard the violence that had accompanied the strike as relevant was somewhat unfair, and caused him to be criticized in the press. The mine owners had introduced the evidence of lawlessness partly with the idea of discrediting the workers, it is true; but partly also with the aim of receiving an undertaking from the workers' representatives that they could and would control and prevent such things in the future. Darrow would not concede this point at all, and the impression that was left was well expressed in *Harper's Weekly:*

> The advocates of the strikers virtually undertook to justify the violence of which the non-union workers complained, by setting up the principle that a man has no moral right to work, if, by his work, he quenches the hopes and levels a death-blow at the interests of his fellow-man. In other words, the liberty to work begins when it can be exercised without impairing what a fellow-worker believes to be his right to labor or abstain from labor. This, obviously, is a new principle which cannot be reconciled with legal right as was hitherto formulated. This principle would give strikers the right to employ the coercion which the law prohibits. It would make them the sole arbiters of right and wrong in their own case. It should be obvious that the principle would justify organized capital in employing force to compel strikers to return to work.

> Mr. C. S. Darrow, the counsel for the mineworkers, took the ground that the boycott was a natural and permissible weapon of partisan warfare.[12]

Harper's deduction of Darrow's position was to be vindicated on many occasions later, but in 1903 it was not clear where Darrow stood. He approached the arbitration board in a severely practical manner, refusing to be drawn on questions of social philosophy. The mine owners had charged that he, and those who stood behind him, were socialists and anarchists. His reply was a superb way of cutting through the employers' flummery:

> We are here asking for money, independent of any theories of political economy. We are here asking for shorter hours, and it has nothing to do with Socialism or Anarchism, excepting as every demand that the poor makes from the rich is to be construed as socialistic. And in so far as that, why, let it go; we are willing to accept it. In discussing this question of wages it might be a good idea to find out what we are getting. What we are getting has something to do with whether we ought to have more or not.

By some witty calculations, Darrow determined that a fair average of the wages of a miner would be $528 per year, less $40 a year because a miner bought his own tools, making a net of $488; the below-ground coal loader averaged $333. He then made a very telling point. Child labor was in use throughout the coal region of Pennsylvania—the boys as slate pickers in the coal fields, and the girls in silk mills. Even though the boys were within the terms of reference of the commission because they were employed by the mines, whereas the girls were not, Darrow chose to emphasize the plight of the girls:

> Is there any man so blind that he does not know why that anthracite region is dotted with silk mills? Why are they not on the prairies of the West? Why are they not somewhere else? Why is it that the men who make money that is spun from the lives of these little babes, men who use these children to deck their daughters and their wives—why is it that they went to Scranton and to all those towns? They went there because the miners were there. They went there just as naturally as a wild beast goes to find its prey. They went there as the hunter goes where he can find game. Every mill in that region is a testimony to the fact that the wages that you pay are so low that you sell your boys to be slaves of the breaker and your girls to be slaves in the mills.[13]

The truth was—in this and many other classic strikes—that the employers were less scared of giving the workers their demands than they were of recognizing the union. Many of the workers at mine sites were on twelve-hour shifts, including the engineers, the firemen, and the pumpmen who kept the mines from flooding. When the UMW asked for the job to be turned into an eight-hour rather than twelve-hour job—to have three shifts instead of two—the employers refused. But by the time they were before the commission, they had conceded the justice of the request. It was not the cost, which could after all be passed onto the consumer, that worried the employers, but the prospect that once the unions were recognized, they would ever more be a thorn in the employers' sides. It was the employers' stubbornness, not the employees' lawlessness, which caused the strike and its resulting coal famine. As Darrow pointed out, unions would not thrive or attract members unless the employers provoked them into being:

> Now, agitators never make revolutions. They are made by the other people entirely. All the pamphlets of all the dreamers and agitators in the days preceding the French Revolution amounted to nothing. It was the tyranny of kings and princes, the blind, lavish expenditures of the rich and great, wrung from the labor of the poor, that gave root to the words of the agitator. So Mr. Mitchell and his "paid agitators" as these gentlemen who work for nothing are so fond of characterizing them—Mr. Mitchell and his paid agitators could never have come into the mining region and rallied these pigs—these men who lived as pigs and dogs, according to Mr. Hewitt, unless through a long series of years they had been compelled to live as pigs and dogs.[14]

It was a theme much in the air in the chic circle of progressives among whom Darrow now moved, and he was always quick to see an argument's uses on behalf of his clients. It explained revolutions, strikes, and wars alike; in a few years, Darrow and others, like Lincoln Steffens, were to explain the Russian Revolution in the same way: "it was not revolutionists who 'make a revolution' but blundering rulers—revolutions were made by Pharaoh, not by Moses; by the Tsar, not by Marx."[15] It was an "explanation" of events adaptable to many uses, a sort of half-baked dialectic that, though stopping short of Hegel and Marx, nevertheless brushed inconvenient details aside. A later generation would meet a rather similar theory in the works of Arnold Toynbee, who eschewed the terminology of provocation and reaction in favor of challenge and response.

The domination achieved by employers in some parts of the anthracite region was indeed incredible. Samuel Gompers reported:

> the shacks and huts in which the anthracite miners lived and the "pluck me" stores were in full blast. The miners' families had not only to pay rent to the corporations which owned the shacks but they had to make their purchases of all the necessaries of life, meager as they were, from the company stores at double the prices for which they could be had elsewhere. If the full amount earned had not been purchased, they were haled before some overseer and threatened with eviction and discharge. The tools, gunpowder and clothes, such as they were, all had to be purchased from the company. There was the company doctor for which men had to pay, the company graveyard, the company parson or preacher, so that it was a common saying that children were brought into the world by the company doctor, lived in a company house or hut, were nurtured by the company store, baptized by the company parson, buried in a company coffin, and laid away in the company graveyard.[16]

In some instances mine owners insisted that their employees live in a company-owned home under a day-to-day lease. This arrangement was one Darrow had come across in 1894 when investigating George Pullman's dual capacity as employer and landlord to the railroad workers, but even Mr. Pullman had not thought of leasing by the day. It gave the employer the immense advantage that, if his employee gave notice, he would be evicted. With biting sarcasm Darrow remarked, "I have no doubt that a situation like that would conduce to the independence of the contracting parties."[17] The employers who wielded such complete power over their employees could scarcely be expected to pay more than they needed to, dealing with the men individually.

Darrow's presentation before the commission resulted in solid gains for the miners. When the commission's findings were released in March of 1903, they awarded back pay and pay increases, and in other ways recognized the justice of the miners' complaints. Notwithstanding Gompers's unwillingness to leave the case in the hands of lawyers, he concluded that the outcome of the anthracite arbitration was "the most important single incident in the labor movement in the United States. . . . The strike was evidence of the effectiveness of trade unions even when contending against trusts."[18]

On the other hand, the miners' victory was a moral one, rather than one which gave them what Darrow believed was their right in financial terms. The arbitration had given Darrow himself tremendous publicity and the opportunity to make an impressive argument, for which he was widely applauded. But the results—from his point of view—were trivial. The actual settlement of the anthracite case took place months after Darrow's speech, and though the miners made gains they were by no means spectacular. Conditions were better afterward, but they were nothing like good. Furthermore the deprivation which the men and their families had suffered during the strike was never fully made up. Finally, it was President Roosevelt who got the credit for the settlement; he was hailed as a great conciliator. But Darrow knew enough about politics to realize that Roosevelt had managed to keep his friends in the business community too, for he had seen to it that the miners did not get a very great improvement and that the capitalists on the whole got off cheaply. When Darrow fell to thinking about this, he probably felt he had been duped along with the miners. His speech had made out a case for giving the miners millions more; in fact they got only thousands.

Back in his law office in Chicago, his colleagues felt it unfair that Darrow should have received the public credit for his work in the arbitration and then left the mundane details for other minds to worry over. By going off on his honeymoon, he had forced the less glamorous tasks onto others. And the anthracite arbitration was not the only file on which he had done this: there were many matters Darrow had quite simply dropped to go on his tour of Europe. Though it was conceded that a honeymoon was a special occasion, which deserved particular indulgence, there were those, even in 1903, who admitted this only grudgingly. They already suspected that Darrow's precipitous departure, leaving both partners and clients in the lurch, was likely to be the rule rather than the exception in his professional activities. It did not take long for these suspicions to be confirmed and dissension within the firm to become rampant.

18

Darrow, Masters & Wilson: "An Alliance Calculated Greatly to Instruct a Man"

Neither the longevity nor the tranquility of his second marriage was to be paralleled by Darrow's new law partnership. From the start, relations among the partners were marred by a dispute over the addition of another partner and whether his name should appear on the firm's letterhead. Both Darrow and Wilson wanted this, but Masters objected strongly. The lawyer concerned had recently been convicted of jury bribery and Masters would not hear of him becoming a member of the firm until the scandal had subsided; later, the lawyer was dismissed for cheating.

Masters started work with zeal, working until ten or midnight every night, largely with the motive of making enough money to retire and devote himself to literary pursuits. Even before he had joined the firm, he had shown some distaste for the practice of law, and profit was his aim, which did not bode well for his future happiness or the firm's unity. It was primarily over money that Masters and Darrow quarreled. In Masters's view, Darrow was taking too much money out of the firm and doing too little of the work—a resentment of a kind frequently encountered in legal partnerships.

On the surface, Darrow was a diligent lawyer. He arrived at the office promptly every morning at 8:30, traveling the same I.C. train. He worked straight through the day, taking no lunch, except for a snack at his desk unless he went out on business. There was no turbulence here, but rather respectable regularity. The difficulty arose from his tendency, once inside the office, to do anything but practice law. There were occasions in the courtroom where he could use his histrionic abilities, and feel at one with his profession, but they comprised a small part of practice. In truth, the nature of law practice was changing so that the trial lawyer became less important in Chicago; a contemporary identified 1903 as the year in which office work began to replace

192

litigation as "the large income-producing business" of the bar. In this respect Chicago was succumbing to the same forces New York had seen at work twenty-five years earlier—the transformation of the lawyer from advocate to technician. Thus the "showy" aspect of the bar—which Darrow had always acknowledged as a factor that had drawn him to his profession—was measurably declining in importance as the dull perusal of fine print and columns of figures increased. Darrow had no patience with such detail, and the larger it loomed as a lawyer's function, so in proportion did his disenchantment grow. He was happier as a writer, a speaker, a publicist, a behind-the-scenes manipulator.

A friendly critic with much opportunity to observe him in practice admitted: "Darrow never consumed midnight electricity on his cases. He depended on inspiration, on impulse and improvisation, on the powers of eloquence, and on the blunders of the prosecution."[1] The fact was that a case in progress never received his undivided attention. It was not that he was incapable of doing the painstaking pre-trial research—his early skirmishes in *Brockway* v. *Jewell* had shown that—but that he was impatient of it and tended to leave it to others to do, or to leave it undone entirely. Masters had reason to reproach Darrow for this neglect within a year of the founding of their partnership. The firm had been retained to represent John Turner, the English anarchist, in the deportation proceedings started against him. Turner's defense had been underwritten by the New York Free Speech League, which fought the case all the way to the Supreme Court. Masters was asked many difficult questions by the justices, then Darrow was called upon to address the Court. He started off well, but then, "his wings wobbled, and in five minutes more he came down. He made a very bad talk." The justices sat impassively as he referred them to Spencer's *Principles of Ethics,* Mill's *Essay on Liberty,* Montesquieu's *Spirit of Law,* Locke on *Civil Government,* and Kant's *Philosophy of Law.* It was not the sort of defense likely to avail the client; the justices were less in need of a sophomoric reading list than a firmly based legal argument. "The members of the League trailed out of the room disgusted. And in a few days the court ruled the exclusion law to be constitutional."[2]

Darrow's choice of professional associates reflected his yearning to avoid the humdrum aspects of law practice. He did not like lawyers who were merely lawyers; he preferred men with wider interests in the political and literary field. But what he needed was to form a partnership with the kind of lawyer who had no outside interest apart from his profession and who would deal with the affairs of the partnership with dispatch and without distraction from politics, literary societies, or philosophical discussion. Such men existed and they would have compensated for Darrow's own penchant for neglecting the detailed aspects of his practice. Instead, Darrow gathered round him men like himself, with ambitions in other directions.

Thus the criticisms Masters leveled at Darrow were equally applicable to those around him. It was not as if Darrow's character and propensities had been concealed from him; Darrow was the first to acknowledge that he was pulled in many directions outside the practice of law. For all his collectivism and his scoffing at Victorian precepts of diligence, clean-living, and virtue rewarded, Darrow was a self-made man, with many of the attitudes to prove it. As he acknowledged, he devoted much energy in his early years to "getting on." He did not believe in collective decisionmaking, and in all his cases, people knew who was boss. He was self-reliant when it came to taking responsibility, with the ruthlessness that implied; he also had a streak of cruelty and rapaciousness, which came out in his treatment of subordinates who crossed him. There is abundant testimony that he was not only a man to be reckoned with, but one to be feared. Success, however defined, was important to him and, like most successful lawyers, he was a user of other men's talents—sometimes with, and sometimes without, acknowledgment. In pursuing his goals he was lavish with money, putting together expensive and able teams to back him up. He was not intimidated by big figures, or bashful about asking high fees, or afraid to sue for them if they were unpaid.

Darrow often dismissed the suggestion that he was "successful" in the conventional sense, professing puzzlement about the meaning of success. He did not want riches, he said. But the fact that he craved other things, like fame and admiration, and that he was engaged in a highly competitive profession, meant that financial success was a necessary part of establishing himself. During his career he was much more successful, even financially, than the average Chicago lawyer, at times reaching financial peaks where he was in sight of being rich. He never kept strict account, but there is little doubt that his practice was prosperous, notwithstanding his tendency to devote more time than wisdom would dictate to nonpaying activities. In a sense, the amount of charitable practice he engaged in was a measure of his financial success, for ultimately the paying work had to subsidize the *causes célèbres*. This was one reason why he discouraged description of himself as a "criminal" lawyer; he wanted it known that he would put his hand to almost any type of work, recognizing that criminal cases did not provide the regular work and steady fees of civil cases. On the other hand, the *pro bono publico* work attracted paying business from liberal interests, of which there were many.

It particularly irked Masters that, on one pretext or another, his partner was a chronic absentee from Chicago. There was no doubt that Darrow was frequently away. One explanation was that he gave much time to lecturing against prohibition. During this period many communities were considering the passage of legislation to enforce prohibition through "local option" provisions, and Darrow was energetic in opposing such moves. He was the most popular of anti-prohibitionists, able, for instance, to fill the Youngstown Opera House to capacity when he spoke there one Sunday afternoon, May 2, 1909. Masters called this "speaking for the liquor interests," although there is no evidence that Darrow was courting them. He was acquainted with several men in the business of brewing such as Conrad Pabst of Milwaukee, but in no way beholden to them. He happened to disapprove of prohibition and hoped to head the movement off. But it was by practice in public opposition to prohibition during these years that he finally settled his style of address, which repudiated most of the precepts of nineteenth-century good form.

Apart from these activities—which took him away from the practice of law and contributed no income to the firm—even when he was in Chicago, almost no day went by that Darrow was not engaged in some political meeting. Yet Masters could scarcely complain of this, for it was through such interests that Darrow drummed up the avalanche of work available to the firm. At luncheons, over a drink in the Palmer House bar, after addressing a meeting in the suburbs, it was common for a political admirer to catch Darrow's arm and ask whether he was in a position to take on a legal problem; and Darrow rarely said no. Both by personal self-advertisement and by the careful cultivation of his wide acquaintanceship, Darrow enhanced his firm's business to the benefit of his partners. Naturally he took on much more work than he could possibly handle alone, and it was not expected that most of it would receive his personal attention; he left it for others to do, and it was inherent in his position as business-getter that that should be the case. In this respect Darrow did well by the firm. The work flowed in without cessation, much of it from directly political sources, as can be illustrated by his retainer in the Iroquois Theater litigation, as counsel to the Hearst newspaper chain, and as traction counsel to the city of Chicago.

In 1904 he was involved in the investigation that followed the Iroquois Theater disaster. On December 30, 1903, during a matinée performance of a children's musical called *Mr. Bluebeard* starring Eddie Foy, a fire had broken out. The fire exits were barred and 596 people were killed in the blaze, or trying to escape from it. The case was referred to a grand jury, and prominent officials, including the mayor of Chicago, were subpoenaed.

The Iroquois fire was stunning in its horror. The theater was a modern one, which should have had up-to-date and efficient fire protection. The victims were the families of some of Chicago's leading citizens. The Chicago *American* started an immediate campaign for the indictment of the owners and managers of the theater for criminal negligence, and in fact five men were indicted. An atmosphere of sorrow and recrimination had been created by the tragedy, which made the search for scapegoats intensive. Darrow was always suspicious of the desire of the public to blame someone for misfortune, and on behalf of the indicted men he argued, "it is not just to lay the sins of a generation upon the shoulders of a few." As the initial public revulsion subsided, Darrow, working behind the scenes, managed to get the indictments quietly dismissed.

The Hearst newspaper chain was another source of work so long as Darrow had power. He received a substantial amount of business from the newspaper magnate, who was constantly expanding his empire by buying out the "independents," and who also gave him the chance to contribute a regular column to his papers and always gave his cases huge publicity. In return, Darrow was to second Hearst's nomination on behalf of the Illinois delegation as Democratic candidate for President in July 1904 at the Convention Hall in St. Louis, in opposition to another man who was to play a big part in his life—William

Jennings Bryan. He nearly lost his chance, however. Hearst was bucking the
Democratic machine, and at the last minute the Illinois delegates, under the
direction and control of Roger C. Sullivan and John P. Hopkins, party bosses,
had decided in caucus that their own man, Fred P. Morris of Watseka, would
make the nominating speech instead of Darrow. When Moses Koenigsberg,
editor of the Chicago *American*, went to get an advance copy of Darrow's
speech in the afternoon before the speech was to be delivered, he found Darrow
sitting alone in a dark corner of the auditorium during a convention recess "in
a grouch too thick to talk." Only after a threat from Koenigsberg that he
would expose the dirty internal politics of the Illinois delegation did Hopkins,
who was delegation chairman, back down and allow Darrow to make the
speech after all. As it happened, it did not avail Hearst, who lost the nomination to Bryan by a wide margin.

Darrow's support of Hearst was an outgrowth of his admiration of strong
political figures, who were prepared to suffer unpopularity to realize their
ambitions. The mainspring of Darrow's attraction to Hearst was not dissimilar
to that which had thrust him into Altgeld's camp: what Altgeld had been,
Hearst in 1904 showed promise of becoming. As Lincoln Steffens put it in
1931: "I cannot describe the hate of those days for Hearst except to say that
it was worse than it is now."[3] It was much the same as Mencken's comment
on Altgeld; and Darrow liked to ally himself with such men. It provides a key
to Darrow's character that he was drawn to heroes who had the strength to
withstand the mob as well as the desire to woo it. And that was not all. Hearst
had that quality of practicality and ability to control a great enterprise that
Darrow liked; just as he admired Marvin Hughitt's ability to run a railroad,
so he admired Hearst's knack of running a newspaper.

The work from Hearst was not merely a reflection of Darrow's political
connections, though there can be no question that his firm became a dropbox
for political favors. It also furthered Darrow's literary ambition. It was this
nascent ambition that brought him into professional contact with Hearst in the
first place, when his Chicago *American* was in the very early years of the
century waging an aggressive circulation war in the city. If Darrow had been
so disposed, he could with good reason have found in Hearst many of the
unpleasant characteristics he described in the street-railway magnate Charles
Tyson Yerkes. It was obvious that Hearst was a man to be reckoned with, and
not a wholly admirable one at that. But there was an attractive aura to
newspaper publishing, which worked its charm on Darrow in a way that
streetcar operations, however profitable, did not. Darrow wanted the chance
to write for a newspaper and was determined to wheedle his way into the
Chicago *American*.

So he acquired Hearst as a client, and very soon found that Hearst's business
put him on entirely the other side from that he proclaimed to be admirable.
Indeed representation of the Hearst interests drew attention to an inconsistency in Darrow's practice and precept that was never resolved and was to
haunt him right up to his final case. He had often spoken as if a lawyer should

only represent clients whose positions he approved, yet found himself taking work from sources seemingly no less objectionable than many he derided. If a lawyer should be judged according to the identity of his paymasters, Darrow was not free from taint; and if he should not become the mouthpiece of those whose worldly positions he disapproved, Darrow transgressed many times. Yet those who shared Darrow's views were a small minority and at that among the least likely to be able to pay his fees—and Darrow wanted to earn a living and more. In consequence he was inevitably drawn into some cases on the "wrong" side. But he was sufficiently imbued with the spirit of Horatio Alger that in the battle between idealism and pocketbook, the pocketbook usually won.

One of the major cases in which Darrow defended Hearst (and lost) posed the dilemma clearly. As part of his promotion of the Chicago *American* Hearst had arranged for an advertising sign 75 by 20 feet, weighing more than 1 ton, and containing nearly three thousand electric lights, to be hung over State Street in downtown Chicago not a quarter mile from Darrow's office. The hanging of a sign over a sidewalk was illegal by city ordinance, but that did not stop Hearst, who managed to "persuade" the City Council (it was eminently persuadable) to license it by resolution. Within a few months the weight of the sign had pulled away some masonry from the building to which it was attached, and the rubble crashing down on State Street far below had injured a lady passing by. When Hearst called upon Darrow to defend the Chicago *American* in the resulting case, there was a sizable irony in the about-turn this meant in Darrow's professional posture. The sign itself was a garish monument to rampant capitalism, which in other circumstances Darrow would have taken joy in berating. It had been put there illegally, and almost certainly the City Council's purported sanction of it (which the courts declared to be of no effect) had been procured by bribery or, at best, some kind of illegitimate pressure. It had been negligently erected, and now an entirely innocent pedestrian had suffered serious injury as a result. But Darrow was not appearing on her behalf. The Cook County jury before whom the case was tried found no difficulty in placing liability on Hearst and awarded the unfortunate plaintiff $8,000. As if that was not enough, it was left to Darrow, that popular champion whose articles in the *American* regularly criticized the callousness of legal doctrine, to appeal against the verdict on the ground that it was excessive. Presiding Justice Frank Baker of the appellate court for the first district, who had offices in the Ashland Block where he regularly passed by Darrow in the hall and rode with him on the elevator, dismissed the claim without the comment that might have suggested itself by saying: "In this case, in view of the nature and effect of the injuries which appellee sustained, the damages awarded to her cannot be regarded as excessive."[4]

Darrow's provision of legal services to Hearst must be seen in the context of his nonlegal ambitions. Hearst was ambitious and ruthless and expected his counsel to be the same. There is some evidence that Darrow bowed as readily to Hearst's excessive demands as he did to the unions'. Indeed one writer has gone so far as to suggest that it was the techniques of Hearst's attorneys, Darrow included, which provided the inspiration for the prohibition mobsters in the 1920s: "All the gunplay of the 1920s had a long dress rehearsal before World War I in the newspaper war. The participants learned through the Chicago newspaper attorneys how 'the fix' worked and, under political protection, they functioned the same way in the prohibition gangland wars."[5] Certainly, what Hearst lacked in taste and moral sensitivity, he made up for in flamboyance and boldness. "A Hearst newspaper is like a screaming woman running down the street with her throat cut," wrote one of its journalists.[6]

Typical of the lucrative work that came from the Hearst connection was the spinoff when his newspapers started a campaign against corporate tax evasion in 1906. In order to further it, the Square Deal Tax League was formed, and its attorney became Charles Erbstein, a clever lawyer of unsavory reputation who appeared in many cases with Darrow over the years. The League decided to concentrate its efforts upon making the International Harvester Company pay more tax. The League bought shares in the company, and then demanded, through Erbstein, a look at the company's books and its shareholder lists. At this stage Edgar Bancroft, counsel to the company, contacted Darrow, indicating a desire to settle the matter and to rid the company of the vitriolic campaign being waged against it in the Chicago *American*. The newspaper had demanded that the company pay taxes on an additional $25 million. Bancroft was prepared to pay taxes on an additional $10 million. Darrow thereupon proposed to Koenigsberg, the *American*'s editor, to work out a compromise on the claim. This Koenigsberg was happy to agree to. Darrow left his office, only to return a few moments later and ask permission to take a fee from the International Harvester Company as well as normal payment from the Chicago *American*. This permission was granted, and Darrow did indeed take $10,000 from the company. Afterward Cyrus S. Simon was to bewail the fact that Darrow had asked only $10,000 of International Harvester: "The job was worth at least a quarter of a million dollars," he said. Darrow did not do the settling personally, because he was away in Boise, Idaho, defending Big Bill Haywood of the Western Federation of Miners (WFM), so the negotiations were left to his partner, Francis Wilson. Wilson bargained hard and finally worked out a settlement by which International Harvester's tax base was increased by nearly $15 million.

Koenigsberg suggests in his autobiography that Darrow's conduct in taking a fee from both sides was outrageous and unethical, and that the quid pro quo of the fee from International Harvester was that the settlement was very favorable to it. He says his opinion of Darrow accordingly went down: "It was less disconcerting to be taken in by the wiles and guiles of a great corporation than to suffer from the misstep of a great humanitarian." On the other hand, the Chicago *American* did consent to the arrangement, which it need not have. It is true, however, that there was a serious conflict of interest in Darrow's position of being paid by both sides.

As for Simon, his main complaint was that Darrow had not charged anything like enough to the International Harvester Company. "I know he's the world's worst sucker," said Simon, "but what I object to is that he works overtime at the job. He should never have accepted that fee from the Harvester people. There isn't any question that he earned it. The point is that if he took anything at all, it should have been his size."[7] So neither his partner nor his client approved of Darrow's disposition of the matter—the former because he had not charged enough, the latter because he had charged too much. It was an occupational hazard of trying to earn a living through the practice of law while professing humanitarianism: clients expected to be let off lightly, while partners expected to prosper—and as often as not, both were disappointed. Practice became a tug-of-war between the desire to help indigents and the need to make money. There is conflicting evidence regarding Darrow's fees, Simon's view being only one of several. Mostly his partners complained not so much that he did not charge enough as that he did not remit his fees to his firm but pocketed them himself. It is certain that in the ordinary course of business he quoted and charged substantial fees. Particularly when he represented labor unions, he insisted on large fees and huge defense funds for expenses, even if it meant that the union membership had to be begged for thousands of small contributions. Unionists who sought his services assuming that he would work for them cheaply were swiftly put right. Darrow's view of labor litigation as an extension of industrial warfare was consistently applied to fees and expenses: sacrifices must be made, contributions must be unstinted, and he must be allowed to spend even to the extent that the financial survival of the sponsoring union might be put in jeopardy.

But at this stage of his career Darrow could afford to turn away business, for he was besieged by prospective clients, including many who came his way through politics. By 1905 Darrow was a member of Mayor Dunne's "kitchen cabinet," a close circle of advisers including Margaret Haley of the Chicago Federation of Labor, Adrian Anson, owner of the White Sox, and others whom one commentator described as "high-principled but inexperienced citizens who proposed to build a new, Utopian Chicago overnight."[8] One important project envisioned was the expansion and improvement of public transport in the city, and with this in view the engineer of the Glasgow tramways, James Dalrymple, was invited over to advise the mayor. It was from his membership in the kitchen cabinet that Darrow achieved the position of traction counsel later in the year and announced that he would give up private practice of the law. However, there is no evidence that he did so; his partnership with Masters and Wilson continued, and the appointment never took up his whole time. The announcement seems to have been a piece of political deception, designed to stifle charges that he was simply receiving a sinecure from the city while continuing to practice law privately. In accepting the appointment, he was furthering a long-standing interest in the uses and abuses of street railway franchises, and renewing his battle with Charles Yerkes, whose extraordinary success in this line of business had made him a fabled anti-hero of the left. If the radicals of those days had their pantheon, they also maintained their communal devils—and prize among them was the remarkable Charles Tyson Yerkes. In the minds of many, the victory of good over evil was by no means assured; as Darrow himself put it in later life, "Altgeld is dead but Yerkes is alive."[9]

19

"A Man of Iron Will"

Most of the radical malcontents of the day admired Yerkes and his ilk for their perfect adjustment to the times. Theodore Dreiser memorialized him in *The Titan* and a whole genre of novel grew up depicting the entrepreneur as anti-hero. This was what the age had nurtured, and it was worth study if not outright emulation. Besides, the critics and their subject had more in common than they acknowledged. Many of them, including writer-lawyers like Edgar Lee Masters, Brand Whitlock, and Darrow himself, had shown as much tenacity in pursuit of their careers as Yerkes had in his. They might not have approved his financial methods, but they shared with him a determination to make a mark.

Charles Yerkes was an entrepreneur of audacity and skill, specializing in the manipulation of streetcar franchises held from various cities, including Chicago, which for his most active years was the center of his operations. In spite of some financial scandals in his past Yerkes held his head high and enjoyed the confidence of the business community. Darrow was already personally acquainted with him, through his earlier employment as corporation counsel of the city, where much of his effort had been directed at keeping predators like Yerkes at bay, and through the Sunset Club, at which Yerkes had on occasion spoken. Although Yerkes stood for all that was corrupt by radical standards, Darrow did not dislike him; his boldness and success amused him. "Mr. Yerkes was a man of iron will, and as bold as any buccaneer who ever sailed the financial seas," he wrote later. "He and his family have long been dead, or I might not like to make these very moderate statements of fact." The truth was that Darrow found such men fascinating. There was something about a man who was ruthless—be it an Altgeld or a Yerkes—that attracted him. Those who acted and made their mark on the world, those who would achieve their ends, even if unscrupulously, could engage Darrow's admiration, grudging or wholehearted according to what those aims were. And there was no doubt that Yerkes acted. There was a sense in which Yerkes was larger than life. He was a man to be reckoned with, whose achievements were notable if not altogether creditable. His works were in some respects greatly beneficial to the public. In October 1897, he donated a refracting telescope with a 40-inch aperture to the University of Chicago, which instantly made the university preeminent in spectroscopy and astrophysics. And it was Yerkes who managed the conversion of the London underground system from steam to electricity, and the consolidation of the various companies running subways there. Careful always to keep the favor of the public, he used his wealth to help subsidize the popular band concerts held in Chicago's West Side parks, giving $1,000 for that purpose in the summer of 1898. He was canny enough to hedge his political bets by contributing to the campaigns of any candidate who stood even a remote chance in the municipal elections; indeed Darrow conceded that he had quite possibly contributed to Altgeld's campaign chest, though without Altgeld's knowledge. Yerkes told inquirers that he was "non-partisan," and that was true in the sense that he would bribe any administration if he could. If he did not get his way, it was dangerous to have him as an enemy: he, more than any other individual, had been responsible for Altgeld's financial ruin, as reprisal for the latter's refusal to sign the bill that would have extended Yerkes's traction franchise. "He had only to sign that traction bill to become a very wealthy man," said Darrow.[1]

The streetcar companies had been awarded franchises along particular streets of the city for fairly short periods, beginning in the 1860s. These franchises, granting as they did a monopoly, became more profitable as Chicago expanded. By the 1880s they were among the most lucrative businesses in town. They issued stocks and bonds, upon which interest had to be paid, and which finally became a heavy burden upon the public through the fares charged. Then Charles Yerkes applied the methods of high finance to the business, and merged nearly all the streetcar companies into one huge monopoly, while successfully lobbying the state legislature and city government for extensions of the franchises. His requests were not modest; instead of asking for a ten- or twenty-year extension, Yerkes proposed a ninety-nine-year franchise. At the same time he continued to issue commercial paper of as many sorts as were legal on the public markets. Darrow did not believe this served the public interest: "Even the city of Chicago, with all its enterprise and industry," he complained, "could not stand under the load of stocks and bonds, and gradually it became evident that enough nickels could not be collected to pay the interest upon the last issues of stock within any reasonable time and keep the property in physical condition to perform decent public service."[2]

Darrow's employment as a lawyer dealing with public transport put him in the forefront of contemporary legal battles. It is difficult for the modern reader to appreciate the extent to which the legal liabilities of railroads and streetcar concerns were a matter of controversy at the turn of the century. The price of a streetcar ride became a touchstone of whether urban democracy was working well or not. In theory, since voters controlled the government, which in turn had the power to grant or withhold franchises, they should have been able to control the streetcar companies. But it did not seem to work that way; if anything, the situation seemed rather the reverse as the companies came in sight of extorting ever larger favors from the legislature. Legal scholars earnestly debated the principles on which companies running these facilities should be accountable to the public. Most railroad and streetcar counsel saw the matter differently, and eminent lawyers such as Moorfield Storey advocated systems of law that would insulate railroads and street railways from more than a fixed limited liability.[3]

In his affiliations first with the railroad and then with the city of Chicago, and in his interest in traction company matters, Darrow had dived into the most agitated legal questions of the time. He was on the front line of legal, as well as political, controversy and at no stage in modern history have legal battles reflected so closely contemporary political disputes as they did during the period from 1890 to the passing of the antitrust laws.

Chicago was the scene of the most important development in mass transit systems. In 1895 the South Side Elevated introduced Frank J. Sprague's "multiple-unit control system," which greatly improved the rapid transit facilities of Chicago.

In retrospect it seems peculiar that municipal transport should have been an important issue of Chicago politics; but Chicago was no different from many American cities. All the great domestic problems of the muckraking era could be debated around the question of mass transit: urbanization, monopoly, the problem of political graft. As America's newly acquired millions arrived, they clustered together in the cities rather than spreading out, new customers for Yerkes's street railways. In one of his best pieces of writing Darrow analyzed the finances of the city's transit system and the machinations of the streetcar companies. And here Darrow displayed one of the characteristics that made him such an effective leader for the powerless: he understood the dynamics of power. This was not merely the result of intuition. In many of his endeavors he was gamekeeper turned poacher. When he lectured before the municipal reform leagues of Chicago, he drew upon his years as corporation counsel. When he helped the American Railway Union in the Pullman strike, he had the advantage of knowing railroad management's attitude from the inside through his work at the Chicago & Northwestern. His experience in the Illinois legislature made him the more canny about politics. He had more than his share of shrewdness before obtaining these experiences; but in many instances he performed effectively in his mission because, although he represented outsiders and their interests, he had once been an insider.

The issue of public transport was one much in the public eye at this time, all over the nation. It was one upon which his friend Brand Whitlock fought a mayoralty campaign in Toledo, Ohio. For many years the "five cent subway fare" was a dominant theme of New York politics, though the public did not understand the intricacies of streetcar finance as well as the intellectual sophisticates, it knew the difference between paying 3 rather than 5 cents per ride in Toledo, or a nickel rather than a dime in New York or Chicago. Hence, franchise renewal became a classic live issue of urban politics. It was debated at an exalted level by the reformers and the muckrakers as an example of the money interests taking over government and bending its resources to their own advantage. The complaint was that the public was being taken for more of a ride than it realized by the traction companies. And these companies, especially as they were combined by Yerkes, were antagonists to be reckoned with. Darrow knew this:

> These companies are in daily receipt of $50,000. Everybody familiar with legal affairs understands that a good many high-priced lawyers can be employed from such receipts. Everybody is also wise enough to understand that under the complex administration of law by our courts high-priced lawyers can make plenty of trouble upon almost any proposition.[4]

In radical circles Darrow's reputation was enhanced by his ability to understand and explain the political shenanigans by which profiteers siphoned off huge profits from the public purse. Reuben Borough, a young reporter with the Chicago *Daily Socialist*, whose offices at 163 East Randolph were only steps from Darrow, Masters & Wilson in the Ashland Block, described the characteristic weakness of the radical opposition: "As a Marxist disciple of cigarmaker Ben Blumberg I could dissect the capitalist system with unerring precision, but traction magnate Charles Yerkes's long-term and short-term franchises and his watered stocks were beyond me."[5] Here Darrow was different and the difference made him indispensable. He grasped the ins and outs of financial manipulation as readily as he had grasped Cook County's machine politics. His 1905 article on "The Chicago Traction Question" traced the series of mergers Yerkes had achieved of the various streetcar companies, and the flotation of bonds on the public markets that followed. The explication was masterful, demonstrating Darrow's technical abilities and showing that, in acting for corporations such as Hearst's newspapers, he was capable of practicing commercial law to a high standard. He was, in his unique position as clever lawyer and political radical, the savant of Chicago muckraking. He understood how graft paid off—not merely by direct theft, but through the use of corporate devices, which pumped up profits that ultimately the public had to pay. He reasoned, exactly as his political mentor Altgeld had, that the street railways should be subject to municipal ownership. Altgeld when governor had vetoed a bill to give Yerkes's companies a fifty-year franchise, which had already been passed by the legislature. Now Darrow was carrying on Altgeld's crusade. Darrow had been in the Illinois legislature with Charles A. Allen, the author of the traction bill, and had not detected in him as much concern for the public as for the streetcar companies' shareholders.

In concerning himself with the details of municipal railway systems, Darrow was neither parochial nor petty. His warning of the ills flowing from private ownership turned out to be prescient: within two years of the publication of his article, the New York Metropolitan Street Railway, in which Yerkes had a substantial interest, was declared insolvent.[6] In nearly every major city in the United States the agitation to retain the 5 cent fare became a focus of popular sentiment against the political machine. It was not merely that an increase would weigh most heavily on the poor, but the feeling that in part the necessity to raise the fare had been created so as to line the pockets of men already rich.

The major product of Darrow's appointment as traction counsel was an eight-page opinion written jointly with Gene E. Plumb, dealing with the rights of various rail lines to cross or use Chicago streets.[7] According to the opinion, the rights of most of the street railways within the city of Chicago had expired or were about to expire. They had been granted for a fixed term and had not been extended. Among the lines affected were those running along or across Dearborn Street, North and South Clark Street, and Rush Street, all of them crucial to the streetcar and railroad franchises. Darrow's intermingling of law and politics was demonstrated by this opinion which, though it came to a conclusion with profoundly political implications (and one that delighted Darrow no end), was couched in the usual misleadingly unemotional style of the city's legal memoranda. In some matters, Darrow was unafraid to admit his view that law and politics were inseparable—even indistinguishable—but he knew that to do so on this question would be to hand the opposition a stick with which to beat him. So he adopted a moderate tone untypical of his private practice as he informed the traction moguls that their entitlement to run Chicago's public transport was running out. It was all very polite. But since the major asset of the streetcar companies was their professed right to run on the city's streets for some time to come, his opinion undermined the entire basis of their prosperity. No wonder that Chicago's traction counsel's conclusions were hotly disputed. Copies of the opinion were probably received by the affected companies' managers in a state of mind that contrasted strikingly with its tone. Of course these conclusions were hotly disputed by the affected companies. That was the desired result, so far as Darrow was concerned, for it indicated that he had touched the streetcar companies on a sore point.

It was one of many distractions from the ordinary work of his law office—where a storm was brewing of awesome proportions.

20

The Haywood Trial

In 1906 Darrow's attention to the Chicago affairs of Darrow, Masters & Wilson was distracted by a request from the Western Federation of Miners to aid the defense of its secretary-treasurer William D. Haywood, who was accused of murdering ex-Governor Frank Steunenberg of Idaho.

The mines of Idaho had seen extreme strife between mine owners and miners. In 1899, there had been a bitter strike in the Coeur d'Alene district, which culminated in the Bunker Hill mine being blown up by extremist strikers. Governor Steunenberg, then in office, saw it as his duty to quell the escalating disorder in the Coeur d'Alene region. Yet his resources were almost nonexistent: there were few policemen in Idaho and the state militia was fighting in the Philippines. In desperation, Steunenberg did what Altgeld would not do in Illinois in 1894 and called in federal troops. This quelled the incipient riot in Coeur d'Alene, but it also had the ancillary effect of defeating the forces of labor in their battle against the mine owners. Steunenberg's act was bitterly resented, especially because before he had become governor he had been a union printer; it was thought he had committed treason to the labor movement. When, on December 30, 1905, he lost his life in a dynamite trap laid at the front gate of his house, it was widely suspected that the responsibility lay with the radical officers of the Western Federation of Miners, who had meted out retribution to him for calling in the federal government to Coeur d'Alene five years before. The state of Idaho sent its agents to Colorado, where Haywood, Charles H. Moyer, the president of the union, and George W. Pettibone, another official, were living, and kidnapped them back to Idaho in order to try them for Steunenberg's murder. At this point, the WFM called upon Darrow to defend its leaders.

Initially, when Darrow was called in, the matter was dealt with on a petition for habeas corpus on the basis that Idaho was detaining Haywood and his co-defendants of the WFM unlawfully. But the writ was denied at every level of application, up to and including the U.S. Supreme Court. The Supreme Court's disposition of the case, *Pettibone* v. *Nichols*,[1] added verisimilitude to the contention of the unionists that it was the government, not they, that was the lawless element. It was true that some ancient authority could be found to support the holding of the court that no constitutional rights were violated by the kidnapping of the defendants from Colorado for the purposes of trial in Idaho, but that scarcely justified the actions of the authorities. Even in the legal press, authors unsympathetic to the defendants deplored the result, one of them concluding that it called for an amendment to the Constitution. After the Court had spoken, Darrow remarked, "there was nothing to do then but fight the case in the Idaho courts."

His partners saw the matter from a different perspective, believing that Darrow could and should have declined to proceed further with the case, so that he could return to the business of his Chicago firm. In particular Edgar Masters was incensed by the way Darrow acted like a free agent and ignored his obligations to the partnership. Nevertheless Darrow proceeded to trial in Idaho without consulting his colleagues. Ultimately his decision to do so would prove the main cause of the breakup of the firm. Yet it was easy to understand why Darrow should wish to take the case on; not only was it bound to generate a great deal of publicity, but it was a development of a long-standing labor-management feud. As *Collier's* magazine put it:

> The Moyer-Haywood Case goes far down into the roots of Western life. When the Rocky Mountain States passed from the pioneer age to the period of indus-trial development they inherited from old years two classes of "undesirable citizens." On the one hand were the bad men, the legitimate successors of Slade, Billy the Kid, and their kind. These, when the period of highway robberies, saloon brawls, and cattle rustling were [sic] no more, settled down to mine and ranch labor, bringing with them their lawlessness and their love of trouble. On the other hand was the reckless and conscienceless entrepreneur, the mine owner or mine buyer eager only to rip his pile out of the earth and hurry East to spend it. The fight between these two classes goes as far back as Leadville in 1880. In the Coeur d'Alene, in Butte, in Cripple Creek, it was the same old fight. This Moyer-Haywood case is only its most recent round. And whether these men are guilty or not guilty, the moral responsibility for this state of affairs in the Rockies hangs in balance between the two classes.[2]

In fact Haywood's prosecution was not the first to arise out of the governor's death; these years saw a succession of criminal prosecutions of members of the Western Federation of Miners and others allegedly connected with the murder at Christmas 1905 of ex-Governor Steunenberg. Many of them have been forgotten, or the memory of them has been supplanted by the memory of the trial of "Big Bill" Haywood, which received most attention. In February and March 1907 a previous trial had taken place of Steve Adams, another WFM member, in Wallace, Idaho. The issues raised were much the same in all the five trials ultimately conducted, but Haywood's has been the focus of attention. "Chronologically it was the second trial, but in order of importance it was paramount," says one commentator. "It captured the public fancy far more completely than the trials of Adams, Pettibone, and Orchard. It seems safe to conclude that no other American trial of that decade or of the Progressive Era approached the Haywood trial in significance and public interest."[3] Neverthe-

less the Adams trial provided an important dress rehearsal for the Haywood
trial, and Darrow's summation in behalf of Adams was itself a masterly piece
of oratory: "it is great as all your speeches are," Brand Whitlock told him.[4]

In many ways the marathon of prosecutions conducted in Idaho in these
years represented the apogee of criminal litigation against union leaders. It
became an orgy of class hatred and doctrinal dispute. There were accusations
and counteraccusations, confessions and retractions, and the intricacies of the
proceedings became extraordinarily difficult to follow because witnesses could
be praised or damned by the same side. In part this was because of the
assumption among many labor leaders that any prosecution of unionists, and
particularly union officials, was a frame-up, without legal or factual basis—a
view that led Eugene Debs into error time and time again. To some unionists
it was a matter of indifference whether the accused was guilty or innocent of
the charges leveled against him; as one commentator put it, "they perhaps
wanted to support the labor movement more than they wanted to see the truth
emerge."[5] The trial of a workingman was in their eyes not a merely individual
matter, but an attack upon his class and the rights of all workers. As for
indictments against union officials, they amounted to a suggestion that labor
organizations were the initiators of sabotage and murder, committed to achieving their ends by any means, lawful or not. This attitude on the part of
unionists had been demonstrated from the very outset of the investigation of
the death of ex-Governor Steunenberg. Charles H. Moyer, president of the
Western Federation, immediately volunteered to provide a defense for the
alleged assassin, one Thomas Hogan, out of union funds, though Moyer admitted that no inquiry had been made to ascertain whether Hogan was guilty or
innocent. The act was in furtherance of labor's interest, and that was sufficient.[6] Similarly the A.F. of L. (to which the Western Federation of Miners
did not belong, having withdrawn some years before) contributed to the defense of the men under the prompting of Samuel Gompers. "It was my feeling
that regardless of whoever might be responsible for the Steunenberg murder
the American labor movement could not abandon the labor men helpless to
the vengeance of employers who were in control of the machinery of the state,"
Gompers wrote. "I felt that the accused men ought to be assured fair trial
which I knew they could not have without the financial assistance and backing
of the labor movement."[7]

It was this view of the rights and wrongs of such prosecutions that turned
public opinion against the unionists quite as much as the merits of the workingmen's case. The New York *World* expressed the majority's feeling, which was
not antilabor:

> The labor unions have been making fools of themselves over Moyer and Hay-
> wood. They have attempted to turn a murder trial into a great state case in which
> the principle of constitutional government was at stake. With no knowledge of
> the facts except such as any newspaper reader can possess, they tried and acquit-
> ted the defendants and challenged the courts to set aside their verdict.[8]

But the labor movement was not in the mood for cool reflection. Throughout the nation demonstrators voiced their solidarity with the union officials about to go on trial. On Boston Common, as soapbox orators spoke, "the crowd jeered at the name of the police spy, McParland; and everyone cheered at the names of Eugene V. Debs and Clarence Darrow. . . ."⁹ There were those who looked upon demonstrations with trepidation, fearing that they represented the beginning of a class war:

> Even in New York, two thousand miles away, Fifth Avenue was jammed, one day in May, 1907, with thousands upon thousands of workmen marching to the thrilling music of the *Marseillaise* and carrying banners which announced their sympathy for Haywood. It was a sight to make financiers, looking down from the windows of their great houses and their comfortable clubs, more than a little uneasy. Not only reform appeared to be gathering headway, but proletarian revolt of the most aggressive and vindictive sort.¹⁰

In the face of this emotional and partisan public interest, it was clear that the Idaho trial of Haywood would attract widespread attention. Neither the prosecution nor the defense stinted upon legal talent. Not content to rely upon the local district attorney, Owen M. Van Duyn, the state had retained two of the top lawyers in Idaho to aid him: James M. Hawley, an experienced and successful trial lawyer who had acted for the Western Federation of Miners some years before and drawn up its charter, and William E. Borah, a much younger man who had already been elected to the Senate, though he did not take his seat until after the case was finished. Darrow described Borah as "a hard worker, astute, and in every respect an able adversary. He was always wary and cautious and thoroughly familiar with his case."¹¹ There was one blot upon Borah's otherwise impressive record: while prosecuting the Haywood case, he was himself under indictment by a federal grand jury for land frauds allegedly committed by one of his legal clients. The indictment put Borah in a difficult position for, like anyone in public life, he could be hurt by the accusation regardless of whether it was substantiated. Besides, it came as an uncomfortable distraction from the task of prosecuting Haywood, which he was already trying to accomplish simultaneously with going through the preliminaries of taking his seat in the Senate. It says much for Borah that he remained calm and collected through this ordeal. He did not stint upon his duty as prosecutor or ask for pity. He made a short statement denying the charges of land fraud totally, and carried on as if nothing had happened, though his credibility as a representative of the public's interest in the Haywood affair was compromised. But in this respect help came from an unexpected source: Darrow himself made a statement to the press indicating his complete confidence in Borah's innocence and integrity.*

If, as the unionists claimed, the trial was an attempt to pillory the labor movement, it was clear that labor would not lack for lawyers. The defense staff

---

*For the remainder of Borah's life, Darrow was on good terms with him, and visited him in the Senate whenever he was in Washington.

was not as compact as the prosecution, partly because several local attorneys had been recruited to tell the principals what the state law and procedure were. But in addition, various lawyers of radical sympathies associated themselves with the defense without anyone calling a halt before the situation became unmanageable. The defense team swelled to sixteen lawyers, plus casual helpers, whereas the prosecution was conducted by only four lawyers. Still, the defense seemed to have an impressive array of legal talent, and was at the beginning credited by the press with extraordinary competence and power: "One of the attorneys, Darrow of Chicago, has for years appeared for the defense in great labor cases. He slips into his present duties naturally. There is not a move with which he has not become familiar from long experience."[12] Similar bouquets were handed to some other members of the defense, notably Edmund F. Richardson and John Nugent.

On the other hand, the state machinery for prosecution was grotesquely under provided for. As late as 1892 the Idaho Attorney General (with supervisory control over all district attorneys) had had no staff whatever and answered all correspondence himself in longhand. The incumbent asked plaintively for a stenographer and typewriter, explaining that "If, when his mail arrives, he could call a stenographer to his assistance, dictate his replies and have them run through the typewriter, much valuable time would be saved to the officer in the performance of mere clerical labor, the performance of which might well be shifted to other hands." Idaho was only just moving out of the period of frontier lawlessness, as successive reports of the Attorney General demonstrated, and law and order was still not well established. Thus the defense was probably less hampered in its work by financial difficulties than the average Idaho prosecutor—and though it is true that the state made a special effort in the Moyer case, there is no reason to suppose that the defense was at any financial disadvantage whatever.

At this time, egged on by his friends, Darrow was in the grip of an almost manic sense of destiny. "How full your hands and your heart are just now!" wrote Brand Whitlock. "We think of you daily and watch the progress of the trial with the greatest interest. You are making history out there in Idaho, and the newspapers show that the minds of men are awakening to the real issue involved."[13] His conviction that he was engaged in a form of warfare led Darrow to insist that the labor movement commit inordinate resources to the litigation, in a spirit of "do or die." The costs incurred in supporting the accused men rendered the Western Federation of Miners insolvent, and besides drew heavily upon its reservoirs of membership loyalty in a way that compromised its future ability to accumulate another war-chest or fight another battle on the same scale. Darrow complained that the mighty power of government had been brought to bear upon the task of railroading his clients to their death or to the penitentiary. But the preparations for trial made by the prosecution were by no means as lavish as those of the defense, and actual resources mustered by the defense clearly much exceeded those of the state. The huge campaigns of investigation and counterinvestigation, of check and double check, which Darrow instituted and directed had as their justification the belief that governmental power was being exercised with unparalleled malignancy— that, at root, the prosecutions were treacherous plots to frame innocent men, which would be exposed if only by huge expenditures of time and money. This was the reason that union coffers were emptied in fighting the cases, and that union officials' energies were deflected for months at a time in following cases with which neither they nor their unions had any direct connection. Virtually the whole attention of the labor movement became riveted upon the litigation, as the pitch of the contest heightened and more and more money was poured into it. No stone was left unturned as the defense attempted to trap the prosecution in dishonesty or misrepresentation, and to find a weak link in the chain of proof. The ideal of solidarity was taken to extremes as the labor movement underwrote the costs of defending almost any laboring man accused of violence. In these circumstances the cause of socialism came to be as much a preoccupation as the rights of the defendants.

Yet it very soon became clear that the defense was not going well—and newspaper comments, which had begun so favorably, rapidly became adverse. There were many rumors of discord and stories were filed of defense wastefulness, clumsiness, tactlessness, and confusion. It seemed to some correspondents that the large reservoir of legal talent was acting against the interests of Haywood, not for them. Within a month it was reported, "The organization of the prosecution is perfect; the organization of the defense at times seems to be about as bad as it could be."[14] The adjectives applied to the defense were nearly all belittling: "blundering," "rambling," "confused," and "misguided" were the epithets journalists blazoned across their newspapers as the trial progressed. The consensus was that too many cooks were spoiling the broth.

The abilities of the men conducting the defense of the case were great as individuals, but cooperation was not their strong suit. Relations among them were about as cordial as those of the principals of Darrow, Masters & Wilson back in Chicago. From the beginning there was disagreement between Darrow and Edmund F. Richardson on the course that the defense should pursue, and their relationship was strained by the fact that they had equal rank in the defense camp, an arrangement fraught with danger of friction. No clear chain of command had been set up, and though many newspaper reports referred to either Darrow or Richardson as "chief counsel for the defense," the very existence of such a status was denied. Darrow told the Idaho *Daily Statesman:* "As far as chief counsel are concerned, there is no chief counsel on our side. We are all on equal footing . . ."[15] The clash between the two men had been noted even before Adams's trial in a confidential Pinkerton report to the prosecution on January 2, 1907. The *Statesman* drew attention to the bad blood that developed between the two by publishing a cartoon showing Darrow as a puppet of Richardson's; but in fact the trouble was that neither man could control the other. The result was that defense efforts were uncoordinated and often at cross-purposes. There were rumors that some of the pre-trial statements issued by Darrow had only reluctantly been approved by his co-

counsel and his clients.[16] There was an open breach in court on the question
of whether the defense stood ready for trial; Darrow told Judge Wood on May
6 that it was not, whereupon Richardson jumped to his feet and contradicted
him. "Mr. Darrow's face flushed with deep annoyance and, when he left the
courtroom shortly afterwards, he was manifestly agitated," reported the
Oregonian. "The incident would not have attracted so much attention had it
not been for other straws pointing to feeling between Mr. Darrow and Mr.
Richardson."[17]

Darrow had come out from Chicago expecting to be in complete charge of
strategy, but it was precisely on this question that he and Richardson disagreed. Fundamentally Richardson wanted to play down the political aspects
of the case, whereas Darrow wanted to play them up. Either method of trying
the case had its advantages, but the two did not go together. Both Darrow and
Richardson were men of strong will, and neither would budge from his position. Haywood himself observed that the procession of lawyers coming to his
aid "came by ones and twos" like the animals into Noah's Ark, "until we had
a strong array of legal talent."[18] But it was not working together; it was not,
and never became, a team. Hugh O'Neill, correspondent of the Denver *Post,*
felt that "in employing so many attorneys for the defense the persons who are
managing the defense fund have thrown much money away. So many lawyers
are entirely unnecessary."[19] Darrow himself had observed during the 1903
anthracite strike arbitration that the mine owners had been handicapped by
too many lawyers. Now the tables were turned on labor, but Darrow could not,
or would not, remedy the situation. The verbal fireworks normally sparked by
the adversary system were greatly augmented by the discord in the defense's
own ranks, so that an extraordinarily bitter and rancorous trial ensued. Judge
Wood's daughter recalled that "The whole procedure sounded as though it
were taking place in an insane asylum."[20]

Throughout the trial it was almost as if two separate and inconsistent
defenses were being entered for Haywood, one of which proceeded on the
theory that Haywood was unjustly accused of complicity in the death of
Steunenberg, the other seeking to persuade the jury to acquit on political
grounds even though they might think Haywood guilty. It was not an efficient
way to defend three alleged murderers.

The case was one that worried Darrow greatly, and he provided no comfort
to his clients, whom he often visited in jail. Already he was exhibiting to a
dangerous degree his tendency to become obsessive in his involvement with his
clients' cause so that calm, dispassionate evaluation of the best course of action
had become difficult. He was so preoccupied with his legal problems that
George Pettibone had to remind him, "You know, it's us fellows that have to
be hanged." Haywood sarcastically suggested to him that when things got
gloomy round the office, he should visit his clients in jail to cheer himself up.[21]
Darrow's general unhappiness was compounded by the animosity between
himself and Edmund Richardson, and later by the rift that developed between
Haywood and Moyer. The clashes of personality and the rivalries that devel-

oped during the proceedings made what went on out of court almost as explosive as what went on inside. Besides, he had embarked upon the cases in a frame of mind that rebelled against his professional obligations. He wrote enviously to Brand Whitlock only a month before the Haywood trial began: "You can see your finish as a lawyer, and I hope you will not long need to be bothered with your profession."[22] It might have been thought that Darrow, disturbed and depressed, was unable to perform. In fact he needed to feel beleaguered before he could get up steam. Thus it augured well for his clients that he was so out of sorts.

In anticipation of the trial, newspapermen descended upon Boise in readiness for a spectacular battle between capital and labor that was slated to provide a great deal of copy. Most of them had no previous acquaintance with Boise and expected to find a community in turmoil, but their visions of Idaho as a survival of the Wild West were quickly shattered. Instead, they found a calm, orderly community able to undertake the trial without demonstration or civil disorder. "Considerable disgust is expressed by some of the newspapermen who have come from distant parts," reported the *Oregonian*. "They appear to have thought they were coming to an armed camp, where sensations were likely to be constant, and they have been surprised and disappointed to find a community as quiet as one in New England, and so perfectly composed that no one uninformed would suspect anything of great importance was going on here."[23] The journalists found that the most exciting distraction available for their idle moments was a fishing trip. Some of the reporters assigned to the case were soon withdrawn when it was perceived that local color was lacking; also it was felt that their presence in Boise was superfluous in view of the arrangements for comprehensive coverage which the Associated Press had made.

The trial was one of the first covered by wire services and as such marked an important event in the history of American journalism. In February–April 1907 AP had carried on its wire reports of the Thaw case in New York, in which a millionaire had been tried and convicted for the murder of the architect Stanford White, but its impact on the newspaper industry was much less, because most newspapers already had representation in New York, whereas they definitely had none in Boise. Darrow was fortunate to come to prominence as an advocate in the first great age of national reporting. His rise coincided with the formation of the national wire agencies: in fact Associated Press's single greatest reporting success was the Haywood trial, which persuaded many newspapers to subscribe to its service. The age of the telegraph and the telephone was sufficiently far advanced that the wide dissemination of domestic news became possible on an unprecedented scale.

But that was not all. The reporting style of Darrow's times was to concentrate on detail; the minutiae of a trial became fit subject for reportage and comment. The major journalists of the era deliberately gave critical sketches of advocates that latterly would be considered out of place in an item of news, though suitable for a column of editorial or opinion writing. Hence an advo-

cate might achieve a distinctive public image, and become familiar in print to
many Americans who had never seen him in person. Moreover the ability to
reproduce photographs added a new dimension to newspaper journalism at the
turn of the century.

The relative calm of Boise was generally considered to be a benefit to the
defense, and steps were taken not to stir the community up. So far as possible,
the strategy of the defense was to portray the accused as decent, ordinary,
humane men. So, when Haywood, Moyer, and Pettibone were interviewed in
jail, their statements were good-natured and unpolitical. To the query: "How
have you been treated?", the three answered: "All right."

"We have absolutely no complaint," said Haywood.

"No men were ever treated better under like circumstances," said Moyer.
While the picking of the jury was going on, Darrow lectured at the Unitarian
church on Walt Whitman. Altogether, the desire was to create an impression
of civilized moderation on the part of the defense. There were, however, two
impediments to maintaining this unruffled front. The first was the threat that
Eugene Debs would come to Boise as the personal representative of the socialist newspaper *Appeal to Reason*. The *Appeal* was covering the trial anyway,
all the time loudly proclaiming the innocence of the accused. It had already
had a great success with a special issue called the "Kidnapping Edition,"
which Haywood reported sold 4 million copies, and it was determined to
capitalize still further upon events in Boise. Darrow—remembering Debs from
the ARU Pullman strike days and knowing that he would not conciliate or
compromise—did not relish the idea of Debs visiting Boise. He therefore
requested that Debs should not come to Idaho during the trial, and Debs
complied. Haywood believed that Darrow had a selfish motive for discouraging Debs from visiting Boise: that he did not want Debs to steal the limelight.
"I searched my mind for Darrow's reason for objecting to Debs' presence, and
could think of nothing but his desire to be recognized as the most prominent
person in the trial." But Darrow's fear that Debs would aggravate the situation
and say silly things against the interests of the defense was well founded. Debs
was a partisan who could never concede that the other side might be telling
the truth. He suffered from a paranoid inability to see virtue in his adversaries
that was to lead him into untenable positions throughout his life. It even
happened during the Haywood trial, though he never visited Boise. In early
May the Chicago *Journal* alleged that Charles Moyer, the president of the
Western Federation of Miners, had served time as a convicted burglar in Joliet
Prison—a fact that had not been known to the public or the defense and that
punctured somewhat the image of respectability the defense had been cultivating. Debs, contacted by the press in Topeka, made an immediate statement:
"I have known Mr. Moyer for years," he said, "and it is as impossible to
connect him with burglary as it is with the crime for which he is being tried,
that is, complicity in a plot to assassinate."[24] What Debs said was designed to
help the accused, but its effect was the reverse when it became clear beyond

any question that Moyer was indeed the ex-convict identified by the Chicago *Journal.* Foes of the defendants pointed with glee to the logic of Debs's statement: if Moyer could be connected with the burglary, might he not also be connected with the plot to assassinate? Debs, of course, had no way of checking the facts independently, and it was typical of him to make an assertion of fact on blind faith, which turned out to be misplaced.

From the start the defense placed great importance upon jury selection, a matter upon which Darrow prided himself. His handling of *voir dire*—the questioning of prospective jurors to ascertain bias or interest—was one of the very few accomplishments that his professional peers conceded to him. Large sums of money were paid out by the defense for investigations of the background and disposition of men on the jury panel, and dossiers (referred to jokingly by Darrow in court as "dope sheets") were compiled on a large number of those actually called. Rumor had it that sometimes the investigative agents of the defense did more than solicit views. "Each evening at the dinner table father and mother discussed the latest developments," wrote Kendrick Johnson, who lived in Boise and was fourteen at the time.

> I can still feel the delicious thrill of fear and excitement as they commented on the rumor that families of the jurors were being called upon by men affecting to be peddlers or book salesmen and being subjected to only thinly veiled threats in the form of reminders that in similar trials in Colorado, jurors whose vote was adverse to the miners unaccountably did not long survive.[25]

Apart from intimidation, the defense was suspected of retaining expert jury bribers to ensure a verdict in favor of their clients.

Jury selection became a long-drawn-out interrogation of each man on the jury list, conducted by both prosecution and defense. Two entire jury panels were exhausted and another had to be produced by the sheriff before twelve qualified men could be found. This was partly attributable to the care taken by both sides to object to an unfavorable-seeming juror, but partly also, as the newspapers pointed out, to a marked disinclination of many of those called to sit on the jury. A very large number of them deliberately disqualified themselves from service by professing a conscientious objection to capital punishment, or a fixed opinion on the case that was not amenable to contrary evidence. This unwillingness to serve became a subject of jest by the time the third and last panel of talesmen was called. "That the sheriff and his deputies certainly had all kinds of trouble in summoning many of the talesmen . . . is no secret," wrote the *Daily Statesman.* "The sheriff denies that he had to pull a gun on several to hold them still long enough to serve the subpoena on them or that several were chased down on horseback and finally 'roped' like wild range steers, but he admits that several of the deputies had to, in a number of instances use very strategic tactics to land their men. . . ."[26]

Darrow took a considerable amount of the business of jury selection upon himself. Hugh O'Neill noted critically, "Neither Darrow nor Richardson has ever apparently taken the trouble to learn the statutory form for challenging

jurors for direct bias or implied bias, and in that matter Nugent has had
invariably to come to their rescue," but this advice did not save Darrow from
occasional faux pas.[27] For instance, he instigated his co-counsel Richardson to
ask a question of a prospective juror regarding a letter written by President
Roosevelt in which he had condemned the attitudes of certain businessmen and
labor leaders—specifically mentioning Moyer and Haywood—and branded
them "undesirable citizens": "If the President should write any more letters
on this subject, as my co-counsel suggests, would they influence you?" The
juror replied, amid laughter, "I wouldn't get a chance to see them." The
question was a pointless one: the law of Idaho kept prospective jurors under
lock and key and they were not allowed to see newspapers. However, outside
the juryroom the President's statement was so well known that the defense
capitalized on it by distributing lapel buttons to sympathizers which read: I AM
AN UNDESIRABLE CITIZEN. They were often to be seen around Boise during
the trial, and became a much-prized souvenir.

Haywood described Darrow's performance on *voir dire* admiringly:

> The examination of the jurors was a broad education in the class struggle. In the
> panels selected, all the bankers of the county had been called as jurymen, but
> Darrow disposed of these in short order. He would begin by asking if they were
> acquainted with the case; if they read the newspapers; if they had formed an
> opinion; whether evidence would be required to change this opinion. Then he
> would show by his questions that there was little difference between a banker and
> a burglar; one worked in the daytime with interest and stock-juggling as the
> means of robbery, while the other worked at night with the jimmy and nitroglyc-
> erin. He would challenge them for cause. It was like killing snakes.[28]

This cannot be regarded as either an accurate or exhaustive description of what
actually occurred, but no matter. Was Haywood right in believing that the jury
selection was in his best interests? It is true that the defense had challenged
many jurors; but the jury that resulted was not necessarily the best to try a
case which, on the defense's own theory, reflected a current industrial dispute.
It was composed predominantly of farmers, with no experience of, closeness
to, or sympathy with the mining industry, who had been pressed into jury
service in the middle of summer when "the irrigated cropland of the Boise
Valley needed constant . . . attention."[29] Was there any reason to believe that
this jury was favorable to Haywood? True, it could have been worse, but the
achievement of the defense can only be regarded in this negative vein. The
suggestion that the defense achieved some miracle on *voir dire* must be discounted; in a farming community, it got a farming jury. The defense admitted
this result in a statement that was much criticized by the press. "The jurors
appear to be men of honest purposes, determined to give the defendant a fair
trial, but it is uniformly made up of a class to which none of the defendants
have ever belonged and who have no natural kinship to organizations," declared Darrow and Richardson.[30] This was regarded as needless hostility toward the jury that would sit in judgment on Haywood, and inappropriate in

view of the failure of the defense to challenge the entire panel of talesmen from which the jury had been selected.

Before the trial proper, it was reported that Richardson and Darrow were at loggerheads over whether to challenge the entire jury, the former being for doing so, the latter against. As it was, it appeared that each attorney was reveling in the mistakes of the other. Commenting upon a difficulty Richardson had faced during *voir dire,* a journalist reported: "Perhaps—we don't know—but perhaps Darrow felt just a little bit elated by Richardson's discomfiture. At any rate he didn't hand the Denver attorney any smelling salts. He just sat back in his chair and let his associate work out his own salvation if he could."[31] Then it was reported that the arrival of a militantly radical attorney from Butte, Peter Breen, "has given rise to further friction among attorneys for the defense. Mr. Darrow wants Mr. Breen entered at once as one of counsel, but Mr. Richardson objects, and there is a clash, the settlement of which is not yet in sight."[32] During the course of the trial Darrow and Richardson issued a joint statement that "at no time has there been any disagreement upon any point in the case we are now trying"; but that was so palpably false it was not taken seriously by observers, and indeed was thought to be a tacit admission that problems did exist.[33]

It would not have been surprising if Richardson and Darrow had clashed on the merits of the jury, for they intended to present completely different theories to the court on behalf of their clients. As the trial progressed, it seemed almost as if the two were appearing for different defendants, so great was the contrast between their approaches. It was a wonder that the jury felt able, at the end of the trial, to render a verdict one way or the other, for it heard three versions of the events leading to trial—the prosecution's and two from the defense.

The state's case stood or fell on Harry Orchard's testimony: he alone could link Haywood to the death of Steunenberg. Closely shielded from public view for over a year before the trial, he had met the press only once and little was known about him. When he was called as a witness for the prosecution, there was an anticipation of extraordinary drama. His appearance and manner were the first surprise: "Far from being the furtive weasel of a man that his story would lead one to expect, Orchard was well set up, bluff, with an apparently open manner," conceded Haywood. Judged by appearances, Haywood with his one eye and lopsided face was a desperado, while Orchard was a picture of respectability. Everyone knew that Orchard's testimony could hang Haywood, and as Orchard entered court the spectators awaited the face-to-face confrontation of the two enemies. Accounts differ as to who got the better of it. Haywood said Orchard never met his eyes, but the Idaho *Daily Statesman* reported entirely to the contrary:

> The eyes of Orchard and the one eye of Haywood met. For a moment Orchard's
> face flushed, but he did not remove his gaze. For several seconds the two men
> seemed to be trying to stare each other out of countenance . . . Orchard's gaze

was unflinching. It was as if he was being challenged. In a moment Haywood dropped his gaze to his lap. . . .[34]

Haywood could be convicted only if the jury believed that Orchard was a professional killer, paid by the WFM, directed particularly by Haywood. The case was a classic trial of credibility, in which the verdict depended on whether the jury decided Orchard was telling the truth. From the start Orchard impressed observers as a truthful witness. Quietly and undramatically he told his story with a wealth of convincing detail. His performance on examination-in-chief conducted by Hawley was extraordinarily persuasive.[35] He sat in the witness chair alert, well mannered, and unruffled as he told the long story of his own infamy. He had killed many men for money over the previous ten years. It almost seemed as if every explosion ever to have rocked the West in the recent past had been engineered by Orchard: at Bunker Hill and Sullivan Mill in the Coeur d'Alene, in the Cripple Creek district and at the Vindicator Mine and the Independence depot, Orchard had dynamited men and women to their death. In addition he had laid traps for judges, opponents of the WFM (including officials of other labor organizations), and two state governors, one of whom was Steunenberg. He never wavered or prevaricated even while admitting the worst of his deeds. They were recounted impersonally, resignedly, as the court listened in horrified fascination. All of this had been done, he alleged, at the behest of officials of the Federation. As Hawley drew out admission upon nightmarish admission from his witness, the newspapers ran box scores of Orchard's crimes that grew longer after each court session. With reference to the murder of ex-Governor Steunenberg, he testified that Haywood placed a high priority upon his death, and that Haywood had told him that he had already tried unsuccessfully to have Steunenberg killed.

What explanation did Orchard have for confessing? That was the million-dollar question. Orchard said he had reformed as a result of a religious conversion, and having seen the light had decided that he must confess everything. The defense suggested that he was cooperating with the prosecution to save his own skin.*

When, at the end of direct examination, Orchard was turned over to the defense for cross-examination, a strong prosecution case had been made. Naturally the crucial question was whether Orchard could be caught in contradiction, or impeached in any substantial way. Edmund Richardson conducted the cross-examination. The strategy of the defense was not known in advance and could only be guessed at. Various possibilities existed: Orchard might be shown to be totally unreliable, because of deceit or madness; his story might turn out to be fantasy, or any number of other revelations might be hoped for upon cross-examination. What happened was summarized in the *Daily Statesman*'s headlines of Sunday, June 9, and Thursday, June 13, the former of which

---

*The defense tried unsuccessfully to show that Orchard had received a definite promise of clemency for his cooperation, but its existence was consistently denied by the prosecution and was not shown.

described Richardson's efforts to discredit Orchard as ABSOLUTELY UNSUC-
CESSFUL and the latter stating simply: RICHARDSON FAILS UTTERLY. The
attack on Orchard was a miserable failure—an anticlimax that made the
prosecution look impregnable and the defense very weak. The *Statesman*
regarded Richardson's cross-examination as "disastrous to the interests of his
clients." It actually strengthened and reinforced the apparent reliability of
Orchard's testimony. Darrow afterward repudiated Richardson's methods as
foolish:

> He was a man of much force of character and full confidence in his own ability
> to accomplish whatever he set out to do. So, in a loud voice and antagonistic
> manner he re-examined Orchard for several days on every detail of his direct
> examination. Orchard remained perfectly cool and, like most witnesses, repeated
> on cross-examination the story already told. . . . As a rule, it is futile to go over
> in cross-examination the testimony already given. But although Mr. Richardson
> was an able man, he was somewhat lacking in subtlety.

But was not Darrow, as part of the defense, responsible for the methods
adopted? Had not the plan of action been sketched in advance? It ought to have
been, especially since Darrow had been delegated to make the opening statement for the accused. If Darrow's criticism of Richardson was just, it was a
reproach to the defense counsel generally that they had permitted the crucial
cross-examination of the trial to be mishandled.

When the defense's turn came, hopes were high for a damning and dramatic
exposure of the prosecution case. Large sums of money had been spent in
seeking to demolish it, but no hint had been given of the line the defense would
take, so it had the benefit of surprise. The courtroom tingled with expectation.
Newspapermen, who on the whole had been disappointed with their gleanings
from the case thus far, looked to the defense to inject something fresh into their
copy. In anticipation of a memorable show, the actress Ethel Barrymore, who
was in Boise appearing in a revival of Clyde Fitch's farce *Captain Jinks of the
Horse Marines,* attended court, a Thespian in search of drama in real life.
Rarely had an advocate stood up to face a court in such opportune circumstances. Everyone was ready to see the defense score points; after Richardson's
disappointing cross-examination of Orchard, Darrow was expected to turn the
tables so that the truth, at last, would be revealed.

Alas, the expectations of court, press, and nation were sadly disappointed.
The defense lawyers had implied that they held a trump card, which they
would play when their turn came, and win. But they were bluffing. The
thousands of dollars spent, the hundreds of hours of lawyers' time, the scores
of protests made, had not produced any evidence of substance with which to
impeach the prosecution's case. The paucity of the defense showing merely
made the prosecution case look stronger. Darrow huffed and he puffed, but to
no avail. He tried to make up for his lack of evidence by his vehemence, but
he convinced no one. His opening statement was a flop. The Idaho *Daily
Statesman* reported the scene:

"We will prove that Harry Orchard is the most monumental liar that ever lived
on earth," said Clarence S. Darrow yesterday in outlining the course of the
defense in the Haywood trial. He talked for three hours and twenty minutes but
that one sentence was the gist of what the defense's course would be. . . . It was
neither a feast of reason nor an oratorical treat. . . . It was a long and rambling
talk that Mr. Darrow made and when he got all through and said he was finished
—and the jury was glad and the spectators were glad, and the judge, too, was
probably glad—not one thing had been added to what the spectators already
knew regarding what course the defense would take.[36]

Hugh O'Neill of the Denver *Post* thought at least as badly of Darrow's performance:

When Clarence Darrow finished his address on behalf of William D. Haywood
yesterday afternoon, he had proved himself perhaps the best witness for the
prosecution who has yet lifted his voice in the courtroom. . . . He had made so
many admissions on matters that the prosecution considered vital that you began
to wonder what portion of Orchard's testimony he was going to disprove.[37]

There was much else in the same vein. No favorable view was expressed of
Darrow's speech.[38] According to Miss Barrymore, "He had all the props, an
old mother in a wheelchair and a little girl with curls draped around Haywood.
I don't know whether she was his daughter or just one of Mr. Darrow's
props."[39]

Once Darrow had embarked upon his summation, there was no holding
him. The fact that the jurors showed signs of boredom, impatience, and outright annoyance did not dissuade him from continuing for many hours. *The
New York Times* recorded the dubious benefit of his second day of summation
as a means of winning the jury:

They were tired of Darrow's talk. Perhaps they were tired of all the talk but
whether it was that they didn't want to hear any more argument at all, or only
that they had heard enough of Darrow's, they certainly took no pains to conceal
the fact that they were bored almost to the limits of endurance. They twisted
about in their chairs, looked everywhere but at the speaker, shut their eyes,
yawned, and in all sorts of ways showed how they felt. Grandfather Russell, who
has been the least fidgety and most attentive man of the twelve up to today,
suddenly found that the spring in his revolving chair would squeak if properly
encouraged, and put in the greater part of the afternoon giving it encouragement,
but Darrow kept at it regardless, and would not have quit when he did if the
Judge had not interfered.[40]

Darrow was far more concerned with saying what he believed than whether
it was falling upon sympathetic ears in the courtroom. He knew that his words
would be reported, regardless of whether people had been listening attentively
when they were spoken. He did not adjust what he said according to audience
reaction as he went along; there were no sensitive impromptu changes of
course. The fact is that at nearly all the trials in which his speeches have come
to be considered classic, the immediate audience did not sit spellbound

throughout. Of course he preferred to have an audience sit riveted in attention, but he had the tenacity necessary to all advocates to persevere undaunted if it did not. So it was in Haywood's defense. The inattentiveness of the jury during parts of what he had to say amounted to outright hostility. It is dubious in the extreme that his persuasive powers with the jurors were particularly strong, or that jury deliberations could have been influenced by a minute consideration of Darrow's arguments. Very little of what Darrow said (though parts of it were said very well) was relevant or helpful to Haywood. A juror who had sought from Darrow a reasonable and reasoned defense on the evidence would have been greatly disappointed. The best that could be said was that his summation contained a number of different, rather unconnected strands of thought, not all of which were likely to help his client. He did not persuade by logic or analysis. David Grover lists the prominent themes:

1. Orchard is a liar.
2. Hawley is crazy for believing Orchard, and is motivated by his own greed.
3. The religious issue in Orchard's confession is a spurious issue.
4. There is a capitalist plot to kill Bill Haywood and the labor movement.
5. Violence done in behalf of the cause of labor is justified.
6. Orchard's greatest crime is in revealing his family background and bringing shame to his relatives.
7. Defense witnesses are more honest looking than the state's witnesses.
8. Orchard had a personal motive to kill Steunenberg.

As Grover comments: "Obviously only two of these themes are germane to the issue of Haywood's guilt or innocence."[41] The rest of his "defense" was an exposition of a political view he had no ground for believing the jurors sympathized with, or could be persuaded of. An eyewitness present in the courtroom remembered: "Although his argument was a defense of 'Big Bill' Haywood as an official of the WFM, conversely, it was a vitriolic and violent attack on the mine owners' association, the public officials of Idaho and Colorado, and social conditions generally as to capital and labor in our United States."[42]

Was such a line of argument helpful to Haywood, on trial for his life, before a jury composed largely of farmers? Was it to the advantage of his client to pour scorn on religion before such a jury? Most observers thought not, especially because its relevance was tangential at best, Darrow's excuse for raising the issue being Orchard's professed conversion. Oscar King Davis of *The New York Times* described Darrow's attitude throughout the trial as "one prolonged sneer, not only at Orchard and his explanation, but at all religion, in general as well as particular." Davis regarded Darrow's attitude as having given William E. Borah for the prosecution an opportunity for one of his best bursts of eloquence in drawing the jury's attention to Darrow's antireligious bent.[43] And, as an added way of endearing himself and Haywood to the jury, he told them what a mug's game farming was.

Some of his themes had nothing to do directly with the guilt or innocence of the defendant and were singularly inappropriate to the case, as was demonstrated by what he said in expanding on Grover's themes six and seven. Darrow contended that it was proof of the depth of Orchard's degeneracy that he revealed he had lived under an assumed name for years, and that he was a bigamist with an illegitimate child. Apparently he considered this argument particularly meritorious, for he referred to it again in his memoirs:

> To close his testimony, Harry Orchard was asked by Mr. Hawley if the name he had used so long was his real name or an assumed one. He replied that it was not his real name, and, in answer to further questions, gave his real name, the place of his childhood, the name of his wife and his daughter, a girl then in her teens, both then living in a far-away place. It would serve no purpose to repeat the information here. In my closing address to the jury I made the most of this gratuitous statement of Orchard's to give credit to his story; I called attention to the countless men in prisons who live out their lives in blank despair and those who die on the scaffold refusing to reveal their names so that their disgrace shall not attach to fathers and mothers, wives and children and others who are left behind.

What Darrow does not recall is that he had much reduced any force this argument might have had by arguing to the jury in his opening statement that it was common for WFM men to use assumed names; that they did so because they were all "fugitives"; and indeed that "everyone" in parts of the West traveled and worked under names that were not their real ones.[44]

But quite apart from this, Darrow had failed to show what else Orchard could have done, except tell the truth on this as on other matters. He was under oath, and questions about his family would undoubtedly have been asked by the defense if they had not been asked by the prosecution. There would have been little to gain by refusing to answer, because the matter could have been put to him on cross-examination. The second argument— of an extraordinarily unscientific variety—was closely associated with theme seven of Grover's analysis: Darrow's insistence that honesty could be deduced from a man's face. He returned to this more than once in his summation, and particularly in relation to Thomas Wood, a key defense witness, of whom he said to the jury:

> . . . I think you gentlemen in your journey through the world, have learned something about human nature and somehow or other, not always, the Lord stamps on the face of a man His stamp if he is genuine, just as much as the minter puts the stamp upon the coin. . . . Now, you saw Thomas Wood. To me, Thomas Wood's face shows that he is an honest man. And I believe that when you heard the story you thought you were hearing the story of an honest man. And for anybody to say that the story should be set aside for a moment to give credit to Orchard is a thing too monstrous for me to consider or talk about.[45]

Yet there had been near unanimity among observers that facially and in total demeanor Orchard made an excellent and truthful-seeming witness. The proposition was a poor one as a generalization, and it was applicable adversely to the particular conflict of testimony to which Darrow was referring. Besides,

Darrow's client, Haywood, had a menacing and violent appearance as he sat
in court, one-eyed, defiant, and a little contemptuous. What if the jury took
Darrow's assumption about the mark of Cain and applied it to Orchard and
Haywood? To whose benefit would such an application be?

The truth was that Darrow, in this case as in others, threw discretion and
tact to the wind; he made, in one form or another, a political speech in all his
trials. There was substantial reason to doubt that he was an asset to his clients,
rather than a liability, once he had mounted his hobbyhorse. His co-counsel
could not control him, or make him conform to an agreed strategy; he simply
let rip as soon as he was on his feet, without regard to previously agreed tactics.
Prior to Haywood's trial there had been a concerted defense effort to make
Haywood, Moyer, and Pettibone seem normal, moderate, and reasonable, to
show them as men it would be unthinkable would turn to murder. But as soon
as Darrow rose to make his summation, that attempt was thrown overboard.
Instead, he made a speech justifying and even inciting violence—defiant, unapologetic, scarcely regretful, and completely incongruous with the efforts
made earlier. Even those who sympathized with labor violence, and who
admired Darrow, saw the drawbacks of having him as counsel. The bourgeois
English Marxist Henry Mayers Hyndman, who knew Darrow from the visit
some years before when Darrow and Ruby were on their honeymoon, reflected
on his Haywood defense: "A more earnest, not to say perfervid, advocate of
the men's case it would have been impossible to find, but I am bound to say
I doubted whether his industry and prudence were equal to his unquestionable
eloquence."[46] In the Haywood trial Darrow risked the necks of the defendants
in promoting the militant unionist world view. His attitude was explicit. He
told the jury:

> I want to speak to you plainly. Mr. Haywood is not my greatest concern. Other
> men have died before him, other men have been martyrs to a holy cause since
> the world began. Wherever men have looked upward and onward, forgotten their
> selfishness, struggled for humanity, worked for the poor and the weak, they have
> been sacrificed. They have been sacrificed in the prison, on the scaffold, in the
> flame. They have met their death, and he can meet his if you twelve men say he
> must.[47]

With this, and several other protestations to the same effect, Darrow proceeded
to discuss the rights and wrongs of industrial conflict in general, making
almost no reference to the facts of the case. Indeed he made astounding
admissions against the interests of Haywood, being tried as he was for a violent
crime. Speaking of labor unions, he continued:

> I don't care how many wrongs they committed, I don't care how many crimes
> these weak, rough, rugged, unlettered men who often knew no other power but
> the brute force of their strong right arm, who find themselves bound and confined
> and impaired whichever way they turn, who look up and worship the god of
> might as the only god they know—I don't care how often they fail, how many
> brutalities they are guilty of. I know their cause is just. I hope that the trouble

and the strife and the contention has been endured. Through brutality and
bloodshed and crime has come the progress of the human race.[48]

These statements were not likely to help Haywood on the facts, and it
seems that they were not authorized by the other counsel for the defense.
Richardson, who quit the defense staff immediately after the trial, complained: "Preaching socialism and trying a law case are entirely different
matters. If you don't believe it, look at Darrow's closing speech before the
jury. It was rank. It was enough to hang any man regardless of the fact of
his innocence or guilt."[49] *The New York Times* concurred: ". . . Darrow
was not making an argument upon the facts that have been presented to
the jury. He was expressing with passionate eloquence his views of certain
phases of life."[50] And yet Haywood himself, whose lawyer Darrow was
and whose life was at stake, approved the speech wholeheartedly. Quoting
the passage in which his lawyer had disclaimed him as his greatest concern, Haywood remarked, "This speech was, I think, one of Clarence Darrow's greatest."[51] As for Darrow, he regarded his performance with great
pride: "In all my experience I never had a better opportunity, and when I
had finished I felt satisfied with the effort I had made." It was, undoubtedly, a good speech, but it was not a good plea.

    Did it benefit his clients to use their cases as opportunities to expound
political and social arguments to which judge and jury were unsympathetic
and which in some cases were not espoused by the clients themselves? Did a
defendant charged with a violent crime gain from having violence in general
justified? And did the cantankerous presentation of cases by Darrow keep the
interests of his client in focus as much as the lawyer's? The use of a criminal
case for soapbox oratory did not strike all lawyers as entirely right. Some
thought that what Darrow said in court, ostensibly on behalf of his clients, was
actually said on his own behalf. It was almost never in their interests; rather,
it was a self-indulgence of Darrow's, fanciful and only superficially connected
to his client's circumstances. The risk that all Darrow's clients took was that
he would say nothing helpful to them and their case. It remains a matter of
dispute in many of his cases whether his handling helped his clients at all. His
tendency to justify violence, to denigrate religion, to preach political doctrines
not shared by the jury, to launch personal attacks on the other side's lawyers
and witnesses, were thought by some to be an unwarranted hazard for the
client and an abuse of his position as counsel.

    All this would no doubt have been the subject of bitter recrimination by the
defendants had they not been acquitted. But by some miracle, they were—
though whether because of or in spite of the efforts of their counsel it is hard
to say. Not everyone was as sanguine as Brand Whitlock about the outcome
after Darrow was done. On November 22, 1907, he wrote to Darrow: "I see
by the dispatches today that you are about through with your trial, and by the
time this letter reaches you I have no doubt you will have won another victory,
and so I send you congratulations on that victory; even if it turns out the other

way, I congratulate you, for you win if you lose. . . . How tired you must be after all your hard work."[52]

Certainly the approach of Richardson and Darrow could not have been more unlike. The greatest manifestation of the differences between Richardson and Darrow was the way in which arguments and theories were presented to the jury. Richardson tried to convince the jury and court that reasonable doubt existed in the traditional way. Darrow, on the contrary, widened the area of conflict between prosecution and defense in order to make the trial even more political than it was.

Why was Haywood acquitted? Did the jury disbelieve Orchard, or did Judge Wood's instructions persuade it that acquittal was the only proper verdict as a matter of law? There is no way, finally, of telling, but the speculations of those who attended the trial have some interest. Of Orchard's credibility, Oscar King Davis, correspondent to *The New York Times,* commented:

> I do not believe any open-minded, honest man could have listened to all the testimony in that case, as I did, without becoming convinced that the story elicited by the prosecution was the truth. The chief witness, Harry Orchard, went through an ordeal which could have been sustained only by a man who was relying solely on his memory of events in which he had taken part, and was relating them exactly as his memory brought them back to him.[53]

Privately, Judge Wood stated his belief that Haywood was guilty.[54] John MacLane concluded that Orchard "convinced the world generally by his quiet and dignified demeanor and courteous treatment of his adversaries that he had experienced a complete change of heart, a spiritual conversion, and a desire to atone for the crimes that he had committed."[55] Professor Hugo Munsterberg of Harvard tested Orchard for veracity and after the trial was over, published his conclusion in *McClure's Magazine* (October 1907) that Orchard was telling the truth. David Grover summarized his method of inquiry: "Apparently the word-association test was the key to Munsterberg's conclusion that Orchard told the truth; very short response times reportedly indicated there was no attempt at fabrication."[56] Whether Munsterberg's hypothesis—that it takes longer to formulate a lie than to tell the truth—was scientifically valid may be dubious; but his conclusion added weight to the huge amount of lay opinion of Orchard's honesty.

Orchard, reviled though he was by the defense, seemed to have made a good impression. This being so, it cannot have been the unsatisfactory nature of his testimony that made the jury acquit, but the judge's instructions. The main criticism of these instructions is not that they were erroneous, but that they overemphasized principles of law that were of benefit to the defense. Judge Wood gave a large number of versions of the well-established principle that a conviction should only be returned if the jury was convinced of guilt beyond reasonable doubt. Some observers believed that he labored the point so much that the jurors interpreted the instructions as a warning to them that reasonable doubt existed. As Davis of the *Times* put it: ". . . out of sixty-four paragraphs, as I recall it, in the charge, forty or forty-two dealt with the subject of reasonable doubt. Under those circumstances it has always seemed to me that it would have been a super-human jury that would not have said that the judge had charged it that there was a reasonable doubt in that case, and so the verdict must be not guilty."[57] Even Haywood himself, not one to give credit to the forces of reaction, realized that the instructions were to his benefit, and that Judge Wood had read verbatim a submission of the defense team which had actually been written by John Murphy, attorney to the Western Federation of Miners, and an old friend of his. The oddity of Judge Wood's position was that it was unnecessary under Idaho law for him to have instructed the jury on this matter at any great length. Only three weeks before he gave his instructions, the Supreme Court of the state had considered the appropriateness of elaborate instructions and had concluded that they were not to be encouraged.[58] Judge Wood would have been perfectly within his rights to have given a simple, one-sentence instruction that the jury must be convinced beyond reasonable doubt, and left it at that. It is possible, though unlikely, that he had not heard of the Supreme Court's decision before he instructed the jury; the Attorney General of the state argued the case on appeal, and presumably informed judges throughout the state of the decision.

Orchard spent forty-seven years in jail after his testimony in the Idaho trials was given, and never retracted what he had said, remaining consistent to the end.

After the trial was over, Darrow tried to persuade Haywood to lie low for a time, but he refused—"Darrow had been employed as a lawyer and not as a mentor." The very next day he took the train for Denver, on which he was accompanied for part of the way by Darrow. "He [Darrow] seemed peevish and sulky," Haywood wrote, "but I knew of no reason for this except my refusal to retire to the mountains as he had advised me."[59] Haywood was free of anxieties for the time being, but Darrow still had Moyer and Pettibone to worry about. Furthermore, throughout much of the Haywood case he had been troubled by a persistent ear infection. He had consulted many doctors without success and was in continuous pain. He and Ruby had developed a necessary but unpleasant ritual of injections in an attempt to combat his suffering, but it seemed to do no good. After about six months of this, a swelling suddenly appeared behind his ear. It was a freak case of mastoiditis. Luckily, Darrow was able to obtain prompt medical attention to see him through the crisis. In the light of existing medical knowledge, mastoiditis was quite likely to prove fatal, but he survived to tell the tale and in 1908 they were able at last to return to Chicago. They had been away for two years and, according to Darrow's own account, "when I reached home I not only had nothing left but was in debt." In the meantime things had gone from bad to worse in his law partnership.

21

Moving to the Left

Darrow returned from Idaho to a law practice that was disintegrating. Masters had become less and less reliable and was spending his time on literary rather than legal work. When *Reedy's Mirror* first published *Spoon River,* Masters was so grateful that almost every issue from 1909 to 1920 contained a contribution from him. It was widely believed in the firm that these contributions were produced on office time. Certainly precious little was done in the evenings, where Masters was often to be found roistering.

It was as if all Masters's initial reservations about his association with Darrow had now come into focus and he had stopped work in protest. In his suspicions of Darrow's honesty, there was also a feeling that Darrow was stepping beyond the pale in adopting extreme positions on behalf of the WFM. However prejudiced Masters may have been, there was some truth to his allegation that Darrow was not "in good odor." It was not so much anything that Darrow had done as it was a coarsening of attitude. He had turned, with experience, from moral outrage to cynicism, and had become hard. Earlier on, Lincoln Steffens had found out just how hard when he called upon Darrow in Chicago shortly after the Darrows' honeymoon. He sent in his card and Darrow came from his inner office, unsure what his visitor's claim to fame was:

> He kept coming toward me till, close up, he threw back his head, looked into my face, and exclaimed: "Oh, I know. You are the man that believes in honesty!" And he laughed, and laughed, and laughed. He took and he shook my hand, but he laughed till tears came into his eyes. And he did not invite me into his office; he did not answer my questions. They only amused him the more, and I—well, I ran away. It was a year or two before I understood what Darrow meant by my belief in honesty; all I gathered at the time was that he, too, despised me as a person prejudiced by a fool conviction of some sort and not worth a moment even of his loafing time.[1]

It was a dangerous attitude for a lawyer to have. Steffens might be absurd, naïve, or just juvenile; but to deride honesty in whatever context was hardly good for Darrow's reputation, however worldly he might be. In the course of time Steffens was to see Darrow in a situation that nearly cost him his license to practice and his reputation, where the key was the suspicion that Darrow did not hold with honesty any longer, and had left the strait and narrow. Certainly it appeared in 1907 that he was in sympathy with the extremism he had rejected in 1903.

At this time more than any other in his life Darrow seemed to be a potential revolutionary—an *enragé* to whom almost any change would be preferable to the continuation of the existing order. His speeches challenged the government's right to complain even of murder, so long as it tolerated such working conditions as were found in the mines. Like many contemporary observers the world over, Darrow found in the mining industry a dramatic illustration of the evils of capitalism. The combination of a high rate of physical injury with low wages and horrible working conditions seemed to inspire bitterness and sympathy beyond other callings. Born midway between the French and Russian revolutions, Darrow was likewise poised between them ideologically. His beliefs were more progressive than the passionate, even eccentric individualism of Rousseau (though he had much in common with Voltaire) in that he recognized the moving force behind social change to be group, not individual, interest; but he recoiled from the collectivism that submerged individuals into expendable groups. That Darrow's drift toward the left took place between 1903 and 1907 was demonstrated by his abandonment of the moderates. Whereas, in the anthracite arbitration, he had represented the UMW under John Mitchell's control before an avowedly peacemaking board, by 1907 Darrow was representing the WFM, which was to all intents and purposes a forerunner of the IWW. Like other radicals of the era such as Mother Jones, he was veering strongly toward the left in a group—the miners—that was noted for its radicalism. The WFM existed in part because the leadership of Mitchell, himself a moderate, was not sufficiently radical for the miners of the West.

The world over, it seemed that the strain of the twentieth century bursting forth from the nineteenth had brought politics to a state of near hysteria—a veritable orgy of complaint and frustration. There was, indeed, much of the excess that accompanies a *fin de siècle* about the age. Darrow's exaggerated diatribes against the rich were just as pointed as their ostentation, which his fellow Chicagoan Thorstein Veblen characterized as "conspicuous consumption." It was as if the times forced citizens to overplay their parts, becoming almost caricatures of themselves. There was a way that anarchists and socialists were supposed to be, just as there was a way that millionaires were supposed to be. Substance and pose had become, in the last years of the nineteenth century, impossible to untangle.

From the perspective of 1907 it seemed altogether possible that the future of labor was with the IWW rather than the AFL, with Haywood rather than Gompers. Both Darrow and Gompers saw this and were in consequence propelled leftward in the next three years, so that when the next incendiary case arose, Gompers himself pleaded with Darrow to enter a defense. Already Darrow was showing signs of rising to the challenge; outside court, he was adopting much of the unflinching revolutionary posture with which the IWW was associated. Easily influenced by the power of words, he became reckless in his *ex cathedra* statements, until he and Haywood seemed to be interchangeable in their views of labor. His speeches were root and branch condemnations of the status quo: law was a massive machinery for oppression—a conspiracy against the poor and guileless, a smokescreen for the plunder of the masses, a justification for social injustice.

There was a relationship between the success of the orators who had wooed so many mass meetings in the last decade and the appearance of violence on the political scene. Their success was founded, not upon dispassionate and scientific discussion of burning issues, but upon thoroughly partisan and emotional tirades. Frequently their message was violent and physical and it swayed the crowd thus. Vivid metaphors of attack, allegations of conspiracy against the public interest, aroused in unsophisticated listeners the self-righteousness and irresponsibility that Darrow himself condemned in crowds. If, finally, lawlessness was legitimized in their eyes, it was done so in part through the urgings of countless public meetings.

As Darrow became more influential and prominent, the question arose again and again among various left-wing groups: Was he with them or not? Was he genuinely committed, or was he merely sitting on the fence? The answer finally, though never given directly, was that he remained uncommitted. In the end, many of the groups with which he associated at one time or another became disillusioned with him. The doctrinaire ones, those closest to fanaticism—who took the view that one who was not with them was against them —had to conclude that he was against them. Ultimately, in his middle age, there would have been a parting of the ways even without the trauma of the McNamara case and his own bribery trials. In a time much given to ideology, Darrow was not ideological. He successfully disguised this in the short term, but in the long term the truth necessarily came out. Yet he delayed the revelation for as long as possible, in the meantime camouflaging his lack of commitment by thundering out statements of position that misled his listeners into believing he was with them. So his inflammatory oratory branded him even if his conduct did not.

There are good grounds for regarding Darrow's entry into the Haywood case as a dangerous step leftward to which his ultimate breach with labor in 1911 is directly traceable. The case raised moral issues which Darrow's precepts of political conduct had not developed far enough to rationalize. Ever since his public espousal of the labor cause in 1894, he had tended to evade moral judgments by taking refuge in a theory of the inevitability of strikes in the face of managerial intransigence and, in turn, of accompanying violence. In this determinist philosophy, there was no room for determining whether an event was right or wrong; it just happened. Yet Darrow had never decided where, if at all, he drew the line with this argument. It was perhaps acceptable to shrug off the sporadic violence that was the unplanned—though preordained—by-product of a strike; many men of goodwill, faced with the brutal economic facts of the machine age, were prepared to overlook momentary lapses into lawlessness. But what of deliberate arson and murder? Did the logic of destiny apply to these too? In the Debs case the circuit court had raised these awkward questions but had of course no means of compelling Darrow to answer them. It had suited him, politically and professionally, not to have to define his position with exactness, for to do so in whatever terms would have lost him the support of one or other of the many organizations of the left upon which his fortunes depended. But the Idaho indictments put him into a dangerous corner. The prosecution alleged that a most horrible premeditated act of revenge had been perpetrated against the ex-governor of Idaho, Steunenberg, procured and paid for by the officials of the miners' union. Was this another of those events that defied moral condemnation because it was inevitable? And if it was inevitable, why should Darrow be so exercised about the prosecution, which must surely be regarded as equally inevitable, as indeed must the verdict? Though Darrow was introduced to dialectic by Hegel rather than Marx, he faced the same dilemma as Marxist activists in explaining the need to attempt to influence the course of history if it was already set. Rather than clinging to the traditional distinction made by advocates between their pleading on behalf of clients and their private views, he had time and again repudiated that view of his duty and insisted that he believed what he said on behalf of his patrons. More by luck than skill, this stance had not caused him great embarrassment before. The labor cases that had brought him into the public eye had either involved relatively minor and unorganized disorder, or fairly moderate challenges to the law. They had never involved hired killers.

Prior to the Haywood case Darrow had last appeared in the national headlines as a labor pleader during the 1903 anthracite arbitration. Then he had presented a case that seemed to many thinking Americans to justify the claims of the miners, before a tribunal that had conciliation as its purpose, and was under the auspices of the President of the United States. His performance had earned him respect and gratitude in all but the most bigoted quarters. By contrast, 1907 saw him defending the most outrageous criminal allegations on behalf of the extreme left wing of the miners' movement, which many Americans believed capable of perpetrating almost any crime. Big Bill Haywood's one-eyed stare was equated by many with the evil eye of anarchy.

This development in Darrow's thinking did nothing to improve his relations with the moderate center of the Democratic Party. Because he had declined several opportunities to run for office since his stint in the state legislature, his influence within the party might naturally have been enhanced by the fact that he was demonstrably not an office seeker and there was no need for prospective candidates to fear him as a rival. But behind the scenes his extreme public statements caused him to lose whatever advantage he might have gained, and indeed his standing diminished as he put himself more and more out on a limb. How far this was a deliberate estrangement from the party on Darrow's part and how far an unwanted side effect is not clear; but his loss of major national importance of the kind Altgeld had wielded in 1896 may be dated to April 1908. Once more William Jennings Bryan was the Democratic favorite, and on a visit to Chicago, Bryan and Darrow were both guests at a breakfast at Edgar Lee Masters's apartment. Afterward, while driving downtown, Bryan asked Darrow if he could rely on Darrow's support. Darrow replied that he would give it only if he were promised the patronage of Illinois. Masters reported: "Bryan's jaws snapped shut, and there was a painful silence."[2] Bryan did not get Darrow's support and Darrow did not get the patronage of Illinois. His potentially powerful position in politics was slipping away.

By 1908 Masters himself was doing almost nothing in the firm, and instead apparently used firm time to write his verses. Masters's admission on this point is quite plain:

> My law partnership lasted for eight years, from 1903 to 1911, but for three years
> of this time it was a dying thing. . . . It was now that I committed the spiritual
> error of falling into indifference, and even casual attention to business. . . . Often
> I went out in the morning thinking, this is the day that I'll drop dead. I really
> expected that I should do so. . . . Altogether just now I was in a half-torpid state
> of life.[3]

The literary circle in which he and Darrow moved was a strange one. They were part-time dreamers, tied to the practical reality of earning a living and the discipline of the daily grind. What did bohemian evenings mean to a man who had to face the morning with a clear head and a businesslike mien? Finally, it seemed, dissatisfaction and impatience with the arduous routine of law practice. The unpleasantness to which Darrow returned in his practice was manifested less by open quarrels than by a strained surface politeness between the two men, while behind each other's backs there were constant complaints and accusations. No direct confrontation ever took place, and even after the partnership had been disbanded, Darrow assumed—or affected to assume—that their personal relationship remained cordial. The resentments which Masters later spilled over onto paper were not expressed openly, but smoldered beneath the surface doing untold damage to the prospects of the partnership's survival. Perhaps too by this stage, when it was manifest that Paul would not follow him into the legal profession, Darrow had become less interested in the possibility of building a dynasty that would perpetuate the Darrow name in the profession.

Paul had left college in 1904 to return to Chicago and work in the McClurg publishing firm, starting in their Chicago store. Darrow had fought valiantly to avoid imposing his wishes upon his son, but the temptation was almost irresistible. He wanted to do well by the boy, and was a doting and even indulgent father. Like his own father, he focused much hope in his offspring, trying to guide him along the path to success. It is evident that Paul felt smothered by his father's solicitude and did not wholly like the reflected notoriety that came with the Darrow name. Throughout his life he would exhibit a desire to stay out of the public eye, seemingly the exact opposite of his father. Late in life he wrote, "I don't know what I have done that would make interesting reading. . . ."[4] His reticence and unwillingness to carry the torch for his father's beliefs was a private source of regret to Darrow, though never a matter of reproach. Regretfully, he reconciled himself to the differences between himself and his son. When it became clear that Paul was not going to be a lawyer, Darrow supported his son's other activities and partially financed a number of his business ventures. Even these caused some resentment in the firm, because Darrow had solicited investments from his partners. In 1905, for example, Masters had put $5,000 into a bank in which Darrow, Masters, and Paul all had an interest; the bank folded and Masters lost his money. This was not the direct responsibility of Darrow or his son, who were likewise victims of the bank's collapse, having been too trusting of its employees, who, according to Paul, "started grafting and putting in bad loans."[5] But Masters added this business failure to the already considerable list of his grudges against his partner.*

According to Masters, Darrow's superb network of contacts as a business-getter was being wasted because the business he brought in was not properly handled: "Several years before this business had poured into our office and we could have become rich on it. But he [Darrow] neglected the most important cases; and the result was that they ceased to come to us."[6] Though this was to some extent a case of the pot calling the kettle black, there was much justice in Masters's criticism, for there were a hundred demands upon Darrow's time outside his law practice to which he often gave undue priority. He had reached a stage where his support was sought for almost every liberal cause. Even though he refused the vast majority of invitations to speak, he became heavily committed—not simply with his antiprohibition speeches, but for other causes such as the advocacy of Negro rights, as well as his literary connections. Days and weeks passed in a whirl, so that matters not dealt with instantaneously would probably not be disposed of at all. Possibly Darrow gave his time to these pursuits as a means of vindicating himself in the eyes of those who thought he should not be engaged in orthodox law practice; speaking for radical causes allowed him to show that he was not a bought mouthpiece, corrupted by corporate clients, but had maintained his independence in spite of all. There was a bravado about his publicly expressed views regarding big business that was meant as much as a reassurance to himself as an attack upon the Titans. His outspoken views on the race question served a similar function.

As Darrow knew, one of the reasons that he was unsuited to a political career was that no one who held elective office could afford—as he put it—to be "too far ahead of the crowd." It was Darrow's knack to be much ahead of the crowd on many questions. While his instinct was not unerring, he managed to leave to future generations a legacy of speeches and writings that retained their modernity for succeeding generations. In his attitudes toward various social questions such as penology and capital punishment, civil liber-

---

*Other investments proved more profitable, in particular one in a utility company in Greeley, Colorado, which Paul spent much of his adult life managing. When the Darrows, senior and junior, sold out in the twenties, the proceeds were substantial and, had it not been for the 1929 crash, would have made both "gentlemen of leisure."

ties, divorce, civic reform, prohibition and labor relations, he was startlingly
ahead of his times. Whether this gift was attributable to the incisiveness of his
analysis, his desire to shock, or his freedom from contemporary sanctimoni-
ousness, it set him apart in his own time and for posterity. In no sphere was
this more clearly demonstrated than in dealing with race.

In May 1910 Darrow addressed the second annual conference on the status
of the Negro in New York City. This conference was the forerunner of the
National Association for the Advancement of Colored People, with which
Darrow was always sympathetic. His speech drew some criticism, however, for
its advocacy of racial intermarriage. Darrow had very liberal views on this,
taking the position that everyone in America was a product of racial mixture
and that racial "purity" was a myth. ". . . I have never known any one who
was not of mixed blood," he claimed. He saw no special virtue in racial purity,
if such existed, and was quite prepared to sacrifice it. In this, as in many other
of his public utterances, he reflected the influence of those theological statesmen whom his father had loved to read. His older brother, Channing, had been
named after William E. Channing, the abolitionist minister who eighty years
before had taken the same attitude toward miscegenation:

> . . . allowing that [racial] amalgamation is to be anticipated [from the abolition
> of slavery], then, I maintain, we have no right to resist it. Then, it is not
> unnatural. If the tendencies to it are so strong, that they can only be resisted by
> a systematic degradation of a large portion of our fellow-creatures, then God
> intended it to take place, and resistance to it is opposition to his will.[7]

In substance Darrow's theme to the conference was the same as Channing's,
minus only the appeal to God's will.

The press took a less than charitable view of Darrow's performance. The
New York *Age* reported his countenancing of interracial marriage and warned
that no good would come from "agitating such a question."[8] Journalists were
right in believing that such themes were unlikely to gain favor for the Negro
cause, although Darrow had received tumultuous applause for his speech.

It was far from clear that these advanced views were shared by the wider
public or by his partners. But his partners wanted less to censure Darrow's
public statements than to get him to do his share of legal work. And if his views
on the Negro question were controversial, they did not seem to stop work from
coming to his law office, at least through political connections. When, in 1910,
the garment workers of Chicago went on strike, Professor Charles Merriam
of the University of Chicago, then a member of the City Council, introduced
a resolution passed on November 29 to attempt to settle it by arbitration. The
original plan was that a three-member panel should be appointed—one person
chosen by either side, and a third neutral. The strikers chose Darrow, and the
employers (Hart, Schaffner) chose Carl Mayer, their attorney. The third,
supposedly neutral member, was meant to be John H. Wigmore, dean of the
Northwestern School of Law, but he refused to serve. Rather than wait,
Darrow and Mayer proceeded to negotiate between the two of them, and found

they could settle most differences quite easily. By March 13, 1911, the basis for a two-year contract had been agreed, and though there were many loose ends to be tied up, the settlement was in sight. When Darrow left for Los Angeles to defend the McNamaras, his law partner William O. Thompson took his place, and he found that there was so much to be done that his position as arbitrator became to all intents and purposes a full-time one, precluding any further practice of law. This was an indication of the sorry state of Darrow, Masters & Wilson. In effect the practice was at an end.

It was Darrow's undertaking of the McNamara trial that provided the occasion for Masters's withdrawal, though it was symptomatic of a dissatisfaction that had grown up long before. It seems likely that there was a restlessness, jealousy, and even paranoia in Masters by this time. He described the autumn of 1910 as "one of the hardest periods of my life, if not the hardest of all," and said he was tired of his partnership with Darrow. Yet the reason for his unhappiness was only partly professional—he was also having matrimonial and other family difficulties (his brother-in-law, a quack doctor, had been in trouble with the law, and his mistress had just left him and he was "utterly lonely").

When Masters heard of Darrow's intention to depart for Los Angeles to defend the McNamaras, it seemed like yet another round in the Haywood case. He suspected that the partners who stayed behind would be left in the lurch. Consequently he used Darrow's announcement as an occasion to announce his own departure from the firm. He refused to run the office while Darrow was away in the West; he did not believe that Darrow should take the case in preference to that of Chicago clients.

In assessing the fairness and accuracy of what Masters says, it should be said that there was much prejudice in his view of the law practice he was part of. At the time he broke with Darrow, he himself had not pulled his weight in the firm for three years. He broke with him only to go into practice under a different banner. And he had come to look upon his situation from a twisted perspective. "I had been in the Ashland Block for eighteen years," he said, "and I wanted to go to a finer building where the tenants were a better class of lawyers."[9] The truth was that he had been in the Ashland Building long before he joined forces with Clarence Darrow, and it was in that building that he had come to know Altgeld. Throughout the relevant period all the judges of the first district of the Illinois Appellate Court had their offices in the Ashland Block, as did the clerk of the court; court was held in the building. There was no ground for Masters's disparagement of the address of choice and convenience of a fair proportion of the Chicago bar. Nevertheless the partnership was bound to founder in view of the acrimony that developed. In 1911 Francis S. Wilson left to become the county attorney for Cook County and the partnership became defunct. Henceforth Darrow's professional associations would be smaller and less formal, leaving no room for any doubt that he was boss. Seeing that Darrow, Masters & Wilson would not survive his absence in California to defend the McNamara brothers against charges of murder, he arranged with another attorney, Jacob L. Bailey, that while he was away his Chicago affairs should be funneled through a new firm, which in theory though not reality would be Darrow's.

The collapse of Darrow, Masters & Wilson was a major event in his professional career. Yet it would be wrong to explain it simply by the personal dissensions of the partners, for it reflected also a more general change in the nature of law practice to which Darrow could not or would not adjust. Darrow's fame was built upon his courtroom performances, but the trial lawyer was being eclipsed in his importance and moneymaking potential by the "office" lawyer. Darrow attracted office work, then refused to bother with it himself, with the result that clients turned elsewhere. Darrow's conception of himself as the kingpin of a law firm was rapidly becoming anachronistic. This love of the limelight ensured that he was doomed in his efforts to keep a large firm under his control so long as his conception of practice harkened back to an earlier age.

Once more, Darrow was to venture far from home in the defense of labor. But this was to be the most dangerous sortie of all, destined not only to destroy his law practice but also to cause a crisis of reputation for the labor movement and him personally. Both had staked their good names on the case. Both were to lose.

22

The McNamara Case

At one o'clock in the morning of October 1, 1910, the downtown plant of the Los Angeles *Times* was rocked by an explosion so great that many Angelenos, roused from their beds, thought it was an earthquake. Since the *Times,* owned by Harrison Gray Otis, was rabidly anti-union, it was immediately suspected that the explosion was caused by unionists. In spite of the disaster, the *Times* managed to put out an edition on October 1 with a banner headline—UNION-IST BOMBS WRECK THE TIMES—that left no doubt of General Otis's opinion as to where responsibility lay. The explosion was dynamite politically as well as in fact. Labor relations with employers were particularly strained in California, a state echoing with the old American ideal of independence, which was still as yet ununionized and somewhat unsympathetic to the labor movement. The bombing—if it was such—was evidence that anarchy had reached America as a political method. The dead and injured numbered nearly fifty, for the paper's full night staff were in the building preparing the morning edition for the presses.

It was indicative of the distrust that existed between capital and labor at that time how quickly the tragedy became distorted by political considerations. Much more culpable than the legitimate suspicions of General Otis (based, as they were, upon the immediate conclusion of the Los Angeles police department that the case was one of arson)[1] was the completely unfounded response of labor leaders, notably Eugene Debs. In the socialist periodical *Appeal to Reason* he denied complicity of any workingman in the explosion and instead, taking it to be another instance of the technique of Nero, who secretly burned Rome and then accused the Christians of the deed in order to discredit them, accused Otis and his businessmen-friends of being "themselves the instigators, if not the actual perpetrators" of the crime. The piece had a hysterical tone that belied the journal's title. As Debs's sympathetic biographer Ray Ginger noted: "This was a clear charge, with no available proof, that General Otis had prior knowledge of the dynamiting."[2] It was typical of Debs that he would make such a statement without any evidence; he did not and could not know for sure that labor men were not involved, nor had he any basis for accusing Otis of setting the dynamite in his own building. It was pure rhetoric, fanning the flames of hatred. Debs was a man of integrity, in the sense that he always believed what he said, but he was so blinded by prejudice that the truth had become irrelevant to him; there was a higher truth in his mind. Life had become a perpetual crusade against Evil Capital on behalf of Virtuous Labor. His inability to doubt that he was right led him frequently into arrogance and error. He was blind to sin in the labor movement, blind to virtue in managers. He must have known that labor was not guiltless—this was not the first time that lawlessness had touched the labor movement; the Haywood case had been tried only four years before.

Nevertheless the fact remained that Debs had lent his huge prestige among laboring men to the view that labor was innocent. From that point on, it was impossible to achieve any fair-mindedness on the part of the public. The insistence by Debs and many others that the labor movement was not involved had its counterpart on the management side. The county of Los Angeles retained the services of Earl Rogers, a well-known criminal lawyer, to investigate the bombing and to prepare a case for presentment to the grand jury if the culprits were tracked down. Rogers was not a man normally to be found on the prosecution side, being, like Darrow, much more comfortable in the role of defender; but his office was only a short distance from the *Times* plant and he had been working there at 1:00 A.M. when the explosion occurred. He had rushed to the scene and seen the suffering of those trapped inside. Harvey Elder, the night editor who was killed in the blaze, was a friend of his. He felt he had to take the position of special prosecutor. He did it effectively and it was his investigation that led, in April 1911, to the arrest of the perpetrators James B. McNamara and Ortie McManigal in Detroit, and two weeks later of John J. McNamara, James's brother. By this time union members had heard for six months the repeated denials of complicity by their leaders, and the arrests came as a great shock, especially because J. J. McNamara was a union official. At once union financial backing of the McNamara defense was pledged, and there were protests that the brothers were innocent. In the labor movement and in Los Angeles politics, their guilt or innocence became, not a matter of proof but of faith. The technique of four years before, when in response to President Roosevelt's statement on the Haywood trial, the labor leaders had worn buttons declaring I AM AN UNDESIRABLE CITIZEN, was adapted to the new circumstances. Thousands of lapel buttons were distributed with the legend: THE MCNAMARAS ARE INNOCENT, and the socialist candidate for mayor, Job Harriman, adopted the statement as his campaign slogan. Harriman was one of the McNamaras' defense team, and his adoption of the slogan was to cost him victory in the election. It was in this atmosphere that Darrow arrived in Los Angeles in April 1911 to head the defense team.

He had not wanted to take the case. It was, in many material aspects, likely to be a replay of the Haywood case of four years before. Darrow's partnership with Francis Wilson and Edgar Lee Masters had been wrecked by his taking on the McNamara defense which would inevitably mean he would be away from Chicago for many months. Besides, Masters was not wholly wrong to accuse him of being out of shape for a battle royal of the kind that the McNamara case promised to be. Masters warned him that he was rusty on the law and that he was not equipped to try a case in California where the rules of practice were not familiar to him. Initially Darrow was swayed by these considerations and, feeling he was not up to the battles he foresaw in Los Angeles, suggested that a younger man be found to fight them. His reluctance to take a case with potential for unpleasant conflict had been building within him since the Haywood trial; now the prospect of fighting an unpopular cause made his heart weary.

Strong pressure was put on him. The request that he should conduct the defense had come from the president of the International Association of Bridge and Iron Workers, Frank Ryan. The case was being financed by the American Federation of Labor and Samuel Gompers personally came to see Darrow to persuade him to act on the McNamaras' behalf. Gompers was not only in favor of labor solidarity, but a foe of capital punishment, who recognized the likely sentence the brothers would draw if found guilty. There was the prospect of a large fee, which was especially appealing in the light of the foreseeable end of Darrow, Masters & Wilson.[3] Lastly, it was a case bound to focus national attention on Darrow once more, which he found alluring; if he did not seize the chance of further fame, it would go to some other lawyer. As it was, rumor had it that he had not been labor's first choice as a defense lawyer and that there were others below Darrow on the list who were eager to take the responsibility.[4] Therefore, although he had initially given Ruby a promise that he would not accept the case, he asked her to release him from it, which she did. It was the most momentous decision of his life, for it was to be the bitterest culmination of the courtroom conflicts of capital and labor to take place prior to World War I—and would almost topple the AFL and Darrow personally at one fell swoop.

Taking the McNamara defense was dangerous to Darrow because it would give the authorities one more chance to test how far his inflammatory viewpoint was matched by reckless conduct. Was he inside or outside the system? Did he believe the ends justified the means? Emotionally Darrow often spoke as if he was prepared to step outside the bounds of propriety to aid the laboring man, but that was impossible while he remained a lawyer who ostensibly "played by the rules." He had prevaricated time and again on the crucial question of how far he would go. The key to his career between 1903 and 1911 must be found in his inability to come down firmly on one side or the other. He was torn between the two possible stances open to him; there was a mercurial element in him that made him a revolutionary one moment and a democratic radical the next. It was this same characteristic that led Lincoln Steffens to describe Darrow as a hero at three and a coward at three fifteen. When it came down to it, Darrow was ruled by the fancy of the moment, not by any rigorous intellectual discipline. He was superb at trotting out addresses that inspired the incendiary and the democrat alike. As time went on, this tactic became a deliberate ploy to marshal disparate groups behind him; he became a master fence-sitter.

There was besides the burden of experience, which had hardened and coarsened him. In his early years, though he had never been free of vanity and ambition, idealism had been a predominant feature of his character. By 1911 that was no longer true. The conditions of practice had sapped his idealism and strengthened his guile. Darrow was getting to the stage where he could not be shocked—even by himself. And now that he was so well established, no one gainsaid him. There was no restraining hand. Darrow, it was thought, could take care of himself.

But could he? Acting on behalf of clients with whom he sympathized politically, and whose cause he believed in, he had lost the fundamental professional quality of objectivity. In his ardent desire that a political persuasion should be vindicated, he had all too often ignored or suppressed the unpleasant particulars of a case in favor of bringing out its supposed political implications. His intensely partisan perspective had taken hold so much that, no matter what his clients had done, he would not condemn them, publicly or privately, but was carried away into dangerous rhetorical fantasies that none of their actions could be as infamous as the wrongs perpetrated by the boss class. Ever since the Debs case, labor had expected him to carry the workingman's standard high, regardless of how sordid or wicked had been the deeds of his immediate clients. He was not paid to place a steadying hand upon them; and on the rare occasions when he attempted to do so, as in the case of Big Bill Haywood, he had been rebuffed: "Darrow had been employed as a lawyer and not as a mentor." In consequence his advocacy went further and further, and in each successive case he felt the combined weight of the previous ones, so that he must rise to ever greater heights of denunciation and accusation. By 1911 it was Darrow as much as his clients who needed a steadying hand as he became more reckless, too sure of himself, and strove at more and more risk for his effects.

In principle, there was no ambiguity about Darrow's acceptance of violence in pursuit of political ends; this dated from well before the McNamara trials. At the base of much that he said was the premise that lawbreaking, threatening, and even murder, were an excusable response to severe social injustice. This aspect of Darrow's thought had first been brought to the attention of the public by his stand in the anthracite coal strike arbitration. Darrow himself tried to put it into fictional terms only two years later in an unhappily contrived novel *An Eye for An Eye* (1905), which, as a perceptive critic observed, showed "how willing to exonerate every law-breaker Darrow was."[5]

Darrow was prepared to countenance violence not only between management and labor, but between worker and worker if need be—the scab, he felt, deserved whatever he got. When he wrote an introduction to the autobiography of Mother Jones, who had many times been to jail for her pro-labor activity, he said of her philosophy:

the purpose was the moving force, and the means of accomplishing the end did
not matter. . . . To her there was but one side. Right and wrong were forever
distinct. The type is common to all great movements. It is essentially the difference between the man of action and the philosopher. Both are useful. No one
can decide the relative merits of the two.[6]

That was a summary of Darrow's attitude to all who violated the law in
vindication of a deeply held principle. He could not decide—he merely accepted.

It was not merely Darrow's words which demonstrated his condonation of
violence, or at least his acceptance that it would happen. Hutchins Hapgood,
who knew him well, perceived a powerful emotional tendency in that direction
too: ". . . there is no doubt that he has this strong, deep, emotional feeling,
which is implicit in what may be called the soul or heart of the labor movement, and which has sometimes, as in the case of the deeper forces behind the
McNamaras, resulted in crimes."[7]

The difficulty of the McNamara case was that it tempted him to go too far
in practice along the route that he seemed to approve in principle and emotion.
Had he passed up the chance to go to Los Angeles, disaster would not have
struck and temptation would not have stared him in the face. But for all the
temptations, the flaw was finally within himself. He allowed himself to go to
ever greater lengths as an advocate. For all his reluctance, once he accepted
a case, he fought with no holds barred; no sign of his initial disinclination to
enter it showed in the way he did battle. On the contrary, he shouldered an
added responsibility, for by taking such cases only with a great show of
reluctance, he further secured an absolute hold over his clients that allowed
him to be in complete command of strategy.

Darrow's instinct not to enter the McNamara case, had it been heeded,
would have saved the labor movement from one of its worst humiliations and
himself from his greatest personal catastrophe. But it was not to be. On May
21, 1911, Gompers confirmed in writing Darrow's appointment as chief counsel and authorized him to hire assistants. In underwriting the defense, the AFL
was making a commitment of money that it did not have, and from the start
the financial position was shaky. It was not until June 11 that the members
of the executive council discussed the financial burden. When they did so, the
decision was made to meet it by asking all chartered national and international
unions within the Federation for a contribution of at least 25 cents per member. If there was total compliance with the minimum—and the AFL had no
power to enforce its request—the Federation would raise $440,000.[8] But this,
though a very large sum, was less than Darrow anticipated would be needed
if the case dragged on. He told a conference of labor leaders in Indianapolis
on June 29 that the absolute minimum he needed was $350,000, a sum near
to the practical limits of the AFL's capacity. That would not itself have been
a problem if the money had come in quickly, but it did not. By October 11,
relations between the AFL and Darrow were already strained because of the

financial situation and he wrote to O. A. Tveitmoe, a San Francisco labor leader, saying bitterly:

> I am going to have assurance of the money that I need or finish up Jim's case without putting any more money into it and then quit the farce. I am simply not going to kill myself with this case and then worry over money and not know what to do. . . . I only wish some of the fellows had my job and had to raise money. Up to February 1st, 350,000 will be needed; we have but 170,000. The case may run two years longer. Jim's probably until April 1st. I could hurry except that the longer it takes the sooner the other side will get tired. After February 1st it will need at least 20,000 a month—if it can't be done for God's sake let me know, so I can fix my plans. If it can be done do it. But if it isn't made definite and quick I am going to assume that it won't come in any considerable amount and will curtail in every direction.[9]

The difficulty of raising funds was acute. Unions had not in 1910 accumulated bloated pension funds, waiting to be plundered at the whim of their top officers, and honest Samuel Gompers had no means of laying his hands on the money needed except by asking the membership for voluntary contributions. This was embarrassing, unreliable, and above all slow. Darrow was proposing to spend on the defense five hundred times as much as the average AFL member earned in a year.

When he took the case, it is extremely doubtful that Darrow could have had any idea whether his new clients were guilty or not. He had not talked to them, or been out to Los Angeles, or contacted the prosecution. The disposition of all pro-labor forces was to believe them entirely innocent; Samuel Gompers, of the AFL, would not have given his support to the McNamaras if he had thought for a moment that they were guilty, as he afterward admitted. Darrow, on the other hand, was experienced enough as a lawyer to realize that they might be guilty, and he knew that whether they were or not, the prosecution meant to convict them. He did not start out for Los Angeles sharing the same presumption of innocence as Gompers did:

> Before I left Chicago I knew nothing about the facts. There were many rumors of dynamiting, and many others to the effect that the explosion was due to gas. The task for the lawyers of the defense was to see that the defendants were not condemned except on clear proof of guilt, and, if guilty at all, to get as small a penalty as possible—especially to save the lives of those on trial.

He did not like to know the truth about what his clients had done—it took some of the fire out of his advocacy of their cause. He denied that he knew that the brothers were guilty from the beginning: "I did not know. I have practiced law for many a year. I do not go to a client and say, 'Are you guilty, are you innocent?' "[10] Even had he done so, it is unlikely that the McNamaras would have responded honestly. His predicament was that labor pinned too much faith upon his entry into the case; they expected miracles from him that he could not perform. *The New York Times* identified the high hopes that

Darrow had brought with him: "The unions expect Mr. Darrow, if employed as counsel, to prove the innocence of the union man [J. J. McNamara] as he did for Moyer, Pettibone and Haywood of the Western Federation of Miners, when tried for the murder of Governor Steunenberg of Idaho."[11] Already doubts about the way he had conducted the Haywood case had been suppressed in the light of its happy outcome. Edmund Richardson, who might have voiced some misgivings about the merits of Darrow's performance in Boise, was silenced by an automobile accident less than two weeks after the appearance of the *Times* story. Rank-and-file unionists never doubted that the McNamara verdict was safe with Darrow and he did nothing to discourage their confidence.

Darrow was keen to enlist the services of his friend Brand Whitlock in the defense of the McNamaras and had already proposed that Whitlock join him in May 1911. But Whitlock was by now inextricably enmeshed in state politics and therefore declined the invitation on the ground that it would require him to resign the mayoralty of Toledo, "which I have more desire than right to do."[12] Once out in Los Angeles, Darrow renewed his invitation by lettergram on November 13, at which time Whitlock was in the throes of another mayoralty campaign. Had he been defeated, he would almost certainly have joined Darrow, but he was reelected, and wrote on November 20 saying it was impossible that he should travel to the West Coast: "What fun it would be aside from all the rest! But I don't have much fun any more and can't have, I suppose, as long as I am in this place and in politics, which is like swimming in a mother of dead dogs."[13]

When he arrived in Los Angeles, it did not take Darrow long to realize that the situation was bleak. Ortie McManigal, arrested with the McNamaras, had turned state's evidence with a detailed confession that implicated the McNamaras not only in the bombing of the Times Building, but in the bombing of the Llewellyn Iron Works in the county. McManigal occupied a position in the McNamara case very similar to that of Harry Orchard in the Haywood case, and *The New York Times* was quite right in explaining the unionist hope that the prosecution would be confounded in the McNamaras' instance just as it had been in Boise. But this time there was a salient difference in the government's reliance on one who turned state's evidence. In Los Angeles, the prosecution had documentary corroboration of nearly every point made by McManigal in his confession. It would be impossible for the defense to discredit him. The revelations made by McManigal were just as blood-chilling as Orchard's, so much so that "it was so fantastic that he was at first regarded [by the prosecution] as a highly accomplished liar."[14] But gradually the prosecution changed its mind. McManigal's story, insofar as it could be checked, seemed to be absolutely accurate. When he told District Attorney Fredericks that nearly all the major orders to sabotage and murder had been in writing, and that documentary evidence was preserved in the vaults of the Iron Workers' Union in Indianapolis, the prosecution realized that it had a watertight case if only the documents could be obtained.

There were two ways in which the documents might be seized: by cooperation from the state of Indiana or the federal government. Neither seemed likely to be forthcoming, since union influence over both governments would prevent it. With great care, the prosecution made a personal approach to President Taft to obtain federal cooperation, and Taft agreed to get it. A couple of days after this, on October 12, 1911, federal authorities seized the records of the Iron ☻ Workers' Union, and the prosecution case was complete. The results of the federal seizure were made available to the Los Angeles prosecutor. It did not take long for the defense to realize that the game was up. The documents made it completely impossible to discredit McManigal as a liar. His confession given before the documents were seized tallied exactly with the documentary evidence.

There were detailed checks on the authenticity of McManigal's confession by the staff of investigators Darrow had put together, but they found nothing suspect about it. Darrow weighed the information brought to him by his staff, and knew it boded ill for his clients. Exasperated, he told James McNamara, "My God, you left a trail behind you a mile wide!"—a sign that he knew perfectly well that the McNamaras were guilty as charged and of a great deal more besides.[15] Of course, guilt-in-fact was something that did not worry an experienced defense attorney like Darrow. The question before him professionally was whether the prosecution would be capable of obtaining a conviction. He started on the assumption that he would go to trial contesting the McNamaras' guilt, if not proclaiming their innocence. The brothers had given assurances to labor leaders who had spoken to them since their arrest, including Samuel Gompers, that they were innocent of the charges against them. So Darrow mounted a massive defense operation, taking a large suite in the Higgins Building in downtown Los Angeles, hiring an army of investigators, and even having a scale model of the Times Building made so that it could be used as demonstrative evidence at trial. He took every possible precaution in the interests of his clients. Realizing that public sentiment in Los Angeles was against the political extremes with which the brothers were associated, he did his best to prevent inflammatory radicalism from prejudicing their chances of acquittal. Remembering how he had kept Debs out of Boise during the Haywood trial so that the possibility of guilt by association was minimized, Darrow repeated his strategy by asking Big Bill Haywood to cancel a planned lecture tour through California that would coincide with the anticipated date of the trial. Haywood agreed, going to Canada instead.

Darrow planned to suggest in court that the tragic explosion had been caused, not by dynamite, but by a faulty gas main and was therefore not arson at all. This theory was from the first indefensible in the light of the investigations of the fire marshals. It had been put forward by a number of people sympathetic to labor, but the fire department knew at once that the ignition had been by dynamite. Furthermore there had been no rupture of the gas lines. Very quickly, therefore, Darrow modified his theory to read that, though dynamite was used, it was only a small charge, which could not have been expected to have caused the holocaust, was set only to damage the building, not to take life, and had started a fire and devastated the building only by accident. He later wrote in his autobiography:

> *The Times* Building was not blown up; it was burned down by a fire started by an explosion of dynamite, which was put in the alley that led to the building. ... Unfortunately, the dynamite was deposited near some barrels standing in the alley that happened to contain ink, which was immediately converted into vapor by the explosion, and was scattered through the building, carrying the fire in every direction.

Darrow concocted this explanation in order to help his clients, but it was unconvincing, as he must well have known. First, the distinction made between the initial explosion and the fire afterward was entirely artificial because dynamiting is often followed by fire. Second, J. B. McNamara had not placed a small amount of dynamite next to the building, designed to scare; he placed sixteen sticks of it. Third, it was not true that the alleyway next to the plant just "happened" to contain barrels of ink; its name was Ink Alley and it was part of the plant itself—not a public right of way—where ink was regularly stored.

By the time Darrow adopted this theory, he was morally sure of his clients' guilt, for it conceded the fact that the dynamite had been placed by the accused men. The evidence was overwhelming, and many of those interested realized that the McNamaras were liars. The truth was so patent that Lincoln Steffens proposed to cover the trial for the New York *Globe* (and another syndicate) on the assumption "that organized labor has committed the dynamiting and other crimes charged against it." This procedure was approved by Darrow and by the McNamaras, and the intention was to persuade the readership that the behavior of employers had driven laboring men to it.[16] At this point Darrow had come to the conclusion that it was hopeless to expect an acquittal if the case went to trial. His investigations had shown that the McManigal confession was true and his clients' protestations of innocence were false. Public sentiment in Los Angeles was much aroused against the bombings and the likelihood was that any jury which the McNamaras faced would be a "hanging jury." Darrow had had several interviews with his clients, and he found that his initially favorable impression had changed, particularly about James, the younger of the brothers: ". . . we could not put the younger brother on the stand, for he would not be able to sustain himself on cross-examination, even should he attempt to deny the evidence of the State." Thus it was that Darrow started secret negotiations to obtain a bargain from the prosecution in exchange for a plea of guilty. Darrow's major concern, as ever, was to save his clients from the noose—and if he could not save both, to save one.

Editorially *The New York Times* took Darrow to task over his negotiations with the prosecution regarding sentence. Darrow had said that his primary concern was to save both his clients' lives. But Judge Bordwell (who accepted the pleas of guilty) made a public statement that the defense had proposed that if John was allowed to go free, the defense would acquiesce in James confessing and being hanged. The *Times* called for "a further explanation from Mr. Darrow," and suggested that "there will be keen impatience to hear how Mr. Darrow harmonizes" his own statement and Judge Bordwell's.[17] The strain of the case came to be so great that Darrow was only capable of working on it intermittently. Most of the time he seemed desperate. E. W. Scripps, the newspaper magnate, who saw him during the latter part of the ordeal, concluded: "Darrow is in no state of mind to try that case. He is beaten by it."[18]

And well he might be. He knew that if the prosecution once started presenting its case, the Iron Workers Union documents would come out, discrediting the union movement totally. Orders to commit arson and murder would be printed in all the newspapers, identified as union documents. No amount of cross-examination and vituperation of McManigal could hide those. His position was an exceptionally difficult one. The financing of the defense came from unions and workingmen who believed honestly, though misguidedly, in the innocence of the defendants. A mayoral campaign was at that time being waged in which one of his co-counsel was a candidate who was running on the platform of the McNamaras' innocence. And, last but not least, if he pleaded the brothers guilty, his reputation with labor would suffer considerably. In fact he was in precisely the position he had dreaded when first approached to undertake the case. His primary duty was to his clients, but they were not his paymasters. If he had asked the AFL leaders whether they approved of a plan to plead the brothers guilty, they would have surely said no—their conduct afterward demonstrated that. After all, union financing of the defense was in essence an exercise in propaganda. The McNamaras were unimportant and unprepossessing unionists. The purpose of the defense fund was to vindicate labor, not to uncover its excesses. Darrow therefore stood alone in making the decision, but make it he did, and negotiations with the prosecution commenced.

The exact circumstances in which arrangements for settlement of the case were made are not known for certain. Lincoln Steffens made large claims for the credit in the arrangements, but they have been discounted by most commentators on the events.*[19] It seems that preliminary contact with the prosecution was made through an intermediary, Otto F. Brant, general manager of the Title Insurance and Trust Company, and that the McNamaras' plea of guilty was consummated by agreement between LeCompte Davis, a member of the defense team, and district attorney John D. Fredericks.[20] The first proposition made by the defense was that in exchange for J.B.'s plea of guilty to murder, all other indictments against both brothers would be dropped. The district attorney refused this offer of compromise, saying that J.J. must also plead guilty. After protracted dickering, the arrangement was made that J.B. would

---

*Max Eastman described Steffens as "a sprightly and rather self-pleased cork bobbing about on currents of which it had no understanding and upon which it had no effect."—Eastman 1948, pp. 430–431.

plead guilty and take a life sentence, and J.J. would plead guilty to dynamiting and take ten years' imprisonment.[21] The district attorney did not, of course, have the power to bind the judge in any offer of compromise, and later the judge before whom the pleas were entered refused to accept J.J.'s plea in exchange for ten years, saying it was not enough in view of the heinousness of his crime. Instead, fifteen years was imposed.

Professionally, Darrow was lucky that the McNamara brothers, whether out of loyalty to each other or political solidarity, did not challenge his right to barter their respective fates simultaneously. As soon as plea bargaining started, there was a necessary conflict of interest between the two brothers, and in the event J.J. achieved a much less favorable disposition than had originally been sought. Darrow had hoped to avoid his conviction entirely and had only reluctantly accepted an offer of a ten-year sentence for him. Later J.J. was actually sentenced to fifteen. Both the prosecutor's office and Darrow as chief defense counsel treated the two brothers as rightly bartered as a pair, with the inherent danger that one's interest would be sacrificed to the other. If anyone had a complaint on these grounds, it was J.J., who for reasons of magnanimity or naïveté did not raise one. But his case considered individually might be regarded as serving fifteen years in order to save his brother from execution. He might have done this willingly. Certainly he was under no duty to do so, and had he been represented by separate counsel, it is quite possible that the matter would have become an additional issue in an already difficult case.

All this was entirely unknown to anyone except the defendants themselves, the defense attorneys, the district attorney, and a few trusted confidants. The huge majority of union members, who had contributed from their hard-earned wages to provide for the McNamaras' defense, expected a glorious courtroom fight that would totally absolve them from blame and reflect glory on labor. At worst, the capitalist-dominated courts might convict the men, but—as all true unionists would know—unjustly. It was unthinkable and unthought of that the McNamaras should plead guilty. The crime of which they stood accused was a vicious one, without support among the mass of decent people. America had been told they were innocent by Debs, Gompers, and Mitchell, and America had believed.

The price of such belief was the possibility of betrayal. Darrow knew that —and that pleading the McNamaras guilty would be the end of his career as a labor lawyer, just as surely as pardoning the Haymarket anarchists had been the end of Altgeld's political career. On the other hand, the record shows that he attempted to bring the officials of the AFL into his confidence when he foresaw the possibility of a guilty plea. On November 23 he wired Gompers asking for a high union official to be sent to Los Angeles forthwith, but the request was ignored. So he was forced to act without having first softened the blow. He telegrammed Gompers on the day of the guilty plea: "There was no avoiding step taken today. When I see you I know you will be satisfied that all of us have done everything we had to to accomplish the best. Hope you will believe we realize our responsibility and did the best that could be done."[22]

On December 1, 1911, Darrow went into court to plead his clients guilty, knowing that the masses would turn on him as soon as the news spread. It was one of the worst days of his life and he never forgot it: ". . . if perchance I allow myself to slip back the bolt, with which all mortals seek to lock away some of the sad and unpleasant memories of the past, at once my mind goes straight to the courtroom in Los Angeles on the evening of the plea of 'Guilty.' "[23]

When the defendants were taken into the courtroom, the more acute newspaper men realized that something special was about to happen, for trial had only been set for J.B. McNamara, yet both brothers were there. But none of them expected the guilty pleas, which caused first a stunned silence in the courtroom and then pandemonium. Darrow delegated the unpleasant business of changing the pleas to LeCompte Davis, who actually made the dramatic statement:

> Your honor . . . we have concluded to withdraw the plea of not guilty, and have the defendant [J. B. McNamara] enter in this case a plea of guilty. A like course we intended to pursue with reference to J. J. McNamara.[24]

Indictments 6939 and 6944 were disposed of. Sentencing was set for December 5, and court adjourned. The journalists besieged the defendants and their counsel for explanations, were told that "the prosecution had it on us," then scrambled to broadcast the news to the world. Darrow had not changed the plea in court, but it made no difference to the attitude he faced outside the courthouse; everyone knew he was the chief counsel and that the decision must have been made with his approval. He was cursed and threatening gestures were made against him as he left the court, but he refused the chance to avoid the crowds and leave by a back entrance. Was not this confirmation of what he had always known about the fickleness of public sentiment? It was not pleasant, but he determined to face the crowd's vituperation as he had faced its cheers. If the hisses of the crowd had been his only worry at this time, he would have been lucky. But more, much more trouble was brewing.

He had arranged, in the circumstances, a desirable end to the McNamara cases. He had saved J.B. from hanging and had persuaded the prosecution to accept a statement from him that was presented on the day of sentence and read:

> On the night of September 30, 1910, at 5:45 P.M. I placed in Ink Alley, a portion of the Times Building, a suit case containing sixteen sticks of 80 per cent dynamite, set to explode at 1 o'clock in the morning. I did not intend to take the life of anyone. I sincerely regret that these unfortunate men lost their lives, and if giving of my life could bring them back I would freely give it.[25]

It is a wonder that the prosecution accepted this statement denying an intention to take human life, for if J.B. did not intend to take human life, he certainly acted as if he did. He knew that people would be in the building at 1:00 A.M., the time he set the dynamite to explode; he had himself been a pressman and was acquainted with the normal hours of a morning paper like the *Times*. Furthermore, as the statement itself demonstrated (aside from the substantial amount of evidence amassed by the prosecution), the crime was one of callous premeditation. J.B. was prepared to kill; he was full of hatred, as he admitted himself. When he was asked by Darrow why he had done it, he replied, "There was a labor parade. The police beat up some of the boys. The next morning the *Times* praised those cops for their heroic work. It was more than I could stand."[26] His emotions provided him with a justification for putting the lives of *Times* workers in jeopardy and he had acted in wanton disregard of their safety, which in fact and law was a murderous state of mind. Quite apart from this, J.B. had killed in the course of arson and California law treated death inflicted in such circumstances as murder under the so-called felony murder rule.

There were thus two approaches to the case open to the district attorney which could result in J.B.'s conviction for murder without proof that he intended to kill. Darrow maintained that "none of the perpetrators of this deed was ever morally guilty of murder,"[27] but most Angelenos believed that a man who dymamited an occupied building was guilty of murder if the occupants died. McNamara claimed: "I sincerely regret that these unfortunate men lost their lives, and if giving of my life could bring them back I would freely give it," and perhaps it was true at the time of his statement, over a year after the dynamiting. But how much had he regretted it at the time? He set the charge at 5:45 P.M. to go off at 1:00 A.M. the next day. Did he take care to check at 10:00 P.M., or 11:00 P.M., or midnight that no one was liable to be hurt? Did he make an anonymous call to the building shortly before the explosion to warn people out? The *Times,* being a busy newspaper, had its telephones manned throughout the night. Did he, immediately upon apprehension by Earl Rogers's agents, show contrition?

The answer was that he did none of these things. On the contrary he smoothly lied to everyone—friends, well-wishers, counsel—saying he had no complicity in the crime at all. He was prepared for the *Times* employees to be sacrificed for the cause. After the McNamara guilty pleas had been taken, most unionists repudiated the brothers. A notable exception was Big Bill Haywood, who was prepared to shed blood, to kill, injure, or maim in the cause and who made a resounding statement endorsing the McNamaras' actions.

The last words of the confession statement were undoubtedly pure Darrow —he was later to use the same formula in 1924, when he defended Leopold and Loeb. It may be doubted that he served his clients' interests very well by putting such words of feigned remorse into their mouths, for they compounded rather than mitigated the crime by their insincerity. They were met with scorn by Judge Bordwell in court. In passing sentence, he remarked: "There is very little or no ray of comfort, Mr. McNamara, in the assertion by you that you did not intend to destroy life. The widows and orphans and the bereaved parents will look upon that statement at this time as a mockery." William J. Burns, who had done much of the detective work upon which the prosecution was based, made an even more pointed response to McNamara's claim: "Why don't Jim McNamara tell how he knocked off the gas cocks and flooded with gas the place where the suitcase filled with dynamite was put?" he asked.[28]

The reaction of organized labor to the McNamaras' guilty pleas was—with the exception of Haywood's frank endorsement—to abandon the brothers, to repudiate their methods, and to turn upon them. No longer were they labor heroes, loyal unionists, or symbols of the workingman's struggle. They were as vermin. Throughout the land leaders of unions denounced the McNamaras, professed deep shock, declared the peaceful intentions of workingmen, and disapproved loudly of violence and anarchy. The propaganda sheets of the left —not least *Appeal to Reason*— had spent months building up the McNamaras as symbols of the American workman. Now they turned tail and set about discrediting the two men. The machine went into reverse gear at full power; it was newspeak in action. It was abundantly clear that Debs's previous allegations were false in all material respects, yet he never admitted error. Instead, he sought to deny the McNamaras' association with the labor movement— though J.J. was secretary-treasurer of the International Association of Bridge and Structural Workers—by the absurd excuse that they were Catholics, not socialists. Debs and the others had all changed their tune, without acknowledging the change: yesterday's truth was not today's, and today's might be obsolete tomorrow. The workingman's credulity was to be severely tested.

While many labor leaders were undoubtedly shocked to hear of the guilty pleas, it was inconceivable that they were unaware that there were violent groups within the ranks of labor. There was scarcely a local in the nation at which violence had not been discussed as a means of achieving union purposes. And in some cities the most active unionists were those who scorned peaceful methods. Everywhere there were men willing to kill and burn to achieve revolution. There were union officials (like J. B. McNamara) who would break the law without compunction to further the labor cause, and this was well known among all those who took an interest in politics. Most union leaders genuinely abhorred violence, but it was impossible that they did not realize their leadership was being challenged by men who justified it. Within a year, on October 1, 1912, a trial was begun in Indianapolis against fifty union officials and members for illegal transportation of dynamite, which demonstrated that a national network of unionist dynamiters had been formed; thirty-nine of the fifty were found guilty, including Frank Ryan, president of the Bridge and Iron Workers Union, who had suggested Darrow's name for the defense of the McNamaras in the first place and who received seven years imprisonment. As it was, in the last dozen years many major unions had suffered power struggles within their own organizations between groups that advocated peaceful means of achieving labor's ends and groups that supported violence. Every union leader knew this, and it was cant for them to act as if violence had never crossed any laboring man's mind. This was the age of dynamite, an era in which (in the United States and elsewhere) the use of dynamite to achieve political ends was approved by many. Admittedly the McNamara cases were among the first in which the undercurrent of violence had surfaced. As Adela Rogers St. Johns put it, the McNamara case "was evidence that anarchy, as a method, had crept into the ranks of organized labor, however much labor repudiated them. . . . This could be the beginning of terrorism, it must be checked before it got a foothold."[29] A man who, in 1911, did not know this was either too stupid or too artless to have become a union leader.

Nevertheless union leaders professed shock and horror and many blamed Darrow. Was this what he had been paid for? He had been hired as a miracle worker to get the McNamaras off, yet he had pleaded them guilty. Darrow suffered the wrath of many for his action. The unions had insisted that the McNamaras were innocent on blind faith, and therein lay the seeds of the ugly situation that developed. Just as Job Harriman had run as socialist candidate for the mayor of Los Angeles on the campaign slogan: THE McNAMARAS ARE INNOCENT, so the unions supported their defense upon that supposition. The scheme had been fraught with danger if the McNamaras turned out not to be innocent. Darrow, as head of the defense team, had not objected to Harriman's politicization of his clients' case; indeed he condoned it and possibly encouraged it. When he fell foul of it, he could not complain.

Almost alone in this storm of condemnation, Louis Brandeis gave public support to Darrow. He wrote to the Boston *Globe* on December 2:

> the unions as well as the public are to be congratulated on the wise and coura-
> geous action of Clarence S. Darrow in inducing his clients, the McNamaras, to
> plead guilty. Unionism and the able, honest, law-abiding labor leaders would
> undoubtedly have suffered greatly from the prejudice created against unionism
> by a continued contest which must have resulted in a verdict of guilty.[30]

It was a well-meant effort to conciliate and tame the passions of all sides, but it failed.

The bitterness engendered by the McNamara case took years to dispel. Samuel Gompers ceased all communication with the brothers as soon as they had pleaded guilty. Job Harriman had been ruined politically. As a result of a press vendetta that had its origins in the McNamara case, Joseph Scott, one of the attorneys who was a member of the defense team, sued the Times-Mirror Company for malicious libel in a litigation which dragged on until it reached the Supreme Court of California in October 1919, where judgment for Scott of $67,500 (including $30,000 in punitive damages) was affirmed.

Much was made then and later of the sudden abandonment of Darrow by labor and its leaders. As Gertrude Barnum was to lament: "It is the old story. The masses ever deserting their leaders; with petty criticisms excusing their base ingratitude."[31] But some serious misapprehensions of the position of labor's leaders have resulted, in particular regarding Samuel Gompers. It has repeatedly been suggested that Gompers refused to communicate with Darrow after the guilty plea or even acknowledge his existence. Stone wrote of Gompers's attitude: "So outraged was he that in his autobiography, *Seventy Years of Life and Labor,* he completely omitted mention of labor's greatest legal defender, in spite of Darrow's monumental work for the American Federation of Labor."[32] The statement is false in fact and spirit. Gompers's autobiography refers to Darrow by name three times, twice in the context of the McNamara trials. Further, when Darrow requested financial aid from the AFL to pay for his own defense on the charges of jury bribery which were preferred against him in the wake of the McNamara convictions, Gompers replied civilly and sympathetically:

> Believing, aye, almost firmly convinced of the innocence of the McNamaras, we strained every nerve to raise as near as possible the amount of money you suggested would be necessary for their defense. Upon learning that they were guilty, the first intimation of which was conveyed to the rank and file as well as the officers of the labor movement through their confession, I am free to say to you that in my judgment any general appeal for funds to defend you or the men under indictment would fall upon deaf ears and elicit little if any response at this time. If I had the means or the control of means, I should be glad to place it at the disposal of you and the other men, but I have none.[33]

Gompers's letter marked the end of Darrow's reign as labor's legal darling. The movement to which he had given his best since 1894 no longer wanted him. It was not that he had deserted the cause—though in the long term, his ardor for unionism would cool—but that the cause had deserted him. Now he faced the loneliness of adversity and the shock of abandonment. In a matter of weeks, what might have been his greatest triumph had turned into his greatest disaster; from being the leader of a powerful legal team defending against one of the most sensational prosecutions ever to have been brought, he had been reduced to a clientless, moneyless, and seemingly futureless suspected jury briber. He did not need to read Gompers's letter a second time to recognize the truth: he had been ditched.

23

"Pretty Near Done"

When Darrow reluctantly accepted Gompers's invitation to defend the McNamaras, he knew that the fight would be a tough one. The prosecution had public sentiment and business capital behind it. Los Angeles was a "scab-town"—one in which unionism scarcely had a foothold—where the chances of obtaining a jury sympathetic to labor were rather small. It was for this reason that Darrow had demanded, as a condition of taking the case, a large fund for expenses. Knowing that long, hard work was ahead, he took with him to the West Coast John Harrington, an ex-investigator for the Chicago City Railway who had been fired for insubordination, and whom Darrow had known from the days when he had been engaged in railroad law himself. He looked upon Harrington as a friend; he and his daughter lived with the Darrows in the home they set up in Los Angeles for the duration of the McNamara trial. Harrington acted as manager and coordinator of the nonlegal staff of the defense team, and Darrow trusted him. Mrs. Darrow's brother, Burt Hamerstrom, was also recruited onto the team, but neither Harrington nor Hamerstrom were local men, and what the defense really needed was people familiar with the local conditions in Los Angeles. Detective work relies heavily upon informers, and upon an intimate knowledge of local personalities, which neither Harrington nor Hamerstrom had. Shortly after setting up headquarters in the Higgins Building, therefore, they hired two local detectives, along with a host of assistants, for the purpose of providing local liaison: Bert Franklin, once a member of the U.S. Marshal's office, and Captain Tyrrell, late of the Los Angeles district attorney's staff. Both Harrington and Tyrrell were eclipsed quite rapidly by Bert Franklin, whose competence commended itself to Darrow. Soon Franklin was in charge of investigations.

As mentioned, the prosecution had a strong case before Darrow arrived on the scene. It had the detailed confession from McManigal, implicating the McNamaras in startling and accurate detail, but even so it was taking no chances. Darrow's reputation was as a fighter, who had a record of success behind him in winning acquittals against all odds. He came from a city known for the immorality of its legal and civic life. In view of this, both sides were from the first prepared to use unscrupulous means to win. They spied on each other and placed informers in each others' offices; they read each others' telegrams, passed to them by paid collaborators in the telegraph office; they planted recording devices in offices and hotel rooms; they tried to buy off the opposition's witnesses. It was, as Lincoln Steffens remarked, a dirty business.[1]

At an early stage, Darrow directed Bert Franklin to investigate every man on the jury list from which the McNamara jury would be selected, to find out his political, religious, and other beliefs so that when the case came to jury selection, the defense could object to any prospective jurors known to be antagonistic to the McNamaras or labor interests. This practice was perfectly legal, though hugely expensive. No ordinary defendants could have afforded such a luxury, but with union money behind them, no expense was spared to do everything that might aid the labor champions the McNamaras were thought to be. Franklin went about his task efficiently, providing Darrow with useful background information about many of the jury prospects. He was apparently entirely in Darrow's confidence.

Then, on November 28, 1911, on Third Street near its intersection with Los Angeles, Bert Franklin was apprehended for the attempted bribery of a prospective juror, George Lockwood, which had taken place only minutes before Franklin's agent, White, was caught redhanded. Neither White nor Franklin denied the charges. The amount of the bribe was $4,000. Just as the two men were about to be arrested, Clarence Darrow had run across the road toward them, obviously in a great state of excitement, waving his hat. He arrived, panting, and they were led away as Darrow, still catching his breath, watched. Three days later the McNamaras were pleaded guilty; two months later Franklin pleaded guilty to attempted bribery and was fined the exact amount of the bribe; and three months after that Darrow was indicted for suborning bribery. The question was: What was he doing at Third and Los Angeles on that November morning and how much did he know? It was a golden opportunity for the office of the Los Angeles district attorney to discredit Darrow, and with him his supporters.

Embarrassing as the incident was, it was one of many problems facing Darrow at the time, and not the most urgent. Negotiations for pleading the McNamaras guilty in return for leniency were already under way. As things turned out, only four days afterward the guilty pleas were entered. This was later to become a matter of controversy, for the suspicion arose that Darrow had finally agreed to the deal by which the brothers pleaded guilty in order to save his own skin. Darrow claimed he had not, but many parties who were privy to the full story thought otherwise. Judge Bordwell, who accepted the pleas and pronounced sentence on the McNamaras, issued a statement suggesting that the bribery arrest was the catalyst of the defense's willingness to reach agreement. On December 5, the day he sentenced them, Judge Bordwell said: "As to the defense, the public can rely on it that the developments last week as to bribery and attempted bribery of jurors were the efficient causes of the change of pleas which suddenly brought these cases to an end."[2]

The description of the bribery revelations as the efficient cause of the pleas

may be accurate, but it does not follow that Darrow authorized them because
of any personal fear that he might be in trouble. But Judge Bordwell's imputation was unmistakable: Clarence Darrow had put his private interest above his
clients' and sold them down the river in an attempt to save his own skin. In
this, as in some other aspects of the case, Lincoln Steffens's account is quite
different from Judge Bordwell's. Steffens claimed that the charge against Darrow had no substance, and that Darrow had refused the opportunity to have
it included in the settlement of the McNamara prosecution with the words:
"Tell the prosecution to leave my case out of the settlement. They can have
me—to try, if they'll let these prisoners off." And Steffens goes on:

> This may have been an expression of his assurance that he could not be convicted,
> but as a lawyer he knew that a criminal case is not a matter of fact, but of
> evidence. Innocent or guilty, he might be convicted and sent to prison; and
> Darrow would die in a prison cell. He was determined, however. He gave me
> his orders, and I did leave his case out of the settlement. And Fredericks rejoiced;
> he said that it was all the compensation he desired for giving up the trials of the
> McNamaras, to have the chance to "get" Darrow.[3]

The prosecution, cheated by the McNamaras' guilty pleas of the chance to try
them, fell back on the next best thing, which was to try their chief defense
counsel. If the prosecution had adopted an argument that the defendants had
no respect for law whatever, and would lie, cheat, steal, bribe, and kill to
achieve their ends, the defense could have been further discredited by Franklin's arrest.

Had the McNamara case been neatly ended by the sentencing of the brothers
on December 5, Darrow's sojourn in Los Angeles would have been relatively
short. Darrow chose to regard his own trials for bribery as part and parcel of
the McNamara case. But the unions that had financed the original McNamara
defense took a different view and felt no responsibility to contribute to Darrow's own defense. His position was suddenly changed in a most unenviable
way. He no longer had the financial support of the unions, yet the prosecutor
continued to be as well provided as he had always been, and had the accumulated evidence from the McNamara trials at his disposal. Whatever the
rights and wrongs of the case, it was clear that Darrow could not compete with
the district attorney's expenditures. Indeed he was from the first short of
money, and very little was spent upon preparing his defense by way of investigation. Yet he bore the burden not merely of defending himself, but of having
many elements germane to the McNamara case dragged out to reflect adversely on him.

Now that he needed help, Darrow reaped what he had sown over many
years of practice. So often when he had sallied forth to debunk, to scoff, to
denounce and revile his opponents' ideas, he had aroused deep dislike. He had
tried to apply Shakespeare's admonition to lawyers to fight as enemies but eat
and drink as friends with only limited success—his personality was too strong,
his tongue too hurtful for him not to have offended many. He had never fully

acknowledged the extent of the enmity his public pronouncements aroused. Now that he was down, there were precious few who came forward to rescue him. The bosses, of course, relished his fall from grace. But even the interests he had at one time or another served were not about to rush to his aid; the unions did not, and no more did the socialists after what he had done to Job Harriman's campaign for the mayoralty of Los Angeles. Even many of the literati sided with Edgar Lee Masters rather than him. Thus most of his natural allies were alienated from him. Instead, he was left with the aid of a few individuals who were unmoved by the passions of group interest and the hysteria of the moment. When his true friends had to stand up and be counted, they were few enough and there were many disappointments.

The result was that a severe financial strain was put upon him, which meant in turn that there were hard feelings amongst the lawyers retained to defend Darrow. He knew that Franklin's plea of guilty meant trouble and was determined that (though he had not yet been indicted) he would stay in Los Angeles. He feared that if he returned to Chicago, it would be said he had fled the jurisdiction and the California prosecutor would institute extradition proceedings against him in Illinois, so he and Ruby took an apartment in Los Angeles for $50 a month and waited for the worst. This was a sensible economy forced upon them by the expectation that they would have to stay in Los Angeles, but it also reflected another uncomfortable fact. At some point Harrington had been "turned" by the prosecution, so that he spent a large portion of his time trying to trap his employer. With the aid of the district attorney's office, a Dictograph was hidden behind a bureau in his room where he and Darrow often talked, so that Darrow's words would be recorded, in the hope that he would incriminate himself. Brand Whitlock witheringly described "the apotheosis of the Puritan ideal" as having "a Dictograph in every bedroom and closet,"[4] and Darrow later waxed eloquent on the matter before the jury. Anticipating future legal controversies, he argued: "Wouldn't it be better that every rogue and rascal in the world should go unpunished than to say that detectives could put a Dictograph into your parlor, in your dining room, in your bedroom, and destroy that privacy which alone makes life worth living?"[5] Harrington had impeached Darrow while still living under his roof, though he and his daughter moved out after Harrington had given a statement to the district attorney that Darrow had solicited him to perform bribery during the course of the McNamara trial. Darrow later complained: "A man sleeping in your house, eating at your table with yourself and your wife, and betraying you! Is there any crime more heinous than that?"[6] Yet it was Darrow who had trusted him, brought him out from Chicago, and chosen to put him in charge of his office. Harrington's accusations were more damaging in one respect than those of Franklin because Harrington had been known to Darrow for years, whereas Franklin was only recruited locally.

In late January 1912 the indictment was presented and Darrow gave himself up and posted bail. Then he knew for sure that he needed a lawyer, though even before the prosecution had formally begun, he had been taking steps to ensure that he would be well represented. His choice was the very man who, as special prosecutor, had indicted the McNamaras: Earl Rogers. Darrow retained him after having made a trip to Hanford, California, to see Rogers appear in court, where he was litigating a will case. What he saw impressed him, and that very night Darrow consulted Rogers about acting on his behalf. Rogers, who admired Darrow greatly, was tickled pink and initially relations were cordial. But there were four serious obstacles to things remaining that way during Darrow's protracted first trial. First, although Darrow himself wanted Rogers's services, Ruby did not; she thought him theatrical and lacking in substance. Second, Rogers had a drinking problem, which would cause him to be absent without notice at crucial times in the case on secret binges. Third, no clear agreement was reached between Darrow and Rogers about how far, if at all, Darrow should participate in the legal work of his own defense. And fourth, no understanding was reached between the two men about Rogers's fees and expenses—what they should be, who should pay them, and when. As the trial progressed, money would become a constant source of friction.

None of these things boded well. Darrow watched his own case like a hawk and, as a sick doctor makes a truculent patient, so he made a difficult client. He thought he knew better than Rogers. "I . . . looked after every detail myself," he claimed. This conviction was by no means vindicated by subsequent events; Rogers was an extremely able lawyer, though his style was different from Darrow's, and contributed much to the first trial.

The initial necessity was to develop a plausible and consistent theory of the case, which the defense could argue to the jury—a basic responsibility of any defense counsel who expects to go to trial. Alas, at this initial stage a proper resolution was never made, though preparation to meet the prosecution went on apace. Darrow wanted to argue, first, that he had been framed and that his prosecution was all part of a cruel vendetta against labor; that the prosecution was out to "get" Darrow because he was sympathetic with the labor cause and to maul him in the public gaze. This argument had some attractions, especially because Darrow was at the time full of self-pity and could expound it convincingly. Its fatal defect was that there was abundant evidence of defense misconduct; the central fact of bribery could not be denied, and by itself this argument would not carry the day. Second, Darrow wanted to justify the McNamaras' position as part of his own defense, to suggest, as it were, that the defense should be forgiven because it did what it did for an honorable cause. This would have been disastrous and Rogers tried to talk him out of it. Third, Darrow was convinced that Franklin and Harrington could not possibly be believed against him, and that the evidence was too flimsy to stand up in court. In this he made a sad mistake, and Rogers told him so: "It's not as simple as that. You hired Franklin as your chief investigator, as they can prove; you trusted him with vital matters over a long period. His reputation here as a United States marshal was good. He'll be a competent, cagey, cold, careful, tough witness."[7] Last, Rogers wanted the defense theme to be the lack of proof connecting Darrow with Franklin's actions, or even showing knowledge of them, and the inherent unlikelihood of Darrow appearing at Third and Los Angeles while the bribery was in progress if he was implicated in it. The defense would hammer home the point: A guilty man would have stayed away.

It was this last theory which was by far the strongest, and which Rogers used as the basis of his defense of Darrow. The only evidence the prosecution could muster of Darrow's involvement with bribery was Franklin's and Harrington's word—and they were, by their own admission, accomplices to the crime of which Darrow was accused. As such, their testimony needed corroboration. It was probably this, above all, that led to Darrow's acquittal on his first trial. The presiding judge, Judge George H. Hutton, gave the jury a very strong direction on the necessity for corroborative evidence linking Darrow to the bribes. On the other hand, it was undisputed that the bribe had been $4,000, and that the money had to come from somewhere. Franklin himself clearly did not provide it. It was also rather difficult to believe that Franklin would have initiated the bribery himself, without direction or at least acquiescence by his boss.

The impending prosecutions dazed Darrow and put him into a deep depression, so that he was incapable of acting in his best interests. The case hurt. Darrow took it very hard, and it counted as the single most painful experience of his life. He suffered the more because he lacked the support of close friends near at hand. Lincoln Steffens later wrote to Brand Whitlock, "Poor Darrow. He had missed you. But it is all right now."[8] He felt sorry for himself, and with reason. He had been drawn into the case unwillingly and now that he was in trouble, many of his friends had deserted him. Financially, he was crippled. His name was mud; he had disillusioned labor by pleading his clients guilty, and now was widely thought to be crooked.

The enforced sojourn in Los Angeles between the end of the McNamara case and the beginning of his own gave Darrow much opportunity to ponder his position. Even his tenacious spirit was not equal to this crisis and he fell into the lassitude of extreme adversity. He was fifty-five, had made his own way, built his own reputation, but now all that he had built up over the years seemed to have been shattered. Then, too, he was becoming generally less sympathetic to the labor movement. The Haywood case had left him with substantial doubts about some of the men involved, though he never questioned the justness of their cause. He was unable to believe in Debsian simplicities, or that all virtue was in the laboring poor. If this was a Holy War, which was the massacre of the innocents: the employers paying their workers a wage insufficient to live on, or the anarchists blowing up buildings? When Darrow had first moved to Chicago, an anarchist bombing of the Haymarket had been the focus of attention. It appeared that labor politics and violence were inseparable; arson had been a constant preoccupation of his throughout his career as a labor lawyer. He wanted no more part of it, though much of his professional energy had been devoted to defending it. But what else was there for him? He was ill-prepared to start a new career. Darrow became convinced that he was finished.

It was an irony of fate that disgrace and humiliation should be the watershed between his two careers at the bar, and that his "comeback" would be bigger and better than anything that had gone before. But Darrow had no crystal ball; he saw nothing good to come and had constantly to be shaken out of the lethargy of depression. In those weeks he traveled all the sad highways and byways of self-pity. Psychologically it was but a short step from his strong sympathy with the underdog to an even stronger sympathy with himself as underdog. He saw his career and savings being sacrificed to the Los Angeles district attorney's office. He took to drink, was fretful and ill-tempered, and lost his powers of concentration. Had not his idol, Altgeld, died a broken man after the public turned against him? Like him, he felt the urge to crawl out of sight to nurse his wounds in private.

At this point an ex-client of Darrow's, whose conviction for murder he had managed to get reversed two years before in Chicago, appeared with an offer to kill Franklin, the chief witness for the prosecution. The means was to be dynamite. The McNamaras had wished to further the socialist cause with it: why should not labor's champion be saved from the penitentiary by the same means? So reasoned George Bissett, gambler, burglar, professed socialist, and bum, who appeared in Darrow's office shortly before his first trial. "It was one of a long series of days when I was very sad . . . ," wrote Darrow.

> All along through my life I have had many warm demonstrations of friendship, but this was the first time any man had offered to kill someone for me. . . . I had known all sorts of men. I had so often found the good and the bad hopelessly mixed in almost all the people that I knew; I wondered if any human being really could pass judgment on another.

Tactfully, Darrow declined the offer and persuaded Bissett to leave Los Angeles by the next train.

Rogers, valiantly trying to defend his famous client, saw that Darrow's despair was bound to rub off in court and give the impression of guilt. He reprimanded Darrow, cajoled him into action, tried to bolster him, but with limited success. When the trial opened, Darrow was not the man he once had been. The Los Angeles *Herald* reported that "his voice appeared to have lost its resonancy and piercing caliber, and his manner . . . was considerably different from that shown during the McNamara case. His arrest upon the bribery charge appeared to have left its indelible imprint upon him."[9] Darrow's demeanor in court was to be a point of violent disagreement between him and his counsel before the end of the trial.

For all his torpor, Darrow had nevertheless enlisted aid from back east. Before the indictment he had not wished to visit Chicago for fear that he would be regarded as fleeing California, and once indicted he was prohibited from doing so as a condition of his bail. But he wrote to Lincoln Steffens and Edgar Lee Masters for help. It is an indication of how low his reputation had fallen that both men thought him guilty of bribery. Steffens disguised the conclusion he had reached when he wrote his autobiography, explaining: "I went out there to testify that the settlement had been agreed to before the date of the alleged act and that Darrow knew it; there was no motive for jury-fixing."[10] Not only was this statement inconsistent with his claim that Darrow had the opportunity to have his case "settled" along with the McNamaras, but it is quite different from what Steffens said privately while the drama was actually being played out. On June 25, 1912, Steffens wrote to his wife:

> . . . I do feel that when that fight is on [with one's soul] there is a call, not for an umpire, but a friend. That's why I'm here with Darrow. He is scared; the cynic is humbled, the man that laughed, sees and is frightened, not at prison bars, but at his own soul. Well, then, what do I care if he is guilty as hell; what if his friends and attorneys turn away ashamed of him and of the soul of Man,—Good God, I'll look with him, and if it's any comfort, I'll show him my soul, as black as his; not so naked, but—Sometimes all we humans have is a friend, somebody to represent God in the world.[11]

Darrow had written on February 27 asking Steffens to testify on his behalf. It turned out to be unnecessary, as the prosecution subpoenaed Steffens on May 17.

Steffens was not the only loyal friend. Fremont Older, managing editor of the San Francisco *Call-Bulletin,* proposed to Darrow that he should join a cooperative community of intellectuals Older was to set up north of San Francisco, and like Steffens he testified at the bribery trial. The invitation came as a refreshing confirmation that some remained true.*

Of Masters, Darrow had a different request. He wanted him to collect testimonials to his honesty from all those who knew him in Chicago. Masters resented having the task imposed upon him. He was far from an admirer of Darrow's, believed him to be untrustworthy, and thought it "obtuse" of Darrow to write to him as if they were still friends. Nevertheless Masters did what was asked of him, and many judges, lawyers, and politicians attested to their belief that Darrow was honest.[12] What could such documents prove? At best, that he had friends in his home town who would rally round when he was in a mess. But they knew nothing about the facts underlying the indictments; they did not contradict the prosecution's clear proof that the defense team of which Darrow was the head had been engaged in bribery, or the evidence that Darrow had been on the scene just after money had changed hands. The common reasoning was that Darrow was the big city lawyer come to bamboozle a small town—for Los Angeles was still tiny by comparison with Chicago. And the reputation of Chicago was notoriously unsavory, its politics and law practice alike thought to be corrupt.

There was some justification for the suspicion Darrow faced. He was being brought in for a large fee to confound a Los Angeles court, and it was a fair

---

*Although Darrow had always been attracted to the romantic Tolstoyan notion of rural cooperation and self-sufficiency, he never seriously considered joining Older's Los Gatos venture.

assumption that he would fight hard. It was true that he had been associated for nine years with a lawyer who had been convicted of jury bribery and that his reputation was, whether justly or not, suspect in the minds of many Chicagoans. Many wondered whether a lawyer practicing in the city of magnificent sin could attain prominence without a bit of sin himself. A current story told of an Illinois judge who was asked about the success of a lawyer who had been in practice in the state for five years. The judge said the young man was doing well, though he admitted he knew nothing of his work. "You seem to think he is doing well and yet you know nothing about his practice or business. What do you mean?" he was asked. "I mean just this," replied the judge, "that any man who practices law in Illinois five years and keeps out of the penitentiary is doing well whether he has a practice or not."[13]

When Rogers had first considered Darrow's case, he had put forward the argument that Darrow had acted in a manner that showed foolishness, but not guilt. Darrow's story was that he had received an anonymous telephone call in his office at the Higgins Building telling him to go down to Third and Los Angeles quickly if he wished to help Bert Franklin keep out of trouble. This call had propelled him helter-skelter toward the scene of the crime. Rogers questioned Darrow on this, taking into account his own repeated statements that the prosecutor wanted to "get" him:

"If you were the man they were after, didn't it occur to you that your presence might put you in the frame-up?"

"Not at the time," replied Darrow. "If I hurried I might prevent it. I never think of myself in a crisis."[14]

Rogers saw that it was not enough to defend his client by saying, "He is of good reputation, and therefore it is impossible he would stoop to bribery." There were too many dangers to such a course. It invited the prosecution to bring evidence that there were those who thought poorly of Darrow. Not all the people in Chicago who were invited to attest to his good character did so. (Judge Kenesaw Mountain Landis for one refused.) Now that Darrow was in trouble, there were many who reveled in his discomfiture. He had exercised the power, in politics and professionally, of raising people up and smiting people down, and enough men in Chicago had suffered at his hands for an undercurrent of hostility to emerge at the bar. Darrow, it was said, was about to get his come-uppance.

All told, there was much that a determined investigation could uncover in Chicago which would neutralize any favorable effect to be expected from the testimonials to Darrow's honesty.[15] Rogers saw the grave dangers of precipitating a courtroom battle on the subject of Darrow's trustworthiness. Rather, he wanted to argue that Darrow would have covered his tracks better if he had meant to commit bribery, and would not have made so many blundering elementary mistakes. This line of approach, sensible as it was in not putting Darrow's character in issue, galled Darrow. But Rogers refused to change tactics. He saw that, on the evidence, the jury might plausibly believe that Darrow was a knave, but not that he was a fool. Realizing this, he wanted to play upon the jury's predisposition to thinking Darrow was intelligent while distracting them from the question whether they believed him morally capable of the crime charged. "We must insist that if you, Clarence Darrow, had taken to crime you would have been as good as Caesar, Borgia or Moriarty. You couldn't have left such a trail."[16] Darrow only grudgingly accepted this strategem.

When trial began on May 5, 1912, the defense made an outward show of unity but many knotty problems had not been resolved. The knottiest was the defendant's attitude to the proceedings, and his alternating moods of listlessness and hyperkinetic paranoia. His moodiness was well known even at the best of times, but in adversity his oscillations robbed him of all stability. "When people ask me what sort of man Darrow is," Lincoln Steffens was to say, "I ask them the apparently irrelative question: When. And my answer is that at three o'clock he is a hero for courage, nerve, and calm judgment, but at 3.15 he may be a coward for fear, collapse, and panicky mentality."[17] Too often, Rogers had to battle his 3:15 moods, which had to be dealt with as they arose, and it was surprising that more harm was not done to Darrow's case than actually occurred. Rogers, Darrow, and Ruby walked into court trying, with some success, to look brave and confident. It did not last long. Ruby dissolved in tears almost as soon as she sat down. Darrow had to be prompted by his counsel to stand in order to hear the charge read against him.

It had been agreed that Darrow would conduct the selection of jurors. Although this was regarded by many lawyers as his particular forte, there was nothing distinguished about his technique on this occasion; he seemed but a shadow of his former self. A full jury was chosen by May 24, after many objections from both prosecution and defense. Then the district attorney, Captain Fredericks, made his opening address to the jury. He was pulling no punches. He pictured Darrow as crooked, hypocritical, cynical, and treacherous, making as violent attack upon his integrity as imaginable. It was a prosecution with a vengeance, which startled Darrow, who complained of it bitterly:

> I think I can say that no one in my native town would have made to any jury any such statement as was made of me by the district attorney in opening this case. I will venture to say he could not afterward have found a companion except among detectives and crooks and sneaks in the city where I live if he had dared to open his mouth in the infamous way that he did in this case.[18]

But Fredericks's speech merely put in strong terms the case for the prosecution: Darrow was accused of corrupting justice, and Fredericks said Darrow was corrupt. The prosecution reflected the revulsion of many people from the dirty business which had been engaged in during the preparation of the McNamara cases. Fredericks's sentiments were shared by many, including some of Darrow's erstwhile friends.

The indictment on which Darrow was being tried was for the attempted bribery of George Lockwood, former policeman and jailer. It was for this man that the scene at Third and Los Angeles had been enacted. Franklin, who knew

Lockwood personally, had visited him at his ranch in Covina in the third week in October, and informed him that his name was on the roll of prospective jurors in the McNamara case, which Lockwood did not know. Franklin then offered him a total of $4,000 to vote for McNamara's acquittal in the event that his name was drawn, $500 to be paid as cash in advance, the balance after the verdict had been returned.[19] Lockwood told Franklin he would think it over. After Franklin left him, Lockwood went to the district attorney and revealed the bribery offer. The district attorney told him to act as if he accepted the deal, keeping the office informed, with the idea of catching the defense team in the act of passing the money—in which aim he was entirely successful.

On Saturday, November 25, George Lockwood's name was drawn for jury service and Franklin again went to see Lockwood. He arranged that Captain White, a mutual friend of Franklin and Lockwood, would act as depository of the money owed to Lockwood in the event that a verdict of acquittal or a disagreement was returned. The next day final arrangements were made for the transfer of money. Franklin asked Lockwood on the phone whether he ought to bring the "big fellow" along, and Lockwood said yes. Lockwood understood that phrase to refer to Darrow, but Franklin testified that he meant Captain White. This was plausible, since Captain White had been Lockwood's boss at one time. When Franklin turned up at Lockwood's home without Darrow, the misunderstanding was discovered. Franklin explained that he had meant Captain White and had intended to bring him, but White had not been able to come.[20]

Arrangements were then made for handing over the money next morning in downtown Los Angeles. Franklin would meet Captain White at the corner of Third and Main at 8:45 A.M. and give him $4,000 in cash, $500 of which he would turn over to Lockwood at Third and Los Angeles at 9:00 A.M. Lockwood reported these plans back to the district attorney, so that the next morning Third Street was infested by plainclothes policemen waiting to make an arrest. After the transaction between Franklin and White was completed, White, under the surveillance of Franklin and, had he but known it, about twenty policemen, met Lockwood. There was a misunderstanding about the amount of money to be handed over, but that was resolved. Then followed a complaint from Lockwood that the $500 advance should not be paid in one bill; he wanted smaller, less conspicuous denominations. Next Lockwood dropped the bill. Franklin came out of the bar from which he was watching and joined the two men. They exchanged a few words before walking down Third Street. It was then that they saw Darrow coming toward them, and it was as he drew close to them that Franklin was arrested by Captain Sam Browne of the Los Angeles police department.

When Franklin was arrested he admitted the bribery, but consistently denied that Darrow had any part of it. Yet he could give no plausible explanation of where the money came from, or of how attempts at bribery were first suggested to him. Darrow furnished the $10,000 bail for Franklin from the McNamara defense account and waited. After two months Franklin changed his tune, and attributed both the inspiration and financing of the bribery to Darrow. It never became entirely clear what had prompted Franklin's change of story, though it was suspected that the district attorney had offered leniency to him in exchange for implicating Darrow—and in fact Franklin never served time for his offense. Without such testimony, there was no way to link Darrow with what had been done. Lockwood could not do so, because all his dealings had been with Franklin, as he admitted on the stand.

It was Lockwood's testimony that caused the first of many disagreements between Rogers and Darrow on the way the trial should be conducted. Darrow was becoming irrational in the circumstances of stress and wanted to accuse Lockwood of lying and being part of a conspiracy to "get" him. Rogers spent long hours dissuading him from this course, arguing that Lockwood was telling the truth, that he was not part of any conspiracy, but that he was merely confirming what Franklin had admitted. The better approach, Rogers maintained, was to cross-examine in order to bring out Lockwood's inability to show that Darrow was implicated. Rogers prevailed. During the examination of Lockwood Darrow began to cry, creating a picture of misery some observers thought embarrassingly unmanly. Rogers suggested that the district attorney's office had set a trap for Darrow by telephoning Darrow anonymously in order to get him down to the scene of the bribery, and therefore implicate him. So far Rogers was doing a good job on behalf of his client.

But things did not go well thereafter. The most important witness in the entire trial was Bert Franklin. Of this there can be no conceivable doubt in view of the prosecution's statements. District Attorney Fredericks—no friend of Darrow's—had told the press prior to Franklin's change of story: "Regardless of my own opinion in the matter, we have no case against Darrow."[21] Only after Franklin changed his tune was there the possibility of conviction. It was he who had given the damaging testimony that Darrow stood behind the attempts at bribery, had approved and encouraged them. The night before Franklin was due to be cross-examined, Rogers disappeared on a drinking binge. He had done so periodically, but this was the first major occasion on which it had happened. Darrow was understandably irate. He was on trial for bribery and his counsel had disappeared. It was the culmination of a series of disagreements between them. After frantic efforts by his staff Rogers was found and appeared in court the next day without visible signs of the previous evening's debauch. But relations with his client, and with Ruby, who had not liked Rogers from the start, were not improved.

For all these setbacks, Rogers managed a superb cross-examination of Franklin. Questioned by the district attorney, Franklin testified that Lockwood was only one of half a dozen prospective jurors that he "got to" on Darrow's instructions. The prosecution had proved in detail the fact that Franklin had passed money to White and White had passed it to Lockwood; it brought in witnesses galore to the illegal propositions which Franklin had made at various times to prospective jurors. There was no need for this. The defense conceded openly that Franklin had done these things, and Franklin had already been convicted of attempted jury bribery. But it was a way of spreading the dirt to Darrow, because Franklin claimed that Darrow had provided him with the bribe money only five minutes before he had met Captain White at Third and Main. This was the crux of the case. If the jury believed Franklin, they would convict. Rogers made the most of Franklin's change of story regarding Darrow's guilt:

"The district attorney told you he didn't want you. We want Darrow, isn't that what he said?" asked Rogers.

"They said if Darrow had been in this they wanted me to tell them."

"And you said he hadn't?"

"At first I did,"

"That was a lie?"

"Well—"

"Then you said he was in it?"

"Yes."

"Which one was the lie—one or the other was a lie—you lied sometime, Bert, didn't you?"

"I didn't tell the truth when I said Darrow didn't know about it."

"But how can we tell? How can we be sure which time you lied? They told you they wanted to get Darrow."

Even at this stage Darrow was totally despondent and Rogers found it hard to bear. One evening at dinner, after he had been cross-examining Franklin all day, he complained to his client.

"I am not Houdini. I cannot do this without some cooperation. Time and again, juries bring in verdicts against all evidence, and the judge's instructions. The impression the accused makes on the jury can be fifty per cent of the verdict?" Darrow nodded.

"Then, you lugubrious wretch, you are going to jail."[22]

In fact it was impossible for Darrow to correct his fault even if he had wished to, as Lincoln Steffens saw all too clearly: "He can say anything he wants to say, but he cannot conceal much; his face is too expressive."[23]

Later there were to be disputes about another aspect of Darrow's demeanor —the fact that he openly cried in court. Such a display of self-pity was believed to be unacceptable in the West and embarrassing to the jury. As Adela St. Johns put it:

> In those days before the First World War, we weren't far out of the old West and its rules and codes of conduct. . . . We were a fairly simple, emerging pioneer people, the sight of a man *crying* about himself for hours in public was unfamiliar to us. In time it came to be a gag, that "out where men are men," but then we simply took it as a basic fact of life that if possible a man faced a firing squad with dry eyes and fought at Dodge City the same way.[24]

It is difficult to avoid the conclusion that the circle of people around Darrow in Chicago were much given to feeling sorry for themselves. Indeed there was a tendency to self-dramatization in the literary and intellectual life of the city, whatever the mores of the West might be—Theodore Dreiser and Edgar Lee Masters both displayed it unattractively in their writings.

The fact remained that Rogers had Franklin—and the prosecution—over a barrel. To convict, the prosecution had to convince the jury that there was no reasonable doubt about the words of an admitted liar. After Rogers's cross-examination, the prospects of that had dwindled considerably. Nevertheless there was evidence that looked bad from Darrow's point of view. The prosecution showed that a check for $10,000, which had originated from the defense office, had been made out to O. A. Tveitmoe—the union official shortly to be convicted in Indianapolis for illegal transportation of dynamite—and cashed in San Francisco. This was the money, said the prosecution, that Darrow had used to bribe Lockwood and others.

When Darrow himself took the stand, according to his own account, "I had no more trouble about answering every question put to me than I would have had in reciting the multiplication table." Yet observers agreed that he was a poor witness to his own defense, who did not answer questions directly. It was too much for Ruby, who suffered a breakdown that made her unable to stay at her husband's side or to be present during his cross-examination. As Adela St. Johns, Rogers's daughter, says: "Ruby Darrow, thin, angular, old-maidish yet obsessed by a *grande passion* she had probably feared in her youth would pass her by, saw the man who had been her life being burned at the stake. Her desire to help him made her jump off into space once in a while."[25]

There were no notable exchanges in the three days Darrow was on the stand, no flashes of the old brilliance, no clever highlighting of the issues. Bert Franklin and Lincoln Steffens made a greater impression on the witness stand than Darrow, who avoided saying anything to incriminate himself but failed to convince of his innocence. At best his testimony was neither a gain nor a loss for his side, but indecisive. It might have been thought, then, that the verdict hung upon the final addresses of both sides. Unquestionably Darrow thought so himself. However, two eyewitnesses to the trial have since claimed that the jury had made up its mind to acquit Darrow even before the closing speeches were made. Both Hugh Baillie and Adela Rogers St. Johns say they had prior knowledge of the jury's verdict, Baillie from a juror named Golding, and St. Johns from bailiffs and deputies who had the responsibility of sequestering the jury.[26] If this is so, the jury had the benefit of listening unnecessarily to two of the best defense summations ever heard in an American court of law. For both Rogers and Darrow, in spite of all their differences, excelled themselves.

Rogers made a summary of the evidence that was concise and logical. He picked holes in the prosecution's case and discredited each of its witnesses. He relied, in the final analysis, on the argument that he had favored from the start: that Clarence Darrow was too intelligent to have made such a mess of a bribery as this one, and that it was unbelievable he should have been involved. "Will you tell me," he demanded of the jury, how any sane, sensible man who knows anything about the law business—and this defendant has been at it for thirty-five years—could make himself go to a detective and say to him: "Just buy all the jurors you want. I put my whole life, my whole reputation, I put everything I have into your hands. I trust you absolutely. I never knew you until two or three months ago and I don't know very much about you now, but there you are; go to it!"[27]

It was a cunning argument, well put. The trouble was, it answered only part of the prosecution's case. It focused upon the testimony of Bert Franklin, but ignored that of Harrington, whom Darrow had known for years and had trusted so much that he had brought him all the way from Chicago and had him to stay in his own house. Harrington had said that Darrow asked him to bribe jurors. Was not Harrington precisely the kind of man a dishonest lawyer would choose to do his dirty work?

In spite of Rogers's useful marshaling of the evidence, and the information that the jury would acquit, Darrow was still deeply depressed on the evening before the trial. He had adopted a fatalistic attitude of seeming indifference, which made it appear to the defense team that he was incapable of making an effective plea on his own behalf. Almost the entire night before the final speech, until dawn was breaking, Darrow spent in the office of his chief defense attorney. In view of his performance in court the next day, there is no better proof of his astonishing ability to forego sleep in an emergency. As he put it, he needed eight hours of sleep every twenty-four, but could make do with much less if he had to. What went on at that all-night session was to be crucial in his relationship with Rogers, and its product was one of Darrow's greatest speeches.

It has been alleged, notably by Irving Stone, that on that fateful night Rogers and Darrow argued as to which of them should make the summation to the jury. Should Rogers continue, having made his summary of evidence, or should Darrow take over and speak in his own defense? But Rogers's daughter states categorically that her father was happy that Darrow wanted to speak to the jury, and gracefully relinquished the spotlight to him, and that the real cause of the breach that occurred that evening was Rogers's horrified discovery that Darrow was in fact guilty of jury bribery. Rogers had believed in Darrow, thought him too great and moral a man to stoop to bribery, and had worked for his defense on that basis. The disillusionment that Rogers suffered then was ten times worse than the petty quarrels over money, over strategy, over his drinking, or over precedence in court. Many times during the proceedings Rogers had complained to Darrow that he presented a picture of guilt. Now, it seemed, that picture was true. The disillusionment of honest trade unionists had come with the realization of the McNamaras' guilt; Rogers's came with the conviction of Darrow's guilt.

But this horrifying blow only came after many hours of discussion, during which Rogers had to rouse Darrow out of a blue funk and give him the confidence to speak for himself on the morrow. It was not a pretty sight—a great man at his lowest ebb. Jerry Giesler, who was there as junior counsel, recorded: "One of the things I wish I could forget about that first trial was the consternation I felt at seeing my boyhood hero, Darrow, so discouraged that Earl Rogers had to give him fight talks to keep him from giving up the battle."[28] Darrow saw himself as a martyr to a cause in which he no longer believed, persecuted and reviled for doing what was right. He was very, very nervous about his final plea. Rogers coaxed, bullied, and shook him that night, bringing out the themes of the final address from the depths of Darrow's soul. They were all there, almost entirely unmodified from the time when Darrow had first engaged Rogers. He still argued that he was part of a vicious conspiracy; that the McNamaras' actions were excusable; that he had told the truth and all others were knaves and liars; and that the prosecution had no proof that he had any knowledge of or involvement in the bribery. And still Rogers made the same objections and suggestions, pointed out the same weaknesses, discouraged Darrow from treading the infirm ground that would justify the arson of the Times Building. Darrow would not, perhaps could not, take advice. He would plead in his way, as he saw the case. Rogers might have the better line of defense, the one most appealing to a jury, least vulnerable to objection, but it was not one with which Darrow felt at home. Darrow was not going to defend himself with someone else's script.

In the course of that long grueling night with Rogers, Darrow emerged from the paralysis of despair. When he arrived at court, literally thousands of people were waiting to see him, hoping to get in to hear him. The greatest orator of his time, come to speak in his own defense, was an attraction many people in the small city of Los Angeles did not want to miss. There were scuffles as men vied with one another to obtain a place in court and the police had difficulty in keeping even a semblance of order. When Darrow stood up to speak on August 14, he did not lack for witnesses to his fate, whatever it might be.

It was arguably the most brilliant speech he ever made. It soared, it uplifted, it entranced: a tour de force admired by friends and enemies alike. Adela St. Johns, who despised and reviled Darrow, described it as "one of the great all-time performances ever seen and heard in any courtroom since Cicero."[29] He carried the audience with him as he railed against his accusers:

> Suppose I am guilty of bribery, is that why I am prosecuted in this court? . . . No, that isn't it, and you twelve men know it. I have committed one crime, one crime which is like that against the Holy Ghost, which cannot be forgiven. I have stood for the weak and the poor. I have stood for the men who toil. And therefore I have stood against them, and now this is their chance.

He denied, he justified, he denounced, he persuaded. His audience was spellbound. Jurors cried as Darrow catalogued the injuries done to him, the injustice and humiliation he had suffered. He described the prosecution and its allegations as preposterous: "I am as fitted for jury bribing as a Methodist preacher for tending bar." He chastised Franklin, Harrington, and William Burns of the detective agency as perjurers and contemptible tricksters. It all flowed, point after point, in his favor. He put into his speech all those arguments which had looked so dangerous to Rogers, even down to the unpopular assertion that the McNamaras were not morally guilty of murder. Yet in Darrow's hands the arguments ran together and worked for him; he had synthesized them and made the whole greater than the parts. It was his greatest speech up to that time, and he had put into it some of his favorite oratorical material. For instance, one of his most effective stories was used to describe Harrington:

> They used to have a steer down in the stockyards of Chicago, where Harrington came from, that had been educated; they had educated the steer to the business of climbing an incline to the shambles. There was a little door on the side so that the steer could dart through this door and not get caught in the shambles, and his business was to go out in the pen and lead the other steers up that incline to the shambles, and then just before they reached the place he would dodge down through the door and leave the rest to their destruction. That is Harrington.[30]

In his final, personal plea to the jury he characterized himself as a martyr, a victim of his enemies and deserving of sympathy, not scorn. Certainly Darrow had his enemies, and they wanted to "get" him, but legally that was beside the point. The crux of the matter was whether the jury believed that, in trying to get him, his enemies had framed him, or whether they had merely exposed Darrow's own folly. Darrow was right that they were out to trap him. The question for the jury was whether they had grounds to do so. There are also the seeds of Darrow's later triumphs in this speech, including his defense of Leopold and Loeb. The product of months of brooding, misery, and self-pity was distilled into magnificent prose. Darrow had not written it down, but it had come to him complete, almost poetic, in form: "Even those who thought him guilty or had called him traitor were stilled and tranced."[31] Darrow himself knew that he had done well: "My argument occupied a day and a half. It was a good argument. I have listened to great arguments and have made many arguments myself, and consider that my judgment on this subject is sound." Not since his first great triumph at the Central Music Hall with Henry George in 1888 had he been so satisfied with a speech. Indeed he used the same description of the sensation both speeches gave him—that it was as if he was visiting with his audience and talking to them round a fireside.

After Darrow's summation Judge Hutton, visibly moved, instructed the jury very shortly. It retired and returned in just over thirty minutes to record a vote of not guilty.[32] This was the signal for hysterical joy in the courtroom, joined in by Judge Hutton himself, who showed himself to be on Darrow's side. From the time court was adjourned until midnight, Darrow was not free of well-wishers and supporters come to congratulate him. His success was sweet, but there was a bitter aftermath to the trial too. Many acquaintances had avoided Darrow since the shadow had fallen over him. Labor had turned its back on him; seeming friends had treated him as a pariah. Even those who had stood by him, like Lincoln Steffens and his ex-policeman friend Billy Cavenaugh, had thought him guilty. Now, with a verdict of acquittal in, they came to pay homage, to protest undying support, laden with insincere good wishes. But Darrow could not help but wonder: What if the verdict had gone the other way? Who then would have stood by? "Now that the news had gone out, I received telegrams from people who had been silent until then," Darrow wrote. The experience was confirmation of all he had believed about human nature; it was a lesson he was not to forget. Few men are given such a yardstick by which they can measure those who call themselves friends, but how many would wish to have one?

For the moment, however, all was joy. Darrow had survived his ordeal and no one expected that the district attorney would proceed with the second indictment against him, which related to the bribery of Robert Bain, another juror. "The acquittal of August 17 is thought by the press to end the case against Darrow," observed the *Literary Digest*. "For, while he faces another trial under a second indictment, the press generally believe that even should it be found worthwhile to bring the case before a jury, an early acquittal would be practically assured."[33] It was assumed that the stronger case had been prosecuted first, as is normal practice, and that the district attorney would not persist. But the press were wrong.

Three months later the prosecutor proceeded to trial on the Bain indictment. "I did not consider it seriously," said Darrow, "for everything possible had been brought out in the first trial. No one regarded the second as serious, so far as I could learn." So far as his own group of friends was concerned, that appeared to be the case. "It shocked me, but it may have another effect on you," wrote Lincoln Steffens to his wife on November 26, 1912, "to hear that Darrow is to be tried again at Los Angeles and that I may be called as a witness. I had a letter from him today, dated November 11, warning me that 'they' propose to put him on trial soon and asking me if I'd not come. I can ill afford to go."[34] Steffens did go nonetheless and gave testimony on February 22, 1913, on Darrow's behalf. As things turned out, the second trial was more serious than the first, and Darrow was misguided in believing that it could be taken lightly. Several differences existed between the Lockwood and the Bain indictments. In the Bain case, the bribery had taken place long before the settlement of the arrangement by which the McNamaras had pleaded guilty. It was therefore not open to Darrow to argue, as he had in the Lockwood case, that he had no incentive to bribe jurors since things had already been settled. Also, by the time the second trial was under way, a sensational dynamite conspiracy trial in Indianapolis had implicated many unionists in a criminal plot to terrorize the public to get concessions for labor. Again, in the second trial, Judge Hutton was replaced by Judge Conley of Madera, California, who was not so favorably disposed toward the defense as his predecessor. Lastly, Earl Rogers was no longer Darrow's counsel and the defense was conducted by Darrow personally.

The rift between Rogers and Darrow had been apparent only to those behind the scenes during the first trial. Rogers and Ruby did not get along and she disapproved of his drinking; there was Rogers's unhappy belief that his client was guilty; and there was the question of fees and expenses. Money had become a bone of contention that soured the proceedings more and more as time went on. Rogers resorted to refusing to go into court each day without first being given cash on the nail. It was sordid, but there was fault on both sides. Darrow did not volunteer the money, or offer to regularize the position. According to Adela St. Johns, when Rogers died $27,000 in expenses from the trial still remained unpaid by Darrow. Perhaps Darrow could not afford to pay, perhaps he begrudged having to pay members of his own profession. But whatever the reason his financial recalcitrance caused much of the ill-feeling that arose on the defense benches. Jerry Giesler, who was junior counsel in both bribery trials, confirmed that he received no payment for his work from Darrow.

Without Rogers at the second trial, Darrow was left to his own devices and he went into court with Jerry Giesler as his counsel. Darrow explained the situation by saying that Rogers was taken ill and not able to continue, but Adela St. Johns gives a different version. In any event, apart from a brief appearance at the beginning of the second trial Rogers did not play any further part in the proceedings. Darrow conducted his own case and deliberately set about defending his erstwhile clients, the McNamaras. This Darrow had done briefly in the summation at the first trial, but he had not made it the centerpiece of his argument. In the second trial he did so, consciously taking "the chance of saying something in defense of the McNamaras and their real motives, which I felt I should say." The argument was adapted from Lincoln Steffens's articles on "justifiable dynamiting" and was a good one. Yet this course of action was so antithetical to Darrow's interests there must be a suspicion that he had looked forward to making a speech to the jury at the trial of the McNamaras, which the guilty pleas had prevented, and was determined not to waste all his efforts in preparation for that speech.

It was not a wise decision, for it needlessly brought upon him some of the unpopularity of the McNamaras' crime and was utterly irrelevant to the issues of his bribery case. It made a good speech, but not a good defense. Overconfident as a result of the first trial, Darrow failed to assess the seriousness of his situation accurately. Writing to Carl Eric Linden during his second trial, he told him:

> I have been busy dodging the pen, where a lot of rotten sons of bitches want to send me purely because I have been for the exploited. . . . I don't think they can ever put it over, but even if they could it wouldn't look so bad for me. Everyone that knows me understands and trusts and the rest wouldn't anyhow—and think how many books I could read in a year or two. . . . [T]his will someday be over. As Swinburne says "Even the weariest river winds somewhere safe to sea. . . ."[35]

The jury did not, as in the first trial, acquit. It disagreed, eight jurors out of twelve believing Darrow guilty. Darrow put the result down to ill-chance, but many put it down to his misjudgment in his line of argument, while some attributed it to Darrow's guilt. The hung jury left a cloud over Darrow's reputation; it was much less satisfactory than acquittal. Darrow therefore asked for yet another trial (which surely he did not truly want) in order to leave the record as clean as it could be. It was understood that his case would be continued and then quietly dismissed, and it was on that basis that Darrow returned to Chicago, in early 1913. But it was not dismissed, and as the year's end drew closer, Darrow was depressed enough to complain to Steffens about it.

The humiliation of the proceedings and the damage they did to Darrow's professional reputation and practice were slightly abated when the Becker trial in New York began to provide some new spice in the lives of newspapermen and their readers. A corrupt policeman was accused of killing a gambler who had threatened to squeal. By early summer of 1912 there was much good copy to be had from that trial and it was new, whereas Darrow's second bribery trial merely repeated most of what had come out in his first. So Darrow was able to lick his wounds outside the full glare of publicity. But it was small consolation—he had already had more than his fair share of that.

By this time the district attorney had unsuccessfully tried twice to put Darrow behind bars. The verdict on the Lockwood indictment having been an acquittal, it could not be retried; but the possibility still existed of retrying the Bain indictment. It appeared that the district attorney was considering that course of action, but after the hung jury was dismissed, he announced in December 1913 that further proceedings against Darrow would be discontinued.

Darrow had been through much in his two years in Los Angeles. He had lost friends, money, and reputation. It had been the bleakest segment of his life, providing fuel to feed the flames of cynicism. Yet his ordeal also provided him with an instance of generosity and nobility never to be forgotten. From out of the blue, on the very day that the jury in the second trial reported disagreement, he received a telegram from a total stranger:

I NOTICE FROM THE DAYS PAPERS THAT YOU HAVE EXHAUSTED YOUR LAST DOLLAR IN YOUR DEFENSE STOP YOU HAVE SPENT YOUR WHOLE LIFE TRYING TO SEE THAT THE POOR GOT A SHOW NOW YOU SHALL HAVE EVERY CHANCE THE LAW AFFORDS TO PROVE YOUR INNOCENCE STOP IF YOU WILL WIRE ME THE AMOUNT YOU REQUIRE I WILL SEND IT TO YOU

FRED D. GARDNER [36]

After all Darrow's disappointments, this marvelous act of charity touched him deeply. His eyes filled with tears as he read it. He replied that he was, indeed, in dire straits, but did not wish to take money unless he knew how much hardship it would mean to Mr. Gardner. Within a few days Gardner had sent Darrow $1,000, and Mrs. Gardner had added her own check for $200. Gardner was a self-made businessman who had read of Darrow's plight while on vacation in Hot Springs, Arkansas. (Later the Darrows and the Gardners became friends, Gardner was appointed governor of Missouri, and Darrow wished that he might become President of the United States.) As it happened, Gardner's offer came after the worst was over, but it was as valuable for its psychological uplift as for the debts it would pay. The noble gesture balanced out some of the squalor of the spying, perjury, and baseness that had filled the previous eighteen months.

Both his trials had been full of irrelevance and pyrotechnics. While the prosecution had gleefully proved, re-proved, and proved again the admitted fact of bribery in the defense camp, Darrow had expanded his arguments about the rights and wrongs of the McNamaras' actions far beyond what was called for by the rules of evidence. He had discussed motive, but motive was only secondary to the question of what he had actually done. Darrow claimed it was improbable that he would stoop to bribery—but improbable things can happen, nevertheless. Much of the evidence in the first trial had been ruled inadmissible by Judge Hutton. Its length had been the subject of bitter complaint by the press. "It is unlikely," the New York *Herald* pointed out, "that it would have consumed in England or Canada more than seven days to hear a case similar to Darrow's."[37] Jerry Giesler described the proceedings as a thicket of "legal tanglefoot."[38] The right to a day in court had been extended to ninety days in court—but was anyone the wiser or justice more effectively served? After those millions of words had been poured out, was the truth illuminated or obscured?

In one sense Darrow was correct in saying it was unlikely he would bribe. It would have been reckless of his reputation and far beyond the call of duty. Yet the battle was fierce, men's lives were at stake, and the undisputed conduct of the defense showed a willingness to resort to extreme measures. In the many labor cases he had tried he had consistently become emotionally involved in the issues and personally concerned with the outcome. From the time of the Pullman strike on, he had treated the cause of labor as a crusade more than a litigation. His defenses had been mounted on ever more lavish scales, until, on behalf of the McNamaras, there was a just suspicion of megalomania. If the prosecution had spies, the defense had its counterspies. There was scarcely an employee of the defense staff that the district attorney's office had not tried to corrupt, or a member of the prosecution team that the defense had not tried to "get to." In addition the Burns Detective Agency, hired to conduct independent investigations for the prosecution, was setting up its own system of paid informers under the direction of Joseph Ford, assistant to Fredericks. "Before long some of the private detectives were drawing three separate salaries, passing around their information in a daisy chain; Darrow, Fredericks, the prosecuting attorney, and Ford knew what each other had had for breakfast."[39] Nothing was secret, nothing sacred. Both sides were spending huge amounts of money.[40] The defense adopted a code with which to send telegraphic messages and the prosecution deciphered it; it recorded Darrow's conversations on hidden Dictographs; it threatened witnesses sympathetic to the defense with prosecution.

Darrow claimed that he had "played according to the rules of the game." But what were the rules, and was it a game? If there were any, they were made up by the players as they went along, and what was done was in deadly earnest. Witnesses were kidnapped and attempts made to buy off the inconvenient ones. A particularly damaging instance was one Darrow must have known about because the contact involved his brother-in-law.

One of the strongest elements in the prosecution's case against J. B. McNamara was its ability to corroborate Ortie McManigal's confession. McManigal had described McNamara's movements in the weeks before the dynamiting in considerable detail. At various hotels McNamara had checked in as J. B. Bryce, and it was possible to identify the handwriting, and in some instances desk clerks were able to make a positive identification of the guest who had signed in under the name of Bryce. One of these was Diekleman, who had registered McNamara under the name of Bryce in Los Angeles. Since that time Diekleman had moved to Albuquerque, New Mexico. There he received a visit from Burt Hamerstrom, Ruby's brother, who was now working on Darrow's defense team. Hamerstrom tried to persuade Diekleman to change his identification of McNamara, but Diekleman refused. Hamerstrom then said:

"Now you are a valuable witness to us, and whatever your price is we will give it to you. Do you know Rector's Restaurant in Chicago?"

"Yes," replied Diekleman, who by this time was in the restaurant rather than the hotel business.

"Well," said Hamerstrom, "I think Mr. Darrow is interested in that. How would you like to be assistant manager there?"[41]

Diekleman refused this offer, and others made later by Hamerstrom, but finally agreed to visit Chicago when Hamerstrom said he would pay the expenses of Diekleman and his girlfriend. Diekleman made the trip, but proved no friend to the defense, not retracting his identification of McNamara one bit. This episode told heavily against Darrow in his own trial for bribery, because it looked as if he had attempted to pay Diekleman to perjure himself. Darrow said only that he "hoped" Diekleman would alter his testimony, but that there was no corrupt deal. Diekleman said bluntly that there was a clearcut proposition offered to him to change his testimony.

Altogether, the conduct of the defense was not above criticism. Bribery might only have been a small step after many big steps had been taken. It is as impossible to be sure what happened in retrospect as it was impossible at the time—but nearly everyone acquainted with the circumstances, or who was present at the trials, thought that Darrow was guilty. The list of journalists, lawyers, and others who were involved and believed him guilty is a long one: among the lawyers, his own counsel, Earl Rogers and Jerry Giesler; Oscar Lawler of the prosecution team; among the journalists, Hugh Baillie of United

Press, James H. Pope of the Los Angeles *Times*, Fletcher Bowron of the Los Angeles *Record* (and later the *Examiner*), Lincoln Steffens, then writing for the Los Angeles *Express*, and Adela St. Johns, Earl Rogers's daughter, later to be a Hearst reporter; and among well-wishers, Billy Cavenaugh and Paul Jordan Smith, a friend of Darrow's in Chicago.* W. W. Robinson, historian of the Los Angeles Bar Association, reported: "I have been unable to find a lawyer or anyone else directly connected with, or an observer of, the McNamara and Darrow trials who believed in Darrow's innocence,"[42] and Adela St. Johns said: "A press-box vote would have convicted him, that's for sure."[43]

A review of the known facts does not prove Darrow's guilt beyond reasonable doubt, as the law requires for conviction, but neither does it give confidence that he was innocent. On the contrary, it demonstrates that Darrow, like his opponents, was fighting dirty. When asked about the case shortly after his return to Chicago, Darrow commented, "When you're up against a bunch of crooks you will have to play their game. Why shouldn't I?"[44] Victor Yarros, his associate for eleven years, reported:

> I never asked him directly what the facts were in that notorious case but he said to me: Do not the rich and powerful bribe juries, intimidate and coerce judges as well as juries? Do they shrink from any weapon? Why this theatrical indignation against alleged or actual jury tampering in behalf of "lawless" strikers or other unfortunate victims of ruthless Capitalism?[45]

In the case of the McNamaras, in which Darrow was so much concerned with ends that did or did not justify the means, perhaps he became convinced that his ends as an attorney justified the means. (Later, in another context, he was to say: "A great many people in this world believe the end justifies the means. I don't know but that I do myself.")[46] He wanted to win. He had always advised people who played poker to keep the limit down, but it was advice that he could not translate into his own professional life. In the McNamara case and the series of labor cases that had preceded it, he had anted up the odds until he had gambled everything—the future of the AFL, his professional reputation, even the well-being of the labor movement itself—upon the outcome. In these circumstances, with the stakes so high, might he not have taken a final, reckless gamble?

It should be remembered that jury bribery was by no means unknown in criminal cases. It took place from time to time in every locale in the United States and happened often in Chicago. In 1910 and 1911 a well-known Chicago attorney with whom Darrow had often associated was prosecuted for that very offense and acquitted. Darrow had himself associated with an attorney convicted of jury bribery. The circumstances indicate that the best verdict in the bribery trials might have been, in the Scottish style, "not proven." Perhaps an

---

*It is also possible to infer from the carefully guarded words of Victor Yarros that he suspected Darrow was guilty.

excess of enthusiasm for his cause led Darrow astray: he was no saint, but felt the pressures like any other participant. And is there a man who ever lived who has not at some time been guilty of an act of dishonest folly? Darrow himself put the position well, knowing that there were many who could not believe him innocent:

> There was . . . one view that I was sure practically every one would agree on —that, whatever the facts might be, there had been no sordid or selfish motive connected with the affair. They would know if the charge was true it was because of my devotion to a cause and my anxiety and concern over the fate of some one else.

There was something else that could be agreed upon. Whatever the facts, Darrow had little excuse for being caught in an admittedly compromising situation. He was not an innocent abroad; nearly all the unpleasant features of the McNamara affair had appeared in the Haywood trial in Idaho over four years earlier. There, too, vast sums of money had been spent by both sides; detectives had been active in following up all kinds of leads and had acted as double-agents; interception of defense telegrams had been successfully tried; intensive pre-trial investigation of the jurymen had taken place, which some believed to have amounted to intimidation—it had been alleged on the front page of the Portland *Oregonian* that "an expert jury fixer from Chicago" had been imported to Boise.[47] All the elements that could cause combustion were there. Yet Darrow took no precautions to avoid getting burned. Certainly the failure to take account of the close scrutiny that he was under and the animosities inevitably engendered by the kind of fight he put up must be accounted a lamentable piece of negligence, even if he was completely innocent.

24

Picking Up the Pieces

Although Darrow's reputation had been tarnished in Los Angeles, it had not been ruined; and although it would have been better if the second trial had resulted, like the first, in an acquittal, the important thing was that he had not been found guilty. If he had been, his legal career would have ended in 1912 with disbarment and imprisonment. As it was, he emerged from the ordeal without any formal constraints upon continuation of his career, but nevertheless with a fear that, practically speaking, it was over. The publicity from Los Angeles had done him no good, for though fame is an asset to a lawyer, notoriety is not, except with the most undesirable kind of client. He could no longer expect cases from the labor movement and he did not want them. His partnership with Edgar Lee Masters and Francis Wilson back in Chicago had been dissolved. The trial had made him feel that his best years had been spent and he was near the end of the road. He had told the Los Angeles court, ". . . I am pretty near done, anyhow. If they had taken me twenty years ago, it might have been worth their while, but there are younger men than I . . . who will do this work when I am gone,"[1] and he had believed it. It was the theme of his reply when Gompers had pleaded with him to take the McNamara case. He felt he was on the brink of obsolescence, broken and declining, with no future.

Darrow's eighteen months as a defendant had accentuated the feeling of deep depression that had set in at the onset of his first bribery trial, which Rogers had fought day after day to remedy. After the acquittal he had shaken it off, and become more like his old self. Whereas many months had been spent without any outside interest or activity, and the trial and its ramifications had become an obsession, he was able, gradually, to find time for other matters. By December 1912 he had sufficiently recovered from his anguish to address the San Francisco Radical Club on one of his favorite themes: John Brown. It was one of his set pieces, delivered to many audiences all over the country; he was getting into the swing of things once more. He was further encouraged by the support given him by his old friend from Chicago, Gertrude Barnum of the Ladies Garment Workers' Union, who spoke out bitterly against labor's abandonment of Darrow in his hour of need. Referring to Darrow's many services to labor, she wrote:

> Has he been rewarded by our faith in return, by our loyalty, when the opportunity was given us to lay them at his feet? No, all through those bitter months of his trial organized labor, for the most part, has timidly cowered before the very shadows of the mighty antagonists Darrow rose to meet undaunted. It is the old story. The masses ever deserting their leaders; with petty criticisms excusing their base ingratitude. No wonder Darrow cried out in his last suspense, "I know the crowd. I love them. In a way I despise them." Yet he knows and we know that the treachery of the crowd is neither here nor there with such men as Darrow.[2]

Many had felt that Darrow's address in Los Angeles had been marred by its egotism: "Because of its excessive self-pity, many men that day did not admire it."[3] Darrow's analysis of his position was not wrong, but it came ill from him. Gertrude Barnum painted an idealized picture; Darrow had in fact been daunted, and the treachery of the crowd did make a difference, which he felt deeply.

He and Ruby returned to Chicago, the scars of battle still unhealed. Some old acquaintances—including Edgar Lee Masters—burned with hostility toward him. Masters complained that Darrow visited him, "never suspecting that I was not friendly to him." But in this Darrow was justified, for Masters had complied with his request to supply testimonials to his good character without disclosing his underlying malice.[4] There were others, friends and admirers, who welcomed him back from the fight. "One who has serious trouble always has two surprises: one over the friends who drop away, and another at the supposed strangers who stand by him in his hour of need," Darrow reflected. Mr. Gardner of St. Louis was an example of the second— a Good Samaritan of biblical stature. The crisis showed Darrow both good and evil in his fellow men.

Darrow learned the extent of Masters's animosity only with the publication of Masters's *Songs and Satires* in 1916. It contained a poem entitled "On a Bust" that Masters as good as admitted to be an attack on Darrow—an amazing admission, for the poem is as vicious a piece of writing as could be imagined, the venom of which far surpasses its literary merit. It attacks the character of Darrow through a consideration of a bronze bust of him:

> You can crawl
> Hungry and subtle over Eden's wall,
> And shame half grown up truth, or make a lie
> Full grown as good. . . .
>
> A giant as we hoped, in truth a dwarf;
> A barrel of slop that shines on Lethe's wharf . . .
> One thing is sure, you will not long be dust
> When this bronze will be broken as a bust
> And given to the junkman to re-sell.
> You know this and the thought of it is hell![5]

It says much about Masters's state of mind that he could publish this attack. It is clearly malicious, and reflects his belief (afterward repeated in prose) that Darrow was guilty of the crimes with which he had been charged in Los Angeles.

On his return Darrow was a sitting target for the many who had, or thought they had, old scores to settle. Many who had felt the lash of Darrow's tongue were happy at his downfall and even added to the tragic allegations made in Los Angeles a few from nearer home. As usual in the wake of disgrace, a large number of new imputations were made by a whispering campaign it was impossible to counteract. The accumulated hatreds and resentments of thirty years of lawyering and politicking in Cook County mustered forces to form a daunting wall of disapproval.

Ruby and Clarence settled down once more in their apartment in the Midway. It was with a sense of profound relief that they found they retained some friends. Gertrude Barnum reassured them that they were still *persona grata* with her circle. There were private parties in his honor and the Lawyers' Association of Illinois held a dinner to mark his return. Only a month after the second trial, he and Ruby were guests at dinner along with Hamlin Garland and his wife at the home of Mr. and Mrs. Angus Shannon, whom he impressed with his resilience. Garland noted in his diary for May 19, 1913:

> We dined at night with the Shannons. The Darrows were there and we heard a good deal of the trial through which Darrow has passed. He seemed very well and carefree so far as this trial is concerned. He said he was to get forty-four thousand dollars out of the McNamara case but his own trial had cost him twenty thousand so that for two years' work and all his worry he had only twenty-odd thousand dollars. He was in debt, too, he said. He did not look old or broken; on the contrary, he was vigorous and full of fight.[6]

He had been tested, but he had survived to come out fighting. Once again he could face the world. But he had the immediate concern of earning some money. The only law partnership to which he now belonged was the one he had entered with Jacob L. Bailey, two years before, to keep his name on the bar list. It had no business for him, and he dissolved it. He was not sure he wanted to practice law any longer, but he had to do something. At least the option of practice was still open to him; the Illinois bar had not revoked his license.

Darrow put a bold face on it. When he appeared in court, he was to be found in the corridors, puffing at a cigarette, laughing and joking with the younger lawyers. Yet they all knew that something grave had happened—and for all the outward show, some saw a chastened and embarrassed soul beneath the surface. As older practitioners recognized him, they usually acknowledged him and hurried by, not wishing to look as though they were being friendly. The young men noticed, and Darrow noticed, making the brave pretense that nothing was wrong.

Once the worst was over, a sprightly defiance returned to him. He resumed his inflammatory public addresses. On May 4, 1914, he told the Women's Trade Union League tenth aniversary meeting at the Cooper Union that in the war between capital and labor, "it is worth while to sacrifice anything, even life." The meeting shortly afterward broke up in disorder after a petition was read asking that the Colorado mines should be confiscated by the government "because of the murders that the Rockefellers have been committing there."[7] Darrow's belief in and even encouragement of class warfare had deepened as a result of his trials, so that the newspaper entrepreneur E. W. Scripps confessed that he and Darrow were motivated more by hatred and contempt for the upper class than by any altruistic concern for its victims.

His clients of palmier days did not come back to him. Even his old associates did not want to link their names with his in the practice of law. To earn money, he signed up for a series of Chautauqua appearances, forced like such different figures as Debs and William Jennings Bryan to act as a crowd-pleasing entertainer, in danger of becoming an empty windbag, sandwiched between quacks, revivalists, and juggling acts. His first bookings were provided by Caroline McCartney of the International Lyceum Association, who recognized Darrow's crowd-drawing potential. Both Debs and Darrow knew the price to be paid. It was said that Bryan had delivered his address on "The Prince of Peace" over a thousand times, as frequently as Russell Conwill, the founder of Temple University, had delivered "Acres of Diamonds." It was well enough paid for a "name" such as Darrow, but it was unedifying and stultifying. Glenn Frank, editor of *The Century Magazine,* described it as "intellectual masturbation." Yet Darrow took to it well and came to rely upon it for a large portion of his income for the remainder of his active life. Whatever reservations others had about it, he had little hesitation in delivering the same lecture or debate over and over, as a vaudevillian performed the same act.

Finally he formed a partnership with a socialist lawyer, Peter Sissman, who nineteen years before had been his employee. Sissman, an immigrant Russian Jew, was not particularly successful himself, but this was the best opportunity Darrow could find and Sissman was sympathetic. Later, they were joined by William H. Holly and William L. Carlin; the firm of Darrow, Sissman, Holly & Carlin practiced law from 140 North Dearborn Street until 1925. Many of the lawyers whom he had counted as friends in better days no longer wanted to associate with him, while those few who did Darrow did not wish to disadvantage themselves by linking his name with theirs. For all his reservations about the bar, it hurt him to be an outcast in the profession of which he had been a leader, but he steeled himself to his embarrassment. A dozen years earlier he had counseled readers to acknowledge their skeletons in the closet, rather than hiding them, but when he had written that, the only skeleton in his closet was his divorce—then considered quite shocking enough. Now that another skeleton had invaded his closet, he tried to take his own advice:

> . . . [T]here was but one thing to do. I must go back to work. So I went to my office without delay. I made no statement, gave no explanations, I offered no

excuse or extenuation. I said nothing about the matter unless someone asked me, and then I avoided their queries as much as I could. I went straight ahead as though nothing had interrupted my course, but I was conscious that something had taken place. I offered no occasion for snubbing me, if perchance anyone might have been so inclined. If people wanted to see me, my door was open; if they did not care to come I never knew it. Every house has skeletons in its closets grinning and struggling to come out. It is doubtless better that they should be free and roaming in full light of day.

The adversity of his new circumstances in Chicago nevertheless brought him to a pattern of practice that suited his nature much more than his previous partnerships ever had. Darrow and Sissman were dissimilar in legal talents. Sissman made no pretense at being a trial lawyer; as he told Darrow at the beginning of their association: "I have only a small Jewish practice, a small office business. I can't bring you anything."[8] What he did provide was moral support, a base of operations, and the words of encouragement that his erstwhile mentor sorely needed. Sissman took care of all the mundane points of organization by keeping the accounts, and tolerated Darrow's casual financial ways without complaint. Though the two men were partners, Sissman treated Darrow, the older man, with respect and as a superior, deferring to his wishes in a way that no previous partner had. The arrangement, by which to all intents and purposes Darrow went his own way and Sissman acquiesced, provided Darrow with a much better-run law firm than he had known before. It was not mere egotism that made him work best like this—though that was undeniably a part of it—but that he was incapable of running a well-organized law practice. It was therefore a blessing in disguise that his Los Angeles débâcle had dislodged him from the respectable or high-class practice of law, and that he had alighted at a level much better suited to his tastes and abilities.

Gone was the lucrative business from the Hearst newspaper chain; gone was the patronage which unions were able to lavish upon their favorite lawyers. Gone, even, were the smaller, private clients, who had visited Darrow's firm in better days. Before his disgrace, Darrow had generated more work than could be handled. Now he could not find enough paid legal employment even to keep himself busy. No one wanted his services who could afford to pay for them, though his abilities were undiminished and perhaps even enhanced by the storm he had weathered. Darrow put it simply: "I had to begin anew"—not an easy task for a man of fifty-five. He tried to regain his prior position as a lawyer by offering to work free for people, rich or poor, who were defendants in criminal trials raising issues of principle. In 1915 he offered his services to Margaret Sanger, who was under federal indictment for contravening postal regulations by advocating birth control in *Woman Rebel*. She turned his offer down, repeating a refrain that Darrow had heard from other radical clients: "I was convinced that the quibbles of lawyers inevitably beclouded the fundamental issues. . . ."[9]

In order to support himself, Darrow found himself taking more purely criminal cases than he ever had in the past. He defended the small fry of the underworld against charges which had, by any stretch of the imagination, no political or ideological overtones; they were straightforward, run-of-the-mill prosecutions. Even in the palmier days only a small proportion of the cases handled by his office had had political aspects. The bulk of his work, like that of any other lawyer, was bread and butter, and the cases that attracted some public attention were the exception rather than the rule. But this was the stage of his career in which he was most involved in criminal practice, and from which his reputation as a criminal lawyer stemmed. He was successful in defending small-time criminals and attracted attention from those higher up the criminal ladder. By 1916 he had rehabilitated himself sufficiently that good, paying clients were coming to him for criminal defense work. When an investigation of illegal gambling was organized under Judge Kenesaw Mountain Landis, the notorious kingpin of betting at the Hawthorne Race Track, Mont Tennes, retained Darrow as special counsel. On Darrow's advice, Tennes appeared voluntarily and took the fifth amendment in answer to nearly every question. In so doing, he was better advised than the many other witnesses called, who revealed the extent and methods of the gambling network in Chicago. As the Illinois Crime Survey reported:

> Tennes alone was obdurate. Though the court spoke in friendly terms, Tennes insisted on his constitutional right not to incriminate himself. He testified that his real estate business was on the square; that his News Bureau was law-abiding; that he had been in California and had just returned; and that . . . his bookkeeper took care of his real estate business.[10]

Darrow's advice was so successful that it frustrated the federal inquiry entirely. His utility was thereafter acknowledged by the underworld, which was growing increasingly prosperous in this era and provided him with several lucrative cases. He might have become a gangster's mouthpiece—but that fate he was saved from by World War I, though for the next ten years his clientele would include more than a sprinkling of professional criminals.

Now, after two years in which luck had run against him, one stroke of good fortune came to him. Victor Yarros, then a reporter in Chicago, volunteered his services to Darrow free. Yarros did not need the money, but wanted the occupation for his mind and the human interest involved in the practice of law. "In five minutes, the arrangement was agreed upon," he wrote. "This informal relationship lasted 11 years, until Darrow dissolved his partnership with Peter Sissman and W. H. Holly, and joined a firm of popular and prosperous criminal lawyers who needed his advice and cooperation, as well as his prestige."[11] Yarros was an able and energetic man, of great use to Darrow as an investigator, researcher, and advocate; he had a quick mind and broad education. His assistance was a valuable asset in handling the cases, charity or otherwise, which came to the office, not least because Darrow had never been inclined personally to do the detailed work inevitably involved in preparing a case for trial.

Still, he needed clients and fees; he was more than $20,000 in debt from his fight in Los Angeles. Fee-paying clients were not easy to come by, but there were the poor who came, as they had always done, to Darrow's office. He helped them if he could, though he was almost as impoverished as they were. If he could not sell his time, he preferred to give it for nothing rather than remain idle. It was a strange situation; one of the nation's most famous lawyers, who but a short time before had commanded $50,000 fees, now unable to make ends meet yet giving his services to the poor. Many had cause to thank him. One of the first was a Negro named Isaac Bond, who was convicted of the rape and murder of a white nurse.

If any proof were needed that Darrow was, for the moment, without much legal business, his taking of the Bond case supplied it. The prosecution's case was a strong one, with a substantial amount of circumstantial evidence against Bond and a number of positive identifications of him. Darrow believed it worth fighting on the ground that identification evidence was always suspect. "Most identifications are of little value unless a witness has been acquainted with the subject," he wrote. "It takes a close acquaintance when the meeting is casual, unless there is something specially noticeable about the person; if a man is black that is identification in itself, in most minds." Notwithstanding that, Victor Yarros, his own associate, was very reluctant to believe Bond innocent, and so was the jury, which convicted him of murder. Remarkably, Darrow persisted in pressing Bond's appeal to the Supreme Court of Illinois, which reviewed the record in considerable detail and affirmed the conviction. At his trial Bond had produced alibi witnesses who contradicted the state's evidence and Darrow sought to persuade the Court to reverse the conviction, apparently on this ground alone. But the Court, basing its decision on a well-known principle of law, reminded Darrow that it could not usurp the function of a jury. Darrow could scarcely have expected any other result. Had he been busier, the pressure of work would have forced him to exercise more critical judgment in espousing an indigent's cause. Yet he remained undaunted, and continued his efforts on Bond's behalf until Bond died in prison of tuberculosis.

Sometimes men he had helped in better days came and asked for help once more. One was George Bissett, who had offered to kill for him, and whose conviction for murder Darrow had got reversed years before. Bissett came back for advice after Darrow's return from Los Angeles. He was accused (rightly) of stealing half a million dollars from a government building. Darrow once again gave his services free, this time recommending that Bissett plead guilty. There were others, too, whose work was done as an act of charity and could not be the foundation of a practice. But as long as there was nothing more profitable to do, Darrow did it. Meanwhile Peter Sissman continued with the routine business of a small firm—wills, contracts, the occasional divorce.

In giving his time to those unable to pay for his legal services, Darrow frequently found himself confronted by black clients in dire circumstances, brought to him by black lawyers who knew of his sympathy with their race. Darrow's charity in taking such cases did not redeem him in the eyes of the profession. On the contrary, it made him more suspect, for the majority of

the bar did not see Darrow's association with Negro attorneys as either enlightened or altruistic. Cook County had no racial barriers to admission to
the bar and it is probable that more black lawyers were to be found in Chicago at the turn of the century than in any other part of the United States.
There was no formal impediment to a Negro obtaining the same legal education as anyone else, though the quality of education in the few black law
schools left much to be desired. The difficulties came for a black attorney
after he was admitted to the bar, for he could obtain almost no white clients
and black clients of substance preferred to take their business to a white
attorney. The result was that black lawyers eked out a marginal living by
taking the least desirable cases of the least desirable black clients. Inevitably
they were shunted into criminal defense work, like it or not. Even there,
however, they did not have the field to themselves, for there were many
hungry young white lawyers who would take criminal defense work on assignment from a judge. Such assignments tended to be highly political in
Cook County, and all the best of these cases, whether involving black defendants or not, were given to lawyers with connections—which by definition
excluded black attorneys. It thus came about that black lawyers were the last
in line for the most hopeless cases.

The fact that Darrow accepted referrals from Negro practitioners was attributed by many not to high-mindedness but to lack of scruple; to most
members of the bar it was a sign of hitting rock bottom. Unfortunately he
provided some factual basis for these suspicions. In the Isaac Bond case, he
had agreed to defend on the ground of an alibi to be proved by some black
witnesses. As the case proceeded, the trial judge called Darrow to a bench
conference outside the hearing of the jury and complained to him that "there
is a whole lot of clumsy perjury in this testimony." Darrow chose not to have
regard to that aspect of the case he was presenting. Even his protégé Victor
Yarros, who was acting for him at the time, recorded that "I had my doubts
about the veracity of the witnesses."[12] None of this eased Darrow's path back
to respectability.

During this period he was able to help other outcasts from society, one of
whom was the architect Frank Lloyd Wright. Wright's difficulty was women.
He liked them, but did not have the art of leaving one for another without
creating violent and acrimonious disputes. He could not keep on good terms
with ex-wives and lovers, and this defect had a disastrous effect upon his
architectural practice. As one biographer put it, his "great allies had been
women; now they had reason to look on him with caution as one who would
put aside the conventions provided for the protection of their marriages and
their children. As a result, commissions for houses, once so plentiful in
Wright's office, became noticeably scarce; and while Wright's income dropped,
his expenses rose."[13] Wright resorted to borrowing money. He spent grandly,
if not wisely, had a large family by his first marriage to support, and in
consequence was severely at the mercy of his creditors. On one occasion
Orchestra Hall in Chicago was almost closed and padlocked by the sheriff

pursuant to a judgment. Wright forestalled this disaster by borrowing $1,500 only thirty minutes beforehand.

The result of these experiences was to engender in Wright a hatred of lawyers, and a suspicion of the world that verged upon madness. He did not see that his difficulties were largely of his own making. He was burdened with genius, but banks make no allowance for that. He was loved too much, so that women grew spiteful when he abandoned them. His autobiography is permeated with his contempt for lawyers and their clients, especially creditors, wives, and ex-wives. Wright did not understand money—or debt. He came to accept it as inevitable that wives, friends, lovers, relatives, colleagues would all commit treachery against him. Darrow knew Wright, and saw that his problems with the law were the product of his attitudes—to people, to money, to convention. Like many other defendants before and since, Wright had a self-punishing streak, a desire to be a martyr, to feel persecuted. Darrow was not without that himself, as he had demonstrated in Los Angeles, but it never became a dominant part of his character. Tactfully, he tried to give Wright some self-knowledge, telling him: "Your case is not a legal case, Frank. What you need is the advice of some wise man of the world who will be your friend and who will see you through. Keep away from lawyers."[14] It was good advice, but impossible for Wright to follow. He did not know the men who were "wise" in the sense that Darrow meant.

The crisis came in 1915, when Wright was prosecuted for violation of the Mann Act, which makes it a federal offense for a man to cross state or national boundaries with a woman for an immoral purpose. The statute was originally intended to penalize commercialized vice, but the courts held that it applied to interstate transportation of a woman regardless of whether there was payment involved. Wright had traveled with a lady who was not his wife, and, being famous and having many enemies, he was prosecuted. The scandal was immense even though the allegation was a humdrum one. Wright's relationship with the woman concerned was well known, and he had been living apart from his lawful wife for some time before he formed the liaison. Yet the offense had been committed, and Wright was not one to deny it. It took some considerable behind-the-scenes negotiations by Darrow to dispose of the matter without it coming to trial.

Meanwhile Darrow had tried to put his unaccustomed spare time to good use. Apart from his lecturing, which paid the rent on the Midway apartment, he enjoyed his association with the Walt Whitman Fellowship, which had welcomed him back to Chicago by inviting him to be chairman of its annual banquet. On May 31, 1913, he gave a paper speech to the Fellowship entitled "Whitman in Literature," which showed that he had lost none of his pugnacious wit. He started off: "Whitman was not a religious man. Few great men have been," and got a laugh and applause.[15] That audience, at least, was reassured that Darrow had not changed.

He used some of his time learning to type, though not in any scientific way. He bought a typewriter and pecked at the keys, rather than learning the proper fingering, and managed to hit the key he intended about three times out of four. Nevertheless the results were an improvement upon his handwriting, which was often impossible for him or anyone else to read. The art of typing would be useful in his legal practice (if ever it flourished again), but more importantly it was a symptom of the resurgent desire for literary recognition in which he sought refuge from the law. He wrote to Brand Whitlock on December 13, 1913, "I have heard a good many literary fellows say that they could write better by using a typewriter; so it has recently occurred to me that this was just what I lacked, so I am practicing on my friends and here goes with you."[16] However his good resolutions in this respect came to nothing. His typing remained rudimentary and his handwriting execrable. In 1928 Charles G. Shaw would report: "He is unable to use a typewriter, though his long-hand is so illegible that he himself is at times unable to read it."[17] It was therefore a mercy to his friends and associates that many of his letters were dictated to a typist and that the duties of correspondence of the Darrow household were taken over by Ruby, whose handwriting was large and clear. Until the end of his life Darrow wrote some of his own correspondence and it was frequently a puzzle to his friends and himself, but he never entirely mastered the type-writer.*

The lighthearted tone of his letter to Whitlock soon changed to seriousness as he broached an idea that had been in his mind before he went to Los Angeles, and was more attractive than ever now that he had lost everything he had in Chicago: "I am strongly thinking of leaving here [Chicago] before very long and going probably to New York. Would have done it before if I had not lost all my money a few years ago and did not dare risk it, but I can do it very soon."[18] He had toyed with the prospect of moving to New York several years before, writing to William E. Walling of the NAACP, "as soon as I am out of the woods I intend moving to New York," but the California excursion had intervened.[19] At this stage in his career, it was not fanciful. Perhaps because his early years had been characterized by a special fascination with Chicago, his enthusiasm had waned in maturity; he had lost the feeling of excitement it once brought him. The professional and political goodwill carefully built up over the years was gone, and seemingly irreplaceable. Before he had been welcome in the jovial gatherings of lawyers and politicians with which the city abounded. Now he was a pariah, shunned by some, avoided by many, and acknowledged only by a few courageous men in public life. They were afraid of guilt by association, even though he had not been found guilty.

Darrow could no longer hobnob on equal terms with those who ran Cook County, who dispensed its abundant political patronage, and who could mate-rially aid or hinder a Chicago lawyer's practice. He was not even very welcome at City Hall any longer, though successive mayors of both political parties had

---

*Although the age of the typewriter had dawned by 1890, there was still a willingness to insert holography for last-minute changes. Darrow's pleadings are full of modifications, compromises, stipulations, and dismissals by consent, entered after a hurried courtroom conference and scrawled in longhand on a piece of paper for the court files, never reduced to neatness.

always had time for him before. His contacts had turned sour on him. It looked as though he might just as well start over elsewhere rather than rekindle them. There were many incentives to do so. A number of the Chicago luminaries of the 1890s had already moved eastward and Chicago was no longer the literary center of the United States. The vision of men like William Stead, who had forecast that Chicago would become the center of federal government and true capital of the United States, had been discredited by events. Darrow was not alone in feeling that ennui had enveloped Chicago in this era. "I have lost the power to work in Chicago," Hamlin Garland recorded in his diary. "I have shifted ground. I have now a sense of impermanency, a desire to get back to New York where my real home now is. As soon as we can sell the house we shall move."[20] Already the literari were developing the conviction that the muses dwelt almost exclusively in New York's West Village, and even members of Darrow's own profession like Jerome Frank were leaving "for the greener pastures of New York City."[21]

Furthermore some of Darrow's best audiences were those in New York and many of his friends were there. And it would be a change, an opportunity to start anew. From Darrow's standpoint in 1913, it looked most attractive. The pall over the intellectual community of Chicago in this period is not easy to explain, but long-time residents of the city, who had witnessed its stupendous growth at the end of the century, felt that somehow the city was slowing down and that the spirit that had carried it along during those years had been lost. As the decade progressed, its literary luminaries clustered around Greenwich Village rather than the near North Side. The urge to move to New York infected Darrow like the rest. The change came rather suddenly. The sculptor Jo Davidson had to move from New York to Chicago in 1911 to gain recognition, yet as soon as he had been accorded it he found it preferable to migrate back to New York in 1913; Margaret Anderson made the same journey in 1917. Just when Darrow returned from Los Angeles many young artists and writers were experiencing a reversal of winds, from west to east. To Chicago's benefit and New York's loss, nothing came of it, and like his friend H. L. Mencken in Baltimore, Darrow remained to the end one of the few literati who resisted New York's blandishments, and could say with him, "for twenty-five years I have resisted a constant temptation to move to New York."[22]

Nevertheless he visited it frequently, making speeches. On January 24, 1914, he was there to address the United Hebrew Trades, and again on May 4 he spoke at Cooper Union. People seemed just as keen to hear him speak as they ever were, even if they did not want to consult him as a lawyer. He had not lost his sparkle, or become bitter, and he was still among the most entertaining platform speakers in the country. All in all, circumstances were set fair for his slow reclamation of reputation and business, while the passing of time healed his wounds and obscured unpleasant memories. But it was the outbreak of the European war in 1914 that would act as a catalyst to the rehabilitation of his reputation, and America's entry that would propel him from the outer to the innermost circles of power.

25

Doing Well Out of the War

Darrow's stand in August 1914 on the outbreak of World War I marked a drawing of lines such as he had never confronted before. It was the first time he had taken a position against many of those with whom he had been a friend and colleague. It also indicated a moral outrage Darrow had rarely shown in the last few years, during which a moral fatalism had set in.

His sudden "recovery" from pacifism marked the end of his alliance with many sections of the left. His warlike attitude seemed to many of them a most unholy apostasy from basic principles. And indeed it was a remarkable about-face: only five months before, in April 1914, Darrow had publicly objected (with a number of others, including Judge Ben Lindsey and Jane Addams) to the formation of the "Buster Brown League"—an organization designed to promote good citizenship among young boys and girls, and sponsored through the press—on the ground that it promoted "regimentation" of the young and was likely to produce militarist attitudes. But Darrow's apparently sudden shift was not unique; he only did what many other American and British intellectuals were doing at the time. Bertrand Russell complained of the overnight metamorphoses in his friends in London. Lloyd George himself changed from pacifist to advocate of conscription.

Up to the German invasion of Belgium, Darrow had managed to be at one and the same time a pacifist on international affairs and a believer in the inevitability of violence in domestic labor disputes. It was a feat of intellectual juggling that the fundamental inconsistency of these positions did not become troublesome to him until 1914. In the face of reproaches that he countenanced and even encouraged labor to achieve its ends by violence, there was a certain convenience for him to be able to claim that he was a man of peace who consistently supported pacifism. Time and again he had appeared on the lecture and debating platform urging the "theory of non-resistance," quoting Tolstoy as his mentor. Yet the arguments raised in those debates had a peculiarly American isolationist twist. They were the product of America's innocence, before its fall, and implicit in Darrow's pacifism was an aloofness from international squabbling that World War I would belie. In spite of their professed internationalism, American radicals had little insight into the mechanisms by which violence erupted in international politics. On the other hand, the vocabulary of radicalism was replete with the language of battle in describing the clash of capital and labor, as Darrow recognized. Coming quite close upon the heels of his Los Angeles dénouement, Darrow's reversal terminated his ability to hold together the various persuasions of Utopianism that made up the legacy of the founding fathers' idealism. The ease with which Darrow had moved among diverse sorts of visionaries was shattered now for all time; the cornerstone of their vision had been harmony and a world without war, enforced by the refusal of good men to fight or to support fighting. Neither the origins of the Republic nor the Civil War deflected them from their view that there was no principle worthy of vindication through the shedding of the people's blood. Was it not the history of war that those who had nothing were sent to die on behalf of those who had all? And here was an erstwhile champion of the workingman leading them into the valley of death.

The revulsion from Darrow as a turncoat was strong—and indeed, his new position sharply contradicted his recorded support of "non-resistance." Bellicose as his positions on domestic issues had often been, he had never approved international violence. It was strange, to say the least, that a man who had made a name for himself in exposing the follies of government and the mendacity of power should now lend himself to a wholesale campaign of propaganda. He seemed another idol with feet of clay.

In large measure, those who had been shocked by Darrow's position in the McNamara trial had been within the labor movement. But now his position for the first time alienated many on the left whose views were independent of unionism, who were radicals born of a preindustrial, more romantic tradition. The left, ever more divisive, was confounded by seeing one of its leading figures exit from its midst.

Among the small circle of socialist intellectuals, World War I was Darrow's undoing. They could tolerate, even admire, his troubles with the ordained government of the day for which they had no respect, but his abandonment of a fundamental precept of their belief was inexcusable. In the wider world, however, his bellicosity went far to rehabilitate his reputation. His words in favor of American intervention were music in the ears of authority, which could be (and were) readily adapted to use as governmental propaganda. Along with Douglas Fairbanks, Charlie Chaplin, Jack Dempsey, and many other "names," he was pressed into service to encourage the public to support the war effort.

Pacifism as a movement was not hugely influential in the United States, because until the outbreak of World War I in Europe American critics had had the benefit of being on the sidelines. George Jean Nathan spoke for many Americans when he confessed:

> I do not care a tinker's damn whether Germany invades Belgium or Belgium Germany, whether Ireland is free or not free, whether the Stock Exchange is

bombed or not bombed, or whether the nations of the earth arm, disarm, or conclude to fight their wars by limiting their armies to biting one another.[1]

The United States had not been challenged by any substantial external enemy since it gained independence from Britain. Partly this was a product of isolation, partly of isolationism. American radicalism, in almost all its forms, had been concerned largely with domestic policies, and only peripherally with international affairs. Socialism, communism, anarchism, and syndicalism had as their concern international change—but in America the international aspects of the matter did not loom large.

World War I revealed divisions which until then had been concealed, or at least ignored, in the American left, and splintered it irreparably. The war, more than any other single factor, caused the demise of ideological radicalism in America. As Darrow's association with countless different progressive groups in the 1890s and 1900s demonstrated, there was a feeling of good fellowship among progressives of all persuasions, and their tendency was to emphasize points of accord rather than their differences. Advocates of violent revolution and change by peaceful means, Christian socialists and humanists, single taxers and anarchists could rub shoulders in prewar Chicago without worrying about the practical implications of their differences. It was easy to be in favor of truth, beauty, and justice, of good rather than evil, as long as those terms were not defined. But the war confronted radicals with actual, not merely hypothetical choices, by which men would live or die and nations win or lose independence; faced with such choices the old affiliations crumbled and the radicals split.

America's intellectuals were by and large unprepared to react to events on the other side of the Atlantic. Darrow, on the other hand, saw a moral issue in the war over German violation of Belgian neutrality, and was from the first in favor of aiding the Allies. Throughout the period 1914–1918 he would be outspoken in his condemnation of the Germans and his support of the Allied cause. For this he received much criticism from radical friends, especially for allowing a capitalist war to spill workingmen's blood. Many members of America's *avant garde,* such as Eugene Debs and John Reid, favored revolution but not war. Revolutions stood for progress and the proletarian interest, but wars were bad because they were battles in the interest of big business, not of the people.

Darrow had recognized the contradictions within the left for years. Always he had been "sympathetic" to each group without ever embracing its ideology; he wanted to make up his mind according to the facts, not to rely on ready-made mechanical answers. But many of his radical associates lacked his prescience and were puzzled and shocked by the schism that war created. Almost all socialists in the United States at this time included pacifism among their tenets. And foremost among the socialist-pacifists was Darrow's first major client, Eugene Debs, who combined his pacifism, logically enough, with opposition to conscription, and was arrested under the Sedition Act on June 30,

1918, for his inflammatory attacks upon United States policy.

Darrow sympathized deeply with the desire to avoid violence, but was much more pragmatic than his socialist associates. When the European war broke out, he was visiting his son in Estes Park, Colorado. He was at once horrified and fascinated, and

> eagerly sought and consumed every word I could get on the subject. . . . It appeared plain to me that Germany wanted the war and that all other nations, excepting possibly Austria, did everything in their power to avoid it. When, in violation of their express treaty, Germany sent her great army into Belgium, I at once felt that the whole world should help drive her back to her own land. . . . Up to this time I had believed in pacifism. . . . When Germany invaded Belgium I recovered from my pacifism in the twinkling of an eye.[2]

Darrow belonged to a generation that had not known war, conscription, or military service; he was too young to have any clear impression of the Civil War and too old to fight in World War I. His nation's economy had expanded without depletion by military expenditure—the U.S. Army was minute by European standards. Darrow had no wish to see it expanded, or that the spirit of militarism should grip the country. But he did not believe that an aggressor should go unrepelled, and from the start he believed Germany to be an aggressor. Furthermore, although his avid support of the Allied cause divided him politically from many who had previously stood with him, it in no sense marked an abandonment of the workingman. On the contrary, he believed that war generally had an advantageous effect on the conditions of life of the working people. War, he argued, promoted the interests of the working class in two ways. It destroyed labor, thereby tending to increase wages; and by destroying property, it provided added employment. Darrow saw that a nation which has accumulated capital in the form of buildings and luxuries has less need for labor than one without. War equaled destruction—and destruction would stimulate new demand for replacements of what had been destroyed. Here Darrow was voicing an idea then prevalent among intellectuals; but more than that, he was drawing upon his own knowledge of the effects of the Great Fire of Chicago in 1871, which produced a massive rebuilding program that raised wages, and provided employment for a large number of workers for years. He advanced this theory in a lecture given shortly after the outbreak of war, and expanded it in a letter to William Kent:

> The destruction of property as property, does not directly affect anybody, excepting the owner of the property destroyed, and the workingman practically has no property to destroy. The question is as to its indirect effect. Most property destroyed must be re-built, as for instance, Chicago and San Francisco after the fire. The funds to rebuild this property must come from the capitalist and the land owner. This lowers the price of land, possibly raising the price of interest, which is not so serious a matter. It also increases the amount of work to do, and therefore forces wages up. . . . I think the history of Chicago, San Francisco, and our own country during the Civil War, shows that the destruction of property adds to the share that labor is able to take.[3]

He discounted suggestions that war was a capitalists' conspiracy: "Our friends, the pacifists, tell us that this war is a creation of Wall Street; in other words, that it is a rich man's war. How any sane man can make such a claim as this, I do not see."[4] His argument, though true, was an opportunist one valid in aid of any war, and ignored the number of workingmen whose lives would be sacrificed in fighting. But on this, as in other matters, Darrow was a shrewd advocate. In declaring immediately in 1914 for American intervention on the Allied side, he had been greatly ahead of public opinion, but the next two years saw a substantial shift to his viewpoint, even in the Midwest. By June 3, 1916, designated "Preparedness Day," a large segment of the American public favored the Allies. The parade along Michigan Avenue was one of the largest in Chicago's history up to that point or since. Only in the face of this action did the federal government become somewhat more belligerent. Darrow's attitude had been ahead of the public and the public in turn was ahead of the government.

The war was momentous for Darrow personally, for it not only hastened his reputation's rehabilitation, but propelled him into eminent circles in which he had never before been welcome. The president of the National Security League, under whose auspices most of his pro-war speeches were made, was the venerable Joseph H. Choate, who had been respectable even longer than Darrow had been notorious, and whose patrician background was not generally to be found in the courts in which Darrow practiced. Choate's last public speeches, delivered when he was eighty-four, were devoted to encouraging the United States to enter the European conflict, a cause he supported until his death on May 14, 1917. The presidency was then assumed by Elihu Root, who belonged at Choate's end of the legal profession rather than Darrow's.

Darrow's early stand for American aid to the Allies anticipated American foreign policy by nearly four years and reflected his realization that, like it or not, the United States had become a world power. This he recognized with greater readiness than Woodrow Wilson, and for a time he lost patience with the President, though he later admitted that Wilson had been wise, and became a defender of his reputation. In most matters Darrow was in complete agreement with the President, so for the first time he found himself on the side of the powers-that-be. On only two issues was Darrow to find any fault with Wilson: his treatment of the Negroes, and his refusal, after the war, to give clemency to people like Debs who had been imprisoned under the Espionage or Sedition acts.[5] But these matters were in the future; on the war Wilson and he were utterly agreed. As to such imprisonment for the duration, Darrow had no objection whatever. He argued that in time of national emergency, defiance of the will of the majority was justifiably visited with sanctions—"so, during the war, I can find no honest criticism, from my point of view, for the forcible detention of those who were actually in the way of carrying it on."[6]

This hastened Darrow's reinstatement into the ranks of respectability. He came to have the ear of the government on such questions as the censorship of the mails and freedom of the press during wartime, discussing these matters with Wilson and the Postmaster General. At the same time his strong views

on the war led to a realignment of his domestic sympathies, which made him
yet more acceptable to the establishment. He found himself disapproving
socialist candidates for public office. When Morris Hillquit ran for mayor of
New York City in 1917, Darrow opposed him because he ran on a pacifist
program, though he was supported by Dudley Field Malone, later to be an ally
in the evolution trial in 1925. As Darrow stomped the country making pro-war
speeches, he became a spokesman for government policy. By 1918 he had even
become a part of the government's propaganda machine, in the most curious
turn of his career. He was the darling of the establishment, courted by high
government officials and by the President of the United States himself, with
whom he had a private meeting on August 1, 1917, less than one month after
America entered the war. Mutual admiration resulted, and William Kent
wrote to President Wilson that the meeting had gained Darrow's "entire
confidence and backing."[7]

The subject of discussion had been how best Darrow could help the government, but he had also asked the President to ensure that socialist periodicals
would not be intercepted by the Post Office as part of the war censorship. In
spite of his support of American entry into the war, Darrow had objected to
the Post Office's denial of mail privileges to pacifist and socialist newspapers.
He had visited Postmaster General Albert Sidney Burleson along with Roger
Baldwin, using—in the latter's words—"all his folksy talents of persuasion on
the postmaster general. Burleson just refused. . . ." Baldwin concluded that the
Post Office Department "was a graveyard for us."[8] The next port of call was
the Department of Justice, this time with Baldwin and Morris Hillquit, where
they met exactly the same response. As they put it to Robert La Follette, they
had been told to "cut out war criticism or stay out of the mails."[9] President
Wilson wrote to Darrow about all this on Thursday, August 9:

> I agree with Mr. Kent that you could probably do a great deal of good by
> speaking on the East Side of New York and, as we agreed in our recent conversa-
> tion, that is a place where wise work is very urgently needed.
>   You may be sure I will try to work out with the Postmaster-General some
> course with regard to the circulation of the Socialistic papers that will be in
> conformity with law and good sense.[10]

Once the United States entered the war, Darrow devoted almost all his time
to promoting the war effort. He became even better known as a persuasive
advocate of the energetic pursuit of victory than he had as a proponent of
America's entry into the war. The skill with which he threw himself into the
business of propaganda was merely a slight adaptation of his professional
abilities as an advocate. He was good at constructing arguments that fitted the
conclusion he wanted to reach, and his war effort won him the approval of the
masses. But among those with whom he had stood earlier in innocent idealism,
his metamorphosis from fervent supporter of the rights of man to war propagandist was more difficult to stomach. There was something tawdry about his
addresses, which appealed to a baser side of his audiences than he had attended

to before. On September 15, 1917, he spoke to a mass meeting of the American Alliance for Labor and Democracy in bellicose terms:

> There are those who say that we should not have sold ammunition to the allies. I agree with them. They are correct. We should have given it away. The United States was slow to enter this war. She was long-suffering. But now that she is in she will remain until German autocracy has been destroyed.[11]

His effective presentations of official policy drew praise from unexpected quarters. On May 18, 1918, *The New York Times* commented:

> Some of us have not found, in the past, as many opportunities as we would have liked to agree with the opinions and assertions of Clarence Darrow. That is because he has so often chosen to devote his well-recognized abilities to the upholding of causes that either were lost or in course of deserved defeat. But one statement in a recent speech of his has at least as much of truth as can be possessed by any epigrammatic presentment of a generalization, and after only a little cogitation the majority of people will admit that Mr. Darrow was quite right. . . .
>
> What he said was that nobody else was or could be so far wrong on any great question that involves the rights and liberties of men as he who remains neutral. "If you are a partisan," he declared, "you have at least one chance in two of being right: if you are neutral you have no chance to be right."[12]

Darrow's facility for what the *Times* called "epigrammatic presentment of a generalization" drew the government's attention to him, so that when the Allied governments, notably the British, asked for the names of suitable distinguished Americans to undertake a tour in Europe, his was one of thirty put forward, and he accepted. Darrow took it as a great honor, and perhaps sincerely believed it to be so, but it is difficult to credit that he did not realize the dangers inherent in acceptance, as most of the others who were asked to participate did. As James Weber Linn put it, "Not many of the original list of invitees accepted; in fact the scheme as a whole petered out. It was perhaps too obviously propagandist in intent: a wholesale drive on public opinion, without subtlety."[13] Others faced with similar invitations to join the government's propaganda juggernaut had shown themselves more fastidious; for instance, when President Wilson's Committee on Public Information had invited Lincoln Steffens to join its Foreign Press Bureau, he had declined, recognizing that "the demand is for liars and lying."[14]

But July 21, 1918, found Darrow in New York, about to sail for Europe. "I shall tell the people over there that while America was very slow in getting into the war, there were a great many people here, outside of those who were hereditary friends of the Central Powers or enemies of England, who had always been with the Allies, and who were impatient to get into the war earlier," he told reporters. "I believe we should have gone in when Belgium was invaded. . . . And no matter how long it takes, this country will never stop until Prussian militarism has been destroyed."[15] His visit lasted three months, and gave him the opportunity to meet many English literary and political figures he admired—H. G. Wells, Sidney and Beatrice Webb, Keir Hardie. He also visited France. There he was convinced that the accusations of war atrocities against German soldiers were the inventions of the Allied propaganda machine, and he came back to the United States somewhat disgusted by the lies spread by the British and French governments. He knew that "nothing is easier or more contemptible than stirring the masses with commonplace ideas and trite expressions." Yet he had become a part of that propaganda machine himself, and during his absence in Europe the American Alliance for Labor and Democracy issued an article under his name that was, in sentiment and tone, indistinguishable from current government exhortations.

It seems likely that, had not the armistice intervened very soon after Darrow's return to the United States, he would have been faced with a severe crisis of conscience. He was disillusioned by the discovery that tales of war atrocities were not true, and began discouraging the public from investment in another series of Liberty bonds, on the ground that the war could be expected to be over by Christmas. He was right—the armistice was signed on November 11.

This last-minute apostasy went unnoticed in the joy of victory and Darrow kept the renewed respectability he had achieved by lending his skill to the government. The memory of the Los Angeles bribery trials was all but expunged by his conspicuous showing of patriotic fervor. As his stature as war propagandist had grown, he was admitted once more to the circles of domestic politics that had shunned him in 1914. In the spirit of "forgive and forget" engendered by war fever, Darrow was rehabilitated. He was, in fact, one of those who had done well out of the war.

PART THREE

From Disgrace to Distinction

26

Rehabilitation

When Darrow had returned to Chicago in 1913 he was a discredited lawyer of fifty-five, his practice lost, his fame changed to notoriety, and his fortunes professionally at their lowest ebb. Yet from the point of view of posterity, his greatest achievements were still to come. Respectability was to be regained during World War I by donning the tawdry mantle of patriotism; prosperity was to be attained in the twenties (though lost in the depression); and canonization as a radical saint was assured before his death in 1938. How did this magnificent recovery come about?

The answer did not lie simply in the passing of time. It was rooted in the revolution in manners and morals that followed World War I. The intensity and bitterness of prewar politics had been dissipated; the spiritual fatigue of conflict was impossible to sustain into the twenties. Much was forgiven and forgotten in the postbellum years, when many a tub-thumper felt sheepish about his uncritical acclaim of America's war aims. In consequence, prewar scandals lost their interest: war, as the pursuit of politics by violent means, had discredited vigorous ideological efforts in the eyes of many. "Normalcy" meant caring less about issues. In particular, the passions of the struggles of labor seemed a long time gone from the standpoint of 1920.

The catharsis of war had somehow made prewar transgressions seem irrelevant by comparison with the enormity of intervening events, while Darrow's association with patriotic causes in the war had reestablished him as a public figure. Apart from that, he was the beneficiary of the revolution in morals and manners that the war had accomplished. "Men who follow war have neither faith nor piety"—but neither do they have the will to judge their fellow men. The scandal of two trials for bribery, especially when neither had resulted in conviction, was dwarfed by the scandal of the war. Then again, Darrow's trial seemed far distant in the postwar years. Events before the war seemed to belong to ancient history when America was a different, simpler place. The permissiveness of postwar America was accompanied by a remission of past sins. The enormity of the war, and the social and political reconstruction it had wrought, accentuated the present and made prewar events seem totally remote.

Darrow's rehabilitation stemmed from his stand on international affairs, but it took effect in domestic politics too. The internationalist pretensions of the left had repercussions at home that forged new links between Darrow and the establishment while discrediting much of the isolationism of both right and left. For example, much of the wind was taken out of the sails of the left by the patent fact that President Wilson was a sincere and avid supporter of the Russian Revolution, which caused Darrow to fall into the government camp yet more and to sympathize with American radicals like Debs even less. For America initially supported the Russian Revolution and was the first Western power of any significance to recognize the provisional government. On April 2, 1917, President Wilson made an official call for war against the Central Powers, speaking of "the wonderful and heartening things that have been happening in the last few weeks in Russia."[1] The President was appealing to a sentiment in America that was against oppression yet peculiarly ill-informed. American sympathies were to take a completely different turn within a very short time, and this, among other things, was to recoil upon Wilson, of whom Debs would shortly say: "No man in public life in American history ever retired so thoroughly discredited, so scathingly rebuked, so overwhelmingly impeached and repudiated. . . ."[2] But for the moment it was Wilson who appeared to be on the side of the angels, while Debs seemed churlish if not downright treasonable.

The stumbling block of American radicalism was that in its redder hues at least it did indeed involve rejection of America in preference for some other locale. In the immediate postwar period a number of well-known radicals such as Big Bill Haywood and John Reid chose to emigrate to Russia, while others, though not convinced of Russian virtue, contrived in the postwar years to remain for long years abroad. The supposed internationalism of the radicals, no longer sustainable by an illusion of solidarity, was revealed as an urge to escape from the United States. Brand Whitlock, once aide to Altgeld, later mayor of Toledo, Ohio, was one of those in Darrow's circle. "Since the war," wrote Darrow, "Mr. Whitlock has virtually remained abroad. He finds more freedom in Continental Europe than in his native land, with its bigotry and intolerance." There was an affinity between the generation of Darrow, Charles Edward Russell, and Brand Whitlock and the generation of Sinclair Lewis and Scott Fitzgerald. Whitlock was the older generation's representative in France, as Fitzgerald was the younger's; some of the brightest lights in both generations tended toward expatriation in that era, finding abroad a freedom and gaiety they could not attain in their homeland. "Their anguish fills the Liberal weeklies, and every ship that puts out from New York carries a groaning cargo of them, bound for Paris, London, Munich, Rome and way points—anywhere to escape the great curses and atrocities that make life intolerable for them at home," wrote Mencken with his customary vigor, then reflecting that it was "easier for him to stay than to join the exodus."[3] Darrow fell into Mencken's category. He frequently asserted that he stayed in America because he chose to do so: "if I did not like the United States better than any other country, I would not stay here because I could go away; in that regard I have an advantage over some others who must stay."⁴ He preferred to remain and fight the characteristics that he disliked. Nevertheless, like Mencken, he understood the motives that prompted his own and later generations to move abroad.

In this respect, the war caused a parting of the ways and a fragmentation of the left in America from which it was never to recover. It was the end of the age of innocence, for it showed that platitudes of international brotherhood turned out to mean different things to different groups when a practical political decision must be made. Darrow was not so blinded by ideology or in the thrall of faith for his views to follow a cause slavishly. This was his difference with Debs, and with many of those with whom he had sympathized in the labor movement. He was not a believer, either religiously or politically. He would never have emigrated to Russia, as Bill Haywood and John Reid did; he saw too many difficulties with all-embracing theories, too many blemishes on the complexion of radicalism. And this gulf between him and the left was widened, or at least uncovered, by the war.

On the domestic front, Darrow had made a rapid transition from opposition to the militarist aspects of the Buster Brown League to membership of the National Security League, an organization primarily concerned with "Preparedness" and opposition to local political figures who were not supportive of the Allied cause. In 1917, this meant opposition to Big Bill Thompson as mayor of Chicago. And as the course of Chicago politics was consistent during peace or war, a number of political defenses came Darrow's way.

The Chicago political machine was running profitably in 1917, with graft keeping many people, including Chief of Police Charles Healey, quite happy, but this state of affairs came to an end when the state's attorney of Cook County, Maclay Hoyne, started an investigation of corruption in City Hall. From his investigation came indictments charging a number of politicians and officials with corrupt practices. The defendants in two of the most sensational trials retained Clarence Darrow's services.

In January 1917 Alderman Oscar DePriest, the first black alderman of the city, was indicted by a grand jury for "conspiracy to allow gambling houses and houses of prostitution to operate and for bribery of police officers in connection with the operation of these houses." The evidence against DePriest was strong, because witnesses who had turned state's evidence testified that he had accepted money from gangsters to be used as bribes and paid it to policemen. DePriest was acquitted thanks to Clarence Darrow's contention that the payments made were campaign contributions, not bribes. One commentator on the trial remarked: "the evidence tended to support the indictment." Another simply quoted Professor Merriam as a comment on the case: "Chicago is unique. It is the only completely corrupt city in America."⁵

Darrow had secured his client's acquittal by a speech to the jury warning them against convicting DePriest through a prejudice against his race. In fact, evidence in the trial seemed to point to DePriest's deliberate peddling of police protection in the second ward. In another trial arising out of the Hoyne raids, Darrow defended the chief of police, Charles C. Healey, on the same charges as were levied against DePriest. Healey, like DePriest, was acquitted.

In securing the acquittals of Healey and DePriest, Darrow shared the defense with Charles E. Erbstein, a very successful criminal lawyer, and one trusted by criminals themselves. Darrow several times in the ensuing years would cooperate with Erbstein, who was a notable member of the Chicago legal fraternity. Erbstein shared a special bond with Darrow: like him, he had been prosecuted unsuccessfully twice for jury bribery.

Darrow's reputation as a criminal, rather than a labor, lawyer dates from this period. Although he had always done some criminal litigation, it was not the major part of his practice from 1894 to 1912, which had encompassed many civil matters, notably corporate and labor work. In rebuilding his practice after the Los Angeles disaster, however, he had needed work and took whatever came. The result was that he undertook the defense of many disreputable defendants. He was not proud of it, and rather shrank from the reputation he built up as a good crook's mouthpiece, a miracle worker, who could and regularly did snatch the guilty from the clutches of justice. Being a criminal lawyer paid, but he knew it was not a compliment to his integrity; "though the professional thief uses lawyers . . . and tries to get the most capable lawyers available when he needs one, he believes that few lawyers in the city are honest and that most of them win their cases by using crooked methods."[6]

Darrow did not like to be known as a criminal lawyer because of the stigma it carried, and he did not want to be known as a labor lawyer now that he had been repudiated by the labor movement. He wrote to Henry Mencken about his dilemma when he contributed to the *American Mercury*:

> It has occurred to me that you have a Who's Who business in the back of your magazine giving a sketch of the contributors. Less said about me the better. Please *don't* say I am a "labor lawyer." If anything you can say I am a lawyer. . . . Please *don't* say I am a criminal lawyer—although I am both. Still, as to law, I have done *all sorts.*[7]

Darrow had been trapped by his own past; it was far too late for him to complain of being described as a labor or criminal lawyer. He was reaping what he had sown for many years, and in spite of his protests, posterity would remember him for his primacy in these spheres. In fact Darrow was doing nothing different from any other lawyer engaged in criminal defense work in Chicago, but it was at this point that he began to be criticized for putting his talents to the use of professional criminals. Previously he had represented defendants whose political affiliations he had approved, or at least sympathized with. Now, his immediate radical justifications having gone, he expanded his view that no one was guilty, and hence an all-purpose rationale was concocted which bore no reference to an accused's motive or situation. It was this revision of his principles, forced largely by circumstances, that would reach its apogee in 1924. In the postwar period, Darrow was to make a slow, almost imperceptible shift from being an advocate who was a passionate believer to one who believed in nothing at all. His critics did not immediately perceive this change, and while grudgingly admitting that criminal defendants had a right to a defense, did not want them to have a good defense.

Yet, in this respect, the critics did not really have a much different view from Darrow himself; it was merely that they did not see eye to eye regarding who deserved a good defense and who did not. Darrow did not conceive his duty as being simply that of a mouthpiece. He believed that he must deliver speeches on his clients' behalf that were of a humanitarian and progressive tendency. Thus, whether he could deliver depended upon choosing a client for whom a liberal argument could be made, and that in turn meant that he had to prejudge his client's case. Was he merely a victim of circumstances, or was he an incorrigble rogue? Had he told his lawyer the truth or had he not? The stumbling block of Darrow's theory was that once committed to a client, it was difficult to withdraw even if the facts turned out to be very different from what he had first supposed. In consequence he sometimes found it necessary to paint a picture of his clients that was far too rosy.

On the theory that he should not lend his talents to clients of whom he disapproved, Darrow originally withheld his services from conscientious objectors who refused to submit to the draft. "Luckily, as I felt, I was not invited into any of the cases of the conscientious objectors. Most of them, for the time, realized the gulf between us."[8] Besides, his work on behalf of the government became more and more time-consuming. When 165 leading members of the Wobblies were indicted for conspiracy to hinder the war effort on September 28, 1917, their first thought was to hire Darrow. But he was too busy in Washington to undertake the work, though he offered some assistance from his office; the services of George F. Vanderveer were retained instead.

By this time Darrow's new-found status as darling of the Wilson government had had its repercussions in the rank-and-file of the IWW, where—as Ralph Chaplin put it—"unconfirmed rumor had it that Darrow's 'war work' consisted of helping to draw up the Espionage law under which we were to be tried."[9] Whether or not this was true, it was manifest that he had allied himself with the government. Nevertheless Darrow offered Bill Haywood the use of his investigating staff, which was considered "second to none in the city."[10] As it turned out, the defendants probably fared no worse at trial with Vanderveer than they would have with Darrow, especially in view of the fact that it took place before Judge Kenesaw Mountain Landis, whose disapproval of Darrow had made him refuse to sign a testimonial for him during the Los Angeles jury bribery cases, and whose investigation into illegal gambling Darrow had confounded only the previous year by advising Mont Tennes to take the Fifth. The IWW for its part began to doubt its wisdom in being so doctrinaire about the necessity of having lawyers to represent it who were personally committed to IWW policy.

The issue raised by the IWW prosecution was a fundamental one, symptomatic of the splintering of the extreme left: some of those prosecuted really did have contempt for the law and its machinery, believing that to reply to the accusations made against them was to dignify them. Their view in World War

I was both contemptuous and resigned, and treated the law as an instrument of oppression, manipulated to make it a crime to speak the truth. There was something of this in the attitude of Emma Goldman and Margaret Sanger; but its most articulate exponent during the war was Eugene Debs, whose pacifist stance was uncompromising and who did not want to be acquitted, except on the ground that the Sedition Act was unconstitutional. He did not wish to benefit from "lawyers' tricks," and was prepared to admit that he gave the speech alleged by the prosecution. Darrow offered his services to Debs, but they were refused in favor of representation by a number of socialist-pacifist attorneys, including William Cunnea, who had run for state's attorney in Chicago in 1916 on the socialist ticket and was a friend of Darrow's. Darrow could forgive Debs's pacifism, but Debs could not compromise with Darrow's belligerence. It was a foregone conclusion that Debs would be convicted, as his attorneys told him. The militance of some labor clients before the war had been manifest in their determination not to bow before the courts even by defending themselves—and the war brought out a similar attitude in many others.

There were many less famous defendants, however, who were glad to accept Darrow's services, and these Darrow helped. "Over and over I went to the government offices in Chicago to save someone from imprisonment that I knew was not hostile to the United States, but who was accused of disloyalty. In most cases I succeeded because the authorities knew that I was for the war and they could trust my honesty in the matter." Official acknowledgment of his honesty was important to a man whose honesty had been impugned in a court of law only six years before. On Darrow's birthday in April 1918 a large dinner was given in his honor at the Auditorium Hotel, which was attended by civic and literary leaders alike. He had achieved an almost total comeback. He told the crowd: "No one ever gave me a dinner like this before, and I really do not know how my friends happened to take into their heads to do it this time."[11] But, of course, it was as a public mark of his return to respectability—an outward sign that the past had been buried and that he could hold his head high once more. His birthday was a convenient occasion to mark the fact that his own return from the wars had been helped by the change of attitudes and determination that America's war had brought about. In the spirit of wartime, the charges against Darrow seemed to dwindle into pettiness and unimportance. What counted was what he was doing now, not what his past had been.

Because of the reevaluations the war had forced upon his attitudes, Darrow himself took the opportunity to take stock of his own career and the motive force behind it. For a few moments, that evening at the Auditorium Hotel, the mask was lifted to reveal the man's true identity. What made him tick? He supplied an answer that came nearer to candor than any other public statement he ever made; it was the testimony of a mature man, already old enough to recognize in his life a discernible pattern.

Even while I have fought for freedom, the freedom of others and the freedom of myself, I have always had a consciousness that I was doing it to amuse myself, to keep myself occupied so I might forget myself; which after all is the best thing that any of us can do as we go along. . . . I have always yearned for peace, but have lived a life of war. I do not know why, excepting that it is the law of my being. I have lived a life in the front trenches, looking for trouble. . . . There, for a short time, you really live. It is hard, but it is life. Activity is life.

This is life and all there is of life; to play the game, to play the cards we get; play them uncomplainingly and to play them to the end. The game may not be worth the while. The stakes may not be worth the winning. But the playing of the game is the forgetting of self, and we should be game sports and play it bravely to the end.[12]

Darrow's self-knowledge and insight revealed in this speech were profound and notably free from bombast. Passivity made him unhappy, and therefore he had been active. There were no false claims of charity here; the analysis was not marred by conceit. His low opinion of the human psyche and his disbelief in the perfectability of man turned out to be based in part upon introspection. He saw in himself those forces of darkness that had a place in all humanity and made human beings as dangerous as they were. He had not murdered, but he had read some obituaries with a good deal of satisfaction.

Indirectly, Darrow owed his capacity for unflinching self-appraisal to his bribery case. Prosecution brought with it a reordering of priorities borne of introspection. As the painful memory of the Los Angeles ordeal faded, he was able to evaluate himself and his motives with a startling candor. In many ways this was the period of his best, most truthful work. Stripped, for the moment, of his position of public honor, he was able to see himself more clearly, and to communicate better the mainsprings of his character and persuasions. It was now, until the twenties reestablished his celebrity and replaced introversion by ebullience once more, that he explained himself best.

He had been a controversial figure, not from moral principle so much as from the love of the heat of battle and out of a fear of idleness. By joining the fray, he induced what he called "forgetfulness," his confessed need for which explained his perverse delight in unpopular causes as much as idealism. The need to avoid melancholy brooding was the mainspring of his energies. Like Scott Fitzgerald, he found that in the dark night of the soul it is always three o'clock in the morning. He sought refuge not from a cruel world but from his own mental agonies. Unlike Fitzgerald he did not drink, but his addiction was just as compelling. Immersed in controversy, he was as surely drowning his unhappiness as with a bottle of booze. His support of the "wets" reflected his understanding of the inner pain that led men to seek the temporary oblivion of a drunk. His psyche was strong enough to find forgetfulness by rushing into the fray, but he understood the opposite desire to escape. Fitzgerald expressed the sentiments of a generation deprived of stability and standards, whereas Darrow, having had those things, preferred to reject them.

As a whole generation threw over the conventions of the prewar era, Darrow's tenets seemed to have great sophistication. The social dislocations of war caused a lapse of piety—and he was the great agnostic. His derision of Ben Franklin's precepts of thrift seemed justified in a postwar boom unparalleled before; even his hypothesis that work was a silly way to become rich seemed to be validated. Alone among the stuffy older generation, he was in tune with the times. The young found so little to praise and so much to debunk that Darrow's persistence on the "off" side of everything put him in the *avant garde,* and his anti-authoritarianism was such that youthful psychopath and devil-may-care debutante alike might approve. His antagonism to prohibition made him an ally of the smart set, while the open flouting of the Volstead Act, passed in 1919 to prevent commercial sale of alcoholic beverages, brought the virtues of obedience to a new low estate. Even to those few who were still plagued by occasional pangs of conscience Darrow offered solace, for his determinism left no room for praise or blame or any moral responsibility.

A war had been fought, supposedly upon a great issue, and in retrospect the great issue had been dwarfed. The nation was impatient with great issues, fearful that they might turn out to be, as had World War I, smaller than they appeared at first glance. In consequence, even serious issues were treated lightheartedly or cynically; somehow the war had drained politics of much of their prewar intensity. Writing to Negley Cochran, writer on the Toledo *Blade,* in 1921 of Vincent St. John, the one-time leader of the IWW, Darrow recognized this: "He is probably like you and me," he confided, "and got over his illusions that he could do much good and has embarked on the laudable business of getting money. . . ."[13] A quarter century had passed since Brand Whitlock had chided Darrow himself for being "under the awful compulsion of the age, to make money." Now making money seemed a harmless preoccupation by comparison with violent politics.

It was the attitude of many people, Darrow included. And in postwar America he, like many others, would prosper as never before.

27

The Early Twenties

Darrow immersed himself in the problems of postwar reconstruction at home and abroad. As soon as the war was over, he campaigned for the release of those who had been interned and defended those who had been charged with war-related crimes—notably under the Espionage Act.[1]

His aid to the Allied governments had put him in a stronger position than ever to use his influence with government officials on behalf of clients and others whose welfare interested him, and he did so on several occasions in the postwar years, beginning with President Wilson and later with Harding. But he was wary of enmeshing himself too much in his new-found affiliation with the establishment. Unlike others, he wanted neither place nor title:

> When the war was over, and so many orators found themselves out of employment, I was urged to help form an organization of those patriots who, like myself, were safe in America making speeches with a view to inducing young boys to fight. It didn't appeal to me. I sensed that most of the members of the organization would be looking for office after they were all organized, and many of them did not wait that long.
>
> Almost every day some of my friends came along parading the titles of "Colonel" and "Major" and so forth, who had been nowhere near the war, as every one knew. Thereupon I suggested that no American should have a war title if he had been anywhere east of Washington D.C. during the struggle.

By this time, too, he was confident of his ability to earn a living from the practice of law once more. By the beginning of 1918 he had achieved a continuous flow of work, mostly criminal, which he found interesting and lucrative, and which put him back in the swing of things, legally and politically.

As a lawyer, Darrow was already beginning to find that the younger generation starting out in the profession looked to him as a kind of hero, undaunted by the embarrassments of the prewar era. And in spite of his uncomplimentary attitude to his own profession, he always found the time to talk with young aspirants who came to his office to pay homage. Darrow never forgot that he got his first chance because of the kindness of men who were already estab-

lished, and even at the pinnacle of his fame he would put work aside to help
a young unknown.

Behind the scenes he continued to aid radicals entangled with the law at the
same time he was actively engaged in the war effort. When Emma Goldman,
the anarchist, and Alexander Berkman were convicted of conspiracy to violate
the Selective Service Law, he accepted the invitation to help with their appeal
to the Supreme Court, challenging the law's constitutionality, but wrote to
Harry Weinberger, the lawyer in charge of the case, that he did not want his
name on the brief.[2] No doubt he wanted to avoid both stealing the thunder of
the other lawyers involved and the difficulty of explaining to the public how
he could advocate the energetic prosecution of the war and defend Goldman
and Berkman at one and the same time.

After the war, Darrow was able to use some of the fees paid by prosperous
clients to subsidize cases involving worthwhile causes. Nearly all of the latter
involved incidents arising out of wartime restrictions on free speech. These
provided him with a substitute for the labor cases he had given up; they were
a new crusade. By their very nature, however, they were a dwindling species
—though they were augmented by the "red raids" of the postwar Attorney
General Mitchell Palmer who, relying on fears brought on by the success of
the Russian Revolution, instituted a campaign of suppression of radical
groups. The year 1919 marked the watershed of America's distrust of foreign
radical ideology. Anarchism had been the hobgoblin; now it was communism.
Until the end of World War I the chances were that if a radical got into trouble
with the law, he would be an anarchist—and even if he was not, he would be
branded one. But the passion for arson that anarchism stood for in the public
mind became diverted by the war, which was another, better way of releasing
destructive energies. Only the excesses of the overthrow of czardom supplanted anarchism's first place in the public wrath by communism. Of course
both anarchists and Communists were reviled, but the shift in emphasis was
undeniable. Two of the cases arising out of the war taken by Darrow illustrate
the trend.

The first case involved eleven alleged anarchists, who had each received
sentences of twenty-five years' imprisonment as a result of a wartime clash in
Milwaukee involving rival groups of Italians. In August and September 1917,
a minister by the name of August Guliani took to holding Sunday meetings
at the corner of Bishop and Potter avenues in Milwaukee. These meetings were
entirely legal and he had obtained permits for holding them in advance. At the
meetings held on the last Sunday of August and the first two Sundays in
September, Guliani encountered strong opposition from a group comprising
the defendants in the later trial. It was never established whether the opposition was stimulated by Guliani's alleged anti-Catholicism or by his speeches
in favor of the war, but it appears likely that the hostility was mainly due to
his pro-war views. One of the defendants, Amedeo Lilli, was proved to have
said: "We don't believe in this war. You came here because you want to preach
about the war, we don't believe in any government, Wilson is a pig, the

American flag is a rag, and this country is a jail." Guliani, realizing that trouble was brewing, asked for police protection at his meeting on September 9. The meeting had not progressed very far before attempts were made to break it up by the same group that had heckled Guliani on previous Sundays. One of them, Tony Formaceo, was asked to move on by a policeman. Formaceo pulled a revolver and a gun battle started, resulting in his death, among others. As a result, all the members of the opposition group were arrested on the theory that each of them had conspired to assault with intent to murder. On that theory, all were convicted after a fifteen-day trial.

Darrow had not represented the defendants at trial, but there were several aspects of the case that encouraged him to appeal it on their behalf. Once more he was up against his old enemy the conspiracy theory, which imputed the actions of one man to another through the use of doubtfully admissible evidence. The sentences were not only harsh, but demonstrated no effort by the sentencing judge to distinguish the culpability of different defendants, who all got the same term of imprisonment. Finally there was an aspect of the case that struck a chord of sympathy with Darrow because of his own experience as a defendant in Los Angeles. He had always felt that he had been unable to obtain total acquittal in his second trial for bribery because of the prejudicial effect of the publicity given to an anarchist case just before his own trial, in which the defendants had been found guilty. Here precisely the same kind of possible prejudice might have been at work. Four days before the trial of these defendants began, a bomb explosion occurred at the central police station in Milwaukee which killed several people. The Milwaukee papers attributed the explosion to groups associated with the defendants, thereby turning public opinion even further against them.

On his return from Europe, Darrow, with his partner Peter Sissman and local Milwaukee counsel, set to work on a brief for the Wisconsin Supreme Court. It argued that the evidence did not justify imputing the shooting to the defendants generally, and that no conspiracy to assault with intent to kill had been shown at all. The real offense of the majority of these defendants, it said, was that they held unpopular opinions. Darrow went to argue the case orally before the court in March 1919 and achieved remarkably favorable results for his clients. He succeeded in overturning the conviction of nine out of the eleven, the only two whose convictions were affirmed being men who had weapons and who did not disperse after shooting broke out. Two others had their cases remanded for a new trial; the other seven had their convictions reversed and were completely discharged. Inevitably, the Wisconsin court had not adopted all of his arguments in the anarchists' favor—in particular, it had not accepted his contention about the prejudicial effect of the bombing of the Milwaukee police station just before the trial—but in a number of respects he had convinced the court of the dangers of the allegation of conspiracy, and the court held that, on the evidence, no conspiracy was proved.[3]

By contrast, the case known as *People* v. *Lloyd* involved the newer obsession with communism, and twenty Communists were prosecuted for violation of the Espionage Act of 1919. Communism had not been greatly feared by the American people at the time of the Russian Revolution; indeed, American entry into World War I had been linked in President Wilson's official statement on the subject on April 2, 1917, with his approval of it. But the mood of American diplomacy and the American people had changed sharply when they heard of the revolution's excesses. There had been a romantic association in the minds of some Americans between the revolution that had thrown off the yoke of King George III and the revolution against Czar Nicholas II. Events proved that the better analogy would have been to the French Revolution. Instead of the terror, there were pogroms; instead of the guillotine, the firing squad. The very mistake that had led Americans to see similarities between Russia and America now repulsed them, and a fear spread that events in Russia were a premonition of the shape of things to come. This apprehension was in the back of many minds when Attorney General Palmer began his "red raids."

The Lloyd case gave Darrow an opportunity to defend freedom of belief, of speech, and association. His speech to the jury combined an eloquent justification of the right to dissent with a denunciation of the conspiracy laws, which allowed the acts of one defendant to be attributed to another if both acted with common purpose. A charge of conspiracy in restraint of trade had been the traditional prosecutor's tool in suppression of trade unions, and many of his most hard-fought cases had been indicted as conspiracies. Here, once again, was a chance to speak out against the conspiracy laws. The fact that Darrow himself was fond of imputing a conspiracy, as he had done in the Haywood case and in his own trial, did not deter him from decrying laws that made conspiracies crimes. (It was an irony of history that, though he had opposed business cartels and monopoly throughout his life, the antitrust laws passed at the turn of the century—the Sherman and Clayton acts—had relied upon the very conspiracy theory he had so often criticized.)

The Chicago Communists were prosecuted for advocating the overthrow of the government by force. The Communist Labor Party had just been formed, with a strong sprinkling of the foreign-born, though it also included native-born Americans like William Bross Lloyd, son of Henry Demarest Lloyd. Much of the evidence was designed to show that the defendants had endorsed and encouraged, if not inspired, a general strike in Seattle in 1919, with the intention of taking political control of the city; the chief witness for the prosecution was Ole Hanson, a former mayor of Seattle. Darrow made one of his best arguments founded in logic, rather than emotion, in defense of the Communists, telling the jury:

> I shall not argue to you whether the defendants' ideas are right or wrong. I am
> not bound to believe them right in order to take their case, and you are not bound
> to believe them right in order to find them not guilty. I don't know whether they
> are right or wrong. But I do know this—I know that the humblest and the
> meanest man who lives, I know that the idlest and the silliest man who lives,
> should have his say. I know he ought to speak his mind. And I know that the
> Constitution is a delusion and a snare if the weakest and the humblest man in

the land cannot be defended in his right to speak and his right to think as much
as the greatest and the strongest in the land. I am not here to defend their
opinions. I am here to defend their right to express their opinions.[4]

From this standpoint he went on to argue that the defendants were entitled
to think and speak as they had done, taking one by one the complaints of the
prosecution. The prosecution complained they did not believe in the Constitution—but they were not on trial for that. There were many people who criticized it, from the foundation of the Republic down to Professor Charles Beard,
whose economic interpretation of the Constitution had recently been published. The prosecutor complained that the defendants owned red flags—but
they had as much right to that as to a green, or a yellow one, or one of any
other color. They were accused of being sympathetic with the Russian Revolution—but was not President Wilson one of the first to applaud the overthrow
of tyranny that it involved? The Communist Labor Party was said to seek the
control of industry. "Is there any reason on earth why the poor should not
control industry if they can? I submit there is none." They were said to have
incited and encouraged a general strike, but that was not illegal: "I say again,
that a strike, a general strike or a special strike, is perfectly lawful. If a general
strike results in violence, you may punish the violence, and that is all."

He attacked the prosecution on two fronts. First, he hammered home the
point that the evidence for the prosecution was illegally procured. The police
had entered Lloyd's home without a search warrant and rifled through his
papers. If the prosecutor stood for constitutionalism, how could this happen?
"What right had a state's attorney, who ought to support the Constitution of
the United States and the state of Illinois, what right had he to violate the law
in this way?" Indeed this complaint was one frequently to be levied later at
the "red raids"—that, in the name of the law, the conduct of the authorities
was lawless.

Second, Darrow poured scorn on the testimony of Mayor Hanson. Hanson
had told the court that his city was in danger of being taken over by the
Communist Labor Party agitators. But Darrow introduced into evidence Hanson's statements at the time, none of which referred to the danger of a Communist takeover. Hanson had left his job as mayor of Seattle to join the lecture
circuits to make money. How dedicated a public servant was he?

> Is Ole Hanson hard to understand? Is he? Doesn't he show, all over him, the
> marks of a cheap poser? Doesn't he show all over him evidence of a lightheaded
> notoriety hunter? . . . When he was advertised from one end of America to
> another for his fool proclamation because he was the jumping-jack mayor of
> Seattle, when his advertising was worth thousands in lecture courses, he forth-
> with lays down his job and leaves Seattle to go to the dogs, or to the workingmen,
> as the case might be.

But Lloyd was convicted. Darrow's skillful arguments did not touch a jury in
Chicago criminal court in 1920. The defendants were unattractive—Darrow
knew this, and avoided appealing to the jury on their behalf:

If you want to convict these twenty men, then do it. I ask no consideration on behalf of any one of them. If you have any idea in your heads that I want you to protect them or save them, forget it. . . . I am not interested in them. . . . I am interested in the policy of the country. I am interested in the verdict of this jury as to whether this country shall be ruled by the conscienceless men who would stifle freedom of speech when it interferes with their gold; or whether this jury will stand by the principles of the fathers and, whether so far as you can, you will stop this mad wave that threatens to engulf the liberty of the American citizens.

The jury took Darrow's invitation, convicting the defendants. The case went on appeal to the Illinois Supreme Court, which refused to overturn the convictions, with one justice dissenting.

The bench that heard the Lloyd appeal had known Darrow for a long time. Judge and jury were in age if not disposition his peers. Gleefully they quoted precedents to him bearing upon his client's case that had been created by previous *causes célèbres* in which Darrow had appeared. It was almost as if they were telling him that a lifetime of law practice in his state had not convinced them one whit of his radical opinions. Perhaps the result would have been exactly the same no matter who the lawyer representing Lloyd had been. But it added a special sense of occasion to quote back to Darrow the Debs case and others.

Darrow was concerned with results, though, and not legalisms. As in other cases, he took the battle into the political sphere and sought executive clemency. His political "pull" was considerable as a result of his war efforts, and on November 29, 1922, the governor of Illinois pardoned sixteen of the defendants.

Meanwhile the number of clients with problems arising out of their wartime activities was dwindling rapidly and his peacetime practice necessarily found new directions. Three strands to his court work may be traced in the early twenties: his continuing aid to the poor or misguided defendant he believed he could help; the defense of the rising breed of Chicago gangster; and the equally entertaining defense of political grafters. His reputation for taking the cases of the poor and the hopeless meant that he got referrals from other lawyers faced with seemingly insoluble predicaments. Always Darrow replied, and if there was the slightest hope, took on the case. Not a generous man with money, Darrow never stinted with his time; he answered even casual inquiries from people he did not know carefully and at length.

The problems presented were often psychological or social—and the solutions were common-sense more than legal. In the course of his long career Darrow had picked up a substantial acquaintanceship among the incorrigible criminals of the nation, and it often happened that, when apprehended in some strange city, a criminal would reveal that sometime in the past he had been defended or helped by Clarence Darrow. More often than not this prompted someone to write to Darrow for help. An example is the case of John R. Randolph, who was arrested for burglary in Denver, Colorado, in 1922. His case came to the attention of Judge Benjamin Barr Lindsey, who wrote to Darrow because Darrow had already helped Randolph before. Judge Lindsey was mainly concerned about Mrs. Randolph, a woman of good family who had met her husband while she was engaged in prison and reform work. Darrow's reply illustrates the care with which he dealt with such inquiries:

My Dear Judge Lindsey:

Your letter of May 2nd is received. I know John R. Randolph, if that is his name. I do not suppose even he remembers what his name is, and I likewise know his wife. I think you know me well enough to know that I will be very careful not to do an injustice to anyone who might suffer on account of it.

Randolph was in the penitentiary in Missouri, if I recall it, for burglary. His wife and his wife's mother whom I have known for many years, were instrumental in getting him out. He then married the young woman. Her mother later came to see me because she could not get track of the daughter. I looked him up and found the evidence to show that he was a professional burglar. I advised her mother that he would turn up sooner or later to see the outcome of things. Not long after that, early in December last, the wife came to me in great trouble because her husband had been arrested and was in the lockup for burglary. I told her that there was nothing that could be done for him and that she ought to get a divorce and get it at once. There were many charges against him here at the time and there was no sort of question about his profession, but she succeeded in getting bail for him and they came to my office, together. I told him what I had told her, that it would be impossible for him to change and that if he really cared anything about his wife he should leave her. He said if he ever got into trouble again he would. I urged him to do it at the time but of course he did not. I am not certain what was done with the cases and he went somewhere else to ply his trade. If he is released in Denver, we will hear of him in some other state. I say all this without the slightest feeling against him. I am sorry for him, but it is out of the question for him to change. If he were sixty years old and somebody would take care of him, he might not have ambition enough to engage in business any further, or if there should be such a change in society that he would get as much as I do in a safer trade, he would follow that, but with society as it is, he never can do anything else.

He seems to me to be a nice fellow and under other environment in his early life, might have been a good respectable hodcarrier, getting $50.00 a week and being satisfied, but he is too ambitious to hold any job that is recognized by society, with the attainments he has. Of course there is no other place for him than prison, although I wish there was.

His wife is all right. She comes of a good family, has been in newspaper work; has written some good short stories. She has ability and is a fine person. Of course she is not guilty of any crime. I am certain of it. It may be that any wife of the right sort would get remotely implicated with something the husband did, if the husband was this sort and she most certainly will if she sticks to him, but everything ought to be done that is possible to help her to leave her husband. I told her this when she was here and I told it to her in his presence, with the best intentions to both of them. If he had the right kind of feeling, he would tell her the same. He has absolutely no business to have a wife.

I am willing to do anything I possibly can to help her in her difficulty and if there is any danger of her suffering any through this, let me know and I will see that anything that I can do is done.

You are at perfect liberty to show her this letter and to show it to her husband. She has no chance whatever unless she quits him.

I expect to be out your way this summer and shall call and see you.

With kindest regards, as ever,

Your friend,

Clarence Darrow[5]

Even sorting through referrals such as this in order to decide whether anything could be done for the unhappy defendants took a great deal of time, which was uncompensated. Throughout his years of practice Darrow arranged that about one-third of his clients received his services free. But he did not take their cases simply because they were poor; there had to be some aspect of their situation that was challenging and some prospect that his intervention would achieve good results. He claimed never to have taken a charity case by assignment from a judge. Always he screened the case himself.

In this particular case, the charges against Mrs. Randolph were dismissed. Randolph pleaded guilty to burglary and robbery and was sentenced to not less than five years or more than nine, which meant that with remission for good behavior he could get out in two to three years. On hearing this news, Darrow wrote back to Judge Lindsey: "Randolph is certainly lucky. Possibly too lucky. I don't see anything in him that shows the possibility of his recovery. I wish there was but he can't do it."[6]

The continual referral and re-referral of this sort of case was one of the reasons that Darrow did not retire or wind down his practice; without trying, he found his time occupied. Yet he was sixty-five in 1922, with no incentive to keep his practice going for the benefit of his child. As his reputation grew, he paid the penalty of success. Clients and would-be clients came to him because they believed he could help them, but more than that, that he could save them. The onus upon him grew with his reputation: he was believed to be a miracle worker, a genius who could snatch success from adversity. Rich and poor alike displayed a touching faith in his abilities. Yet Darrow, the realist, knew full well that he could not win losing cases and that inevitably some clients would be convicted. The burden of dealing with desperate, trusting clients became greater and greater, and he became less and less willing to remain at the center of the struggle.

Nevertheless, so long as he remained in harness and took such cases, he faced the problem of subsidizing the nonpaying clients by charging high fees in the paying cases he took. And so Darrow found ways to make one client pay for another's litigation as well as his own. Wealthy clients in the criminal arena came from the ranks of professional criminals and—what often amounted to the same thing in the environs of Chicago—professional politicians.

Chicago was a city in which money had come easily to many people. Unexplained wealth attracted less attention than elsewhere, with the advantage that the Great Fire of 1871 had destroyed birth records and questions of identity were rather harder to prove there than in other places. Many incorrigibles were proud to call themselves graduates of the Chicago school of crime. Yet although Darrow received a considerable amount of business from the notorious criminals and grafters of Chicago's most spectacular era, his forensic talents were never monopolized by gangster clients. If any one type of client can be singled out as typical for him, it must be the political grafter rather than the mobster.

The twenties provided an entertaining and scandalous pageant of politics in Chicago that has not been rivaled since. The era was one that repaid Darrow's assiduous cultivation of behind-the-scenes political contacts, for the tales to be told were far more extraordinary than anything revealed to the public. The cynical plunderings of everything the city or county could lay hands on—from the school board to the tuberculosis sanitarium to the Department of Parks and Recreations—exceeded the worst nightmares of civic corruption of the muckrakers. And the muckrakers were now gone. True, the Chicago newspapers still complained and exposed and reprimanded, but the moral indignation of the muckraking era had dissolved in postwar prosperity.

In 1922 Mayor "Big Bill" Thompson's campaign manager, Fred Lundin, was indicted with others for conspiracy to misappropriate more than $1 million of school funds. Lundin, a seasoned performer in the high comedy of Chicago politics, even managed to look the part of its chief comedian: in his old-fashioned morning-coat, his jauntily knotted bowtie, and wire-rimmed spectacles, he might more readily have passed for a music-hall "turn" than adviser to a mayor. Darrow and Erbstein defended him. The testimony tended to show that the school board had bought supplies at rather more than their market price from suppliers with connections with City Hall. For instance, contracts for doors in new school buildings were awarded to the Central Metallic Door Company, owned by Lundin. Notwithstanding a considerable amount of testimony to this effect, Lundin was acquitted. There were some splendid moments, as when Darrow called on Thompson to testify as to Lundin's honesty. Then Darrow put Lundin on the stand and guided him through his testimony so that he appeared an honest but misunderstood man. Finally, Darrow told the jury: "If Fred Lundin or any other man in this case could be convicted on this evidence, made up of suspicions and cobwebs, then I want to retire to a cannibal island and be safe! This is an infamous conspiracy against the liberties of man."

During this entire performance a delegation of Japanese jurists attended the trial, studiously watching the proceedings for pointers on the improvement of the administration of justice in their native land. "What weird and unbelieved tales they must have told their friends of the state of civilization in the Land of the Free when they returned home," remarked one commentator. As the jury went out, a circle formed around Darrow, laughing and joking while awaiting the verdict. And when an acquittal was returned, it was said of Lundin, "only with the help of God and Clarence Darrow did he escape the penitentiary."[7]

The trial had two points of special interest in the light of Darrow's career. First, even at this stage, a number of prospective jurors in the trial expressed strong views about Darrow reflecting upon his integrity and beliefs, and were excused for cause; thus, even ten years after his Los Angeles encounter, the mud stuck. Second, the prosecution was put in motion by Robert Crowe, the state's attorney whom Darrow was later to attack bitterly in the Leopold and Loeb trial.

Perhaps of all his clients, Fred Lundin was the one with whom Darrow could identify best. Darrow understood the role that Lundin had played behind the scenes of successive administrations—it was not unlike his own role in advising Altgeld twenty years before. Lundin, as he said, played politics as a game, but his attorney had long been an enthusiast of it as a spectator sport. He could not find it in his heart to condemn the "poor Swede"; his sins were far outweighed by his skills in Darrow's eyes. Darrow had been a member of nearly every reform league that had abhorred Lundin and his ilk—and there were many—but he was also human enough to take secret delight in the ingenuity with which Lundin picked the public pocket. There was an aspect of Lundin, as there was of the radical's devil Yerkes, that appealed to Darrow's instinct for individualism: a roguish, world-wise ability to take from the world what he wanted. Even Lundin's attitude toward politics as a game struck a chord of sympathy. After all, Altgeld had declared politics to be his recreation. With less ideology and more humor, Altgeld might have been quite close to Lundin.

Yet the defense of Lundin could not be depicted as a moral crusade, any more than the defense of Chicago gangsters. In the early twenties Darrow's practice was—except for its large number of charity cases—indistinguishable from that of any successful criminal lawyer. There was much less of a political slant to his practice, and the days of great issues seemed to have vanished. Now more than ever, Darrow filled the role of the "mouthpiece" lawyer, taking on clients whose cases could not be dressed up with political significance.

28

Return to Normal

Darrow, like everyone else, had adjusted to the mood of postwar America. The issue of capital versus labor was still important, but lacked the intensity of prewar years. The end of the war had jolted the intellectuals out of their heavier political preoccupations and into Menckenesque dalliance. In a time for reassessment, the savants of the age were throwing off the stodgy German and Russian ideologies, choosing to denounce absurdity rather than injustices, and to use ridicule as a weapon rather than dynamite.

No better illustration of the change the war had wrought can be found than the response to prohibition. Darrow had long been its foe, though—with the exception of the short period during the bribery trials in 1912—he was a very moderate drinker himself. He did not believe in many governmental restrictions or much respect their promoters. Even before the war he had been active in opposing prohibition; his partner Edgar Lee Masters had complained that "speaking for the liquor interests" caused him to neglect his work.[1] In the twenties Darrow became one of the most fervent opponents of the eighteenth amendment, debating and writing on the subject frequently. While the issue lent itself to much jesting, it had an undercurrent of seriousness since it involved the right of the majority to impose its will on the minority. Its proponents were associated with much else that liberal intellectuals found unsatisfactory; and, perhaps most significant of all, it prompted, like the automobile, the situation in which lawlessness became a middle-class commonplace.

The seeds of Darrow's utter cynicism about the law were planted during his battle against prohibition. He came to see prohibition as a demonstration that the law was devoid of moral content, and purely an exercise of power. In the course of a debate with the Reverend John Haynes Holmes on prohibition, sponsored by the League for Public Discussion, he stated flatly: "I never talk about the 'rights' of anybody. There is no such thing as 'rights' anyhow. It is a question of whether you can put it over. In any legal sense or practical sense, whatever is, is 'a right.' If you can put it over, all right!"[2] It was a short step from this to his later conclusion that "there is no such thing as justice, in or out of court."[3] In his crusade against prohibition Darrow was continuing his

315

alliance with Woodrow Wilson, who had vetoed the original Volstead Act but
to no lasting avail. Both men found prohibition anathema.

On other issues he found himself at loggerheads with Wilson. He opposed
the League of Nations on the ground that it would be an instrument of the
great powers against the small. And early on he repudiated the principle of
reparations enshrined in the Treaty of Versailles. By 1920 he was already
persuaded by John Maynard Keynes's *Economic Consequences of the Peace*
that the United States must modify its attitude toward the war debt. He wrote
an article on this which, as Max Putzel observed, was one of the very few
American considerations of the difficulties of postwar economics to have appeared. He continued to advocate cancellation of the war debt throughout the
twenties, his most widely circulated plea being published in the magazine
Vanity Fair in 1927. There he argued for cancellation not only to speed
European recovery, but also on the moral ground that America "should do
something to redeem herself from her reputation as a Shylock and a usurer."[4]
And part of Darrow's dislike for Coolidge rested upon his inflexibility in
demanding total repayment, with interest, of American war loans.

Yet, if the spirit of the age was less intense, the return to "normalcy"
necessarily meant a return to some prewar themes. In consequence, Darrow's
repertoire of advanced views could be regarded as coming back into fashion,
and he made the most of this return. It took him no time at all to shift from
making propaganda speeches on behalf of the war effort to brushing up his best
liberal homilies on the speculative questions at which he excelled. At the
Chicago City Club on March 29, 1919, he delivered an address on the subject
of inheritance: "There is not the simplest thing in the world that a man can
do today except he uses the brains and efforts of countless men, many of whom
are dead and gone, and some for ages." In this way, the dead ruled the living,
like it or not. "There is, as I can see, no logical reason to limit a man's power
to give away property after he is dead that would not equally apply to his giving
it away while he still lives."[5] The theme, beloved of radicals through the ages,
was an indication of how swiftly America had returned to peacetime preoccupations—just four months after the armistice. Darrow's participation
reaffirmed that his advocacy of the war had not been accompanied by any
diminution of his left-wing fire. He was still the same, even if the world had
changed; and if the world had changed, it still retained many of its older
features.

An example was the Irish question. In 1895 Darrow had published his
pamphlet entitled *The Rights and Wrongs of Ireland,* favorable to the Irish
desire for independence. In consequence, he had become well known to Irishmen as a sympathizer—so much so that one of the few moments of humor at
his first trial for bribery came during the examination of a prospective juror
by the name of Mullchaney, who was asked:

"Did you ever meet this defendant?"

"No."

"Did you ever hear him speak?"

"No."

"Did you ever read any of his books?"

"I read one."

"Which one?"

"The Rights and Wrongs of Ireland."

"What do you think of him?"

"He is a fine man!"[6]

A settlement of the Irish question was desirable, if not imperative, for the British in 1919. The Irish turned to the United States for support and advice in dealing with Lloyd George, the British prime minister. The leader of the Irish at this time was Eamon de Valera, himself an American, and 1919 found him in consultation with Darrow in Chicago only a few weeks after his escape from an English prison. Moses Koenigsberg met both of them in earnest discussion in the lobby of the Auditorium Theatre during the intermission of an evening performance. Because of his help to the Irish cause, Darrow was always received well by Irishmen on his trips to Europe. In 1920 he defended James Larkin, an Irish agitator charged jointly with Benjamin Gitlow for criminal anarchy, and his association with the movement to obtain a pardon for Thomas Mooney gave him credit in the minds of some Irishmen, though Mooney's conviction had little to do with Irish independence. In the late twenties Darrow visited Ireland and was an honored guest in many Dublin houses, including that of Oliver St. John Gogarty, the surgeon and writer, on Ely Place.

As Darrow responded to the lowering of pressure that the twenties represented, he became ever more the public figure and less the straightforward lawyer. He devoted more time than ever before to platform speaking and journalism. If the way he spent his time in the early twenties is any index of his true priorities, it must be said that he was much more interested in being famous than in furthering his legal practice. He was besieged by well-wishers on the street wherever he went, the volume of his correspondence was enormous, and the autograph seekers persistent and never-ending. But he made only token objections to these burdens, while attracting and encouraging more and more publicity. Once he gave a statement to the press that put his position in a thoroughly exaggerated and intemperate light. "You don't really believe that, do you?" he was asked. "No," he replied, "and neither will the readers —but at least they'll have read it."[7]

The attitude was becoming increasingly typical of him. He dressed up his public pronouncements to make them sound shocking because he enjoyed the notoriety they brought him. It is doubtful that he completely believed in his own platform or journalistic stances, which were adopted more as a way of being conspicuous than because of their truth. There had always been a streak of perversity in Darrow's character that made him strive mightily to avoid a conventional conclusion. Even on those topics that most touched his professional experience, his sorties into print seemed ill-considered. His book *Crime: Its Cause and Treatment,* which had been inspired by Altgeld's *Our Penal*

Machinery and Its Victims, was published in 1922 but was a disappointing product in both substance and form. Many of his readers found its perspective unsatisfying because it failed, except in a few vague passages exhorting society to improve itself, to suggest any means of curing crime. While justly criticizing prevailing methods of treatment, it unhelpfully provided no alternatives. In spite of his fame, editors were not always willing to accept such work. When Darrow submitted an article derived from *Crime: Its Cause and Treatment* to the *Saturday Evening Post,* the editor, George Horace Lorimer, was greatly disappointed by its lack of balance. He wrote to Thomas Costain: ". . . I have turned down the Darrow article, because it is thoroughly one-sided and gives a false picture of the criminal classes as a whole. We could agree with what he says about one class of criminals, but he took the position that practically all crime was entirely due to early environment and poverty."[8]

In some ways, Darrow's dual ambitions as speaker and writer were in conflict, for what made him impressive as a speaker made him disappointing as a writer. As a rhetorician, Darrow's ability to persuade was as much theatrical as intellectual; performing, he could engage his auditors' emotions as well as their brains and distract them from his dubious first premises, his logical faults, and his factual inaccuracies and exaggerations. The surface clarity of what he said did not persuade so well in print. His statements were striking and his arguments ingenious, but his substance rarely equaled his eloquence and even his admirers were sometimes puzzled upon reflection to know what he stood for. He thrived on debating points, seemingly preferring them to more reflective arguments with less dramatic impact; these did not translate from speech to print at all well, but they crept into his work ever more frequently as he turned to the lecture circuit. There, his display of an entertaining but rather unadmirable point-scoring cleverness brought him the applause he savored, but in print it raised doubts whether real intellectual achievement was compatible with the incessant practice of public debate. He seized upon the weakest point in an argument and, finding it unsatisfactory in one particular, rejected it entirely. Conversely, on his own favorite themes he was given to an over-reliance that appeared foolhardy when published.

The defect of overwide generalization that struck Lorimer was compounded by Darrow's lack of care in revising his manuscripts. As one critic remarks of *Crime: Its Cause and Treatment*: "In places, the writing seems almost haphazard, as if the author were making an impromptu speech."[9] Stylistic imperfections that passed unnoticed on the platform were very apparent on the printed page, and contrary to Darrow's ardent desire his publications probably detracted from his reputation among those he most wished to impress.

Perhaps the most significant revelation of these writings was that Darrow's attitude toward criminals was almost completely uncensorious. They were criminals through no fault of their own. Heredity and environment had shaped them to be what they were, and that was that. He therefore believed that no personal blame attached to crime; his attitude was, at least philosophically, entirely fatalistic. His was a generation that believed in a "destiny" for all sorts of things, and so Darrow could not condemn a man for acting out his destiny. He was wonderfully suited to defense work, because a defense lawyer's duty is to produce reasonable doubt—and his turn of mind was inherently skeptical. He had merely to express his doubts to put forward an attractive argument. The criminal law was predicated on a theory of individual moral responsibility. Most judges believed, like the public, that crimes were committed by "bad" men. Darrow's theories, on the contrary, ascribed criminality to anything but immorality: if society could not be blamed directly, then crime was due to an accident of body chemistry. Darrow tended to present a world view in general to his audience and then to apply its logic to the case in such a way that there was no point in conviction at all. The general-to-particular style suited him well, especially since he generalized about the universe and man on a largely fatalistic level. These fatalistic arguments were easily adapted to a criminal defendant in such a way as to present his actions as the inevitable outcome of the human predicament. There was an inherent *reductio ad absurdum* to all Darrow's later thought which many found distasteful.

But the objection to Darrow's pronouncements on this, as on other public questions, went beyond logic. For though he spoke and wrote fatalistically, he did not seem to practice law that way. There was, for instance, an inconsistency between Darrow's professed view that a criminal's course was charted and the great care he took in the process of jury selection, where he manifestly did not believe that veniremen were interchangeable or that it was a matter of indifference who took which historical role.

> In selecting a jury [says one eyewitness], he conversed with a juror over the jury rail as would two neighbors talking over a fence. It was not uncommon for him, when he had finished "visiting" with a prospective juror, to make some such remark as: "And if you are selected as a juror in this case, you will do the best you can, won't you?" When a juror answered he would, I suspect Mr. Darrow had made a friend.[10]

On a more general level, his attention-getting pronouncements seemed to sit badly with his fighting instincts as an advocate. "There is no such thing as justice, in or out of court," he proclaimed. But if that were true, what sense did it make to seek it, or complain of its absence? His jury speeches became so openly deterministic that a reflective juryman might have wondered why Darrow believed a jury was open to persuasion; judging from his words, he subscribed to a doctrine of predestination every bit as rigid as Martin Luther's. According to him his clients, like all men everywhere, were merely puppets of history, not accountable for their actions. He did not explain why he nevertheless found it necessary to strive mightily for them, using every trick he knew to gain their acquittal. He seemed to believe in his ability to influence events by personal effort, as if he alone possessed the secret of free will. It was this contradiction between precept and practice that would be dramatically highlighted when a case unparalleled in forensic history came his way.

29

The Crime of the Century

On June 2, 1924, the doorbell of Darrow's apartment rang violently in the early hours of the morning. Ruby answered it. It was a deputation from the family of Richard Loeb, son of a vice-president of Sears, Roebuck and Company. Darrow knew the Loeb family reasonably well; the president of the Sears company was Julius Rosenwald, a liberal philanthropist who had financed several worthy causes with which Darrow had been associated, including the costs of the unsuccessful appeal on behalf of Isaac Bond. Rosenwald was a figure of immense charity in Chicago, of whom all philanthropists were in awe: "In the Book of Good Deeds, his name deserves to be written in gold. Of all Chicagoans of great wealth, and there have been many, Julius Rosenwald heads the list of those who understood and acted upon high concepts of the stewardship of wealth," wrote the Reverend Preston Bradley of the People's Church of Chicago.[1] (One of the horrible ironies revealed by the Leopold and Loeb trial was that the victim of the crime might easily have been Rosenwald's own grandson, whom the teenagers had considered but rejected because it might hurt the Loeb family business.)

Darrow had read in the papers of young Loeb's arrest on a charge of murder but had thought it inconceivable that he was guilty. He was wrong. Loeb and his friend Nathan Leopold, Jr., had confessed to the crime that afternoon. Darrow's reaction was typical of all those acquainted with the well-connected Loebs—Mary Garden of the Chicago City Opera, for instance, heard of the crime and found it impossible to believe. Although the Loeb family knew many lawyers better than Darrow, they had decided that they needed him, and had come round as soon as the decision had been reached (they could not telephone him, for his home number had been unlisted for several years).[2] The facts of the case were such that no comprehensive theory of the psychology of crime seemed to explain them. Certainly the case showed that poverty and lack of opportunity were not the only causes of crime.

Richard Loeb was eighteen and Nathan Leopold nineteen. Both belonged to rich Jewish families, and both were extremely successful academically. They conceived a plan to commit the "perfect crime" and put it into effect by first kidnapping and then killing a fourteen-year-old boy

320

called Robert Franks, who was a neighbor of theirs and whom they chose at random from a number of boys who attended the Harvard Preparatory School in South Side Kenwood, a high-class local boys' school across the street from Nathan Leopold's home. It was, as the defense alleged, a motiveless crime, done for its own sake. The boys had set themselves a game to play, and had played it rather badly.

When Bobby Franks failed to return home from school on May 21, his parents mounted a fruitless search for him and were on the point of calling the police when they received a telephone call.

"This is George Johnson," the caller said. "You know by this time that Robert has been kidnapped, but you needn't worry. He is safe and unharmed. We will let you know what we want. If you refuse or report to the police, we will kill the boy."[3] The line went dead. For the Franks family, this disturbing call had only one consolation—it contained an assurance that Bobby was alive and well. No member of the family wanted to do anything to jeopardize the boy's life or safety, so the warning not to report to the police was taken seriously. Mr. Franks called his attorney and asked advice; the attorney recommended that the police be told, in spite of the warning, and they were. It must have been with much heart-searching that the family decided to inform the police. What if, somehow, the kidnappers found out that they had been informed? The police had promised not to publicize the case until the kidnappers had been heard from further, but there could always be a leak or a mistake. Had the unhappy family known all the facts, it would not have found the decision so hard to make. For when "George Johnson" called, Bobby Franks was already dead, bludgeoned to death with a chisel.

The call had been made by Leopold from a pay phone a block from his house. Afterward the boys mailed, by special delivery, a ransom letter which they had prepared the day before. Then they tried to clean the blood from the rented car they had used for the kidnapping and murder. The special delivery letter was delivered by post office messenger at 9:30 A.M. the following morning, Thursday, May 22. It was typewritten on plain, white paper, and read:

Dear Sir:
    As you no doubt know by this time your son has been kidnapped. Allow us to assure you that he is at present well and safe. You need fear no physical harm for him provided you live up carefully to the following instructions and such others as you will receive by further communications. Should you, however, disobey any of our instructions, even slightly, his death will be the penalty.
    1. For obvious reasons make absolutely no attempt to communicate with the police authorities or any private agencies. Should you already have communicated with the police allow them to continue their investigation but do not mention this letter.
    2. Secure before noon today $10,000. This amount must be composed entirely of old bills of the following denominations:
        $2,000 in $20 bills
        $8,000 in $50 bills

The money must be old. Any attempt to include new or marked bills will render the entire venture futile.

3. The money should be placed in a small cigar box or if this is impossible in a heavy cardboard box, securely closed and wrapped in a white paper. The wrapping paper should be sealed at all openings with sealing wax.

4. Have this money with you prepared as directed above and remain home after one o'clock P.M. See that the telephone is not in use. You will receive further instructions then instructing you as to your final course.

As a final word of warning, this is a strictly commercial proposition and we are prepared to put our threat into execution should we have reasonable grounds to believe that you have committed an infraction of the above instructions. However, should you carefully follow out our instructions, we can assure you that your son will be safely returned to you within six hours of receipt of the money.[4]

On Friday, while Jacob Franks waited for the promised phone call, another call came through from the police. A boy's body had been found in a swamp on the outskirts of the city near the Indiana state line. Would Mr. Franks come to the mortuary to see whether it was his son? Franks refused to believe it could be, because the kidnappers had assured him, both by their phone call and in their letter, that Bobby was alive and well. But to satisfy the police he sent his brother-in-law. He himself was determined to stay by the phone.

At 3:00 P.M. the telephone rang, and once again it was "Johnson." "I am sending a Yellow Cab for you," he said. "Get into it and go to the drugstore at 1463 East 63rd Street. Have the money with you." That was all. Mr. Franks, already tense and distraught, was not sure that he had got the address correctly, and was puzzling over it when the Yellow Cab arrived. He was just leaving when the phone rang again. It was his brother-in-law. The body at the mortuary was that of Bobby Franks.

This, of course, was not what Leopold and Loeb had planned. They believed they had devised a foolproof scheme for collecting the ransom without revealing their identity. If Mr. Franks had gone to the drugstore at once, he would have received another phone call there. This would have directed him to take the southbound train at 63rd Street Station, close to the drugstore, go to the last Pullman car on the train, and retrieve a note, previously planted there by Loeb, from the telegraph-blank box. This note instructed Franks to throw his package of ransom money off the train as soon as it passed the Champion Manufacturing Company's factory at 75th Street. By the time Leopold made the three o'clock phone call to Mr. Franks, both boys already knew that Bobby's body had been discovered by the police, because Leopold had chanced to see the early afternoon edition of the Chicago *Daily Journal,* with its headline: BODY OF BOY FOUND IN SWAMP. But the body had not been identified, and they gambled that Mr. Franks would not yet know. "It's a cinch there's only one thing to do," Leopold told Loeb; "play the string out. No sense assuming they know yet who it is. Remember, they think he's alive."[5] They waited by the Champion factory for the southbound train and it came right on time, but no package was thrown out as it steamed by. It was still in the Franks home, where a heartbroken Jacob Franks now knew that he would never get his boy back.[6]

The discovery of the body less than twenty-four hours after the crime was the first of many discoveries which indicated that, notwithstanding the boys' superior intelligence and their months of planning, their crime was far from "perfect." The police had broken the case within ten days of its commission. Leopold complained to Loeb as soon as they read the *Journal* story, "That was a swell damn place you picked to leave him. They'd never find him, huh? Not for twenty minutes anyhow!"[7] But if Leopold had reason to complain, Loeb had at least as much, since it was Leopold's mistake that led the police to suspect them. Leopold had dropped his spectacles near the body and they were found. The district attorney's office checked the origin—they were a common enough prescription, and the horn-rimmed frames were of a standard pattern, but the hinges were a special type, patented by the Bobrow Optical Company of Rochester, New York. This company had only one outlet in Chicago, Almer Coe & Co. of the Loop. Only three pairs of spectacles of this type had ever been sold in Chicago: one pair to an attorney who, when the police inquired, had been on vacation in Europe for six weeks; one to an elderly lady; and one to Nathan Leopold, Jr., of 4754 Greenwood Avenue, near both the Harvard School and the Franks's home. The murder had been committed on Wednesday, May 21. By May 30, Friday morning, those glasses had led the Chicago police to Leopold's doorstep.

The boys had started preparations to commit a murder months before. They had established an account at the Hyde Park Bank under an assumed name in which to deposit the ransom and to pay for a rented car so that they would be able to hire a murder vehicle easily when the time came. They had dreamed of it and planned it together as an adventure which, by the necessity for secrecy it created, would bind them even closer in friendship. They had not decided the exact circumstances of their crime, or who the victim should be, but they knew that they would commit it. They had previously committed petty crimes together, including the theft of the typewriter on which the ransom letter had been written, but nothing on a grand scale. This was to be their *pièce de résistance.* On May 20, final preparations were made for a murder. They purchased a chisel and some rope from a hardware store, and some hydrochloric acid from a drugstore. The chisel was to be used as a weapon. The rope was to strangle the victim, Leopold pulling one end of it and Loeb the other, so that they had an equal part in the killing; and the acid was to be used to obliterate the features of the corpse prior to its disposal.

The next morning, taking their tools with them, they drove downtown and hired a light blue Willys-Knight at a firm where they had previously done business under assumed names. After lunch, in the late afternoon, the pair cruised round the vicinity of the Harvard School looking for a victim. It seems clear that they were looking for a young boy, but that it was pure chance that settled them on Bobby Franks; they had no special reason for singling him out, except that he happened to be there. They had considered a boy named Rubel, but rejected him because they feared his father would not pay ransom, and they had wanted to kill a boy named Levinson, whom Loeb had talked to earlier, but could not find him. All three of the boys were known personally to Leopold and Loeb. It was easy for them to invite Franks to get into the car as they drove alongside him on Ellis Avenue. Franks accepted, unsuspecting, and got in. As soon as the car moved off, he was struck several times on the head with the chisel, gagged with a rag soaked in hydrochloric acid, and wrapped in a rug.

The crime was committed, perfect or not. There could be no turning back, and the only question was whether they could escape detection. Loeb was the youngest graduate on record of the University of Michigan; Leopold was a Phi Beta Kappa graduate of the University of Chicago, currently enrolled at its law school. Loeb, too, intended to go to law school. Surely these two bright young men could fool the district attorney of Cook County and the Chicago police force? In fact they bungled, and when confronted with their bungling, they cracked. They had invented a childish alibi both were to tell, but had not fixed with sufficient specificity when it should be told or the details. Leopold, who had studied criminal law and procedure for a year, did not even use his knowledge to his own advantage while he was being questioned by the state's attorney, Robert Crowe. All told, the perfect crime fell far short of perfection.

Their immediate problem was to dispose of the body. The boys had already agreed that this should be done in a marshy, undeveloped corner of the city, near the state line, where Leopold often went birdwatching. But they could not safely go there until after dark. Leopold drove through Chicago, along the Midway and other major streets, with Loeb on the back seat beside the corpse, until they got to South Chicago. There they stopped and went into a restaurant for a meal, leaving their ghastly cargo in the car. Then they drove on to the grave they had chosen for Bobby Franks, between 118th and 123rd streets. They stripped him naked and deposited his body in an open culvert where they had both concluded it would not be found for months, if at all.

They tried to hide some of Franks's clothing and threw the chisel out of the car on their return journey. They headed for Loeb's home, where they burned the rest of the clothing and the rug in which the body had been wrapped. But there remained a problem they had apparently not foreseen: the floor carpeting of their rented Willys-Knight was covered with blood. They tried, unsuccessfully, to remove the bloodstains, then abandoned the attempt in order to make the phone call to the Franks home under the alias of George Johnson. They parked the rented car, its interior still badly stained, on a quiet street near their homes and went back as normal for a night's rest.

The next morning, Thursday, was spent in further efforts to clean the carpet of the Willys-Knight in the Leopold garage. The afternoon was taken up with the plot that misfired for the throwing of the ransom money off the train at the Champion factory. After that, the car was returned to the rental agency.

On Friday they disposed of two more pieces of incriminating evidence. First, they took the stolen typewriter on which they had typed the ransom note to

Jackson Park and twisted off the keys with a pair of pliers. They threw both the keys and the typewriter into the lagoon. Then later they burned the car rug used to wrap the body in, which had got blood on it during the murder. This completed their dispersal of the evidence.

Presumably, if this crime had really been perfect, the boys' endeavors would have stopped here. The crime was accomplished and according to their own calculations, it should have taken months for the authorities to discover the body. Meanwhile Bobby Franks would become yet another adolescent whose name was added to a list of missing persons. The rapid discovery of the body and almost immediate identification of the victim put a rather different slant on the situation, because it brought the perpetrators dangerously close to discovery. Any evidence there might be was still fresh when the investigation was mounted with full vigor by State's Attorney Robert Crowe. Here an element appeared in the behavior of the boys that went far beyond bungling and incompetence. Loeb actually volunteered his services to the newspaper reporters covering the case, taking an active part in an investigation of the drugstores up and down 63rd Street that he himself had suggested, playing the role of amateur sleuth and flying closer and closer to the flame. Darrow was later to say of this extraordinary conduct: "My experience is that the last person that a conscious criminal associates with is a reporter. He shuns them even more than he does a detective, because they are smarter and less merciful."[8] Yet Loeb's conduct throughout the police hunt for the killers showed him to be under a compulsion to lead a double life, to thrust himself into the bosom of the enemy and to revel in his shocking secret. But in so doing, he let the secret out.

Leopold, too, demonstrated the same desire to fly close to danger. The day after the murder, he propounded a question in his class in criminal law at the University of Chicago Law School: What criminal liability would result if X forcibly seized a person with intent to kill, or with intent to hold him for ransom, or with intent to commit indecent liberties upon him, and in fulfillment of that intent killed him? The law professor believed at the time that the question was a hypothetical one, such as law students often ask in class discussion; later he realized that it was far from hypothetical.

Loeb and Leopold had made plans to give each other a false alibi. In the event that either of them was arrested within a week of the crime, they should tell a story about picking up two girls and driving out to Lincoln Park. If either was arrested after that, they should say they had no recollection of what they were doing on the relevant days. The theory was that the police could not expect them to remember what they were doing more than a week before, but that it would be strange if they could not remember their activities within the week. It was a theory of obviously doubtful validity, for it was unlikely that, in pursuing a murder investigation, the authorities would be satisfied with a suspect who simply could not remember what he had done more than eight days ago. In its foundation the plan was startingly weak. Furthermore the alibi about picking up the girls was risky. It was entirely untrue and, as was later revealed, the boys had left important details undecided so that their stories when pressed were alarmingly and suspiciously inconsistent. Besides, the police would try to trace the girls or witnesses to the foursome. But worst of all was the failure to decide on the crucial timing of the alibi.

Leopold had been picked up at 2:30 P.M. on May 29. In the evening he was taken to a room in the La Salle Hotel to be questioned by Robert Crowe and two of his assistants, John Sbarbaro and Joseph P. Savage.* The questioning was polite but relentless and finally Leopold told them that, yes, actually he had been with another fellow that day—Richard Loeb. At 2:15 P.M. on the same Thursday, Loeb was also arrested, but the two suspects were kept apart and had no chance to compare notes or reconcile their stories. By 3:00 A.M. on Saturday, May 31, Richard Loeb had made a detailed confession while Leopold stuck to his threadbare alibi, believing that his confederate would have corroborated it:

> When, precisely, was "a week after the crime"? There was a period of some twenty-six hours that remained in doubt. It depended entirely upon what specific act you took to date the moment of "the crime." As it turned out, Dick and I interpreted it differently. He reckoned from the beginning of the chain of events; I, from their termination.[9]

The Loeb confession for its part was truthful in all respects but one—he attributed the death blows with the chisel to Leopold, though it seemed fairly certain that Loeb himself had dealt them. Confronted with Loeb's confession the next day, June 1, Leopold also confessed, though disputing the allegation that he had used the chisel.

The confessions were, of course, damning evidence, especially since they were given independently. But even without them, the evidence against the boys was piling up rapidly. Leopold denied owning a typewriter such as the one used to type the ransom note, but classmates from law school were able to produce carbon copies of notes made by him on the typewriter. And even without the mistake about when the alibi should be used, it was independently proved false. The fictitious pick-up was, by prior agreement, supposed to have taken place with Leopold's car. But the Leopold family chauffeur, Sven, was able to say positively that the car had not been removed from the garage on May 21; he remembered the day well because his wife had been ill and had gone to the doctor. He also recalled that on Thursday, May 22, he saw the boys trying to wash red stains from the carpet of the rental car. He was surprised, because the boys never normally did any work. They told him they had spilled some wine in the car the day before. Sven told this to the state's attorney and his young master's story was destroyed.[10]

It was not until the state's attorney had a watertight case that any legal advice at all was taken. Leopold, particularly, was perfectly well aware of his

---

*The hotel room had been taken to avoid the publicity that activity at the prosecutor's office would inevitably attract.

right to a lawyer at any time after his arrest, as he himself admitted, but chose not to obtain one. He considered and rejected the possibility shortly after his arrest, and again during the course of the state attorney's questioning that evening. Even after he was charged, he was reluctant to accept the assistance of counsel and had to be persuaded to enter a defense. It is almost certain that, had either of the boys obtained a lawyer, they would have been advised to say nothing. Instead they chose to say more and more, without duress, incriminating themselves by the hour. When, finally, the advice to remain silent was given to them on Monday, June 2, by Benjamin Bachrach, who was a lawyer and relative of the Loebs retained along with his brother Walter, it was too late to be much use.

Darrow met the defendants for the first time the next day, gaining access to them only after bringing a writ of habeas corpus against the state's attorney. If ever there was a hopeless case, this was it. Nevertheless he had agreed to take it on. By the time he was engaged as counsel, both boys had made a full confession. As Nathan Leopold himself put it: "What could a lawyer do now? They had the facts—all the facts. A lawyer couldn't make them unhappen. There didn't seem to me to be any contest left: There was nothing to contest. The police had won, completely and utterly; the battle was over."[11] Added to that, Leopold had no desire to avoid the death penalty. He asserted then and thirty years later when he came to write his autobiography that he believed it would have been better to hang than to be imprisoned for life. The crime was the more horrifying for its absence of apparent motive. The world was used to depraved adults but depraved youths, in a generation of flaming youth, seemed more ominous.

In these circumstances, apparently devoid of hope, the boys' families turned to Darrow. He had never believed in the "cab-rank" principle by which a lawyer took on any client with the ability to pay. On the other hand, it was a question of impulse just where he drew the line. Besides, he was intrigued by the facts. Predictably there was criticism of him for even undertaking to represent such clients, and he found his own reproach of Robert Ingersoll for prostituting his talents thrown back at him. Several of his friends chided him for having been "bought off"; they pointed out that the defendants were privileged scions of rich and indulgent families. Not for the first time, Darrow's decision prompted more misgivings among his well-wishers than he felt himself. He apparently felt no unease about reserving to himself the ultimate decision whether to accept or reject a case, without articulating his reasons. Furthermore, there was a sense in which the very extremity of the case helped reduce the burden upon him. An acquittal in such a seemingly hopeless situation would be seen by all as a professional triumph. A failure, on the other hand, would be but the inevitable.

Every parent was brought face to face in this case with his powerlessness to mold his children. These boys had not come from broken homes, they were not the sons of alcoholic fathers or promiscuous mothers. No skeleton in the family closet could be resurrected. The parents had acted in approved style and still their sons had turned out to be murderers. Had the two boys gone wrong because their parents had spoiled them? And if that was the explanation, why were more spoiled children not murderers? Had the new manners and morals of the twenties caused America's youth to grow callous and corrupt? The crime shocked an abandoned era like an accident during a frivolous party game. Respectable bourgeois America could harbor the worst crime of all—murder. Inevitably Leopold and Loeb were regarded as examples of a golden generation gone wrong, symbols of a postwar emancipation that was both envied and feared by their elders. This was the view taken by Benjamin Barr Lindsey of Denver, a friend of Darrow's:

> It is a new kind of murder with a new kind of cause. That cause is to be found in the modern mentality and modern freedom of youth, with the misunderstanding between parenthood and childhood. Thus we have the modern misdirection of youth. Do you not, then, see this is more than the story of murder? It is the story of modern youth, the story of modern parents, the story of modern education, even though it is an extreme and exceptional episode in the stream of modern life. There are lesser offenses that come from the same causes and pass us by almost daily. The indifference to the rights of others in stealing of automobiles, in joy rides, jazz parties, petting parties, freedom in sex relations and the mania for speed on every turn. They do not gain our attention, because they are not so startling, so terrible.[12]

Behind the attitude of some of Darrow's erstwhile admirers that his acceptance of the Leopold and Loeb defense was treachery to his supposedly altruistic principles was a darker suspicion. Rumor had it that the reason for retaining Darrow in the first place was that the Leopolds had hired him, frankly, to put in the fix. His defenses in 1923 of gangsters and politicians had convinced some members of the Chicago bar that he could buy "justice." In particular the suspicion was strong because the Bachrach brothers, Benjamin and Walter, knew, as lawyers, what Darrow's reputation was. Why else, it was asked around the newspaper offices of Chicago, had Darrow been brought in except for his supposed ability as a fixer? The combination of rumors of a very high fee and the blackness of the defendants' case caused many to suspect that Darrow was being brought into the case to corrupt justice. This suspicion would turn the newspaper fraternity against him for the duration of the case. It was one of the few occasions when he could not bend the press to his own side.[13]

The case was one that lent itself easily to "sensationalist" coverage and the press understandably made the most of its chance, though in part the massive journalistic coverage of the case depended on a coincidence of timing, since the trial date was set just after the Democratic convention. "There were six hundred journalists at the Democratic convention in New York," remarked one correspondent. "It is apparent they all came here."[14]

In ten days the two defendants had lost privileged positions with golden futures and become reviled criminals, whose best hope was life imprisonment and whose likely fate was hanging. From his entry into the case, Darrow's only aim was to prevent the sentence of death from being imposed—it was with the aim of saving the boys' lives that the Loebs had approached him in the first place. Both murder and kidnapping were capital crimes in Illinois, punishable by death at the court's discretion. In view of the awful acts the boys had done, Darrow was faced with only two possibilities. He could accept conviction, but hope that the sentence imposed would not be death; or he could plead insanity which, if found, would result in institutionalization but not hanging. It was dubious whether either defendant could be shown to be insane within the legal definition, though they were grossly abnormal. But even if evidence could be adduced that satisfied the law's requirements, it was doubtful that a jury impaneled in Chicago would accept the evidence and return a verdict of insanity—and in Illinois, the question was one for a jury to pass upon. The outcry against the defendants was tumultuous. The crowd was, by a large margin, in favor of the death penalty for both of them. If Darrow pleaded a hopeless case on the trial for murder and the inevitable verdicts of guilty were returned, there was no real doubt that a death sentence would be imposed. Even if it was not, the boys could be tried again for kidnapping and the prosecutor would have a second chance to see them hanged.

There was only one other course open to Darrow: to plead his clients guilty, and attempt to persuade a judge, sitting without a jury, not to impose the death penalty. The normal procedure in Chicago at this time would have been for the defense attorney to try to make a deal with the prosecutor. In exchange for the defendants pleading guilty, the prosecutor would intercede with the judge to obtain an undertaking that the death penalty would not be imposed. But Darrow did not trust the prosecution to offer such a bargain in a situation like this, and did not want to show how hopeless he thought the position of his clients to be. Besides, he saw a tactical advantage in not broaching the subject in advance, which in all probability saved the boys' lives. If he had opened negotiations for a sentence less than death in exchange for a plea of guilty, the judge might have refused to allow such a bargain. And his refusal might have reduced any compunction he would have about passing the sentence of death later. Darrow wanted to pile all the responsibility on one judge without the possibility of evasion or dilution.

The judge to whom the case fell was well known to Darrow professionally. John Caverly, Chief Justice of the criminal court of Cook County, was the son of Irish Catholics. Born in London in 1861, he had been brought to the United States as a young boy and educated in Catholic schools in Chicago. Like Darrow, he had seen city politics from the inside, having served as municipal attorney in the early years of the century. Twenty years ago Darrow had sued the city of Chicago on his own behalf when Caverly was the attorney defending on the city's behalf. Darrow knew that he was up against an unusually fair-minded and scrupulous man, with whom the death penalty weighed heavily. Already, Caverly had had some involvement with the Leopold and Loeb case, for it had been he who had issued the writ of habeas corpus ordering the state's attorney to allow Darrow to see his clients.

If Darrow's plan for changing the pleas was to succeed, absolute secrecy was essential. The case was the best publicized ever up to that time. It had caught the public's attention, firing its worst fears, and not a day went by without some item on the murder in all the major newspapers from the time of its discovery until the date set for trial. Public interest was so great that the Chicago *Tribune* offered to broadcast the proceedings over its radio station; the *Evening American* disparagingly countered the suggestion by offering to hire the White Sox baseball stadium for use as an open-air courtroom. Then the *Tribune,* not to be outdone, offered to pay any sum Freud cared to name to come to Chicago and psychoanalyze Leopold and Loeb. When Freud refused, the paper's proprietor, Colonel R. R. McCormick, asked him for an opinion of the boys' mental condition based upon newspaper accounts. Freud replied: "I cannot be supposed to be prepared to provide an expert opinion about persons and a deed when I have only newspaper reports to go on and have no opportunity to make a personal examination." Of course even this correspondence made good copy.[15]

It was agreed that the trial would not be broadcast, since Darrow argued that pre-trial publicity had condemned the defendants beforehand, giving no chance of an impartial jury. "We knew that seldom had a case been handled like this one; and every one, far and near, had made up their minds what should be done." In these circumstances he felt that a full trial would inflame public opinion further and cause pressure for the imposition of the death penalty it would be impossible for a judge to resist. That he was determined to prevent.

It was the state that had first called in experts to consider the mental condition of the accused. Naturally enough, it had called in local men, who found the defendants to be sane. Psychiatry was not as yet generally recognized, and its professors were known as "alienists." The inquiries of the state's investigators were directed toward the question whether either defendant had any ground for pleading the insanity defense. It was not considered at all surprising that the defense called in a number of outside experts who had been recruited by Walter Bachrach, as assistant defense counsel, during the National Conference of Psychiatrists then being held at Atlantic City. Altogether Leopold and Loeb were examined by eighteen alienists, four on behalf of the state and fourteen on behalf of the defense. It was assumed that the defense was running through one psychiatrist after another in an attempt to find one who would testify that the boys' mental condition amounted to legal insanity. This was exactly the impression that Darrow wanted to create. He was so anxious his tactics should not be anticipated that he did not even tell his clients of his plans. He knew State Attorney Crowe well—so well, in fact, that when Crowe arrived for the first day of the trial, both greeted each other warmly and sincerely. In part this was the tradition of all lawyers, but it was also based on sincere mutual admiration.

Indeed it was impossible for anyone in Cook County not to know Robert

Emmet Crowe. He was among the most powerful Republicans in the state, whose career has been described by one serious commentator as "a great epic in American politics," and by another contemporary as having "more polish than most of the politicians of the period."[16] He was the joint controller of an extraordinarily successful Republican machine, which had brought him to the forefront of Chicago's public life. Like Darrow, he had started off as assistant corporation counsel, but thereafter had chosen the G.O.P. rather than the Democratic Party, and prosecution rather than defense. There was no question that the Leopold and Loeb trial afforded him great political opportunities, not least for personal publicity. Crowe was the kingpin of a huge patronage empire and had soon to fight for his reelection. Opinions differed as to the effectiveness of the office over which he presided in enforcing the law in the average case; but in a headline-capturing murder, Crowe could be relied upon to spare no effort. He was widely recognized to be capable of extremely good work. He differed from most of the lawyers in Chicago politics in having received his legal education in the East, at Yale Law School, rather than at one of the night law schools in Chicago whose main purpose seemed to be to breed Cook County's political bagmen. Even in this tragic case politics played a very significant part. As many insiders saw the case in terms of a contest between incumbent Republicans and reform Democrats as saw it as an epoch-making decision of law.

Crowe and Darrow had appeared against each other in Fred Lundin's trial. Both were important figures in the criminal courts of Cook County and took an interest in politics—Crowe from necessity since the office he held was elective. Darrow's knowledge of Crowe's methods told him that he would do all he could to get the "popular" sentence on both boys: the death penalty. In the past Crowe had instigated campaigns designed to enhance his own popularity and had been involved in crucial decision making at the very center of Chicago politics. There were points upon which Darrow and he were in complete agreement; for instance, Crowe was an articulate opponent of prohibition and was sympathetic to the Negro race. But there was one issue crucial to the Leopold and Loeb trial on which the two men disagreed fundamentally: Crowe was an advocate of capital punishment who publicly demanded it in nearly all murder cases, believing it to be a deterrent to future potential murderers. During his first two terms as state attorney of Cook County, the number of murders had almost doubled. It would therefore be a matter of consistent policy for Crowe to do all in his power to obtain the death penalty for Darrow's clients.

On the morning of July 21, 1924, the date set for the trial, the older brothers of both defendants went to see them very early in their cells. Both brothers stressed that when the defense lawyers saw them later, they should do precisely what they were told without questioning it. Leopold and Loeb were taken over to the court building early, and there they saw Clarence Darrow and Benjamin Bachrach. Nathan Leopold described what followed:

"Boys," said Mr. Darrow, "we're going to ask you to do something that may strike you as very strange. Believe me, we have all thought hard about this for weeks, your families and Mr. Bachrach and I. We haven't arrived at the course of action we're going to outline without deep thought. We are all convinced it is the best way. Hell, boys, it's the *only* way. Now, have your brothers told you that we would have a suggestion that might strike you as absurd? And have you agreed to follow our instructions exactly? And will you live up to your promises?"

We both nodded.

"Boys," said Mr. Darrow solemnly, "we're going to ask permission of the Court to withdraw our pleas of not guilty. We're going to plead you guilty!"

Mr. Darrow paused a moment to see how we would react. We didn't. I wasn't even surprised; it was what I had expected. As for Dick, from the very start he had been willing to leave everything to the lawyers—to make no suggestions or objections.

I think Mr. Darrow was a little surprised at our lack of protest. Perhaps he thought that the implications had not really sunk in. After a moment he continued:

"After I have made the motion to the judge that we be permitted to withdraw the pleas and plead guilty, he will, if he allows it, ask each of you whether this is, in fact, your plea to each of the two charges. He's going to be very solemn about it. When you answer that it is, the judge will warn you in formal language of the consequences of your plea. He will list all the possible sentences, including death. And then he will ask you once more if, in face of this, you still persist in your pleas.

"Believe me, boys, it is absolutely essential that you answer yes. Your lives depend upon it.

"I feel that I ought to apologize to you for springing this on you at the last moment, for not telling you earlier. I feel that I've gotten to know both you boys well in these short six weeks. I like you both. I hope that you like me, and I think you do. I think you both trust me. Believe me, it hasn't been easy not to tell you of our plans in advance, not to give you a decent chance to weigh the matter and to consent or refuse only after you had had a reasonable interval to think about it. But, boys, we had to do it this way! There is only one legal matter, one point of strategy involved. In Illinois there are only two crimes punishable by the death penalty. You were unfortunate to commit them both. Mr. Crowe, not satisfied with what he calls his 'perfect hanging case,' wanted two bites at the apple, not one. He had you indicted both for murder and, separately, for kidnapping for ransom. We pleaded not guilty. All right. He'd try you on one charge, say the murder. If he got less than a hanging verdict, he'd turn right around and try you on the other charge. He'd have two chances for the price of one!

"There is only one way to deprive him of that second chance: to plead guilty to both charges before he realizes what is happening and has the opportunity to withdraw one of them. That's why the element of surprise is absolutely necessary. And surprise depends upon absolute silence. He mustn't know until we actually make the motion in court that we have in mind changing our plea.

"Now I want to be absolutely honest with you. I try to be honest with everyone. It's all the more important when the other fellow's life is in my hands. I was convinced, and I am convinced, that we could have told you this a week ago and that you would not have breathed a word of it. I hated being, in a sense, hypocritical with you boys, not telling you all that was in my mind. But so many things could have happened. Maybe one of you talks in his sleep. Maybe you might have been tempted to discuss it together—after all, it's a pretty important decision—and you might have been overheard. What the newspapers wouldn't have paid for a scoop like this!

"Boys, this was the only sensible, the only safe way to do it. I bowed to the dictates of prudence. But I apologize for doing it. I am truly heartily ashamed."[17]

30

The Million-Dollar Defense

Having explained his strategy to the defendants, Darrow, accompanied by Benjamin Bachrach, made his way into court. The courtroom was packed tight —in the hubbub it was difficult for everyone, including court officials, to get in. After the usual preliminaries Darrow stood and made a carefully prepared statement, indicating that the defendants wished to change their pleas to the indictments from not guilty to guilty. It took a moment for the significance of this announcement to sink in, then the prosecutors were on their feet objecting all at once. It took a moment longer for the press to understand what had happened, then they ran for the telephones. By the time the members of the public had realized what had happened, Judge Caverly had directed that they should remain in court until the hearing was completed. The case was adjourned until July 23.

On that day the court convened without a jury, Judge Caverly presiding. The state's attorney had put an immense amount of work into preparing the prosecution's case, but it was all premised upon trying the case to a jury after a plea of not guilty. His experts were ready; among his young assistants, John Sbarbaro, who had studied medicine for three years, was ready to speak up on all the grisly details of the killing in case the defense sought to deprecate the medical evidence. Now the carpet had been whisked from under Crowe's feet. The defense tried to avoid the presentation of the evidence of the crime by offering to stipulate the facts of the case by agreement with the prosecutor, but Crowe did not want that. He wanted to bring out the shocking details of the crime just as he would have done before a jury. He had all his witnesses prepared, and not to do so would waste his effort. By proving the prosecution's case, he hoped to demonstrate how this, of all cases, should draw the death penalty for the defendants. So, by means of 102 witnesses, plus documents and physical evidence, he went ahead and proved the gruesome facts.

Because the defense did not dispute what was said, it did not cross-examine the lay witnesses. It wanted to minimize its impact by showing that the defense did not consider it important enough to challenge. Darrow had done all he could to eliminate inconvenient testimony. He made a proposition to the state: "Don't you call any of your lay witnesses and I won't call any of mine." He even arranged that the Loebs' old nurse should be sent to Europe rather than testify, for fear she would inadvertently harm the case by saying that the boy was normal. In so doing he steered close to committing an offense of obstruction of justice. But finally his strategem was to deflect attention from the devastating lay testimony by introducing experts. Even in doing this, however, Darrow knew that he had to be highly selective. The comprehensive report on his clients' psycho-sexual history, which had been prepared at his request by Drs. Harold S. Hulbert and Carl M. Bowman, did not improve their chances of sympathy. As one observer put it:

> . . . probably the most fascinating revelation of the Hulbert and Bowman report was that the Franks murder was not an isolated incident in the lives of two otherwise innocent thrill-seekers, but served as a climax to criminal careers that had been developing over a period of years.[1]

When the prosecution had finished its case in chief, the defense produced its first witness, Dr. William A. White, director of St. Elizabeth's Hospital for the Insane in the District of Columbia, a nationally recognized expert on mental illness. He got no further than giving his name and occupation before the prosecution had objected vigorously to his presence, on the ground that any testimony he could give would be immaterial; the defendants had not pleaded insanity and expert opinions on their mental condition had no bearing upon the only question before the court: the penalty they should pay.[2] If the prosecution's contention was accepted, the defense would have no evidence whatever to offer. In essence, the prosecution's contention was of the "all or nothing" variety. If a defendant wished to introduce evidence of his mentality into his trial, he had to plead insanity. If not, he was not entitled to adduce any evidence regarding his mental condition at all and the law presumed him sane. The defense, without conceding that contention, said that it was inapplicable. Rules of evidence only applied to trials. But the present proceeding was not a trial. The guilt of the accused was not in issue; they were there only for the purpose of sentencing, and such proceedings were not bound by the rules of evidence. In retrospect, it is clear that the defense view of the law was correct; but at the time of the trial the question was undecided, and it was a close fight, for three days, before the judge ruled in favor of the defense and admitted the evidence.[3] The argument on the legal precedents in this matter, conducted by Thomas Marshall for the prosecutor and Walter Bachrach for the defense, was a comprehensive rehearsal of the state of the law up to that time.

Once admitted, the experts testified for the sides that had called them— defense experts for the defense, prosecution experts for the prosecution. By far the most thorough examination of the defendants had been made by the defense experts, and Darrow made the most of this, challenging the validity of conclusions based upon a few hours' observation of the boys. One of the experts had not examined the boys at all, but merely observed them in court. Darrow's technique in cross-examination of the prosecution witnesses was exceedingly effective. His first strategy was to get them, so far as possible, to agree with the defense experts upon principles. This was relatively easy in most cases, because psychiatric principles were couched in vague terms. As soon as a point of disagreement was reached, either in principle or application to the defendants, Darrow would try to catch the witness in a contradiction, either directly by quoting the witness's own book at him, or indirectly by Jesuitical interrogation, inveigling the witness to concede the argument step by step until caught in contradiction.

His last thrust was of the Morton's fork variety. Did the witness believe the defendants to be insane? No. Did the witness believe they were mentally ill? If the answer was yes, the defense had won its point. If the answer was no, Darrow would cover the witness with ridicule by asking whether the witness believed that the admitted crimes of the defendants were the acts of people in a healthy mental state, insisting (as he was entitled to do) on a yes or no answer. Whatever the witness said, Darrow could use to his clients' advantage. But there was one state expert upon whom this technique could not be used. Dr. William Krohn was an experienced witness and would not fall into any of the traps Darrow had set. He consistently maintained that the defendants were entirely sane, with no mental abnormality whatever, and that yes, people who were completely sane could and did commit disgusting, immoral, and callous crimes such as the defendants had admitted. He was a strong witness and refused to be diverted. Darrow mounted an attack upon him on cross-examination impressive in its wild force. Said Nathan Leopold:

> I hesitate to describe the carnage that was Mr. Darrow's cross-examination of Dr. Krohn. He threw away his rapier and pulled out his bludgeon. Furiously, even crudely, he attacked. He tried to beat the witness down, sometimes resorting to actual insult. Dr. Krohn did not retreat from his position. We were still the sanest, mentally healthiest individuals he had ever examined. But I think there was little doubt in anyone's mind who emerged as the victor from that Armageddon. And little doubt as to the caliber of the two antagonists.[4]

But Darrow was not satisfied, and Dr. Krohn would reappear later. After the experts had testified, there was little more left but the closing arguments. The prosecution stressed the vile nature of the crime committed, and the hoped-for deterrent effect that a death sentence would have. All the arguments that might have been anticipated were made, forcefully and competently. But it was upon Darrow that the world waited, knowing that whatever he said, it would be memorable.

On August 22, the crowd outside the criminal court building of Cook County was the largest ever assembled there. All the personnel connected with the case had been under police protection for some weeks, and on the day that Darrow was to begin speaking, there was a grave danger that the mob would go out of control. "At times the crowd swept away officers and ran over each other in frantic efforts to get inside the trial room," he said. The proceedings had been running for three weeks, and although there had been a constant press to get into the courtroom, nothing like this had happened before. Clearly Darrow was the crowd-drawer.

It was from this day that Darrow acquired truly national fame, which he would retain to the end of his life. Before then he was a well-known lawyer but his name was not a household word. From now on, he would be in a class of his own, with no living lawyer to compare with him. Indeed no lawyer since has achieved the fame that came to Darrow. Yet he achieved recognition on this scale only at the age of sixty-seven, a man already weary, and wracked by rheumatism and neuralgia, who had been trying to give up the necessity of law practice for thirty years in favor of writing, and who had taken the case only with the greatest reluctance. All this is necessary to understand the impact of what Darrow said then. He was not already known to the masses for what he believed, and the greatness of what he said had added effect because of its surprise to the world at large. Darrow's views were known to the intellectuals and the informed middle class, of course, but the public generally knew only vaguely of his previous career and did not appreciate the measure of the man.

It was a sweltering summer day. Straw hats were festooned round the courtroom on pegs, giving an incongruously jaunty appearance to the scene that contrasted oddly with the macabre recital upon which Darrow was about to embark. He was not comfortable and had wanted to take off his jacket during his final address, but did not do so in deference to Nathan Leopold's wishes. The months of tension had reached their climax. He knew that his clients had employed him to work miracles. The effort was enormous—never again was he to reach such heights. "From that day I have never gone through so protracted a strain, and could never do it again, even if I should try," he wrote later.

He referred to this strain at the opening of his speech, saying that it had not been due to "the facts that are connected with this most unfortunate affair, but to the almost unheard-of publicity it has received."[5] The case had attracted publicity not because of the nature of the crime, but because the defendants were rich:

> If we fail in this defense it will not be for lack of money. It will be on account of money. . . . I insist, Your Honor, that had this been the case of two boys of these defendants' ages, unconnected with families supposed to have great wealth, there is not a state's attorney in Illinois who would not have consented at once to a plea of guilty and a punishment in the penitentiary for life. Not one.

It was a superb reversal of the state's attorney's arguments in his statements to the press. Crowe had argued that the riches of the boys' families were being used to evade justice. Now Darrow had turned the tables. As for his argument that a plea bargain could have been arranged if the defendants were not rich, it was cleverly put. Darrow had never approached State Attorney Crowe to see whether such a bargain could have been made. Yet it seems likely that, had negotiations for a plea begun, they would have been rebuffed, not on the ground of the defendants' wealth, but the atrocious nature of the crime.

He dealt with the precedents in Chicago, saying that there had never been a case in which a human being under twenty-three had been sentenced to death, and poured scorn on the wealth of authorities produced by Assistant State's Attorney Marshall for the execution of minors, calling them "cases from the Dark Ages." Then he turned to the question of why he was before Judge Caverly:

> My friend, Mr. Savage, in as cruel a speech as he knew how to make, said to this court that we pleaded guilty because we were afraid to do anything else. Your Honor, that is true. . . . Your Honor will never thank me for unloading this responsibility upon you, but you know that I would have been untrue to my clients if I had not concluded to take this chance before a court, instead of submitting it to a poisoned jury in the city of Chicago.

But as Darrow well knew, Illinois law countenanced and even encouraged prosecution speeches in aggravation of sentence, just as it permitted the defense to mitigate. In this respect Illinois practice carried the logic of the adversary process to an extreme. Still he appealed to Judge Caverly not to be swayed by inflammatory rhetoric as a jury might be. Deftly, he juxtaposed this reminder of the judge's exclusive responsibility against the picture of a trapdoor being sprung under the feet of the two manacled boys if sentence of death was passed.

The rest of his speech, magnificently lucid, lasted all of that day and all of the next. It minimized the horror of the crime, which many commentators, at the time and since, believed to have been the only weak line of argument in the summation:

> They call it a cold-blooded murder because they want to take human lives. . . . Was it a cold-blooded murder? Was it the most terrible murder that ever happened in the state of Illinois? Was it the most dastardly act in the annals of crime?
>
> No.
>
> I insist, Your Honor, that under all fair rules and measurements, this was one of the least dastardly and cruel of any that I have known anything about.
>
> Now, let us see how we should measure it. . . . I would say the first thing to consider is the degree of pain to the victim.
>
> Poor little Bobbie Franks suffered very little. There is no excuse for his killing. If to hang these two boys would bring him back to life, I would say let them hang, and I believe their parents would say so too. . . . Robert Franks is dead, and we cannot call him back to life. It was all over in fifteen minutes after he got into the car, and he probably never knew it or thought of it. That does not justify it. It is the last thing I would do. I am sorry for the poor boy. I am sorry for his parents. But it is done.

Many felt that to describe the murder as "one of the least dastardly and cruel of any that I have known anything about" was a serious overstatement, more likely to outrage public opinion than to placate it, and that Darrow's strongest tactic would have been to acknowledge without reservation that it was all the prosecution claimed it to be. The thrust of all previous defense energies had been that, because of the mental state of the boys, it would be unjust to punish them by death for their actions. But if that principle was sound, it would follow that the horror of what they had done was totally irrelevant. Darrow's argument minimizing its cruelty seemed inconsistent with what came both before and after. Whether or not he was wise, however, it afforded him an opportunity to use the form of argument that he had thirteen years before put to the use of J. B. McNamara: " . . . if giving of my life could bring them back I would freely give it," McNamara's statement, drafted by Darrow, had read. And now, an era later, "if to hang these two boys would bring him [Bobby Franks] back to life, I would say let them hang. . . . But it is done"—a reminder that what had been done was irrevocable, and that revenge could never amount to restitution.

This followed an earlier shaft directed against the obvious determination of the prosecution to secure the hanging of the defendants. Knowing that popular sentiment would support the death penalty, the prosecution had been strident in its demand for hanging: "It seems to me," Darrow said somberly,

> if I could ever bring my mind to ask for the death penalty, I would not do it boastfully and exultantly or in anger or in hate, but I would do it with the deepest regret that it must be done, and I would do it with sympathy even for the ones whose lives must be taken. That has not been done in this case. I have never seen a more deliberate effort to turn the human beings of a community into ravening wolves and take advantage of everything that was offered to create an unreasoning hatred against these two boys.[6]

It was a sharp rap over the knuckles for Crowe, Savage, and Marshall, and the public opinion they were deliberately trying to represent. Probably it was one of the arguments that weighed most heavily with Judge Caverly, who was known to have serious moral doubts about the spirit in which the death penalty was sought by Crowe.

Darrow complained bitterly about the prosecution's unnecessary proof of the crime in an effort to inflame feeling against the defendants. But he, too, painted vivid word pictures of the two boys' fate if sentenced to be hanged: how they would be led to their death handcuffed, guarded, without hope of escape; how their heads would be cowled, the nooses placed around their necks, and how the trap would be sprung. He depicted it with just enough horror to remind the judge of the consequences if he declared the penalty to be death, but not so much as to give grounds for accusing him of dwelling on it.

The chief thrust of Darrow's argument was the one that had caused a major battle on the question of admissibility of evidence: that the boys, though not insane in a way amounting to a defense to the crime, were nevertheless so mentally diseased that they were not morally blameworthy. Darrow had three strands to his argument here. First, he knew that the acts of the boys were such as to raise a most serious doubt about the sanity of the perpetrators in most men's minds. Second, he was prepared to argue that the crime was motiveless. Third, he argued that the testimony of the alienists showed that the boys were mentally abnormal.

The first point was less a matter of argument than a constant reminder to the judge throughout the two days he spoke. At various times Darrow referred to the crime as senseless, motiveless, and mad. On the second point, the prosecution had handed him a golden opportunity. It had argued that the motive of the boys was the ransom money demanded, which was $10,000, to pay gambling debts. But at the time of the crime Loeb had $3,000 in his checking account and three Liberty Bonds, on all of which the interest was past due, and one of which had matured. He had not even bothered to collect. In addition, he was entitled to draw checks from his father's private secretary on request. Leopold had a monthly allowance of $125 and his father had been about to give him $3,000 to make a trip to Europe when he was arrested.

It was the argument of mental disease that caused most furore, partly because of its novelty and partly because of an unexpected turn to Darrow's address. The hypothesis he developed from the alienists' testimony was very simple: that both boys had an abundance of brains but were devoid of normal human emotion; that they had much intelligence but little feeling. This, Darrow claimed, was a gross mental abnormality. Such a theory had been adopted by the defense because it was compatible with the reports of the state experts, Drs. Church and Patrick—it was a way of spiking the state's guns. Indeed the hand of the defense was forced, because this was the only abnormality acknowledged by the prosecution reports. Darrow used it brilliantly to contend that neither boy was blameworthy:

> I know that they cannot feel what you feel and what I feel; that they cannot feel the moral shocks which come to men that are educated and who have not been deprived of an emotional system or emotional feelings. I know it, and every person who has honestly studied this subject knows it as well. Is Dickie Loeb to blame because out of the infinite forces that conspired to form him, the infinite forces that were at work producing him ages before he was born, that because out of these infinite combinations he was born without it? If he is, then there should be a new definition for justice.[7]

Yet there were only two pieces of evidence supporting Darrow's contention that the boys were mentally abnormal: first, their undoubted intellectual gifts, and second, their commission of the crime. His argument came dangerously near to the circularity of saying that anyone who committed a horrible crime was mentally abnormal, and therefore should not suffer the death penalty even though it was reserved by the law for just such offenses. Of course the intent of his argument was narrow; it was designed exclusively to avoid capital punishment. He conceded several times during his summation that neither of the boys should be set free. The only expert called by the state who did not agree with the view that the boys were emotionally undeveloped was Dr.

Krohn, who was known as a frequent witness in the courts. Darrow described him contemptuously as a man "who by his own admissions, for sixteen years has not been a physician, but has used a license for the sake of haunting these courts, civil and criminal, and going up and down the land peddling perjury."

The one other strand of Darrow's argument regarding the mental condition of his clients came as a surprise to many. He argued at considerable length that Leopold had been corrupted by reading Nietzsche's philosophy, taught to him at the University of Chicago. There was evidence that Leopold had, indeed, been influenced by the philosophy which preached that some men were beyond the confines of morality:

> Is there any blame attached because somebody took Nietzsche's philosophy seriously and fashioned his life in it? And there is no question in this case that it is true. Then who is to blame? The university would be more to blame than he is. The publishers of the book—and Nietzsche's books are published by one of the biggest publishers in the world—are more to blame than he. Your Honor, it is hardly fair to hang a nineteen-year-old boy for the philosophy that was taught him at the university.

He was to have his own words quoted back to him in an entirely different context within the year. Still, the fact remained that Darrow, the great libertarian, had conceded a great part of the classical argument in favor of censorship and moral supervision. No matter that the University of Chicago had not taught Nietzscheism as an official credo; the fact that it had put it into circulation among its students made it, said Darrow, at least as blameworthy as the perpetrator of a horrible murder. The argument failed to explain why more of Nietzsche's readers had not committed murder, or why many more alumni of the University of Chicago were not murderers. If even the critical faculties of a brilliant boy could not save him from the immoral influence of the liberal arts syllabus, surely the dangers to less able minds than Leopold's were great. And was it not a fact that Darrow had written admiringly of Nietzsche himself without going out to kill? Extending his argument beyond the particularly sinister effect of reading Nietzsche, Darrow also made much of the boys' incessant reading of detective stories as a factor that had induced them to commit their crime.

The peroration of the speech made a magnificent appeal to Judge Caverly and ended with a quotation from Darrow's favorite poet, Omar Khayyám. Darrow, the judge, and many in the audience were crying. Darrow had taken the case far beyond the bounds of reason and logic, moving his listeners to a pity for the human race as a whole. It was his most masterly oration, rousing his audience to display emotion openly beyond what the conventions allowed. After the raucous cries for blood that had emanated from the prosecution, the gentleness of what had been said had immense appeal. A correspondent wrote: "There was scarcely any telling where his voice had finished and where silence had begun. Silence lasted a minute, two minutes. His own eyes, dimmed by years of serving the accused, the oppressed, the weak, were not the only ones that held tears."[8] The spellbinder had cast his spell once again, saved from cheapness by his ability to move not just others but himself, and from tawdry sentimentality by his own spontaneous emotions.

The next day Darrow's entire speech was reproduced in many of the newspapers all over the country. Its impact depended in large measure upon the novelty of his perspective on the crime. It was widely agreed that he had given everyone food for thought about the nature of crime, criminals, and punishment. But it was also widely agreed that he had convinced almost nobody on a number of points. His description of the crime as "motiveless" did not altogether satisfy many members of the press. Was not the motive for what was done pleasure? Was not the public outrage about this crime the brutal selfishness of it all—a hedonistic excess of the gay twenties? True, the boys did not need money, but there were strong undertones of sexual perversion in the relationship of the two accused. Details of these aspects of the crime and its perpetrators were heard in chambers, and therefore not reported; but many thought Darrow's failure to discuss this aspect of the case was an indefensible evasion.[9]

There were others who doubted the proposition Darrow had advanced about the boys' riches being a disadvantage. He had said there was no doubt that an ordinary, obscure pair of boys would immediately have got an agreement for a non-capital sentence in exchange for pleas of guilty. Some thought that this was untrue; but even if it was true, it was a sad reflection on the administration of justice in Cook County. The legal fraternity in Chicago was mildly shocked at Darrow's open references to plea bargaining in his summation, which was a somewhat clandestine part of the system of criminal justice in those days, almost never acknowledged in open court. More than that, Darrow's statement of the position was doubted by many regular practitioners in the Chicago criminal courts. It was not their experience that the state's attorney would negotiate a plea of guilty to murder when he was in possession of evidence on which he could unquestionably convict by trial. Robert Crowe had refused to do so in previous cases where he wished to obtain a sentence of death. As it turned out, Judge Caverly explicitly rejected Darrow's contention when he pronounced sentence.

Another aspect of Darrow's plea that displeased some members of the Chicago bar was his harsh treatment of Assistant State's Attorney Joseph Savage, to whom he made several slighting references. Savage was widely regarded as a competent and effective prosecutor, who had honorably represented the interests of the people. The *cognoscenti* knew that one of Darrow's standard techniques was to find a "butt" among the prosecuting attorneys to distract attention from his clients' ill-doing. But even if that practice was justifiable before a jury, it was totally senseless before a judge sitting alone. Some thought that Darrow was smearing Savage—who was only twenty-nine and had been a member of the bar for only three years—gratuitously.*

---

*However, when Savage ran as a Republican candidate for county court judge with John Sbarbaro in November 1926, neither was recommended by the nonpartisan Chicago Bar Association,

In nearly every major trial in which he had participated, Darrow had deliberately singled out a prosecution figure upon whom to vent his wrath. By now the wording and imagery of his harangue were well tested. It had been his stock-in-trade for a quarter of a century, though his brilliant ability to extemporize gave his words an appearance of freshness. As phrase followed vivid phrase, he painted a picture of Savage as a despicable, blood-hungry bully. But there was something wrong. Though the description was superb, the monster Darrow portrayed bore no resemblance to Joseph Savage as he actually appeared. Darrow's exaggeration was a caricature almost unrecognizable as human, so that but for the solemnity of the occasion it would have been laughable.

In other respects the speech was a tour de force for what it did not say. No mention was made of the sexual perversion of the crime or of the fact that his clients were Jews. The families of the defendants had feared that anti-Semitism would result from the trial, and though the ostensible reason for Darrow's avoidance of jury trial was the public's willingness to hang, an unpublicized element was the fear of anti-Semitism in the jury.

In effect, the Darrow speech was for much of the public the climax of the proceedings—and it is often forgotten that after Darrow, the state's attorney had the final word, speaking for two further days. Crowe was a clever, hard-working man, who put all he had into his closing address, but Darrow was too hard an act to follow, and his speech seemed dull and uninteresting by comparison. At the close of the prosecution case, court was adjourned until September 10, at which time Judge Caverly hoped to be able to render his decision. His was not an enviable position, as Darrow had said, but for the rest there was nothing to do but wait.

The waiting was hard for all concerned, not least Darrow. He had wound himself up over a period of three months in dealing with the case, and it was difficult to unwind. He hated capital punishment and was scared that he would have to face its reality in this case. He received, as did the judge and the defendants, a huge number of crank letters, some of them threatening and all of them abusive. He went back to his office and tried to pay attention to other matters, but could not. He chain-smoked through the days, slept only fitfully during the night. All other activity was suspended until the result in the Leopold-Loeb trial was known; there could be no distractions. Nearly all the editorials that appeared on the subject of the trial were against Darrow's view, and the weight of public opinion was clearly on the side of hanging. In addition, he had to contend with the fear that one of his many anonymous correspondents might carry out their threats against him. The Chicago police department treated the danger to Darrow and all principals in the case as substantial, and when finally the judge delivered his verdict, court and lawyers alike were heavily guarded.

---

though Savage's Democratic opponent was overwhelmingly approved. Whatever fault the bar found with Darrow, it was not enthusiastic about the team behind Crowe, or for that matter about Crowe himself.

When the day came, another crowd besieged the courthouse wanting to hear the result of Judge Caverly's deliberations. He entered the court looking visibly nervous, though neither prosecution nor defense knew whether that was favorable to their side. Judge Caverly was not required under Illinois law to do anything more than pronounce sentence, but he chose to give his reasons for his decision. He started by saying that the defendants were entitled to no special consideration because they had pleaded guilty. It later appeared that Caverly had laid deliberate and particular emphasis on this point because he felt that, if the law were otherwise, those accused of especially outrageous crimes would always be able to avoid the death penalty by entering a plea of guilty and, as suspected by some of the regular lawyers, he had been rather annoyed with Darrow for suggesting it. It was a somber opening to the opinion, and did not bode well for Leopold and Loeb.

He then went on to repudiate Darrow's argument that, because the defendants were mentally abnormal, they should be exempt from paying the penalty of death. Leopold and Loeb were, he said, no more abnormal than many criminals. Again, if the defense contention were correct, the death penalty would be effectively abolished in Illinois. Here he demolished in a paragraph the centerpiece of Darrow's defense and accepted instead the objections to it that had appeared in many newspapers. At this stage Nathan Leopold concluded that Judge Caverly was leading up to the imposition of the death sentence, and so, apparently, did the prosecution, if their reaction of stunned silence when the judge finished may be regarded as evidence. But then the opinion took a rapid turn in the opposite direction. The judge did not like to impose the sentence of death on juveniles. The boys would each receive a sentence of life imprisonment for murder and ninety-nine years for kidnapping, the sentences to run concurrently. The defendants were to be treated as equally guilty in the eyes of the law, with no difference in their punishments.

"The reversal in the concluding paragraphs had come as suddenly and unexpectedly as a flash of lightning out of a clear sky," wrote Francis X. Busch, Chicago's corporation counsel at the time.[10] The news was the hottest ever to come out of a courtroom, and was flashed across the world within minutes of its announcement. Darrow waited until the courtroom had cleared, then left for a period of rest and recuperation.

Darrow had saved his clients' lives, but he had not saved their reputation or that of their families. After the trial rumors circulated freely of other fiendish acts perpetrated by the boys, which had not been disclosed in open court. Leopold protested consistently thereafter that no sexual perversion had been involved in the case: "There wasn't a scintilla of evidence in all the hundreds of thousands of words of testimony to support such a charge," he alleged in 1958.[11] But this was, at best, a half truth. Letters that the boys had written to each other were quoted in court by Darrow himself to indicate the abnormality of their relationship, which clearly had sexual overtones. Furthermore some of the findings of the alienists engaged by the defense, explained privately in Judge Caverly's chambers, directly alleged sexual oddities. For the rest of their lives Leopold and Loeb were to fight the persisting stories of their sexual atrocities. A Chicago newspaperwoman recalled that after their sentencing, a number of other local crimes were attributed to them: ". . . they had done some preparatory practice work in crimes by maiming a few Hyde Park residents, including at least one castration."[12]

Although the boys and their representatives vigorously fought these rumors, events were against them. Loeb was stabbed to death on January 28, 1936, in prison, in circumstances that strongly indicated a homosexual *crime passionel*. The prisoner who had struck the fatal blows, James Day, was later tried for murder, but was acquitted after he had alleged that a homosexual assault was made on him by Loeb in the shower stalls at Stateville Prison. Leopold protested that Day's story was utterly untrue.*

This was not the last of the damaging pieces of publicity the boys were to receive. In October 1956 *Compulsion,* Meyer Levin's fictionalized version of their crime, was published. It described explicitly in print (as never before) how they had mutilated their victim's naked body by pouring acid over his sexual organs. Nathan Leopold alleged that the book "is perhaps 40 per cent fact, 60 per cent fiction. . . . It made me physically sick—I mean that literally. More than once I had to lay the book down and wait for the nausea to subside."[13] He prevailed upon his lawyer to write to a publisher considering the manuscript, warning that he would sue for any libelous statement in the book. Meyer Levin resisted Leopold's claims, "considering the suit an outrageous attempt a third of a century after the deed to collect the ransom money for Bobby Franks."[14] Later, on a different legal theory, he attempted to prevent the release of the movie based on Levin's book. But the crime was too horrible for complaints of misrepresentation to be effective, and the public presses stuck to the view they had taken from the beginning.

The contemporary reaction of the American press to Judge Caverly's decision was almost universally adverse. Many objections were made, some of them in general terms—that if this was not a crime for the death penalty, then no crime should merit it. But some made telling specific points about the precedent, pointing out that Leopold and Loeb would become eligible for parole under Illinois law regardless of Judge Caverly's wishes in the matter. Others referred to the position of Bernard Grant, a nineteen-year-old convicted of murder in Chicago who, at the very time Leopold and Loeb were sentenced, was awaiting hanging pursuant to a sentence of death. The New York *Herald-Tribune* disapproved the professed principle of Judge Caverly, saying: "The Illinois law makes no twenty-first birthday distinction in murderous intent or responsibility. But if such a distinction is to be drawn in favor of some minors it ought to be drawn in favor of all. And the rule should be embodied in the law itself, not left to the hazards of individual judicial enforcement."[15]

---

*Darrow, by that time seventy-eight years old, typically tried to help by making a statement deflecting public attention away from the immediate facts of the case by blaming the slaying on the inhuman conditions in American prisons.

Some journalists believed that the case had been fixed, not to the Leopolds' and Loebs' satisfaction, it was true, but nevertheless the possibility that Judge Caverly had been reached did not seem entirely far-fetched. Newsroom speculation took into account that Darrow, the great jury advocate, had seen fit not to go before a jury. By presenting the case to a judge, it was said, he needed only to influence one man, not twelve; and Caverly was a Democrat whom Darrow had known over a long period. Victor Yarros, himself a journalist who had worked extensively in Darrow's law practice, discreetly suggested that Darrow had been "lucky" with Judge Caverly, who "had nothing to lose politically."[16] The only newspaper reaction favorable to Judge Caverly in Chicago was from the Jewish press, which was relieved that neither the hearing nor its result pointed to anti-Semitic influence.*

The consensus agreed with Yarros that the defendants had been lucky Judge Caverly was Chief Justice of the criminal court. This was a one-year appointment rotated among the judges of the circuit and superior courts of Cook County, and it was pure coincidence that Judge Caverly happened to be one of the most open-minded of judges then presiding. He knew that the clamor of the mob for vengeance was the enemy of justice, but his view was not typical of his fellow judges. A much more typical attitude among the judges was that death was the proper, logical, and just penalty for Leopold and Loeb. Ironically, only four years before, Judge Caverly's position had been held by Robert Crowe. Judge Caverly himself had campaigned on the platform that every criminal should be sent to the penitentiary and every murderer should be hanged—a position that helped get him elected.

Judge Caverly's colleagues on the Cook County bench maintained a proper reticence about their views on what had been done. They were not going to second-guess their Chief Justice's decision, whatever their own feelings might be. But judges elsewhere did not hesitate to indicate that, had the case come before them, the result would have been different. One such was Judge Alfred J. Talley of New York's Court of General Sessions. Darrow had made a statement to the press indicating that he hoped the Leopold-Loeb case would occasion further research into the psychology of crime and possibly the foundation of neuropathic hospitals across the country. Although he specifically mentioned the instances of his young clients, he avoided saying that he believed treatment would have prevented their crimes. But this was too much for some critics, and Darrow's support for preventive mental medicine brought a remarkable retort. Judge Talley issued a counterblast, aimed at Darrow. "It is not the criminals, actual or potential, that need a neuropathic hospital. It is the people who slobber over them in an effort to find excuses for their crimes. There are lots of sick people who concern themselves with crime, but the criminals are not numbered among them."[17]

This statement was the beginning of a torrent of criticism released after the

*On this basis Judge Caverly became one on the very few non-Jews to receive the endorsement of the Jewish press when he ran for reelection.

14. *Darrow sorting through some of the mail received during the Leopold and Loeb case, 1924. "I seldom went to my office in those troublous days, and rarely read any of the letters that came in stacks," he recorded. "These were usually abusive and brutal to the highest degree."*

15. *America's last "village atheist" objects to opening court with a prayer, Scopes trial, Dayton, Tennessee, 1925.*

16. *The drugstore where the Scopes case all started. Sitting at the table are Arthur Garfield Hays and Clarence Darrow, Scopes's counsel, 1925.*

17. *Darrow in action at the Scopes trial. The man standing in the right foreground is Dudley Field Malone, co-counsel with Darrow.*

18. Rivals face-to-face: Darrow with William Jennings Bryan, Scopes trial, 1925.

19. *Clarence and Ruby Darrow on vacation in Paris, 1929.*

20. *Clarence and Ruby Darrow in the garden of Sinclair Lewis's home in Barnard, Vermont, 1930. The Darrows and Lewis became good friends.*

21. *Darrow sampling the pleasures of island life during the Massie case, Honolulu, 1932.
In explaining why he took the case, he said: "I had never been to that part of the Pacific
and longed to sometime see it."*

22. *Darrow with Thalia Massie and her mother, Mrs. Grace Fortescue, outside the Judiciary Building, Honolulu, 1932.*

23. *Charles Edward Russell* (seated, left) *and Darrow, chairman, at the Willard Hotel during the hearings on the workings of the National Recovery Administration, 1934. H. G. Wells described the pair as "fine flowers of American insurrectionism....They were 'agin the government' all the time and the wildfire of freedom shone in Darrow's eyes."*

24. Darrow leaving Chicago for Washington, D.C., March 16, 1935, to give testimony before the Senate Committee on Finance investigation of the Review Board of which he had been chairman.

25. *Darrow poses with his wife on his seventy-ninth birthday, 1936, in the Chicago apartment in which they had lived for thirty years.*

verdict was handed down, criticism directed not so much at Judge Caverly or the laws of Illinois as against Darrow—for it was he who was blamed for cheating the public out of hanging Richard Loeb and Nathan Leopold. It is a measure of Darrow's reputation that he was credited with "pulling off" the sentences of imprisonment where really there ought to have been sentences of death. This confusion arose from public misunderstanding. Many believed that Darrow had somehow evaded a statute that imposed a mandatory sentence of death on murderers and kidnappers. In fact, the sentence was at the discretion of the court. Darrow's eloquent plea had been an attempt to persuade the court not to impose the sentence of death, but the decision itself had not been his. That made no difference in the minds of many—he was the one who had pleaded for mercy, which was tantamount to condonation, even approval, of what the boys had done. As always myth-making depended on the will to believe.

Most abhorrent to many who considered the verdict was the "psychiatric pardon" that Darrow's presentation of the case had seemed to give. And for this he *was* responsible, since the court repudiated all the alienists' evidence as a ground for mercy. It seemed that Darrow denied individual moral responsibility for action, which was both frightening and horrifying. Yet in this respect Darrow's views had scarcely changed in twenty-five years, and he had expressed them frequently. It was not that he had forged a novel plea for the boys, but rather that he had adapted his standard line of defense. There was scarcely any part of the Leopold-Loeb defense (with the exception of his references to Nietzsche) which Darrow had not presented before, more or less identically, to other courts, or in other contexts; but it was the Leopold-Loeb trial that brought them most dramatically to public attention. In part, Darrow brought the public wrath upon himself because he propounded the same view of human conduct in and out of court. His defenses were not artificially contrived orations for the sake of clients. They represented, in the main, his real attitude. Darrow the advocate and Darrow the man were in important respects the same. But he was right to say that much contemporary hostility came from the public view that Darrow and the Bachrachs "were committing a crime in defending two boys, who probably needed it as much as any two defendants ever on trial for their lives."

Having appeared for the boys in court, Darrow stood up for them out of court. Much that he did in the next few months was still done in their defense. The League for Public Discussion had noted Judge Talley's forthright challenge of Darrow's position and invited both protagonists to debate the matter in New York. Darrow had no hesitation in accepting. In justification of his position with respect to juveniles convicted of murder, he undertook to take on the case of Bernard Grant, the young man who was under sentence of death for murder at the very time that Leopold and Loeb drew life imprisonment for their offense. His intercession on Grant's behalf won a three-month reprieve, in order that an appeal could be prepared for him.

Immediately after Judge Caverly's opinion was rendered, Darrow repaired to Charlevoix, Michigan, as the Loeb family's guest. Albert Loeb's superb estate included a section dotted with replicas of French and Norman castles put up at huge expense in 1918; the circumstances underlined, as emphatically as they could, that "Dickie" Loeb did not come from a deprived background. Charlevoix was a lavish playground of the Jewish rich. Apart from the Loeb home, the country houses of E. J. Block of Inland Steel, David May of the St. Louis department store, Cy Lazarus of Federated department stores, J. Godchaux of a New Orleans sugar company, and Albert Wachenheim of the shoe business were in the area. Every season from Independence Day to Labor Day the owners of some of the greatest business wealth in the nation congregated there. But now the season was finished and the Loebs and Darrow could rest quietly, away from the press. Darrow was seriously overtired, sustained only by the victory he had achieved. He did not know that there would soon occur a breach between himself and his hosts on what might have been thought a most unlikely subject in the circumstances—money.

In the meantime, all seemed well. He did what he could to minimize the apparently favorable position of his clients by comparison with Bernard Grant. Having prevailed upon Governor Small to grant a temporary reprieve from execution to the boy, he gave it out to the press that he intended to prepare an appeal for him. He followed his normal practice of treating his ex-clients like friends and did his best to cheer up his young clients, now already serving their sentences, by writing them letters. He wrote to Nathan Leopold:

> Charlevoix, Michigan
> Sept. 20th [1924]
>
> Dear Nathan
>
> I have been up here for about ten days getting some rest. Shall be back in Chicago on Monday & will arrange to go & see you soon after arriving. I wont take the trouble to give you advice now & anyhow I presume I know less about it all than you do. Although I am not a Christian Scientist (or anything else) I know that the most of life is within us and man is a wonderfully adaptable animal. I think you know this too. Of course you will be there for a long time & will naturally figure out the best way to make things tolerable, as I have tried to do, with poor success, on the outside. I can help you figure this out & will make it my business to do it for both you and Dick. I am ambitious for you to write your bird book. I have had a good deal of pleasure, or rather forgetfulness in writing books which no one reads, & I want you to write one which will be read. Anyhow I wont forget you and I am sure I can help you in many ways.
>
> Always your friend
> Clarence Darrow[18]

A similar letter of comfort was written to Richard Loeb. Until his last year Darrow kept in contact with the boys as they grew toward middle age behind prison walls. He never let his dispute with the Loeb family interfere with his relationship with the two convicts.

From the outset of the Leopold and Loeb trial there was a suspicion that because the families of both defendants were rich, attempts would be made to "buy off" the prosecution. State's Attorney Crowe had characterized the trial as a contest between "five million dollars and justice."[19] He described Darrow as "a paid advocate whose profession it was to protect murder in Cook County, and concerning whose health thieves inquire before they go out to commit crime."[20] As soon as he entered the case, Darrow had seen this fear that the defendants' riches would save them as one of the most dangerous to their interests, yet he was caught in an insoluble dilemma. This was not a charity case or one which he would have taken on but for the fee, and to that extent it was clear that the Loebs, in purchasing Darrow's services, were in reality purchasing privilege. Darrow had sold his services high before, but normally not to clients whose money was fairly honestly made, as the Loebs' was. He did all in his power to dispel the impression that large fees were being spent to save the boys, although the impression remained, regardless of all denials.[21]

Difficulties had been inherent in his relationship with the Loebs from the time on June 2 when they solicited his aid. Then no fee was fixed, though a $10,000 retainer was paid; two o'clock in the morning was not a time to start drawing up a fee agreement with a desperate, horror-struck family. Next, it was by no means clear what Darrow was expected to do, except that it had to be a miracle. Was he merely to avoid the death penalty being imposed, or try to gain an acquittal? From the start Darrow acted as if the former was the agreement with the Loebs, who were consulted throughout; but in retrospect they seemed not to be satisfied with that achievement.[22] Lastly, there was an ambiguity about the lawyer-client relationship: Darrow had been hired by the Loebs, but to defend both their kin and Nathan Leopold. Thus the only redress Darrow had was against the Loebs, not the Leopolds. The Bachrach brothers, too, were relations of the Loebs, and it was therefore to the Loebs that Darrow had to look for payment.

The feeling against the Loeb and Leopold families was so great that one of Darrow's major arguments to Judge Caverly was that his clients were being prejudiced in their rights because they were rich. Among the representations made to the court on August 22 was that "The attorneys, at their own request, have agreed to take such amount as the officers of the Chicago Bar Association may think is proper in this case."[23] This was an indication that as late as the beginning of the summation, no agreement had been reached on the amount of the fee. After the trial the Loebs made no overture with a view to settling their debt, much to the distress of Darrow's partners, whose office had borne the burden of much of the work and expenses that went into the conduct of the trial. It also appeared that the Chicago Bar Association was making no move, and had not at that stage even been invited to pass on the appropriateness of a fee. Darrow had committed the classic mistake. He had given services to a criminal defendant on credit, without any firm written agreement for payment.

The exact circumstances of the rift remain uncertain, with conflicting accounts by well-qualified and sympathetic parties.[24] But there are at least three hypotheses that seem probable. Possibly the Loebs' failure to pay Darrow was an extension of a dispute between them and the Leopold family about the amounts each should contribute. As has been pointed out, the initiative to hire Darrow had been the Loebs'. Second, it may have reflected an objection on the part of the Bachrachs, who were the Loebs' relations, to the amounts allotted to them and to Darrow. Third, there is every probability that the Loebs resented Darrow's inclination to blame Loeb more than Leopold for the crime, insofar as he blamed anyone. It was clear from his summation and his subsequent statements that he regarded Richard Loeb as the architect and instigator of the crime, and Leopold merely as a follower.[25] The Loeb family probably resented this perspective on the crime, even though the facts seemed to support it, and felt that it gave them an excuse, if not justification, to avoid paying Darrow. When finally the family met with Darrow, they asked him what he would consider a reasonable fee, and Darrow replied $200,000, which the Loebs thought far too high. They indicated the next day that $100,000 was the most they were prepared to pay. Darrow accepted. It is at this stage that there is a material difference in the accounts of what took place. According to Charles Yale Harrison, an admirer with whom Darrow discussed the dispute, the Loebs sent a check for $70,000, which Darrow shared with his partners. According to Irving Stone, the Loebs deducted from the $100,000 a total of $70,000: $10,000 already advanced and a third of the remainder for each of the Bachrach brothers—who were not Darrow's partners. Darrow accepted $30,000 rather than have it be said that he quibbled over the fee.[26]

Years before Darrow had complained that defending the poor did not pay. Now he knew that it did not always pay to defend the rich either. Many Chicago lawyers felt that Darrow should have refused to accept the $30,000 and made a complaint to the Chicago Bar Association about the Loebs. After all, their agreement was part of an uncontradicted record of the trial proceedings. But Darrow would not make an issue of it and the families accused of spending millions in defense of their murderous sons spent very much less than anyone would have expected.

Darrow returned from Charlevoix to Chicago and then went on to New York to face Judge Talley in the debate on capital punishment on October 26 sponsored by the League for Public Discussion. It took place in the Manhattan Opera House, which was packed with people who had paid up to $4 for a ticket. It is possible that the families of the two boys believed Darrow's public debating on the issue of capital punishment so soon after the trial was a means of getting paid twice over for his forensics, and that this too disinclined them to pay him. In any case he was a singular success, and lambasted Judge Talley to the point of ridicule. Capital punishment had never prevented murder, he said, but that was not something he was concerned with. "There is just one thing in all this question. It is a question of how you feel, that is all. It is all inside of you. If you love the thought of somebody being killed, why, you are for it. If you hate the thought of somebody being killed, you are against it."[27] It was clear that Judge Talley was outclassed in the debate and did not live up to the promise of his most provocative challenge of the month before, which had suggested a talent for vituperation worthy of Darrow's combat.

Darrow's success immediately brought him offers of many other engagements, including two more in New York City. Under the auspices of the League, he debated the Reverend John Haynes Holmes on prohibition, and on November 30 at Town Hall he debated Professor Scott Nearing of the Rand School on whether life was worth living. An audience of 1,700 paid between $1 and $3 to attend. He was a box-office "draw" and went on to deal with themes not associated with the plight of his late clients. The public, especially in New York, wanted to see at first hand who this remarkable man was, and Darrow was pleased to let them. He had more interest in lecturing and writing than he did in practicing law, and the Leopold and Loeb trial, as he knew, had taxed him to the limit. From now on he would be scarcely involved in the regular practice of law at all. He became a regular on lecture tours, debating the same theme with the same adversary in different cities, as he did with Dr. Nearing. There were more invitations to "pair" with an antagonist than he could possibly accept. One night in Rochester he debated the open shop question with Noel Sargent, a representative of the National Association of Manufacturers, and was so successful that he was then and there offered a contract for a tour of debates with Sargent. An eyewitness reported:

> While Sargent was speaking that night—he was speaking first—Darrow sat slouched in his chair without taking a single note, apparently quite oblivious to all that was going on. When his turn came he slowly unwound his long legs, walked to the lectern, and one by one repeated almost word for word all the essential points of Sargent's speech, then demolished them so completely that the great audience screamed in delight. It was the finest forensic feat I had ever witnessed.[28]

Afterward Darrow was entreated to agree to similar appearances throughout the United States. He refused. He was going to enjoy his celebrity but not overdo it. Besides, top billing on the lecture and debate circuit could not, in Darrow's mind, be considered altogether respectable.

Although he was engaged in a fee dispute with the Loebs, Darrow was not in bad financial condition and had no need to seek the income that lecturing and debating could provide. The twenties had been good to him. Neither did he wish for another professional opportunity like the Leopold and Loeb case, of which he was to say: "When I closed I had exhausted all the strength I could summon." Thus, as 1925 approached, it seemed unlikely that he would enter another major case unless it promised less anguish and more amusement than his recent experience. Remarkably, such a case was to come.

31

"As Old-Fashioned as William Jennings Bryan"

Darrow's participation in the Leopold and Loeb case had cemented his association with Chicago more firmly than ever in the public mind. "Clarence Darrow was so much a part of Chicago and had such a wide horizon of contacts that any young person on a newspaper was bound to cross his path," wrote Fanny Butcher.[1] He was a familiar figure in the Loop, greeted by all and sundry. "When he invited me to lunch we were hailed so many times by well-wishers, most of them strangers, it would take us thirty minutes to advance two blocks," Matilda Fenberg recalled. "I accused him once of loving the limelight, and he answered, 'No, but I find I work best under direct light.' "[2] The identification with Chicago was completed when Maurice Watkin's play *Chicago*—a bitter comedy about a female murderer who is acquitted by a jury of halfwits after her defense attorney describes her as "a brave little woman"—was produced in 1927. It was widely believed that the defense attorney was a composite character, one of whose main ingredients was Darrow.[3]

Judge Talley's condemnation of the result in the Leopold and Loeb case was only the first of many responses. It caused a serious reexamination of *Crime: Its Cause and Treatment,* which was itself a derivative work. Since neither Altgeld's original (which even Darrow acknowledged to be "somewhat crude") nor Darrow's work was very carefully written, it became a rich mine for his critics against the backdrop of the Leopold and Loeb case.

One of the most thoughtful refutations of Darrow's position came from Horace James Bridges in his book *The God of Fundamentalism,* published in 1925. Assessing Darrow's fatalism, he concluded: "The whole argument is constructed for the sake of the criminal, but its benefits are ruthlessly denied to all other men."[4] On a slightly different tack, Christopher Hollis, visiting Chicago only a little while after the Leopold and Loeb case, expressed his exasperation with and suspicion of Darrow after talking with him:

He started off as a conventional liberal by condemning Southern prejudices, but then, as a determinist, he had to concede that Southerners, creatures of heredity and environment, could not help having these prejudices, and Clarence Darrow, one could not but reflect, being Clarence Darrow, could not help talking like Clarence Darrow, and, that being so, it was really very difficult to see what was the sense in his talking at all, if all he had to say was that nobody could help being as they were.[5]

Others were struck by the hopelessness of Darrow's logic. A retired school-teacher wrote to Benjamin Barr Lindsey: "I had just been reading Clarence Darrow and had about come to the conclusion that we were a fixed species like the ants and the bees, and that there really was no hope of our further improvement."[6] The debate went back and forth, adding to Darrow's opportunities to speak publicly. Addressing the Nebraska State Bar Association in Lincoln in 1926, he told his audience: "I am much more interested in this subject than in any other. . . . The principal thing to remember is that we are all the products of heredity and environment; that we have little or no control, as individuals, over ourselves, and that criminals are like the rest of us in that regard."[7] And though his views came under fierce attack, he had many defenders, one of whom was to become of great importance in his old age. In 1926 Harry Elmer Barnes published a book entitled *The Repression of Crime,* which had as its central tenet the same premise as Darrow's: "There is not the slightest iota of freedom of choice allowed to either the criminal or the normal citizen in his daily conduct."[8] Barnes, at thirty-six a professor of history and sociology at Smith College, was a prolific writer who had already tackled some of the subjects that most interested Darrow: in time, criminology, penology, organized religion, party politics, and the evils of monopoly were all to be grist for his mill. His outpourings appealed to Darrow; they were, perhaps, the kinds of work he would have liked to produce himself if his energies had not been dissipated in debating, speaking, and lawyering. Darrow and Barnes became brothers-in-arms, and in him, Darrow was to see a spiritual heir.

Darrow himself was not specially trustful of criminals, but his conclusions about the causes of crime were remarkably like the reminiscences of a good number of recidivists—a resemblance that did not add to public sympathy with Darrow's fatalistic explanation of criminality. The beleaguered citizenry, daily told by the newspapers that the crooked had inherited Chicago, if not the earth, sought immediate deliverance and were not willing to abandon their treatment of criminals unless and until some better way was suggested. Darrow provided no solution except a radical, vaguely defined reordering of society; like many iconoclasts, his métier was finding fault rather than devising means of improvement.

The reproach that he had no blueprint for the future did not alter the fact that many of his observations on the human condition were exceedingly acute and startlingly ahead of their time. Darrow was by no means the first social critic to take the view that things were sufficiently bad that a move forward —no matter where—was better than no move at all. His wholehearted espousal of modernity was, whether he acknowledged it or not, influenced by the idea of progress: that improvement was a natural if erratic consequence of change. Was not this, after all, the underlying premise of Darwinism? There might be false starts, uncomfortable transitions, even aberrational throwbacks, but somehow the race got slightly better as it blundered on. In retort to objections such as that of Hollis, Darrow would have replied that his obligation was to think, not to think creatively, and to follow the truth wherever it might lead.

The extreme public reaction against Darrow's fatalistic explanation of criminality was intimately related to his identification with Chicago, which throughout the twenties was gaining a reputation for the most unsavory and brutal of gangland criminals. No American could ignore the growing litany of repulsive crimes centered in the city. Beginning with the murder of Big Jim Colosimo on May 11, 1920, less than four months after the Volstead Act had gone into effect, the twenties were punctuated by crimes that have remained the most notorious in America's history: the death of Frank Capone in March 1924; of Dion O'Banion in his North State Street flower shop in November of the same year; Angelo Genna's murder in the following year; and the culminating St. Valentine's Day massacre in 1929. These things did not provide a sympathetic background for Darrow's doctrine of *non culpa*.

In any event, Chicago's underworld and its politics—and there was little discernible difference between them—did provide him with all the legal work he wanted. Throughout the 1920s the largest prosecuting office in the country was that of the state's attorney of Cook County, considerably surpassing New York in size. Additionally his close connections with the Cook County Democrats could have ensured a regular flow of work if Darrow had needed to rely on contacts. But the publicity that the Leopold and Loeb case had given him was national, even international, and though Darrow was by this time well on in years, he showed no sign of losing his appetite for the limelight. While he was still riding on the crest of publicity created by his efforts for the two boys, an opportunity arose that he found irresistible. A young Tennessee schoolmaster, John T. Scopes, had defied his state's law prohibiting the teaching of evolution. In May 1925 the American Civil Liberties Union (ACLU) was offering to defend Scopes, and Darrow urgently wished to act as counsel. The case appealed strongly to Darrow's anti-religious bent as well as his impatience with rural America; and to add further spice, there was the chance to confront William Jennings Bryan in the courtroom challenge to Scopes's prosecution. He was able to boast, more or less truthfully, that "I have never had to look for clients." But there were cases that he actively sought out and the Scopes case was such a one. He said: "For the first, the last, the only time in my life, I volunteered my services in a case . . . because I really wanted to take part in it." And he went on: "One can easily understand that lawyers are generally slow to offer their services; at best, it is a delicate step to take, for they might not be wanted, and that would be embarrassing."

Darrow no doubt wrote that with feeling, for the offer of his own services in the Scopes trial was very nearly turned down, in spite of his agreeing to waive a fee and undertaking to pay his own expenses. When a meeting was held to consider who should be employed by the ACLU as counsel, there were bitter arguments over Darrow's possible appointment. John Scopes, who was present, reported: "These were arguments—not discussions. Any vote taken during the first thirty or forty minutes would have gone against Darrow two to one." He went on to explain: ". . . the main problem was that some felt Darrow was a headline chaser, and as a consequence the real issue would be obscured. If Darrow were injected into the case, the trial would become a carnival and any possible dignity in the fight for liberties would be lost."[9] As it was, Darrow was only grudgingly accepted as counsel at the end of the meeting—and then, according to Scopes, only because Dudley Field Malone said that unless Darrow was employed, he, Malone, would not serve on the defense.

The wisdom of the ACLU in "buying" the Scopes case was at the time, and remains, open to question. The ACLU had wanted to bring the issue before a federal rather than a state court. Had it chosen, it could have agreed to support Scopes's defense only if its attorneys were successful in obtaining a transfer of the proceedings to the federal jurisdiction. It had no wish for a jamboree in the backwoods of Tennessee, but in this respect the interests of the ACLU and Darrow diverged. Darrow was primarily a trial lawyer at his best in a state court, which would give him more leeway than a federal court. Although he was unquestionably competent to argue the constitutional point—he had been counsel in a number of cases appealed before the Supreme Court—this was not the area in which he excelled. An application was made to the federal courts for removal, but it was Scopes's opinion that Darrow was secretly pleased when the application was denied. If the ACLU had refused to proceed further, the world would not have been treated to such an entertaining trial. But it persisted, with the predictable consequence that the union's good name suffered in the eyes of the mass public. Many people heard of the ACLU for the first time in connection with the Scopes trial; it had changed its name from the National Civil Liberties Bureau only five years before when it looked beyond the preservation of civil liberties in wartime to the problems of peace. The Scopes litigation neither struck a sympathetic chord with the American masses nor introduced the ACLU as a serious and idealistic organization; it smacked too much of an attack on Old Glory, motherhood, and apple pie.

Even if the decision to support the litigation at trial level could be justified in terms of the ACLU's desires, it might reasonably have dropped the case once William Jennings Bryan announced, in April 1925, his intention to join in the prosecution. His entry into the case ensured that many of his admirers would conclude that the Union was anti-religious. For of all public figures, Bryan best represented rural piety. He was its spokesman and even its personification. As such he was Darrow's pet aversion, and the Scopes trial was a dream-come-true for Darrow. In a sense, he had been preparing for it all his life; certainly he had been preparing for it long before actual proceedings were ever contemplated.

Bryan had become the butt of intellectual opinion well before Scopes had ever been heard of—"By early 1923 Bryan was the prime target of criticism for so many philosophers, historians, and literary figures as well as Modern churchmen that a few examples must suffice," says his leading biographer.[10] But Darrow was a long-time challenger. On July 4, 1923, the front page of the Chicago *Tribune* carried fifty-five questions about the Bible, composed by Darrow and addressed to Bryan. These questions, which Bryan ignored at the time of their publication, were to become the basis of Darrow's cross-examination of him at the trial two years later. But the derision with which intellectual America treated Bryan did not alter the fact that Bryan commanded the respect of a large segment of the general public. In spite of all efforts Darrow had never managed to dislodge Bryan's hold upon the popular imagination, though he had tried many times; and the ACLU necessarily sacrificed goodwill by being the sponsor of the Scopes defense after Bryan entered the case as a prosecutor.

In the absence of an established church empowered to set up an official doctrine and suppress heresy, sects proliferated in the rural United States with startling diversity. Churches were set up by the personal enterprise of one individual and the teachings that emanated from them were completely at the whim of their founders. In the rural areas of the nation private enterprise had formed many congregations whose version of the "true gospel" would have astounded theologians brought up in a conservative tradition. In the days of the frontier, religion had provided a friend in the wilderness to lonely people who had no roots and had left family and relatives behind, stressing that "God is always with you," that He might be talked to, that He was an ever-present friend. Yet the authority of churchmen was declining steadily. New advances in secular knowledge were causing more and more doubts to be raised in the minds of the erstwhile faithful. The self-ordained clergy of the backwoods were incapable of responding intellectually, and so resorted to dogmatic assertion and, when that failed, to a blatant appeal to the emotions through hysterical sermons. In its extreme form the retreat from rationality was accompanied by snake-handling, orgiastic touching of members of the congregation, and an incoherent babbling justified as the biblical "speaking in tongues." The credulous could believe the incredible. Every device was used to promote free enterprise Christianity, including even the adaptation of the recently electrified artifacts of show business so becomingly demonstrated by Aimee Semple McPherson. Yet the very fundamentalism with which Darrow would battle was not uplifted by the new sophistication of man's ingenuity. McPherson with her colored lights was followed by a series of radio preachers whose vacuous sermons did not improve one iota with the dawning of the technological age. It was this fundamentalism that Bryan stood ready to defend.

Bryan was the incarnation of all those aspects of rural America from which Darrow had escaped so many years ago. All that the prosecution stood for was anathema to Darrow. It brought back the narrowness of Kinsman, his father's unpopular positions, the mustiness of the McGuffey Readers. Darrow blamed the McGuffey Readers for the attitudes that he combatted at Dayton, and in a sense he was right. In Tennessee in 1925, religion meant the Protestant version of Christianity and the King James Version of the Bible. That was what it meant to McGuffey too, and in Darrow's eyes he was fighting all the forces of complacent reaction that held men back. As historian William E. Leuchtenburg put it: "Immigration restriction, the Klan, prohibition and Protestant fundamentalism all had in common a hostility to the city and a desire to arrest change through coercion by statute."[11] Bryan kindled a spirit of solidarity among a mass of people whose way of life seemed in jeopardy. The difference between Darrow and Bryan was reflected in their choice of home: Darrow had headed for a great city, while Bryan remained in a small town to the end. Yet all in all it was not so much their differences that made for animosity as their similarities. Hatred only thrives on common ground. Darrow understood Bryan too well to remain a dispassionate critic, sensing perhaps that his background need only have been a little different for them both to be on the same side of the fence.

In addition there were purely political reasons for opposing Bryan. He had confused every national convention of the Democratic Party since 1896 by his support of bimetallism, prohibition, pacifism, and piety, and had lost every election in which he had been its presidential candidate. The two men disagreed profoundly about the control of the national Democratic Party—Bryan standing for agrarian control, Darrow for domination by industrial labor. Bryan had left the country and gone to Chicago earlier than Darrow, but had returned to the land, believing that "the people" lived there, whereas Darrow had preferred the town. Darrow saw Bryan's success with baleful eyes. But did he have reason to object? Had he not seen long ago, back in Andover, that the people would listen to empty orations? Did they not listen to him when he was young? No one who understood Darrow could believe that his dislike of Bryan merely reflected political disagreement; Darrow entered the lists with too much relish for that.

There was a further, more sinister animosity between Bryan and the defense. Bryan, failing though he was, was still probably the greatest public speaker then living in the United States. The defense team (including Darrow) wanted to pitch themselves against him so as to seize the crown. Darrow recognized Bryan's power over his audience. He was a worthy competitor, to be confronted in a final battle in which Darrow's superiority would be displayed. Thus the entire Scopes trial was colored by a personal rivalry as well as a difference of opinion. The proceedings would represent a pitched battle of town against country, North against South. The assumptions of superiority that Darrow and his co-counsel Arthur Garfield Hays brought to Dayton displayed a Northern arrogance worse even than that of the postbellum carpetbaggers. At many stages it would be difficult to distinguish attacks on Bryan from attacks on his religious beliefs, since Darrow's anti-religion became a matter of baiting his rival. Waldo Frank remembered that Darrow and Hays "worried the poor man like terriers with a wounded buffalo. . . . My sympathy was with Bryan. The rationalist liberals could never know that the Old Testament story was a myth whose truth lay beyond reach of their sneers."[12] There were indeed serious objections to rural fundamentalism. But for that matter, so there were to Darrow's childish conception of theology, which was in its way as dated as Bryan's. Mrs. Frances Taylor-Patterson, who heard Darrow debate G. K. Chesterton on religion at the Mecca Temple in New York, summed up the misgivings of many: "He seemed to have an idea that all religion was a matter of accepting Jonah's whale as a sort of luxury liner."[13]

If Darrow's appreciation of religious subtleties left something to be desired, it was because his antagonism was less to religion as such than to its Bible Belt version. He was an agnostic, but he was careful in the targets he singled out. He never made a frontal attack on the well-established churches and frequently debated religious subjects with assorted rabbis, clerics, and other establishment figures. Although he took great pains to single out the Lord's Day Alliance and fundamentalism for scorn and attack, he did not do the same with the Catholic church. Darrow disliked religion, but more, he disliked the way in which religious undercurrents sanctified other, secular views. He saw that for the mass of the people a minister's view was worthier of credence than any others, whereas for him it was less worthy. He believed that religion was a sanctifier of bigotry, of narrowness, of ignorance and the status quo. In this respect as in so many others, he reflected the antislavery tradition of northern Ohio; in particular, the view of Frederick Douglass, the ex-slave whose *Life*, published in 1845, was one of the favorite texts of the abolitionists:

> I assert most unhesitatingly, that the religion of the south is a mere covering for the most horrid crimes,—a justifier of the most appalling barbarity,—a sanctifier of the most hateful frauds,—and a dark shelter under which the darkest, foulest, grossest, and most infernal deeds of slaveholders find the strongest protection. Were I to be again reduced to the chains of slavery, next to that enslavement, I should regard being the slave of a religious master the greatest calamity that could befall me. For of all slaveholders with whom I have ever met, religious slaveholders are the worst. I have ever found them the meanest and basest, the most cruel and cowardly, of all others.[14]

Darrow shared this animus against Southern religion, which he had practically imbibed with his mother's milk. It was stock talk among antislavers. Yet the battle played out on the Dayton stage was essentially *le fin-de-siècle*. Both the elderly stars were fighting their own generation's fight rather than that of the radical twenties. If Bryan was the last of the great fundamentalists, Darrow was the last "village atheist."[15] And while fundamentalism refused to acknowledge the discoveries of the modern age, a new, successful kind of religious huckster was already emerging who utilized the newest methods of publicity. Aimee Semple McPherson, who dedicated her Angelus Temple in Los Angeles in 1923, was enthralling thousands. Billy Sunday was having huge success at his rallies round the country. Old-style fundamentalism was being overtaken by a newer fashion, but Darrow chose to pay it no attention.*

Bryan had started on the evangelical trail when it was still untainted, but by the time he reached Dayton, America had been provided with the allurements of the Sears, Roebuck catalogue and the silver screen, and preaching had taken on the trappings of show business. On the issue of evolution itself, very few contemporary churchmen any longer sought to obstruct the teaching of Darwinism. Woodrow Wilson reflected this when he replied to an inquiry about his beliefs by saying "he was surprised at this late date that anyone would question" the tenets of Darwinism. Darrow was lambasting an era of ignorant piety that was already disappearing and his suggestion that free thought would be suppressed in America if the anti-evolution law was not struck down was nonsense. The fact that the law was on the books meant little —its counterpart remained until the 1970s in several states. The law was not being enforced in Tennessee in 1925. Scopes had deliberately brought prosecution upon himself. When the bill making the teaching of evolution an offense came before the governor of Tennessee for signature, he indicated that he did not expect it to be enforced. Nevertheless he signed it and it became law. The governor's words at the time of signature had no legal effect whatever, and his signature made it theoretically enforceable like any other law. Yet Darrow and the ACLU exaggerated its practical importance; they wanted it to be the last great heresy trial.

Thus, for all Darrow's ostensible modernity, he would be fighting a passing generation's fight. The Scopes trial was not so much a modern phenomenon as a period piece, not least because both its major participants, Darrow and Bryan, were in their way relics of the past. During the trial Darrow turned to Arthur Garfield Hays and said: "Isn't it difficult to realize that a trial of this kind is possible in the twentieth century in the United States of America?"[16] It was indeed. But in truth it was Darrow and the ACLU, not the dark forces of intolerance in Tennessee, who had made it happen. No prosecution would have been brought had it not been arranged. The Scopes trial was a great set piece. From first to last it was contrived—by the ACLU, by Scopes, by Mencken, by Darrow, and by the residents of Dayton, avid for the business that would be brought to their community.[17] Adela Rogers St. Johns was right in concluding that "Darrow was as old-fashioned as William Jennings Bryan."[18]

As Darrow had gained in years and confidence, he became not merely an unbeliever but a militant agnostic. His antagonism was directed to that multitude of clerics who, in the face of scientific knowledge, adopted absurd positions on the truth of the Bible. It was one thing to preach that the Bible was true, but entirely another to say it was the only source of truth. The latter position became an excuse for boorish ignorance—anti-educational, anti-progressive, and anti-

---

*The new-style preachers believed that Bryan was their ally—both McPherson and Sunday sent effusive messages of support to Bryan in Dayton.

intellectual. For if the only truth was to be found in the Bible, there was no reason to look elsewhere—to do so could only lead to error. Bryan apparently was inclined to this extreme position; certainly many of his supporters were. It maddened Darrow and he fought it fiercely. But Darrow had a counterbalancing intellectual weakness in that he was inclined to rely overmuch on the impartiality of science and the immutability of its conclusions. He asserted that "no one can gainsay" these conclusions, or "the scientific truth is there for all to see." In this reliance there was an inconsistency with his own skepticism about most matters. He did not believe in the impartiality of expert witnesses, including scientific ones. He was inclined to think that humanity generally was not to be trusted. And he was a wise enough lawyer to know that the selective use of data can distort the truth just as much as actual lying. His certainty that science (meaning the conclusions of science) was infallible was a naïve one, which would badly mar the persuasive force of some of his arguments. His experts in the Scopes trial all relied in part upon the evidence derived from the Piltdown man—which in turn was found to be a fraud of just the kind that Darrow might have expected. Science, in its superiority to religion as a means of establishing truth, was not perfect, did not have all the answers. In this respect Chesterton had genuinely identified a weakness in Darrow's mental framework when, after a power failure had cut off the microphones at their debate, he cried out: "You see, science is not infallible."

On the other hand, though Darrow could go overboard in his attacks, nothing he said against religion was anything like as stupid as the things the fundamentalists said in its favor. The paraphernalia of speaking in tongues, the paroxysms of spirit possession, the rituals of backwoods revivalism, the ecstatic snake-handlings and moonlit incantations surpassed by far any idiocy that the agnostics could dream up. And, like Satan, he had read his Bible well, combing it for evidence of inconsistency, absurdity, cruelty, and obscurity. His Bible was as well thumbed as any preacher's; even his anti-religion fed upon a curiosity and thirst for explanation of a peculiarly religious character. Like George Bernard Shaw, he gave biblical study as much priority as a preacher.

In the face of Darrow's well-rehearsed derision, Bryan was not an ideal champion of the fundamentalist cause. Even some of his admirers were uneasy about his ability to present it with dignity—he had a tendency to commit faux pas. Several stories against him on this score reflected on his common sense. For example, in 1903 some observations appeared in the *Saturday Review* signed by "A Chinese Official." These moved Bryan to write a book in refutation that boasted the superiority of Christian culture, and particularly Christian American culture, to that of the Chinese. Bryan remarked that the "Chinese official" had obviously never seen the inside of a decent Christian house; had he done so, he could not have taken the attitude he did. This and other of Bryan's statements indicated that he believed the writer of the Chinese official's views was a Chinese. In reality the author was Lowes Dickinson, a fellow of King's College, Cambridge. Bryan was the subject of much derision when the true identity of the author was revealed.

A decade later, when Woodrow Wilson appointed Bryan "the most improbable Secretary of State America ever had,"[19] he continued during his term of office to appear at Chautauqua between acrobatic and conjuring acts. Such activities were felt to demean his role as Secretary of State and to be particularly inappropriate while World War I—a matter of prime concern to his government department—raged in Europe. Still later he became involved in a promotion of Florida land sales that further reduced his standing. Altogether Bryan was slightly absurd: a figure of fun, standing for an awkward lack of sophistication and characterized by a lack of *savoir faire*.

Finally, between Darrow and Bryan, the clash was not merely between ideas, or even between two famous platform speakers. It was a clash between the old and the new style of public debate. Bryan's speeches were grandiose and flowery. Darrow's, though moving, achieved their effect by understatement and good argument. Darrow excelled in facing audiences that started out being unsympathetic to him, Bryan with audiences who were already with him. Both were supreme in their own spheres. As Mencken, who was normally one of Bryan's detractors, wrote:

> . . . when he had a friendly audience he was magnificent. I heard all the famous rhetoricians of his generation, from Chauncey M. Depew to W. Bourke Cockran, and it is my sober judgment, standing on the brink of eternity, that he was the greatest of them all. His voice had something of the caressing richness of Julia Marlowe's, and he could think upon his feet much better than at a desk. The average impromptu speech, taken down by a stenographer, is found to be a bedlam of puerile cliches, thumping nonsequiturs and limping, unfinished sentences. But Jennings emitted English that was clear, flowing and sometimes not a little elegant, in the best sense of the word. Every sentence had a beginning, a middle and an end. The argument, three times out of four, was idiotic, but it at least hung together.[20]

Soon talents like Bryan's would lose their usefulness, as the radio and the talking pictures demanded a different style and technique. But until that time Bryan stood supreme, and against him all other orators had to measure themselves. It was manifest that the country, and in particular the South, was Bryan's natural constituency. The war had loosened many of the old moral certainties and accelerated the rise of the city. But in its death throes, the country would cling so tenaciously to Bryan's platitudinous reassurances that even Darrow found it difficult to loosen its grip.

32

The Trial of the Century

The circumstances were odd. The defendant, John Thomas Scopes, was actually a physics rather than a biology teacher; his experience in teaching biology had come to him only when he served as a substitute for the regular teacher, who was ill. Furthermore, although he had assigned reading to his class dealing with the theory of evolution, he never taught a class based on that assignment because he himself was sick on the day for which it was scheduled. He had not been disciplined or warned to desist from his teaching by the local school board, and on the contrary did not feel his academic freedom to have been threatened or restricted by Dayton. After his conviction the Dayton school offered to take him back in the same position.

From the start, the trial was influenced by the presence of the two rival celebrities. Just as Bryan was popular because he was a man of God, so Darrow was disliked as the Devil. His representation of Leopold and Loeb had cast him in the role of defender of the indefensible in the eyes of many. His final address to the judge in that case was on sale in Dayton for 50 cents while the Scopes trial was taking place. Few of those in Dayton who bothered to read it were likely to sympathize with the views propounded there.

Once Dayton was inundated by celebrities, Scopes himself was forgotten. He became a mere cipher, overtaken by the leading counsel for the prosecution and defense alike. He attended the proceedings only to be ignored. His trial became a vehicle of sophisticated America's sport at the expense of the Southern simpletons. The spirit of the defense was frivolous and self-indulgent, each lawyer in turn vying for press attention and credit in the eyes of posterity. As they preened themselves and postured, the serious-minded schoolteacher saw that the momentum of the case was such that he might just as well not have been there. He liked Darrow when he was "off-stage," finding him kind and humorous; but his public antics he found hard to bear. Indeed John Scopes suffered at his hands much as Darrow's son had done, and Darrow in turn could identify in Scopes much of Paul's early reticence when he was the same age.* Nearly everybody else associated with the trial, from Judge John Raul-

*In later years Scopes showed the same dislike of the glare of publicity. The trial was enough to give him a lifelong distaste for it.

362

ston to H. L. Mencken, was in some sense cashing in. Scopes refused all offers to do so except those that furthered his academic chances.

The trial demonstrated how a simple criminal case can be complicated by the introduction into it of determined and competent defense counsel. Points of procedure and evidence were argued in the Scopes trial that would not have arisen in most trials, citations of authority made and witnesses prepared in a way that would have been inconceivable in a trial that had not attracted such wide attention. Little of the proceedings involved a dramatic cut-and-thrust on the merits, and fully two-thirds of the transcript is taken up with arguments of law that shed no light upon the clash between religion and science which most people took the trial to be about.

The proceedings took place in the midst of the chaos produced when the world descended on a country courthouse, interrupted by train whistles from the nearby railroad, by the crash of a camera falling from its tripod, and by the intimation that a clergyman was wanted to conduct a funeral for one of Dayton's long-time residents.

Scopes's fate was to be decided by a jury comprised of farmers. All twelve of the selected men described themselves as farmers, though four of them gave occupations in addition to farmer—U.S. marshal, merchant's shipping clerk, cabinetmaker, and carpenter. One of them, Jim Riley, was illiterate. All but one had been born, raised, and worked in Tennessee all his life; the exception was the carpenter, who was a union member and had worked in Ohio for three years.

The trial opened on July 10 in sweltering heat. From the first day Darrow and former Attorney General Ben McKenzie of the prosecution had discarded their jackets. It says much for Darrow's flair for publicity that it was he, and he alone, who was pictured by posterity displaying his suspenders. The concern of those in the courtroom was more with the discomfort from the heat than the issues. Apart from the fact that the trial was taking place during a very hot summer, the courtroom was packed full—so much so that Judge Raulston warned the assembly of the danger the floor might collapse, and finally adjourned the court to the yard outside the courthouse. There were several suggestions that Rhea County invest in some electric fans to cool the court, including a unanimous request from the jury. They were installed on the fifth day. Throughout the trial Bryan fanned himself with a fan provided gratis by a local funeral home. Some of the sharper exchanges owed their sharpness to the weather; Darrow acknowledged during the trial that "the weather is warm, and we may all go a little further at times than we ought."[1]

The discomfort was added to by the constant bustle of activity. Press and radio were represented fulsomely, undiscouraged by Judge Raulston, who was rather partial to having his picture taken and invited the press to do so more than once. Darrow himself displayed a lively interest in keeping the reporters informed, both during the proceedings and outside, and he frequently asked witnesses to speak louder for the benefit of the press. Although the press was at one time called upon by Judge Raulston to explain a "leak" of information, he continued to look after its interests by being solicitous of its easy access to the court.

Most of all, the proceedings were punctuated by lively audience participation which the court was unable (and perhaps unwilling) to control. The first demonstration of the sympathies of the crowd came on the first day, when a jury was being picked. A prospective juror was a minister, who was asked by Darrow whether he preached for or against evolution. His reply: "I preached against it, of course," was greeted by applause. At that stage (and several times thereafter) Judge Raulston threatened to exclude the public if the applause was repeated, but in truth the trial transcript reveals that there was a lively crowd throughout. In the early stages almost anything that William Jennings Bryan said was greeted by thunderous applause. Judge Raulston also made a vain effort to prevent laughter in court, but this was doomed to failure.

The first great maneuver of the proceedings came when the defense objected to the fact that Judge Raulston's court followed custom by opening with a prayer. It could have come as no surprise to Darrow that the court was opened with prayer each day. The Democratic conventions he had attended all his life were opened with prayer; the Illinois legislature of which he had been a member opened with prayer (and then, he quipped, "a large part of the assembly proceeded to look around to find some one to hold up"); and many courts did so, as Darrow well knew.

According to Arthur Garfield Hays (the junior counsel for the defense), an attempt was made privately to dissuade the judge from opening with prayer, but to no avail. Only then was objection made in open court. Of course, the stratagem seemed to many onlookers to confirm that Darrow was indeed anti-religious. As it was, continual references to the defense counsel as being "gentlemen from Chicago" or "gentlemen from New York" were reminders for the rural faithful that the defense came from the big city, cauldron of sin and ungodliness.

But the next revelation of the proceedings was the most important of all, and one that colored all subsequent events. It was the fact that the defense wished to call William Jennings Bryan, who was acting as prosecution counsel, as a defense witness, and that Bryan rose to the bait. Arthur Garfield Hays claimed that the idea of calling Bryan as a witness for the defense was not Darrow's and came as a complete surprise; that Darrow was not prepared and had no wish to examine Bryan:

> In response to a query as to whether the defense had any more evidence to offer, I stated that we wished to call Mr. Bryan as an expert on the Bible. I have never yet discovered whether this was a greater surprise to Darrow or to Bryan. Darrow turned to Malone: "You examine him, Dudley." Malone answered, "Oh, no." Darrow turned to me. I shook my head.[2]

In the light of Darrow's interest in the matter, his immediate skillful cross-examination, and abundant evidence to the contrary from other sources, Hays's claim must be discounted. More plausible is the account of the defendant, John T. Scopes, of this dramatic moment:

I did not look at Darrow. I knew he wasn't surprised, for although I hadn't been to the Mansion for the past two days and hadn't known precisely what was afoot, I knew that Bryan's being called as a witness had been contemplated; the defense staff had already discussed what could and couldn't be asked.[3]

Darrow had appeared in many trials in which more was at stake than this one. Scopes had little to lose. It was Bryan who would lose most in the end, for though he was not the accused and suffered no legal penalty, he lost a reputation, was humiliated in public, and was shown to be a man of clay even to his ardent supporters. Darrow's cross-examination and the scorn to which Bryan was subjected in the newspapers—especially by H. L. Mencken—broadcast to the nation that his time had passed. There was something cruel about the proceedings. Bryan appeared trapped, like a dumb animal. The truth was that he was too far removed from the modern world, from intellectual exercise, to put up a decent fight. He was used to popular adulation, and had grown flabby. Darrow, accustomed to adversity and fighting public opinion, had grown strong—and hard.

True, Darrow knew very little more about the Tennessee anti-evolution law than Bryan did. Most journalists who covered the Scopes trial saw that his co-counsel knew more than he did; he did not care about Tennessee's rules and precedents, which he left to his colleagues. But on the intellectual issues he was beyond compare. No matter that this was the Darrow who had coyly refused to act as prosecutor of a Chicago policeman at the request of the good ladies of Hull House; who had boasted that he always took the side of the defense; and who only the year before had berated the Cook County prosecutor's office for making a "cruel" speech at the sentence hearings of Leopold and Loeb. In the Scopes case he came as near as he could to being a prosecutor without taking that title, and he gave no quarter.

The theory of evolution was close to Darrow's philosophy about life in general, not merely to his anti-religious bent. He believed life to be cruel, and mankind to be unregenerate. Darwinism provided an explanation for human nature. It was part of the urge to life that human beings should fight their way to survival. Darwinism emphasized discord, not cooperation, among the animal kingdom. Today there is less certainty that the animal kingdom is uncooperative, and more emphasis on the collective cooperation of humanity and interdependence of men.

Darwinism also had appealing deterministic aspects. No man could step aside from the march of history, which was inexorable and inevitable, and Darwinism was the idea of progress translated into biological terms. Indeed H. G. Wells had characterized the 1890s, the apogee of Victorian optimism, as the age of "aggressive Darwinism."[4] All this Darrow was prepared to defend. The arguments did not take him by surprise. He had bided his time. The Scopes trial was an ideal chance for him to defend science, revile William Jennings Bryan, and refute fundamentalism, the Bible Belt, and Southern justice all at once. For many years the forces of anti-religion had scoffed behind Bryan's back, but never before had Bryan been brought face to face with his detractors. Yet Bryan voluntarily exposed himself to Darrow's cross-examination; he was not subpoenaed. He genuinely believed himself able to withstand Darrow's taunts, perhaps encouraged by the popular support of Dayton's residents. In this he made a grave mistake. For Darwinism had reached Tennessee only in adulerated form, through *Hunter's Biology,* just as the Bible was known only in its King James Version. The initial popularity of Bryan was therefore based on a rather restricted understanding of what was at stake, and it did not take long before the locals began to root for Darrow and his team as much as for Bryan.

Much of the examination was conducted by Darrow "slouching back in his chair." But later personal animosity was revealed between Bryan and Darrow, and "at times Darrow and Bryan rose and glowered at each other, shaking their fists."[5] From an early stage the audience applauded the defense as well as the prosecution, and in particular the statement of Dudley Field Malone, co-counsel for the defense, on the fifth day that if a religious belief like Bryan's was true, it did not need the protection of the law, is noted as having been received by "profound and continued applause."[6] The early exchanges between Darrow and Bryan during Bryan's cross-examination displayed enough wit from both men to evoke a duo of cross-talk comedians, and the audience frequently showed their appreciation. It is a peculiarity of that famous cross-examination that it took place outside the presence of the jury. The judge had only agreed to hear it in order to ascertain whether it was competent evidence —and after hearing it, decided it was not. Thus a rather freer rein was given to the discussion, which was held in the open air with nearly every person in Dayton listening. Small wonder that a public discussion between two great celebrities should be accompanied, as Darrow put it, by "great applause from the bleachers."[7]

Further spice was added to the proceedings by complicated crosscurrents of rivalry, competitiveness, and personal dislike. Many antipathies were memorialized during those sticky, sweaty days, both publicly and privately in diaries.

Owing largely to the writing of Henry Mencken, the impression was created that the exchanges between Darrow and Bryan were entirely one-sided; that Darrow outshone Bryan every step of the way. In fact this was far from the case. The sparring of the two men reflected some credit on Bryan as a tactician, though his position weakened as cross-examination continued. On points Bryan was not a total loser, and during the course of the examination he showed himself capable of incisive barbed ripostes, effective and quite witty. Some of his retorts to Darrow were well deserved. Darrow did not succeed in showing that Bryan was a blithering idiot—for indeed he was not. His weakness was a nonrational faith. He was an easy target because, unlike Darrow, he had not prepared his tactics, believing perhaps that the righteousness he perceived in his cause would see him through. He was ravaged, outclassed, outmaneuvered, and out-argued by the defense team. But the very awesomeness of his defeat, his inability to defend himself, took away some of the sweetness of victory.

It must be granted that Bryan was exceedingly foolish to open himself up to Darrow's cross-examination; the defense itself had been much more guarded. For instance, it had done all it could to prevent the defendant Scopes from being a witness and thus open to cross-examination by the prosecution. Scopes himself recalled: "Darrow had been afraid for me to go on the stand. Darrow realized that I was not a science teacher and he was afraid that if I were put on the stand I would be asked if I actually taught biology."[8] But once Bryan had agreed to testify, he opened himself up to a whole series of debunking questions: If God is good, why does He permit pain? If the universe reveals a divine purpose, what is it? Is it immoral to learn a foreign language because, since the fall of the Tower of Babylon, God has intended that we speak different languages? How long is it since the Creation? Was Jonah really swallowed by a whale?

Not only was Bryan faced with the inherent difficulty of giving answers to these questions without prevarication, but his attitude toward the defense was not one likely to lead to the most effective kind of rejoinder. Up to the end, Bryan tried to deal with Darrow more in sorrow than in anger. On the fifth day of the trial, Bryan explained his attitude to his foe:

> Mr. Darrow says he is an agnostic. He is the greatest criminal lawyer in America today. His courtesy is noticeable—his ability is known—and it is a shame, in my mind, in the sight of a great God, that a mentality like his has strayed so far from the natural goal that it should follow—great God, the good that a man of his ability could have done if he had aligned himself with the forces of right instead of aligning himself with that which strikes its fangs at the very bosom of Christianity.[9]

Yet the lament that Darrow was not a man of God scarcely met the case; it was merely a reiteration of what was manifest. And in his strongest lines of attack on the defense Bryan was defeated by procedural considerations. Had he had the opportunity to cross-examine Darrow as Darrow cross-examined him, he could have found points of weakness. For example, Bryan wanted to explore the statements made by Darrow in the Leopold and Loeb case about the corrupting influence of Nietzsche's writing. If Nietzsche corrupted Leopold and Loeb, was there not a chance that Darwin would corrupt the schoolchildren of Tennessee? This line of inquiry would have been a two-pronged attack on the defense forces, for the leading popularizer of Nietzsche's philosophy in the United States was Henry Mencken, much in evidence as a reporter of the Scopes trial. But Bryan was not able to put these questions to Darrow directly because he was not a witness, and Judge Raulston, realizing that Bryan was getting the worst of the exchange, finally ruled that such testimony was inadmissible anyway.

Ill-feeling was generated also between out-of-state counsel and the court. Darrow, never notably deferential toward the bench, was asked at one stage by Judge Raulston whether he intended to cast aspersions on the competence of the court. "I hope not," said the judge. "Your honor has a right to hope," retorted Darrow. As a result, Judge Raulston cited Darrow for contempt. This was given added drama by the fact that the court adjourned for the weekend between the contempt and the citation, thus leaving everyone in suspense. It is quite obvious that some of the defense, at least, enjoyed the matter and did not take it seriously at all. On Monday, at the opening of court (says Hays), the judge "read aloud his version of the occurrence. When the matter appeared in consecutive fashion, it seemed to us of the defense even more satisfactory than did the original colloquy."[10]

Darrow avoided punishment by an apology which, it must be said, did not seem to be very sincere—it had something of the spirit of a schoolboy cocking a snook. However Judge Raulston accepted it and the case continued. In fact, contrary to the impression the defense's many journalist sympathizers tried to create, Judge Raulston did rather well considering the trying circumstances in which the proceedings took place. Far worse judicial performances could have been encountered in more exalted courts than the criminal sessions of Rhea County. The North wanted to believe that Raulston was a ludicrous boob and Darrow an all-conquering hero. The truth was that Raulston was a simple man, doing quite creditably under serious provocation.

Darrow's ability to make a general point almost regardless of the particulars was demonstrated when he produced a short homily on the accusation that he himself was an "infidel." Mencken's newspaper reports from Dayton and indeed his writings on religious topics generally are peppered with the word, which was one of his favorites. Darrow was completely undaunted in producing an argument he had used many times before; accusing the prosecution of using the word, he introduced his statement by sleight of hand, then plunged in with his statement that the word's only meaning was "someone whose views you didn't like." It was important to him personally, for he too had been an infidel, just as his father had been Kinsman's infidel. In a trial that was the culmination of Darrow's labors, he was now trying to explain, not just the religious aspect of his dissidence, but the motive force behind so much of his thinking. And he was doing it in the milieu that he understood best and that had nurtured him—small-town, rural America. In vindicating John Thomas Scopes, he was vindicating himself and his father before him, who had asserted the right of inquiring minds to roam where they pleased. The backwardness of the South, deriving from the Civil War, meant that Dayton resembled spiritually the Ohio of Darrow's youth. Darrow reveled in the scene because his life had come full circle. He was finally vindicating his youthful rebellion.

No doubt Darrow was right that "infidel" had no precise meaning, but was the charge that the defense were "infidels" unfair? It was clear that the leading personalities among the defense lawyers were an alien breed to the citizens of Dayton. All were from the great cities, and even those among them who professed religious belief were of different persuasions from those found in rural Tennessee. Dudley Field Malone was a divorced and excommunicated

Roman Catholic, whose second wife had caused scandal by checking into the Hotel Alta in Dayton under her maiden name. She did not wear a wedding ring and caused great speculation as to her true status. Darrow was, of course, notoriously irreligious. Finally, "At the end of the line is the Jew, Hays, who reeks of East End impertinence. His dark hair is standing pompadour and his eyes are full of shrewdness and brightness."[11] It was not a team with which the Dayton populace could be expected to have a great deal of sympathy.

The prosecution was aware that the defense was importing to Dayton a number of distinguished scientists it intended to make witnesses in the case. After consultation, it was decided that a motion should be made to exclude all such expert evidence, on the ground that it was incompetent. Naturally, this motion was resisted by the defense, which had gone to considerable effort and expense to find these witnesses. On the sixth day of trial—Friday, July 17— Judge Raulston ruled in favor of the prosecution, holding that the use of expert evidence was only permitted under Tennessee law when the facts were so complex that a man of ordinary understanding would not be competent to form an opinion on them.

As soon as Judge Raulston's ruling was handed down, the defense realized that the main benefit of the proceedings had ended from its point of view, and its remaining efforts were devoted to preventing the prosecution from being able to "get back" at the defense. In this respect Bryan was also procedurally outwitted. Darrow, realizing that Bryan might make a comeback by giving a final address to the jury, pleaded Scopes guilty and waived the defense's right to a closing speech, thereby under Tennessee law depriving the prosecution of the chance to address the court. And with that the trial ended, leaving only the much less spectacular appellate proceedings to be taken. Thus Darrow deliberately refused to make a closing speech for the defense, so as to avoid giving Bryan the opportunity to give a peroration which, he knew, had already been prepared. He had on his side a friendly press; and in particular Mencken gave Darrow's short speech about marching with banners back to the Middle Ages a disproportionately prominent place in his dispatches. Many different observers noted that the defense team were trying to outdo each other in their speeches to the jury, and their conceit was manifest.

Bryan had been beaten ignominiously, and the ignominy would reflect on his taunters. It is difficult to disagree with the verdict of Andrew Sinclair that the defense showed in the trial "a pride and complacency and vindictiveness as mean as the bias of a dry fundamentalist."[12] It was a victory for modernity —but was it victory with honor?

For a brief period Darrow was the hero of the case, notwithstanding that Scopes had been convicted. He captured the imagination of the young. Immediately after the trial the youngsters of Dayton High School gave a dance in Darrow's honor—"he attended, danced and even smoked cigarettes with them."[13] Professionally, the image projected by the Scopes trial was to be his for posterity: that sweaty week in July left an indelible picture, which not even subsequent different publicity could erase. This reflected the huge quantity of favorable publicity that the trial had generated, which had done much to polish his image beyond what his performance deserved. The public from all sections of the community recognized the Scopes trial as an epitome of much that America was and felt in those years, and insofar as it could be personified, Darrow did it. The Scopes trial provided a rallying point for freethinkers. The fact that Darrow ludicruously overstated the dangers of Tennessee's law did not diminish his reputation as a liberal hero. The trial coincided with a huge increase in the number of college students and journalistic panderers for whom Darrow was a natural hero, so that the twenties gave him, though he was already well into his sixties, the appearance of dashing modernity. At retirement age he was being identified with bright young things a third of his age, many of whom were his ardent admirers.

Meanwhile Bryan smarted under the humiliation of the abrupt termination of the case; he had lost much ground without having had the chance to regain it. He had prepared a rebuttal of the defense position as a final speech in the case and felt cheated that he could not deliver it. Instead, he made the best he could of the situation by using the text of the speech at a public meeting. His biographer remarked of an address he gave immediately after the trial: ". . . it was evident that, despite his use of remarks pleasing to a rural audience, he had been deeply hurt by the accusation by Darrow and others of his bigotry and by the ignorance he had revealed concerning every subject about which he was questioned except the text of the Bible."[14] It was easy to laugh off Bryan —he was a simple target, too foolish to recognize his foolishness, too set in his ways to adopt new arguments or new tactics. Yet there had been something very cruel about the way he was ravaged by the new thinkers, which was suddenly and dramatically highlighted by Bryan's death only five days after the Scopes trial had ended. The cause was never entirely clear; some ascribed it to overeating, for it was well known that Bryan was a glutton. But many others remembered with sorrow the way that he had been worried and taunted by Darrow and not a few believed, with Fulton Oursler, that Darrow had "cross-examined the helpless William Jennings Bryan into his grave."[15]

So ended the career of one of America's most famous failures. He had been in the forefront of the nation's public life for nearly three-quarters of the century, but never achieved the high office or universal respect he craved. In part, it was because his contemporaries could not credit him with sincerity, believing him to be a cynical manipulator of the ignorant. In this vein both N. D. Cochran and Eugene Debs cast aspersions on his integrity shortly before the Scopes trial. Cochran wrote privately on May 22, 1925:

> Bryan, as leader of the Fundamentalists, is a clever demagogue. He is either ignorant or is deliberately playing upon the ignorance of the great mass of the people—for he deliberately misrepresents the theory of evolution. I think he understands the ignorance of the majority and plays on it.[16]

And Eugene Debs used less temperate language in writing to Darrow:

> When I think . . . how petty, mean and contemptible Bryan was and is . . . and
> that Bryan was popularized almost to idolatry and glorified by press and pulpit
> as an apostle of truth and an evangel of religion, this shallow-minded mouther
> of empty phrases, this pious, canting mountebank, this prophet of the stone-age,
> my blood runs hot in my veins with indignation and resentment at the utterly
> cruel and perverse ways of the world in which we live and the age-old rule of
> crowning frauds, hypocrites, time-servers and scoundrels, and murdering proph-
> ets, pathfinders and all other true leaders of the people and saviors of the race.[17]

This extreme assessment of Bryan was one that would be tempered only by
time. He was a man who excited strong antagonisms just as he did strong
loyalties. But by 1928 Darrow was acknowledging Bryan's sincerity in a way
he had not done during Bryan's lifetime:

> All of his political activities, as well as his religious endeavors, show sincerity
> to the verge of fanaticism. And a fanatic I believe Mr. Bryan was. Fanatics in
> any age are dangerous to the peace and pleasure of the world, but there is a very
> clear distinction between the fanatic and the charlatan.[18]

Even Mencken, who had been one of Bryan's most persistent critics, finding
it impossible to believe that Bryan could be silly and sincere at the same time,
finally retracted:

> After the death of William Jennings Bryan, in 1926, I printed an estimate of his
> life and public services which dismissed him as a quack pure and unadulterated,
> but in the years since I have come to wonder if that was really just. When, under
> the prodding of Clarence Darrow, he made his immortal declaration that man
> is not a mammal, it seemed to me to be a mere bravura piece by a quack sure
> that his customers would take anything. But I am now more than half convinced
> that Jennings really believed it, just as he believed that Jonah swallowed the
> whale.[19]

The Scopes trial left much anger and bitterness in its wake. Mencken was
threatened with lynching. It was believed that some members of the outdoor
audience were ready to shoot Darrow during his cross-examination of Bryan.
Yet all this turmoil achieved nothing legally. Scopes's conviction was reversed
by the Supreme Court of Tennessee on nonconstitutional grounds in January
1927, and the case actually stimulated other states—like Arkansas in 1928—
to pass anti-evolution laws which they had not had before. The Dayton jamboree had provided entertainment and scandal without clear legal results. Subsequent history proved that such laws would not, as Darrow had warned, cause
all liberties to wither.[20]

The ACLU, which had contributed $1,400 to the defense fund, published
a four-page pamphlet on the trial and an explanation of the strategy of the
Scopes defense. In addition it offered its members Leslie H. Allen's pamphlet
Bryan and Darrow at Dayton. Never before in the history of the ACLU had
one case attracted so much of its attention and effort. This list of publications

was added to in the following year when a thirty-six-page pamphlet was published giving the views of prominent people on anti-evolution laws.

The union had shown from its inception a special interest in laws touching schools and colleges, and efforts were made for many years afterward to confront the fundamentalist position as a matter of constitutional principle. The Annual Report for 1927 informed members that "efforts are in hand to bring in the courts of Tennessee a new case under the evolution law for the purpose of getting to the U.S. Supreme Court for a final ruling on an issue still pushed by the Fundamentalists."[21] This turned out to be a more difficult task than might have been foreseen since a latter-day John Scopes could not be found. In 1931 it was reported:

> We kept up our search for a teacher, willing to make a test of the anti-evolution law in any one of the three states with that legislation—Tennessee, Mississippi and Arkansas. Circular letters and public offers of legal service brought interested inquiries, but nobody willing to make the sacrifice. The Fundamentalist drive on the teaching of evolution has somewhat let up; the laws are not effective in the state universities; and our counsels are divided as to the wisdom of taking the issue to the Supreme Court of the United States. But we intend to do so if a teacher for a test case is found.[22]

The Annual Report of the ACLU for 1931–1932 was the first issued since 1925 that did not mention the union's intention to challenge evolution laws afresh. By that time there were more pressing practical issues raised by the Depression for the ACLU to face.

Posterity has been left with the idea that the Scopes trial made Tennessee justice a laughing stock. But the fact that Scopes's conviction was overturned on appeal does not support that view. For one thing it was the Tennessee courts themselves, not the federal Supreme Court, which reversed the result. Furthermore, the issue on reversal was a technical one, which it was not within the trial judge's power to control and which had not been raised by the defense at trial level. The constitutional issue was finally decided in 1968, when the United States Supreme Court held that an Arkansas statute that forbade the teaching of Darwin's theory of evolution was unconstitutional because it violated the prohibition on the establishment of a state religion.[23] In many respects, the 1968 case reflected the same artificiality as the Scopes trial. The case had been "set up" for the purpose of obtaining a decision from the Supreme Court. The Arkansas "monkey law" had never been enforced since 1928, and the state indicated that it "would make no attempt to enforce the law should it remain on the books for the next century." Mrs. Epperson, the teacher concerned, had not been prosecuted for violating the statute, but on the contrary had herself instituted proceedings for a declaration that the statute was unconstitutional. In addition, there was a suspicion that Mrs. Epperson was no longer a teacher at the time of the Supreme Court hearing, and therefore could not be said to be endangered by the alleged unconstitutionality of the statute. The litigation was lifeless and of little practical consequence. But in any event, the Supreme Court rendered an opinion that civil libertarians had been seeking for the past fifty years, though in the intervening decades none had managed to come close to Darrow's week of glory in Dayton.

33

The Sweet Trials

The Scopes trial had been an attack on the old South, singling out for scorn its narrow bigotry, although scarcely raising the issue of race, which had been the most bitter source of disagreement between North and South. The Sweet trials in 1925 and 1926 were a reminder that the racial issue was not one confined to the South—indeed Darrow himself called them a saga of "the Negro in the North."

A huge migration had taken place as the wages of industrialism in the Northern cities had tempted thousands, both black and white, to leave the rural South behind. As more and more Negroes arrived in Detroit, Chicago, and St. Louis, the favorable attitude toward them crumbled. There was no enthusiasm in welcoming many. It appeared that the North had been well disposed toward Negroes as long as they stayed down home. Once they came north, attitudes hardened. In 1923, when Lord Birkenhead visited the United States, he was struck by the phenomenon in Chicago, where he said

> Almost like a horde of locusts the Negroes of the South are invading city after city of the rich and indiscriminating North. A whole area of Chicago—and a not disreputable one, fifteen years ago inhabited exclusively by a white population —has now been handed over in undisputed possession to the dark invader.[1]

In some ways a change in attitude was understandable. The Southern immigrants were unused to city living, simple and uneducated, and had little in common with the industrial North. They were unsightly and of the roughest kind. By definition, they were poor—they had come to make Henry Ford's $5 a day. Not all Negroes were like that, but they were treated that way. That was the complaint of the NAACP, which sought to dramatize the plight of the educated black man in the North through the trials first of Dr. Ossian Sweet for conspiracy to murder and then, after a jury disagreement, of his younger brother Henry Sweet, a student, for murder.

The trials acquired the reputation of being a vindication of the rights of a black family who had done nothing wrong and whose conduct throughout was entirely justified. That was the version of the matter promulgated by the NAACP, Darrow, Marcet Haldeman-Julius, and the history books. But as in so many of Darrow's cases, the defendants were not entirely faultless, and the facts were such as to be cumulatively damaging to the Sweets. Before they moved into their new house in a white neighborhood, they had armed themselves extensively. One of the white men killed in the incident that gave rise to the trials, Leo Breiner, had been shot in the back and therefore could not have been an aggressor. It could be shown that the occupants of the house initiated the shooting and were not merely responding to fire from outside; that no evidence existed that the crowd was armed with guns; and that statements given by the defendants to the police after arrest were not merely untrue, but could be interpreted to mean that they had sought the opportunity to start a fight. None of these factors would make Darrow's task an easy one when he undertook the cases. He believed passionately in the rights of black Americans, but the Sweet trials were not an ideal vehicle with which to vindicate them. Still, like any good trial lawyer, he made the very best he could of the facts, and his performance and the result finally reached were widely regarded as a victory.

The Sweets were a remarkable family. Ossian was a physician who, after having received a medical degree from Howard University, had pursued his studies in Vienna and Paris. His younger brother Otis was a dentist, and Henry was a student at Wilberforce College in Ohio. Together they had acquired far more education than most of their generation, black or white. They represented a determined upward social mobility, and an American desire to "get ahead" that showed they had imbibed the spirit of their age and nation as much as any white family. Ossian Sweet explained why he had started a practice in Detroit in 1921 by saying that he thought it was a good place to "make a little money and get ahead in the world."[2] Sweet did manage to make a little money and his practice flourished. In 1922 he met and married Gladys Mitchell, and decided to take a protracted honeymoon in Africa and Europe while studying radiology. He and Gladys did not return to Detroit until 1925, by which time they had had a child, born in Paris. Back in Detroit they faced the problem of finding somewhere to live. Temporarily they solved it by moving in with Mrs. Sweet's family on the near northeast side, but almost immediately they looked around for something more permanent. It was not easy. The section of the city that had become home for most colored residents of Detroit was Paradise Valley, which was far from paradise. It was rapidly becoming a verminous, decadent slum, overcrowded and ugly, not the sort of area in which anyone who could afford to do better would stay. The Research Bureau of Associated Charities of Detroit had reported in 1919: "Seventy-five percent of the Negro homes have so many lodgers that they are really hotels. . . . The pool rooms and gambling clubs are beginning to charge for the privilege of sleeping on pool room tables overnight."[3] The difficulty of the black bourgeoisie was to escape from this.

Ossian Sweet could afford to buy a house, but he wanted it to be outside the blind-pig and brothel belt that the black area of Detroit had become. The problem, of course, was that money was not enough. Even though he could

pay the asking price of many houses in the white areas of Detroit, the color
line was resolutely held and he was not welcome. Only shortly after Sweet had
returned from his year abroad, another black physician—a friend of his—had
found out exactly how resolutely. The same summer that the Sweets were
looking for a home, Dr. A. L. Turner had moved into a white area on Spokane
Street, Detroit, and Vollington Bristol, a black mortician, had settled on
American Avenue. In both instances there had been large demonstrations in
front of the homes, and both Turner and Bristol had decided that discretion
was the better part of valor and vacated their homes. It was particularly clear
in Dr. Turner's case that racial battle lines were being drawn. The neighborhood's white residents had formed an organization called the Tireman Avenue
Improvement Association through which, in effect, they were determined to
keep the area all white. On June 22, 1925, the police responded quickly to
Turner's request for protection in the face of a large white crowd, but advised
him to return to his old home if he did not want a repetition of the incident.
It was therefore felt by the black middle class that their aspirations were
frustrated. They were not welcome in the white middle-class areas of the city,
and there were no black ones.

Just before this, in May, Dr. Sweet looked at 2905 Garland Avenue, a house
on the corner of Charlevoix that a black realtor had interested him in. The
house was on the market because its owner, Mrs. Smith, intended to move to
California. Mr. Smith was a Negro, but so light-skinned that he passed for
white; he had made no effort to proclaim his race in the neighborhood, and
there had been no comment or recognition of the fact in the two years that
he had lived there. Nevertheless it appears that Dr. Sweet regarded this as a
good omen, although Mrs. Smith had received threatening telephone calls
warning her not to sell to a black family. Undeterred, she sold to Sweet for
$18,500. The area of Garland and Charlevoix was not an especially distin-
guished one. It contained modern single and double family dwellings, but they
were not of high quality, and represented respectable but not outstanding
accommodations for the rising middle class. Most of the white residents were
foreign-born or first-generation Americans, and there is no evidence that any
white professionals lived in the immediate vicinity, or would have chosen to.
Indeed, few of the white residents had the education of the Sweets.

Dr. Sweet was certainly not unaware of the potential conflict that would
arise from his purchase of a house in the area. The interesting question is
whether he bought the house with the deliberate purpose of forcing the issue
of housing segregation. And on this point the evidence is conflicting. According to his brother Otis, "He wasn't looking for trouble. He just wanted to bring
up his little girl in good surroundings." And he himself said: "If I had known
how bitter that neighborhood was going to be, I wouldn't have taken that
house as a gift."[4] On the other hand, if that was so, one must conclude from
his subsequent statements and actions that he was determined to go through
with the deal once he had entered into it. The experiences of his own friend
Dr. Turner, and of Mr. Bristol in June made the climate of white opinion

abundantly clear. But unlike both of them, he was not going to take the line of least resistance. Instead, he prepared to fight it out.

Once it became known that Mrs. Smith had contracted to sell the house to Sweet, a Waterworks Park Improvement Association was formed after the pattern of the Tireman Avenue Association. At a meeting of the Waterworks Association on July 14, just prior to Dr. Sweet's scheduled taking of possession, the principal speaker was provided by the Tireman Avenue Association. There seemed little doubt that the Sweets would find their new house surrounded by a hostile mob if they moved in, just as Turner and Bristol had done. What was in doubt was the form that the confrontation would take—and its outcome. In the previous incidents that summer there had been stone-throwing and name-calling, and a small amount of property damage, but nothing more; but that was because Turner and Bristol vacated their houses. In a sense the Sweets were testing whether or not the freedom acquired by the Civil War was equal with that of the whites. There was no doubt that the freedom to acquire education and wealth existed. But was a black man's dollar to be accepted on the same terms as a white's?

Sweet's preparations for his move into Garland Avenue indicate that he believed serious violence was a possible result if he refused to evacuate the home. He bought nine guns and sought the assistance of nine male friends and relations in moving on September 8, besides asking for police protection. This move was accomplished during the daylight hours and there was no response until the evening, when a crowd gathered outside the house and a wary police force of eight men watched and waited. The size of the crowd remained ever afterward in dispute, but on the night of the eighth no violence took place. The next night was different. By mid-afternoon on the ninth another crowd had gathered (the one from the previous night having dissipated). At 8:15 P.M. Otis Sweet (the dentist) and a family friend, William Davis (a federal narcotics agent), returned to the house by cab. It was dusk but not yet dark. As they went inside amid hostile murmurs from the crowd, a barrage of gunfire emanating from inside the house shattered the evening peace. Both Otis Sweet and Davis got safely into the house. But Leo Breiner, resident of 2906 Garland, lay dead outside, and Erik Halberg of 2910 Garland was shot in the leg. Up to that time no crime had been committed. Now the case had become one of homicide.

Altogether, circumstances point strongly to the conclusion that the Sweets intended to force a showdown and, using a pretended need for self-defense as pretext, resorted to aggression. Probably there was no intention to kill Breiner. But by firing into the crowd they deliberately took the risk that someone would be shot. Throughout the evidence presented in two trials, no explanation was produced for the barrage of shots being released when it was. Since the shots came from the house in rapid succession, it may be deduced that an unprovoked decision was made to scare and presumably scatter the assembly outside. It was, as it were, a private attempt to "read the Riot Act," though there was as yet no riot. There was no reason for singling out Breiner as a target, and it was accidental that he was hit. He became the Waterworks Association's martyr.

At first the police were not aware that anyone had been hit; they had merely seen the shots coming from the Sweet residence. Police Inspector Norman Schuknecht then went to the front door and knocked, identifying himself as in charge of the police detail. Ossian Sweet, complaining that his property was being damaged, gave an undertaking that there would be no more shooting, and Schuknecht retired. Only then was he informed that two men had been shot. In the company of five other policemen, he returned and arrested all the occupants of the house. From these events the Sweets and their friends were charged with conspiracy to commit murder in the first degree.

From the start, the case was a politically charged one. Judge Frank Murphy, presiding judge of the Detroit Recorder's Court (the court of criminal jurisdiction in which it would be tried), stated: "Every judge on this bench is afraid. . . . They think it's dynamite. They don't realize that this is the opportunity of a lifetime to demonstrate sincere liberalism. . . ."[5] Murphy took the opportunity of a lifetime: he assigned the case to himself and presided over both the trials arising out of the events of September 9. The case became a *cause célèbre* in Detroit and the nation. It was taken up by the NAACP, and the Sweets were painted by their supporters as brave heroes of the black cause. The suggestion was made that the Sweets had done nothing cognizable by the criminal courts, and were being prosecuted purely as a means of racial oppression. Conversely, it was said that the police had conducted themselves in a scandalously partisan manner, so as to become the true instigators of what happened. One commentator has written that: "Inspector Schuknecht and his men not only tolerated but in a sense took part in the two day siege of the Sweet house. The police did nothing to discourage the mob and violence became inevitable."[6]

When the Sweets were arrested, Mrs. Sweet's mother, Mrs. Mitchell, retained the firm of Rowlette, Perry & Mahoney to defend them. On September 16, Rowlette in vain applied for bail for them before Judge Faust. This was one of the leading firms of Negro attorneys in the city, but the NAACP were investigating the case with a view to making it their own. James Weldon Johnson, the head of the national NAACP office, made a trip to Detroit and decided that the case would be better handled if the Association threw its prestige behind the defense, retained nationally prominent lawyers, and, above all, provided money. This last was most important; the Association raised more than $75,000 to defend the Sweets—enough to buy four 2905 Garland Avenues. With that money the NAACP proposed to defend the Sweets using Clarence Darrow as their chief counsel, assisted by Arthur Garfield Hays. It happened that at the time they sought to retain Darrow, he was staying with Hays in New York City, and so when they caught up with Darrow they found Hays too. The NAACP cannot have regarded the Sweet trial as an ideal vehicle for their cause, but—like the ACLU in the Scopes litigation—they made the best of what fate had handed to them. The fact was that it would have been more embarrassing for the Association to stay out of the Sweet case than to go into it.

There was an irony in the way in which the NAACP got involved. To begin with, its retention of Darrow had a strange twist to it. He was to represent the Sweets in a case in which a prominent firm of black attorneys had already been retained, not one where the defendants were without the means to pay or the sophistication to retain counsel. And Darrow was to supplant the Rowlette firm. Furthermore Darrow himself was at loggerheads with some of the founders of the NAACP, notably its first president, Moorfield Storey, who had said he had "no sort of respect" for criminal lawyers like Darrow.[7] More importantly, the NAACP was only with difficulty presenting a united front to the world, for it was touch and go whether it should tread a path of moderation or militancy. The compromises that were necessary to satisfy both groups were reflected in its handling of the Sweet case. The NAACP stood in relation to its actual and potential supporters in much the same way as the AFL had to its supporters—it was perpetually under pressure to take extreme measures from a group which, although it did not speak for the majority, was vocal out of all proportion to its numbers. And just as Gompers had been derided by the left wing as a collaborator and a toady, so Walter White and the restrained leaders of the NAACP were denounced by radicals like W. E. B. DuBois. Indeed the rivalry between White and DuBois became thoroughly acrimonious.

There was a feeling that the NAACP could with advantage be more assertive of the rights of colored Americans, and for some time the left wing had wanted to find a case that would vindicate the right of Negroes to "fight back." It was felt that the NAACP's careful statistical compilations of lynchings and other episodes demonstrated a submissiveness that degraded the race. A. Philip Randolph had commented on one aspect of this submission when in 1919 he wrote in the *Messenger:* "Anglo-Saxon jurisprudence recognizes the right of self-defense. . . . The black man has no rights which will be respected unless the black man forces that respect. We are consequently urging Negroes and other oppressed groups concerned with lynching and mob violence to act upon the recognized and accepted law of self-defense."[8] The underlying suggestion of this and similar statements was that the victims of lynchings had somehow acquiesced in their fates, though it seems far more likely that they had realized resistance was useless and might have made matters worse. But it gave the impression that the right of self-defense which the law accorded could be transformed into a weapon in the black man's hands, without warning that that right was strictly limited and was altogether lost if, going beyond defensive measures, it turned into aggression. The dilemma of the Sweet case was that it was doubtful whether, in law, the Sweets did have any legally recognized right of self-defense in the circumstances. Nevertheless, under pressure to do something, and using the slogan that "A man's home is his castle," the NAACP turned the case over to Darrow and Hays to let them make what they could of it.

When Darrow arrived in Detroit in September 1925 to take charge of the first Sweet trial, he was already a hero among the black community and for that very reason unpopular with large sections of the city's white society. But he swiftly corrected that imbalance of sentiment by a speech to the local Negro clergy at the YMCA, in the course of which he said: "You might still be savages in Africa . . . and at that you might be better off there."[9] This was not what his audience wanted to hear and the Presbyterian Ministers' Association issued a statement of disapproval. Darrow, ever the shrewd publicist, was no doubt quite pleased with this result, which reassured the white community that he did not accept the Negro cause uncritically. He hoped that the speech would soften the attitude of prospective jurors, who were bound to be mainly white. The defendants needed all the advantages they could get.

The prospects looked poor for a number of reasons. The defendants had told conflicting and palpably untruthful stories while in police custody, including some absurd denials. These statements, if admitted at trial, would give a thoroughly negative impression to a jury. Furthermore they removed much of the heroic quality from the trial, which would otherwise have allowed public sympathy to be harnessed on their side. The autopsy on Breiner showed that he had been shot in the back, which made any defense based upon an attack by him personally exceedingly far-fetched. Last but by no means least, Michigan law lent little support to an expansive view of the right of self-defense, which would be desirable to show the Sweets excusable under the law. The leading authority in Michigan stated that one who was assaulted in his dwelling "may use such means as are absolutely necessary to repel the assailant from his house, or to prevent his forcible entry, even to the taking of life."[10] But it was difficult to show any assault or attempt at forcible entry, let alone that Breiner had made one. The facts strongly suggested that those inside the house had resorted to indiscriminate and deadly force without any legal justification. Of course, their purpose had been to scare the crowd away—but was that lawful? The strong likelihood was that it was not. Certainly, in view of the police presence there, the resort to gunfire was hard to justify.

Arthur Garfield Hays, once again co-counsel with Darrow, identified other difficulties, the main one being that the defendants had not told the truth to their counsel and that, even during the trial, he doubted that all of them were telling the truth.[11] At the first trial Mrs. Sweet created a bad impression on the stand by her denial that she could recollect where her husband was at the time the shooting began. When pressed, she said: "I don't remember because I don't remember," and the examining attorney gave up. Then Henry Sweet tried to take responsibility for the shooting by saying that he had fired from a front window, though Hays thought the evidence pointed to his being on the back porch. Furthermore it was incontrovertible that the Sweets had moved in with a huge amount of ammunition and sufficient firearms for all.

At least one of the defendants was spoiling for a showdown: "He was rather proud of the fracas—the whites had learned a lesson. They couldn't tread on a negro with impunity," was how Hays expressed it.[12]

Notwithstanding these problems, Darrow determined to try the case before a jury and, in his customary manner, embarked upon a large-scale investigation of the jury rolls. The victory, if there was to be one, would be so much more impressive to the public if it were won before a jury, especially because any jury that could be summoned would inevitably be white. The purpose of the investigation was to give the defense information that would, according to Darrow's preconceptions, rid the panel of jurors who might be antagonistic to black defendants. He did not want a fair jury, as he admitted: ". . . no one ever wanted a fair juror; at least, no lawyer ever did. The State wants a juror who has grown cold, serious, unimaginative, and, a Presbyterian, if possible. The lawyers for the defense want a man who is alert, witty, emotional, and who is a Catholic, or without any religious faith whatever." So he did his best to eliminate Presbyterians and succeeded pretty well. He told Judge Murphy privately that he thought he had got a good jury. The judge asked why.

"Well," Darrow replied, "six of them are Irish Catholics." Judge Murphy asked him whether he meant by that that Irish Catholics would not find a hanging verdict. "No, it isn't that," replied Darrow. "It's just that I never met an Irish Catholic yet who didn't think that someday he might be in trouble himself."[13] It was typical of Darrow to believe that the law and the facts could be overcome with the right jury. Having only recently come from his triumphs at Dayton, and having spent many hours in the blaze of publicity following from that trial, he had been busy classifying particular denominations according to a stereotyped profile. Presbyterians were the least attractive of all, because they were strongly identified with temperance. Roman Catholics, by contrast, he considered relatively harmless. In part, this was because back in Kinsman when he was a boy they had been in a minority and therefore often his father's only allies in debate; but more recently he had been impressed by the fact that the Reverend John A. Ryan, a Roman Catholic priest who was on the board of the ACLU, had acquiesced in its fighting the Scopes case, even though it might mean embarrassment to organized Christianity in general. In any event, Darrow was devoting much of his spare time to stalking various brands of religion, and his interest spilled over into the Sweet trial. On *voir dire* he managed to keep Catholics on the jury while eliminating the Presbyterians, not because questions were permitted to be asked on religion, but because he had obtained such information through pretrial investigation.

The first trial proceeded with three main lines of defense:

1. Darrow's usual objection to the use of a conspiracy charge;
2. A strong objection to the conduct of the police throughout;
3. The contention that what had been done by the Sweets had been done in self-defense.

The main effective use of the objection to the conspiracy charge was to bring home to the jury that the prosecution could not show who had fired the bullet that killed Breiner. The only Sweet who admitted firing his gun at all was Henry; but it could not be shown that it was a bullet from his gun that had killed Breiner, because no bullet had been found in or near the body, though unquestionably Breiner had died by shooting. The defense properly made the most of this gap in the prosecution's proof, casting doubt on whether the bullet had emanated from the Sweet residence at all. Since two police officers had admitted shooting over the heads of the assembled crowd to keep them in order after the shooting first started, it was at least a possible inference that a police bullet had caused the death. Judge Murphy did not prevent the trial being continued on the conspiracy theory, wisely leaving the question to the jury to decide, but in so doing he gave Darrow the chance to complain of the Star Chamber origins of the charge.

The attack upon the Detroit police force was handled with great skill, for the truth was that the police had done little that was wrong on either September 8 or 9. Their mistakes were made not then, but at the stage when they prepared for trial, and on the witness stand. In his handling of the police conduct and testimony in issue, Darrow showed himself once again a master tactician. It had been suggested that the police were derelict in failing to disperse the crowd that assembled in the neighborhood of the Sweet home on September 8 and again on the ninth. Kenneth Weinberg complains: "There is no record that the police, at any time, did anything to disperse the crowd or restrain any member of it. Had that been done on the eighth, none of the events of the ninth would have occurred."[14] But even assuming that the crowd was a large one, the police had to deal with it cautiously; their powers in dispersing a crowd that was apparently unarmed and not riotous were strictly limited. As long as the individuals in it were not disorderly, there was nothing the police could do. The offense of unlawful assembly was probably not committed on the ninth, for there was no reason to fear that the assembly would commit a breach of the peace, especially in the light of the relative quiet of the previous night. There was nothing unlawful in the mere fact that a crowd had formed. It accorded with sensible police practice not to confront a crowd unless absolutely necessary. If there were any unlawful incidents, the police were at best entitled to arrest the persons responsible; short of riot (a very specific and narrowly defined sort of disturbance), the police had no inherent power to disperse a crowd. The criticism to which they were subject in failing to "deal" with the crowd was therefore insupportable in law.

Nevertheless the police seriously damaged their case by denying that, on either night, there had been a crowd at the corner of Garland and Charlevoix at all, and further, by apparently suborning the perjury of other witnesses to corroborate their own view. Darrow worked crossword puzzles while the prosecution brought enough witnesses to testify that there was no crowd outside the Sweet residence to make it seem highly likely that there had been one. Darrow capitalized on this foolishness when he came to summation, telling the jury: "I say that a man who has been on the police force thirty years and who comes here as your assistant commissioner and swears that there was no crowd at the Sweet house is not to be trusted. He lies."[15] And so it appeared. For the evidence seemed to indicate, contrary to police estimates, that a large crowd had assembled. Particularly telling was the cross-examination of a youth of fifteen by Darrow, who asked him how many people were in the vicinity:

> *A:* There was a great crowd—no, I won't say a great crowd, a large crowd—well, there were a few people and the officers were keeping them moving.
> *Q:* Have you talked with anyone about the case?
> *A:* Lieutenant Johnson.
> *Q:* And when you started to answer the question you forgot to say "a few people," didn't you?
> *A:* Yes, sir.[16]

The conclusion was inescapable that the police had coached witnesses to deny there was a crowd. The police had put their own integrity in issue, and the prosecution lacked moral fiber as a result.

A less happy example of Darrow's strategy was the way in which he contrasted the educational levels of his black clients with their white neighbors to the latter's disadvantage. He made capital out of the mispronunciation of the name of a street near Garland and Charlevoix called Goethe, to highlight the lack of sophistication of the local residents. In this emphasis upon the ignorance of the working-class residents of Charlevoix and Garland, Darrow was repudiating to a large extent his remaining ties with labor. Twenty, even ten years before, he would have thought twice about a public attack on people who were union rank-and-file. Now he had no hesitation at all. Darrow's identification had ceased to be with the working class and his ideals were only in a vague sense political. The passion of his life now was literary, and he was far more interested in the intellectual circle that gathered in his apartment near the University of Chicago than in politicians or labor leaders.

Darrow's performance did prevent a conviction. When, after forty-eight hours' deliberation, the jury failed to agree, Judge Murphy called a mistrial. The probability is that this happened in the first round of the Sweet trials because the prosecution misjudged the public's and the jury's mood. It took what was a rather strong case on its facts and overstated them. The argument it used to the effect that everyone has rights, which they should not exercise in all circumstances, was fraught with danger. It was not entirely absurd, for it is true that though one has a right to walk out into the road when the "Walk" signs are on, one is foolish to do so if manifestly they are not functioning properly, or if a reckless driver is ignoring them. But it invited the jury to have nagging doubts—and Darrow made quite sure that they were implanted and reinforced. He ridiculed the prosecution suggestion. If rights meant anything at all, he said, they meant that one could assert them at any time. A qualified right was not a right at all. Had the prosecution contented itself with saying that such rights as the right to self-defense unquestionably existed, but that on the evidence the Sweets were not in a position where self-defense applied

(having on the contrary turned the tables and resorted to aggression), the jury
would probably have been readier to convict.

The other mistake of the prosecution—and one it sought to remedy in the
second trial—was the indictment and trial of so many people at one time. This
allowed the defense to make comparisons of culpability which, from a prosecution standpoint, were odious. Some defendants were the subject of more evidence than others, and the defense effectively cast doubt on the validity of
convicting all of them, with the result that the jury was reluctant to convict
any. In particular, it was probably a very unwise move to have indicted Mrs.
Sweet, against whom there was almost no direct evidence. Darrow, old war
horse that he was, seized the chance to use her plight to great advantage.
Exploiting the notorious tenderness of juries to female accomplices, he painted
a picture which almost inevitably ensured that she would not be convicted, and
then made the tactical extension of the argument to embrace all the rest. If the
prosecution could so irresponsibly indict poor Mrs. Sweet on no evidence, was
there not a real doubt as to all the rest? Lastly, a young and inexperienced
prosecutor made the suggestion to the jury (legally improper and tactically
unwise) that he "held a brief for the deceased." Darrow did not omit to tell
the jury that this was quite wrong, and again to impute sinister motives to the
prosecution, including an imputation of breach of the public trust. Altogether,
it may be concluded, Darrow achieved a hung jury by the prosecution's
mistakes rather than from any very forceful or cogent material he produced
in his clients' behalf. Like all defense lawyers he had learned long before that
the best friend of the defendant often turned out to be the prosecutor.

A hung jury was a kind of victory. It brought respite from the case for the
defendants and Darrow. The prosecutor reviewed the failing of his first attempt to convict and decided to go forward on a second attempt in April and
May 1926 by trying Henry Sweet alone, using the same evidence and witnesses.
In the meantime Darrow returned to Chicago, where his law practice, his
public speaking, and several essays into journalism occupied his time. As if that
were not enough, he developed a marked interest in Mrs. Sally Russell, a lady
he met in Chicago at this time and to whom he wrote several times from
Detroit when the Sweet trial was being replayed. After seeing her he wrote:

> I have not forgotten you. . . . It was mighty nice to see you but the time was all
> too short. . . . A girl like you will always have sympathy and understanding.
> Really, I hated to leave myself . . . it has been lonely all afternoon. I don't care
> how you fix your hair. You are all right and dangerously lovable.

During the second trial, which followed much the same course as the first, he
kept Mrs. Russell abreast of its progress. "You ought to be here and see what
a terribly hard time the colored people have. It looks as if I will be back in
about ten days. If you haven't gone west will see you immediately."[17]

Perhaps because of his new-found romantic interest (which almost certainly
was concealed from Ruby), Darrow's physical appearance at the Sweet trial
seemed to have improved markedly over the Scopes trial. Marcet Haldeman-

Julius reported: "The famous galluses were safely hidden under well-pressed vest and coat. Almost invariably his gray hair was neatly brushed," and this impression of neatness was confirmed by Mrs. Josephine Gomon, who sat next to Darrow during part of the Sweet proceedings.[18] He made virtually the same peroration to the jury in the second trial as in the first and this time achieved an acquittal. He wrote jubilantly to Mrs. Russell: "Was in Detroit four weeks and won my case. It was really exciting and very gratifying," adding on a more personal level, "I have thought of you many times. . . . I really want to see you again."[19]

Predictably, the acquittal of Henry Sweet was regarded as a great liberal triumph. Bartolomeo Vanzetti, then in Charlestown Prison, wrote of the case to a friend: "Darrow said, 'if you are not worse than your fathers, if you have progressed a little, you shall acquit these negroes.' And the jury acquitted them."[20] Probably, however, the real reason for the acquittal of Henry Sweet was that identified by Arthur Garfield Hays in the first trial: the evidence put him on the back porch at the instant when the shot that killed Breiner had been fired from the front. Thus the acquittal may have stemmed from insufficient evidence rather than from anything Darrow had said. But the result was one pleasing to the NAACP and to Darrow personally, and did much to cement his friendship with the leading lights of that organization, especially when his speech was printed and widely distributed by it, in much the way that the Woodworkers' Union had published his speech in the Kidd case a quarter century before. In the next few years much of Darrow's time would be spent furthering the cause of Negro rights from the lecture platform.

34

The Greatest Box-Office Draw
in America

In the wake of the exhilaration of his triumph at the second Sweet trial, serious illness now descended upon Darrow for the first time since his attack of mastoiditis in Idaho twenty years before. It was perhaps a warning that his stamina was diminishing and that he could not continue to face the demands of a trial practice on a regular basis. In October 1926 his doctor ordered him to take a thorough rest and to give up his normal stream of visitors. He was fatigued to the point of depression and unreasonableness, and Fay Lewis reported to Walter White that he "seems to be carrying on sort of a propaganda for an early exit from this 'bloody world.' "[1] It was a signal from nature that he must reduce his pace. And indeed, though the illness was happily brief, 1926 was the last year in which he could be regarded as being in the practice of law in any regular way. Darrow placed his formal retirement in 1928, but he had been winding down for the two years before that, devoting more time to other pursuits.

Had it not been for the influence of Arthur Garfield Hays, with whom he had become firm friends, it is doubtful whether Darrow would have taken any further cases after the Sweet trial. But Hays was active in cases of the type that interested Darrow and furthermore could be relied upon to do the spadework that Darrow himself was not prepared to do. As a consequence of his connection with Hays, he appeared for the defense in two cases in 1927—in New York and Boston, respectively—which can be regarded as the last in which he engaged in regular practice.

The first of these indicated how little patience Darrow had with the law and how irresponsible he had become. The defendant, Donald Friede, was accused of selling an obscene book in Boston, Theodore Dreiser's *An American Tragedy.* But the entire proceedings were lacking in seriousness, for Dreiser's work had never truly been "banned in Boston," and the prosecution had been engineered by the defendant himself: the sale of the book had taken place in a police station. (The policeman who bought it at its cover price of $5 com-

plained constantly thereafter that the Boston police department failed to reim-
burse him for it.) After the transaction was completed, the defense offered to
sell the same policeman Shakespeare's *Complete Works* and Hawthorne's
Scarlet Letter, but his superior officer stopped further purchases. The defense
team then asked whether the refusal to buy meant that the Boston police
department approved of them, but no opinion was given as to their legality.
"I am not saying anything and won't say anything about those books," said
the superintendent of police. "I have refused to buy them and that is all."[2]

A deliberate attempt to set up a prosecution of Dreiser's work could have
been a serious decision to test the law, but it did not turn out that way. One
problem was that an offer of a bribe was made to the judge as a way of
achieving an acquittal. Darrow had nothing to do with this attempt, which was
the dreamchild of "well-meaning friends" of the defendant. Later the judge
told Donald Friede that the attempt had hardened his attitude toward the
defendant, partly because of the affront of trying to bribe him and partly
because the amount offered—$500—was so paltry. A more fundamental diffi-
culty was that counsel for the defense had the wind taken out of their sails by
the palpable evidence that the authorities were not in earnest in suppressing
free speech by use of the obscenity law. Darrow had shown by his performance
in the Scopes case that he was much given to exaggerating the dire consequences that would follow from a failure to render a verdict for his side. He
did the same in the *American Tragedy* case, as if the Boston police department
was about to suppress all truth—the witch-hunt and the censor, Darrow
implied, were the only alternative to acquittals for his clients. The incredibility
of Darrow's dark picture of doom was heightened by the fact that the prosecutions had been initiated by the defendant himself, who had not merely cooperated with the authorities, but goaded them to prosecute. The commonwealth
of Massachusetts was not especially interested in devoting time to such matters, but was baited by the defendant. This is not to say that the laws concerned
did not deserve testing; it is to say that the arguments presented by the defense
did not ring true.

Darrow did not improve his chances of gaining an acquittal for his client
by appearing at a public meeting at Ford Hall during the proceedings and
saying some derisory things about the authorities and his own attitude to the
Boston police. Then, before the verdict was rendered, he departed, leaving a
local attorney to carry on. The hapless man said, with truth, that the defendants had been ill-served by their friends. Darrow had simply washed his hands
of the case, and when the convictions were appealed, he took no part. His
conduct in the *American Tragedy* trial indicated that he no longer had the
patience or commitment to his client's cause to sustain himself in the regular
practice of law. In a general sense he was genuinely interested in the issue of
freedom of speech; but in a legal sense he really no longer cared. It was the
penalty of growing old. The old moral fire had gone, to be replaced by a
somewhat cantankerous and self-indulgent hell-raising, which probably did
more harm to his causes than good. The outcry against the obscenity laws in

the twenties was a minority concern. The majority, especially in the heavily
Roman Catholic cities like Boston, supported book censorship and was unim-
pressed by the arguments of Darrow. It desired neither the vices of the intellectuals nor their mockery. There had always been obscenity laws, just as strict
or stricter than those of the twenties, but social restraint had prevented the
candor of Sinclair Lewis or Theodore Dreiser from surfacing, and probably
lack of sophistication had prevented vigilante groups from interpreting it
correctly. Then America lost its innocence in the war, and manners and morals
changed, just as literature changed.

The only explanation to hand for Darrow's entry into the *American Tragedy*
case was that the issue of book censorship had arisen in an entirely different
form in Chicago, as a result of some convoluted local politics. In 1927 Chicago's Mayor "Big Bill" Thompson was having a final fling before retirement
by alleging that Americans were being undermined by British propaganda. He
decided to check the books of the Chicago Public Library to determine
whether they were pro-British or anti-American. Thompson's campaign
caused a great deal of entertainment around the world. Clarence Darrow
commented: "When Thompson gets through throwing out books written with
a bias in favor of England, in the end he'll have nothing left but fairy tales."[3]
Thompson had not read the books he condemned, nor had he reason to believe
that the pernicious English influence was more widespread in Chicago than
elsewhere. Rather, the move was part of a strategy designed to oust a school
superintendent, William McAndrew, who refused to bend before the political
machine. In an effort to discredit McAndrew, allegations were made that he
was "anti-American" and poisoning the minds of the American young. From
that point the theme had spread, until it became grotesque even by the standards of Chicago politics. If Darrow was moved to participate in the Dreiser
case in Boston because of these points of high comedy in Chicago, he showed
less than his usual good sense.

His other major trial of the year had a more serious side to it. On Memorial
Day, two Fascists were murdered while boarding the Third Avenue El in the
Bronx after taking part in a parade. The well-known anti-Fascists Calogero
Greco and Donato Carrillo were indicted for the murders three weeks later.
A defense was organized for them by an anarchist, Carlo Tresca.

Arthur Garfield Hays, Isaac Schorr, Vito Marcantonio, and Carolyn Weiss
King all offered their aid as counsel, but Tresca insisted that Clarence Darrow
was also needed to insure victory. He urged Norman Thomas to approach
Darrow, who did so by telephone. Darrow said he would have to ask a $10,000
fee. Since the committee was running largely on nickels and dimes from poor
anti-Fascists, Thomas hesitated. But Tresca literally shoved Thomas in the
back and ordered him to say yes.[4]

The defense was contrived to obtain jury sympathy rather than anything
else. The jury was told that the defendants were anti-Fascists, but nothing else
about their views. Formally the defendants claimed an alibi, but the thrust of
the defense was sympathy for Greco's mother, who described on the stand how

worried she had been when her son had not come home after his arrest (the police not having told her). As Hays said, "the story, which had nothing to do with the charge of murder, was most effective." She gave an alibi for her son on the day of the murder, and then asked in court: "May I embrace my son?" A touching scene ensued, with Greco Junior in tears.[5]

After the acquittal, Tresca provided the strategy for avoiding paying Darrow the agreed fee for his services. Norman Thomas saw little chance of the defense committee's managing to raise the money. But once again, "Tresca saved the day. He said, 'Tonight we'll go to the victory party at Art Hays'.' After Darrow has had a couple of drinks to mellow him, you tell Clarence how things stand. He's proud of the victory and I'm sure he'll forget the fee."[6]

Those ex-clients of Darrow's who had been sued for nonpayment of fees back in the nineties when Darrow was practicing law in earnest would have reflected that he had mellowed in his old age. Indeed he had. He no longer really cared about the law, and his defense of the anarchists was planned to be his last major trial. In writing to Harry Elmer Barnes, who by now had become one of his most valued and regular correspondents, he referred to himself as "a man of leisure."[7] To prove it, he and Ruby set sail from Montreal on a protracted vacation directly after the acquittal of Greco and Carrillo. In large part this trip was a "second honeymoon," which retraced their sojourn through Europe twenty years before even down to the detail of embarking from Canada, "where you can get a drink from the start," just as they had in 1903.[8]

On their first honeymoon, Darrow had occupied himself by writing *Farmington*. On their second, true to form, he commenced his autobiography while Ruby and he were visiting Charles Edward Russell and his wife, Teresa, in Switzerland. Ever helpful, Ruby typed his manuscript in the Russells' garden as Charles Russell finished his *Life of Charlemagne*. Thus by a strange quirk of fate the story of a self-appointed guardian of the Christian faith was written in the very same spot as that of one of its most famous reputed attackers. Darrow's book, to be called *The Story of My Life*, was less autobiographical than many of his readers hoped; as Irving Stone justly remarked, "it might more accurately have been called *The Story of My Philosophy*."[9] It was noticeably reticent about many aspects of his private and professional life. He explained the lack of details about his legal career in a letter to Arthur Spingarn of the NAACP:

> I did not, and do not feel that anything in the nature of a life-story should go further into my cases than I have done. I could not publish a volume of such stories without the consent of those involved who are living, unless sort of common property, and this would handicap me.
>
> And then,—I could not write about how I tried my cases. I cannot brag about what I have done, and anything one would write about cases not known about would show that attitude. Really, I cannot imagine doing such a thing. You *know* how modest (?) I am![10]

Both Darrow's forgiveness of his defense fee in the anti-Fascist case and the European trip were born out of the same euphoric sense of prosperity. For the first time in history it appeared that a substantial segment of the population, apart from those who inherited wealth, would be relieved from the necessity of working—money came so easily by other means. As in every boom era, heroes appeared whose virtue resided mainly in being the beneficiary of a bonanza. The stock market was the urban counterpart to a gold rush. For a time it worked. Few challenged the assumption of prosperity. Certainly Darrow did not. In its wake many Americans were learning with Scott Fitzgerald how to go broke on $50,000 a year. Darrow had often disparaged Ben Franklin's *Almanac,* "with its foolish lessons about industry and thrift," and now the whole nation was joining him.

In 1928 the Greeley Gas & Fuel Company, which had been Paul Darrow's full-time interest since 1908 and in which Clarence had a large amount of stock, was sold at a substantial profit to the National Gas & Electric Corporation. The Greeley Company was a modest business; it employed only about sixteen people and Greeley was a small community. Its sole function had been to supply the town of Greeley, Colorado, with gas. Still, its disposition put both father and son in a comfortable financial position, giving them a substantial nest egg. The company had been taken over in an era of consolidation in the public utility field; by 1930, National Gas & Electric Corporation had itself become a subsidiary of National Gas & Power Corporation, which was in turn controlled by American Commonwealth Power Corporation. As a result, things looked so rosy that not only did Darrow feel confident that his and Ruby's needs would be taken care of, but that he was rich enough to make some charitable bequests. As it turned out, this was premature, for the crash of 1929 was to affect him like so many others. But for the moment all seemed bright.

In the meantime his new lifestyle left more room than he had had since his youth for social pleasantries and nonlegal distractions. Crosswords became a constant amusement for him; he described his life after his seventy-fifth birthday as sleep, reading, and crosswords. But he also spent much time with members of the University of Chicago community who came to his apartment for discussions. He refueled his literary and debating activities with the new literature of which they kept him abreast. The university was cast much more in the mold of modernism than any of his formal education had been, and he felt far more favorably disposed toward Chicago than to any institutions of learning he had himself attended. Besides, he was reaching an age of reflection, and had lost some of the impatience of impetuous youth.

When Henry Ford announced that he would spend $100 million on promoting "practical education," Darrow was delighted. He forgave him his capitalist excesses, his anti-war stand, his alleged anti-Semitism, and wrote to him from Cannes: "If schools of this type could reach all the youth of America, in time it would result in the abolition of crime and poverty, both of which are a disgrace to civilization."[11] (He might have been rather less sanguine if he had

known that Ford was an ardent admirer of McGuffey, who claimed to have
drawn more from Longfellow's *Psalm of Life,* reproduced in the sixth
McGuffey Reader, than from anything else he had ever read.) Ford and
Darrow both perceived that the irrelevance of much American education left
many schoolchildren incapable of earning a living except at totally unskilled
jobs. Darrow wanted to teach them to think; Ford wanted to teach them a skill.
United in their belief in the necessity of change, the two men might have
reflected that whatever the shortcomings of their country education, it had not
stifled their own personal genius or their will to succeed. For all its impracticality, the schooling provided by the Midwest in the mid-nineteenth century when
both Darrow and Ford were boys had not stopped them from achieving
success.

Darrow was not relying only on the profits from the sale of his son's
business. He was also doing very well personally out of journalism and the
lecture circuit. He was now very famous indeed and commanded attention in
print and on the platform as a grand old man. He pursued his pet themes
through the written and spoken word to great effect. As a journalist and critic
he came into his own during the twenties, making it his business to cultivate
literary men whom he admired. In this way he came to know the rising literary
set as well as the more seasoned professionals, and by the later twenties these
contacts were bearing fruit. In 1921 Darrow had written to Sinclair Lewis to
praise *Main Street,* then a best-seller. He understood its theme of the clash of
town and country and the inapplicability of rural standards to modern society:
"I am a confirmed pessimist and think the people have no brains. Now [that
Main Street is successful] I must either change my opinions as to the people
or give up the idea that I am a judge of literature."[12] He could identify with
Lewis's despair over the narrowness, parochialism, and ignorance of large
tracts of America. Lewis, though much younger than Darrow, was likewise
in rebellion against small-town values, and after Darrow initiated a correspon-
dence they rapidly became friends. By 1928 Lewis was staying in the Darrows'
apartment and announcing that he was about to write a novel based upon
Darrow's career. The novel he envisioned never materialized, but in a sense
Main Street was a fictionalized version of many of Darrow's life battles. The
character of Jackson Elder of the Gopher Prairie planing mill was much like
George M. Paine, the real-life owner of the Paine Lumber Company whom
Darrow had confronted in the Kidd case. Asked whether he approves of labor
unions, Elder replies in almost exactly the terms that Paine in fact used:

> Me? I should say not! It's like this: I don't mind dealing with my men if
> they think they've got any grievances—though Lord knows what's come over
> workmen, nowadays—don't appreciate a good job. . . . But I'm not going to
> have any outsider, any of these walking delegates, or whatever fancy names
> they call themselves now—bunch of rich grafters, living on the ignorant
> workmen! Not going to have any of those fellows butting in and telling *me*
> how to run my business! . . . I stand for freedom and constitutional rights. If
> any man don't like my shop, he can get up and git. Same way, if I don't like

him, he gits. And that's all there is to it. . . . They like what I pay 'em, or
they get out. . . .[13]

This type of "realist" fiction had the strongest appeal to Darrow. There was
an affinity of experience between Lewis and Darrow that more than made up
for the difference in age. Both had been imprisoned by the conventions of
small-town life and had set themselves free by making a reputation in the wider
world. Both knew that rebelliousness was an important spring of their achievement, but equally wisely recognized that a successful rebel has to have something substantial to rebel against. Darrow's enthusiasm for Lewis's work led
him to discuss it at length with friends.

A similar overture to Henry Mencken also resulted in a firm friendship.
Darrow had made his first contribution to the *American Mercury* in 1924,
when he wrote introducing himself: "I have long wanted to know you and have
read most everything you have written and find little of your stuff I do not
believe is true. This of course will show you that your views are logical and
correct."[14] Like Mencken, he could see too much wrong with everything to
think much good of anything, and from then on the two men were nearly
always in the same camp. Mencken virtually acted as his publicity manager
for the Scopes trial and continued to accept pieces from Darrow. Even in
August 1925—a period of intense legal work for Darrow—the *Mercury* published an article by him debunking the art of salesmanship.

His withdrawal from active practice allowed him to make more frequent
and longer trips to New York, where most of his writer and editor friends
(though not Mencken) were based. His older brother Edward lived on
West 111th Street, near Columbia University, until he died on September
28, 1927, and this too provided an incentive to travel. Darrow had a number of articles published in the "smart" magazines, including *Vanity Fair*,
the *American Mercury*, and the *Saturday Evening Post*, but the pieces did
not do him justice. In the main they lacked style and pungency. Some, for
whatever reason, seemed to lack polish, as if they were first drafts rather
than finished products. He chose themes unassociated with issues of law,
as a number of his contributions to *Vanity Fair* reflect. Many of them
were notably unpolemic and even nostalgic, the works of a man who has
had, for the moment, too much controversy and seeks peace—or, as he so
frequently referred to his quest, "forgetfulness." They succeeded in entertaining, but lacked redaction.

Even when he presented themes in print that had been part of his stock-in-
trade for his entire career, Darrow seemed to miss his target. As he grew older,
his anti-religious bent grew stronger and stronger. He wrote to Mencken in
1927 about the Lord's Day Alliance, an organization he had seen in action in
Mobile, Alabama:

> The Lord's Day Alliance, with Headquarters in New York, are raising H—l
> generally, especially in the Bible Belt. Wherever they see anyone having any fun
> on Sunday, they are introducing laws to prevent it; theatres, Sunday baseball,

etc., etc.. They have a good deal of literature that could be used to good effect. If you want me to do it, and can manage to get their literature in New York and send it to me, I will see what I can make out of it.[15]

With Mencken's blessing, Darrow embarked upon his analysis of the Alliance materials. It seems likely that Mencken believed the major thrust of Darrow's piece would be a complaint that Sunday laws were inappropriate to a pluralistic society like America. But when he received the manuscript from Darrow on August 2, he found that it said much more than that. It was a diatribe not only against the lobbying techniques of the Alliance, but against much of the fundamental tenets of Jewry and Christianity alike. He flayed the "bloody, barbarous, tribal God of the Jews," deriding the Old Testament as a collection of cruel superstitions. But it was Christianity that provoked his wrath the most. He described the shorter Westminster Catechism as "the horrible creed of the twisted and deformed minds who produced this montrosity which has neither sense, meaning, justice nor mercy, but only malignant depravity. A devilish creed which shocks every tender sentiment in the human mind."

Such strong stuff was not at all what Mencken had bargained for. While he was privately somewhat of the same mind as Darrow, he knew, with the instinct of a good editor, that Darrow's piece was a humorless tirade that would harm the *Mercury*'s reputation, and he rejected it. Darrow clearly had no comprehension of why it was rejected, believing it to be a well-done piece. He submitted it to *Plain Talk,* where it was published as the lead article of the March 1928 number, with an editorial introduction praising its "priceless irony."

He continued to sift through the religious outpourings of the day, intent upon uncovering literalism, absurdity, and contradiction with the same energy that a devotee of the faith might seek out heresy; he seemed, in fact, to be in danger of the fanaticism on this issue that he ascribed to his late foe William Jennings Bryan. The fires were stoked by various friends in different parts of the country who catered to his taste for sectarian tracts. "It was nice of you to send those Methodist pamphlets," he wrote to Harry Elmer Barnes, after receiving one such gift. "I am going to send for the whole set and have something to say about them."[16]

On the lecture circuit, Darrow remained a stunningly successful speaker on the same themes. Yet here another similarity with his erstwhile adversary appeared; for he was becoming more and more a performer, a mouther of scripts, and less a thinker. If Bryan had been at fault in riding the Chautauqua circuit, Darrow was open to much the same criticisms in 1927 and 1928, as he fed his appetite for glory while traveling from city to city for one-night stands.

Platform speaking did for Darrow what Dr. Johnson believed the prospect of hanging did for a condemned man—it cleared the mind wonderfully. He had a magical ability to rise to an occasion. Before an audience he became a giant. He was less interested in applause—which he frequently wrung out of even antagonistic audiences—than in attention, in occupying many minds at one time. Always he liked the drama of advocating an unpopular position. Then the adrenalin flowed. The pressure of performing urged him on like nothing else, and he relied upon it. He shared the mysterious, obscure gift of "presence" that all public figures have or attain. Something brought out the best in him and caused people to listen. Of course some preparation had to be done; but he had developed his repertoire to perfection well before middle age. Scarcely a thing changed in his addresses for over thirty years—though always he adlibbed something new, with a gift for improvisation and topical humor—but lecture audiences listened attentively to ideas which they would have scoffed at as anachronistic had they been presented in print.

There were dangers inherent in the lecture circuit. The public usually came not to think and listen, but merely to gape at the famous participants as they gaped at exotic animals in a zoo. So far as the promoters were concerned, that was all right as long as they paid. But what did it make of the lecturers? How were they different from freak shows at fairgrounds, shown off in captivity where they could do their audience no real harm? Or in a circus, put through their tricks like trained bears? There was something distasteful about being a pundit in a traveling roadshow, just as there was something a little pathetic about an undeniably great but elderly pleader shadowboxing around philosophical issues for his living. The lecture circuit was where the radicals of a previous age could cash in on the remnants of their fame—where old war horses bucked and snorted harmlessly just before being put out to pasture. It was saved from being embarrassing only by the fact that Darrow was not the slightest abashed; he had lived by his wits long enough not to feel himself demeaned. Lecturing and debating were easier than litigation and provided as much, or even more, gratification. He felt he was retaining the "showy" aspects of public speaking, which he had always enjoyed, while avoiding the grind of law practice and the responsibilities of having clients. In his youth his advocacy had sprung spontaneously from the wells of emotion and had the intensity of psychic energy behind it. As the years progressed, he became less the impassioned advocate forced forward by moral outrage and more the measured, practiced performer. As age dimmed the passions while sparing the intellect, reason took precedence over fervor, and his arguments became more polished, his effects more calculated. He learned by experience to contrive the effects he wanted, becoming such an actor that even the appearance of spontaneity was contrived.

This metamorphosis from driven idealist to cool professional was neither complete nor sudden. Probably it was not deliberate or conscious, but it was accelerated by the demands of the lecturing roadshow. When nature robbed Darrow of the psychic energy that had seen him through in practice, he had to develop a substitute to make good the deficiency. Nothing had been completely spontaneous even when he first drew the world's attention. Now more was already worked out beforehand so that if inspiration should fail, there was preparation to fall back on. In consequence, as he reviled hogwash, claptrap, blarney, and buncombe, he evolved his own litany of commonplaces and platitudes. Like all practiced speakers, he developed stock responses to the challenges he most frequently encountered. They appeared to some to be more notable for their dramatic or diversionary qualities than for their relevance or intellectual rigor. Darrow had always had a tendency to say things more for their effect than because they were true. These aspects of showmanship and egotism irritated some who encountered him almost beyond endurance. His greatest intellectual defect was that the stock responses had nothing behind them; he was satisfied with them as they were, and they were not simply a prelude to an enlightening or creatively developed argument. They were the end product, the finishing point, not the start. Only narrowly did he miss becoming still more like his adversary Bryan as he traveled from one town to another. He was almost the itinerant preacher of the nonbelievers as he traipsed round the countryside producing at will a few set speeches or debates. Yet always there was a substance and quality to what he said—though he had said it so often before—that elevated him above the normal run of hacks.

Darrow had been eagerly sought after by the agencies ever since the end of the Boise trials, at which period his bookings were handled by the Bryant-Spence Agency, together with those of George Burnam Foster of the University of Chicago, with whom he appeared until Foster's death in 1919. There was something undignified about the proceedings that nearly all sensitive men recognized. When Joseph Labadie inquired of Eugene Debs about the possibilities of the lecture circuit, Debs replied:

> I can hardly find it in my heart to cheer you on. There is so much to contend with and to overcome in the present condition of things that the undertaking is fraught with all that is calculated to make a man think a second or third time before engaging in it. If you were a quack revivalist, or sensationalist, or fantastic humbug of some sort, starting out to pander to the ignorance of the people, it would be different.[17]

But if Darrow felt the same way, he gave no sign of it. On the contrary, he was avid for the chance to lecture or debate throughout his final years. The tendency was for the commercial promoters to favor debates rather than lectures, though habitués of the debating circuits were perfectly capable of putting their points of view by a lecture, and did not need to have an adversary to pump their views out of them. But debate was the popular format of the era, providing a dimension of entertainment as well as education such as a simple lecture could not achieve. The agents of the debating circuits believed in it wholeheartedly, knowing debate had the same element of combat that attracted audiences for cockfights and boxing matches alike.

In Darrow's case it was a foregone conclusion how the contest would turn out. Almost any opponent was merely "a foil to give Darrow a chance to exhibit his forensic powers."[18] Dozens of people who heard him perform have left their testament that he was extraordinarily cogent. Samuel T. Williamson, describing Darrow's debate in Rochester, New York, with the Reverend Clin-

ton Winder of the Baptist Temple on the subject "Is There a Hereafter?,"
commented: "If the Lord was on his side, as the clergyman intimated, it must
have been an off day, for Darrow wiped the ground up with his opponent, not
only demolishing the hereafter, but denying the existence of the Deity."[19] His
skill overwhelmed even those predisposed against him, like Thomas G. Higgins, who saw him debate prohibition in Columbus, Ohio. "My instinctive
reaction to Darrow was completely negative, and I imagine he made the same
initial impression on others," he confessed. Yet, when he got up to speak, he
overcame this antagonism:

> . . . Darrow understood people, individually and collectively; how they react;
> what they are like. Within a matter of minutes—and this was the amazing thing
> —he seemed to have the entire audience in the hollow of his hand. . . . As he
> progressed in his talk the audience became spellbound; you could quite literally
> have heard a pin drop. I never saw such a demonstration of the power of
> personality.[20]

At this time Darrow was already well over seventy years old, but his oratorical
powers showed little sign of diminishing. Those who saw him debate detected
no lack of zest. He was ferocious and merciless, exhibiting neither apathy nor
dearth of spirit. His reputation was such that an invitation to meet him on the
platform was not always accepted with alacrity. When Harlan Fiske Stone was
Attorney General in 1924–25, he refused to meet Darrow, recognizing that he
was not his equal as "a popular speaker."

There was some justification for the view that Darrow was not a wholly fair
or honest debater. When Judge Michael Musmanno debated him on one of his
stock themes, "Does Man Live Again?", at the Carnegie Music Hall in Pitts-
burgh, Darrow challenged a quotation given by Musmanno in the course of
debate, attributed to Voltaire, to the effect that "If God did not exist, it would
be necessary to invent Him." Since Darrow had written a short study of
Voltaire, it was likely that the two thousand people in the audience would
think Darrow right and Musmanno wrong. But Musmanno was able to au-
thenticate his quotation: ". . . I crossed over to Darrow's side of the stage and
thrust the book before his eyes. His courtroom aplomb did not desert him. He
glanced at the open page, shrugged his shoulders, and grinned. The audience
broke into good-natured laughter and further applause."[21]

The debate form suited Darrow for the very reason that others found it
unsatisfactory. T. V. Smith, who often debated Darrow, feared that the art of
debate was to overstate a case, simplifying untruthfully in order to carry the
audience. Darrow did not mind doing this; he painted with a broad brush,
putting across the general theme without worrying about its total consistency.
This was demonstrated in many of his confrontations with the press. After the
Scopes trial he held a press conference in which he made a number of unqualified pronouncements on a variety of public questions. When the reporters
had gone, H. E. Colton, a journalist himself, who had been present throughout,
pointed out that before in private conversation Darrow had been cautious in

qualifying his generalizations about the very same issues. "That's quite true," admitted Darrow, "but . . . if you qualify your main point the thing you wish to emphasize loses its news value; it loses its interest to the public."[22]

This tendency to overstatement on a number of themes close to the heart of middle America brought him further notoriety, which was formally marked in 1928 (to his great satisfaction) by his being blacklisted by the Daughters of the American Revolution, and later when he was listed in Elizabeth Dilling's *Red Network* as an un-American radical. The DAR represented especially an extravagant reverence for the superficial half-truths of glory which, in large measure, were the backwash of the government's wartime propaganda machine. The DAR was a self-defined elect, with birth as its reference point, and by implication hostile to recent immigrants whom it suspected of subscribing to "foreign" doctrines of subversion.

Actually the DAR was out of date, for Darrow's politics throughout the twenties were channeled into the entirely orthodox machinery of the Democratic Party. Though he still paid lip service to the possibility of revolutionary change, he did not really expect to end up at the barricades. When Sinclair Lewis bracketed him with Lincoln Steffens and Norman Thomas as "obvious anarchists and soreheads," Steffens put his finger on the truth by observing: "Lewis puts me in a group not worth killing."[23] In 1924 he was a delegate to the Democratic convention in Madison Square Garden, and in the presidential election he voted for the official Demoratic candidate, John W. Davis, rather than Robert La Follette, who ran as a Progressive. In 1928 he supported Frank Lowden for nomination on the Democratic ticket, and having failed to achieve that, remained philosophic about the Democratic defeat in the ensuing election. He wrote to Harry Elmer Barnes: "I hope you will not be too disappointed over the election. I have been with the loosers [sic] so long on every question that it never bothers me."[24] The focus of his "subversion" by the twenties was much less in formal politics than in his anti-religious and pro-Negro efforts, which were in reality two sides of the same coin. Almost the entire leadership of the NAACP was hostile to religion, regarding it with some reason as the bulwark of ignorance and superstition in the Negro race. Of course this was not an official position of the Association, because it had to work largely through the network of black churches that provided the only social link among black communities. But the aim of its intellectual supporters was without important exception against the church. Walter White wrote to Darrow a little over a year after the Scopes trial that "The great work of de-religionizing the Negro moves on apace! Allah be praised."[25] In the same vein Darrow told James Weldon Johnson of the NAACP, "I am not interested in God and he is not interested in the colored people."[26] The truth was that most of the circle interested in improvements for the Negro to which Darrow belonged regarded the black churches as forces of reaction, often riddled with the frauds of their mostly self-proclaimed ministers of the Gospel. They scoffed at the promise of joy in the hereafter and the bankruptcy of the religious ecstasy that provided Sunday relief from the drudgery of the average Negro's

lot. This became a common bond between Darrow and the Harlem intelli-
gentsia, and provided an almost inexhaustible vein of humorous discussion
when they got together. Darrow regarded the clergy, whether black or white,
as generally "hot-air artists without any ideas,"[27] but of course the NAACP
officials were especially critical of members of their own race. Most of them
believed that emancipation from slavery was only a legal formality compared
with the necessity of emancipating their race's mind from the religious junk
with which it had been filled. Like Frederick Douglass, the great black intellectual of the antebellum years, they saw religion as the enemy, not the friend,
of the Negro people.

The strong sympathy with the Negroes that Darrow evinced involved a
complex set of shared values. As a race, they had been excluded from full
participation in society and in consequence had developed an anti-culture in
which the conventional virtues of the dominant whites were disparaged, failure
was excused, and the outcast was a hero. With all this Darrow had strong
emotional sympathy, for it was a part of challenging orthodoxy. He himself
had always been, as Hamlin Garland had remarked, "on the 'off' side of
everything," and there he found many more black intellectuals than white
ones. In a sense they were involved, as Darrow was, in a continued campaign
of subversion. In this limited sense the propagandists of the DAR were correct
in identifying Darrow as part of the "Red network."

Feeling himself to be financially secure, Darrow chose the NAACP as the
beneficiary of some of his prosperity. Under an arrangement he initiated in
January 1928, he gave up certain of his lecture fees to the organization,
apportioning three-quarters to its general fund and one-quarter to the erection
of a monument to John Brown. Since he commanded a fee of $500 in smaller
towns and not less than $1,000 in larger ones, this was a considerable source
of revenue. On top of that, in April 1929 he made further charitable provision
for the Association, writing to Walter White: "As you know I am getting damn
old. And like all people who have no other outdoor sport I am making a will.
I want to include your organization in it. There won't be enough to make it
of any great consequence. But still enough to show how I feel and possibly
attract some others to do likewise."[28]

But the illusion of financial security that the proceeds of the shares of
Greeley Gas & Fuel had given was soon shattered. Both Darrow and his son,
Paul, had invested those proceeds in exchange-listed securities that were to
suffer the ravages of the great crash of 1929, with the result that the income
upon which Darrow had relied to see him through his declining years was
drastically reduced. By an extraordinary piece of ill-timing, Paul associated
with a stockbroking firm on his return to Chicago from Greeley, and thus faced
five lean years between 1930 and 1935 that were financially far more precarious
than any of his twenty with the gas company. So freedom from financial worry
eluded Darrow even in his old age.

As things turned out, the Darrows would have done better to leave their
money in the Greeley Company, whose bond ratings had become AA under

Paul's management, and the income from which would have been secure. Had they wished, they could no doubt have negotiated with the National Gas & Electric Corporation that their shares of common stock were exchanged for the Greeley's secured debt; but Paul had decided to pull out entirely. He believed that investment in the market was likely to produce better returns than a conservative bond holding, and his father bowed to his judgment. Then the crash came, and Darrow found himself as an old man forced to hit the lecture and debating circuits to survive. Like many another lawyer he had never had a pension scheme, or any retirement plan worth anything, and there was no cushion for him to fall back on. Within three years Darrow's share of the proceeds of the sale—approximately $300,000—had shrunk to $10,000.

Though the crash was serious for the Darrows, its impact was softened by Clarence's lifetime habits. He had never believed in using credit and therefore did not have a large debt to pay off. And the paternal example had left its mark, for (except for book-buying) he had no tendency to extravagance. His lifestyle was unostentatious to the point of austerity. Ruby and he had lived in the same Midway apartment throughout their married life, never caring to flaunt any prosperity that might come to them. The success Darrow sought was not material. Reputation had always come before riches, fame before fortune. His only interest in money was to have enough not to need to think about it. Alas, after 1929, he did need to think about it once more.

Darrow now became even more the performer, and his attraction was as an entertainer more than as a pleader of causes. In the search for income he turned more naturally to exploiting his celebrity. His fame had become "official" only shortly before Wall Street crashed, when the *Encyclopaedia Britannica* brought out a new edition in which his name appeared as a separate entry. He was a star, promoted by agents and traveling a circuit much like a vaudevillian. With the brash, entrepreneurial spirit of the decade in his favor, he became a box-office "draw." *Variety* described him as "America's greatest one-man stage draw," and this was not mere hyperbole (for which *Variety* already had a reputation). T. V. Smith recorded that "he alone was enough to draw a crowd anywhere in America. . . ."[29] By 1931 when he was feeling the adverse effects of the crash acutely, Darrow was primarily an entertainer. He lectured regularly. He was also working on a movie documentary entitled *The Mystery of Life* that explained the theory of evolution to nonscientists, and was considering an offer, which he subsequently accepted, to participate in a two-part radio show in which he would "defend" Benedict Arnold in a mock trial for "a considerable fee."

Darrow had the distinction of being almost the last public figure able to make something of a career out of the debate circuit, for at the very time that *Variety* was describing him as the greatest box-office draw in America, the competition of the radio and the talkies was supplanting personal appearances as an attraction and source of fame. The lecture circuits were declining, and their last bastion was the South. Attractions such as Darrow were being eclipsed, and he was, in his last years, making his living in a declining industry.

True, it was still possible to find willing listeners for the famous, but the time was not far off when the fame would have to come from appearances in movies or on radio and it would be impossible to use the same material time and again, as Darrow had done. As one to whom it came naturally to repeat, in one city after another, the same lecture or debate, with only minor variations, he was a relic of a past age. But the documentary *The Mystery of Life* and his radio "Defense of Benedict Arnold" remained unique. The radio "jury" convicted Arnold (like many of Darrow's real-life clients) in spite of the defense; and the National Dairy Association, which had been the program's sponsor, was content to stop at having one traitor tried.

He departed on his whirlwind lecture tours with rather less regret than Ruby might have wished. In spite of the creature comforts provided on East 60th Street, he seemed to welcome the break from routine that his travels meant, even relishing sleeping each night in a different hotel room and living out of a suitcase. Once, he revealed his attitude to a lecture manager, George White-head, who was traveling with him and whom Ruby had asked to look after him. "If you're going to take such good care of me there's no reason for me to leave home," he complained. Tranquility did not come easily to him and he fretted under the loving care of his wife. The security he could have under his own roof appealed to him much less than the excitement of being on the road.

His travels afforded him some opportunity for extramarital dalliance of a discreet kind; his interest in Mrs. Russell during the Sweet trial was not a unique episode. As a star, he even met stars to whom he paid court, reputedly vying with Reynald Vanderbilt for the attention of Kay Laurel of the Ziegfeld Follies. Ruby was understandably not tolerant of such conduct, so Darrow had to seek his chances out of her sight: "Apparently she believes that eternal vigilance is the price of a husband," he wryly observed.[30]

But he did not ignore Ruby or forego the freedom of retirement entirely. As a couple they made social trips to see various friends. They were the guests of Sinclair Lewis and Dorothy Thompson at their farm in Barnard, Vermont, in 1930. In the same year the curmudgeonly Henry Mencken married. Darrow wrote to him with a certain relish:

> I knew it would happen. It always does. Still, I want to compliment you on the long, brave fight you made. That is all a man can do, for the foul race must be preserved, and this is the way that has been ordained for its preservation. Any-how, I hope to see both you and Mrs. Mencken before very long. Give her my kindest regards and best wishes; also my sincere sympathy.[31]

Shortly afterward he and Ruby went to the Menckens' house in Baltimore. Mencken had just achieved the ultimate in iconoclasm by publishing *On the Gods,* retailing his view that theism, like much else, was buncombe. The recent marriage was celebrated by reminiscences of the Scopes trial and several drinks over which the company pledged its antagonism to prohibition.

Darrow became a practiced traveler, familiar with hotels in all the major stops on the circuit and known to their staff. In New York, when he did not stay with friends, he favored the Murray Hill; in Washington, D.C., the Willard; and the Fenway or Princess Martha when down in the St. Petersburg-Tampa area of Florida. Since he was constantly on the move, his correspondence was written without reference to files or notes or even to the letters to which he was responding. They were the products of memory, and became less and less "lawyerlike" in their precision even when dealing with legal matters. And in his spare moments on the road during most of 1930 and 1931 he finished putting together his autobiography, *The Story of My Life,* confessing that he was not sure "how much of it can be called biography and how much propaganda. I have fully discussed my ideas in law, courts, crime, Religion, God etc."[32] It was manifest that he regarded his years as a lawyer as behind him. Biography writing already appeared to be the vice of his generation. He complained to Brand Whitlock that "everyone was writing his autobiography nowadays . . . everybody was standing on the street corner beating a bass drum and crying: 'For God's sake, look at me for a minute!' "[33] The thought did not discourage Darrow from doing the same. On the contrary, he took special pains to see that he had every possible exposure in a market glutted by his contemporaries and already somewhat sluggish because of the Depression.

The autobiography was not, as Darrow himself admitted, truly a self-portrait. It was concerned much more with his views than with the way that his life had been led. He acknowledged that embarking on an autobiography at all was evidence that he did not expect his life to hold much more excitement than it had already. Certainly he did not expect that he would ever again appear as counsel in a major case. While he was writing, his economic circumstances changed much for the worse. For Christmas of 1931 he and Ruby sent out peculiar home-made cards, executed in several different inks by Ruby. Each must have taken a considerable time to pen, and though it is not known how many were sent, the total effort expended on them must have been huge even if they were confined to an inner circle of friends. The results could not be said to be pleasing aesthetically, for Ruby's work was untidy and somewhat childlike, but the cards emphasized that the Darrows were feeling the Depression's pinch. They expressed the secular rather than religious hope that the coming year would be better than the one just suffered.

At the beginning of 1932, at an age when many of his less famous colleagues at the bar had retired in comfort, Darrow was forced back into harness. He had neither the patience nor energy to run a law office of his own; but in search of a place to hang his hat, he joined a law partnership with three much younger lawyers who had set up practice after having been in the state's attorney's office under Robert Crowe. The younger men were pleased to be able to use his name, and printed up their letterhead as Darrow, Cronson, Smith & Smith. It was to be the last professional affiliation in Darrow's career. Now was the time that he might repent his insouciant assumption that accumulating wealth and squirreling it away was mere avarice. Had he practiced for purely commercial motives and taken the conventional steps to perpetuate his practice, he would have been much better prepared for old age. He would have been less than human if he had not felt some bitterness and self-pity at his lot. Still, he braced himself to enter the lists once again and found thankfully that his services were still in demand.

35

The Last Big Case

It was the NAACP that initiated Darrow's reentry into practice, when five black teenagers were accused of raping two white girls in Alabama. The Scottsboro case, as it became known, was a *cause célèbre* in which the proceedings remained an issue throughout the thirties and even beyond, largely because the allegations of rape were not believed by many Northerners. It became a case symbolic of the clash between the North and the deep South, in which an extraordinary mélange of ill-feelings developed among many organizations that had no direct interest in the proceedings. The normally sober and factual ACLU reports started referring to the imprisoned defendants as "political prisoners," though their cases actually did not fit the Union's own definition of that term. In view of the racial aspect of the case, the NAACP at once considered hiring counsel; but it did not turn to Darrow immediately because it feared his known atheism might prejudice even black Southerners against the defense. Walter White, secretary of the Association, wrote to Dr. Charles A. J. McPherson of Birmingham, Alabama, regarding the possibility of such feeling against Darrow "because of his religious and other views which are, as you know, anathema to the reactionary South."[1] However Dr. McPherson was able to reassure White that Darrow was not disqualified in this way. By a strange irony, he used as evidence Darrow's reception on the lecture circuit:

> We do not believe that his religion will be so very intolerant in these cases, once it is known that he is not allied with the I.L.D. or the Communists.
> I went to hear Mr. Darrow last week when he spoke here, as you may know, on the religious question "Why I am an Atheist." There were [sic] very little heckling from the large audience which heard him. He received more applause, possibly, than any of the five speakers who spoke.[2]

Encouraged by Dr. McPherson's report, Walter White approached Darrow. Financially the opportunity looked very attractive, coming as it did after a very austere Christmas and with no other prospect in sight; so without committing himself, Darrow agreed to look into it. In early 1932 he went down to Birmingham with Arthur Garfield Hays, at the request of the NAACP, to see what could be done for the Scottsboro defendants. By that time the International Labor Defense (ILD), a Communist organization, was already involved with

403

the case, which it wanted to retain control of. In 1926 this same organization had tried unsuccessfully to take over the defense of Sacco and Vanzetti from the Boston Defense Committee. With the Scottsboro case, it was more successful.

When Darrow and Hays arrived in Birmingham, the question of legal representation for the Scottsboro boys was already complicated. The ILD's lawyer, George W. Chamlee, Sr., was in dispute with the local NAACP lawyer, Stephen R. Roddy, who had been retained earlier in the proceedings. As soon as Darrow and Hays came on the scene, they received a telegram signed with the names of all the defendants, which read: "We do not want you to come and fight the I.L.D. and make trouble for Mr. Chamlee just to help the NAACP. If you want to save us and to help us get a new trial please help the I.L.D. and Mr. Chamlee."

It was not then clear, and never subsequently became clear, whether the telegram was actually from the defendants. It was generally believed that the boys were malleable in the hands of the last people they talked to, and that the telegram was concocted by the ILD. Certainly the ILD's conduct seemed to indicate that. The Communists did not want to turn away the two distinguished Northern lawyers, for that would seem to be much against the boys' interests. The ILD recognized that Darrow's reputation was worth having; it had tried to hire him for Sacco and Vanzetti several years before. On their side Darrow and Hays were mainly interested in doing what they could for the defendants, and were prepared to cooperate with the lawyers already in the case. When they offered their services, one of the ILD lawyers, Irving Schwab, having apparently taken instructions from the ILD's organization in New York (but not from the defendants), turned to Darrow and said, "Mr. Darrow, we will be glad to have you and Mr. Hays in this case, but on certain conditions."

Darrow, at that time seventy-five years old and the most famous living American lawyer, took this quite well from the young Schwab.

"Young man," he said, "it is a long time since anyone has invited me into a criminal case on conditions, but what are they?"

"First," Schwab replied, "you must repudiate the NAACP. Secondly, the tactics of the case must be left to the ILD."

"You mean," drawled Darrow, "that if you people choose to send insulting telegrams and letters to all the judges and even to the Governor to whom we may have to appeal for a pardon you'll do it and I shall have nothing to say about it."

"That is just what we mean," said Schwab.[3]

On these conditions neither Darrow nor Hays could serve. They made an effort to persuade the ILD lawyers to agree to work for the benefit of the boys, regardless of the organizations that backed them, but in vain. Darrow and Hays reported back to the NAACP that it was impossible to help.

The confusion and unpleasantness that resulted from competing claims to be the legal representatives of the Scottsboro boys cannot fairly be blamed on the NAACP. Nevertheless its practice of stepping in and taking over a case of interest to its management was one that was to cause trouble one way or another for many years to come.* Certainly, had a private attorney (including Darrow) stepped in and offered his services directly to the Scottsboro boys, a question of professional ethics would have been involved. But although the NAACP acted from the best of motives, it should be recognized that the dispute arose from a characteristic desire of the times to make an issue if one could possibly be made. In its sphere the NAACP was seizing the opportunity to "take on the old South" in much the same way as Darrow himself had seized an opportunity—manufactured it, even—to take it on at Dayton six years before. It should be mentioned that, wretched though the treatment of the Scottsboro boys had been, the conditions of the female accusers were as sad as those of the accused, and the background investigation conducted by the ACLU into conditions in Huntsville, Alabama, where the girls came from, revealed simply amazing circumstances. At least one of the accusers had the courage and decency to admit the falsehood of her accusations at a later date.

Just as the Scottsboro case fizzled out from Darrow's point of view, an entirely different opportunity presented itself. The relatives of Lieutenant Thomas Massie, U.S.N., approached Darrow asking him to defend against a charge of homicide of a native Hawaiian. The case had arisen out of an incident at the naval base in Hawaii where Massie had been stationed while undergoing submarine training.

Massie was a Kentuckian from a comfortable but modest background, who would have gone to the United States Military Academy if an acceptance from Annapolis had not come through first. At the Naval Academy, a penniless but ambitious cadet, he gained an entrée into Washington society and met Thalia Fortescue, a pretty but troubled adolescent on bad terms with both her parents.

In 1927, when she was sixteen, Thalia ran away—to Thomas Massie. She had not gone to him because she pined for him, but merely to escape her parents; it was an act of adolescent rebellion. But it looked as though everyone might gain if Massie would marry her. The parents could rid themselves of a difficult daughter; Thalia could rid herself of difficult parents; and Massie would climb the social ladder several rungs by marrying into the Fortescue family. But Tom Massie found that the marriage he had entered in the hope that it would advance him socially was doing rather the reverse in the wake of Thalia's profoundly unsociable bent. She was a misfit in the gregarious naval life of Pearl Harbor. Arguments, awkward silences, and unspoken reproaches became the common coin of their marriage together, especially after Thalia suffered a miscarriage. Massie tried to deal with this situation as a gentleman; for while he could not alter the character of his wife, he could do his best to keep up appearances. He liked to attend those social occasions to which he could persuade Thalia to

---

*It was not until 1963 that the Supreme Court held conclusively that the NAACP's practice did not constitute unlawful soliciting of legal business.

accompany him, as if all were going well. It was a pretense, and recognized as such by his brother officers, but it was not the first time that they had seen a young couple's marriage flounder in Pearl Harbor.

On Saturday evening, September 12, 1931, Massie had an invitation to join an informal party of naval couples at the Ala Wai Inn, at the point where Kalakaua Avenue met the Ala Wai Canal. He wanted to go; Thalia did not. After much bickering, she capitulated. In company with other naval personnel they drove to the Ala Wai Inn, which was already hot and crowded. In the mêlée Tom and Thalia parted, each probably glad to avoid the other. Tom joined a boisterous party of classmates from Annapolis. Thalia left the dance floor for a private room where a dinner party among some acquaintances was just ending. In less than an hour she had become involved in a violent altercation with another Navy lieutenant whom she slapped hard across the face, ending the dinner peremptorily. The guests left.

Shortly after 11:00 P.M. Thalia, finding herself without company, decided to take a walk outside. There is no reason to think that she was slipping away to a prearranged rendezvous, though that rumor made the rounds subsequently. Three-quarters of an hour later, when her husband went to look for her, he was baffled. He concluded that she must have gone on to someone's house for a nightcap and proceeded in company with friends to the most likely home he could think of, that of "Red" Rigby and his wife; but neither the Rigbys nor Thalia was there. It was nearly 2:00 A.M. when he asked to use the phone to call his own home, and Thalia answered, obviously in a dreadful state. "Come home at once," she implored. "Something terrible has happened!"

He was there within minutes. Her face was bruised and bleeding, and she was hysterical. It was only then that she told her husband that she had been raped by several natives. She had been deserted, managed to find her way to the nearest road, and had flagged down a passing car whose driver had, at her request, driven her straight home. The horror of the charges and his wife's serious state did not distract Massie from his duty: he called the police, asking them to come immediately. But the Hawaiian police were not the most efficient in the world and that Saturday night they had some reason to be confused. Massie had reported on the telephone that a woman had been "assaulted"— and that was not the first assault complaint they had that night. Finally three policemen went to Massie's address. When they heard Thalia's story, the case took on a much more serious complexion. They proceeded to interrogate her, but it became obvious before they got far that she was in need of medical attention; her jaw hurt so much that she could not speak. Besides, it was standard procedure that a medical examination should be given to the victim of an alleged rape, so Thalia, together with the police and her husband, went to the Queen's Hospital at once. There she was ascertained to have a broken jaw but not the usual signs of rape, especially on the scale of which she had complained.

But at the hospital a confusion arose that was to have much greater significance. In the comings and goings of the police in the emergency room, the automobile license number given by another woman, Mrs. Peebles, was repeated in Thalia's hearing several times. After she was treated and released, she went to police headquarters. There, for the first time, she claimed to recollect the license number of the car that *her* assailants had used—it differed from that given by Mrs. Peebles by only one digit. This reinforced the assumption already made by the police that Mrs. Peebles and Mrs. Massie had been victimized by the same men. The driver of the car with the number given by Mrs. Peebles had already been identified and rounded up. His name was Horace Ida, and he had been driving his sister's car earlier that night; he did not deny that he had been present when the incident with Mrs. Peebles took place. He was brought in for identification by Thalia, who, after asking him a few questions, tentatively identified him as one of her assailants. Ida vehemently denied any knowledge of Thalia's attack, and after some prevarication, admitted he had been accompanied by David Takai, Henry Chang, Joe Kahahawai, and Benny Ahakuelo. He had not revealed this at first, he said, because he did not want to get his friends into trouble.

The police tracked down the other four men without much difficulty, and interrogated each of them separately. All told the same story regarding the altercation with Agnes Peebles, but all steadfastly denied any knowledge of the assault of Thalia Massie. Furthermore, according to their own account of their late-night actions, they could not have been at the scene of her assault at the relevant time. If they were liars, they were very skilled ones, who had concocted an amazingly convincing alibi. All of them were examined at the Emergency Hospital and none showed any signs of having taken part in a rape. With this evidence the five young men would ordinarily have been well on the way to exoneration, but Kahahawai and Ahakuelo both had criminal records, and they were both excellent boxers. Moreover, Thalia had made a positive identification of Chang as one of her attackers. This posed a dilemma for the police. All the men said they had been together. Thalia said she could identify Chang, but not the others. It was decided to hold them all. The most powerful factor influencing the police was not the available evidence, but the confident assumption of the Navy personnel that the men apprehended were guilty. For the naval establishment was up in arms about the incident, and wanted summary justice. Even in this strained and excited climate of opinion, however, there were cooler heads. Obviously something terrible had happened; Thalia's wounds were real enough. But was it rape, and were the five boys guilty of it? In quiet private conversations away from the immediate parties, the answers to both questions seemed less than a certainty.

In the midst of this, Thalia's mother and sister arrived in Honolulu. They had been summoned by Thomas Massie when disaster first struck, but his cable gave no hint that the attack had been a sexual one. Mrs. Fortescue's arrival in Honolulu sealed the fate of Tom Massie and was destined to change the course of events much for the worse. If Massie found his wife difficult to handle, he found her mother quite impossible. She took charge as soon as she stepped ashore, reducing all the other participants to mere acolytes, and she became outraged when she heard of the sexual aspect of the assault. Massie had already suffered greatly and was not strong; the last thing he wanted was a contretemps with Mrs. Fortescue. He let her have her way. It was doubtful that he could have stopped her even if he had wished. But in the stress of events, he could scarcely think straight. When Thalia was recovering slowly from her broken jaw, the doctors became more concerned about Tom's health than hers: he was clearly headed for a breakdown. As an officer, his profession was leadership; but as an unhappy husband faced with a difficult wife and an imperious mother-in-law, his part was submission. So Mrs. Fortescue took firm command. She had the confident recklessness of a mad general and the moral certainty of God—and she led her group into deep, deep trouble. Among other things, she ruined her son-in-law's career by obtaining his cooperation in a venture that put him, for the first time, clearly in the wrong. She transformed a relatively trivial incident, which could have remained a local affair, into one that would attract national, and even world attention. And she recruited Tom Massie and two sailors into a kidnapping that ended in murder.

Mrs. Fortescue entertained none of the doubts that circulated round the island and set it in an uproar. She was sure that her daughter had been raped, and she was sure that the men being held for the crime were guilty. By Monday, November 16, when the trial was to begin, the native defendants had been provided with two competent and well-respected lawyers—Territorial Senator William Heen and William B. Pittman, brother of the U.S. senator from Nevada. Of course, they had not been in a position to pay for this representation themselves, but sympathetic forces on the island had seen the danger that they would be railroaded to conviction by Navy pressure and racial prejudice on slender evidence.

It was quite certain that Mrs. Fortescue and the Navy identified their interests with those of the prosecution. Rear Admiral Yates Stirling went to lobby both the governor and the Attorney General to urge the importation of the best possible legal talent to prosecute the case. Thomas Massie himself procured extra legal talent to assist the public prosecutor. The trial lasted three weeks, and the jury deliberated for ninety-seven hours but could not reach a verdict. This was immediately interpreted by the Navy and by the Massie-Fortescues as a defeat for justice. Admiral Stirling believed that the mixed jury had divided on racial lines, saying, "the defendants were not men who might be given the benefit of a reasonable doubt."[4] In reality the evidence on the charge of rape was slim, and it is in many ways surprising that the verdict was not one of outright acquittal rather than a disagreement. The crucial difference between these results was that it was still open to the prosecution to retry the case.

In naval circles, feeling ran very high against the defendants. Mrs. Fortescue twice asked the trial judge to keep the defendants in jail by refusing them bail, which he told her he had no power to do. A gang of naval men tracked down Horace Ida, who was at liberty, and severely beat him up. The Massie-Fortescues were deeply convinced that a retrial should be had, because now the public record showed that Thalia had not been believed under oath.[5] It was a further slur on her honor, already badly tarnished by island gossip. But the authorities were extremely reluctant to go before a jury again without more evidence. Unlike the Massies, they did not attribute the jury's disagreement to the incompetence of the prosecution, but rather to the inherent weakness of the case. There was the chance that a retrial would result in total acquittal. Just one thing would alter matters: a confession by one of the accused.

This intelligence was received glumly by Massie and Mrs. Fortescue, for none of the defendants showed any sign of confessing. They had throughout been vehement in their denials, and for that matter were thought by observers to be extremely good witnesses on their own behalf. But over Christmas and New Year Mrs. Fortescue formulated a plan to see justice done. She must arrange to extort a confession. After January 1 she became a woman possessed, bent upon a mission which, though wholly futile legally, clearly gave her then and later enormous psychological satisfaction. She determined to abduct Kahahawai and force him to confess. He, like the other defendants, had to report at the courthouse every day. She found out at what time, and procured a photograph of him from the *State-Bulletin* offices to make sure she would recognize him. She studied the lay of the land around the courthouse square. She arranged to dismiss her maid for the day, so that her house would be available as a prison for Kahahawai. She drew up a crude imitation of a summons to Kahahawai to appear in the name of Major Ross, who had recently been appointed commander of the Territorial Police. To this Massie added a paper gold star from a diploma of his, to give the superficial impression of authenticity. He also procured the assistance of two sailors, Edward J. Lord and Albert O. Jones, both members of the submarine base boxing team, who could help overcome Kahahawai's resistance, if any. The date of the abduction was set for January 8. On January 7 Lord and Jones rented a Buick sedan.

According to the participants, the aim of the abduction was to obtain a signed confession that would "vindicate" the Massies; but there was an obvious risk that in the course of attempting to extract a confession, considerable violence might develop. All those involved (including Mrs. Fortescue) were armed with revolvers or pistols. Feeling against Kahahawai ran very high. Mrs. Fortescue wrote in her narrative of the case: "All now depends on finding Kahahawai. I take his picture from my purse. Again I study that brutal, repulsive black face."[6]

If evidence were needed that Massie had been badly affected by his wife's experience, it is provided by the way he fell in with his mother-in-law's scheme for kidnapping Kahahawai. He knew it was criminal and could not have seriously believed that any statement extracted from the man would have legal value. Kidnapping was a felony, which the Navy could not overlook even if the civilian authorities did not prosecute him. And the plan called for him to solicit the collaboration of two enlisted men under his control—a startling abuse of his rank and arguably a court-martial offense in itself. It was true that no order had been given to the sailors, or coercion used. But reprisal and lynch law were in the air. The naval base had made outrage *de rigueur* for officers and men alike; an atmosphere had been created in which unmistakable, if oblique, encouragement was being given to resort to extralegal means to redress the wrong as a matter not only of individual but naval honor. The request for aid amounted to incitement. Massie, as an officer ostensibly seeking a favor from two ratings, had the weight of naval opinion as an invisible but powerful ally, and the chances were rather strong that Jones and Lord would not refuse. He knew this. Yet, in awe of Mrs. Fortescue and unhinged by the strain of dealing with his wife's predicament, he joined in a tragic madness that would bring with it much more attention than the story of his wife's assault had done.

On Thursday, January 8, Lord, Jones, and Thomas Massie slept the night at Mrs. Fortescue's, and rose early on Friday morning, determined to catch Kahahawai as he reported to the courthouse at 8:00 A.M. Massie, disguised as a chauffeur, drove the Buick to the courthouse, and Mrs. Fortescue followed in her Durant. Just before eight Kahahawai appeared, in the company of a cousin, Edward Ulii. Jones stopped him, saying: "Major Ross wants to see you," and bundled him into the back of the Buick, which drove off leaving Ulii standing puzzled on the square.

It did not take long for Ulii to realize that something seriously irregular had just happened. He reported what he had seen to a policeman on duty in the court building, who suggested, reasonably enough, that he check with Major Ross himself. Ross, at the armory, immediately suspected that the abductors who had used his name in vain were the Massies and he alerted the island authorities to search for a Buick sedan. Only a short time later it was spotted on Waialae Avenue by Detective George Harbottle, who gave chase and identified himself to the occupants as a police officer, though in view of who they were and the fact that he had been the first policeman to interview Thalia Massie after her assault, it was probably unnecessary. He had caught Thomas Massie, Mrs. Fortescue, and Edward Lord. There was one other captive— Joseph Kahahawai—but he was dead, bundled up in the rear of the Buick on the floor. A short while later Jones was found drunk at Mrs. Fortescue's rented home. Dried blood, pieces of rope, and a stained towel were found there, and he too was arrested.

In custody, none of the prisoners gave the authorities any aid. Massie offered only his name and rank, declining to say anything more. The others merely evaded and rambled, but the result was the same for all. They were charged with murder in the first degree. The autopsy report on Kahahawai showed that the cause of death was a shot in the left lung from a .32 gun.

Even in these dire straits, the suspects were in a better position than most, for it was arranged that they should be held captive by the Navy, to be produced on demand of the territorial authorities. Their time as prisoners was spent in relatively congenial circumstances aboard a decommissioned hulk lying in Pearl Harbor, the U.S.S. *Alton.* There they enjoyed privileges that few other murder suspects before or since have had. They received newspapers, letters, and telegrams at will, and were even given the opportunity to speak to the press, though this last turned out to be a mistake for the defendants as much as for the authorities, since Mrs. Fortescue said some thoroughly unwise things.

As soon as the news was reported, an avalanche of congratulatory messages poured in to the prisoners from the mainland. In particular, Mrs. Fortescue's friends seemed to regard it as a foregone conclusion that she had arranged for Kahahawai's killing, and that it was a subject for jubilation. By contrast, the mood in Hawaii itself was uncertain. The Navy confined all men to base and there was some fear, which turned out to be unfounded, that the funeral of Kahahawai would spark demonstrations. But the most bitter aspect of the publicity from the Hawaiians' viewpoint was the scarcely disguised innuendo that the native population was given to molesting white women in a way that made the alleged rape of Thalia Massie a typical incident.

Now that the formal processes of law were moving against the prisoners, the need for a defense loomed large. Massie had consulted with his local lawyer, Frank Thompson, but felt that he needed greater support. In this he was encouraged by his sympathetic naval jailer, Lieutenant Old, who believed that a legal luminary from the mainland would best be recruited. It was apparently he who came up with the name of Clarence Darrow, with which all the prisoners concurred.

It was all very well for Old to make plans to engage the best legal talent to defend his friend, but it was another matter to find the wherewithal to pay for it. Mrs. Fortescue's haughty manner and aristocratic self-confidence turned out not to be backed by cash—she could scarcely raise $10,000. It must have been an ordeal for her to approach friends on the mainland for financial aid, but she chose to do so rather than rely upon local counsel. Thumbing through the many cables of support and commiseration, she decided on Mrs. Eva Stotesbury of Philadelphia, who had earlier telegrammed:

> Dear Gracie: This brings you my love and heartiest sympathy, also my admiration and respect for your magnificent courage in this overwhelming misfortune. I would have done the same in your place and so would any other good mother. If there is anything I can do for you and yours, count upon me.[7]

Mrs. Stotesbury was in Havana when Mrs. Fortescue sought her aid. But she asked her son, lawyer James Cromwell, to do what he could to help. And in the third week of February Cromwell contacted Darrow through Dudley Field Malone.

The overtures on behalf of Mrs. Fortescue came at a time when Darrow was counting his money and lamenting how little of it there was. The year 1932 was the nadir of his finances, and it appears that he was close to the line. That was the year in which he was unable to repay $1,000 to the NAACP. He saw his retirement disappear as the national economy went from bad to worse. He could not pay debts and had to search round for new ways of raising money. Ruby, writing to Harry Elmer Barnes, made the situation sound grim indeed:

> *Not a thing* for C[larence] and only a few spools of thread for myself for making
> over my old *really ragged* clothes. Have turned over my worn-out coat-collars,
> and have not had a new hat for four years, (winter and summer combined).
> . . . We get along with what others would not consider good enough to give away.[8]

Altogether Darrow's fortunes were at a low ebb. In spite of his age and the
fact that he was definitely not well, he needed paid work badly.

When Lieutenant Old suggested Clarence Darrow as the right defense attorney for Mrs. Fortescue, he was not producing a premeditated plan. He realized
that his friends were in a mess and that they needed the best available help.
Darrow's name came to his mind as it would have to any American thinking
of well-known trial lawyers—Darrow was the most famous of them all. He
probably had only a vague notion about Darrow's age, and did not realize that
he was already effectively retired from the practice of law. But there was some
irony in the approach. The Fortescues' many ill-advised statements to the press
made it rather obvious that their views on race, among other things, did not
exactly coincide with those of their prospective counsel. The defendants were
by now justifying their slaying of Kahahawai on a racial theory and were
saying things that were certain to intensify the latent animosity between the
races. It seemed exceedingly unlikely that Darrow and his would-be clients
would see eye to eye.

Probably Darrow would not even have been prepared to consider the matter
but for his acute financial difficulties. In any event, he did not feel that he was
so desperate that he must enter the case. When first approached, it was the
opportunity to visit Hawaii that attracted him as much as the fee. Yet he
initially turned the case down, not because of his disapproval of the defendants'
moral position, but for fear that his own previous pronouncements would
redound to their detriment. On March 5 he wrote in a letter to Barnes:

> Without expressing any opinion on the matter I learned that one who tried this
> case could scarcely avoid discussing race conflict in the trial of the case. I had
> so long and decidedly fought for the negro and all so-called "foreigners" that I
> could not put myself in a position where I might be compelled to take a position,
> even in a case, at variance with what I had felt and stood for. . . .[9]

And he sent the defendants a copy of his argument in the Detroit Sweet trial,
as published by the NAACP, to emphasize the apparent inconsistency between
his views and theirs.

No record exists of the persuasion used between March 7 and March 10 to
reconcile Mrs. Fortescue to Darrow's attitude, but miraculously it was done.
Possibly Thomas Massie himself was able to act as mediator on the question.
Word was sent to Darrow that he would have complete control of the strategy
of the defense, that the defendants recognized the possibility of being hindered
by his past expression of views on the race question, and that they accepted
that danger and nevertheless wished him to represent them. On March 12,
Darrow reported to Barnes: "After a day or two they wrote me that they
thought I was right in my position on the race question, and they wanted that

attitude maintained in court, and all would be as I wished. Which left nothing for me to do but go."[10]

Immediately Darrow had to deal with an avalanche of reproachful mail from friends and strangers alike,* who were scandalized that he had apparently sold out to the forces of reaction. He was taken to task for betraying a reputation built up over fifty years for being on the side of the angels; the fact that he had many times in his long career defended clients who did not have a respectable progressive argument in their favor was entirely overlooked. Darrow was caught in the predicament of any lawyer who has professed only to take "just" cases. Having for so long proclaimed that he passed judgment on the worthiness of his clients before he accepted them, he had to explain why the Massies qualified. The lurid facts of the case and the opinions of the defendants as reported in the press had convinced many of his friends that the Massie-Fortescues represented much that was deplorable in the contemporary United States. That Darrow would lend his skills to their defense seemed totally uncharacteristic. It was believed that he was committing a kind of treachery; that his undeniable talents were being used for inexcusable ends— as Oscar Cargill put it, speaking of Darrow's career, "Fairly won prestige was used, perhaps unconsciously, in ways that bred disrespect for law and condoned anti-social acts of impulse."[11]

When Harry Elmer Barnes himself wrote very critically on the matter, both Clarence and Ruby were stung to reply at length. Ruby's position was particularly difficult because she had grave reservations about her husband's entry into the case. She loyally justified his decision:

> C.D., as no one else, should be able to go to Honolulu and handle this case in such a manner that—as an outcome—there would be established a bridge between the white and brown folk, a new understanding, a better code of conduct on the part of the brown people, back and forth, a lessening of that element termed "color-line" in the minds of both. . . . I am sure that C.D. has been made to feel that *he might* do a *great kindness* to *the natives by going,* and doing the job HIS WAY and thus preventing some lawyer of the other "school"—or what is it?—from going there and stirring up a worse hatred between the two kinds of people.

But she went on: "I feel dreadfully uncomfortable about it all! I can hardly take a positive stand against whatever decision is to be or not to be. . . ." In fact, the decision whether or not he should participate in the trial precipitated a minor domestic crisis in the Darrow household. Darrow was by now an old man, his health was none too good, and Ruby appreciated far less than he the true dimension of their financial plight. "I am gingerly about indicating that I might have definite ideas of my own on any point arising in our little family; after all, I am living with this man, and want to go on to *the end* of our *remnant* of life together, of course," she wrote, indicating her fear that the exertion might kill him, "and should hesitate to even hint that any notion of mine

---

*Some of it addressed simply: "Clarence Darrow, Chicago."

should be weighed against any of his. I just never do that. It wouldn't flatter C.D., and I am anxious not to offend him, in my old-fashioned wifely way."[12]

Darrow was perhaps less concerned with posterity than his friends were. Only three months before he had written ruminatively of his early interest in the labor movement and the equal distribution of wealth, confessing: "As the years have passed, I find my zeal in this and many other causes has gradually disappeared."[13] He could still burn with moral fervor on occasions, but there had always been more of the pragmatist—opportunist, even—in him than some of his acquaintances discerned. He had not spent a lifetime in the public view without learning how to handle such things adroitly. He wanted to see the Hawaiian Isles: "I had never been to that part of the Pacific; I had heard of and read about its unusual charm, and longed to sometime see it, but whenever I could go so far away, for so long a time, I found myself embarking for Europe instead. . . ." But perhaps the most important reason for his taking the case was one he could least explain to his wife. Since he had ceased active practice and stayed home more, time had hung heavy on his hands—he was bored. Although he had spent most of his life looking forward to the time when he could discard the law, when finally he did so, he missed it: "So, altogether, loafing is not so ideal as it seemed to one who was anxious to welcome it as a dear dream come true. Four years of freedom from work, seemingly doing as I pleased, gradually grew monotonous and dreary. I was tired of resting." Often he had complained that the law was a jealous mistress whom he wished to discard. Once he had done so, he found that he was thrown back into the arms of his wife and wanted his mistress again. No doubt it was a delicate matter to tell his wife that he did not find it entirely satisfying to be at home, especially since he was seventy-five and Ruby had a tendency to treat him as a semi-invalid. But the Massie case provided a chance of adding some spice to life which Darrow felt he sorely needed.

As for explanations to his friends, Darrow did not want to confide quite how serious his finances were, though he hinted at how handy the fee would be, writing to Barnes on March 12: ". . . of course, I have occasionally in the past represented people of wealth, and there have always been criticisms when I have done this; especially was this true in the Loeb-Leopold case. I don't know what I should have done if now and then a fairly well-to-do client had not come my way; the ravens have never called on me."[14] It was Darrow's confident expectation that his new clients were the kind to whom "money was no object." In this respect, he was wrong. He was more explicit in his memoirs when, explaining his interest in the newspaper reports of the case, he wrote: "Then, too, the so-called 'depression' had swept away practically all the savings that I thought I had for keeping me comfortable to the end, and I needed the fee. This was not at all large, but it was sufficient."

It may not have been large, but it was more than the defendants, including Mrs. Fortescue, could afford. Jones and Lord were totally unable to contribute. The result was that a collection had to be taken on the naval base, causing the case to be further identified as a naval rather than a personal trial. Darrow wanted $30,000, and his doctor insisted that he be allowed an assistant. Dudley Field Malone offered to take the job for $10,000, but even this was too much and Darrow was asked to find an assistant who would come cheap. Malone suggested that he consult "Wild Bill" Donovan, the hero of World War I who was later to found the Office of Strategic Services and was then building a law practice in New York. Donovan in turn recommended his young partner, George S. Leisure, who had returned from conducting litigation in Hawaii on behalf of the Castle family only a short time before. Darrow, by now anxious to settle the matter, thereupon telephoned Leisure. It so happened that Leisure —though a very different sort of character—was an admirer of Darrow's. He had taken his undergraduate education at the University of Chicago before going to Harvard Law School, and had known of Darrow's achievements and reputation in Chicago, but had never met him. It was therefore natural that when he picked up his phone and heard a voice at the other end say: "Good morning, this is Clarence Darrow speaking. I was wondering whether you might be free to join me at the Colony for lunch to discuss your working on a case of some importance shortly to be tried in Hawaii?" he should assume that he was the victim of a practical joke. However, within the hour Leisure made his way uptown to meet the hoaxer. He had only a pang of doubt as he strolled through the midtown throng. Could it possibly be that the call was genuine? At that moment a lank figure appearing in the restaurant doorway answered the question. Darrow was accompanied by the mayor of New York, Jimmy Walker. Over lunch Darrow proceeded to explain that he had been engaged in the Massie case. Leisure did not need to be told the essential facts any more than anyone else who read the newspapers, but Darrow told him anyhow. He regaled him with his plans, various theories, and his view on the racial situation in Hawaii from soup through to coffee. Then Walker suggested that the three of them should attend a matinee performance of George Gershwin's *Of Thee I Sing.* By the end of the performance Leisure had agreed to assist his idol virtually without fee (though he had not consulted his partners to seek their permission), and it was arranged that he would rendezvous with Darrow and his wife in Chicago within a week.

Throughout the boat trip to Honolulu Darrow steadfastly declined to say anything about the case he had taken on, in spite of repeated questions from journalists along the way. Darrow handled them well; he told them nothing of importance while at the same time giving them some copy about prohibition. The journey provided Leisure with his first real opportunity to observe Darrow in action. He was impressed with how much the old man had his wits about him, but he was also impressed that he was indeed old. It became clear that Darrow knew rather little about the clients he was engaged to defend. It appeared to Leisure that Darrow expected his defense to rest in large measure upon the mistakes of the prosecution. Surprisingly little work of any description was done on the voyage out to Hawaii, and when the party disembarked on March 24 to be met with the formalities of baggage declarations and the traditional flowered necklaces, it was still an open question what tack the defense would take. Avoiding the press, Darrow went directly to meet his clients.

The Leisures had caught some of the vacation spirit Darrow had shown while traveling to Hawaii, and wanted to check into a fashionable hotel near the beach, but on his return from seeing his new clients, Darrow vetoed that idea. Instead, they all registered at the Alexander Young Hotel in downtown Honolulu, near the courthouse and favored by commercial travelers much more than tourists. It was austere and unromantic, and not quite what Mrs. Leisure had envisioned, but it had the virtue of being cheap.

Darrow had no sooner arrived in Hawaii than he announced that he had settled upon his defense strategy, but this announcement was at best premature and at worst sheer bluff. The number of plausible defenses was extremely limited, as any lawyer could tell from reading the newspapers. The nearest possible defense was provocation. But that would not aid the accused because the provocation must be immediate and grave; here Massie had not killed "in hot blood," as the law required, but had planned the kidnapping carefully. It is unlikely that Darrow had finally decided on a line of defense (which turned out to be temporary insanity) so soon after his meeting with the accuseds for several reasons. First, it was widely believed that Darrow's decision to make such a plea was influenced by Dr. John Porter, the gynecologist who attended Thalia Massie and who had examined her after she was assaulted. Second, a plea of insanity was quite incompatible with Mrs. Fortescue's insistence upon her family's honor and for that matter would do no good to Massie's future career, in the Navy or out. But third and most important, a plea of temporary insanity would involve considerable extra expense, and he could not possibly rely upon his already debt-ridden clients to underwrite this. Darrow wanted to have two psychiatrists brought from the mainland on behalf of the defense. He could produce an unanswerable argument in favor of doing so: if it was worthwhile getting him from the mainland for the advice he gave, his advice must be followed. So he proposed the retention of Thomas Orbison and Edward Huntington Williams, who had earlier testified in the murder trial of Mrs. Judd.* The defendants were talked round to this scheme, and the cost was ultimately covered by another appeal to the Pearl Harbor base. Once this was done, the defense arranged to have the two doctors embark for Honolulu in secrecy so that by the time they arrived, the prosecution would have no chance to import rebuttal witnesses even if it wished to do so.

The proceedings began on Monday, April 4, with selection of a jury. But here the first of many peculiarities in Darrow's situation came to the fore. His theory of jury picking, as already mentioned, was entirely based on the quick classification of prospective jurors into stereotypes, which were then used as a yardstick of their desirability. He liked jurors who were Irish, English,

---

*Winnie Ruth Judd was tried in Phoenix, Arizona, for the double murder of one of her doctor husband's female patients and a nurse in 1932. Her defense, based on psychiatric testimony by Drs. Orbison and Huntington Williams (the same ones used to defend Massie), was insanity. She was convicted on May 11—Van Slingerland 1966, p. 190.

German, Jewish, and male, but avoided Scandinavians, Presbyterians, Baptists, and women. Yet these categories had almost no relevance to the Hawaiian population of Asiatic descent, and even those supposedly European were of mixed national origin. Darrow himself apparently saw the futility of applying his normal rules, and after the jury had been chosen (including five Chinese), he whispered to George Leisure that the defense might as well concede defeat. Of course, he did not mean that literally, and when on the following Monday the prosecution was opened by John C. Kelley, Darrow was determined to give nothing away, even the advantage of surprise. He reserved his opening statement.

Kelley proved the events leading up to the killing of Kahahawai with painstaking detail, taking most of the week. It appeared that his case had been most carefully prepared and was inherently a very strong one. He did not seek to show which of the four defendants had fired the shot that killed Kahahawai, but he was not required by Hawaiian law to do so; all were equally guilty of homicide.

When the prosecution closed its case, the excitement of expectation was in the air. The courtroom was packed with people wishing to hear Darrow. But he once more seized the benefit of surprise by waiving his opening statement and immediately calling Thomas Massie to the stand. It was from this point that the full strategy of the defense was revealed, because after some unimportant preliminaries, Darrow invited Massie to give his own account of the night on which his wife had been assaulted. Kelley objected to this evidence on the ground that it was only relevant if the defense intended to rely upon insanity and therefore the defendants' mental state was in issue. Darrow said that was the aim of the defense. Kelley then asked which of the four defendants was to be shown to be insane, to which Darrow responded, "The one who shot the pistol," but without saying who that was. Since all four defendants were equally guilty under Hawaiian law, they ought equally to be innocent if there was a defense.

Kelley could see the trap being sprung and tried to avoid it. He asked that the Territory's expert witnesses be permitted to examine the defendant who Darrow claimed had fired the shot, but Darrow refused, pointing out that Hawaiian law did not oblige him to submit the defendants to examination by rebuttal witnesses. In retrospect, it was a serious error of the prosecution that it had not examined the four accused psychiatrically before trial; but that would not have been easy while they were in Navy custody, and Kelley had not been in charge of the prosecution at an earlier stage. The judge allowed Darrow to continue eliciting the harrowing details of Thalia's assault from her husband. The effect was just as Darrow intended—Massie's anguished sincerity brought him pity and sympathy, and many in the courtroom cried as he recounted the ordeal.

To consolidate the defense's newly improved position, Darrow spent that Thursday evening with the newsmen, when he imbibed a sufficient quantity of the local *okolehao* to prevent him from appearing the next day in court, which had to be adjourned until Saturday. It was indicative of Darrow's casualness that he would take this risk and one of a number of signs noted by his junior counsel that he was not overconscientious. His eminence allowed him to get away with it; the lapse could be explained by his failing health. But it also revealed his blasé attitude. Part of the reason he had taken the case was to see Hawaii: he could enjoy the holiday spirit even while conducting a murder trial.

When Darrow reopened on Saturday, he made a statement that, from a less revered figure, might have been regarded as a sleight of hand designed to mislead the court. In order to set right any misunderstanding, he said, he wanted to assure the court that the evidence would show that Thomas Massie "held the gun in his hand from which the fatal shot was fired." This did not amount to an admission as to who fired the shot that killed Kahahawai, though it sounded as if it did, and it is difficult to see that it had any other purpose than to confuse. It appeared that Darrow did indeed succeed in confusing both the prosecutor and himself, and he never clarified his real meaning, even after the judge had tried to pin him down. But when Massie's testimony resumed, it became clear that Darrow had been laying the groundwork for Massie's statement that he had no recollection of Kahahawai's actual killing. He remembered interrogating Kahahawai in Mrs. Fortescue's house after the abduction, with a .32 automatic supplied by Jones in his hand. After considerable questioning, Massie testified, Kahahawai admitted that he and his gang had beaten and raped Thalia. Darrow asked him: "Do you remember what you did?" Massie replied, "No, sir."

"Do you know what became of the gun?"

"No, I do not, Mr. Darrow."

Darrow asked a further poignant question: "Do you know what became of you?" In deep emotion, Massie answered, "No, sir." He remembered nothing thereafter until he was in police custody.[15]

It came as no surprise to anybody that Kelley was prepared to take an aggressive cross-examination. He asked Massie if he were proud of being a Southerner. Darrow objected that the question was prejudicial in implying that Massie was racially prejudiced. The judge ruled the question out of order. It did not take long for Kelley to confront Massie with some of the unwise statements made by Mrs. Fortescue to the press after she had been arrested, which he used to good effect. But on all crucial points about the killing of Kahahawai Massie consistently protested that he had no recollection, and on this inconclusive note the proceedings were adjourned for the weekend.

As things stood, the defense position was not promising even before the prosecution had made much headway with the cross-examination of the first defense witness. Massie claimed to be suffering from amnesia regarding the actual killing of Kahahawai, but that was not insanity in the eyes of the law. Furthermore the story he had told on the witness stand amounted to an admission that the essential facts alleged by the prosecution were true. All told the Massie-Fortescues had no cause for jubilation at the end of the second week of proceedings.

When cross-examination resumed on Monday, April 11, the ammunition in Kelley's hands was soon spent, though to some effect. He extracted from Massie two denials: first, that he had ever been implicated in a kidnapping plot before; and second, that he had heard some ill-chosen statements made by Admiral Pratt on the attitude of American men to the rape of their women by Hawaiians, which strongly suggested that the admiral condoned or even encouraged immediate reprisal against the natives without waiting for the sanction of the law. Kelley was able to show that Massie and Thalia (then still his fiancée) had been arrested in 1927 on Long Island for wheeling off a baby in a carriage that had been left outside by its mother. The charges were later dropped, but Massie's emphatic denial on the witness stand damaged his credibility—the arrest was not something he was likely to have forgotten. Similarly it seemed far-fetched that Admiral Pratt's statements, inspired by and apropos Massie's wife's ordeal, should not have reached his ears. But Massie insisted that he had not heard of them until after the killing of Kahahawai. Of course, Massie's credibility had a bearing on whether the jury believed his claim to remember nothing about what happened at the crucial time. Kelley, in insinuating that the killing had been in accord with the admiral's view, was also casting doubt on the claim that Kahahawai's killing was not premeditated.

The next important witnesses after Massie were the two imported psychiatrists to testify that, at the time of his participation in the kidnapping, he was insane. It can have only confirmed Darrow's low opinion of experts that they testified as the defense wanted them to—though of course he did not express that opinion to the jury. With minor variations both conveniently suggested that Massie, though insane at the time of the kidnapping, was now once more sane, and Williams labeled his diagnosis "chemical insanity," brought on by sudden changes in body chemistry in the excitement.

Then Thalia was called. Darrow asked her to recount her sad tale, beginning with the incident at the Ala Wai Inn, but the prosecution successfully objected. The judge allowed her only to recount *what she had said* at the time of the incidents leading to Kahahawai's death. Under Darrow's questioning she gave a sob-racked account of what had happened, ending with Jones coming to her to tell her that Kahahawai had been killed. The pathos of her crying and the circumstances of her assault had a huge effect in the courtroom, with many of the audience sharing her tears of grief. Darrow sat down.

When Kelley started to cross-examine her, however, her demeanor changed astoundingly from pathos to anger before he had asked any questions. The cross-examination swiftly reached an impasse of extraordinary dimensions. Kelley had in his possession a psychological self-analysis made by Thalia when she was a part-time student at the University of Hawaii. He put it to her, asking, "Is this your handwriting?" As she was passed the document, she became a woman possessed. Deliberately, she tore it into little pieces. "I refuse to say whether that is my handwriting or not," she hissed. "What right have you to bring this into a public court?"

The effect was stunning. It was obvious that no one—judge, prosecution, or defense—had expected this. Thalia stumbled away from the witness stand toward the hapless Massie, and as she reached him, cried out hysterically: "What right has he got to say that I don't love you? Everybody knows I love you."[16]

The situation was extraordinary. Thalia had been in blatant contempt of court in destroying the document handed to her by Kelley, whatever it contained; and as a result of her hysterical outburst, many people would obviously be likely to doubt her credibility. Kelley announced that he did not have a copy of the document and therefore could not give any further clue as to its contents. That was not likely, but Kelley was smart enough to know that he could not achieve a better effect than Thalia already had. As for Darrow, he must by this time have recognized—if he had not earlier—that the defense was lost. In all his experience he had not seen anything so bizarre in court. He told reporters afterwards, "I never saw anything like it. I've seen some pretty good court scenes but nothing like that one. I was pretty limp when it was all over." He decided not to take further chances with his madcap clients, and announced he had no further witnesses.

Kelley now had only his rebuttal testimony about the state of mind of Massie to produce. By this time he had imported some experts from the mainland to counter Orbison and Williams, but of course they had missed the trial and Darrow would not allow them to examine Massie, so their testimony was of even less value than their opponents'. Darrow treated it as such, contenting himself with asking Dr. Paul Bowers, appearing for the prosecution, only one question: "Doctor, I assume you have either been paid or expect to be paid for coming down here and giving your testimony?" The doctor replied affirmatively. As for Dr. Faus, the city physician whom Kelley called, under Darrow's cross-examination he admitted to very little psychiatric experience. The testimony in the entire case ended with Darrow's distrustful probing of the knowledge, clinical assumptions, and judgments of the medical witnesses.

The next day—the seventeenth day of the trial, calculated from the beginning of jury selection—the jury speeches began. It had been arranged that there would be two on each side, with the prosecution having first and last place. It was hot and humid as Barry Ulrich stood up to make the first presentation on behalf of the prosecution. He argued predictably that there was no justification for the killing of Kahahawai, that Massie was not insane and might not even have been the killer anyway. George Leisure followed him, making a speech that in the main followed the expected pattern, except for its suggestion that the cause of all the trouble was Kahahawai's enormous sexual appetite —a fact neither proved in evidence nor very relevant in law. Both Ulrich and Leisure finished their presentations without surprising or exciting anyone. They were, of course, not the stars of the show. It was for Darrow that the jury and the press waited, the next day. His speech was to be broadcast live to the mainland—the first occasion on which this had been attempted—and technicians set up their equipment in the court before its session the next morning.

An expectant crowd waited to hear the plea that Darrow would make. The defense he entered, like so many in his past, was notable for its eloquence rather than its overall logic, and—again, as so often in the past—he rose to make it in sweltering heat. Understandably, he pulled out all the organ stops for sympathy for both Thalia and Tommy. Thalia had suffered a dreadful ordeal of multiple rape, he said, and here he made a slip of the tongue that may more truly have represented his private assessment. Describing to the jury how, after her assault, she had told her husband what had happened to her, he called it "an unbelievable story." But he recovered as soon as he realized what he had said by continuing, "almost . . . at least an unthinkable one . . ." Turning to Tommy Massie's predicament, he painted the picture of him as shocked by his wife's rape, then by the possibility that she was diseased and pregnant, then by the tide of malicious rumor about his wife and himself, and finally by the acquittal of Kahahawai. "Our insane institutions are filled with men and women who had less cause for insanity than he had," he told the court.

He made a somewhat perplexing statement about the firing of the fatal shot, which cannot have impressed the jury with the defense's candor. Having argued Massie's insanity for some time—though not giving any good reason why that should protect the three other defendants—he went on: "It's of no consequence who fired that shot—I am arguing the facts, and the only facts as you get them. Is there any reason in the world why Massie, on top of all these other troubles, should assume the added burden of assuming the responsibility of this killing?" And later, when he was evidently wilting and tired, Darrow said: "Again, I say I cannot understand why the prosecution raises a doubt as to who fired the shot and how."[17] Of course, the prosecution raised the doubt because of the earlier fancy footwork of the defense, which had left the question unanswered.

The jury saw an old man pleading before them. Darrow lacked the energy that had sustained him in his younger days. When he had completed his first hour, a recess was called and the jury excused so that he could rest. Praise was generously given by all, including the prosecutor, as he tried to recuperate in his chair. Then he took up arms again and the jury were recalled until the lunch adjournment, at which time Darrow went back to his room in the Young Hotel, accompanied by George Leisure. As he went into his suite, he asked George to call him when it was time to go back to the courthouse. It had not been his practice to eat lunch for forty years, but even Leisure was surprised to find that Darrow slept soundly for the whole adjournment, not attempting to do any last-minute preparation for the speech after lunch. Leisure had suspected before Darrow spoke that little thought had been given to the precise nature of the speech he would deliver—and now that he had heard most of it, he was convinced. Darrow had a way with him, and commanded respect as a trier, but he had not gripped his audience as legend had him do. He had admitted after the Leopold and Loeb trial in 1924 that he could never again make a comparable effort. The eight years that had elapsed had taken a further toll: he was nothing like as good as he used to be. Not that he was incompetent, or that he could not be effective at points; but the themes he developed and the moods he evoked lacked the unity that in his younger days he would have managed. There had been a time when his skill in presentation was such that his jumps from emotional appeal to logic and back again seemed to be woven out of whole cloth, and when he could hold a jury entranced with his fluency and sense of the dramatic. It was evident that that time had passed.

When Leisure roused him so that he could return to court, he wondered whether Darrow would reach a magnificent climax and astound everybody. But in spite of his sleep Darrow was not refreshed, and his performance in the afternoon was short and somewhat discursive, consisting of a mélange of sentiments about racial harmony, the delights of Hawaii, and the virtues of his clients: honor in the case of Massie; loyalty for Lord and Jones; and in Mrs. Fortescue the best qualities of motherhood.

There was little more of a convincing nature that he could say. He had made a valiant effort, but one that he probably knew was wasted with the jury, one of whom complained that "he talked to us like a lot of farmers."[18] When Kelley stood up, knowing now the complete defense presentation and knowing, too, that he had the last word, his course was clear. Quickly, efficiently, he pointed out the weaknesses in the defense argument. He asserted that none of the defendants was insane, that there was no evidence that Massie fired the fatal shot, and characterized the suggestion that the crime was an "honor" slaying as being another way of saying the defendants had resorted to lynch law. He was terse, controlled, and convincing, speaking for less than an hour.

It only remained for Judge Davis to instruct the jury on the law, which he did in an entirely proper and orthodox manner, leaving the jury in no doubt that the law applied to Thomas Massie, Mrs. Fortescue, Lord, and Jones as much as to anyone else. The jury deliberated for nearly fifty hours before reaching a verdict, but when it came, it was a finding that all four defendants were guilty of manslaughter. Recalling the trial, Darrow claimed that everyone connected with the case was surprised that the jurors' verdict was not an acquittal. "We could hardly believe we heard them aright!" he said. But that was not Darrow's real reaction, even if it was true of his clients. He had told Leisure several times during the trial that he did not think the defense stood a chance. In point of fact the jury had deliberated long and hard, not on the question of innocence or guilt, but on whether to convict of murder rather than manslaughter. Had it chosen murder, its verdict would have been inviolable legally. Darrow admitted as much when it was all over. "Of course," he confessed, "all the attorneys for the prosecution, and those for the defense, as well as the judge, knew that legally my clients were guilty of murder." Nevertheless he stood by his clients in their moment of need, even issuing a somewhat extravagant statement about the "surprise" verdict:

I can't understand it. The verdict is a travesty on justice and on human nature, and on every emotion that has made us what we are from the day the human race was born. . . . On top of all that these people have suffered it doesn't seem possible that anyone should say that the black gates of prison should close upon them. They are not that type.[19]

Perhaps that was the key to the wave of feeling that the Massie trial had caused. For there were many people who felt that the Massie-Fortescues were "not the type" who should go to prison. In Hawaii itself, aside from the naval base, the verdict was considered a just one. But the mainland interpreted it differently. The flames of indignation were stoked even higher when Judge Davis sentenced each of the defendants to ten years hard labor on May 6. The cry went up on the mainland for an immediate pardon for the four. Some of the reasons for this gave abundant justification to those friends of Darrow who had discouraged him from taking the case in the first place, for they were based upon the proposition that the natives were not fit to govern themselves. The question had now become a directly political one, and the possibility of a pardon was explored by the governor's office. It was rejected as impossible, but executive clemency was not. The governor was prepared to grant it if he could see an end to the continued upheaval caused by the various trials. There was the risk that the rape case would be tried again, and he wanted an assurance that, if commutation were given, it would not be pressed. The prosecutors were agreeable to this, and Thalia Massie became so after Darrow talked to her. So it was arranged that, immediately after the sentencing, Governor Lawrence Judd would commute the sentences to one hour, which he did.

Most Hawaiians were relieved that the matter had been buried. The party of defendants left the islands, and there was an unsuccessful attempt to serve Thalia with a subpoena as she departed. Darrow left with them, having ended his trial career with a highly unusual case. He could have had the chance to prosecute Thalia's assailants had he wished, for it was offered to him by the Attorney General, but he declined, explaining that prosecution was not his line of business. Besides, he did not believe that Thalia should be asked to go through the ordeal of testifying a third time.

As usual Darrow had given diplomatic reasons for not falling in with the possibility of a third prosecution, but they were not the whole story. He distrusted Thalia's testimony. This distrust had grown as a result of the friendship he had struck up with her gynecologist, Dr. John Porter, to whose home he made his way several times to escape the turmoil of the trial. Porter had very carefully not committed himself to any public opinion on Thalia's story of rape, but he said much later, "If I had had to get up and tell everything I knew it would have made monkeys of everybody. It would have been awful."[20] What, if anything, he told Darrow to elaborate on this, has never been revealed; but it convinced Darrow that the less Thalia Massie was trusted the better. Even without Porter's doubts, the public record was strange.

After the end of the litigation Governor Judd commissioned the Pinkerton Detective Agency to make its own investigation into the affair. Pinkertons summarized the evidence in a 279-page report that contained much veiled criticism and doubt about Thalia Massie's testimony, while supporting the alibis of those she accused. Most crucially, Pinkertons concluded:

> We have found nothing in the record of this case, nor have we through our own efforts been able to find what in our estimation would be sufficient corroboration of the statements of Mrs. Massie to establish the occurrence of rape upon her. There is a preponderance of evidence that Mrs. Massie did in some manner suffer numerous bruises about the head and body but definite proof of actual rape has not in our opinion been found.[21]

As soon as Darrow was back in Chicago, he wrote up his experience in Hawaii for addition to *The Story of My Life*, which had recently been published. It amounted to twenty-four pages, which his publishers rapidly distributed as a kind of appendix while the public still remembered the case. Initially this was issued as a separate pamphlet, which was inserted into the existing stock of hard-bound copies until they were exhausted, after which a new printing gave the chance to bind in the extra pages as a final chapter. It was not inappropriate since Darrow never again engaged in a significant trial. The book's sales were considerably boosted and it became the number-one best-seller in Hawaii as a result. Darrow was as pleased with its acclaim as that of anything he had written: "I realize that my story has been criticised, but, at that, on the whole it has been remarkably well received. If the times had been anywhere near good, it would have had more than a fair sale, I think."[22] He presented the case in a tactful narrative that put his clients in the best possible light, coupled with fulsome praise for Honolulu and its residents. Those Hawaiians who eagerly bought up the new printing in the hope of fresh insights into the trial were disappointed. Darrow gave nothing away. His discretion was impeccable. He breached no confidences, and neither did he voice any suspicions. His account gave the impression that everything about the case was clear and straightforward and that there was nothing left to discuss.

Darrow had entered the case with the avowed intention of reducing conflict and promoting racial harmony in the Territory. It seems clear that he succeeded. He restrained his clients and their relations from making more ill-advised comments about lesser breeds, barbarians, half-breeds, and natives. He stopped some of the silly talk about the protection of white women. He accepted a jury with a majority of colored members. He managed to avoid references to the racial overtones of the case during most of the testimony, and when he referred to race in his speech to the jury, he did so in moderate terms, encouraging cooperation and mutual trust. His courtroom career, which had been distinguished in the main by its hell-raising, therefore wound up with a conciliatory plea to bury the hatchet.

The newspapers were already providing an alternative distraction for the public. On March 1, the Lindbergh kidnapping took place, a sensation that commanded headlines for the next two years. It was the kind of case Darrow might have been offered ten years before, but now—perhaps especially in the light of his performance in the Massie case—he was not in the running. So by a strange coincidence Darrow's last case was eclipsed by another kidnap-murder that aroused precisely opposite emotions in the public mind. The Massie case had played on the sympathies of the public for the defendants; but the trial of Bruno Hauptmann harvested sympathy for the victims and would leave a permanent mark upon federal law and the American psyche.

36

Battling the Blue Eagle

When Darrow returned from Hawaii, his financial situation was very serious indeed. While in Honolulu defending Massie, he had been asked to return the $1,000 retainer the NAACP had paid him but could not do so. He wrote back to Walter White: "I had intended returning the $1,000 but it looks from here as if I was broke entirely. Can't tell until I get home and will write you at once from there about the situation. Will leave here by the time you get this letter. If I am broke I think I can raise $1,000 very soon. Always your friend. Darrow."[1] And again a month later, as soon as he got back to Chicago, he wrote:

> Dear Walter:
> I am awfully sorry that I could not help out on the thousand that I owe. I haven't been able to do it. The truth is that before these terrible times I had about $300,000 in what seemed perfectly good securities. They are now not worth more than ten and are not paying dividends. Then Paul had about the same but he owed quite a large amount and for a year I have been giving him every cent I could to save what he had. The debt is now reduced to about $10,000 but the value of his stock has been reduced much more. I believe I can begin paying soon. If I don't in the next three weeks to July 1st I will take some means to make a substantial payment. This is the first time in fifteen years that I have had any trouble about finances, and I am terribly sorry but I will arrange some way to make a substantial payment. I expect to get to N.Y. before then and will see you.
> With all good wishes.
>
> > As always,
> > Your friend
> >
> > Clarence Darrow

Walter White showed Darrow's letter to Arthur Spingarn, with the comment: "Here is a most pathetic letter from Clarence."[2] White was right: it was pathetic. He could not even travel to New York to explain the position more fully, though he had professional and business incentives to do so. "I haven't felt like spending the money for a trip to New York," he wrote, "but hope I will not always be broke; and, likewise, I hope the rest won't be either."[3]

Darrow was now an old man—even a grand old man—but he had to keep

426

going in order to make money. His only other source of income, apart from his law practice and his investments, was the fees he received for lecturing and debating. But the halcyon days of the lecture circuit were already done. The world was closing in around him. Things were so tight in May of 1933 that on a trip to the East Coast, Ruby regretfully declined an invitation to visit the Barneses because they were traveling on round-trip summer-rate tickets and could not afford the extra fare to the Barneses' home.

Matters were not helped by the fact that, from about 1930 onward, Darrow's health had become a constant rather than an intermittent preoccupation. Now, whenever any proposition was put to him that involved a departure from routine or a trip outside Chicago, it was a concern whether he was robust enough to stand the strain. The ravages of time were becoming more evident, and although he let Ruby do most of his worrying for him, he began to recognize that old age must perforce limit his activities. For years he had been used to an energetic régime that left less time for meals and sleep than most people needed. He had had to thrive on a hectic schedule. Now those days were over; he no longer had the stamina for such a life. Even when he was not positively ill, he lacked the buoyant energy that had sustained him through most of his career. Querulously, he wrote to Fremont Older: "Do you think your will to live grows stronger or weaker as you grow older? I believe mine weakens, but am not quite certain."[4] Though he had often taken the negative in debates on the question "Is Life Worth Living?" he still sought to evade the grim reaper; and though many times he had railed against doctors as quacks, he took the precaution of consulting them nonetheless, preferring even quackery to nothing at all. He even tried rejuvenation through monkey-gland treatments—surely a fit therapy for America's most highly publicized defender of Darwinism—but it did not help him.

There was a special cruelty, therefore, in the decree of fate that he should not enjoy an old age free from financial worries as he had expected. And when Darrow was invited to undertake the chairmanship of the National Recovery Review Board in Washington in 1934, it was a godsend. He accepted with alacrity. He had some interest in the subject matter and needed the money. The position would pay him as chairman and, though it was of indeterminate length, seemed likely to provide a substantial amount of employment. He was appointed by presidential order on March 7, 1934, and began work immediately, moving to the District of Columbia with Ruby for the duration, taking a suite at the Willard Hotel. Darrow reveled in his new position, even to the extent of forgetting his increasing physical frailty. Ruby wrote from the Willard to a friend: "In April Clarence will celebrate his 77th birthday. . . . He isn't too robust, but is getting a lot of 'fun' sitting on the throne in the ballroom here being called *judge* because he is chairman of the Review Board of the N.R.A. and the decisions are up to him."[5]

Roosevelt's administration was facing mounting criticism from Congress and elsewhere for the operation of the NRA. To placate and deflect some of its most strident critics, and to buy time, FDR agreed to appoint an investigative body to pass upon the justice of the criticisms. From the President's point of view, the very best that could happen would be that such a body would be composed of members respected enough by the informed public to be credible, would investigate, and would report favorably on the NRA. In order to give credibility to such an investigation, however, someone had to be appointed as chairman who was demonstrably not in the administration's pocket. That credential Darrow certainly had, but he was not likely to produce a tame, uncontroversial report. He was no supporter of FDR. "Mr. Darrow never had much enthusiasm for President Roosevelt and the New Deal," recalled Harry Elmer Barnes. "He was long an admirer of Al Smith and wanted him to be President."[6] Nevertheless Roosevelt suggested Darrow's name to General Hugh S. Johnson, head of the NRA, who approved it, as he later recalled, in "a moment of total aberration." It is revealing that Roosevelt did not make the appointment until the chairman of the very body that was to be investigated had "approved" it.

In spite of Johnson's misgivings, Darrow was not a totally implausible nominee for a position of responsibility in dealing with the crisis of the thirties. The mistake was to put him to work in the industrial sphere rather than in coping with the rural depression. Conditions in the countryside offered opportunities well suited to Darrow's talents, which he might have grasped with honor. His beliefs were rooted in populism, not socialism. There were those who thought he would have been an appropriate spokesman for the farmers who had been reduced almost to starvation by the Depression. Even his opponents saw this. Eugene Manlove Rhodes wrote to Theodore Van Soelen: "I have damned Clarence Darrow for thirty-five years—but he had the chance to go out with honor defending the Iowa farmer. By all the gods, I do believe he is the best man to do it—and to earn love by it."[7] And Darrow himself wrote to Irving Fisher of Yale on the farmers' plight in 1933:

> My suggestion is that you make as one of the bases of your defence the point that the real debt of the farmer has been greatly magnified—three to five times —when translated into farm products. Whatever may be said technically against the farmers' actions in resisting the creditor, there has been fundamentally a great injustice done to all debtors through the appreciation of the dollar.[8]

But he wrote this advice in recognition that it would not be he who carried the banner in the courts. He was out of the arena of litigation by now, never to return.

By 1934 Darrow had achieved radical eminence. He represented an older American tradition of politics than that which inspired the New Deal. His choice to investigate the National Recovery Administration was therefore a dangerous one, for he was totally out of tune with its ideology. His political idols were Altgeld and Grover Cleveland. Small wonder that his perception of the issues gave away his age. He spoke as a voice from the past, analyzing current events from an outmoded set of assumptions: his framework of ideas, his preoccupations, and his destructive distrust of government betrayed him as a member of a generation no longer in control. As a public figure of long standing, he had some aptitude for giving his old ideas the appearance of newness; but finally he could not conceal that he was dated. It was almost as if a time machine had miraculously transported a representative of mid-nineteenth-century radicalism forward into the 1930s to provide some old-fashioned antidote to the wild new ideas being propounded to deal with the country's economic woes. And in truth, though he was blithely unconscious of it, Darrow had become a piece of living history. In spite of his many young admirers and the efforts of a wife considerably younger than he, old age was isolating him. The temper of the thirties was much different from that of the 1890s in which he was spiritually rooted. He was becoming an outdated figure to whom radicals of a younger generation paid respectful homage but without adopting his theories. Nothing could better have highlighted the gulf between his preconceptions and the thirties than his service on the Review Board.

The NRA had already been subjected to strong criticism as the tool of big business. It regulated, through complex "Codes," nearly all the key industries of the United States. Altogether over 600 of these Codes were in operation. The existence of the NRA was itself evidence of how much the Wall Street crash of 1929 and its aftermath had discredited the ideal of free enterprise, for it represented a drastic reaction against tradition. It exerted the power of the federal government in spheres where it never had entered before. By the time the Review Board was set up, it was arguable that the worst of the economic crisis was over, though whether the NRA could be credited with turning the corner was then, as it has always been since, a matter of controversy.

Darrow's opposition to the New Deal was spiritual as much as intellectual. He had made his name by asserting his independence during a lifetime that saw a huge growth in governmental regulation. His conceptions of liberty and self-fulfillment were rooted in individualism, even though he understood the economic interdependence of mankind. His fear of too much of government was greater than that of too little. He was, from the start, antagonistic to the NRA, as the course of his investigations and his reports reflected. He built a case along lines already decided in an investigation that was neither open-minded nor sympathetic. The spirit of the whole thing was to raise Cain. Darrow's entire life had been spent as a partisan, and he was not about to take on the mantle of a neutral or become impartial overnight. He surrounded himself with friends of similar views, including Charles Edward Russell, and went to work with a will. When visited by H. G. Wells, then on a tour, the impression they made was unmistakable:

> In the New Willard, in Washington, I found myself in contact with those fine flowers of American insurrectionism, my old friends Clarence Darrow and Charles Russell. They had been summoned to the capital to report on the working of various codes and they were reporting as unhelpfully and destructively as they knew how. They were "agin the government" all the time and the wildfire of freedom shone in Darrow's eyes."[9]

Darrow was determined to upset the applecart, and there was a psychological need to vindicate himself. In the twenties he had sung the blues in an era of ragtime; now, in an era of depression, the people wanted messages of hope, not doom, and his tune seemed strangely discordant. Yet, in attacking the monopolies, he was in some intellectual difficulty. He did not like monopolies, but neither did he like competition. He would use strong words in condemning competition in his first NRA Report. If the natural tendency to monopoly existed in all businesses, how was it to be stopped without competition? Darrow left that to others to figure out; he wanted to make things difficult for the government, not easier. Seventy-six years had persuaded him that governments were usually up to no good. As soon as he had arrived in Washington there was a confrontation that did not bode well for relations between Darrow and the NRA. Its administrator, Hugh Johnson, had provided offices for the Review Board next to his own. Darrow declined them, feeling that the board might be too much under the influence of the organization it was meant to be investigating. Instead, he set up headquarters at his hotel, which provided him with space free. Relations between Johnson and Darrow did not improve thereafter.

The hearings that were held by Darrow involved a large number of industries—electrical manufacturing, footwear, motion picture, retail solid fuel, steel, ice, cleaning and dyeing and bituminous coal, among others. The avowed purpose of the Review Board was to discover whether the Codes for these industries that had been promulgated by the NRA promoted monopoly and oppressed small business. Without exception, it was found that they did.

But the disposition of the board was predetermined. Regulation was bound to be in favor of the larger enterprises in the industry because they had greatest influence in Washington. This attitude received much bolstering from the fact that very few industries would cooperate with the Review Board. It had no powers of subpoena, and appearance before it was strictly voluntary. Thus the industries could ignore the board if they wanted to. It did not help that, though Darrow had visited Washington many times during his long career, he had never actually worked there before; he did not know its milieu and ground rules. In the Washington of 1934 and 1935, his indignant rantings against big business and monopoly were peculiarly incongruous with the spirit of the times.

The first Report of the Review Board was quickly suppressed. It reviled the trusts, characterized the NRA as a conspiracy against the poor, and rehearsed the arguments of a bygone age. It was a document that reflected Darrow's conditioned reflexes of a quarter-century before, unsuited in both tone and substance to the early thirties. Darrow had well and truly "dated" himself. In this respect he shared a bond with his friend and collaborator in the NRA investigation, Charles Edward Russell, one of the first of the muckraking journalists, whose articles on the trusts became classics of their genre. The report did not reflect governmental policy and it incensed General Johnson, who wrote to President Roosevelt on May 15, 1934:

A more superficial, intemperate, and inaccurate document than the report I have never seen. . . . In my judgment, this Board has missed a great opportunity for a real public service. As it is now acting, it is of no service to anybody—it is a political sounding board. In view of its fixed prejudices and partisanship and its unfair methods of taking and reporting on testimony, the conclusion is inescapable that the Board is not proceeding in good faith to fulfill its public obligations. . . . I recommend that it be abolished forthwith.[10]

The mandate of the Review Board had been to report to the President, and the first Report was sent to him, but nothing happened: "I do not know what the President was supposed to do, whether he would put it in the closet with the clothes, or what he would do, but the report was to be made to the President."[11] It had been assumed by many people that the reports would be printed, but they were not. Friends and interested parties such as Salmon O. Levinson, the Chicago lawyer, wrote to Darrow asking for copies of the Report on that assumption. But Darrow's reports were not what FDR wanted and Rexford Tugwell claims that the President "wanted to play [the reports] down."[12] Although they did not receive any official publication or circulation, their general theme was well known and important people on the Hill knew that serious charges were made against the NRA. The first Report appeared in the newspapers. Subsequently the Review Board produced two further reports, both of which Darrow personally leaked to the press. The administration had decided that the reports were too embarrassing to be released to the public, so the committee did it themselves. Once released, they did not fall on deaf ears. There were those who had opposed the scheme from the start and were prepared to feast on the political ammunition that the Review Board was providing. The National Industrial Recovery bill had been spoken against in the Senate by Hugo L. Black:

This bill if it shall pass and become law, will transfer the lawmaking power of this nation, insofar as the control of industry is concerned, from the Congress to the trade associations. There is no escape from that conclusion. That is exactly what has happened in Italy, and as a result, the legislation passed by the parliamentary body of Italy, as expressed by one economist, has reached the vanishing point.[13]

Later when General Johnson, the administrator of the National Recovery Act, testified before the Senate Committee on Finance (coincidentally, on Darrow's seventy-eighth birthday), he returned to the attack on the Darrow Board:

It was a political wailing wall and it came out and recommended Communism. There was not one fair hearing before it. . . . They disregarded the N.I.R.A., packed the record with framed testimony, disregarded every judicial rule of fairness known to man, solicited and accepted unsupported statements, restricted or ignored testimony unfavorable to their purposes, hazed witnesses on that other side, insulted N.R.A. officials, and for that spent $50,000 of Government money.[14]

Much the same conclusion was reached by a sober study published by the Brookings Institution and written by men of an entirely different bent from Johnson's. While both Darrow and Johnson were in their element in the thick of things, the Institution was dedicated to contemplative, unpolemic assessment. In taking a wider view of what happened, its study concluded:

> An outgrowth of the attack in Congress was the appointment by the President on March 7 of the National Recovery Review Board, the so-called Darrow Board. . . . This board was ill-equipped, on the side of fact-finding and procedure, for effective accumulation and analysis of evidence. Nevertheless, its existence was of very great importance. Throughout the spring of 1934, it kept before the country, the President, and the NRA itself the idea that all was not well with the codes. It dramatized the need for internal re-examination of the results of code making.[15]

The rising tide of sentiment against the National Recovery Administration, which the Brookings Institution described as "an outgrowth of the attack in Congress," itself fanned the flames of discontent within Congress, and this culminated in the passing of Senate Resolution 79, which in effect meant that the Senate Committee on Finance would investigate the Review Board. Its hearings began in March 1935.

Darrow had originally been scheduled to give his testimony on Monday, March 18, 1935, but at the request of Senator McCarran—one of the co-authors of the resolution that brought the hearings into being and who could not be present on that day—Darrow's testimony was deferred until Wednesday, March 20. It was a nice compliment. When Darrow arrived in the Finance Committee room, he received all the attention due to a celebrity and the cameras flashed around him.

With almost no variation, he gave his standard performance before the Senate Committee, reciting all the reasons for gloom and regret without bothering with the particulars of the subject at hand, any more than he had dealt with the particulars of some of his most famous cases. "I have been a lawyer so long that I am suspicious of almost everything," he told the committee. He displayed a rigidity in his hopelessness and his conviction that things would not improve, coupled with the muckraker's certainty that maggots and decay could be found under every stone. The best that humanity could do was bear its burden; even reform was an illusion, merely replacing one evil with another.

On March 20 he was questioned about the effect of the Codes promulgated by the NRA on child labor. Senator Barkley asked him about the elimination of child labor and whether the Codes had speeded it up. Darrow replied:

"I don't know. I hate to give them any credit." A ripple of laughter went round the Finance Committee Room.

"That may furnish a key to your whole attitude toward this thing," retorted Senator Barkley.

The Senator asked him, pointedly, "You are opposed to the whole theory of the N.R.A.?"

"Yes," replied Darrow, "I do not think it is the right theory."[16]

When pressed for his own views on the present discontents, Darrow inclined toward socialism:

> I think that something like a socialistic system would be the only thing that would make anything like an equal distribution of wealth . . . it would be a help toward some day when people will be ashamed to be rich. . . . I would say that the best theory to get would be that of some of the old philosophers, William Morris among the rest, "to everyone according to his needs, and from everyone according to his capacity."[17]

The whole pattern of economic regulation envisaged by the enabling legislation of the NRA was difficult for Darrow's generation to accept. The great fight of their day had been against "the trusts"—and their commitment had been in favor of competition and against monopoly. Yet, it seemed, the NRA was designed to promote cooperation between competitors, and price fixing, which was the first step toward monopoly. There was a contradiction between the antitrust philosophy and that of the New Deal that was almost entirely a clash between generations of American economic thought. For this, however, it is harsh to belabor Darrow. Precisely the same failing (if failing it was) led the Supreme Court to invalidate most of the major statutes upon which the New Deal rested between 1933 and 1935, the National Industrial Recovery Act included.* The leading lights of the Supreme Court were Darrow's age and shared his assumptions. It was no accident that Roosevelt's Court-packing plan was designed to reduce the power of "nine old men"—for the clash of ideologies was also in large measure a clash of the older and younger generations. Darrow's comrade-in-arms in the campaign against the trusts and his representation of the anthracite miners of Pennsylvania, Louis D. Brandeis, had taken a leading part in dismantling the New Deal legislation. And indeed there were practical objections to it; for all its heroic radicalism, the legislation marked the passing of many important liberties in compromise with the economic crisis. As Chief Justice Hughes confided in his autobiographical notebook, "whatever grounds for criticism of these decisions the partisans of particular theories may find, certainly when Justices Brandeis, Stone, Cardozo and Roberts, or three of them, to say nothing of myself, concurred in the decisions, it is idle to charge that they were attributable to an illiberal bias."[18] William O. Douglas, a rising star of the New Deal and soon to be a Justice of the Supreme Court himself, shared that view: "Any Supreme Court that ever sat would have so ruled, because lawmaking under the Constitution is a matter for Congress, not for private parties."[19]

Notwithstanding the Supreme Court's willingness to strike at the same legislation that Darrow had attacked, there was a sense in which Darrow's work was more influential than the Court's. The Court passed upon the

---

*The act was struck down by the Court without dissent in *Schechter Poultry Corporation* v. *United States*, 295 v.s. 495, on May 27, 1935, only two months after Darrow had given his unfavorable testimony.

constitutional validity of the legislation, but Darrow's report, albeit not published, influenced the political climate profoundly. The considered conclusion of a close aide of the President at this time is that the reports "had a good deal to do with Johnson's rapid decline in prestige and his replacement a few months later" in September 1934. So Darrow in a sense "won" a Supreme Court case in which he had not appeared.

It was to be positively his last. The NRA hearings and its Report were Darrow's swan song. Like Bryan before him, he had outlived his time. His rantings about monopoly were not in tune with the people any longer, and his themes struck no chord of sympathy. He had not lost eloquence, or intellect, but the passing of time had robbed him of relevance. His rhetoric was that of a radical individualist, but Washington was dominated by collectivist bureaucrats. Like his old foe William Jennings Bryan, time had overtaken him, and he was now a historical curiosity, a leftover from the past.

Ironically Darrow's unfavorable attitude to the New Deal brought him closer to his conservative son than he had been in many a year. The Depression moved Paul to write a pamphlet, *What Shall We Do for the Poor?*, in which he explained his dislike of the New Deal. It showed how little like his father Paul was. His writing lacked the sure touch of his father's rhetoric, and conspicuously avoided pointing the finger of blame. Its main recommendation was to establish an "unemployment wage," but along the way it criticized wage and hour laws as a diminution of freedom, and stated that "the ability to produce at a profit is an ability which society should encourage and not hinder by excess profits taxes, capital gains taxes and innumerable other interferences."[20] At Paul's age Clarence had been without peer in the brilliance and trenchance of his statements on social questions, but the gift had not been transmitted. Where Clarence's prose had sparkled, Paul's lacked style and form and even lapsed occasionally into incomprehensibility. Paul's work was proof that he had not been merely wilful in refusing to follow in his father's footsteps; he could not have done so. Indeed he saved himself from a life of disappointment and even humiliation by refusing to become a lawyer. His inclinations were so much at variance with his father's that he would have been under perpetual pressure to explain himself. In almost every way, father and son contrasted; the father, a risk taker to the point of recklessness, a gambler and an extrovert extremist, had spawned in Paul a moderate, conservative, cautious, and reticent man. He was not a chip off the old block in anything but his determination to go his own way.

Clarence Darrow had emerged from a family that had never attained fame; he was a shooting star in an otherwise stable constellation, neither preceded nor followed by any other stars. Paul had merely reverted to the norm of his heredity.

37

Peace at Last

Darrow had one more chance to sit on a board, though an entirely unofficial one. Both Dudley Field Malone and Arthur Garfield Hays were active in trying to arouse public sentiment about what was happening in Germany. They were members of a committee designating itself the American Inquiry Commission, which held hearings modeled after typical congressional inquiries. They prevailed upon Darrow to take the chair at its first session on July 2, 1934, held at the New York County Lawyers' Association at 14 Vesey Street, only a few doors away from where the NAACP had been founded. Darrow listened to a morning of volunteer testimony before taking lunch with Mayor La Guardia. There he made it clear that he did not need to inquire further in order to make up his mind. He told the mayor that "Herr Hitler is a very dangerous man and should be destroyed."[1] Many would have said that this was merely a continuation of his modus operandi at the NRA—he made up his mind before he had heard the evidence.

It was positively his last public performance. Now at last his body showed the ravages of age. Up to this point the signs had been gradual—first the glasses, then the false teeth, then the thinning hair and twinges of arthritis, then the deep furrows on his forehead and folds in his cheeks. But around 1935 there was a sudden and dramatic speeding up of the aging process, which left none in doubt that the flesh was weakening. From being an old war horse, he became only a shadow of his former self. The seventh age was upon him. In June he went into hospital for observation: "thru all of the modern tests they have given him, he now has a lot of fine, new strength," reported Elizabeth Quereau to Benjamin Barr Lindsey. "There really was no disease, but he was tired and a little below par; they do so much good now-a-days for people with the gland extracts."[2]

But Darrow was getting beyond the stage that monkey glands could help and he knew it. He looked in vain for a successor to keep the flag flying. Twenty years before, in the midst of his Los Angeles ordeal, he had cried out confidently that even if he were destroyed, other men would rise up to carry on in his place. But where, in the event, were they? As Darrow surveyed the new generation of lawyers and scholars, he saw few made in his own image. After much dalliance he pinned his faith on Harry Elmer Barnes, who in 1930 had resigned his position as a professor at Smith College in order to devote himself entirely to free-lance lecturing and writing. The fruits of Barnes's expensively gained independence were in general less worthy of attention than Darrow's words. In focusing on Barnes, he was choosing a man who, though much inferior in platform ability and without legal background, was in one respect more successful. Barnes was a prolific writer, turning out work that was better received than any of Darrow's sorties into print. This Darrow noted in his letters, ruefully admitting that he wished he had the facility and ability Barnes displayed. Posterity would judge Barnes's work of only mild interest, in spite of its quantity; but Darrow regarded it highly and accorded it an educational importance.

Darrow expressed his need to feel that he had a successor as an assurance that his mission in life should be carried on. But what was his mission? It was, of course, consistent with his determinist philosophy to think that history had given him an appointed role to play. The difficulty was to define that role. Barnes, though an articulate, "advanced" thinker, was not an iconoclast in Darrow's tradition and represented the very college training Darrow had so often knocked. His writings, while competent, lacked the quality of drama that nearly all Darrow's best work displayed. If Darrow was hoping to ensure that his work would be carried on, it must be said that his appointed inheritor was not hewn in his own image. He badly missed his own strengths and weaknesses in treating Barnes as such; and indeed Barnes never filled a position comparable to Darrow's. Darrow looked round in frustration for a more appropriate protégé. He had willingly taken Altgeld's mantle. Why was it that no one— not even his son—stepped forward to take his? He was almost inclined to attribute the problem to some personal failing on his part. But the reasons were much more deeply rooted in history. The nation had changed, so that men of his stamp were no longer being produced or afforded the opportunity to come to the forefront of American life. The rural tradition had degenerated, and by now the cities were crucibles of vested interests far bigger than anything Darrow had grown up with. The memories of the Civil War with which Darrow was raised had long since faded, and the mobility of the motor car combined with the growth of speedy communication had left the countryside fighting an unequal battle in the cultural life of the nation as its newspapers, books, and radio programs emanated from the cities. Darrow's career had been made by his adaptation of country virtues in the city; now the city had absorbed those virtues and moved on. Yet as Darrow got older, he dwelt in the past. The clearest reality seemed to be that early time in Kinsman when he and America were much younger. There was a security in the return to his youth, and the continuity of his memories was reinforced by the unchanging appearance of his native state:

> Go out through the country where I came from and where I go to every chance
> I have to get out, because I love the country, and there is hardly a new farmhouse

anywhere in this northern country. . . . I took a trip of considerable length not long ago near my old country home in Ohio. I travelled a great many miles and I knew pretty nearly every house. I left it 50 years ago, but the houses did not. Everyone of them wants a new house.[3]

In his native village his fame had reached the stage of geometric progression where myths about his early life fed upon one another, so that, like a saint, artifacts of his boyhood were presented. Darrow acknowledged toward the end of his life that he heard tales about himself he knew to be untrue. He did not, by and large, take the trouble to correct them. When returning, as he liked to do, to the village in which he he had grown up, he found that "Now and then some old native shows me a bed or a table or chair said to have been made by me . . . but though I never contradict the statement, but rather encourage it instead, I am quite sure that the claim is more than doubtful."

Darrow's last public pronouncement of any consequence was made in January 1936, shortly after his client Richard Loeb had been stabbed to death in Joliet prison. Darrow told the press: "He's better off than Leopold. He's better off dead."[4] After that morose pronouncement, he never again showed himself to be in touch with reality; the reveries of old age enveloped him.

As the last years came upon him, he dwelt more and more in the past. His recollections were bathed in sunlight as he watched himself as a boy in the familiar haunts of boyhood—the paths he had walked, the waterholes he had swum, the streams he had fished. It was *Farmington* all over again, where he heard the echoes of childish voices. A flood of memories came back, of events far less consequential than many that had occupied his active years, but which commemorated moments of importance in the making of the man. Across the decades he reached, ignoring the tumult of a controversial and embattled life, to the only time of peace that he had known. Sitting up as he looked over the Midway, or dozing halfway between consciousness and sleep, the balm of childhood images came more and more to soothe his old age.

It was, of course, a sign of dotage. The past now meant more to him than the present. He had always evoked fond images of his growing years, romantically and even sentimentally picturing the adventures of the countryside. Now they became his major solace. The triumphs of his checkered career counted for little by the side of those carefree days he shared with Tom Sawyer and Huck Finn. The last trip in 1937 was taken to indulge the whim of an elderly invalid, old enough to take his final pleasure in revisiting childhood haunts. In Darrow senility was the more painfully obvious since above all he had lived by his wits, and now they were gone. The local newsman saw it clearly: "The old man didn't have all his buttons."[5]

Darrow had long brooded upon death. From his earliest years its dreadful fascination had been impressed upon him by his father's part-time undertaking. Always, lingering in the back of his mind was a knowledge of the inevitability of death. At his birthday celebration in 1918, he had proclaimed: "There is not so much difference as you get older; at least so far as I can see but little.

I am not sure how it would be if I really should get old."[6] Now he was finding out. Mixed with his pessimism there had always been a morbid streak, which stressed futility and fatality as the background to all human endeavor. As he approached the time when he was "near done," he tended to alternate between moods of hope and despair. "I find that at seventy I am scarcely conscious that the end grows near," he had informed readers of the *Christian Century* in 1928.[7] But he was conscious of the odds lengthening against him, and by 1931, when he took a lengthy holiday in Florida for the winter, had confessed: "The calendar and various other hunches constantly warn me that there are only a few more 'speeches' and debates left for me. . . ."[8] He had dabbled in spiritualism and visited mediums "in most American cities of any importance, and many in Europe. I really have wanted to believe it all and therefore tried to, but in vain." He had even prompted Nathan Leopold to draw up a list of questions to answer from the dead in the event that Leopold was executed— a macabre arrangement to have made with a client in serious jeopardy of having the death sentence imposed upon him, but one that revealed the hold which the possibility of life after death held for him.

On the occasion of Darrow's eightieth birthday, Henry Mencken wrote: "I gather from the public prints that you are claiming to be eighty. I refuse to believe it. Your actual age is what it has always been—about thirty—which is prime for homosapiens."[9] Alas, the facts belied Mencken's kind words. Darrow was faltering toward the end, and time was catching up with him; his eightieth birthday was to be his last.

If Clarence suffered during those last, cruel months, so did Ruby. For thirty-five years she had lived vicariously through her husband. His triumphs had been hers and now his pain was also hers. She had no children to lend her moral support in the difficult months in which Clarence approached death, nor had she any realistic hope that he would be reprieved. The joys of his companionship became less as the grim, depressing regimen of an invalid's demands swallowed up her days. His progress toward death was gradual, and sometimes for weeks at a time imperceptible as his condition seemed to stabilize. But slowly his strength and faculties left him, and though it sometimes seemed that he was not getting worse, it never really appeared that he was getting better. The protracted process of dying without hope of a return to good health made death, when it came, almost a relief. But in the meantime there was the sad processional of terminal illness: the inquiries of friends, the grave conversations with doctors; the false and real alarms of Clarence's fluctuating vital signs; the ever-present fear that any given day would be his last. The sense of foreboding was as bad as the grief of death.

He had walked in the valley of the shadow of death too long. When the end came, on March 13, 1938, it was a release for his family and friends, who knew at first hand that his final months were pitiful and ugly. It had been his own suggestion that Judge Holly should speak at the commemoration service at his death: "He knows everything there is to know about me, and he has sense enough not to tell it."[10] But the man who had spoken at Altgeld's funeral and in memorial for nearly all the great radicals of his age—Ingersoll, George, and Trumbull among them—had no valedictorian left who could be his equal.

The final memorial service was held in the Bond Chapel at the University of Chicago, where Judge Holly, not trusting his own eloquence, used the text of the funeral oration that Darrow himself had given nearly forty years before at the grave of John Peter Altgeld. So Darrow unexpectedly enjoyed the privilege of writing his own funeral speech—almost as good as having written his own epitaph and obituary. No one begrudged him that, though the use of an oration designed to describe the virtues of another lent a strangely impersonal note to the ceremony.

Darrow had been steadfast in pursuit of many of the same ends as his mentor and had shown at least as much courage. Yet there was a great difference between Altgeld and Darrow, in spirit if not in principle. Though thousands filed past Altgeld's casket when it had lain in state in Chicago's public library, his methods and character had stirred animosities so deep that there were many who could not bring themselves to mourn him. But a seemingly never-ending throng had gathered to pay their last respects to Darrow, waiting in line on the sidewalk in the pouring rain outside the funeral home. Darrow left much less bitterness in his wake. There were some, it was true, who, having crossed swords with him, never found it in their hearts to forgive; but there were far more who, at the end, were able to put aside their differences and do homage to a unique spirit. Darrow had a human warmth that far surpassed that of his political mentor.

As those anonymous thousands queued in the Chicago rain to pay their last respects, they mourned the passing of an age as well as a great American. For the forces that had contributed to Darrow's character had been transformed in his lifetime, and would not again converge. His strengths and weaknesses he had gained from conditions that were gone forever. And as they stole a last look at a giant stilled by death—a reminder of mortality as poignant as any speech he had ever delivered—they knew the truth of a conventional memorial address with unconventional strength. They would not see his like again.

Darrow was unique. Neither before nor since has any man arisen with his particular greatness. He carved his own niche in history, a voice for the inarticulate, the oppressed, the poor, and besides a figure of genuine intellectual importance and an artist with words who in America has never been surpassed. When he was down, in 1912, he told the court: "I am pretty near done anyhow. If they had taken me twenty years ago, it might have been worth their while, but there are younger men than I . . . who will do this work when I am gone." He was wrong; nobody took his place. There was no successor worthy of the name. Not many men have left a void that posterity could not fill. Darrow did—and his robust independence left an example for later generations to admire.

Notes

All quotations from Clarence Seward Darrow that are not footnoted come from *The Story of My Life* (New York: Charles Scribner's Sons, 1932). Where possible, quotations from Darrow's other writings and speeches have been taken from Arthur Weinberg, ed., *Attorney for the Damned* (New York: Simon & Schuster, 1957) and Arthur and Lila Weinberg, eds., *Verdicts out of Court* (Chicago: Quadrangle Books, 1963).

All books quoted, cited, or otherwise relied upon are cited by the surname of the author (or editor where indicated), followed by the date of publication. The full citation may be found in the bibliography, which also contains a complete list of the MS collections consulted. The only exceptions are references to Darrow's autobiographical novel *Farmington* (Chicago: A. C. McClurg & Co., 1904), which is cited by name. In the case of multi-volume works, the volume number precedes the author's (or editor's) surname.

PART ONE: FROM VILLAGE TO CITY

CHAPTER 1

1. *Biographical History of Northeastern Ohio* (Chicago: The Lewis Publishing Company, 1893), p. 849.
2. Letter, Darrow to Dr. Alex Dienst, Temple, Texas, February 21, 1935, quoted in Hamilton Catalogue 30, lot 94.
3. *Farmington,* p. 266.
4. Golden 1969, p. 333.
5. Edward attended the University of Michigan from 1866 to 1868, and Mary from 1871 to 1872; neither graduated.
6. See Clarence True Wilson in 21 *Unity,* no. 6 (May 16, 1938), 96; Stone 1941, p. 470; and Weinberg 1971, p. 68. Albert Mordell, describing the mistake as "a frightful boner," observed that "An elementary knowledge of American history would have made him [Stone] aware, for example, of a well-known date in American history, December 2, 1859, when John Brown was hanged"—Mordell 1950, p. 17. However it ought in fairness to be added that the story appeared in 21 *Unity,* no. 6, in an issue dedicated to Darrow's memory.
7. *Farmington,* p. 268. See also Darrow's speech in the Kidd case, 1898, Oshkosh,

Wisconsin: "I well remember when scarce a babe . . . I heard my people tell of those brave men and women, Garrison, Kelley, Foster, Pillsbury and others of their kind who took their fortunes, their lives and their reputations in their hands, who traveled up and down the land the best they could, preaching their doctrines to all who would stop and hear"—reproduced in Weinberg (ed.) 1957, p. 323.

8. *Ibid.*, p. 19.
9. *Farmington,* pp. 218–219.
10. *Ibid.*, p. 82.
11. *Ibid.*, p. 59.
12. Darrow and Holmes 1924, p. 60.
13. *Farmington,* p. 105.
14. *Ibid.*, pp. 108–109, 123.
15. Darrow and Holmes 1924, p. 60.
16. *Farmington,* p. 177.
17. *Ibid.*
18. *Ibid.*, pp. 12–13.
19. *Success Magazine* (Christmas 1924), p. 31.
20. *Farmington,* p. 261.
21. George S. Leisure, "Reflections on Clarence Darrow," 45 *Virginia Law Review* (1959), 418.
22. *Farmington,* p. 265.
23. Steffens 1931, p. 666.

CHAPTER 2

1. *Farmington,* pp. 27–28.
2. *Ibid.*, pp. 25–26.
3. *Ibid.*, p. 30.
4. *Ibid.*, pp. 131–132.
5. *Ibid.*, p. 267.
6. Harrison 1931, p. 23.
7. Ashtabula *Sentinel,* August 16, 1884, p. 2.
8. *Darrow 1924,* p. 16.
9. *Farmington,* pp. 169–170.
10. *Ibid.*, p. 7.
11. Arnold 1965, p. 252.
12. Brown 1959, p. 269.
13. Henry Wade Rogers, "The Law School of the University of Michigan," 1 *Green Bag* (1889), 197, 198.
14. See, e.g., the Ashtabula *Sentinel* for June 11, 1881, p. 1, reporting that eight applicants out of forty-two had been failed at Columbus on June 7. There was, indeed, no uniformity of standards in Ohio at this time. A contemporary survey found that the character of examination given in that state "varies constantly with the different examiners"—Francis L. Wellman, "Admission to the Bar," 15 *American Law Review* (1881), 303.
15. Apparently there was considerable migration from northern Ohio to McPherson during this period. The local press recorded several marriages in McPherson involving ex-Ohioans; see, e.g., Ashtabula *Sentinel,* March 30, 1881, p. 3.

16. Letter, Darrow to Ralph Johnson of McPherson, Kansas, January 30, 1932, quoted in Weinberg 1963, p. 22.
17. Ashtabula *Sentinel,* May 23, 1883, p. 1.
18. Quoted Kempf 1965, p. 346. Lincoln said this between 1848 and 1856.
19. Letter, Darrow to William McKnight, April 15, 1936, in possession of addressee.
20. *Farmington,* pp. 203–205.
21. Ashtabula *Sentinel,* July 2, 1881, p. 1; August 25, 1881, p. 1.
22. Whitlock 1925, p. 28.
23. *Ibid.,* pp. 13, 25.
24. Ashtabula *Sentinel,* June 18, 1884, p. 1.
25. Ashtabula *Sentinel,* October 8, 1884, p. 1, and October 11, 1884, p. 1.
26. Ashtabula *Sentinel,* November 27, 1884, p. 5.
27. Quoted Ashtabula *Sentinel,* November 27, 1884, p. 1.
28. Lynn 1971, p. 66.
29. Whitlock 1925, p. 28.
30. Steffens 1931, p. 666.
31. Clarence Darrow, "Why I Have Found Life Worth Living," *The Christian Century,* April 19, 1928, p. 505.
32. 52 Ohio 187 (1894).
33. See Ashtabula *Sentinel,* February 17, 1887, p. 8, reporting that each man was paid $32.50 for this purpose.
34. Barnard 1938, p. 88.
35. Interview with Clarence Darrow, November 9 and 10 [1936?], Illinois Historical Survey, p. 4.

CHAPTER 3

1. Harrison 1931, pp. 47, 48.
2. Taeuber and Taeuber 1971, p. 45: "Chicago had grown from a town of fewer than 5,000 in 1840 to a city of more than a million in 1890." Darrow incorrectly states in his autobiography that he arrived in Chicago in 1888; the Lakeside Directory of 1887, p. 419, gives his address for 1887 as 94 La Salle.
3. Stead 1894, pp. vi, viii, 56, and 410.
4. Lewis and Smith 1929, p. v.
5. 25 *Central Law Journal* (1887), 289, 481.
6. 1 *Harvard Law Review* (1888), 307.
7. It was subtitled *A History of the Red Terror and the Social Revolution in America and Europe.*
8. Anderson 1942, p. 107.
9. The appellate court had the power to admit to the bar by examination in open court, and set aside the first Friday of each term for the purpose—1 Ill. App. 28, and see Joseph Burke, "History of the Appellate Court," 44 *Chicago Bar Record* (1963), 239. Within five years of Darrow's admission the president of the Illinois State Bar Association, James M. Riggs, was calling for higher standards for admission—34 *Central Law Journal* (1892), 189.
10. *18 Central Law Journal* (1884), 2.
11. Letter, Darrow to William Kent, December 19, 1914, Kent Collection.
12. Linder 1879, p. 163. The building was 115 Monroe Street.

13. Quoted Destler 1963, p. 168.
14. Chicago *Record-Herald,* September 22, 1900, quoted in Hutchinson 1957, p. 60.
15. Quoted Stead 1894, p. 147.
16. Chicago *Tribune,* November 5, 1893, quoted in Barnard 1938, p. 258.
17. Interview, November 9 and 10 [1936?], Illinois Historical Survey.
18. Farrell (ed.) 1958, p. 202; reprinted from the *American Mercury* (October 1924).
19. Barnard 1938, p. 64.
20. Shannon (ed.) 1963, p. 101.
21. Barnard 1938, p. 121.
22. *Ibid.* p. 184.
23. Holly 1937, p. 2.
24. Interview, November 9 and 10 [1936?], Illinois Historical Survey.
25. Quoted Gertrude Barnum, "Darrow the Great Defender" (n.d.), to be found in Whitlock Papers, box 26.
26. Barnard 1938, p. 152.

CHAPTER 4

1. De Tocqueville 1945, pp. 191–192.
2. Wells 1934, p. 142.
3. *Echoes of the Sunset Club,* 1891, unnumbered front pages. The club kept transcripts of its proceedings, which are a remarkable verbatim source of contemporary thought. These transcripts were published in summary form. The years 1889–1891 were covered by the *Echoes,* and the subsequent years by *Year Books* in a slightly different format, which appeared until 1901, with the exception of the years 1895–1897 when the club was not active.
4. Frank J. Loesch, "The Chicago Bar in the Seventies and Eighties," 21 *Chicago Bar Record* (June 1940), 358, 363–364.
5. Altgeld spoke in 1890 on "What Shall We Do with Our Criminals?" (reproduced in Altgeld 1890, pp. 283–296); Charles T. Yerkes in 1894 on "The Disposition of Cities of Corporate Privileges"; and Jane Addams in 1892 on "How Would You Uplift the Masses?"—see *Echoes* and the *Year Books* for the relevant years.
6. *Year Book* 1892–1893, p. 148. This was the fifty-seventh meeting, held at the Grand Pacific Hotel on February 23, 1893, on the subject of "Municipal Government."
7. *Year Book* 1891–1892, report of meeting 35; *Year Book* 1892–1893, report of meeting 53. For the prohibition speech, see Darrow 1909, applying the same arguments to prohibition laws as to Sunday laws. (Darrow regarded the impulse behind both sorts of law as the same.) For the attack on the Lord's Day Alliance, see *Plain Talk* (April 1928).
8. See Darrow 1899. Darrow applauded the novels of both Lewis and Dreiser because they had the virtue of "realism." He wrote to Upton Sinclair, about his book *Oil,* that from a purely "realist" viewpoint, "it should help the public to see how constant and insidious have been the encroachments upon thought and speech since the war"—Letter, Darrow to Sinclair Lewis, June 30, 1927, reproduced in Sinclair 1960, pp. 330–331.
9. Chicago *Tribune,* January 15, 1886, p. 2.
10. 37 Ill. App. 206 (1890); 135 Ill. 552 (1891).
11. Whitlock 1925, p. 336.

12. Quoted Stead 1894, p. 170, fn. 1.
13. *Ibid.*, pp. 11–13.
14. Debs 1908, p. 321. But compare, for example, Baedeker's *United States* for 1893, pp. 281–282: "Great injustice is done to Chicago by those who represent it as wholly given over to the worship of Mammon, as it compares favorably with many American cities in the efforts it has made to beautify itself by the creation of parks and boulevards and its encouragement of education and the liberal arts."
15. See Fiedler 1973, p. 368: "In January 1905 an explosion and fire rendered it unfit for further occupancy. . . . The contract for wrecking the old building was let on August 16, 1905, and the demolition began on October 1, 1905."

CHAPTER 5

1. *Chicago and Northwestern Railway Company, Annual Report, 1894*, p. 27, gives "law expenses" for 1893 as $121,540.07.
2. Barnard 1938, p. 59.
3. 3 *Chicago Law Times* (April 1889), 179.
4. Frank J. Loesch, "The Chicago Bar in the Seventies and Eighties," 21 *Chicago Bar Record* (July 1940), 399.
5. 21 *Central Law Journal* (1885), 60, reviewing Hiram T. Gilbert, *Railroads and Courts* (1885).
6. Cullom 1911, p. 237. As a result Melville W. Fuller was appointed instead. (Cullom erroneously spells the name "Gowdy.") Frank H. Brooks, who was with Fuller when he received official news of his appointment at the Iroquois Club in Chicago, says that he was never a politician, and that the only way Cleveland would have known of Fuller was through Goudy, to whom Fuller was "a friend and adviser" —22 *Green Bag* (1910), 486.
7. 4 *Central Law Journal* (1888), 339.
8. Stead 1894, pp. 174–175.
9. *Ibid.*, p. 181.
10. Darrow incorrectly spells the surname "Hewitt" in his autobiography.
11. Interview, November 9 and 10 [1936?], Illinois Historical Survey.
12. Cullom 1911, p. 270.
13. Barnard 1938, p. 160.
14. Interview, November 9 and 10 [1936?], Illinois Historical Survey.
15. Stead 1894, p. 169.

CHAPTER 6

1. Barnard 1938, p. 165.
2. *Ibid.*, p. 253.
3. Interview, November 9 and 10 [1936?], Illinois Historical Survey.
4. *Cerveny* v. *Chicago Daily News Co.*, 139 Ill. 345 (1891).
5. Quoted Barnard 1938, p. 138.
6. *Chicago* v. *Altgeld*, 33 Ill. App. 23 (1889), at 25.
7. Quoted Barnard 1938, p. 141.
8. Interview, November 9 and 10 [1936?], Illinois Historical Survey.
9. This account combines Darrow 1932, pp. 100–101, and Interview, *op. cit.*
10. Quoted Barnard 1938, p. 217.

11. 5 *Green Bag* (1893), 470–473.
12. Interview, November 9 and 10 [1936?], Illinois Historical Survey.
13. Francis F. Browne, "John P. Altgeld," in *The National Review* (December 1896), reproduced in Memorial 1910, pp. 23–28, at 30.
14. *People* v. *Coughlin,* 144 Ill. 140 (1893). The Supreme Court of Illinois had achieved a certain reputation for inconsistency in its chequered history; in the sixty-seventh volume of its reports, two of its decisions were reported that had been rendered at the same term of court, which considered the same jury instructions. One of them held the instructions proper, the other improper. In 1876 one of Chicago's leading lawyers had told the Chicago *Tribune* in disgust that "even Alabama, Texas and Arkansas reports are considered better authority"—Quoted 3 *Central Law Journal* (1876), 646–647.
15. Interview, November 9 and 10 [1936?], Illinois Historical Survey.
16. Harrison 1935, p. 210.
17. Interview, November 9 and 10 [1936?], Illinois Historical Survey.
18. Clarence Darrow, "Nietzsche," 1 *The Athena* (1916), 6, 16.
19. Shannon 1963, p. 102; Samuel Alschuler, Memorial 1907 (n.p.).
20. Memorial 1907. Address by Hon. Edward F. Dunne (n.p.). Dunne expressly refutes the widely circulated rumor that $1 million was offered.

CHAPTER 7

1. Reproduced in Destler 1963, pp. 243–244.
2. *Biographical History* 1893, p. 849.
3. 2 Bryce 1888, p. 625.
4. Fiedler 1973, p. 239.
5. "The Administration of Justice in Chicago," February 12, 1889, reprinted in Altgeld 1890, pp. 50–51.
6. 3 *Central Law Journal* (1876), at 345.
7. Fiedler 1973, p. 247.
8. Quoted Stone 1941, p. 72.
9. Stead 1894, p. 242.
10. Stone 1941, p. 165.
11. Pizer (ed.) 1968, p. 122.
12. Bradley 1962, p. 114.
13. Stead 1894, p. 144.
14. *Ibid.,* pp. 145–146.
15. Clarence Darrow, "Whitman in Literature," delivered before the Walt Whitman Fellowship, transcript, Darrow Papers.
16. Darrow 1909, p. 11.
17. Gertrude Barnum's unpublished autobiography, quoted in Stone 1941, pp. 115–116.
18. Sharpe 1928, p. 37.
19. Kaplan 1974, p. 91.
20. Quoted *ibid.,* p. 137.
21. Quoted *ibid.,* pp. 117–118.
22. Darrow 1899, p. 56. ("Some Paragraphs Addressed to Socialists.")
23. Stead 1894, p. 380. See also Edward Noyes Wescott, *David Hansen* (1898), ch. 20: "Do unto the other feller the way he'd like to do unto you and do it fust."
24. Whitlock 1925, p. 114.
25. Russell 1910, p. 301.

26. Whitlock 1925, p. 220.
27. Winter 1963, p. 119.

CHAPTER 8

1. Harrison 1945, p. 111.
2. Sharpe 1928, p. 37.
3. Gertrude Barnum's unpublished autobiography, quoted in Stone 1941, p. 116.
4. Stead 1894, p. 218.
5. *Ibid.,* pp. 75, 77.
6. See, e.g., *The New York Times,* May 22, 1894, p. 1.
7. Stead 1894, p. 73.
8. Holly 1937, p. 17.
9. Browne 1924, pp. 95, 129, 130, and 133.
10. Stead 1894, p. 292.
11. Browne 1924, p. 142. It is possible to interpret Darrow as believing this the true reason for local failure to seek state aid—see Darrow 1932, p. 59.
12. Nevins (ed.) 1933, p. 358.
13. Letter, Florence Kelley to Henry Demarest Lloyd, August 1, 1894, quoted in Blumberg 1966, p. 153. The meeting was never actually held.
14. Whitlock 1925, p. 85.
15. 39 *Central Law Journal* (August 10, 1894), 110. Three weeks later the editor was disposed to doubt whether the civil injunctions being issued against unions were not too wide in that they included "enticing" workers away from employers' employment and picketing—39 *Central Law Journal* (August 31, 1894), 177.
16. Radosh 1971, p. 18, quoting Eugene Debs from the New York *Comrade* 1902.

PART TWO: FROM SUCCESS TO DISASTER

CHAPTER 9

1. See, for example, Debs's own testimony before the President's Commission on the Pullman Strike, reproduced in *United States* v. *Debs,* 64 F. 724, at 759 (1894).
2. Eugene Debs, *Walls and Bars,* quoted in Coleman 1930, p. 150.
3. Coleman 1930, pp. 157-158.
4. Debs's out-of-court statement, quoted in *United States* v. *Debs,* 64 F. 756.
5. *Ibid.,* 733.
6. Mayers 1964, p. 350.
7. *United States* v. *Debs,* 64 F. 724, at 757-758.
8. *Ibid.,* 758.
9. *In Re Debs,* 158 U.S. 565, at 600 (1895).
10. *Ibid.,* 583.
11. *Ibid.,* 598-599.
12. *Ibid.,* 584.
13. Quoted *United States* v. *Debs,* 64 F. 759.
14. Masters 1904, pp. 16-17.

CHAPTER 10

1. Quoted in Weinberg 1963, p. 58.
2. Cole 1931, p. 15.
3. Whitlock 1925, p. 163.
4. Bernard M. Baruch, foreword, to Mackay 1932, p. vi.
5. Farrell (ed.) 1958 p. 172.
6. Kaplan 1974, p. 119.
7. Chicago *Times,* June 26, 1896, quoted in White 1913, pp. 425–426.
8. Interview, November 9 and 10 [1936?], Illinois Historical Survey.
9. Koenig 1971, p. 253.
10. Quoted in Koenig 1971, p. 194.
11. *Ibid.,* p. 148.
12. Francis F. Browne, "John P. Altgeld," in *The National Review* (December 1896), reproduced in Memorial 1910, p. 23.
13. *Ibid.,* p. 27.
14. Coolidge 1897, p. 34. There were in addition a number of independent candidates: an Independent Gold Standard Democrat, a Prohibitionist, a Socialist Labor Party candidate, and a Middle of the Road candidate—but their total votes combined would not have tipped the balance in favor of Darrow if cast for him. Darrow somewhat exaggerated the closeness of the election, stating: "My opponent was elected by about one hundred votes"—Darrow 1932, p. 93.
15. Cullom 1911, p. 263.
16. Edgar Lee Masters, quoted in Coleman 1930, p. 209. Masters was much more sympathetic to Bryan than Darrow. Koenig 1971, p. 257, has Bryan devoting Jackson's birthday in 1897 to free silver.

CHAPTER 11

1. Letter, Brand Whitlock to Moses Block, November 6, 1896, reproduced in 1 Nevins (ed.) 1936, pp. 4–5.
2. Letter, Brand Whitlock to Octavia Roberts, August 2, 1898, reproduced in 1 Nevins (ed.) 1936, pp. 15–20.
3. Hapgood 1939, p. 297.
4. Harrison 1935, p. 213.
5. See, for example, letter, Benjamin Barr Lindsey to Darrow, May 2, 1922, Lindsey Papers, box 66.
6. For an offer to shield Darrrow from "the avalanche of calls and telephone messages and other annoyances when you are here [in New York]" see letter, Walter White to Darrow, January 14, 1926, NAACP administrative files, box c–93.
7. Severn 1967, p. 35.
8. Goodhart 1949, pp. 27, 71.
9. Stone 1941, p. 71.
10. Letter, Brand Whitlock to Octavia Roberts, August 2, 1898, reproduced in 1 Nevins (ed.) 1936, pp. 15–20.
11. Letter, Darrow to William McKnight, April 15, 1936, in possession of addressee.
12. Hamilton 1943, p. 77.

13. Stead 1894, pp. 246, 298.

14. Reproduced in Weinberg (ed.) 1957, p. 12.

15. Winter 1963, p. 118.

16. *Darrow* v. *Darrow,* divorce no. 168056 Chancery, filed March 12, 1897, Cook County, Illinois.

CHAPTER 12

1. Quoted Stone 1941, p. 114.

2. See 4 Foner 1965, p. 56 (allegation made during trial of Big Bill Haywood, Idaho, 1907).

3. Butcher 1972, p. 209; Gertrude Barnum's unpublished autobiography, quoted in Stone 1941, p. 115.

4. Stone 1941, p. 471. This was high praise indeed from DuBois, who by his own account, admitted: "I did not seek white acquaintances, I let them make the advances, and they therefore thought me arrogant"—DuBois 1968, p. 63.

5. Letter, Darrow to Alfred E. Arnold [Chicago, 1909], Hamilton Catalogue 2, lot 55.

6. Letter, Brand Whitlock to Octavia Roberts, August 2, 1898, reproduced in 1 Nevins (ed.) 1936, pp. 15–20.

7. Nevertheless Darrow's efforts on Whitlock's behalf bore fruit. Howells commended some of Whitlock's work to Harper & Brothers, and it was published as *The 13th District*—see 1 Nevins (ed.) 1936, pp. 31, 33–34.

8. Letter, Brand Whitlock to Octavia Roberts, June 27, 1899, reproduced in 1 Nevins (ed.) 1936, pp. 20–24.

9. Darrow 1899, p. 21.

10. Hapgood 1939, p. 190. See also Ravitz 1962.

CHAPTER 13

1. Darrow's speech to the jury, reproduced in Weinberg 1957 (ed.) pp. 271–273.

2. Weinberg (ed.) 1957, pp. 282, 297–298.

3. *Ibid.,* p. 310.

4. *Ibid.,* p. 271.

5. *Picturesque Chicago* 1893, p. 128.

6. Weinberg (ed.) 1957, p. 303.

7. Leopold 1958, p. 71. See also Judge Michael Musmanno, quoted in Stone 1941, p. 491: "On the platform he was utterly different from the man who had been conversing intimately with me a few minutes before. He was the antagonist, the fighter, the inexorable adversary."

8. Weinberg (ed.) 1957, p. 269.

9. *Ibid.,* pp. 288, 298, 301, 306, and 309.

10. *Ibid.,* pp. 325–326.

11. *Ibid.,* pp. 270–271, 299.

12. Despite wide circulation immediately after the trial, by 1909 it was out of print— see letter, Brand Whitlock to Charles H. Kerr, September 22, 1909, Whitlock Papers, box 18.

13. Quoted Weinberg (ed.) 1957, p. 267.

14. See Grover 1964, pp. 217–219, and note 48, Chapter 20. But Grover demonstrates

that the prosecutor, William E. Borah, also changed his summation substantially in proof form—pp. 248–251.

CHAPTER 14

1. *The New York Times,* February 13, 1898, p. 13.
2. Chicago *Evening Post,* September 1, 1898, p. 3.
3. Barnard 1938, p. 61.
4. White (ed.) 1969, p. 362.
5. Letter, Darrow to John J. Meehan, January 30, 1934, Illinois State Historical Society Library.
6. *Ibid.*
7. Ernst 1968, p. 81.
8. Nelles 1940, p. 59; Hixson 1972, p. 152.
9. Letter, Darrow to William Kent, December 9, 1914, Kent Collection.
10. Quoted Stone 1941, pp. 482–483.
11. For a remarkably favorable appraisal of the literary merits of these pieces of journalism, see Ravitz 1962, pp. 43–69.
12. Quoted Weinberg (ed.) 1957, p. 526, from his speech to the jury in his own defense, Los Angeles, 1912.
13. Kobler 1973, p. 13.
14. Goldman 1931, p. 304.
15. Kellogg 1967, p. 17.
16. Yarros 1950, p. 9; Harrison 1932, p. 334.
17. Mason 1946, p. 321.

CHAPTER 15

1. Darrow 1899, p. 64 ("Some Paragraphs Addressed to Socialists").
2. Whitlock 1925, p. 238.
3. Stead 1894, pp. 99, 215.
4. Bright 1930, p. 68.
5. Letter, Darrow to Brand Whitlock, March 17, 1902, Whitlock Papers, box 9.
6. Masters 1936, p. 273.
7. 17 *Chicago Bar Record* (1935), 15.

CHAPTER 16

1. Chicago *Evening Post,* July 18, 1903, p. 8.
2. Letter, George Bernard Shaw to Henry S. Salt, August 19, 1903, reproduced in Laurence (ed.) 1972, p. 348.
3. *Man and Superman,* Act 4.
4. Letter, Darrow to Arthur Spingarn, September 25, [1931], in possession of the author.
5. Steffens 1938, p. 459.
6. Johnson 1933, p. 379.
7. Interview with author.
8. St. Johns 1964, p. 480.
9. Haldeman-Julius 1936, p. 17.

CHAPTER 17

1. Quoted Weinberg (ed.) 1957, pp. 285–286.
2. Letter, Henry Demarest Lloyd to Mrs. Lloyd, November 4, 1902, Lloyd Papers, reproduced in Chester McArthur Destler, "On the Eve of the Anthracite Coal Strike Arbitration: Henry D. Lloyd at United Mine-Workers Headquarters, October-November, 1902," 13 *Labor History* (1972), 279, 290.
3. 2 Gompers 1925, p. 124.
4. Letter, Walter E. Weyl to Henry Demarest Lloyd, October 29, 1902, in Destler, "On the Eve . . . ," 289.
5. Quoted Harvey 1935, pp. 157–158.
6. Bruce Wyman, "The Coal Mines and the Law," 14 *Green Bag* (1902), 514, at 519.
7. Letter, Henry Demarest Lloyd to Mrs. Lloyd, October 18, 1902, in Destler, "On the Eve . . . ," at 284.
8. Destler, "On the Eve . . . ," at 294.
9. Quoted Weinberg (ed.) 1957, p. 337.
10. See letters, Darrow to Louis D. Brandeis, November 28, 1902; Brandeis to Darrow, December 2, 1902; and Darrow to Brandeis, December 13, 1902, reproduced in 1 Urofsky and Levy 1971, pp. 210–218.
11. Quoted Weinberg (ed.) 1957, p. 336.
12. 47 *Harper's Weekly,* March 7, 1903, at 372.
13. Quoted Weinberg (ed.) 1957, pp. 336, 348.
14. *Ibid.,* p. 359. "Mr. Hewitt" was Abram S. Hewitt, an industrialist.
15. Kaplan 1974, p. 220.
16. 2 Gompers 1925, p. 126.
17. Quoted Weinberg (ed.) 1957, p. 361.
18. 2 Gompers 1925, pp. 126, 127.

CHAPTER 18

1. Yarros 1950, p. 6.
2. Masters 1936, p. 275. The case is reported as *United States ex rel. John Turner* v. *Williams,* 194 U.S. 279 (1904).
3. Steffens 1931, p. 540.
4. *Hearst's Chicago-American* v. *Mary E. Spiss,* 177 Ill. App. 436 (1904), at 440.
5. Lundberg 1969, p. 120, and see also his footnote to this statement.
6. Quoted Higdon 1975, pp. 27–28.
7. Koenigsberg 1941, pp. 310–313.
8. Wendt and Kogan 1943, p. 247.
9. Interview, November 9 and 10 [1936?], Illinois Historical Survey.

CHAPTER 19

1. Interview, November 9 and 10 [1936?], Illinois Historical Survey.
2. Clarence S. Darrow, "The Chicago Traction Question," 12 *International Quarterly* (1905), at 17.
3. Storey 1911, pp. 81–85. In particular he advocated that street railways should charge

extra for insurance against injury, and that their liability to passengers who paid only the standard 5 cent fare should be limited to a "small sum" if they chose not to buy the insurance.

4. Darrow, "The Chicago Traction Question," at 20.
5. Reuben W. Borough, 59 *Journal of the Illinois State Historical Society* (1966), 126–127.
6. For an account of the financial collapse, see O'Connor 1963, pp. 265–274.
7. Clarence S. Darrow and Gene E. Plumb, "Opinion on Exclusion Act and Abandoned Rights to Mayor and Transportation Committee," Chicago, 1905.

CHAPTER 20

1. 203 U.S. 192 (1906).
2. *Collier's,* May 11, 1907, quoted in 19 *Green Bag* (1907), 435.
3. Grover 1964, p. 292.
4. Letter, Brand Whitlock to Darrow, May 11, 1907, reproduced in 1 Nevins (ed.) 1936, p. 78.
5. Grover 1964, p. 154.
6. *Ibid.,* pp. 129, 155. This came out in the testimony during the Haywood trial. It was especially telling because Hogan was an alias of Harry Orchard, whose testimony linked the top officials of the WFM to Steunenberg's "contract killing."
7. 2 Gompers 1925, pp. 182–183.
8. Quoted Idaho *Daily Statesman,* May 2, 1907, p. 8.
9. Blankfort 1947, p. 86.
10. Idaho *Daily Statesman,* May 10, 1907, p. 1.
11. See also letter, William Allen White to Senator Marcus Hanna, November 29, 1902: "Now about Borah: he is a young man, was the attorney for the Coeur d'Alene mine operators during their trouble; has the best corporation practice in the state; is shrewd, levelheaded and true"—Johnson (ed.) 1947, pp. 50–51.
12. Idaho *Daily Statesman,* May 10, 1907, p. 1.
13. Letter, Brand Whitlock to Darrow, May 11, 1907, reproduced in 1 Nevins (ed.) 1936, p. 78.
14. Denver *Post,* June 2, 1907, p. 1.
15. Idaho *Daily Statesman,* May 21, 1907, p. 1.
16. See the *Oregonian,* May 3, 1907, p. 1, for a suggestion that the statement criticizing President Roosevelt was Darrow's brainchild, not concurred in by Pettibone or Moyer. For a contrary assertion that the statement was published "after being approved by all the attorneys for the defense," see Idaho *Daily Statesman,* May 2, 1907, p. 4.
17. *Oregonian,* May 7, 1907, p. 1.
18. Haywood 1929, p. 206.
19. Quoted in Idaho *Daily Statesman,* June 3, 1907, p. 1.
20. Quoted Stone 1941, p. 235.
21. Haywood 1929, p. 206.
22. Letter, Darrow to Brand Whitlock, April 8, 1907, Whitlock Papers, box 12.
23. *Oregonian,* May 12, 1907, p. 2.
24. *Ibid.,* p. 1.

25. Kendrick Johnson, "Trial of 'Big Bill' Haywood," 24 *Nevada State Bar Journal* (July 1959), 124.
26. Idaho *Daily Statesmen,* May 31, 1907, p. 1.
27. Denver *Post,* June 2, 1907, p. 1, Grover 1964, p. 96.
28. Haywood 1929, pp. 208–209.
29. Grover 1964, p. 97.
30. Idaho *Daily Statesman,* June 4, 1907, p. 1.
31. *Ibid.,* p. 7.
32. *Oregonian,* June 2, 1907, p. 1.
33. Denver *Post,* June 4, 1907, p. 2. The statement identified Hugh O'Neill of the Denver *Post* and F. L. Perkins of the Portland *Evening Telegram* as misreporting signs of a breach between Darrow and Richardson. In fact almost every correspondent had mentioned such signs in his dispatches.
34. Idaho *Daily Statesman,* June 5, 1907, p. 6.
35. Haywood 1929, p. 209, mistakenly attributes direct examination to Borah.
36. Idaho *Daily Statesman,* June 25, 1907, p. 1.
37. Denver *Post,* June 25, 1907, p. 2.
38. Grover 1964, in his otherwise excellent account, makes no mention of the extremely unfavorable reaction to Darrow's first important contribution to the defense.
39. Barrymore 1955, p. 158.
40. *The New York Times,* July 26, 1907, p. 2.
41. Grover 1964, p. 211.
42. Kendrick Johnson, "Trial of 'Big Bill' Haywood," 24 *Nevada State Bar Journal* (July 1959), 127.
43. Davis 1925, pp. 40–41
44. This peculiar line of reasoning was commented on adversely by the Denver *Post* on June 25, 1907, especially by Hugh O'Neill, p. 2.
45. Quoted Grover 1964, p. 221.
46. Hyndman 1912, p. 340.
47. Quoted Grover 1964, p. 217.
48. Quoted *ibid.,* p. 218. It is worth noting, as Grover (pp. 218–219) does, that Darrow's speech in the transcript of this, as in other trials, varies very considerably from what was afterward published as the summation.
49. *Ibid.,* p. 271.
50. *The New York Times,* July 25, 1907, p. 5.
51. Haywood 1929, p. 216.
52. Letter, Brand Whitlock to Darrow, November 22, 1907, reproduced in 1 Nevins (ed.) 1936, pp. 84–85.
53. Davis 1925, p. 39.
54. *Ibid.,* p. 42. The statement was made on a fishing trip Judge Wood took with Davis during the trial, reported in the *Oregonian,* May 22, 1907, p. 2.
55. MacLane 1953, p. 160.
56. Grover 1964, p. 281.
57. Davis 1925, p. 43.
58. *State* v. *Neil,* 13 Idaho 539, at 551. This opinion was handed down on July 6, 1907. Judge Wood did not charge the jury in the Haywood case until July 27.
59. Haywood 1929, pp. 218–219.

CHAPTER 21

1. Steffens 1931, p. 424.
2. Masters 1936, p. 282.
3. *Ibid.*, p. 293.
4. Letter, Paul Edward Darrow to Dartmouth College, [?], 1948.
5. Stone 1941, p. 179.
6. Masters 1936, p. 317.
7. Channing 1849, p. 57.
8. Quoted Kellogg 1967, p. 45.
9. Masters 1936, p. 317.

CHAPTER 22

1. See the Los Angeles *Times*, October 1, 1910, p. 1, for the statement of the police
   department within two hours of the conflagration that dynamite was responsible.
2. Ginger 1962, pp. 323 (quotation from Debs), 325.
3. Robinson 1969, p. 6, states it to have been $50,000 plus $200,000 expenses, but other
   evidence indicates that the arrangement was not as clearcut as that.
4. Such matters are notoriously difficult to check. However James H. Hawley's son
   reported that the McNamara case was offered to his father, who declined it, before
   it was offered to Darrow—see Grover 1964, pp. 265–266, 287. Hawley had prosecuted the Haywood case in 1907.
5. Cargill, 1941, p. 129.
6. Jones 1925, pp. 5, 7.
7. Hapgood 1939, pp. 189–190.
8. In 1911 the total membership of the affiliate unions of the AFL was 1,762,000.
9. Taft 1957, pp. 279, 280–281.
10. Quoted Weinberg (ed.) 1957, p. 520.
11. *The New York Times*, April 26, 1911, p. 3.
12. Letter, Brand Whitlock to Darrow, May 7, 1911, Whitlock Papers, box 23.
13. Letter, Brand Whitlock to Darrow, November 20, 1911, Whitlock Papers, box 24.
14. Cohn and Chisholm 1964, p. 185.
15. Stone 1941, p. 275. The words were recounted by J. B. McNamara himself, and
    uttered when Darrow visited him in prison before the trial.
16. Steffens 1938, p. 280. See Stone 1941, pp. 288–289, for the assertion that Darrow
    was shattered by Steffens's attitude, which gave him his first inkling that the
    McNamaras were regarded as guilty by intelligent people.
17. *The New York Times*, December 7, 1911, p. 12.
18. Steffens 1931, p. 668.
19. For Steffens's account of his role, see his *Autobiography* 1931, p. 670–678. Stone
    1941 concluded: "There can be no doubt but that Steffens blew up his own
    importance in this case to many times the size of its actuality" (note to p. 288).
    Since Stone wrote, W. W. Robinson has published an account of the negotiations
    written by Otto F. Brant, which indicates that though Steffens was privy to some
    of the negotiations, he did not play any substantial part. Judge Bordwell, who
    sentenced the McNamaras, issued a statement that Steffens's claim to have ar-
    ranged the change of pleas was "groundless and untrue. . . . The District Attorney

acted entirely without regard to Mr. Steffens and on lines decided upon before the latter appeared on the scene"—Robinson 1969, pp. 26–27. Adela Rogers St. Johns, who knew the people involved, stated: "I find it possible to believe that Steffens' only great fault as a reporter, his own desire to play God to the story, led him to exaggerate his part as treaty-maker, which Judge Bordwell denied ever happened. To anyone who ever knew General Otis, the picture Steffens gives of meeting with him and winning from him a promise to be kind and lenient to the McNamaras is too hard to swallow"—St. Johns 1962, p. 467.

20. Robinson 1969, pp. 31–33. See also Darrow's speech to the jury in his own defense, reproduced in Weinberg (ed.) 1957, pp. 522–523, which corroborates that Davis made the contract with Fredericks.

21. Weinberg, *op. cit.* Brant's account merely records that the agreement was that the brothers should receive "such sentence as the court may administer (except capital punishment)"—Robinson 1969, p. 33.

22. Taft 1957, p. 282.

23. Darrow says "evening," but in fact the pleas were taken in open court shortly after 2:00 P.M.—see Stone 1941, p. 300.

24. Robinson 1969, p. 16.

25. *Ibid.,* p. 24.

26. Stone 1941, p. 282.

27. Quoted Weinberg (ed.) 1957, p. 513.

28. *The New York Times,* December 6, 1911, p. 2.

29. St. Johns 1964, p. 412.

30. 2 Urofsky and Levy 1972, p. 517.

31. Gertrude Barnum, "Darrow the Great Defender" (n.d.), to be found in Whitlock Papers, box 26.

32. Stone 1941, p. 305.

33. Letter, Samuel Gompers to Darrow, December 6, 1911, quoted in Taft 1957, p. 284. If the same inference from silence was made from Darrow's autobiography as Stone erroneously makes from Gompers's, it would brand as enemies many people with whom he is known from other evidence to have been on cordial terms— including his brothers and sisters and some of his law partners.

CHAPTER 23

1. Details of these strategems can be found in Darrow's speech to the jury in his own defense in Weinberg (ed.) 1957, pp. 495–530. The trial was among the first on record to raise issues of electronic "bugging"—Darrow's conversations were secretly recorded by the prosecution on a "Dictograph" which Darrow referred to as "the wonderful tin box." He described the district attorney's use of it as "infamous"—Weinberg (ed.) 1957, pp. 516–517; see also Steffens 1931, p. 664.

2. Robinson 1969, p. 26.

3. Steffens 1931, p. 681.

4. Whitlock 1925, p. 296.

5. Quoted Weinberg (ed.) 1957, p. 516.

6. Quoted *ibid.,* p. 515.

7. St. Johns 1964, p. 446.

8. Letter, Steffens to Whitlock, June 3, 1912, Whitlock Papers, box 25.

9. Los Angeles *Herald,* May 17, 1912.

10. Steffens 1931, p. 698.

11. Steffens 1938, p. 301. Masters was categorical in his assertion of Darrow's guilt whereas Steffens was not, at least in print. However, fair interpretation of his autobiography and his letters seems to justify the conclusion that he thought Darrow guilty.

12. Masters 1936, p. 385, 386. Some—including Judge Kenesaw Mountain Landis—refused.

13. Wellman 1924, p. 149.

14. St. Johns 1964, p. 447.

15. Masters 1936, p. 292.

16. St. Johns 1964, p. 458.

17. Steffens 1931, p. 664.

18. Quoted Weinberg (ed.) 1957, p. 494.

19. There was some confusion about the money involved. At the initial meeting between Franklin and Lockwood, the proposition was for a total of $2,500, but when Lockwood's name was called for jury service, it became $4,000. When Captain White acted as trustee for the money to be paid to Lockwood, he was under the impression the total amount was $3,500; but in fact $4,000 was the correct figure —see Stone 1941, pp. 287, 295, 297.

20. The prosecution tried to show that the "big fellow" was Darrow, thereby linking him conclusively with the attempts at bribery, but was unsuccessful. Adela St. Johns is wrong to suggest, as she does, that the nickname "big fellow" or "big boy" had been established to be a reference to him—see St. Johns 1964, p. 453.

21. *The New York Times,* December 25, 1911, p. 8.

22. St. Johns 1964, pp. 472, 473–474.

23. Steffens 1931, p. 666.

24. St. Johns 1964, pp. 500–501.

25. *Ibid.,* p. 480.

26. Baillie 1959, p. 21; St. Johns 1964, pp. 481, 505. St. Johns recounts that Darrow was told of this inside information, but did not believe it (p. 483).

27. Quoted Stone 1941, p. 335.

28. Giesler 1960, p. 287.

29. St. Johns 1964, p. 498.

30. Quoted Weinberg (ed.) 1957, pp. 496, 506, 516–517. Darrow had originally used the story of the steer in an article he had written in 1900 with George A. Schilling, Altgeld's secretary of labor, condemning labor leaders who did not truly represent the working man's interests. See MS, Illinois State Historical Library, "The Story of a Steer." This story was not original, but was a commonplace anecdote about the Union Stockyards, based in fact—see Baedeker's *United States* for 1893, p. 286.

31. St. Johns 1964, p. 498.

32. Darrow claimed that the jury was out only ten minutes, which is an exaggeration. He clearly gives this time in order to demonstrate the effectiveness of his argument, but of course that would mean nothing if, as has been alleged, the jury had already made up its mind to acquit.

33. 45 *Literary Digest,* (August 31, 1912), 323.

34. Steffens 1938, pp. 313–314.

35. Letter, Darrow in Los Angeles to Carl Eric Linden, Woodstock, New York, March

20 [1913], quoted in Hamilton Catalogue 70, lot 46 (the catalogue wrongly ascribes the letter to 1924).

36. This version of the telegram is taken from Stone 1941, p. 342. Darrow gives a version from memory that is obviously incomplete—Darrow 1932, p. 190.

37. Quoted 45 *Literary Digest* (August 31), 1921, 323.

38. Giesler 1960, p. 286.

39. Stone 1941, p. 273.

40. ". . . The state of California, the power of the Burns Agency, everything was against us. It needed money on our side, and a great deal of it"—Darrow in his own defense, first trial, quoted Weinberg (ed.) 1957, p. 521.

41. Stone 1941, pp. 283–284.

42. Robinson 1969, p. 46.

43. St. Johns 1964, p. 454. Even Stone 1941, extremely sympathetic to Darrow, shows signs of doubting his defense; see, e.g., pp. 327–328. And he describes some of the defense antics as "dirty and stupid business"—p. 274.

44. Robinson 1969, p. 47.

45. Yarros 1950, p. 9.

46. Quoted Weinberg (ed.) 1957, p. 58.

47. See, generally, the excellent survey by Grover 1964, particularly pp. 94, 95, 105, 107. On the specific allegation of juror intimidation, see Kendrick Johnson, "The Trial of 'Big Bill' Haywood," 24 *Nevada State Bar Journal* July 1959, at 124.

CHAPTER 24

1. Quoted Weinberg (ed.) 1957, pp. 497–498.

2. Gertrude Barnum, "Darrow the Great Defender" (n.d.), to be found in Whitlock Papers, box 26.

3. St. Johns 1964, p. 501.

4. Masters 1936, p. 386.

5. Masters 1916, pp. 98–100. There is much more in the same vein.

6. Pizer (ed.) 1968, p. 122. Mrs. Shannon was Garland's sister.

7. *The New York Times,* May 5, 1914, p. 3.

8. Stone 1941, p. 347.

9. Sanger 1938, p. 183. The government withdrew the prosecution on February 18, 1916, without it ever coming to trial.

10. Landesco 1929, p. 72.

11. Yarros 1950, p. 5.

12. *Ibid.,* p. 50.

13. Farr 1961 p. 131.

14. Wright 1943, p. 294.

15. Darrow Papers, box 1, folder 10.

16. Letter, Darrow to Brand Whitlock, December 13, 1913, Whitlock Papers, box 29.

17. Charles G. Shaw, "Clarence Darrow," in Amory and Bradlee (eds.) 1960, p. 143.

18. Letter, Darrow to Brand Whitlock, July 14 [c. 1910], Whitlock Papers, box 29.

19. Letter, Darrow to William E. Walling, July 14 [c. 1910], NAACP Administrative Files, box 63.

20. Diary, March 2, 1916, quoted in Pizer (ed.) 1968, p. 20.

21. Douglas 1974, p. 267.

22. Farrell (ed.) 1958, p. 206. There are differences of opinion about the date of the end of the Chicago renaissance. Some date it to later than when Darrow considered moving. Kogan and Wendt 1958 say: "The Renaissance that had begun in 1890 had reached its most virulent stage from 1911 to 1920 . . . but it was really in its final phases and the best of the writers were preparing to leave for other climes [in the 1920s]. . . . By 1926 the Chicago Renaissance, except for some valiant diehards who remained, was literally over"—pp. 200, 202–203.

CHAPTER 25

1. Quoted Cairns (ed.) 1965, p. xxvi.
2. Darrow 1932, p. 210. See also his words to the same effect in 1920, quoted in Weinberg (ed.) 1957, p. 125: "From the time Belgium was invaded, long before we got into it, I believed it to be our duty [to go to war]." Stone maintains that "during the early years of the World War he had been an ardent pacifist," and that "for two years [after the outbreak of war] he had maintained that America must remain neutral . . . ," but both these assertions contradict Darrow's own account and the evidence of his pro-interventionist activities—Stone 1941, pp. 356–357.

     As for Darrow's outrage at Germany's violation of Belgian territory, Lloyd George argued that the infraction was a minor one, not worth going to war over, whereas Bertrand Russell argued that no one in public life should have been surprised.
3. Darrow to William Kent, December 19, 1914, Kent Collection.
4. Speech to American Alliance for Labor and Democracy, reported in *The New York Times,* September 16, 1917, p. 1. Later Darrow confessed: "I began to suspect that Big Business was unanimously enlisted on account of the vast financial interests involved"—Darrow 1932, p. 212.
5. Letter, Darrow to William Kent, December 19, 1914, Kent Collection; Darrow 1932, pp. 72–73.
6. Darrow 1919, p. 10.
7. 7 Baker 1939, p. 200.
8. Roger Baldwin, "Reminiscences," 2 *Civil Liberties Review,* no. 2 (1975), 55.
9. 2 La Follette 1953, pp. 739, 780.
10. 7 Baker 1939, p. 210.
11. *The New York Times,* September 16, 1917. pp. 1 and 3.
12. *The New York Times,* May 18, 1918, p. 12.
13. Linn 1937, p. 218. Stone 1941, p. 358, strongly implies that Darrow was the only American so invited, but this was quite untrue. Five were invited from the Chicago area alone—Linn, *ibid.*
14. Steffens 1938, p. 412.
15. *The New York Times,* July 22, 1918, p. 10.

PART THREE: FROM DISGRACE TO DISTINCTION

CHAPTER 26

1. Quoted Moorhouse 1959, p. 166.
2. Quoted Sann 1957, pp. 63–64.
3. Cairns (ed.) 1965, p. 89.
4. Quoted Weinberg (ed.) 1957, p. 126. See to the same effect, Darrow 1932, p. 302: "I had lived in America because I wanted to."
5. Tuttle 1972, p. 195; Kobler 1971, p. 64.
6. Sutherland 1937, p. 139.
7. Letter, Darrow to Harry Louis Mencken, May 11, 1924, Mencken Papers.
8. Darrow 1932, p. 213. Stone says, quite without foundation, that Darrow was involved in their defense. He also implies that Darrow strenuously defended the right of conscientious objection, which is again untrue—Stone 1941, pp. 356–358.
9. Chaplin 1948, p. 226.
10. *Ibid.*
11. Weinberg and Weinberg (eds.) 1963, p. 268.
12. *Ibid.*, pp. 271, 278, 279.
13. Letter, Darrow to Negley Dakin Cochran, October 14, 1921, Cochran Collection.

CHAPTER 27

1. See, e.g., letter, Darrow to Woodrow Wilson, July 29, 1919, pleading for the release of Eugene Debs, Wilson Papers, series 4, file no. 4963, p. 3.
2. Letter, Darrow to Harry Weinberger, August 10, 1917, Weinberger Collection, Goldman Papers.
3. The case is reported as *Bianchi* v. *State,* 169 Wis. 75 (1919).
4. This quotation and the ones that follow are taken from Weinberg 1957, pp. 127–128, 161–162, 130, 160, and 123–124.
5. Letter, Darrow to Benjamin Barr Lindsey, May 4, 1922, Lindsey Papers, box 66.
6. Letter, Darrow to Benjamin Barr Lindsey, August 10, 1922, Lindsey Papers, box 66.
7. Bright 1930, pp. 148, 192.

CHAPTER 28

1. Masters 1936, p. 291.
2. Darrow and Holmes 1924, p. 38.
3. *The New York Times,* April 19, 1936, p. 53.
4. The article to which Putzel referred appeared in *Reedy's Mirror.* A later, fuller article appeared in *Vanity Fair* (February 1927), 39–40.
5. "Inheritance—an address delivered before the Chicago City Club, March 29, 1919," pp. 22, 27, Darrow Papers, box 1.
6. Quoted Stone 1941, pp. 316–317.
7. Stone 1941, p. 173.
8. Quoted Tebbel 1948, p. 233.

9. Donald R. Cressey, Introduction to the reissue of *Crime: Its Cause and Treatment* (Montclair, N.J.: Patterson Smith, 1972), p. vi.
10. George S. Leisure, "Reflections on Clarence Darrow," 45 *Virginia Law Review* (1959), at 417.

CHAPTER 29

1. Bradley 1962, p. 235.
2. Letter, Darrow to Benjamin Barr Lindsey, March 31, 1917, Lindsey Papers, box 55. Darrow's home telephone number was Hyde Park 5657.
3. Busch 1952, p.147. Nataan Leopold, who actually made the call, said that his alias was *Frank* Johnson. Leopold 1958, p. 25.
4. Reproduced in Busch 1952, pp. 147–149.
5. Leopold 1958, p. 26.
6. The account given by Darrow 1932, pp. 226ff., is clearly written from memory and is inaccurate in several respects, including the circumstances in which Jacob Franks learned that a body had been found.
7. Leopold 1958, p. 26.
8. Quoted Weinberg (ed.) 1957, p. 45.
9. Leopold 1958, pp. 39–40. Darrow's recollection is incorrect; he wrote: "It seemed to have been agreed that if anything happened and they were arrested within a week they should tell their pre-arranged story, as afterwards told by Leopold; but if arrested after that they were to say that they did not remember where they drove. As fate would have it, Nathan was arrested before the week was over, and Loeb after its expiration"—Darrow 1932, p. 228.
10. Higdon 1975, p. 107. Many commentators have suggested that the chauffeur had a grudge against Leopold, but Leopold himself suggests that the chauffeur's intention was to exonerate him—Leopold 1958, p. 45.
11. Leopold 1958, p. 49.
12. Quoted Higdon 1975, pp. 167–168.
13. Normally Darrow loved to be in the news, but in defending Leopold and Loeb he was unable to squeeze even a few favorable words out of the press. The verdict of the newspaper jury was unanimous. Fanny Butcher attacked the defendants, suggesting that they were guilty of even worse crimes than that of which they stood accused; and Adela St. Johns, assigned by Hearst to cover the proceedings, disliked Darrow so much that she got herself taken off them.
14. Higdon 1975, p. 169.
15. 3 Jones 1957, p. 103. At the court hearing one of the alienists called by the state gave his opinion without having examined Leopold or Loeb at all—Leopold 1958, p. 73. This set a precedent that has been followed in American courts in a number of controversial trials, including that of Alger Hiss.
16. Moley 1929, p. 87; Bright 1930, p. 163.
17. Leopold 1958, pp. 61–63.

CHAPTER 30

1. Higdon 1975, p. 147.
2. Stone characterizes part of Darrow's argument as being "Mitigation is a defense"

—Stone 1941, p. 407; but Darrow never made any such claim. The opportunity to present a defense had been voluntarily relinquished by the pleas of guilty. Darrow's argument was that the defendants' mental condition was relevant to establishing their blameworthiness, which in turn was relevant to determining an appropriate punishment.

3. In doing so, Judge Caverly imposed a caveat: if the evidence so adduced indicated that the defendants' sanity (within the legal definition) was in question, he would of his own motion direct that a plea of not guilty be entered on behalf of the defendants and empanel a jury—Leopold 1958, p. 73. This was exactly what the defense wanted to avoid, and therefore had to be careful in guiding its expert witnesses. In spite of all efforts to avoid testimony that indicated "legal" insanity, some witnesses insisted on venturing the opinion that the boys were insane—Darrow 1932, p. 239. This gave the defense some tense moments, in case the judge used the testimony as ground for rejecting the guilty pleas and allowing the case to go to a jury. He did not.

4. Leopold 1958, p. 74.

5. The citations that follow are taken from Weinberg (ed.) 1957, pp. 20–21, 23–25, and 26–29.

6. Busch 1952, pp. 163–164. This is one of a number of important passages that is omitted from Weinberg (ed.) 1957. Busch emphasizes, correctly, that it was one of Darrow's most telling points against the prosecution, describing the prosecution's attitude as "a rare opportunity of which he [Darrow] was quick to take advantage."

7. The citations that follow are again taken from Weinberg (ed.) 1957, pp. 55, 58, and 76.

8. Quoted Busch 1952, p. 193.

9. Busch 1952, p. 150. Leopold complained that the newspapers added to the rumors of grotesque sexual perversions by failing to report this testimony, thereby encouraging the public in speculations worse than the truth. The rumors flared up again when Loeb was killed in prison in 1936 by a fellow prisoner who alleged Loeb to have made a sexual advance to him—Leopold flatly denies that this was true. And they again received currency with the publication of Meyer Levin's *Compulsion* (1956), a fictionalized version of the Leopold and Loeb crime that portrays sexual perversion as a motive for the crime. Leopold discredited this book and tried to prevent its being published—Leopold 1958, pp. 79–80, 302, 399–404.

10. Busch 1952, p. 198.

11. Leopold 1958, p. 81.

12. Butcher 1972, p. 208.

13. Leopold 1958, pp. 402–403.

14. Higdon 1975, p. 325. As Higdon observed, everybody had made money from Leopold's crime but Leopold, whose own book did not do well—*ibid.*, p. 326.

15. A summary of newspaper comments that followed the sentencing of Leopold and Loeb can be found in 82 *Literary Digest* (September 27, 1924), 10. Almost every daily newspaper carried a comment on September 10 or 11, 1924.

16. Yarros, who discussed the case at length with Darrow shortly after its disposition, also stated that "Fortune favored Darrow—the judge assigned to try the case was old and not well, having just recovered from a long illness and being in no condition to run again and make a fight. He had nothing to lose politically and very little socially by exercising mercy"—Yarros 1950, p. 8. Like many of Yarros's

statements, this is open to doubt. Caverly was younger than Darrow and lived longer than he. Furthermore contemporaries such as Francis X. Busch described Caverly as "known as a kindly man and a humane judge"—Busch 1952, p. 131.

17. *The New York Times,* September 22, 1924, p. 21; September 23, 1924, p. 25.
18. Leopold 1958, pp. 126–127.
19. Quoted, in another form, Weinberg (ed.) 1957, p. 17; the theme was reiterated in many versions.
20. Quoted Busch 1952, p. 194.
21. Darrow claimed later: "I felt that I would get a fair fee if I went into the case, but money never influenced my stand one way or another"—Darrow 1932, p. 232. Even if this were literally true, Darrow was not a free agent in this respect; he was a member of a partnership, bound to share his fees where, as in this case, partnership office space, facilities, and time were used.
22. Both Stone and Darrow state explicitly that the agreement was couched in terms solely of saving the boys' lives—Stone 1941, p. 420; Darrow 1932, p. 234.
23. Quoted Weinberg (ed.) 1957, p. 20.
24. Two differing accounts are given in Stone 1941, pp. 420–421, based upon personal interviews with Mrs. Darrow and Clarence's legal associates, and in Harrison 1931, pp. 272–273, summarized in Weinberg (ed.) 1957, pp. 17–18, and published with Darrow's knowledge and consent during his lifetime.
25. Leopold maintained this was true throughout. "My motive, so far as I can be said to have had one, was to please Dick. . . . From the first I never really believed that we would go through with it. It was only something to talk about, to plan"—Leopold 1958, p. 50.
26. Both Harrison and Stone agree that Darrow received net only $30,000. Harrison says that the $70,000 check was divided fifty-fifty between Darrow and his partners, and from Darrow's share federal and state income taxes took a further $5,000. But tax would have been paid on the fee regardless of size, so it is not strictly fair for Harrison to take it into account; there was never a suggestion that the fee was to give Darrow a sum net after payment of all taxes. It is believed that the Bachrach brothers did not receive $30,000 each, as Stone's version would imply; but that does not disprove the essence of Stone's story, because the Loebs might have used payments to the Bachrachs as an excuse without paying them.
27. Weinberg (ed.) 1957, pp. 95–96.
28. Blanshard 1973, p. 69.

CHAPTER 31

1. Butcher 1972, p. 209.
2. Matilda Fenberg, "I Remember Clarence Darrow," *Chicago History* (Fall-Winter, 1973), 217.
3. *Vanity Fair* (April 1927), 52.
4. Bridges 1925, p. 135.
5. Hollis 1958, p. 107.
6. Letter, Mrs. Lillian Saunders to Benjamin Barr Lindsey, November 30, 1926, Lindsey Papers, box 355.
7. "What to do about crime?—an address delivered before the Nebraska State Bar Association, Lincoln, Nebraska, December 28, 1926," p. 1, Darrow Papers, box 1.

8. Barnes 1926, p. 24.
9. Tompkins (ed.), 1965, pp. 19–20.
10. 3 Coletta 1969, p. 217.
11. Leuchtenburg 1958, p. 221.
12. Trachtenberg (ed.) 1973, p. 144.
13. Clemens 1939, p. 66.
14. Douglass 1845, pp. 77–78.
15. "The old-time 'village atheist' is a thing of the past, a folk curiosity like the town crier; Clarence Darrow, the last of the 'village atheists' on a national scale, has left no successors"—Herberg, 1960, pp. 259–260.
16. Hays 1928, p. 28.
17. There is no doubt about Dayton's business interest in the test case. The precise circumstances in which Scopes became defendant are well explained in Scopes and Presley 1967, pp. 57, 64, revealing, apparently for the first time, that before Scopes was approached, the school principal had refused to be defendant (p. 62).
18. St. Johns 1964, p. 324.
19. Tuchman 1958, p. 40.
20. From *Heathen Days* 1943, reproduced in Cairns (ed.) 1965, p. 452.

CHAPTER 32

1. The transcript (hereinafter T.) of the Scopes evolution trial is published as *The World's Most Famous Trial* (Cincinnati: National Book Company, 1925), pp. 99.
2. Hays 1928, pp. 71–72. Hays's claim can only be explained by his egotism. He is the sole participant or observer who makes the suggestion which, apart from Scopes's express contradiction, may be regarded as denied by implication by Marcet Haldeman-Julius 1936, p. 17, and Francis McConnell in 121 *Unity* no. 6 (May 16, 1938), 87. It would, of course, be a most irresponsible breach of professional etiquette for Hays to make such a proposal in open court without first consulting his senior counsel.
3. Scopes and Presley 1967, p. 166. The Mansion was the name given to the house in Dayton that became the defense headquarters.
4. Wells 1934, p. 461.
5. Hays 1928, pp. 72, 76.
6. T. p. 188. On the seventh day also he elicited "great applause"—p. 301.
7. T. p. 288.
8. Scopes and Presley 1967, pp. 187–188.
9. *Ibid.,* p. 197.
10. Hays 1928, p. 68.
11. 3 Coletta 1969, p. 256, quoting Mrs. Bryan. See also p. 255, "[Hays] is a Jew and is as forward and self-assertive as the New York Jew can be. . . ."
12. Sinclair 1962, p. 286.
13. Hays 1928, p. 79.
14. 3 Coletta 1969, p. 271.
15. Oursler 1964, p. 235.
16. Letter, Negley Dakin Cochran to G. B. Parker, May 22, 1925, Cochran Papers.
17. Letter, Eugene V. Debs to Darrow, June 4, 1925, Illinois State Historical Library.

18. Review by Darrow of M. R. Werner's "Bryan" in 58 *New Republic* (May 15, 1929), 363–364.
19. From *Heathen Days* 1943, reproduced in Cairns (ed.) 1965, p. 448.
20. The last "monkey law" in the nation was repealed by Mississippi in 1972—*The New York Times,* April 16, 1972, sect. 1, p. 18.
21. Annual Report, ACLU, "The Fight for Civil Liberty, 1927–1928," p. 43.
22. Annual Report, ACLU, "The Fight for Civil Liberty, 1930–1931," p. 27.
23. *Epperson* v. *Arkansas,* 393 U.S. 97 (1968). Mr. Justice Black, although concurring in the result of the case, did so on the ground that the statute was "void for vagueness"—i.e., that its meaning was not clear. In this respect the Arkansas statute reflected some of the same difficulties as the Tennessee law, for the Tennessee law never mentioned Darwin by name and it was never resolved whether it prohibited mere reference to the theory of evolution, or only the teaching of it as true.

CHAPTER 33

1. Birkenhead, 1924, p. 15.
2. Weinberg 1971, p. 6.
3. Quoted *ibid,* p. 5.
4. *Ibid.,* pp. 7–9.
5. *Ibid.,* p. 41.
6. *Ibid.,* p. 31.
7. Hixson 1972, p. 152; letter, Moorfield Storey to Arthur K. Reading, December 15, 1927.
8. Quoted Weinberg 1971, p. 21.
9. Harrison 1932, p. 334.
10. *Pond* v. *People,* 8 Mich. 150 (1860), at 176.
11. ". . . our clients seemed evasive. None was inclined to talk. We took their stories one by one and they didn't wholly jibe. . . . Then they seemed to feel that in spite of our expostulations, we might just as well be pleased if we did not know too much"—Hays 1928, p. 199.
12. *Ibid.,* p. 199.
13. 2 Lilienthal 1964, p. 21. In spite of the judge's reference to a "hanging verdict," the Sweets were in no danger of execution. Michigan had abolished capital punishment long before their trials.
14. Weinberg 1971, pp. 26–27.
15. Quoted *ibid.,* p. 118.
16. Quoted *ibid.,* p. 232.
17. Hamilton Catalogue 17, lot 41.
18. Marcet Haldeman-Julius, *Clarence Darrow's Two Great Trials,* quoted in Weinberg (ed.) 1957, p. 231; information from Mrs. Josephine Gomon, personal interview with author, March 20, 1972.
19. Hamilton Catalogue 17, lot 41.
20. Letter, Bartolomeo Vanzetti, to Mrs. Maude Pettyjohn, December 11, 1926, reproduced in Frankfurter and Jackson (eds.) 1928, p. 223.

CHAPTER 34

1. Letter, Fay Lewis to Walter White, October 14, 1926, NAACP Administrative Files, c-95.
2. Hays 1928, pp. 189–190.
3. Wendt and Kogan 1953, p. 289.
4. Fleischman 1964, p. 110.
5. Hays 1933, p. 349.
6. Fleischman 1964, p. 110.
7. Letter, Darrow to Harry Elmer Barnes, February 21, 1928, Barnes Collection.
8. Letter, Darrow to Walter White, July 12 [1927], NAACP Administrative Files, box c-96.
9. Stone 1941, p. 488.
10. Letter, Darrow to Arthur Spingarn, October 22, 1932, in possession of the author.
11. Nevins and Hill 1957, p. 505.
12. Letter, Darrow to Sinclair Lewis, February ? [1921?], Yale Collection of American Literature.
13. *Main Street* (New York: Harcourt, Brace and Howe, 1920), p. 50.
14. Letter, Darrow to Henry Louis Mencken, May 2, 1924, Mencken Papers.
15. Letter, Darrow to Henry Louis Mencken, January 22, 1927, Mencken Papers.
16. Letter, Darrow to Harry Elmer Barnes, August 29, 1928, Barnes Collection.
17. Letter, Eugene Debs to Joseph Labadie, December 12, 1905, Labadie Papers, reproduced in Ginger 1962, pp. 239–240.
18. Smith 1962, p. 154.
19. Williamson 1940, p. 231.
20. Higgins 1965, p. 134.
21. Musmanno 1958, pp. 186–188. The story is told slightly differently in Stone 1941, p. 491.
22. Stone 1941, p. 173.
23. Kaplan 1974, p. 317.
24. Hutchinson 1957, p. 582. Darrow wrote in support of Lowden in *Scribner's* (April 1928), 395–403. See also letter, Darrow to Harry Elmer Barnes, November 10, 1928, Barnes Collection.
25. Letter, Walter White to Darrow, October 4, 1926, NAACP Administrative Files, box c-95.
26. Letter, Darrow to James Weldon Johnson, April 17, 1928, NAACP Administrative Files, box c-63.
27. Letter, Darrow to Harry Elmer Barnes, August 1, [1931], Barnes Collection, describing Rabbi Mann and the Rev. Preston Bradley.
28. Letter, Darrow to Walter White, April 30, 1929, NAACP Administrative Files, box c-83.
29. Smith 1962, p. 154.
30. Stone 1941, p. 490.
31. Letter, Darrow to Henry Louis Mencken, September 5, 1930, Mencken Papers.
32. Letter, Darrow to Harry Elmer Barnes, August 1, 1931, Barnes Collection.
33. Letter, Brand Whitlock to Albert Bigelow Paine, February 23, 1932, reproduced in 2 Nevins (ed.) 1936, p. 512.

CHAPTER 35

1. Letter, Walter White to Charles A. J. McPherson, May 19, 1931, NAACP Legal Files, box d-69.
2. Letter, Charles A. J. McPherson to Walter White, May 29, 1931, NAACP Legal Files, box d-69.
3. This entire verbatim exchange is based upon Hays 1933, pp. 87–89.
4. Quoted Van Slingerland 1966, p. 119.
5. She had testified that she was pregnant as a result of the rape, which though not challenged by the defense, was almost certainly untrue, and anyway beyond her knowledge—See Van Slingerland 1966, p. 92.
6. *Ibid.,* p. 143.
7. *Ibid.,* p. 167.
8. Ruby Darrow to Harry Elmer Barnes [March ?], [1932], Barnes Collection.
9. Letter, Darrow to Harry Elmer Barnes, March 5, [1932], Barnes Collection.
10. Letter, Darrow to Harry Elmer Barnes, March 12, 1932, Barnes Collection.
11. Cargill 1941, p. 131.
12. Letter, Ruby Darrow to Harry Elmer Barnes, March 7, [1932], Barnes Collection.
13. "Who Knows Justice?," 91 *Scribner's Magazine* (February 1932), pp. 73–77, at 72.
14. Letter, Darrow to Harry Elmer Barnes, March 12, 1932, Barnes Collection.
15. Van Slingerland 1966, p. 252.
16. *Ibid.,* p. 264.
17. *Ibid.,* p. 269.
18. *Ibid.,* p. 269.
19. *Ibid.,* pp. 281–282.
20. *Ibid.,* p. 320.
21. *Ibid.,* p. 326.
22. Letter, Darrow to Arthur Spingarn, October 22, 1932, in possession of the author.

CHAPTER 36

1. Letter, Darrow to Walter White, May 3, [1932], Spingarn Papers, box 65.
2. Letter, Walter White to Arthur Spingarn, June 9, 1932, Spingarn Papers, box 65.
3. Letter, Darrow to Arthur Spingarn, October 22, 1932, in possession of the author.
4. Wells 1936, p. 373.
5. Letter, Ruby Darrow to Carl Eric Linden, Woodstock, New York, [1934], quoted Hamilton Catalogue 46, lot 109.
6. Harry Elmer Barnes, in 121 *Unity,* no. 6 (May 16, 1938), 94.
7. Letter, Eugene Manlove Rhodes to Theodore van Soelen, May 3, 1933, quoted in Hutchinson 1956, p. 349.
8. Letter, Darrow to Irving Fisher, June 6, 1933, Fisher Collection.
9. Wells 1934, p. 672.
10. Reproduced, NRA Report 1935, pp. 2002–2003.
11. *Ibid.,* p. 297.
12. Tugwell 1957, p. 327.
13. Quoted Douglas 1974, p. 346.

14. NRA Report 1935, p. 2447 (Testimony of Thursday, April 18, 1935.)
15. Lyon, *et al.* 1935, pp. 710–711.
16. NRA Report 1935, p. 310.
17. *Ibid.,* pp. 308–309.
18. Danelski and Tulchin (eds.) 1973, p. 307.
19. Douglas 1974, p. 347.
20. Paul Darrow 1941, pp. 8–9.

CHAPTER 37

1. *The New York Times,* July 3, 1934, p. 5.
2. Letter, Elizabeth Quereau to Benjamin Barr Lindsey, June 26, 1935, Lindsey Papers, box 183.
3. NRA Report 1935, pp. 304–305.
4. Higdon 1975, p. 303.
5. Quoted from Willis Thornton in Stone 1941, p. 516.
6. Darrow 1918, p. 14.
7. *Christian Century,* April 19, 1928, p. 504.
8. Letter, Darrow to Harry Elmer Barnes, February 8 [1931], Barnes Collection.
9. Letter, Henry Louis Mencken to Darrow, April 23, 1937, Mencken Papers.
10. Stone 1941, p. 517.

Bibliography

Ahlstrom, Sydney E., *A Religious History of the American People.* New Haven: Yale University Press, 1972.

Allen, Frederick Lewis, *The Lords of Creation.* New York: Harper & Brothers, 1935.

American Civil Liberties Union, *Annual Reports.* New York, various dates.

Amory, Cleveland, and Bradlee, Frederic, ed., *Vanity Fair, Selections from America's Most Memorable Magazine.* New York. The Viking Press 1960.

Altgeld, John Peter, *Our Penal Machinery and Its Victims.* Chicago: Janson, McClurg & Co., 1884.

————, *Live Questions.* New York: The Humboldt Publishing Co., 1890.

Arnold, Thurman, *Fair Fights and Foul.* New York: Harcourt, Brace & World, 1965.

Baillie, Hugh, *High Tension.* New York: Harper & Brothers, 1959.

Baker, Ray Stannard, *Woodrow Wilson Life and Letters,* Volume 7, April 6, 1917– February 28, 1918. New York: Doubleday, Doran & Co., 1939.

Barnard, Harry, *Eagle Forgotten.* Indianapolis and New York: The Bobbs-Merrill Company, 1962.

Barnes, Harry Elmer, *The Repression of Crime.* New York: Geroge H. Doran Company, 1962.

Barrymore, Ethel, *Memories.* New York: Harper & Brothers, 1955.

Birkenhead, Lord, *America Revisited.* Boston: Little, Brown & Co., 1924.

Blankfort, Michael, *The Big Yankee—The Life of Carlson of the Raiders.* Boston: Little, Brown & Co., 1947.

Blanshard, Paul, *Personal and Controversial.* Boston: Beacon Press, 1973.

Blumberg, Dorothy Rose, *Florence Kelley. The Making of a Social Pioneer.* New York: Augustus M. Kelley, Publisher, 1966.

Bradley, Preston, *Along the Way.* New York: David McKay Company, 1962.

Bridges, Horace James, *The God of Fundamentalism.* Freeport, N.Y.: Books for Libraries Press, 1969, first published 1925.

Bright, John, *Hizzoner Big Bill Thompson.* New York: Jonathan Cape and Harrison Smith, 1930.

Brown, Elizabeth Gaspar, *Legal Education at Michigan 1859–1959.* Ann Arbor, Mich.: The University of Michigan Law School, 1959.

Browne, Waldo R., *Altgeld of Illinois.* New York: B.W. Huebsch, Inc., 1924.

Buckler, Helen, *Doctor Dan Pioneer in American Surgery.* Boston: Little, Brown & Co., 1954.

Busch, Francis X., *Prisoners at the Bar.* New York: The Bobbs-Merrill Company, 1952.

Butcher, Fanny, *Many Lives—One Love.* New York: Harper & Row, 1972.

Cairns, Huntington, ed., *H. L. Mencken: The American Scene—A Reader.* New York: Alfred A. Knopf, 1965.

Carew-Hunt, R. N., *Marxism Past and Present.* London: Geoffrey Bles, 1954.

Cargill, Oscar, *Intellectual America.* New York: The Macmillan Company, 1941.

Channing, William E., *Works*, 11th ed., vol. 5. Boston: Geroge G. Channing, 1849.

Chaplin, Ralph, *Wobbly.* Chicago: University of Chicago Press, 1948.

Chenery, William L., *So It Seemed.* New York: Harcourt, Brace & Co., 1952.

Chroust, Anton-Hermann, *The Rise of the Legal Profession in America,* 2 vols. Norman, Okla.: University of Oklahoma Press, 1965.

Churchill, Allen, *The Theatrical Twenties.* New York: McGraw-Hill, 1975.

Clayton, John, *Illinois Fact Book 1673–1968.* Carbondale, Ill.: Southern Illinois University Press, 1970.

Clemens, Cyril, *Chesterton as Seen by His Contemporaries.* New York: Haskell House Publishers Ltd., 1969, first published 1939.

Cocks, T. Fraser, ed., *Pictorial History of Ann Arbor 1824–1974.* Ann Arbor Mich.: Bentley Historical Library, 1974.

Cohn, Alfred and Chisholm, Joe, *Take the Witness!* New York: Pocket Books, 1964; originally published 1934, with introduction by Adela Rogers St. Johns.

Coleman, McAlister, *Eugene V. Debs: A Man Unafraid.* New York: Greenberg, 1930.

Coletta, Paolo E., *William Jennings Bryan,* 3 vols. Lincoln, Neb.: University of Nebraska Press, 1964–69.

Coolidge, L. A., *Official Directory of the Fifty-Fifth Congress, 2d Session.* Washington, D.C.: Government Printing Office, 1897.

Cullom, Shelby M., *Fifty Years of Public Service* Chicago: A. C. McClurg & Co., 1911.

Curry, J. Seymour, *Chicago: Its History and Its Builders.* Chicago: S.J. Clarke Publishing Company, 1912.

Danelski, David J. and Tulchin, Joseph S., eds., *The Autobiographical Notes of Charles Evans Hughes.* Cambridge, Mass.: Harvard University Press, 1973.

Darrow, Clarence, *Realism in Literature and Art.* Girard, Kans.: The Haldeman-Julius Company, 1899. Contains, besides title essay, "Robert Burns," "George Burman Foster," and "Some Paragraphs Addressed to Socialists."

————, *Farmington.* Chicago: A. C. McClurg & Co., 1904.

————, *Speech of Hon. Clarence S. Darrow of Chicago at the Opera House,* Youngstown, Ohio, Sunday, May 2, 1909 (Prohibition Debate), n.p.

————, *Response to Birthday Greetings.* Chicago: Waldon Book Shop, 1918.

————, *War Prisoners—An Address, Garrick Theatre, Chicago, November 9, 1919.*

————. *The Skeleton in the Closet.* Boston: International Pocket Library, 1924.

————, *Address Before Nebraska State Bar Association,* Lincoln, Nebraska, December 28, 1926. "What shall we do about crime?" Unpublished, in Darrow Papers.

————, *The Story of My Life.* New York: Charles Scribner's Sons, 1932

Darrow, Clarence, and the Reverend John Haynes Holmes, *Debate: That the United States Continue the Policy of Prohibition as Defined in the Eighteenth Amendment.* New York: The League for Public Discussion, 1924.

Darrow, Paul, *What Shall We Do for the Poor?* Chicago, privately printed, 1941. (In Dartmouth College Library.)

Davidson, Jo, *Between Sittings.* New York: The Dial Press, 1951.

Davis, Oscar King, *Released for Publication.* Boston: Houghton Mifflin Company, 1925.

Debs, Eugene, *His Life, Writings and Speeches*. Girard, Kans: The Appeal to Reason, 1908.

Destler, Chester McArthur, *Henry Demarest Lloyd and the Empire of Reform*. Philadelphia: University of Pennsylvania Press, 1963.

de Tocqueville, Alexis, *Democracy in America,* 2 vols., (Philips Bradley edition). New York: Alfred A. Knopf, 1945.

Douglass, Frederick, *Narrative of the Life of Frederick Douglass*. New York: Signet Books, 1968; first published 1845.

————, *Narrative of the Life,* Boston: The Anti-Slavery Office, 1845.

Douglas, William O., *Go East, Young Man*. New York: Random House, 1974.

Drinnan, Richard, *Rebel in Paradise—A Biography of Emma Goldman*. Chicago: University of Chicago Press, 1961.

DuBois, W. E. B., *Autobiography*. New York: International Publishers Company, 1968.

Eastman, Max, *Enjoyment of Living*. New York: Harper & Brothers, 1948.

Eddy, Ruth Story Devereaux, *The Eddy Family in America*. Boston: The Eddy Family Association, 1930.

Ehrlich, J. W., *A Life in My Hands*. New York: G. P. Putnam's Sons, 1965.

Ernst, Morris L., *A Love Affair with the Law*. New York: The Macmillan Company, 1968.

Farr, Finis, *Frank Lloyd Wright*. New York: Charles Scribner's Sons, 1961.

Farrell, James T., ed., *H. L. Mencken Prejudices: A Selection*. New York: Vintage Books, 1968.

Fiedler, George, *The Illinois Law Courts in Three Centuries 1673–1973*. Berwyn, Ill.: Physicians' Record Company, 1973.

Fleischman, Harry, *Norman Thomas*. New York: W. W. Norton & Co., 1964.

Foner, Philip Sheldon, *History of the Labor Movement in the United States,* 4 vols. New York: International Publishers, 1965.

Frankfurter, Marion, and Gardner, Jackson, ed., *The Letters of Sacco and Vanzetti.* New York: The Viking Press, 1928.

Friede, Donald, *The Mechanical Angel* (autobiography). New York: Alfred A. Knopf, 1948.

Frost, Richard H., *The Mooney Case*. Stanford, Calif.: Stanford University Press, 1968.

Giesler, Jerry (as told to Pete Martin), *Hollywood Lawyer—The Jerry Giesler Story.* New York: Simon & Schuster, 1960.

Ginger, Ray, *Alteld's America*. New York: Funk & Wagnalls, 1958.

————, *Eugene V. Debs: A Biography*. New York: Collier Books, 1962.

Goldman, Emma, *Living My Life*. New York: Alfred A. Knopf, 1931.

Goldman, Marion S., *A Portrait of the Black Attorney in Chicago*. Chicago: American Bar Foundation, 1972.

Gompers, Samuel, *Seventy Years of Life and Labour,* 2 vols. New York: E. P. Dutton & Co., 1925.

Goodhart, Arthur L., *Five Jewish Lawyers of the Common Law*. London: Oxford University Press, 1949.

Grover, David H., *Debaters and Dynamiters: The Story of the Haywood Trial*. Corvallis, Oreg.: The Oregon State University Press, 1964.

Haldeman-Julius, Marcet, *Famous and Interesting Guests of a Kansas Farm*. Girard, Kans.: Haldeman-Julius Publications, 1936.

Hamilton, Alice, *Exploring the Dangerous Trades* (autobiography). Boston: Little, Brown & Co., 1943.

Hamilton, Charles, *Auction Catalogues*. New York, various numbers and dates.

Hapgood, Hutchins, *A Victorian in the Modern World* (autobiography). New York: Harcourt, Brace and Company, 1939.

Harrison, Carter H., *Stormy Years*. New York: The Bobbs-Merrill Company, 1935.

————, *Recollections of Life and Doings in Chicago*. Chicago: Normandie House, 1945.

Harrison, Charles Yale, *Clarence Darrow*. New York: Jonathan Cape and Harrison Smith, 1931.

Hart, Sara L., *The Pleasure Is Mine*. Chicago: Valentine-Newman, 1947.

Harvey, Rowland Hill, *Samuel Gompers*. Stanford, Calif.: Stanford University Press, 1935.

Hays, Arthur Garfield, *Let Freedom Ring*. New York: Boni and Liveright, 1928.

————, *Trial by Prejudice*. New York: Covici, Friede, 1933.

————, *Democracy Works*. New York: Random House, 1939.

————, *City Lawyer*. New York: Simon and Schuster, 1942.

Haywood, William D., *Bill Haywood's Book*. New York: International Publishers Company, 1929.

Herberg, Will, *Protestant, Catholic, Jew*. Garden City, N.Y.: Doubleday & Co., 1960.

Hicks, Frederick C., ed., *Arguments and Addresses of Joseph Hodges Choate*. St. Paul, Minn.: West Publishing Company, 1926.

Higdon, Hal, *The Crime of the Century*. New York: G.P. Putnam's Sons, 1975.

Higgins, Thomas G., *An Autobiography*. New York: (no publisher), 1965.

Hillquit, Morris, *Loose Leaves from a Busy Life*. New York: The Macmillan Company, 1934.

Hixson, William B., Jr., *Moorfield Storey and the Abolitionist Tradition*. New York: Oxford University Press, 1972.

Hollis, Christopher, *Along the Road to Frome*. London: George G. Harrap & Co. Ltd., 1958.

Holly, William H., *A Forgotten Governor*. Chicago: Public Ownership League, 1937.

Howe, Henry, *Historical Collections of Ohio*. Cincinnati: Krehbiel & Co., 1907.

Hutchinson, W. H., *A Bar Cross Man: The Life and Personal Writings of Eugene Manlove Rhodes*. Norman, Okla.: University of Oklahoma Press, 1956.

Hutchinson, William T., *Lowden of Illinois*. Chicago: University of Chicago Press 1957.

Hyde, H. Montgomery, *The Cleveland Street Scandal*. New York: Coward, McCann & Geoghegan, 1976.

Hyndman, Henry Mayers, *Further Reminiscences*. London: The Macmillan Company, 1912.

Johnson, James Weldon, *Along This Way*. New York: The Viking Press, 1968; originally published 1933.

Johnson, Walter, ed., *Selected Letters of William Allen White, 1899–1943*. New York: Henry Holt and Company, 1947.

Jones, Ernest, *The Life and Work of Sigmund Freud*, 3 vols. New York: Basic Books, 1957.

Jones, Mother (also known as Mary Harris), *Autobiography*. Chicago: Charles H. Kerr & Company, 1925.

Josephson, Matthew, *Sidney Hillman*. Garden City, N.Y.: Doubleday & Co., 1952.

Kaplan, Justin, *Lincoln Steffens*. New York: Simon & Schuster, 1974.

Kellogg, Charles Flint, *National Association for the Advancement of Colored People*, Vol. 1, 1909–1920. Baltimore: The Johns Hopkins Press, 1967.

Kempf, Edward J., *Abraham Lincoln's Philosophy of Common Sense.* New York: The New York Academy of Sciences, 1965.

King, Ethel M., *Reflections of Reedy: A Biography of William Marion Reedy of Reedy's Mirror.* Brooklyn, N.Y.: Gerald J. Richard, 1961.

King, Hoyt, *Citizen Cole of Chicago.* Chicago: Horder's, Inc., 1931.

Kobler, John, *Capone.* New York: G. P. Putnam's Sons, 1971.

———, *Ardent Spirits.* New York: G. P. Putnam's Sons, 1973.

Koenig, Louis W., *Bryan: A Political Biography of William Jennings Bryan.* New York: G. P. Putnam's Sons, 1971.

Koenigsberg, Moses, *King News—An Autobiography.* Philadelphia: F. A. Stokes Company, 1941.

Kogan, Herman and Wendt, Lloyd, *Chicago A Pictorial History* New York: E. P. Dutton and Company, Inc., 1958.

Krutch, Joseph Wood, *More Lives Than One.* New York: William Sloane Associates, 1962.

La Follette, Belle Case and Fola, *Robert M. La Follette.* New York: The Macmillan Company, 1953.

Landesco, John, *Organized Crime in Chicago.* Chicago: University of Chicago Press, 1968. (This is a reprint of Part III of the 1929 Illinois Crime Survey.)

Larsen, Charles, *The Good Fight.* Chicago: Quadrangle Books, 1972.

Larson, Orvin, *American Infidel: Robert G. Ingersoll.* New York: The Citadel Press, 1962.

Laurence, Dan H., ed., *Bernard Shaw—Collected Letters, 1898–1910.* New York: Dodd, Mead & Co., 1972.

Leopold, Nathan F., *Life Plus 99 Years.* New York: Popular Library, 1958.

Leuchtenburg, William, *The Perils of Prosperity 1914–32.* Chicago: The University of Chicago Press, 1958.

Levy, Newman, *My Double Life.* Garden City, N.Y.: Doubleday & Co., 1958.

Lewis, Lloyd and Smith, Justin, *Chicago—The History of Its Reputation.* New York: Harcourt, Brace & Co., 1929.

Lilienthal, David E., *Journals,* 4 vols. New York: Harper & Row, 1964–69.

Linder, Usher F., *Reminiscences of the Early Bench and Bar of Illinois.* Chicago: Chicago Legal News Company, 1879.

Linn, James Weber, *James Keeley Newspaperman.* Indianapolis: The Bobbs-Merrill Company, 1937.

———, *Jane Addams.* New York: Greenwood Press, 1968.

Lord, Walter, *The Good Years.* New York: Harper & Brothers, 1960.

Lundberg, Ferdinand, *The Rich and the Super-Rich: A Study of the Power of Money Today.* New York: Lyle Stuart, 1969.

Lynn, Kenneth S., *William Dean Howells.* New York: Harcourt, Brace, Jovanovich, 1971.

Lyon, Leverett S., *et al., The National Recovery Administration.* Washington D.C.: The Bookings Institution, 1935.

Mackay, Charles, *Extraordinary Popular Delusions and the Madness of Crowds.* Boston: L. C. Page & Co., 1932.

Markmann, Charles Lam, *The Noblest Cry.* New York: St. Martin's Press, 1965.

Marshall, Carrington T., *A History of the Courts and Lawyers of Ohio,* 4 vols. New York: The American Historical Society, 1934.

Mason, Alpheus Thomas, *Brandeis.* New York: The Viking Press, 1946.

————, *Harlan Fiske Stone: Pillar of the Law.* New York: The Viking Press, 1956.

Masters, Edgar Lee, *Songs and Satires.* New York: The Macmillan Company, 1916.

————, *Across Spoon River.* New York: Farrar & Rinehart, 1936.

————, *The Role of the Bar in Electing the Bench in Chicago.* Chicago: University of Chicago Press, 1936.

————, *The New Star Chamber.* Chicago: The Hammersmark Publishing Company, 1904.

Mayers, Lewis, *The American Legal System.* New York: Harper & Row, 1964.

Memorial Association, The John P. Altgeld, *Memorial Books, 1907, 1910.* Chicago, n.p..

Moley, Raymond, *Politics and Criminal Prosecution.* New York: Minton, Balch & Co., 1929.

Mordell, Albert, *Clarence Darrow, Eugene V. Debs and Haldeman-Julius.* Girard, Kans.: Haldeman-Julius Publications, 1950.

Moses, John and Kirkland, Joseph, *History of Chicago,* Vol. 1. Chicago: Munsell & Co., 1895.

Musmanno, Michael A., *Verdict!.* Garden City, N.Y.: Doubleday & Co., 1958.

National Recovery Adimmistration, *Report, 1935.* Washington, D.C.: United States Government Printing Oice, 1935.

National Recovery Review Board, *First Report to the President of the United States.* Washington, D.C.: Jesse L. Ward, official reporter, 1934

Nelles, Walter, *A Liberal in Wartime—The Education of Albert de Silver.* New York: W. W. Norton & Company, Inc., 1940.

Nevins, Allan, ed., *Letters of Grover Cleveland, 1850–1908.* Boston: Houghton Mifflin Company, 1933.

————, *The Letters and Journal of Brand Whitlock,* 2 vols. New York: D. Appleton-Century Company, 1936.

————, and Hill, Frank Ernest, *Ford Expansion and Challenge, 1915–1933.* New York: Charles Scribner's Sons, 1957.

Nichols, Beverley, *The Star-Spangled Manner.* London: Jonathan Cape, 1928.

O'Connor, Richard, *Courtroom Warrior.* Boston: Little, Brown & Co., 1963.

O'Connor, Ulick, *The Times I've Seen; Oliver St. John Gogarty, A Biography.* New York: Ivan Obolensky, 1963.

Olsen, Otto H., *Carpetbagger's Crusade: The Life of Albion Winegar Tourgee.* Baltimore: The Johns Hopkins Press, 1965.

Oursler, Fulton, *Behold This Dreamer!* Boston: Little, Brown & Co., 1964.

Partridge, Bellamy, *Country Lawyer.* New York: McGraw-Hill Book Co., 1939.

Pierce, Bessie Louise, *A History of Chicago.* New York: Alfred A. Knopf, 1957.

Pizer, Donald, ed., *Hamlin Garland's Diaries.* San Marino, Calif.: The Huntington Library, 1968.

Radosh, Ronald, ed., *Debs.* Englewood Cliffs, N.J.: Prentice-Hall, 1971.

Ravitz, Abe C., *Clarence Darrow and the American Literary Tradition.* Cleveland: Press of Western Reserve University, 1962.

Reed, George Irving, ed., *Bench and Bar of Ohio,* Vol. 1. Chicago: The Century Publishing and Engraving Company, 1897.

Robinson, W. W., *Bombs and Bribery.* Los Angeles: Dawson's Bookshop, 1969.

Russell, Charles Edward, *Why I Am a Socialist.* New York: George H. Doran Company, 1910.

Russell, Francis *Tragedy in Dedham.* New York: McGraw-Hill Book Co., 1962.

St. Johns, Adela, *Final Verdict.* New York: Bantom Books, Inc., 1964.

Sanger, Margaret, *Autobiography.* New York: W. W. Norton & Co., 1938.

Sann, Paul, *The Lawless Decade: A Pictorial History of a Great American Tradition.* New York: Crown Publishers, Inc., 1957.

Scopes, John T. and Presley, James, *Center of the Storm.* New York: Holt, Rinehart & Winston, 1967.

Severn, William, *Toward One World; The Life of Wendell Willkie.* New York: I. Washburn, 1967.

Shannon, David A., ed., *Beatrice Webb's American Diary.* Madison, Wis.: University of Wisconsin Press, 1963.

Sharpe, May Churchill, *Chicago May: Her Story.* New York: The Macaulay Company, 1928.

Sinclair, Andrew, *Prohibition.* Boston: Little, Brown & Co., 1962.

Sinclair, Upton, *My Lifetime in Letters.* Columbia, Mo.: University of Missouri Press, 1960.

Smith, T. V., *A Non-Existent Man.* Austin, Tex.: University of Texas Press, 1962.

Staley, Eugene, *History of the Illinois State Federation of Labor.* Chicago: University of Chicago Press, 1930.

Stead, William Thomas, *If Christ Came to Chicago!* London: The Review of Reviews, 1894.

Steffens, Lincoln, *Autobiography.* New York: Harcourt, Brace & Co., 1931.

———, *Letters.* New York: Harcourt, Brace & Co., 1938.

Stewart, John Struthers, *History of Northeastern Ohio.* Indianapolis, Ind.: Historical Publishing Company, 1935.

Stone, Irving, *Clarence Darrow for the Defense.* Garden City, N.Y.: Doubleday, Doran & Company, Inc., 1941.

Storey, Moorfield, *The Reform of Legal Procedure.* New Haven, Conn.: Yale University Press, 1911.

Sunset Club, *Echoes, 1889–1891.* Chicago, n.p..

———, *Yearbooks.* Chicago, n.p., various dates.

Sutherland, Edwin H., ed., *The Professional Thief.* Chicago: University of Chicago Press, 1937.

Swanberg, W. A., *Dreiser.* New York: Charles Scribner's Sons, 1965.

Taeuber, Irene and Conrad, *People of the United States in the 20th Century.* Washington, D.C.: United States Department of Commerce, Bureau of the Census, 1971.

Taft, Philip, *The A.F. of L. in the Time of Gompers.* New York: Harper & Brothers, 1957.

Tebbel, John, *George Horace Lorimer and the Saturday Evening Post.* Garden City, N.Y.: Doubleday & Co., 1948.

Tompkins, Jerry R. (ed.), *D-Days at Dayton.* Baton Rouge: Louisiana State University Press, 1965.

Trachtenberg, Alan, ed., *Memoirs of Waldo Frank* Amherst, Mass.: University of Massachusetts Press, 1973.

Tuchman, Barbara, *The Zimmerman Telegram.* New York: The Viking Press, 1958.

Tugwell, Rexford G., *The Democratic Roosevelt.* Garden City, N.Y.: Doubleday & Co., 1957.

Tuttle, Jr., William M., *Race Riot—Chicago in the Red Summer of 1919.* New York: Atheneum, 1972.

Upton, Harriet Taylor, *A Twentieth Century History of Trumbull County, Ohio,* Vols. 1 and 2. Chicago: The Lewis Publishing Company, 1909.

Urofsky, Melvin I. and Levy, David W., *Letters of Louis D. Brandeis.* Albany, N.Y.: State University of New York Press, 1971– .

Van Slingerland, Peter, *Something Terrible Has Happened.* New York: Harper & Row, Publishers, 1966.

Wade, Louise C., *Graham Taylor Pioneer for Social Justice, 1851–1938.* Chicago: University of Chicago Press, 1964.

Weil, "Yellow Kid," *Autobiography,* as told to W. T. Brannon. Chicago: Ziff-Davis Publishing Company, 1948.

Weinberg, Arthur ed., *Attorney for the Damned.* New York: Simon and Schuster, 1957.

Weinberg, Arthur and Lila, ed. *Verdicts out of Court.* Chicago: Quadrangle Books, 1963.

Weinberg, Kenneth G., *A Man's Home, A Man's Castle.* New York: The McCall Publishing Company, 1971.

Wellman, Francis L., *Gentlemen of the Jury.* New York: The Macmillan Company, 1924.

Wells, Evelyn, *Fremont Older.* New York: D. Appleton-Century, 1936.

Wells, H. G., *Experiment in Autobiography.* New York: The Macmillan Company, 1934.

Wendt, Lloyd and Kogan, Herman, *Big Bill of Chicago.* New York: The Bobbs-Merrill Company, 1953.

White, Horace, *The Life of Lyman Trumbull.* Boston and New York: Houghton Mifflin Company, 1913.

White, Ray Lewis, ed., *Sherwood Anderson's Memoirs.* Chapel Hill, University of North Carolina Press, 1969.

White, William Allen, *Autobiography.* New York: The Macmillan Company, 1946.

Whitlock, Brand, *Forty Years of It.* New York: D. Appleton and Company, 1925.

Williams, T. Harry, *Huey Long.* New York: Alfred A. Knopf, 1969.

Williamson, Samuel T., *Frank Gannett.* New York: Duell, Sloan & Pearce, 1940.

Winter, Ella, *And Not to Yield.* New York: Harcourt, Brace & World, 1963.

Wright, Frank Lloyd, *An Autobiography.* New York: Duell, Sloan & Pearce, 1943.

Yarros, Victor S., *My Eleven Years with Clarence Darrow.* Girard, Kans.: Haldeman-Julius Publications, 1950.

List of Manuscript Collections

Barnes Collection: Papers of Harry Elmer Barnes, University of Wyoming Library.

Cochran Collection: Papers of Negley Dakin Cochran, Toledo-Lucas County Public Library,

Darrow Papers: Papers of Clarence Seward Darrow, University of Chicago Library. (Extremely incomplete; disappointing.)

Fisher Collection: Papers of Irving Fisher, Yale University Library.

House Collection: Papers of Colonel Edward Mandell House, Yale University Library.

Illinois Historical Survey: Illinois Historical Survey Collection, University of Illinois, Urbana.

Kent Collection: Papers of William Kent, Yale University Library.

Labadie Papers: Papers of Joseph Labadie, University of Michigan Library.

Lindsey Papers: Papers of Benjamin Barr Lindsey, Library of Congress. (Some of these papers are restricted.)

Levinson Papers: Papers of Salmon O. Levinson, Joseph Regenstein Library, University of Chicago.

Mencken Papers: Papers of Henry Louis Mencken, New York Public Library.

NAACP [Administrative or Legal] Files: Papers of the National Association for the Advancement of Colored Peoples, Library of Congress.

Palmer Collection: Papers of Paul Palmer, Yale University Library.

Spingarn Papers: Papers of Arthur Barnett Spingarn, Library of Congress.

Storey Collection: Papers of Moorfield Storey, Massachusetts Historical Society.

Trumbull Collection: Papers of Lyman Trumbull, Illinois State Historical Library.

Whitlock Papers: Papers of Brand Whitlock, Library of Congress.

Weinberger Collection [Goldman or St. John Papers]: Papers of Harry Weinberger, Yale University Library.

Wilson Papers: Papers of Woodrow Wilson, Library of Congress.

Yale Collection of American Literature: Collection of American Literature, Beinecke Library, Yale University.

Index

Barnum, Gertrude, 84, 89, 139, 140, 250, 276–277, 278
Barrymore, Ethel, 219, 220
Baruch, Bernard, 119
Beard, Charles, 309
Becker trial, 271
Belknap, Hugh Reid, 125–126
Berkman, Alexander, 306
Bible, 356, 357, 358, 359, 360
Birkenhead, Lord, 374
birth control, 7, 280
Bissett, George, 258, 282
Black, Captain, 88–89, 91, 92
Black, Hugo L., 431
blacks, see Negroes
Bland, Richard P., 122, 123
Bly, Nellie, 120
Boer War, 171
bohemianism, 138, 139–141, 179
Bond case, 282, 283, 320
book censorship, 386–388
Borah, William E., 125, 209, 221
Bordwell, Judge, 244–245, 248, 253, 254
Borough, Reuben, 204
Bowers, Paul, 420
Bowman, Carl M., 335
Bowron, Fletcher, 274
Bradley, Preston, 83, 320
Brandeis, Louis D., 133, 187, 250, 433
Brant, Otto F., 245
Breen, Peter, 217
Breiner, Leo, 375, 377–378
Brewer, David J., 113–114
bribery trials, see Darrow bribery trials
Bridge and Iron Workers' Union, 238, 249
Bridges, Horace James, 352
Bristol, Vollington, 376, 377
Brockway v. Jewell, 30
Brookings Institute, 432
Brown, John, 8, 276, 398
Browne, Sam, 262
Browne, Waldo, 95
Bruce, Andrew, 40, 74
Bryan, William Jennings, 29, 122–126, 143, 146, 196, 279
  background of, 122
  "Cross of Gold" speech of, 124, 142
  Darrow on, 122–123, 124
  Darrow's animosity toward, 127, 142, 355, 357–361, 366
  death of, 370–371
  in evolution trial, 354, 355–370
  intellectuals' derision of, 356, 365
  as orator, 357, 361
  populist platform of, 123
  as presidential candidate, 125, 126, 230–231
  religious beliefs of, 123, 355–360
  as Secretary of State, 361
"Bryan and Altgeld club," 161

Bryan and Darrow at Dayton (Allen), 371
Bryant-Spence Agency, 395
Bryce, J. B. (McNamara), 273
Bryce, James, 78
bugging devices, 255, 272–273
Buncombe County, 26
Burket, Jacob F., 30
Burleson, Albert Sidney, 292
Burns, William J., 248–249
Burns Detective Agency, 272
Busch, Francis X., 344
Buster Brown League, 287, 299
Butcher, Fanny, 140, 352
Butler, Samuel, 32

capital punishment, 92, 238
  in Leopold-Loeb case, 329, 331, 338, 339, 343, 344, 345, 346, 347
Cargill, Oscar, 413
Carlin, William L., 279
Carrillo, Donato, 388
Cavenaugh, Billy, 268, 274
Caverly, John, 329, 334, 338, 339, 341, 343, 344, 346
censorship, in World War I, 291, 292
Central Music Hall (Chicago), 49–50
Century Magazine, 70
Cermak, Anton, 174
Chamlee, George W., Sr., 404
Channing, William, E., 5, 233
Chaplin, Ralph, 301
Chautauqua lectures, 279, 361
Chesterton, G. K., 358, 360
Chicago (Watkins), 352
Chicago, Ill.:
  corruption in, 41, 53, 54–56, 118, 299–300, 312–314
  criminal courts in, 135
  Darrow identified with, 352
  Darrow's feelings about, 129, 285
  Darrow's legal positions with, 51, 53–55, 57, 195, 199, 201, 202–205
  Darrow's move to, 34–35
  in 1880s, 35–36
  1893 World's Fair in, 53, 82, 84, 89
  1894 depression in, 89
  as gangland, 354
  intellectuals' exodus from, 286
  police vs. radicals in, 37–38
  streetcar franchises in, 52, 54, 201, 202–205
  see also Democratic Party; politics
Chicago American, 167, 195, 196, 197, 198, 330
Chicago & Northwestern Railway, 58–66, 91, 129, 160, 203
  Darrow in law department of, 57, 58–59, 65, 77, 81, 92, 93–94, 97, 99–100
Chicago Bar Association, 165, 166, 349
Chicago Commons, 82